THE ROUTLEDGE HANDBOOK OF COLLECTIVE INTENTIONALITY

The Routledge Handbook of Collective Intentionality provides a wide-ranging survey of topics in a rapidly expanding area of interdisciplinary research. It consists of 36 chapters, written exclusively for this volume, by an international team of experts.

What is distinctive about the study of collective intentionality within the broader study of social interactions and structures is its focus on the conceptual and psychological features of joint or shared actions and attitudes, and their implications for the nature of social groups and their functioning. This *Handbook* fully captures this distinctive nature of the field and how it subsumes the study of collective action, responsibility, reasoning, thought, intention, emotion, phenomenology, decision-making, knowledge, trust, rationality, cooperation, competition, and related issues, as well as how these underpin social practices, organizations, conventions, institutions and social ontology. Like the field, the *Handbook* is interdisciplinary, drawing on research in philosophy, cognitive science, linguistics, legal theory, anthropology, sociology, computer science, psychology, economics, and political science. Finally, the *Handbook* promotes several specific goals: (1) it provides an important resource for students and researchers interested in collective intentionality; (2) it integrates work across disciplines and areas of research as it helps to define the shape and scope of an emerging area of research; (3) it advances the study of collective intentionality.

Marija Jankovic is Assistant Professor of Philosophy at Davidson College. Her areas of research are collective intentionality and philosophy of language. She is interested in how thinking about manifestations of collective intentionality can illuminate philosophical problems which are traditionally approached individualistically.

Kirk Ludwig is Professor of Philosophy and Cognitive Science at Indiana University, Bloomington. He works in philosophy of mind and action, especially collective action, as well as epistemology, philosophy of language, and metaphysics. His most recent books are *From Individual to Plural Agency: Collective Action 1* (OUP 2016) and *From Plural to Institutional Agency: Collective Action 2* (OUP 2017).

ROUTLEDGE HANDBOOKS IN PHILOSOPHY

Routledge Handbooks in Philosophy are state-of-the-art surveys of emerging, newly refreshed, and important fields in philosophy, providing accessible yet thorough assessments of key problems, themes, thinkers, and recent developments in research.

All chapters for each volume are specially commissioned, and written by leading scholars in the field. Carefully edited and organized, *Routledge Handbooks in Philosophy* provide indispensable reference tools for students and researchers seeking a comprehensive overview of new and exciting topics in philosophy. They are also valuable teaching resources as accompaniments to textbooks, anthologies, and research-orientated publications.

Recently published:

The Routledge Handbook of Philosophy of Empathy
Edited by Heidi Maibom

The Routledge Handbook of Epistemic Contextualism
Edited by Jonathan Jenkins Ichikawa

The Routledge Handbook of Brentano and the Brentano School
Edited by Uriah Kriegel

The Routledge Handbook of Epistemic Injustice
Edited by Ian James Kidd, José Medina and Gaile Pohlhaus

The Routledge Handbook of Philosophy of Memory
Edited by Sven Bernecker and Kourken Michaelian

The Routledge Handbook of Philosophy of Pain
Edited by Jennifer Corns

The Routledge Handbook of Mechanisms and Mechanical Philosophy
Edited by Stuart Glennan and Phyllis Illari

The Routledge Handbook of Metaethics
Edited by Tristram McPherson and David Plunkett

The Routledge Handbook of Evolution and Philosophy
Edited by Richard Joyce

The Routledge Handbook of Libertarianism
Edited by Jason Brennan, Bas van der Vossen, and David Schmidtz

The Routledge Handbook of Collective Intentionality
Edited by Marija Jankovic and Kirk Ludwig

The Routledge Handbook of Pacifism and Nonviolence
Edited by Andrew Fiala

For a full list of published *Routledge Handbooks in Philosophy*, please visit
https://www.routledge.com/Routledge-Handbooks-in-Philosophy/book-series/RHP

THE ROUTLEDGE HANDBOOK OF COLLECTIVE INTENTIONALITY

Edited by
Marija Jankovic and Kirk Ludwig

Routledge
Taylor & Francis Group

LONDON AND NEW YORK

First Published 2018 by Routledge
2 Park Square, Milton Park, Abingdon, Oxon OX14 4RN
52 Vanderbilt Avenue, New York, NY 10017

First issued in paperback 2020

Routledge is an imprint of the Taylor & Francis Group, an informa business

Library of Congress Cataloging-in-Publication Data
A catalog record has been requested for this book

ISBN 13: 978-0-367-57274-7 (pbk)
ISBN 13: 978-1-138-78363-8 (hbk)

Typeset in Minion Pro and Frutiger
by Sunrise Setting Ltd., Brixham, UK

Contents

PART II: SHARED AND JOINT ATTITUDES

PART III: EPISTEMOLOGY AND RATIONALITY IN THE SOCIAL CONTEXT

PART IV: SOCIAL ONTOLOGY

PART V: COLLECTIVES AND RESPONSIBILITY

PART VI: COLLECTIVE INTENTIONALITY AND SOCIAL INSTITUTIONS

PART VII: THE EXTENT, ORIGINS, AND DEVELOPMENT OF COLLECTIVE INTENTIONALITY

PART VIII: SEMANTICS OF COLLECTIVITY

Contributors

Facundo M. Alonso is Assistant Professor of Philosophy at Miami University, Ohio. He works on issues in the philosophy of action and mind, normative ethics, and epistemology.

Ásta (Ásta Kristjana Sveinsdóttir) is Associate Professor of Philosophy at San Francisco State University. In 2016–17 she has been a Fellow at the National Humanities Center, completing a monograph on the metaphysics of social categories, entitled *Categories We Live By* (OUP).

Saba Bazargan-Forward is an Associate Professor at the University of California, San Diego. He works primarily in normative ethics, with a focus on the morality of defensive violence, the morality of war, and complicity. He also works on a variety of other issues in normative ethics, including: the moral analysis of coercion, the bases of rectificatory liability, and the morality of mediating agency. He is currently authoring a book on complicity and the morality of war.

Stephen Butterfill researches and teaches on joint action, mindreading, and other philosophical issues in cognitive science at the University of Warwick, UK.

John Campbell is the Willis S. and Marion Slusser Professor of Philosophy at the University of California, Berkeley. His main interests lie in the theory of meaning, metaphysics, and the philosophy of psychology. His recent books include *Reference and Consciousness* (OUP 2002), and (with Quassim Cassam) *Berkeley's Puzzle* (OUP 2014).

Sara Rachel Chant is a Lecturer in Business Management at Tulane University's Freeman School of Business, as well as retired Associate Professor of Philosophy at the University of Missouri. She works in philosophy of mind and action, especially the metaphysics and epistemology of collective action. Her recent work focuses on methodological approaches to collective action and corporate leadership.

Jan M. Engelmann is Postdoctoral Research Fellow at the Max Planck Institute for Evolutionary Anthropology, Leipzig, Germany.

Brian Epstein is Associate Professor of Philosophy at Tufts University. His research interests include philosophy of social science, metaphysics, and philosophy of language. Epstein is the author of *The Ant Trap: Rebuilding the Foundations of the Social Sciences* (Oxford 2015).

Salvatore Florio is a Lecturer in Philosophy at the University of Birmingham, UK and specializes in philosophy of language, philosophical logic, and philosophy of mathematics. His recent work has focused on philosophical aspects of higher-order logic and has appeared in journals such as *Australasian Journal of Philosophy*, *Mind*, *Noûs*, and *Philosophers' Imprint*.

Margaret Gilbert holds the Melden Chair in Moral Philosophy at the University of California, Irvine. She has published and lectured widely on all aspects of collective intentionality theory and demonstrated its relevance to central topics in moral and political philosophy and the philosophy of law.

Natalie Gold is a Senior Research Fellow at King's College London, UK, where she leads the European Research Council-funded project "Self-Control and the Person: An Inter-Disciplinary Account." She has published on topics including framing, moral judgments and decisions, cooperation and coordination, and self-control.

Marcus Hedahl is Assistant Professor of Philosophy at the US Naval Academy. His research focuses on collective duties and collective values, particularly in the context of climate change.

Frank Hindriks is Professor of Philosophy at the University of Groningen, the Netherlands. His research interests lie in ethics, social and political philosophy, philosophy of action, and the theory of collective intentionality. He is editor, with Sara Rachel Chant and Gerhard Preyer, of *From Individual to Collective Intentionality: New Essays* (OUP 2014).

Bryce Huebner is Associate Professor of Philosophy at Georgetown University. He is the author of *Macrocognition: A Theory of Distributed Minds and Collective Intentionality* (OUP 2014), as well as several articles in the philosophy of the cognitive, biological, and social sciences.

Marija Jankovic is Assistant Professor of Philosophy at Davidson College. Her areas of research are collective intentionality and philosophy of language. She is interested in how thinking about manifestations of collective intentionality can illuminate philosophical problems which are traditionally approached individualistically.

Jennifer Lackey is the Wayne and Elizabeth Jones Professor of Philosophy at Northwestern University. She specializes in epistemology and philosophy of mind. Her recent research focuses on the epistemology of testimony, norms of assertion, epistemic luck, credit for knowledge, and the epistemic significance of disagreement. She has co-edited (with Ernest Sosa) *The Epistemology of Testimony* (OUP 2006) and is the author of *Learning from Words: Testimony as a Source of Knowledge* (OUP 2008).

Harvey Lederman is Assistant Professor of Philosophy at the University of Pittsburgh. He works primarily on issues in epistemology and philosophical logic.

Øystein Linnebo is Professor of Philosophy at the University of Oslo, Norway and works in philosophical logic, philosophy of mathematics, metaphysics, and early analytic philosophy (especially Frege). He has published more than 50 scientific articles and is the author of two forthcoming books, *Philosophy of Mathematics* (Princeton University Press) and *Thin Objects: An Abstractionist Account* (Oxford University Press).

Kirk Ludwig is Professor of Philosophy and Cognitive Science at Indiana University, Bloomington. He works in philosophy of mind and action, especially collective action, as well as epistemology, philosophy of language, and metaphysics. His most recent books are *From Individual to Plural Agency: Collective Action 1* (OUP 2016) and *From Plural to Institutional Agency: Collective Action 2* (OUP 2017).

Kourken Michaelian is Senior Lecturer in Philosophy at the University of Otago, New Zealand. He is the author of *Mental Time Travel: Episodic Memory and Our Knowledge of the Personal Past* (MIT 2016).

Seumas Miller is Professor of Philosophy at Charles Sturt University, Australia and Senior Research Fellow, 3TU Centre for Ethics and Technology, Delft University of Technology, the Netherlands. His extensive publications include writings on social action and institutions, terrorism, business ethics, and police ethics. His recent books include *Institutional Corruption* (CUP 2017), *Ethical Issues in Policing*, with John Blackler

(Routledge 2017), *Shooting to Kill: The Ethics of Police and Military Use of Lethal Force* (OUP 2016), *Corruption and Anti-Corruption in Policing—Philosophical and Ethical Issues* (Spring 2016), *Investigative Ethics: Ethics for Police Detective and Criminal Investigators*, with Ian Gordon (Wiley-Blackwell 2014), *Security and Privacy*, with John Kleinig, Peter Mameli, Douglas Salane, and Adina Schwartz (ANU Press 2011), and *The Moral Foundations of Social Institutions: A Philosophical Study* (CUP 2010).

Elisabeth Pacherie is a Senior Researcher in Philosophy at Institut Jean Nicod (CNRS UMR 8129, Institut d'Etude de la Cognition, École Normale Supérieure and PSL Research University, Paris), France. Her main research interests are in the philosophy of mind and action, and she has written extensively on individual and collective agency.

Philip Pettit is L.S. Rockefeller University Professor of Politics and Human Values at Princeton University, Fellow of the American Academy of Arts and Sciences and the Australian Academies of Humanities and Social Sciences, and Corresponding Fellow of the British Academy. He works in moral and political theory and on background issues in the philosophy of mind and metaphysics. His recent books include *Made with Words: Hobbes on Mind, Society and Politics* (PUP 2008), *Group Agency: The Possibility, Design and Status of Corporate Agents*, with Christian List (OUP 2011), *On the People's Terms: A Republican Theory and Model of Democracy* (CUP 2012), *Just Freedom: A Moral Compass for a Complex World* (W.W. Norton 2014), and *The Robust Demands of the Good: Ethics with Attachment Virtue and Respect* (OUP 2015).

Hannes Rakoczy is a cognitive scientist at the University of Göttingen, Germany. He is interested in the developmental and comparative study of different forms of individual and shared intentionality over the human lifespan and in non-human primates.

Katherine Ritchie is Assistant Professor at the City College of New York, CUNY in New York City. She has recently published articles on semantics and social ontology in the *Australasian Journal of Philosophy*, *Philosophical Studies*, and *Philosophy Compass*.

Abraham Sesshu Roth is Associate Professor in the Philosophy Department at The Ohio State University. He has taught at UCLA and at the University of Illinois at Chicago, and received his Ph.D. from Princeton. He works mainly in the philosophy of action, focusing on issues concerning intentions, practical reasoning, reasons explanation, shared agency, and related issues in epistemology and moral psychology. He has published in *The Philosophical Review, Noûs, Ethics, Philosophy and Phenomenological Research*, and *Philosophical Studies*.

Hans Bernhard Schmid is Professor of Philosophy at the University of Vienna. He specializes in the philosophy of social science, social ontology, action theory, social and sociological theory, and the history of philosophy, especially phenomenology and existential philosophy. He is the editor in chief of the *Journal of Social Philosophy*. Recent books include *Social Capital, Social Identities*, ed. with Christoph Henning and Dieter Thomä (De Gruyter 2014), *Institutions, Emotions, and Group Agents*, ed. with Anita Konzelmann Ziv (Springer 2014), *Self Evaluation: Affective and Social Grounds of Intentionality*, ed. with Anita Konzelmann Ziv and Keither Lehrer (Springer 2011), and *Collective Epistemology*, ed. with Daniel Sirtes and Marcel Weber (De Gruyter 2011).

Frederick Schmitt is Professor of Philosophy at Indiana University. He specializes in epistemology and the history of epistemology. His latest book is *Hume's Epistemology in the Treatise: A Veritistic Interpretation* (OUP 2014).

John Searle is the Willis S. and Marion Slusser Professor Emeritus of the Philosophy of Mind and Language, Professor of the Graduate School, University of California, Berkeley, and Fellow of the American Academy of Arts and Sciences. His work ranges broadly over philosophical problems of mind, language, action and society. Recent books include *The Mystery of Consciousness* (NYRB 1997), *Mind, Language and Society: Philosophy in the Real World* (Basic Books 1999), *Rationality in Action* (OUP 2001), *Mind: A Brief Introduction* (OUP 2004), *Freedom and Neurobiology* (Columbia 2008), *Philosophy in a New Century* (CUP 2008), *Making the Social World: The Structure of Human Civilization* (OUP 2010), and *Seeing Things as They Are: A Theory of Perception* (OUP 2015).

Paul Sheehy teaches philosophy at The Hollyfield School in south-west London, UK. His research and publications are mainly on the ontology and moral status of social groups. Primarily a one-trick pony, he does, nonetheless, do some work on divine nature and modal realism.

Marion Smiley is J.P. Morgan Chase Professor of Ethics at Brandeis University. She is the author of *Moral Responsibility and the Boundaries of Community: Power and Accountability from a Pragmatic Point of View* (University of Chicago Press 1992), as well as numerous articles on individual and collective responsibility, philosophical pragmatism, democratic theory, group identity, feminism, paternalism, and the ethics of dependence.

John Sutton is Professor of Cognitive Science at Macquarie University in Sydney, Australia. His current research addresses social memory and collaborative recall, expertise and skilled movement, distributed cognition, and cognitive history.

Georg Theiner is Associate Professor of Philosophy at Villanova University. He works on issues in the philosophy of mind, cognitive science, phenomenology and embodied cognition, the extended mind thesis, group cognition, and philosophy of language. He is the author of *Res Cogitans Extensa: A Philosophical Defense of the Extended Mind Thesis* (Peter Lang 2011).

Deborah Perron Tollefsen is Professor of Philosophy and Associate Dean of the College of Arts and Sciences at the University of Memphis. Her research and teaching interests include collective intentionality, social and feminist epistemology, and the philosophy of mind.

Michael Tomasello is Co-Director at the Max Planck Institute for Evolutionary Anthropology and Professor of Psychology at Duke University. His most recent publications include *A Natural History of Human Thinking* (Harvard University Press 2014) and *A Natural History of Human Morality* (Harvard University Press 2016).

Raimo Tuomela is Emeritus Professor of Philosophy at the University of Helsinki, Finland and permanent Visiting Professor at the LMU University of Munich, Germany. His work focuses on the methodology and philosophy of science, especially the social sciences, philosophy of action, social action theory, sociality, and collective intentionality. His most recent books include *The Philosophy of Sociality: The Shared Point of View* (OUP 2007), and *Social Ontology: Collective Intentionality and Group Agents* (OUP 2013).

Paul Weirich is a Curators' Distinguished Professor in the Philosophy Department at the University of Missouri. His research interests lie in decision theory, game theory, and logic. His most recent books are *Models of Decision-Making: Simplifying Choices* (CUP 2015) and *Collective Rationality: Equilibrium in Cooperative Games* (OUP 2010).

Robert A. Wilson is Professor of Philosophy at the University of Alberta and Fellow of the Royal Society of Canada. His research falls chiefly in the philosophy of mind and cognitive science, the philosophy of biology, and general philosophy of science, with ongoing interests in ethics, metaphysics and epistemology, and seventeenth and eighteenth century philosophy. He is the author of *Boundaries of Mind* (CUP 2004) and *Genes and the Agents of Life* (CUP 2005), and most recently *The Eugenic Mind Project* (MIT 2017).

Gideon Yaffe is Professor of Law and Professor of Philosophy and Psychology, Yale Law School. His research interests include the philosophy of law, particularly criminal law; the study of metaphysics including causation, free will, and personal identity; and the study of intention and the theory of action. His 2010 book *Attempts* (OUP) concerns the philosophical foundations of the law governing attempted crimes. His 2017 book *The Age of Culpability* (OUP) concerns the philosophical grounds for leniency toward child criminals. He has held fellowships from the American Council of Learned Societies and the Mellon Foundation, and he was named a Guggenheim Fellow in 2015.

Introduction

Marija Jankovic and Kirk Ludwig

WHAT IS COLLECTIVE INTENTIONALITY?

On July 2, 2003, at 7:07 p.m., at the tail end of the rush hour in Manhattan, the lobby of the Grand Hyatt, fronting Forty-Second Street next to Grand Central Station, was nearly empty. A few guests sat in armchairs around the lobby. In twos and threes and small groups people began slipping into the lobby from the street, milling around the lobby making small talk, until there were around two hundred people in the lobby. All at once, they rode the elevators and escalators to the mezzanine level and wordlessly lined the banister looking down into the lobby, staring at where they had just been. After five minutes staring at the lobby, they erupted into precisely fifteen seconds of tumultuous applause and then scattered downstairs and out the doors to the street. This was one of the first flash mobs organized by Bill Wasik of *Harper's Magazine*. The participants, who did not know beforehand who else would be participating, were recruited by email to participate in "an inexplicable mob of people in New York City." What they did, they intended to do, they did it together, and they did it intentionally. It is possible to imagine the same people entering the lobby in the same way in the same groups and milling around and making small talk in the same way, without the members of that group doing anything together intentionally. It is even possible to imagine them all making their way to the mezzanine at the same time and lining the banister and applauding, without their intending to be doing anything together. The same people, the same movements can on one occasion be a random collection of individual actions and on another a collective intentional activity. Since everything about their behavior can be the same—though on one occasion they act together intentionally, while on another they do not—the difference has to lie in their attitudes. The difference between their forming a group oriented toward joint action, a social unit, and a random group of people rests on how they are *thinking about* what they are doing together. That difference is the central focus of the study of collective intentionality.

Intentionality is the property of being about or directed at something. Intentionality may be original or derived. It is derived if the intentionality of one thing (a sign, e.g.) is explained in terms of its relation to something else with intentionality (a sign maker). Original intentionality is a power of the mind. It is not limited to intentions. Intentions are a particular sort of propositional attitude directed at actions. Intentionality encompass all the propositional attitudes—believing, desiring, fearing, hoping, wishing, doubting, and so on—as well as perceiving (e.g. seeing a sand dollar on the beach), imagining (e.g. the roar of a lion), and emotions directed at objects or events (e.g. being angry at a perceived slight).

The study of *collective* intentionality is the study of intentionality in the social context. It subsumes centrally the intentionality of collectives and intentional phenomena involving groups of agents in contexts in which they are acting or oriented toward action as a group. Understanding collective intentionality is the key to understanding the nature and structure of social reality. What is distinctive about the study of collective intentionality within the broader study of social interactions and structures is its focus on the conceptual and psychological features of joint or shared actions and attitudes—that is, actions and attitudes of groups or collectives, their relations to individual actions and attitudes, and their implications for the nature of social groups and their functioning. It is concerned, as it were, with the atomic structure of social reality. It subsumes the study of collective action, responsibility, reasoning, thought, intention, emotion, phenomenology, decision-making, knowledge, trust, rationality, cooperation, competition, and related issues, as well as how these underpin social practices, organizations, conventions, institutions, and ontology.

Collective intentionality is an interdisciplinary area of research with contributions from philosophy, psychology, political science, legal theory, linguistics, cognitive science, sociology, anthropology, and computer science. Pioneering work by philosophers Raimo Tuomela (Seebass and Tuomela 1985; Tuomela and Miller 1988; Tuomela 1989a, 1989b) and Margaret Gilbert (Gilbert 1983a, 1983b, 1987, 1989) in the 1980s led to a rapid expansion of interest in joint action and intention in the 1990s, with seminal and field-shaping contributions by Michael Bratman (Bratman 1992, 1993, 1999a, 1999b) and John Searle (Searle 1990, 1995), together with additional work by Tuomela and Gilbert and a growing number of researchers, providing additional impetus to the development of research on the topic. Since the beginning of the new century, there has been an explosion of work on collective intentionality, with a significant increase of interest in cognitive science, sociology, legal theory, economics, political science, animal studies, anthropology, and the study of the evolution of language, cooperation, and sociality.

WHAT ARE THE CENTRAL QUESTIONS OF THE FIELD?

The central question in the field of collective intentionality is the extent to which the phenomena under study can be understood ultimately in terms of an ontology of individual agents and their psychological states and interactions. There are ontological, conceptual, and psychological dimensions to this.

On the ontological dimension, to what extent must or should we appeal to an ontology of genuine group agents? When members of a basketball team play a game, is it just a matter of a group of individual agents coordinating their behavior in pursuit of a common goal, or is it the team itself that plays the game? Or, to shift the scale, in what sense could General Motors, which has been in continuous operation since 1908, be seen as nothing more than its shareholders and operators, when it, as we say, plans and executes strategies over periods in which its shareholders, board members, management, and employees change constantly? And to what extent are there irreducibly social facts, objects, and events? Is the fact that Bill and Melinda Gates are married reducible to non-social facts? Is the marriage a new kind of entity on the scene? Is money something real over and above the attitudes and dispositions oriented toward action that people have toward certain pieces of paper, bits of metal, and accounting records?

On the conceptual dimension, how should we analyze social concepts? What are the factors that go into determining social categories? Is it entirely a matter of synchronic facts and relations? Or are all or some social categories historical? What resources are available? Are social concepts reducible ultimately to nonsocial concepts? Even if we decide on a sparse ontology of individual agents and ordinary physical objects with an overlay of social description—as we might think of a chair just as bits of wood, e.g. arranged chair-wise and put to certain uses—are the social concepts under which we bring these things analyzable in terms of the relations of the things we bring under them to individual agents, their attitudes, and interactions? Or are some social concepts irreducibly social?

On the psychological dimension, if we admit genuine group agents, how do we understand their psychology? What sorts of psychological state do we attribute to them and on what basis? What is joint attention and what is its role in relation to the mutual responsiveness characteristic of small-scale social interaction? What is a group intention on this view? What is a group belief? What is it for a group to accept something? Can groups lie? Can their beliefs or acceptances be justified and if so, what does it come to? What is the proper scope of these attributions? Do groups have emotions, do they have regrets, can they, as opposed to their members, be angry, sorry, sad, afraid, or anxious? What about group phenomenology? Is there something it is like to be a group? Is there something distinctive about the phenomenology of acting as a member of a group? And if we attribute psychological states to groups, are they the same sorts of state as those we attribute to individuals? And if we reject an ontology of group agents in favor of multiple agents coordinating their actions, still, what distinguishes their attitudes from those of individuals who outwardly behave the same but who are just acting on individual intentions? Let us call the sort of intention one has when participating with others in joint intentional action a *we-intention*, following Tuomela and Miller (1988). We-intentions are conceptually central to group social phenomena. But what is special about them? Are they distinguished by their mode? Is there a special we-mode of intending and, correspondingly, of believing, hoping, wishing, feeling guilt, and so on? Or are the modes the same as in the case of individual intention and so on, while the we-attitudes are distinguished by something special about their contents? And if by their contents, then how? And can we characterize what makes the contents of we-intentions special while appealing only to concepts already in play in our understanding of individual agency, or must we introduce *sui generis* social concepts of one sort or another in characterizing their contents?

The answers to these questions are relevant to the traditional debate between methodological individualism and collectivism in the social sciences. Methodological individualism carries a commitment to the following two theses:

(1) We can understand and explain individual action on the basis of the individual's own attitudes and reasons (which may refer to other agents and their attitudes and reasons, and to reducible group attitudes and reasons) together with physical and nonsocial facts.
(2) Social ontology consists solely of the actions and activities of individuals and their relations and interactions, and both reference to groups as agents or bearers of attitudes and group social and psychological properties are reducible to the bases in (1) and (2).

Collectivism, in its most general form, is simply a denial of the conjunction of (1) and (2). If collectivism is true, then there are genuinely emergent social phenomena, either social objects (new ontology) or new social states, facts, and events and processes.

HOW IS THE HANDBOOK ORGANIZED?

The Handbook is divided into seven parts. Each part begins with a short introduction that provides an overview of the area that it covers and a brief precis of its contents.

The first part focuses on collective action and intention. Joint action is the glue that holds the social world together. Everything else is understood in relation to it. What is collective action? What is it to share an intention? Are these intentions the intentions of the group as such or is it a matter of distributing we-intentions across members of the group, and what does this come to in any case? What sorts of obligation do participants have to one another and how are these related to the nature of their intentions? How do groups act through individual members or subgroups (proxy agency)? And what is the empirical psychology of joint action?

The second part focuses on shared or joint attitudes beyond intention. What is group belief and acceptance? Are singularist accounts, which understand group belief in terms of attitudes of individuals, adequate? What is it for a group to share values, interests, and desires? What is joint attention? What role does it play in making certain forms of joint action available to us? What is joint commitment and what role does it play in our understanding of collective intentionality? What are collective emotions? What is special about the phenomenology of joint intentional activities?

The third part is concerned with the nature of justification and rationality in social groups. Common knowledge is frequently invoked in understanding joint action or the conditions for rational joint action, at least in some circumstances. What is common knowledge? What is the epistemology of groups? When is a group justified in accepting or believing something, as opposed to its members? What is collective rationality and how is it related to individual rationality? How can team reasoning help overcome collective action problems that pose problems for individualist accounts of decision-making, and what is its relation to joint intentional action? Do groups by a division of labor constitute systems which are able to think and reason in their own right? What is the relevance of procedures designed to resolve judgment aggregation problems, especially in the context of corporate action, to whether corporations are agents in their own right?

Part IV focuses on social ontology. What are social facts? What is social construction? What are social groups and what are social kinds? What are status functions, like being a twenty-dollar bill, or senator, or the white king in chess?

Part V focuses on issues involving responsibility in the context of group action. What is collective responsibility in general? What is complicity and what are its conditions in the context of group agency? What is involved in holding an institution responsible for what it does and how is it related to its organizational structure and the roles of its various members?

Part VI focuses on social institutions. How is collective intentionality related to social institutions understood as organizations? How is it related to the institution of language? How is it relevant to legal institutions? What is its relevance to the methodology of the social sciences?

Part VII focuses on the extent and development of collective intentionality. How does the capacity to participate in collective intentionality develop in human children? What forms does it take in non-human animals? What are its evolutionary and developmental origins?

Finally, part VIII takes up the semantics and logic of plurals, the nature of plural and collective noun phrases, and the event analysis of plural action sentences in relation to collective intentionality.

WHAT IS THE GOAL OF THE HANDBOOK?

The Handbook aims to provide a resource for students and researchers interested in collective intentionality by way of survey of central topics in this expanding area of inter-disciplinary research. This promotes several goals. First, it provides an important resource for students and researchers interested in collective intentionality by providing authoritative articles on the wide range of topics covered in the study of collective intentionality. Second, it helps to integrate work across disciplines and areas of research by affording researchers in different fields and areas of study with an overview of work on collective intentionality in other fields or topics related to their work. Third, it helps to define the shape and scope of an emerging area of research that draws on many different disciplines. The Handbook itself is the product of collective intentionality. It is a joint endeavor, a collectively intentional project, involving coordination and cooperation, larger than any individual could undertake, drawing on a body of expertise beyond that any individual could acquire. It aims to promote a larger project, the collective investigation of collective intentionality and its relation to the social, by providing a reference work that will advance the study of the interconnections between its various questions.

REFERENCES

Bratman, Michael (1992) "Shared Cooperative Activity," *The Philosophical Review* 101 (2): 327–41.

——— (1993) "Shared Intention," *Ethics* 104 (1): 97–113.

——— (1999a) "I Intend that We J," in *Faces of Intention: Selected Essays on Intention and Agency*. Cambridge: Cambridge University Press.

———— (1999b) "Shared Intention and Mutual Obligation," in *Faces of Intention: Selected Essays on Intention and Agency*. Cambridge: Cambridge University Press.

Gilbert, Margaret (1983a) "Agreements, Conventions, and Language," *Synthese* 54: 375–408.

———— (1983b) "On the Question Whether Language Has a Social Nature: Some Aspects of Winch and Others on Wittgenstein," *Synthese* 56: 301–18.

———— (1987) "Modelling Collective Belief," *Synthese* 73: 185–204.

———— (1989) *On Social Facts*. London: Routledge.

Searle, John R. (1990) "Collective Intentions and Actions," in *Intentions in Communication*, edited by P. R. Cohen, J. Morgan and M. E. Pollack. Cambridge, MA: MIT Press.

———— (1995) *The Construction of Social Reality*. New York: Free Press.

Seebass, Gottfried and Tuomela, Raimo (1985) *Social Action*. Dordrecht: D. Reidel.

Tuomela, Raimo (1989a) "Actions by Collectives," *Philosophical Perspectives* 3: 471–96.

———— (1989b) "Collective Action, Supervenience, and Constitution," *Synthese* 80: 243–66.

Tuomela, Raimo and Miller, Kaarlo (1988) "We-Intentions," *Philosophical Studies* 53: 367–89.

I

Collective Action and Intention

Introduction to Part I

Marija Jankovic and Kirk Ludwig

Collective action and intention are conceptually central to understanding collective intentionality and the social world. Without the capacity for collective intentional action there would be no such thing as social reality. In this sense, the basic structure of collective action and intention gives the atomic structure of social reality.

As noted in the general introduction to this Handbook, questions about collective intentionality divide into two basic sorts, and each along two dimensions in turn. There are ontological questions, on the one hand, and psychological questions, on the other. And there are, cross-cutting these categories, conceptual questions, on the one hand, and empirical questions, on the other.

In application to collective action and intention, the main ontological question focuses on whether there are genuine group agents, which we may take to be the question whether groups of agents themselves, as opposed to their members, stand in the agency relation, and what the nature is of such groups. When we assert [1]–[5], intending these to be read collectively, who is the agent, and why?

[1] We built a boat.
[2] They danced the tango.
[3] The boys carried the piano upstairs.
[4] The Supreme Court refused to hear the case.
[5] The government suspended refugee admissions for 120 days.

Is it a matter of just various individual agents making their various contributions to bringing something about, or is there, as superficial grammar suggests, a genuine group agent? And even if there are no group agents per se, there is the further question of what has to be the case for a group of agents to be truly described as having done something together, and then further, having done it together intentionally. What kind of structure has to be in place?

The main psychological question is what is special about the psychology of groups when they engage in joint intentional action. When we assert [6]–[7], for example, who is the intender?

[6] We intend to build a boat.
[7] The government intends to suspend refugee admissions for 120 days.

Do we jointly have an intention in the first case or is it only a matter of our individually having intentions? What do we have in mind in saying that the government intends something? Does the government per se have an intention, or only certain of its operative members, which we express in a shorthand way? If we admit group agents into our ontology, then we have to understand what it means to treat a group of agents as itself an agent and whether we wish to conceive of it as just like an individual agent writ large. In addition, whether or not we reject group agents, we must confront the question of what is special about the attitudes of individuals in groups that engage in joint intentional action. What is special about their participatory intentions, when looking toward, or engaged in, joint intentional action, that is, their *we-intentions*, as it has become standard to call them? What does it take, what sorts of rational structures does it give rise to, what are the forms that group agency can take, and what is the empirical psychological infrastructure which realizes in us human beings what is conceptually required of our acting together intentionally?

This section of the Handbook takes up these sorts of questions. It serves as a foundation for subsequent discussion. There are six chapters in Part I, "Collective Action and Agency," "Non-Reductive Views of Shared Intention," "Reductive Views of Shared Intention," "Interpersonal Obligation in Joint Action," 'Proxy Agency in Collective Action," and "Coordinating Joint Action."

Chapter 1, "Collective Action and Agency," by Sara Chant, addresses the question of how to think about the relation between individual and collective agency. How similar are group agents, however we are to think of them, to individual agents? Should we adopt what Chant calls the "Wash, Rinse, and Repeat" strategy, where we treat collective agents strictly on analogy with individual agents, or does this turn out to be a Procrustean bed which lops off important forms of collective agency or stretches it to conform to some preconceived model that badly fits the reality?

Chapters 2 and 3 take up non-reductive and reductive views of shared intention, respectively. A shared intention is expressed by a sentence like [6], "We intend to build a boat," when it is read collectively, rather than distributively (we intend to build a boat together vs each of us intends himself to build a boat). The main options are to treat [6] as attributing a single intention to *us*, or to treat it as about the *members* of the group having intentions directed toward their performing an action together. In the latter case, the main division is between those who think this can be analyzed wholly in terms of concepts already at play in understanding individual action and intention (reductive views), and those who deny this (non-reductive views). Typically, reductionists locate what is special about we-intentions in their content and in the presence of coordinated beliefs. There are two main options for non-reductionists. The first is to see we-intentions as involving a special, irreducible, we-mode. The second is to see what's special as located in conceptually irreducible content in the we-intentions, often together with a constellation of supporting attitudes.

Chapter 2, "Non-Reductive Views of Shared Intention," by Raimo Tuomela, reviews the main non-reductive views about what it is for a group to share an intention, by Margaret Gilbert (special attitude of joint commitment), John Searle (distinctive mode of intending), and Tuomela himself (irreducible collective action concepts in the content of we-intentions).

Chapter 3, "Reductive Views of Shared Intention," by Facundo Alonso, reviews some of the main reductive positions, by Michael Bratman and Kirk Ludwig, and a prominent interpretation of Tuomela's view as reductive (Tuomela's account interpreted as reductive), which has played a significant role in discussion, though Tuomela has denied it was intended in the spirit in which it has often been taken.

Chapter 4, "Interpersonal Obligation in Joint Action," by Abraham Sesshu Roth changes focus to a different aspect of joint action, the normative relations that hold between individuals in a group who are acting together. On one prominent line of thought, this is the essential glue of joint action. The idea is that there are special sorts of directed obligations to other members of a group with whom one is doing something in virtue of the fact that one is acting together intentionally with them. In recent decades, Margaret Gilbert has championed the idea that the form of obligation is *sui generis*, primitive, and the key to understanding what is special about joint action. Roth's chapter explores a variety of perspectives on what he calls contralateral obligations in joint action. What is their source? What role do they play in joint action? Are they fundamental, or derived?

Chapter 5, "Proxy Agency in Collective Action," looks at a form of group agency that becomes salient in the context of institutional action, in which some individual member of a group, or some proper subgroup, acts on behalf of the group, in a way that licenses saying that the group thereby acts. This prima facie contrasts with cases of informal group action, e.g. rowing an eight-man scull, or carrying a piano upstairs, where it is not the contributions of any one member of the group or a proper subgroup of them that brings about what they do but only their contributions in concert. How is this possible? Ludwig argues that it is possible because what the proxy agent (individual or group) does is given a significance in a social interaction that it could not have absent the group authorizing the relevant agents to act on its behalf in the matter. Proxy agency is pervasive in institutional action and a key component in explaining its flexibility and complexity.

Finally, Chapter 6, "Coordinating Joint Action," by Stephen Butterfill, looks at the empirical work on the psychological and neurophysiological infrastructure of joint action, in cases which require real-time interaction and coordination for success. There are a variety of mechanisms that have been examined which can operate even when agents are not engaged in joint intentional action which facilitate carrying out joint tasks. In entrainment, one or more agents synchronize rhythmic behavior to the same phase, a phenomenon that can occur without its being intended. Motor simulation of others' movement can help one to coordinate one's own with theirs, whether when shaking hands or figure skating. Task co-representation involves two or more agents representing the same task. It may be a joint task that each contributes to. Motor simulation of the co-represented task may then facilitate coordination of their performances when neither takes the lead. It may also be a task which just one is to do, but which the other in co-representing it makes way for, or aids in, the performance of as needed. Collective goal states are representations of collective goals. When they involve motor representations they represent the parts of others as if done by oneself, which may then contribute to correct anticipations of what others do in their roles in the task. Finally, perception of joint affordances is important for many kinds of ordinary joint action. Butterfill suggests that motor representations of collective goals may be part of what makes perception of joint affordances possible.

1

Collective Action and Agency

Sara Rachel Chant

The standard approach to collective action and agency is to take the very best accounts of individual action and agency and simply "collectivize" them. Since the very best accounts of individual action theory depend on an agent's intentions and other mental states, when "collectivized," the result is a collective action theory that depends on *collective* agents that have *collective* intentions and other *collective* mental states. Let us call this collectivizing method the "wash, rinse and repeat" (WRR) approach to collective action theory.

WRR is implicit in virtually every account of collective action and agency. Presumably, this is due to its intrinsic plausibility. After all, collective action and agency are just special cases of action and agency. So if there are collective actions and agents, then what distinguishes them from mere collections of actions and agents would depend on whatever distinguishes actions and agents from non-actions and non-agents more generally.

There are two unfortunate consequences of this approach. First, a unified account of collective action and agency proves challenging because groups are very different from individuals, as well as from each other. Second, the approach creates a dilemma for the metaphysics of collective actions: either there are collective agents, collective actions, collective intentions, and the like, or these concepts are all just convenient shorthand for talk about individuals.

The purpose of this chapter is to call into question the methodological assumption governing the literature and how it is applied. I argue that a particular application of WRR has led to an overly narrow conception of collective action and intention, as well as a correspondingly blunt view of the relationship between collective action and collective agency. Finally, I consider how we might construct a more satisfactory theory of collective action and agency.

1. THE METHODOLOGICAL APPROACH

The study of collective action and agency is governed by a methodological assumption that has been adopted in the philosophical literature with virtually no critical examination. This is the WRR approach to collective action theory. Because WRR enjoys such a high degree of plausibility, it appears never to have been explicitly argued for at all. Its plausibility probably derives from the observation that if one were to propose a theory of collective intention according to which for example collective intentions bore no substantive resemblance to individual intentions, it would not be clear why this was to count as a theory of collective *intention*.

Employing WRR as a method for analyzing group-level concepts such as collective intention is to imply a kind of isomorphism between theories of individual action and theories of collective action. The isomorphism is between the respective sets of individual- and group-level concepts (e.g. "individual agent" and "collective agent"), and the explanatory relationships among them. Taking on WRR is tantamount to assuming that if there is an explanatory relationship between two individual-level concepts, there should be a corresponding pair of collective-level concepts bearing the same explanatory relationship to each other.

As an example from classical 1960's Anscombe–Davidson action theory, recall that what distinguishes individual actions from non-actional events depends on mental states such as belief-desire pairs or intentions (Anscombe 2000; Davidson 2001). In Davidson's example of "sinking the Tirpitz," when the submarine commander causes the Tirpitz to sink, we attribute an action to the commander because there was something he did intentionally. Suppose that the submarine commander intentionally pushed a button, which launched the torpedo, and thereby caused the Tirpitz to sink. The fact that the commander intentionally pushed the button, which thereby brings about the sinking of the Tirpitz is why we say that "bringing about the sinking the Tirpitz," or more colloquially "sinking the Tirpitz," designates an action (Davidson 2001: 46–8). Generalizing this example leads uncontroversially to the following:

> In all cases of *individual* action, something is done *individually* intentionally.

If we follow WRR in our theory of collective action, we are led to the following:

> In all cases of *collective* action, something is done *collectively* intentionally.

The near-universal adoption of WRR explains why collective intention occupies such a central role in the literature on collective action. After all, individual intentions and intentional action are the most important concepts in virtually every analysis of individual action. For those who employ WRR for analyzing collective action, it is practically inevitable that collective intentions and collective action should occupy an equally important place in their analyses.

2. ACTION AND AGENCY

Individual actions depend on intentions and other mental states. But those states are only realized in *agents*. Thus, individual action and agency are also closely linked. In fact,

Alfred Mele (2003) takes the concept of "agent" to be so closely linked to action that a theory of agency is an immediate corollary to a theory of action. Call this the "standard view of agency" (SVA):

(SVA) An agent is nothing more or less than something that acts.

This is a highly plausible view of agency, at least within the domain of individual action and agency. The very idea of a non-agent capable of action, or an agent who is constitutionally incapable of performing any action at all strikes us as not only implausible, but logically contradictory.

WRR, when applied to SVA, implies a "collectivized" version of SVA:

(SVA-C) A collective agent is nothing more or less than a collective that acts.

If we accept SVA-C, then questions concerning the nature of collective agents are settled almost immediately by a theory of collective action. The necessary and sufficient conditions for a group's acting collectively will tell us what it is for a group to be a collective agent, just as a theory of individual action tells us what it is for an individual to be an agent.

Unfortunately, SVA-C faces serious concern owing to the fact that mental states are crucial for understanding individual action and agency. Since mental states are housed in individuals with minds, a straightforward application of WRR entails the existence of collective agents with minds of their own. Since any such requirement could reasonably be taken as a *reductio* of the view, WRR and its first principle, SVA-C, are under serious doubt.

The straightest path through this difficulty is to argue that groups *can* have minds. But such an argument, in order to have any plausibility at all, must employ a highly attenuated sense of "mind." The best example of this approach is Philip Pettit's work on the discursive dilemma in which he argues that groups can be "institutional persons" with "minds of their own" (Pettit 2011, 2007; List and Pettit 2002). This counterintuitive conclusion is supported by the fact that groups can form judgments that are starkly at odds with the judgments of their members. However, the sense of "mind" that Pettit uses is so different from the "mind" of an individual that it is not clear that a "group mind" ought to count as a "mind" at all. As Pettit acknowledges:

> [I]t is consistent, of course, with acknowledging that such institutional persons differ from natural persons in as many ways as they resemble them. As we saw earlier, institutional persons are not centers of perception or memory or sentience, or even of degrees of belief and desire. Institutional persons form their collective minds only on a restricted range of matters, to do with whatever purpose they are organized to advance. And institutional persons are artificial creatures whose responses may be governed by reason, not in the spontaneous manner that is characteristic of individual human beings, but only in a painstaking fashion.
> (Pettit 2011: 188)

So, even on Pettit's theory, "group minds" lack perception, memory, sentience, belief, and desire, which is so far removed from any concept of "mind" that the isomorphism required by WRR and SVA-C is severely diminished. Thus, there remains a tension between two desiderata, rendering analyses of group-level concepts especially difficult:

1. WRR and SVA-C require an isomorphism between group- and individual-level concepts with respect to their explanatory relations.
2. Analyses of these concepts must be extremely different because groups do not have minds or mental states (in any ordinary sense).

In short, whoever accepts WRR and SVA-C must provide an account of how these seemingly "mental" states can be attributed to groups that lack minds.

3. COLLECTIVE MENTAL STATES WITHOUT COLLECTIVE MINDS

Because WRR and SVA-C require attributing mental states (or some group-level correlate of mental states) to groups that do not have minds, advocates of WRR and SVA-C are in a bind. They have to look elsewhere for the mental states required by their methodology. The obvious response to this problem is to look to the individual members of a group, and straightforwardly attribute mental states to those individuals. On this approach, groups have collective intentions largely in virtue of their members' having individual intentions that bear certain relationships to each other. Proponents of this explanatory strategy also add other conditions that vary somewhat among different accounts.

The paradigmatic examples of this approach are the accounts of Michael Bratman (1992, 1993, 2013), Raimo Tuomela (1988, 1991, 1995, 2005), and Margaret Gilbert (1990, 2000, 2009). For example, consider Bratman's definition of so-called "shared intention":

> With respect to a group consisting of you and me, and concerning joint activity, J, we intend to J if and only if: (1) (a) I intend that we J and (b) you intend that we J; (2) I intend that we J in accordance with and because of (1) (a), (1) (b), and meshing subplans of (1) (a), (1) (b); and you intend likewise. (3): (1) and (2) are common knowledge between us.
>
> (Bratman 1992: 333–4)

Bratman's view is an excellent representative of this general approach. According to him, a shared intention is an "interlocking" set of individual intentions that must meet two conditions with respect to their content and their relationships with each other (see Chapter 3).

The first condition is that it is not the case that you and I merely have intentions to do some individual actions that just happen to bring about our J-ing. For example, if we are to have a shared intention to lift a heavy table together, it is not good enough for the content of my intention to be "I shall lift one end of the table." My intention is not merely to do something that is my part of lifting the table. Instead, I intend that *we* lift the table—the content of my intention crucially refers to what we shall accomplish jointly.

In addition, Bratman's account is typical in endorsing what I shall call the "interactive knowledge condition." It states that our individual intentions are public in the sense that each of us knows that the other has the corresponding intention. For Bratman, this condition is iterated so that, for example, I know that you have an intention; you know that I know that you have that intention, and so on. There are disagreements about the exact way to satisfy the interactive knowledge condition. But this condition is required by all theories that identify collective intentions with a structured set of individual intentions (see Chapter 15).

Bratman's account is certainly not the only one to follow this general pattern. Raimo Tuomela analyzes "joint intentions" in terms of each individual possessing the right kind of "we-intention," where we-intentions are related to each other in a specific way (see Chapter 2). Here is a (slightly abbreviated) statement of his view:

> A member Ai of a collective g we-intends to do X if and only if: (i) Ai intends to do his part of X (as his part of X); (ii) Ai has a belief to the effect that the joint action opportunities for an intentional performance of X will obtain . . . (iii) Ai believes that there is (or will be) a mutual belief among the participating members of g . . . to the effect that the joint action opportunities for an intentional performance of X will obtain . . . (iv) (i) in part because of (ii) and (iii).
>
> (Tuomela 2005: 340–1)

Requirement (iii) is Tuomela's version of the interactive knowledge condition. Individuals must have the right "mutual beliefs" about the beliefs of the other members of the group. It is important to point out that Tuomela's notion of a "mutual belief" is what he calls a "loop belief"—not what "mutual belief" means in the technical literature on interactive epistemology (Aumann 1999). Individuals have the "loop belief that p" if everyone believes p, everyone believes that everyone believes p, and so on. In other words, this is just what is standardly known as "common knowledge." Finally, Tuomela agrees with Bratman when he asserts that it is not enough for the individuals to have an intention to perform the actions that could make up a collective action. Rather, they have to possess an intention to do their part *as their part* of the collective action.

4. THE WIDE SCOPE/NARROW SCOPE ASYMMETRY

Theories of collective action relying on group-level correlates of mental states invariably restrict the range of collective action to a very small subset of plausible cases, including moving a table together, going to New York together, awarding someone tenure, building a boat together and so on. The reason analyses are restricted in this way stems from the fact that groups vary considerably. They may be highly organized or totally disorganized. They may involve two agents or two million agents. If the interactive knowledge condition is what ties agents together in lieu of positing group minds, then if that condition were to have purchase in a general theory of collective action, it would have to be flexible enough to accommodate various kinds of groups.[1]

To see the significance of the interactive knowledge condition, let us consider a case in which the group does not have any beliefs about the other agents in the group. In other words, let us consider a case that fails to meet the interactive knowledge condition. For example, imagine a case—call it "Mob"—in which a random mob of protesters suddenly turns violent and destroys a city block. Nearly all theories of collective action would judge that no collective action has been performed.

The argument against such cases counting as collective action falls out of WRR and SVAC straightaway:

1. Collective action requires collective agency.
2. Collective agency requires collective intention.
3. Collective intentions require interactive knowledge.
4. Interactive knowledge requires communication and/or a decision procedure.
5. But disorganized groups have little or no communication and no decision procedure; therefore:
6. No collective action is performed by disorganized groups.

The striking feature of this argument is not the conclusion, but the fact that the first three premises are highly stipulative; they are not the conclusions of arguments. Instead, they are plausible consequences of considering a very restricted range of clear cases of collective action that all happen to display a high degree of deliberate coordination and intentionality. Their support relies on WRR and SVA-C, which are never argued.

Owing to the spontaneous and informal nature of the group in the mob case, standard accounts of collective action will not count it as a case of collective action. This is curious and in stark contrast to the much wider scope of individual action theory, which attempts to distinguish actions—including the most spontaneous actions of individuals—from non-actional events, and this is so even if the "bigger" action is an unintended consequence of actions performed by an individual. So, if mob behavior and other cases of spontaneous group behavior ought not count as collective, then the theory owes us an argument to that effect, not a set of stipulations.

The same claim is made and the same observation holds for cases that are not at all spontaneous. Consider the following example:

> *Bomb Factory.* A factory has been cleverly designed by an evil mastermind who wants to produce bombs. The assembly line requires several workers, who have been deceived into believing that they are each constructing harmless widgets. However, the steps that each worker performs are in fact combined in a clever and subtle way such that it is bombs, not individual widgets, which roll off the conveyor belt at the end of the assembly line.

It is extremely plausible to claim that the workers unintentionally "built bombs" together, and that this is a collective action. After all, their work is highly coordinated, interdependent, requires communication, and so on. But by stipulation, there is no shared intention on the part of any of them to build bombs. Hence, no collective intention to do so; and therefore, no collective action is performed.[2]

A correct theory of collective action and intention may reject Bomb Factory as an example of collective action. But this rejection ought to be the conclusion of an argument, not a definition. In short, existing theories of collective action and intention are far too stipulative. They reject the wide range of plausible cases of collective action too quickly, without providing an argument for doing so.

5. WRR WHAT?

Typically, WRR uses the most basic actions of individuals as its model for collective action, despite the fact that basic actions are the least similar to collective actions. The reason for focusing on basic actions is that these acts help answer the "first problem in action theory": what distinguishes actions from non-actional events (Enç 2003)? If we WRR everything from individual action theory, the first problem in collective action theory is just the question: "what distinguishes collective actions from non-(collective)actional events?" The answer, of course, takes us right back to intentions and other mental states.

Luckily, there are other ways to employ the WRR strategy. Instead of using basic actions of individuals as a model of the collective actions of groups, it is more instructive to think about complex individual actions that have actions as parts. For example, writing a paper, practicing a martial arts routine, taking the Great Danes for a walk, and earning a Ph.D. each comprise more than one component action. Carl Ginet (1990) calls such actions "aggregate actions".

Questions concerning aggregate action are importantly different from questions concerning basic action. The latter concerns the first problem in action theory. But aggregate action concerns the problem of what distinguishes aggregate actions from a mere collection of actions. This is what I call elsewhere "the second problem in action theory" (Chant 2006, 2010). Notice that the second problem in action theory does not consider whether the performance of aggregate action requires a further agent over and above the agent who performed each constituent act. After all, those constituent acts bottom out in basic actions of individuals. And if the SVA is correct, then we have all the agency we need. Thus, a theory of aggregate action does not require a further metaphysics of agency.

If we take *aggregate* action to be the appropriate model for collective action, then it is no longer obvious that a second, "collective agent" must be posited above and beyond the individual agents who are part of the group. Similarly, it should not be a foregone conclusion that a uniquely "collective" form of agency must be present if a collective action is performed, just as there is no uniquely "aggregate" form of agency.

6. COLLECTIVE ACTION AND BROAD SCOPE

So far, it seems that the problem with analyses of collective action and agency is not with the WRR methodology itself, but rather with which form of individual action is being used to WRR. If theories of basic action are used as the model for theories of collective action, then the following methodological assumptions are virtually inevitable:

1. WRR and SVA-C are powerful constraints on any account of collective action and agency. They jointly imply that collective agency is a precondition for collective action.
2. Collective agency is inextricably linked to the ability to form collective intentions. Thus, we are led naturally to the view that collective action requires collective intention.
3. Therefore, an account of collective intention and agency is taken to be the central component of any satisfactory theory of collective action; furthermore:
4. Alleged cases of "collective action" that do not involve collective agency or collective intention are ruled out *a priori*, by stipulation.

If aggregate action is used as a model of collective action, these assumptions are cleared away. The problem is not what distinguishes collective actions from non-actional events. The question is what distinguishes collective actions from a mere collection of actions. Notice that focusing on the second problem in collective action theory is not a post hoc suggestion to sidestep a difficult problem; after all, aggregate actions and collective actions are actions that have actions as parts. Basic and collective action share no non-stipulative similarity.

An important benefit of avoiding these assumptions is that a much broader range of collective actions can be accommodated. Indeed, it is easy to come up with examples of circumstances that are plausible cases of collective action, which fail under traditional accounts to count as collective actions. Such cases may fail to satisfy the requirements of traditional theories for a variety of different reasons. For example:

> *Lost in Paris.* Two friends decide on the spur of the moment to go to Paris. They have no specific plans for where they will stay, or what they'll do when they are in Paris. The friends soon become separated in a crowd, and they are unable to find each other. Each, however, decides that their best bet is to go to the nearest landmark, which happens to be the Eiffel Tower. They are soon reunited.

And consider the following variant of the *Bomb Factory* example:

> *Spy-proof Factory.* Concerned that industrial spies might infiltrate WidgetCo's factory and steal information about their widget assembly process, the assembly line is designed to keep their workers as ignorant as possible. Each knows only the bare minimum necessary to do their part of assembling the widgets. None even know that they are building widgets; workers never see each other or are permitted to communicate. They do not even have an approximate idea of how many workers there are. The workers know nothing except for the simple task that each must perform at their specific station.

In each of the cases I have given so far, the individuals engage in coordinated behavior that intuitively ought to count as "collective action." In *Mob*, the mob destroys a city block despite having no decision procedure; the workers in *Bomb Factory* build bombs despite not intending that their actions should be part of a bomb-building process; in *Lost in Paris*, the friends deliberately reunite even though they had no plan for how to do so; and the workers build widgets in *Spy-proof Factory* despite not knowing anything about the other workers or their overall task. In each of these cases, the agents fail to meet the interactive knowledge condition, but arguably perform a collective action.

7. THE SPECTRUM OF COLLECTIVE ACTION

There is a range of cases of collective action. That range is defined by how much deliberate coordination there is on the part of the individuals who perform the collective action. On one end of the spectrum, we have highly deliberate and carefully coordinated cases of collective action. These are the cases that writers on collective action and agency have typically focused on. They involve participants sharing a common goal, and devising a plan for how to achieve that goal by way of a decision procedure involving communication and deliberation. On the other end of the spectrum, we have spontaneous, less well-structured collective actions. These need not involve a group having a decision procedure. The angry mob is an extreme case. The people in the mob act collectively spontaneously, without deliberating or having a decision procedure for the group. Merely observing the mood and behavior of the other people is enough to initiate mob behavior. The tourists lost in Paris and the widget assembly workers occupy places somewhere between these extremes.

What all of these cases share is that individuals have their own intentions, which somehow bring about coordinated and purposeful behavior on the part of the group. The question that must be answered by a theory of collective action is *how* that coordination is brought about. One way is by having a highly structured group apply a decision procedure to determine what they ought collectively and individually to do. This is an important class of cases. It also happens to be the class in which it is most plausible to attribute collective agency. But it represents only one kind of collective action—indeed, it is an extreme kind of case on the far end of a much broader spectrum.

The analogy to aggregate action is helpful once again. One way that a person can perform an aggregate action is by carefully deliberating about what steps are necessary in order to complete a complex task. For example, "building a rocket ship" designates such an aggregate action. It requires a great deal of planning, and a large number of separate actions must be performed in the right way in order for someone to complete it. Other aggregate actions are much more spontaneous, and do not require such deliberation. They may be habitual, spontaneous, and they may even have component actions that are accidental. Aggregate actions vary along the same spectrum as do collective actions. It would be a mistake to take only the most deliberate cases of aggregate action as genuine examples, and ignore the rest. Similarly, we should not make the same mistake regarding collective action.

8. TOWARD A THEORY OF COLLECTIVE ACTION AND AGENCY

When collective agency is understood to be a non-essential feature of collective action, we can no longer rely exclusively on certain group-level properties when constructing a theory of collective action. We certainly cannot assume that there is a decision procedure for the group as a whole. And it also becomes implausible to require a "group's-eye view" of the situation. One cannot, as Natalie Gold and Robert Sugden (2007) suggest, simply stipulate that the individuals use "team reasoning" to make their decisions from the perspective of the group when deciding what they ought to do. The theory must be thoroughly individualistic if it is to encompass the wide range of cases we actually see. It must explain how the individuals in the group are motivated to do "their part" of (what will be) the collective action.

In other words, a theory of collective action must be essentially *contrastive*, in the following sense. Collective actions take place in the context of a specific kind of choice faced by each member of the group. In a simplified form, this choice is between two actions: c and i. Each action has a potential payoff that is contingent on the actions of the other members of the group. The action c is "cooperative"; that is, its payoff is contingent on the other members performing c. If they do not, then the payoff of c is lower. The "individualistic" action i, on the other hand, has a payoff that is not contingent on the behavior of the others.

We can illustrate this idea with the case of the two friends who are separated from each other in Paris. Let us say that each knows he is capable of having a pretty good time in Paris without his friend. Walking around Paris as a lone tourist is i in this example because it has a payoff that does not depend on what the other friend is doing. But each will have a much more enjoyable time if they are reunited. Hence, going to the Eiffel Tower to look for one's friend is c. It potentially has a higher payoff than i, but that payoff will only be realized if the other person also chooses c.

Each of them will have to decide between i and c by weighing the potential payoffs and risks. The risk is understood to be whatever payoff is lost by choosing c when the other members of the group choose i. More precisely, it is the difference between i's payoff (which does not depend on anyone else's behavior) and c's payoff, given that the other person does not perform c. In this example, it is natural for each friend to try to go to the Eiffel Tower to find the other person because the risk is very low (perhaps even zero)—it is just the loss of a little time in what happens to be a very pleasant location. This is why it is very plausible to suppose that the two friends will be reunited. They will likely be able to act collectively because each person's part of the collective action carries a very low risk and a substantial potential payoff.

A collective action occurs when enough members of a group choose c over i. A theory of collective action must explain *why* this choice will or will not be made. Obviously, explanations of why a specific group cooperated or failed to cooperate in any given situation will vary in important ways. This is consistent with what we recognize about the range of collective actions.

Clearly, a variety of different mechanisms may cause the members of the group to select c over i, thereby bringing about the collective action. Formal decision procedures of the kind that indicate agency are one kind of mechanism. But other mechanisms may be much more informal. And in some cases, the payoff of c is so high compared to i, and the risk is so low, that the collective action is brought about "for free," as it were, without any identifiable coordination mechanism except for the rationality of the individuals. This observation allows us to subsume traditional accounts of collective action and agency under a more general theory, in the following way. Consider the class of high-risk collective actions—cases where the performance of c without the others' also performing c carries an extreme penalty. Ensuring coordination on a high-risk collective action will frequently rely on having a formalized group structure and decision procedure in order to guarantee that the requisite information and incentives are common knowledge within the group. Therefore, high-risk actions are the ones that are more likely to satisfy traditional accounts of collective action and intention. We would also expect groups that regularly face such circumstances to be the ones that are most likely to count as "collective agents." In this way, a more inclusive theory of collective action can accept these specific cases; furthermore, such a theory can explain *why* the group displays the hallmarks of agency.

If we keep to WRR, then we will be led to the view that collective intentions may be present in a much wider range of collective actions, even if there is no "collective agency." This turns out to be a natural position to hold. It is plausible, for instance, to say that the two friends have a collective intention to reunite. If we continue to attribute collective intentions to groups that perform collective actions, then we have to make room for a weaker form of collective intention that encompasses examples such as the angry mob and the factory workers in the spy-proof widget factory.[3] We can embrace a wide range of collective intentions and collective actions, without committing ourselves to implausible accounts of collective agents. This is one of the lessons we learn when we take aggregate action as the appropriate model of collective action. Recall that in aggregate actions, we feel no need to posit an additional agent "above" the one who performs each component action. The same may be true for this wider range of collective action and also for weaker forms of collective intention. There is no contradiction in saying that there can be a collective intention without a collective agent. All the agency required for the collective intention is possessed by the individuals in the group.

REFERENCES

Anscombe, G.E.M. (2000) *Intention*, Cambridge, MA: Harvard University Press.
Aumann, R.J. (1999) "Interactive Epistemology I: Knowledge," *International Journal of Game Theory* 28 (3): 263–300.
Bratman, M. (1992) "Shared Cooperative Activity," *The Philosophical Review* 101 (2): 327–41.
——— (1993) "Shared Intention," *Ethics* 104 (1): 97–113.
——— (2013) *Shared Agency: A Planning Theory of Acting Together*, Oxford: Oxford University Press.
Chant, S.R. (2006) "The Special Composition Question in Action," *Pacific Philosophical Quarterly* 87 (4): 422–41.
——— (2007) "Unintentional Collective Action," *Philosophical Explorations* 10 (3): 245–56.
——— (2010) "Two Composition Questions in Action," in *New Waves in Metaphysics*, London: Palgrave Macmillan.
Chant, S.R. and Ernst, Z. (2007) "Group Intentions as Equilibria," *Philosophical Studies* 133 (1): 95–109.
——— (2008) "Epistemic Conditions for Collective Action," *Mind* 117 (467): 549–73.
Davidson, D. (2001) *Essays on Actions and Events*, Oxford: Oxford University Press.
Enç, B. (2003) *How We Act: Causes, Reasons, and Intentions*, Oxford: Oxford University Press.
Ernst, Z. and Chant, S.R. (2007) "Collective Action as Individual Choice," *Studia Logica* 86 (3): 415–34.
Gilbert, M. (1990) "Walking Together: A Paradigmatic Social Phenomenon," *Midwest Studies in Philosophy*, 15 (1): 1–14.
——— (2000) *Sociality and Responsibility: New Essays in Plural Subject Theory*, Lanham, MD: Rowman & Littlefield Publishers.
——— (2009) "Shared Intention and Personal Intentions," *Philosophical Studies* 144 (1): 167–87.
Ginet, C. (1990) *On Action*, Cambridge: Cambridge University Press.
Gold, N. and Sugden, R. (2007) "Collective Intentions and Team Agency," *The Journal of Philosophy* 104 (3): 109–37.
List, C. and Pettit, P. (2002) "Aggregating Sets of Judgments: An Impossibility Result," *Economics and Philosophy* 18 (1): 89–110.
Ludwig, K. (2007) "Collective Intentional Behavior from the Standpoint of Semantics," *Noûs* 41 (3): 355–93.
——— (2016) *From Individual to Plural Agency: Collective Action 1*, Oxford: Oxford University Press.
Mele, A.R. (2003) *Motivation and Agency*, Oxford: Oxford University Press.
Pettit, P. (2007) "Responsibility Incorporated," *Ethics* 117 (2): 171–201.
——— (2011) "Groups with Minds of their Own," in A. Goldman and D. Whitcomb (eds) *Social Epistemology: Essential Readings*, Oxford: Oxford University Press.
Tuomela, R. and Miller, K. (1988) "We-intentions," *Philosophical Studies* 53 (3): 367–89.
Tuomela, R. (1991) "We Will Do It: An Analysis of Group-Intentions," *Philosophy and Phenomenological Research* 51 (2): 249–77.

——— (1995) *The Importance of Us: A Philosophical Study of Basic Social Notions*, Stanford: Stanford University Press.

——— (2005) "We-intentions Revisited," *Philosophical Studies* 125 (3): 327–69.

NOTES

1. Kirk Ludwig (2007, 2016) circumvents the interactive knowledge requirement by rejecting WRR. According to Ludwig, all collective action sentences can be understood in purely individualistic terms.
2. Bratman et al. will allow that when we act together intentionally we do something unintentionally together as well—that is, what we do intentionally is unintentional under some description. Elsewhere I refer to this as "weakly" unintentional collective action. Here I am suggesting that there are cases in which the group does something together collectively unintentional under every description. I refer to such cases as "strongly" unintentional collective action. See my (Chant 2007) as well as Ludwig's (2007) article, and his recent book (Ludwig 2016) for defenses of these cases.
3. Elsewhere, I have argued for a game-theoretic account that identifies collective intentions with a kind of equilibrium state that supports collective action (Chant and Ernst 2007, 2008; Ernst and Chant 2007).

2

Non-Reductive Views of Shared Intention

Raimo Tuomela

1. INTRODUCTION

This chapter will discuss some of the central currently existing accounts of shared intentions that are available in the philosophical literature on collective intentionality. The focus will be on non-reductive shared intentions, viz. shared intentions that are not individualistically reducible.[1] I will below mainly focus on the non-reductive accounts of shared or joint intention or, more generally, collective intentions by Margaret Gilbert, John Searle, and Raimo Tuomela, who all have defended important accounts of non-reductive shared (or joint) intentions.

What are shared intentions? This is a central question that the above authors are supposed to discuss and indeed do discuss. Another central question that one may expect to be answered is "How do shared intentions function in social contexts?" By functioning, many things can be meant here, most importantly that shared intentions help participants in social activities to coordinate their actions. Below I will largely focus on the aforementioned authors' answers to the first of these two questions.

Before discussing shared intentions, I will briefly indicate what reducibility and non-reducibility amount to in the present context. I will do it partly in terms of supervenience, for supervenience is typically advocated as entailing non-reducibility. Supervenience as such correlates two sets of properties (or states or events, etc.). First, to consider the shared intentions case, there are individual-level mental states held jointly or non-jointly, and second, there are group-level ("holistic" or "collectivistic") states and properties (e.g. group intention, group homogeneity). The correlation in question may depend on conceptual or on nomological factual grounds, broadly speaking. The nomological grounds are typically based on causal laws. To clarify, let B be a set of individualistic properties, e.g. group members' "private" mental states, while A will be a set of group-level properties. Both A and B may contain relational properties, and note that the

25

individualistic properties must not include properties conceptually entailing irreducible group or institutional properties. (See e.g. Tuomela, 2013, chapter 1, for discussion).

We may define generally that a set A (of group-level states or properties) ontologically *supervenes* on a set B of individualistic (viz. "private" individual properties that are not group-dependent) if and only if—either on conceptual or on ontological grounds—for each change in the A-properties (or states) there is some change in the B-properties (or states). Thus, it is necessarily the case that a supervenient group property cannot change without a corresponding change taking place in the participants' (typically group members') relevant individualistic single-agent or multi-agent properties.[2] While the supervenience relation usually is concerned with ontology, it may in some cases hold on conceptual grounds. For instance, group cohesion seems to be an example of this if defined in terms of inter-member attraction. Note that supervenience is compatible with multiple realization or instantiation of a generic group property (e.g. a statement about group cohesion might be satisfied by different kinds of relationships between the members).

As to reduction, we say roughly that the set A of group-level properties is *(either conceptually or ontologically) reducible* to the set B of individualistic properties if the properties in it are respectively definable in terms of the set B or if the best-explaining social theory concerning B-properties entails all the relevant true statements couched in terms of the A-properties. Conceptual reduction may in principle proceed by definition of group-level concepts by means of individualistically acceptable notions. However, because of, for example, the possibility that group-level properties are multiply realized on the individual level, explicit definability may not be possible—it could sometimes result in an indefinitely long disjunction of individualistic realization possibilities. Ontological reduction amounts in epistemic terms to the reduction of an explanatory theory or explanation concerning group phenomena to claims or explanations couched in terms of individualistically acceptable properties. At bottom, ontological reduction may be taken to aim at finding out the fundamental existents of the world. My view is, though, that for the time being there do not seem to be any accounts of shared intentions that are even close to being best-explaining ones and thus approaching truth.

The claims about the generic properties in set A are *(conceptually or nomologically) irreducible* to claims in set B if the best-explaining theory (or account) couched in terms of B-properties does not (conceptually or nomologically) explain all the claims holding true of the A-properties. The set A may contain group-level intentions (intentions of groups or shared intentions presupposing groups). In that case, we are typically dealing with individualistically non-reducible or irreducible shared (or joint) intentions with properties that individual intentions do not have, i.e. shared intentions in these cases are not reducible to individual intentions. Also normatively structured organizations such as business corporations can be viewed basically as (hierarchical) groups of human beings as their parts with the shareholders at the top level.

Groups (including collectively constructed group agents) as social systems (interconnected structures formed out of individuals and their interrelations) seem in many cases to be ontologically *emergent* (viz. involve qualitatively new features as compared with the individualistic basis) and in this sense *irreducible* to the individualistic properties of our common sense framework of agency and persons. As will be argued, already on conceptual grounds collective states are in general not reducible to individualistic states (see Section 5 below).[3]

2. MARGARET GILBERT

Gilbert's "plural subject" theory of collective intentionality that she has been developing in her books and articles since her 1989 book "*On Social Facts*" offers a non-reductive account of shared attitudes including specifically shared intentions. One of her basic ideas is that shared intentions are non-reductive at least in part because they rely on the idea that a shared intention does not require corresponding personal intentions by the participants (see the disjunction criterion below). Perhaps Gilbert would like to say that the "we" in a shared intention case (e.g. "We intend to play a game of tennis today") is non-distributive rather than distributive. (See Gilbert 2009: 168.)

In her 2009 paper, she gives the following three criteria of adequacy for an account of shared intention: the disjunction criterion, the concurrence criterion, the obligation criterion.

As to the *disjunction criterion,* Gilbert proposes this clarification from p. 172: 'An adequate account of shared intention is such that it is not necessarily the case that for every shared intention, on that count, there be correlative personal intentions of the individual parties'. It is somewhat unclear whether some member yet must have it according to this account. Furthermore, in joint action cases the content of such a personal intention can hardly be the same as that of the shared intention involved. The disjunction criterion shows that, if tenable, shared intentions are not reducible to personal intentions, because the latter might not even exist.

The concurrence criterion is this:

> An adequate account of shared intention will entail that, absent special background understandings, the concurrence of all parties is required in order that a given shared intention be changed or rescinded, or that a given party be released from participating in it'.[4]

(Gilbert 2009: 173)

Gilbert's third criterion is the *obligation criterion* (2009: 177): 'An adequate account of shared intention will entail that each party to a shared intention is obligated to each to act as appropriate to the shared intention in conjunction with the rest'.

In Gilbert's account the obligation (a "directed obligation") need not be a moral one, but at least in the 2009 paper no more is said about the underlying ground of the obligation in question than that it is related to Feinberg's idea of owing. For example, if I have the right to your action X then you have the obligation to perform X and owe performing X to me—indeed so that I in a sense own your action X and may rebuke you if you fail to perform X.

Gilbert formulates her *plural subject* account of shared intention as follows (2009: 179): 'Members of some population P share an intention to do A if and only if they are jointly committed to intend as a body to do A'. Accordingly, 'persons X, Y, and whatever particular others share an intention to do A if and only if X, Y, and those other particular others are jointly committed to intend as a body to do A'.

This account seems circular because intending as a body seems clearly to entail shared intention, and thus the present account just adds the joint commitment requirement. Gilbert has discussed plural subjects on several earlier occasions (e.g. in Gilbert 1989).

In her recent account, "plural subject" does not entail the capability to have attitudes or to have subjective experiences but the term refers merely to a set of people jointly committed to some activity. (See Gilbert 2014: Introduction.)

So in her theory there are no plural subjects with consciousness and fully intentional mental states. Her notion of plural subject does not really do more work than joint commitment does. On the other hand, Gilbert's account of collective intentionality strongly depends on the tenability of her account of joint commitment that is ubiquitously present in her accounts of collective intentionality notions.[5] But as the very *jointness* involved in joint commitment is a *collectively intentional* notion, this seems to entail that Gilbert's account is circular in the fundamental sense of her central tool for analyzing collective intentionality being circular. This fact need not destroy her analytic accounts of various collective intentionality notions, for they still seem to function as informative (even if partly circular) *elucidations* of the collectively intentional notions at hand.

3. JOHN SEARLE

In a paper of 1990 Searle presented his first account of we-intentions and in his 2010 book he gives a revised account that I will briefly comment on below. His approach is ontologically individualistic and reductive (see Searle 2010: 47). His view of collective intentionality phenomena is that they are conceptually irreducible but ontologically reducible as, according to him, all intentionality exists in individual human brains. He starts his discussion by offering a general counterexample that should work against all of the attempts to reduce "we-intentionality" (that he also called "collective intentionality") to "I-intentionality" ("individual intentionality"). These kinds of intentionality seem to be only imprecisely linguistically defined in his account. For example, "We will paint the table together" in Searle's account contrasts with "I will paint the table," where the latter intention expression can ambiguously refer either to a pure case of I-intentionality or individualistic intentionality or to a part performance in a joint action and express we-intentionality in a derivative sense.

Searle's counterexample to the reducibility of collective intentionality to individual intentionality concerns an imagined case of Harvard Business School graduates who were taught Adam Smith's theory of the invisible hand. Each of them tries to benefit humanity by being as selfish as he possibly can and by trying to become individually as rich as he can. Searle now emphasizes that no cooperation need take place between the agents, although there is a shared goal and mutual knowledge that it is shared. According to him, this case of shared I-intentionality is not sufficient for collective intentionality. Cooperation is in addition required for collective intentionality in his account. According to Searle's second Business School example, the graduates make a "solemn pact" that they each will try to become as rich as they can and also act as selfishly as they can—in order to help humanity. He claims that in this case there is (a) genuine cooperation and (b) genuine collective intentionality. I will here accept these two claims for weak cooperation and weak collective intentionality, although my we-mode account of cooperation and full collective intentionality requires more (see Section 4 below and my 2007 and 2013 books).

Searle's present argumentation seems somewhat underdeveloped. It does not clarify what the required kind of cooperation amounts to and on what precise grounds it is irreducible. Therefore, one cannot properly evaluate Searle's argument against the reduction of we-intentionality to I-intentionality—which are notions that also require further elucidation. (For a fuller discussion of the above examples, see Searle 2010: 48.)

Searle does not give a detailed analytic account of what we-intentionality and collective intentional states amount to. However, he presents here what is a central idea on which his intuitive view relies: 'There is a ground-floor form of collective intentionality, one that exists prior to the exercise of language and which makes the use of language possible at all'. This seems to me a good idea to work on partly because it does not make language (ontologically) primary for expressing intentionality. See Searle (2010: 50).

To clarify how joint actions may be realized and how shared we-intentions function in that context I will consider a musical example, one similar to that which Searle makes use of. Consider thus you and me playing Beethoven's "Spring Sonata" together, as a duet. Assume that you and I have the we-intention to play the sonata together. This we-intended shared action is our collective goal, call it C. Our means actions are that I play the piano (A) and you play the violin (B). Here is what Searle says of this case (2010: 54):

> I can only cause my piano playing. I have to presuppose your violin playing. Thus for my intentional content we have: ia(intention-in-action) collective C [B in Searle's account] by means of singular A (this ia causes: A piano plays constitutes: C duet is performed).

I also must believe that you participate properly: 'And the corresponding belief . . . is Bel (my partner in the collective also has intentions-in-action of the form (ia collective C by means of singular A (this ia causes: violin plays, constitutes: C duet is performed)))'.

Searle's account assumes that a participant's we-intention does not make essential reference to another participant's intentionality and does not control the other's intentional activity. Yet, while it is right that a person cannot intend what another person intends (e.g. to perform his part of a joint action), he can at least intend to do what is in his power to get the other one to have the intention and to act in accordance with it. For example, he can intend by his actions to contribute to the other one so intending. He even ought to intend so in the context of joint action, and the joint action of duet playing is what we are dealing with here. The participants here are supposed jointly to satisfy their collective intention, and hence they should be engaged in an *interactive joint causal process* purporting to bring about the end result that the duet was jointly played by them on the basis of their joint intention to play the duet.

4. RAIMO TUOMELA

My own account is based on an "I-mode/we-mode" theory of sociality that takes group members' *we-mode joint intention* to be the most central kind of collective intention. In a sense, it mediates between an *intention attributed to a group* and group members' shared *we-intentions*. Although the joint intention consists of we-intentions, the latter depend on the more primitive notion of joint intention.

What are modes of attitudes and actions in my account? Here a mode does not concern the familiar intentional Brentanoan mode which distinguishes between e.g. intending and believing that something is (or is to be) the case. Rather, the we-mode and the I-mode respectively point to a group's background perspective ("we-perspective") and way of entertaining a propositional content and to the individual's "private" (viz. not conceptually group-dependent) perspective and the individualistic way of entertaining a propositional content. (See the "adverbial" account I give on pp. 36–8 of Tuomela (2013) and a discussion of the central criteria of we-mode termed "group reason," "collective commitment" and "collectivity"—see chapter 2 of Tuomela (2013), and below.)[6]

As to joint intention, I take full-blown joint intention to be a strong kind of shared intention, its paradigm form being a *we-mode* joint intention that tightly binds the participants together and under normal conditions leads to "jointly intentional" joint action (action based on joint intention) and not only to shared individual intentional action. Group members' joint intention consists of interdependent member intentions (we-intentions) all of which are also expressible by "We will do X together" by the members. The present expression of intention can thus be used to express we-mode joint intentions that some participants jointly have—the expression can be applied both to you and me considered together and to you and me separately to express our joint intention. Furthermore, in normal circumstances it entails that both you and I intend to participate in our joint performance of X and perform our shares of it.

I have come to regard the notion of *we-mode joint intention as a conceptually primitive* notion, one that is not at least on *a priori* grounds explicitly analyzable in terms of individuals' I-mode mental states, e.g. their shared intentions to perform their parts of the action X. Those shared I-mode intentions need not amount to a joint intention. A joint intention generally is irreducible due to having properties that the individual intentions that form it do not have: Trivially, a joint intention only applies to an n-tuple of individuals $A_1, \ldots A_i, \ldots, A_n$ and is thus a relational predicate contrary to its singular intention "slices." Intentions of groups in general involve joint intentions. As groups capable of having intentions must rationally be capable of acting on them, we are really dealing with a kind of group agents when discussing intentions and actions of groups.

Consider again a group g ("our group"). If we, viz. you and I, jointly intend to perform X together, this requires that you and I, qua members of g, both intend to participate in our joint performance of X for us (qua members of g) while being collectively committed to performing X jointly and, by implication, collectively committed to the process leading to X. You and I mutually know (or correctly believe) all this. That the joint performance of X is an intentional action presupposes in this case that there is a group-based reason consisting of the fact that our group has, typically through our collective acceptance formed the intention to perform X, and thus each participant contributed to X because of the group reason that we (viz. our group) collectively intended to perform X.

To rehash, if the members of a group collectively accept the truth (correctness) of "We will do X together as a group," understood as an expression with the world-to-mind fit, and if the central we-mode criteria of group reason, collectivity, and collective commitment are satisfied, then and only then they jointly intend qua group members in the we-mode to perform X together as a group (see clause (ii) of (WI) below).[7] Given this, the participants get some justification for forming the intention to perform their parts and to actually perform them (clause (i) below). Some doxastic conditions are in addition needed for the account of we-intention below (clauses (iii) and (iv)).

Here is my recent summary account of we-intention:

(*WI*) Member A_i of group g *we-intends* in the we-mode to perform X together as a group with the other members if and only if, given that the we-mode criteria for intending are satisfied (in the sense of WMI of Tuomela 2013: 68),

   (i) A_i intends to participate in the members' ("our") doing X together and to do his part of X as his part of X;

   (ii) A_i truly believes that the group members (including himself) collectively accept "We will do X together as a group" in that context and that thus a joint intention to perform X jointly exists between the participants, and this fact is his main justificatory reason for (i);

   (iii) A_i has a true belief to the effect that the joint action opportunities for an intentional performance of X with some likelihood will obtain, especially that a right number of the full-fledged and adequately informed members of g, as required for the performance of X, will at least with a non-negligible probability perform their parts of X, which under normal conditions will result in an intentional joint performance of X by the participants;[8]

   (iv) A_i truly believes that there is (or will be) a mutual true belief among the participating members of g (or at least among those participants who perform their parts of X intentionally as their parts of X) to the effect that the joint action opportunities for an intentional performance of X will obtain (or at least will obtain with a non-negligible probability);

   (v) (i) and (ii) are in part true because of (iii) and (iv).[9]

(Tuomela 2013: 68–9)

It can be noted that (WI) could equally well serve as an account of joint we-mode intention, for it entails and is entailed by the latter.[10] Clause (ii) in conjunction with (iii) and (iv) gives a *group(-based) reason* for the members to participate in the joint intention and thus to form their part-performance intention and normally to perform their part action.[11] The members thus perform X for the group and are necessarily "*in the same boat*" with respect to X here. This concerns all group affairs, i.e. everything that a group does on purpose, all members functioning as members are in some way affected by or play a role, however small, in the group's activity. This is the basic content of the *collectivity condition*. In the case of, e.g. a group goal, it is necessarily the case that the goal is satisfied for the we-mode group or a group acting as a unit just in case it is satisfied for all members. Similarly, a group's being responsible at least for what it purposively and knowingly causes, every member is to an extent involved and responsible. Or a group's prospering or its having achieved a great victory positively affects the members in the eyes of others, and so on.

As intention entails commitment and, specifically, joint intention entails *collective commitment*, the three central criteria of the we-mode, viz. the group reason, collectivity, and collective commitment conditions, are satisfied and we are thus dealing with a we-mode case.[12]

5. CONCLUSION

The present paper has focused on discussing some prominent philosophical views of non-reductive shared intentions. The philosophers whose views have been discussed in detail are, in this order: John Searle, Margaret Gilbert, Raimo Tuomela. Their approaches are largely different even if they all take shared (or joint) intentions to be individualistically irreducible on conceptual or rational grounds. As to their ontological views, Gilbert's and Tuomela's accounts include collectivistic elements although they can hardly be classified as pure collectivists, at least not ontologically. In any case, they, at least Tuomela's, accept social groups as real entities capable of causally affecting the real world. Searle takes himself to be an ontological individualist in the sense of accepting a version of methodological individualism.

The present account of we-mode joint intentionality relates to a family of rich collective intention notions. It relies on the participants' we-thinking in a strong sense that conceptually requires a rather strong psychological bond between participants, yet a bond that we normally have started to learn, understand, and apply as small children and have come to master as the years go by. The we-mode approach to intentionality gives a foundation for social life in our society that seems needed for the smooth functioning of its institutions and democratic structures on the whole.

ACKNOWLEDGEMENTS

This article owes much to Kaarlo Miller for his excellent points and corrections. I also wish to thank Maj Tuomela for her fine comments on this chapter and for her continuous support of my work.

REFERENCES

Gilbert, M. (1989) *On Social Facts*, London: Routledge.
Gilbert, M. (2009) "Shared Intention and Personal Intention," *Philosophical Studies* 144: 167–87.
——— (2014) *Joint Commitment*, New York: Oxford University Press.
Schmid, H.B. and Schweikard, D. (2013) "Collective Intentionality," *Stanford Encyclopedia of Philosophy*, Palo Alto: CSLI.
Searle, J. (1990) "Collective Intentions and Actions," in P. Cohen, J. Morgan and M. Pollack (eds) *Intentions in Communication*, Cambridge, MA: MIT Press.
Searle, J.R. (2010) *Making the Social World: The Structure of Human Civilization*, Oxford: Oxford University Press.
Tuomela, R. (2007) *The Philosophy of Sociality: The Shared Point of View*, New York: Oxford University Press. (Paperback edition 2010.)
——— (2009) "Collective Intentions and Game Theory," *Journal of Philosophy* CVI: 292–300
——— (2013) *Social Ontology, Collective Intentionality and Group Agents*, New York: Oxford University Press.
——— (2014) "Review of Michael Bratman: 'Shared Agency, A Planning Theory of Acting Together'," *Notre Dame Journal of Philosophical Reviews* August 13. http://ndpr.nd.edu/news/shared-agency-a-planning-theory-of-acting-together/
Tuomela, R. and Miller, K. (1988) "We-Intentions," *Philosophical Studies* 53: 115–37 (first public presentation at the meeting of the American Philosophical Association in Washington in 1985).

NOTES

1. The title of this paper was given to me by the editors of the present volume. Because of the assumption that a view to be presented and discussed below must be non-reductive this leaves out, e.g. the well-known individualistic and reductive account by Michael Bratman, and the same goes for the accounts of Seumas Miller and Kirk Ludwig. Unfortunately, also the recent work by List and Pettit will be ignored because it does not offer a new contribution to our present topic, although it is a major work on group agents and their irreducible features.

2. See e.g. the article "Supervenience" in the *Stanford Encyclopedia of Philosophy*.

3. To comment briefly on Michael Bratman's theory of shared agency, it is an individualistic and explicitly reductive theory. Within it thus no talk about non-reductive shared intentions is feasible, for there is nothing to reduce, given that the setup for reduction in the present discussion has been taken to be the collectivism–individualism scheme where collectivism is supposed to deal not only with individual facts and properties but also with groups and institutions and their properties plus possibly other collective matters. See Tuomela (2014), for my review of his recent 2014 book.

4. Concurrence seems to be a kind of loose counterpart to the kind of group-based *collective* acceptance as for example in my own theorizing (see Tuomela 2013).

5. See Gilbert (2014) for examples.

6. In a recent paper of 2013, Schmid and Schweikard discuss the philosophy of collective intentionality in informative terms. In their comments on collectivity they distinguish—in the case of a collective attitude—between its (i) content, its (ii) intentional "Brentanoan" mode (e.g. that of intending or of believing), and (iii) the subject or holder of the attitude (e.g. a human individual versus a group of individuals).

      See Tuomela (2007, 2013) for my detailed account of these central notions. In my distinction between the we-mode and the I-mode—to be discussed below—a mode is not a Brentanoan mode but rather relates to "groupish" versus individualistic (or "private") ways of having an attitude or of acting.

7. See Tuomela (2007, 2013) for accounts of the aforementioned three central criteria that are argued to be necessary conditions for intentional we-mode mental states, and actions.

8. There is partial circularity here, as we-intention depends on intentional joint action—which in turn depends on joint intention. I have discussed this problem in my earlier work, most recently in Tuomela (2007: 96–8).

9. I have discussed we-intentions in detail already in my 1984 book partly on a Sellarsian basis. An improved account based largely on that account is to be found in Tuomela and Miller (1988), a paper that became a kind of classical account of we-intentions largely because of Searle's criticism of it (in Searle 1990). Perhaps it was in part due to the presentation of the core of the account that led Searle and other later commentators to regard that account as a reductive account, which at least was not the authors' view. Thus, on the very first page, p. 172, of the paper Tuomela and Miller declare that they will give a non-reductive Sellarsian account of we-intentions. None of the discussions of the paper that I have seen has commented on the content from this point of view. I have elsewhere, especially in Tuomela (2009), tried to show why many commentators went wrong.

10. The accounts of collective intention notions of mine referred to in the present paper may not be fully realistic because they might seem to require reflective conscious attendance by the participating agents, assumed to be normal adult human beings. However, as long as for example joint intentions serve their main purpose of leading to joint action, it suffices that the participants function subconsciously rather than fully consciously and reflectively toward the various conditions in the accounts.

11. A *main reason* can be regarded as one that is sufficient for the intention in question if considered alone, absent countervailing factors.

12. Collective commitment in my account is my counterpart to Gilbert's notion of joint commitment. I find it to be a more convenient term to use especially in the case of large organized groups.

Reductive Views of Shared Intention

Facundo M. Alonso

Joint action is pervasive among us. We carry a piano upstairs, dance the tango, paint a house together, go for a walk together, and prepare hollandaise sauce together. Joint action is also something we value or care about—both intrinsically and instrumentally. We enjoy going for a walk together and preparing hollandaise sauce together; and we carry a piano upstairs together and paint a house together because we find it difficult to achieve the intended results on our own. But what is it for us to act together? Philosophers agree that joint action is not simply an aggregation of acts by individuals, however coordinated. People can be acting individually in a coordinated way—acting in parallel, as we might say—but still not be acting jointly in a proper sense. The difference is often illustrated by reference to contrast cases (Tuomela and Miller 1988; Searle 1990; Gilbert 1992, 2000; Bratman 2006, 2014). Consider one suggested by Michael Bratman (2006). Imagine that you and I are walking together down Fifth Avenue. Now contrast this with a case in which I am walking down Fifth Avenue alongside a stranger and in which the stranger and I are walking at the same pace, without bumping into each other. Both cases involve a sequence of individual, coordinated acts. Yet, it is intuitively clear that the case of you and I walking down Fifth Avenue constitutes an instance of joint action, while the case of my walking alongside a stranger does not. It is usually inferred from this that the mark of joint action does not reside solely in its external or behavioral component. It resides also, and more fundamentally, in its internal component, in the participants' having a *shared* (or *collective* or *joint*) intention to so act.

We may distinguish between two opposing views of shared intention: reductive views and non-reductive views. For the sake of consistency, here I follow the conceptualization of such a distinction introduced in Chapter 2 of this volume. Reductive views assert that shared intention is best understood in terms of the properties and concepts already available in our understanding of individual intention and action, while non-reductive views deny this. Our concern in this chapter is with the former views. In what follows I consider key aspects of three main reductive views of shared intention: those offered, respectively, by Raimo Tuomela and Kaarlo Miller (1988),[1] Michael Bratman (1993, 1997, 2006, 2009, 2014), and Kirk Ludwig (2007b, 2016).

According to Tuomela and Miller, one of the features that distinguishes the intention of a group concerning a group's activity—that is, shared intention—from the intention of an individual concerning his own activity is that only the former involves relevant "we-attitudes" on the part of individuals, that is, attitudes of individuals that make (purported) reference to the other individuals in the group (1988: 367). Among such we-attitudes we find not only cognitive attitudes of individuals, such as (mutual) beliefs about each other's future actions. We find also, and perhaps more importantly, relevant conative attitudes of individuals, such as intentions of individuals (1988: 370). Rival approaches to joint action—including game-theoretic approaches—are unsatisfactory, the authors claim, insofar as they fail to acknowledge the relevance of conative "we-attitudes" for shared intention and action (1988: 371–2).

In Tuomela and Miller's view, shared intention involves, principally, attitudes of "we-intention" on the part of individuals. An individual's we-intention is a complex attitude that includes both conative and cognitive elements. Basically, the authors analyze "we-intention" thus: (WI) an individual we-intends to do X—where X is the joint activity— if and only if (i) he intends to do his part of X (as his part of X); (ii) he believes that the other members of the group will do their parts of X; and (iii) he believes that there is a mutual belief among the members of the group that each will perform his part of X (1988: 375). (For discussion of the role of mutual belief and of common knowledge in the context of shared agency, see especially Chant and Ernst (2008) and Blomberg (2016).) Suppose, following an example by John Searle (1990), that you and I have a shared intention to prepare hollandaise sauce and that you will contribute to it by pouring in the ingredients and I will contribute by stirring them. It follows from Tuomela and Miller's view that each of us we-intends to prepare hollandaise sauce—where my so we-intending involves my intending to stir the ingredients (as my part in our preparing hollandaise sauce) and my believing both that you will pour the ingredients and that there is a mutual belief between us that you will pour and I will stir; and similarly for your we-intention.

It is important to highlight some central aspects of Tuomela and Miller's analysis (WI). First, a we-intention has as its content "the full social action," X (1988: 375)—where the concept of joint action that figures in that content 'is understood . . . without reference to the notion of we-intention' (Tuomela 1990: 10). For Tuomela and Miller this conception of the content of a we-intention finds support in our ordinary attributions of intentions to participants in joint action since, they think, it captures the intuition that a participant in joint action will accept the locution "We will do X," rather than merely that of "I will do my part of X," as adequately describing his attitude. Second, clause (i) of (WI) represents the conative aspects of we-intending. By postulating that the we-intending agent "intends to do his part of X as his part of X" the authors mean that such an agent not only intends to do his part of X, but also has the "goal (purpose) that X will be performed" (Tuomela and Miller 1988: 376; Tuomela 2005: 357). Thus, on this view an agent's we-intention involves two conative elements: a strong commitment (intention) to doing his part in the joint activity, and a weaker commitment (goal) to the joint action's coming about. The former attempts to capture the idea that the joint action will come about only if each participant does his part in it and that a robust commitment of each to doing his part is necessary to secure this. The latter is motivated by the thought that the absence of some type of commitment, however weak, to the joint action's coming about is incompatible with joint intention and action, as when a violinist intends to play his part in a symphony but nonetheless acts with the intention of ridiculing the visiting conductor and with no concern as to whether the joint performance comes about (Tuomela and Miller 1988: 376). Clause (i) of Tuomela and Miller's analysis (WI) raises, however, a few questions. What does support the cited asymmetry in commitment of an individual in shared intention to the joint action and to his part in it? Is an individual's commitment to the joint activity in shared intention better conceived of in terms of the notion of a goal than in terms of that of an intention? In particular, is an individual's goal that the joint action comes about a robust enough attitude to facilitate the forms of interpersonal coordination characteristic of shared intention? For example, does it exert rational pressure on, and correspondingly dispose, such individual to eschew other options for action that are believed to be incompatible with the joint action's coming about? (cf. Bratman's alternative conception below. On the general distinction between intention and goal, see especially Bratman (1987) and Velleman (1997).) Third, clauses (ii) and (iii) of Tuomela and Miller's analysis of we-intention (WI) establish "cognitive presuppositions" on we-intending. Tuomela and Miller's idea is basically that in order for a participating agent to be able to form the intention cited in (i), he must have the beliefs cited in (ii) and (iii). Tuomela and Miller describe such beliefs as "conceptual preconditions" for we-intention (Tuomela and Miller 1988: 374, 377), although in later work Tuomela regards them as "minimal rationality conditions" for this attitude (2005: 329–30). This raises the question of whether Tuomela is here conflating too seemingly different issues: metaphysical (or conceptual) conditions for we-intention with normative (or rational) conditions for it.

Other reductive views in the spirit of Tuomela and Miller's have been offered as well. Seumas Miller (2001), for example, agrees that the conative profile of an individual who participates in a joint action X includes his intending to do his part in X and his having X as his goal or—as he puts it—his "collective end." However, Miller sees the connection between such intention and end of an individual as being tighter than Tuomela and Miller seem to assume. An individual intends to do his part of X, Miller asserts, 'because' or 'for the reason that' he has the joint action X as his 'collective end' (2001: 65, 73–4). Miller thinks that capturing this feature in a reductionist account of shared intention allows the latter to respond to several objections that have been levelled against it— including the objection mentioned immediately below. For other views in the spirit of Tuomela and Miller's, see Cohen and Levesque (1991) and Kutz (2000).

Searle (1990) advances one of the most challenging objections to Tuomela and Miller's analysis of we-intention (WI). The challenge concentrates on their appeal to the notion of an individual's "doing his part" in the joint action that figures in such an analysis— although it can generalize to other reductive proposals. If we take this notion to mean, as the authors themselves suggest, "doing his part toward achieving the *collective* goal," Searle says, we will be introducing an element of circularity in the analysis, for we will have included the notion of we-intention in the notion of "doing his part" (Searle 1990: 405 (his emphasis)). On the contrary, if we interpret the cited notion as not making reference to a collective goal, Searle argues, the analysis will be too weak. For there are cases that satisfy the conditions established for we-intentions (clauses (i)-(iii)) thus interpreted, but intui- tively no genuine we-intention exists on the part of individuals (Searle 1990: 404–5). Either way, Searle concludes, Tuomela and Miller's analysis fails. (Tuomela responds to Searle in later work by taking the first horn of the proposed dilemma and by stressing that his earlier account with Miller was not intended as a reductive account. See the discussion in Chapter 2, this volume; see also Tuomela (2005: 355–61; 1995: 427–8, note 6).)

Searle contends that we cannot analyze—as he interprets Tuomela and Miller (1988) attempt to do—an individual's we-intention in terms of, as he puts it, "I-intentions," that is, intentions expressible in the form "I intend to do such-and-such," even when such intentions are supplemented with beliefs about the other individuals' participation in the joint activity (Searle 1990: 404). The reason such reductive analyses fail, Searle maintains, is that the notion of we-intention "implies the notion of cooperation" (1990: 406), whereas the notions of I-intention and of belief involved in the purported analyses need not. This leads Searle to propose instead a non-reductive view of the mental component of joint action and of "we-intention" in particular. According to Searle, a we-intention is a biologically primitive phenomenon in the mind of an individual that involves a commitment to cooperate with others to achieve a goal in a way in which I-intentions plus relevant beliefs need not (Searle 1990: 406). We-intending, Searle maintains, is a "special" kind of intending (1990: 402), distinct from I-intending. We-intentions and I-intentions are thus in Searle's view intentions of different kinds (or "modes"). Searle's non-reductive view involves several complexities and raises many interesting questions, but these are not the object of discussion in this chapter (for discussion, see Chapter 2, this volume). That being said, it is important to mention here a particular worry this view has given rise to. This is that not enough has been said to establish that we-intentions are indeed intentions of a kind different from ordinary I-intentions. Thus, as Chris Kutz has put it, Searle's introduction of we-intention as a new item in our ontology of mental states 'invites charges of proliferating intentional kinds, charges that methodological parsimony encourages us to try to avoid' (Kutz 2000: 3; see also Ludwig 2007a: 58, 61; Bratman 2014: 105–6).

Bratman proposes an alternative reductive view of shared intention that attempts to give an answer to Searle's challenge that reductive views are either too weak or circular, and that also differs in many ways from Tuomela and Miller's view. To understand the main aspects of Bratman's view, it is imperative to locate it within the framework of the author's "planning" theory of intention of an individual. According to Bratman's theory, individual (future-directed) intending or "planning" is at the heart of human agency, insofar as it plays some central characteristic *roles* in one's practical thought and action (Bratman 1987). A distinctive role of intention, Bratman maintains, is to help organize and coordinate one's actions both over time and interpersonally. Intention plays this role in virtue of involving a twofold commitment to action that other conative attitudes, such as desire, normally lack (1987: 15–18, 108–9). First, one's intending to do something involves a disposition to "settle" or "control" what one is going to do: if one intends to perform an action, and one's intention persists until the time of action and nothing interferes, one will proceed to execute it then. Second, intending to perform an action disposes one to take the cited action as a fixed point in one's deliberations and to reason in certain ways. In particular, it disposes one to avoid reconsidering one's intention in the absence of new and significant information, to form further intentions about how to execute one's intended end, and to eschew from deliberation options believed to be incompatible with one's intention. It is one of Bratman's fundamental ideas that such dispositions to reasoning are responsive to or guided by, associated norms of intention rationality such as intention stability, means-end coherence of intentions, and intention consistency.

Bratman contends that in parallel with individual intending, the mark of a group of individuals' shared intention resides in the roles this latter phenomenon typically plays in such individuals' practical reasoning and action, in pursuit of their joint activity (cf. Gold and Sugden (2007: 137) on the alternative claim that the mark of shared intention lies instead in the "mode" of practical reasoning, "team reasoning," by means of which the former is formed; see also Pacherie (2013)). Return to our shared intention to prepare hollandaise sauce together. According to Bratman, our shared intention to prepare hollandaise sauce will typically play three main interrelated roles. First, it will help us coordinate our individual actions: one of us will pour in the ingredients, for example, and the other will stir them. Second, our shared intention will help us coordinate our associated planning—for instance, if I plan to buy the ingredients but not to gather the necessary utensils, I will make sure that you plan to do the latter. Third, our shared intention will provide a background framework that can structure forms of bargaining and deliberation between us about how we will perform the joint activity—say, about what recipe we will follow, and so on. Bratman's idea is that our shared intention will typically play such trio of interrelated roles in ways that lead to our successfully making hollandaise sauce together. When an individual agent intends to perform an action, Bratman claims, she commits to future conduct in ways that help organize, coordinate, and unify her agency over time. Much in the same way, Bratman suggests, when we share an intention to act together we commit to future conduct in ways that help organize, coordinate, and unify our joint intentional agency (Bratman 1993: 112).

It is a key thesis of Bratman's theory that shared intention reduces to—or is realized by—a complex structure of attitudes of individuals and that it is in virtue of this structure of attitudes that such a phenomenon plays the aforementioned trio of roles. For Bratman this complex structure involves, mainly, (a) intentions of each individual in favor of the joint activity itself—where the latter is understood in a way that is neutral with respect to shared intentionality (see, also, Alonso (2009); cf. Ludwig (2007b, 2016) and discussion below). When you and I share an intention to prepare hollandaise sauce together, I intend that we prepare the sauce and you intend that we prepare the sauce. In Bratman's view, an intention in favor of the joint activity is not, unlike Searle's we-intention, a special type of intention. It is, rather, an ordinary intention of an individual. Nor is it, in contrast to Tuomela and Miller's view (1988), an intention in favor of the joint activity only in name—i.e. one that reduces in the end to, among other things, an individual's intention to do his part in the joint activity and a goal of his that the joint action comes about. According to Bratman, what an individual intends in shared intention is, strictly speaking, the joint activity itself. Furthermore, Bratman argues that in shared intention such intentions of individuals are interconnected in complex ways: inter alia, (b) such intentions are "reflexive" and "interlocking" (each intends that both his own intention and the intention of the other be effective); (c) they track the compatibility (or "meshing") of lower-level intentions (or "subplans") of each concerning ways of carrying out the joint activity; (d) they are based on the belief that the intention of each will persist so long as the other's intention persists as well—that is, that the intentions of each are "persistence interdependent"—and that if such intentions persist, they will lead to joint action; (e) they are, in fact, persistence interdependent; and (f) the cited structure of intentions (a)–(e) is common knowledge between the individuals (Bratman 1993: 117–20; Bratman 2014: ch. 2–3).

But how does the cited structure of attitudes play the characteristic trio of roles of shared intention? Bratman's answer involves three basic steps. First, Bratman says, we start by noting that shared intention involves intentions of individuals, intentions with the cited special contents and interconnected in the aforementioned ways. Then, we note that these intentions are, after all, ordinary intentions of individuals, and as such, are subject to norms of intention rationality such as intention stability, means-end coherence, and intention consistency (cf. Roth (2003) on the relevance of alternative norms of "practical intersubjectivity" for shared intention). Finally, Bratman observes, we note that such norms of intention rationality exert pressure on those intentions of individuals— intentions with such contents and so interconnected—in ways that lead to the coordination of action and of planning, and to appropriate bargaining and deliberation, in pursuit of the joint activity (Bratman 1993: 122–5; 2014: ch. 4). Thus, we may read certain aspects of Bratman's view—mainly, his arguments in favor of conditions (a)–(f) being sufficient for shared intention and his appeal to a notion of intending the joint activity that is neutral with respect to shared intentionality—as providing an answer to Searle's challenge to reductive views, mentioned above.

Bratman's planning theory of shared intention is plausibly the most elaborate and comprehensive view of the phenomenon on offer. However, this has not precluded critics from raising several objections to it. One line of objection centers on Bratman's idea that an individual may intend a joint activity, that is, the activity of a group. Some have wondered whether appeal to this idea does not in the end bring in a criticizable form of circularity to the view (Petersson 2007; cf. Kutz 2000). Others have argued that the cited idea is incoherent, since it violates one or another essential condition on intending. For some, the cited condition is that one may only intend one's own actions (Stoutland 1997, 2002; Roughley 2001; cf. Baier 1970); for others, the condition is that one may only intend what one takes oneself to "settle" (Velleman 1997) or "control" (Baier 1997). (See also Schmid (2008); Roth (2014); For discussion of this latter condition as applied to intentions in general, see Alonso (forthcoming)). Yet, others have wondered how intentions in favor of a joint activity could ever be formed (Roth 2004: 373–80). If, as Bratman suggests, my intention that we act is truly interdependent with yours, how can I (reasonably) form my intention before you have formed yours, and how can you (reasonably) form yours before I have formed mine? (cf. Velleman's (1997) conceptualization of the interdependence of such intentions in terms of conditional intentions.) Another line of objection to Bratman's theory holds that it is psychologically too demanding—and, therefore, unnecessary—to suppose that the attitudes of individuals in shared intention are characteristically interconnected in the complex ways the theory describes (See especially, Miller 2001; Tollefsen 2005; Pacherie 2011; Butterfill 2012). Bratman responds to most of the aforementioned objections in Bratman (1997, 2014).

Questions about Bratman's view still remain. Some, for example, have to do with Bratman's later conception (1997, 2014) of the structure of interrelated intentions above, (a)–(f), as being only *sufficient*—rather than necessary and sufficient, as originally suggested (Bratman 1993)—for shared intention. One question here is whether Bratman's identification of one—though, perhaps important—realization of shared intention among many is enough to support his claim to the "primacy of intention" for shared intention, that is, the claim that "intentions . . . are at the heart of the coordination and organization" distinctive of this phenomenon (Bratman 2014: 29). Another related question is whether Bratman's general planning theory of intention does not commit us to a view in which intentions of individuals—albeit, not necessarily intentions of individuals in favor of the joint activity itself—are in fact *necessary* for shared intention. As mentioned above, according to Bratman's theory an individual's intention plays distinctive roles in his practical thought and action, that is, roles that cannot be played by a combination of other attitudes of that individual, including his relevant desires and beliefs (Bratman 1987). But, then, it might be asked, how could shared intention play analogous distinctive roles in the individuals' thought and action in pursuit of a joint activity, according to Bratman's theory of intention, if it did not involve relevant intentions on the part of (at least some of) them? Finally, there is a question as to whether it is a limitation of Bratman's approach that it concentrates on attitudes and interrelations that are only sufficient for shared intention, as this does not seem to offer a principled way of separating out attitudes and interrelations that are essential to this phenomenon from those that are contingently associated with it. For further recent discussion of Bratman's work, see Ludwig (2015), Pacherie (2015), Petersson (2015), Roth (2015), Smith (2015), and Bratman (2015).

Ludwig offers, and has recently elaborated on, a yet different reductive view of shared intention (2007b, 2016). Although Ludwig regards his own view as broadly in the spirit of Bratman's (2016: 231, 271–2), his methodological approach for investigating shared intention differs dramatically from Bratman's. Whereas Bratman's strategy is to theorize about shared intention by reference primarily to the functional roles that this phenomenon plays in the individuals' thought and action, Ludwig's strategy is to investigate it mainly by analyzing the logical form of the sentences that we ordinarily use to express our thoughts about it—sentences such as "We intend to prepare hollandaise sauce." Ludwig thinks that ordinary language represents the contours of the phenomenon of shared intention in a fairly accurate way and also captures what is distinctive about it (Ludwig 2016: 6–7).

According to Ludwig, conceptual analysis of such sentences indicates that a group of individuals shares an intention to perform a joint action if and only if each individual in the group "we-intends" that the group perform such an action (Ludwig 2016: 191). But what does a we-intention amount to in Ludwig's view? Like Bratman, but unlike Searle, Ludwig thinks that "what is special about [we-intention] is to be sought in its content rather than mode" (Ludwig 2016: 182). In Ludwig's view, for me to we-intend that we prepare hollandaise sauce is for me to intend that we prepare hollandaise sauce in accordance with a "shared plan"—where this is, more precisely, for me to have

> an intention whose content is that that very intention bring it about in accordance with a plan [I] associate[e] with [my] intention at the time of action (that is, with [my] intention-in-action) that [I am] the agent of an event which is our coming to [prepare hollandaise sauce] by way of a shared plan.
>
> (Ludwig 2016: 201)

In this way, Ludwig explains, my we-intention that we prepare hollandaise sauce is an intention directed both at my doing my part in and at my contributing to our preparing hollandaise sauce together, in accordance with a shared plan (2016: 201) (cf. Bratman's conception of the relevant intentions of individuals as directed solely at the joint activity and Tuomela and Miller's as involving both an intention directed at one's part in the joint activity and a goal directed at the joint activity itself).

The idea that the joint action I we-intend be brought about *in accordance with a shared plan* is crucial to Ludwig's conception of we-intention. By "plan" Ludwig means basically a recipe for action, involving typically 'a series of actions carried out in a particular order with the goal of thereby bringing about an event or state of affairs' (2016: 213). (cf. Bratman's distinction between two uses of "plan," respectively, as a recipe or abstract procedure for achieving a goal, and as basically the mental state of intending (1987: 28–9). While Bratman uses "plan" in the latter sense, Ludwig does it in the former.) In addition, Ludwig notes, the shared plan component that figures in the content of a we-intention is specifically for bringing the joint action about, and it includes an assignment of roles (however specified) pertinent to its implementation (2016: 201–2). Further, the cited plan is a *shared* plan, Ludwig explains, in that each individual in the group has basically the same plan for joint action—where sameness of plan admits of some discrepancy concerning specific details, usually about the other's part (2016: 214–15). (Thus, Ludwig's "shared plan" does not pick out the same phenomenon that our usual talk of "shared intention" does, namely, the intention of a group.)

Ludwig sees the shared plan component of a we-intention as helping secure two features of joint intentional action. First, the existence of such a component in the content of a we-intention helps ensure that the joint action is brought about "in the right way" (2016: 214). Second, and relatedly, it captures an element of interpersonal coordination essential to joint intentional action. (See Ludwig's discussion of the parallel with Bratman's appeal to "meshing subplans" in the contents of intentions of individuals (2016: 250–4)). This has important consequences according to Ludwig. Once we acknowledge the relevance of the shared plan component of a we-intention, Ludwig claims, we realize that the condition of "openness" or mutual belief commonly attributed to shared intention and action is not essential to them. Nor, Ludwig adds, is the condition of believing that the others (will) intend likewise and/or do their parts essential to an individual's we-intention, either (2016: 194–7, 219–21). Imagine a context of high uncertainty and absence of communication between the members of a group. In such a context, Ludwig exemplifies, each member in the group may intend to do his part in a joint activity, and carry out that intention, in accordance to a pre-arranged shared plan, not believing but yet 'hoping that there are still others who are doing their parts, however unlikely it may seem . . . and so they [may act] together, according to their pre-arranged plan, and . . . do so intentionally' (2016: 221; see also Ludwig 2007b: 387–8). Ludwig's rejection of such cognitive conditions on shared intention thus sets an important contrast with the aforementioned reductive views (and with many non-reductive views as well).

Ludwig's account (2016) is novel and complex, and deserves careful discussion. Here are two issues that invite further exploration. First, it might be insisted, Ludwig's claims notwithstanding, that shared intention necessarily involves some cognitive interdependence between the attitudes of individuals—usually in the form of (mutual) knowledge, beliefs, or assumptions about each other's intentions and the like. For one thing, it might be argued, such cognitive interdependence allows individuals to coordinate their thought and action in ways characteristic of shared intention, for it allows each of them to plan and act on the assumption that the others have the right attitudes and will perform the right actions when the time comes (cf. Hobbs's (1990) critical remarks on Searle's (1990) view). Alternatively, it might be suggested, it is not clear that mere intentions on the part of each individual that they act in accordance with what is in fact the same plan for joint action will provide such a basis for coordination, independently of any cognitive stance such individuals may take with respect to each other's intentions. You and I may in fact each intend that we prepare hollandaise sauce in accordance with a plan for joint action and this turns out to be the same plan, but if none of us believes or assumes that such facts obtain, how can they serve as a relevant basis for coordination? Second, and relatedly, it might be wondered whether Ludwig's conception of shared intention does not involve a cognitive dimension after all. For Ludwig's talk of "hope" in the context of the aforementioned example leaves open the possibility that an individual's we-intention be necessarily framed by a cognitive attitude about the others' relevant intentions and eventual actions, a cognitive attitude that need not be belief. (In relation to this, I have argued that cognitive attitudes subject to less stringent evidential standards, such as the attitude of reliance (Alonso 2014, 2016a), might be better suited to play the role of cognitively framing the intentions of individuals in shared intention (Alonso 2009, forthcoming).)

Critics have also raised worries about reductive views of shared intention in general. Some have argued that neither shared intention in general nor intentions of individuals in particular are necessary to produce joint action, and instead that functionally more limited, and psychologically less demanding, structures of attitudes and relations ("shared goals") may do the relevant motivational work (Butterfill 2012; for discussion, see Blomberg 2014). Others, most notably Margaret Gilbert, have noted that shared intention is tightly connected to interpersonal obligations and practices of holding accountable, and have argued that reductive views cannot appropriately account for such connections (Gilbert 2000, 2009). For responses to these worries, see Bratman (2014) and Ludwig (2016). For two different attempts to combine psychological elements with elements of interpersonal normativity into an account of shared intention, see Roth (2004, 2014) and Alonso (2009, 2016b).

There are interesting open questions for the aforementioned reductive views of shared intention. Views such as Tuomela and Miller's (1988) as well as Bratman's have focused mainly on cases of shared intention involving very few individual participants (typically two), and taking place in a context in which authority relations and significant differences in power between such individuals are absent. It is a vexed question what modifications those views will have to undergo, if any, to accommodate more complex cases of shared intention involving a large number of participants, authority relations, and so forth. For discussions of how an account in the spirit of Tuomela and Miller's view might be extended to cover complex cases, see Kutz (2000) and Miller (2001) (cf. Tuomela's extension of his own, later non-reductive view of shared intention (2007).) For discussion of the prospects for extending Bratman's view, see Shapiro (2014). Ludwig (2014) explores some of these issues.

ACKNOWLEDGEMENTS

Thanks to Olle Blomberg, Michael Bratman, and Kirk Ludwig for valuable comments and suggestions on earlier drafts.

RELATED TOPICS

Collective Action and Agency (Ch. 1), Non-Reductive Views of Shared Intention (Ch. 2), Interpersonal Obligation in Joint Action (Ch. 4), Proxy Agency in Collective Action (Ch. 5), Coordinating Joint Action (Ch. 6), Joint Commitment (Ch. 10), Common Knowledge (Ch. 14), Team Reasoning (Ch. 17).

REFERENCES

Alonso, F. (2009) "Shared Intention, Reliance, and Interpersonal Obligations," *Ethics* 119: 444–75.

—— (2014) "What is reliance? *Canadian Journal of Philosophy* 44: 163–83.

—— (2016a) "Reasons for Reliance," *Ethics* 126: 311–38.

—— (2016b) "A Dual Aspect Theory of Shared Intention," *Journal of Social Ontology* 2: 271–302.

—— (forthcoming) "Intending, Settling, and Relying," in D. Shoemaker (ed.) *Oxford Studies in Agency and Responsibility*. Volume 4. New York: Oxford University Press.

Baier, A. (1970) "Act and Intent," *The Journal of Philosophy* 67: 648–58.

—— (1997) "Doing Things with Others: The Mental Commons," in L. Alanen, S. Heinämaa, and T. Wallgren (eds) *Commonality and Particularity in Ethics*, New York: St. Martin's Press, Inc., pp. 15–44.

Blomberg, O. (2014) "Shared Goals and Development," *Philosophical Quarterly* 65: 94–101.

—— (2016) "Common Knowledge and Reductionism About Shared Agency," *Australasian Journal of Philosophy* 94: 315–26.

Bratman, M. (1987) *Intention, Plans, and Practical Reason*, Cambridge MA: Harvard University Press.

—— (1993) "Shared Intention," reprinted in *Faces of Intention*, Cambridge: Cambridge University Press, 1999, pp. 109–29.

—— (1997) "I Intend that We J," reprinted in *Faces of Intention*.

—— (2006) "Dynamics of Sociality," *Midwest Studies in Philosophy* 30: 1–15.

—— (2009) "Modest Sociality and the Distinctiveness of Intention," *Philosophical Studies* 144: 149–65.

—— (2014) *Shared Agency: A Planning Theory of Acting Together*, New York: Oxford University Press.

—— (2015) "Shared Agency: Replies to Ludwig, Pacherie, Petersson, Roth, and Smith," *Journal of Social Ontology* 1: 59–76.

Butterfill, S. (2012) "Joint Action and Development," *Philosophical Quarterly* 62: 23–47.

Chant, S.R and Ernst, Z. (2008) "Epistemic Conditions for Collective Action," *Mind* 117: 549–73.

Cohen, P.R. and Levesque, H.J. (1991) "Teamwork," *Noûs* 25 (4): 487–512.

Gilbert, M. (1992) *On Social Facts*, Princeton: Princeton University Press.

—— (2000) *Sociality and Responsibility*, Lanham, MD: Rowman & Littlefield.

—— (2009) "Shared Intention and Personal Intention," *Philosophical Studies* 144: 167–87.

Gold, N. and Sugden, R. (2007) "Collective Intentions and Team Agency," *Journal of Philosophy* 104: 109–37.

Hobbs, J.R. (1990) "Artificial Intelligence and Collective Intentionality: Comments on Searle and on Grosz and Sidner," in P. Cohen, J. Morgan, and M. Pollack (eds) *Intentions in Communication*, Cambridge, MA: MIT Press, pp. 445–59.

Kutz, C. (2000) "Acting Together," *Philosophy and Phenomenological Research* 61: 1–31.

Ludwig, K. (2007a) "Foundations of Social Reality in Collective Intentional Behavior," in S.L. Tsohatzidis (ed.) *Intentional Acts and Institutional Facts*, Dordrecht: Springer.

—— (2007b) "Collective Intentional Behavior from the Standpoint of Semantics," *Noûs* 41: 355–93.

—— (2014) "Proxy Agency in Collective Action," *Noûs* 48: 75–105.

—— (2015) "Shared Agency in Modest Sociality," *Journal of Social Ontology* 1: 7–15.

—— (2016) *From Individual Agency to Plural Agency: Collective Action 1*, Oxford: Oxford University Press.

Miller, S. (2001) *Social Action: A Teleological Account*, New York: Cambridge University Press.

Pacherie, E. (2011) "Framing Joint Action," *Review of Philosophy and Psychology* 2: 173–92.

—— (2013) "Intentional Joint Agency: Shared Intention Lite," *Synthese* 190: 1817–39.

—— (2015) "Modest Sociality: Continuities and Discontinuities," *Journal of Social Ontology* 1: 17–26.

Petersson, B. (2007) "Collectivity and Circularity," *Journal of Philosophy* 104: 138–56.

—— (2015) "Bratman, Searle, and Simplicity: A Comment on Bratman, *Shared Agency*," *Journal of Social Ontology* 1: 27–37.

Roth, A.S. (2003) "Practical Intersubjectivity," in F. Schmitt (ed.) *Socializing Metaphysics: the Nature of Social Reality*, Lanham, MD: Rowman & Littlefield, pp. 65–91.

—— (2004) "Shared Agency and Contralateral Commitments," *Philosophical Review* 113: 359–410.

—— (2014) "Prediction, Authority, and Entitlement in Shared Activity," *Noûs* 48: 626–52.

—— (2015) "Practical Intersubjectivity and Normative Guidance: Bratman on Shared Agency," *Journal of Social Ontology* 1: 39–48.

Roughley, N. (2001) "Review of Bratman, *Faces of Intention*," *International Journal of Philosophical Studies* 9: 265–70.

Schmid, H.B. (2008) "Plural Action," *Philosophy of the Social Sciences* 38: 25–54.

Searle, J. (1990) "Collective Intentions and Actions," in P. Cohen, J. Morgan, and M. Pollack (eds) *Intentions in Communication*, Cambridge, MA: MIT Press, pp. 401–15.

Shapiro, S. (2014) "Massively Shared Agency," in M. Vargas and G. Yaffe (eds) *Rational and Social Agency: Essays on The Philosophy of Michael Bratman*, New York: Oxford University Press, pp. 257–93.

Smith, T.H. (2015) "*Shared Agency*, Gilbert, and Deep Continuity," *Journal of Social Ontology* 1: 49–57.

Stoutland, F. (1997) "Why are Philosophers of Action so Anti-Social?" in L. Alanen, S. Heinämaa, and T. Wallgren (eds) *Commonality and Particularity in Ethics*, New York: St. Martin's Press, pp. 45–74.

——— (2002) "Critical Notice of Michael Bratman's *Faces of Intention*," *Philosophy and Phenomenological Research* 65: 238–41.

Tollefsen, D. (2005) "Let's Pretend! Joint Action and Young Children," *Philosophy of the Social Sciences* 35: 75–97.

Tuomela, R. (1990) "What are Goals and Joint Goals," *Theory and Decision* 28: 1–20.

——— (1995) *The Importance of Us*, Palo Alto, CA: Stanford University Press.

——— (2005) "We-Intentions Revisited," *Philosophical Studies* 125: 327–69.

——— (2007) *The Philosophy of Sociality: The Shared Point of View*, Oxford: Oxford University Press.

Tuomela, R. and Miller, K. (1988) "We-intentions," *Philosophical Studies* 63: 367–89.

Velleman, D. (1997) "How to Share an Intention," *Philosophy and Phenomenological Research* 57 (1): 29–49.

NOTE

1. Partly due to criticisms by John Searle (1990), Tuomela and Miller's account has been interpreted by many as a conceptually reductive account. Although Tuomela has since denied that it was so intended (see, e.g. note 9 of Chapter 2, this volume), their account, thus interpreted, has had an enormous influence in the literature. For this reason, among others, I believe it is appropriate in this chapter to consider what their account exactly amounts to, and what problems it faces, when so construed. Henceforth, I will here treat Tuomela and Miller's account as a reductive account.

4

Interpersonal Obligation in Joint Action

Abraham Sesshu Roth

1. JOINT ACTION AND THE TIES THAT BIND

Having just eaten oysters on a small hill overlooking a beach, I toss the shells on a pile and go on my way. Eating oysters here is quite popular. The hill that is a nice spot for a picnic turns out to be made of shells discarded by those who have come before. It might be said that I along with others have made a large midden. But this is not something that we do jointly in any robust sense. The midden is, rather, the accretion of countless individual acts, performed independently of one another. Whereas, we might imagine many individuals jointly deciding to create a pile of shells as a monument, and together setting about to do this. Here, what each individual does is *not* independent of what the others do; they are acting *collectively*. The jointness of the monument building, absent in the midden making, would seem to have something to do with how the agents involved are related to one another. If so, what integrates participants in joint activity? What is the nature of the ties that bind us when we act together?

Joint action necessarily involves some level of coordination between the contributions of the participants; we could hardly be walking together if we constantly trip and fall over one another. Might the integration of participants be understood, then, simply in terms of the coordination they exhibit in their behavior? This won't do for a couple of reasons. First, it gets wrong the order of explanation. Joint action is an achievement, something brought about by the shared agency of the participants. On the one hand, we have the participants and how they're related. On the other, we have the joint action and the coordination essential to it. These are distinct. The former that explains the latter, and not the other way around. Second, coordination is often exhibited by individuals each of whom is acting on his or her own. For example, the bustling of shoppers on a crowded sidewalk is coordinated in that hardly anyone collides with anyone else. But there is no joint action here; no one in the crowd is bound in any special way to anyone else.

If the integration of participants in joint action is not just a matter of coordination, how should it be understood? A variety of proposals point to the psychology of the participants: some distinctive attitude they have in common, or the special ways in which the attitudes of different participants mesh into a coherent outlook and plan of action, or the way in which each participant identifies with the group and thinks about what to do from the perspective of the group, etc. Yet other proposals incorporate social facts, such as the presence of collective decision procedures ensuring some modicum of group level rationality, or governance by social institutions regulating the interaction of individuals in specific contexts.

There are insights behind both psychological and social/institutional approaches to cohesiveness or integration of agents in joint action. But I will set them aside here without prejudice, and focus instead on an influential approach that emphasizes the more distinctly *normative* relationship between participants—the obligations or commitments one has when acting with another.

2. MUTUAL OBLIGATION

a. Suppose A and B are engaged in some joint action, say patching a leak in a cistern and preventing further loss of water. Given that they're doing this together, it is suggested that each has an obligation to do her part. A is not at liberty simply to walk away from the project. Likewise for B. This obligation is distinctive in that it does not derive from the obligatoriness of the action in question. Thus, A and B are obligated even if what they're doing together is something entirely optional, like a stroll (to invoke an example from Gilbert 1990) or some other idle diversion. Being subject to this obligation is what distinguishes A, for example, from some non-participant C. C, of course, may be subject to *other* obligations that pertain to what A and B are doing. Perhaps A and B are having serious difficulty in their repair work and this is an urgent matter, like preventing the waste of water in times of desperate drought. In this case, C might have some duty to help. Or, imagine instead that there is no emergency here, but that C has promised someone that she would contribute to the project A and B are undertaking. Here, too, C might have an obligation. But if nothing like this is the case, then what A and B do is not C's concern, and C has no obligation regarding it. Whereas, the simple fact that A and B are engaged in repairing the cistern *together* is thought to entail that each is subject to the distinctive obligation. Thus, Gilbert says of individuals engaged in the joint action of walking together that, 'they will understand that each has an *obligation* to do what he or she can to achieve the relevant goal' (1996: 184).

b. This obligation is often characterized in terms of doing one's part in joint action. But this is not to say that one's part is always clearly defined or that it cannot change over the course of the activity. For example, A's part in the activity might be to repair the cistern while B's is largely to capture the spilling water. But if B has some difficulty, A might have to take on assisting B, for example by fetching some buckets.

c. More contentious is whether one is obligated to do one's part in joint action *understood as such*. In walking with another, one is obligated to keep pace with her. A natural reading of the obligation is that it requires a performance on one's part—namely, that of keeping pace. A stronger reading requires in addition that one *regard* one's performance in a certain light—as a contribution to joint action. Gilbert might be interpreted this way when she says each participant "understands" that each

> has the standing to demand that he act in a manner appropriate to their joint activity . . . They will understand, moreover, that [a participant] has this standing by virtue of her participation with [the other] in the joint activity of walking together.
>
> (Gilbert 2006: 104; see also 105–6)

And, speaking of the related notion of shared intention, Gilbert says

> . . . an adequate account of shared intention will entail that each party to a shared intention is obligated to each to act as appropriate to the shared intention in conjunction with the rest . . . I take it as read here that the account should be such that the parties to the shared intention will understand that they have the stated obligations, and that they understand that this is so as a matter of what a shared intention is.
>
> (Gilbert 2009: 175)

If the obligation requires seeing one's performance as a contribution to joint action, then fulfilling this obligation would require one to have some understanding of joint action as such. But many lack the conceptual sophistication that this entails—young children, for example. It's unclear, then, that such individuals can be held subject to this obligation. This would imply that young children cannot engage in joint action. But it is clear that they do. So, if obligation is what binds participants in shared activity, it should be articulated in a way that would not require too much sophistication on the part of the individuals involved. Participants should, of course, display some sensitivity in their behavior to playing a role in shared activity. But to require that they understand it as such would rule out joint action for many who do, in fact, engage in it.

d. Another issue concerns what it takes to modify the obligation, or to be released from it altogether. According to Gilbert's *concurrence criterion*, this cannot be done unilaterally. The idea is that one cannot "without fault" withdraw from (or substantially modify) shared activity unless every other participant concurs (Gilbert 1990, 2009: 174, 2006: 106–15).

The concurrence criterion might be too strict. Some joint action is fluid, forming spontaneously and dissipating just as easily. At a large reception individuals circulate among a number of group conversations without seeking permission from all or even any of the individuals involved, and no one is thought to be at fault. Friends may also jointly engage in episodic or recurring activity, such as that of having regular lunches or an exchange of letters. But over time the lunches or letters become fewer and farther between, and finally break off entirely. People grow apart. Was there ever a point that release was granted? Is anyone at fault? Finally, there are also cases where joint action involves consent and it is important for the parties that each individual may on her own withdraw consent and thus bring the joint activity to a close. This is particularly important in cases of intimacy. Sexual intercourse with another is, usually, a form of joint activity. But it is one that allows for—indeed one for which we demand—the possibility of unilateral withdrawal by the revocation of consent.

We might try to accommodate such points by qualifying the concurrence criterion. For example, we might say that unilateral withdrawal is disallowed *absent special background understandings*. It might be added that the individuals involved may be party to some social convention that permits unilateral withdrawal or modification even without any specific agreement (Gilbert 2006: 110, 2009: 174, noting Bratman 1993).

Relatedly, Gilbert notes how different conventions might be prevalent in different societies. Societies that emphasize personal freedom and autonomy may have conventions that allow more occasions for unilateral withdrawal. And patriarchal societies might countenance gendered asymmetry in the extent to which one is subject to concurrence of one's partners for withdrawal.

The suggestion about special background understandings and societal conventions affecting the concurrence condition may allow Gilbert to accommodate the sorts of cases mentioned above. But it raises a dilemma for her. The concurrence condition is fundamental to Gilbert's understanding of joint action. But how can what she takes to be essential to joint action simply be legislated away in some circumstances with the remainder still counting as such? Whatever account we do give for why we *still* have joint action in these cases could very well apply in all cases of joint action and thus displace Gilbert's initial characterization of what it means for something to count as joint action. On the other hand, if one insists that such cases don't count as genuine joint action, then what are we to say about them? Why do they appear to be done jointly? For example, consensual intimacy that one can unilaterally end sure can seem like joint activity and not merely in a superficial way; if it is not, what would account for its similarity to genuine joint action?

The concurrence requirement therefore might be overly strong as a condition on how participants in joint action are related to one another. Might something weaker do better? For example, it might be that one might unilaterally withdraw from joint action if one judges that one has good reason to do so. Perhaps one might owe one's partners some warning, an apology or an explanation, and maybe even some sort of compensation. But, on this alternative, it would not be necessary to secure their concurrence. Being able to revise one's participation does not mean that one is at liberty to revise for no reason at all. So, allowing for unilateral withdrawal with good reason need not be at odds with the fundamental insight of the obligation criterion—namely, understanding the relatedness of participants in normative terms.

Even if unilateral withdrawal is permissible for good reason, this doesn't mean that concurrence or the power of release is without theoretical significance. As we will see below, it is one way to articulate another important aspect of the obligation in joint action—namely, its directedness.

e. Describing the normative relation between participants in terms of obligation might suggest—as it seems to have for Gilbert—the demanding requirement of concurrence in order to withdraw. Talk of obligation can also suggest that the demand in question is strong in another way: namely that it is *moral* in nature, such as the obligation to keep one's promises. Gilbert's view was interpreted in this way earlier on. For example, in response to Gilbert's charge that his view doesn't account for mutual obligation, Bratman (1997) contends that there can be joint action without mutual obligation. Bratman argues that some joint action is directed toward morally reprehensible ends and that there can be no obligation to do one's part in such activity. Moreover, Bratman thinks that on occasions when one does have an obligation, this can be explained by considerations that are not essential to joint activity. For example, the circumstances happen to satisfy *moral* principles concerning what one must do upon intentionally creating expectations in others regarding how one will act (Scanlon 1990, 1998). In all this, Bratman has, not unreasonably, assumed that the mutual obligations Gilbert has in mind are *moral* obligations. Gilbert responds by clarifying that the obligations are not moral but are of a "different kind" (2009: 178). She even argues that one might be subject to this non-moral form of obligation when one has been coerced into acting with another. If this is the view, we might forestall misunderstanding by using the more neutral terminology of *commitment* instead of *obligation*.

3. DIRECTEDNESS OF OBLIGATION: CONTRALATERAL COMMITMENT

There has been a recent emphasis on the *directedness* of the commitment/obligation in joint action. It is not enough to describe the obligation in terms of what it is that one is to perform. In addition, the thought goes, the obligation is *owed* to fellow participants. We understand the obligation in question not as a two place relation holding between the subject and act to be performed, but as a three place relation between subject, act, and *object*—namely, the individual to whom the obligation is directed. Standard examples of directed obligations—such as those arising from promises and agreements—suggest that this sort of obligation entails being substantively related to an individual in such a way that that individual in particular has a claim on you. (May's (2015) is a useful discussion of directed obligation, though not in the context of joint action; see also Kamm (2007: 230), and Wallace (ms.); an important precursor is the notion of claim rights in Hohfeld (1964)).

If this is right, then the participants in joint action are bound together not only because they each are similarly subject to the obligation to do their respective parts, but also because each figures as an "object" of obligations to which each of the others is subject. Or, to put the point in the more neutral terminology of commitment, it is to say that a participant's commitment to doing her part is, more specifically, a commitment-to-her-partners to do her part. One's commitment is *contralateral* when it spans across to other participants in this way.

Recall A and B who are acting jointly, and C who is not a participant. Each of A and B has an obligation-*to-the-other* to do his or her share; this is what binds them as participants in joint action. C has no such obligation. We have seen that in some circumstances, C may have an obligation to lend some assistance, but presumably this obligation is a two-place relation holding between C and the act to be performed (lending assistance to A and B). It is also possible that C's obligation is directed. For example, if C has promised yet another person D to help A and B, then C's promissory obligation is said by some to be directed to the promisee, D. In any case, for our purposes, C's promissory obligation is not directed to A and B.

The directedness of the obligation in joint action is arguably implicit in early discussion from Gilbert (1990, 1999), but emphasis on it has grown in subsequent work (Gilbert 2006, 2009; Roth 2004). But just what is it for an obligation to be directed, and what exactly might prompt us to think of the interrelatedness of participants in terms of directed obligations? That is, why think of the commitments in joint action as *contralateral* commitments-to-fellow-participants to do one's part?

a. Sometimes the directedness of obligation is explicated in terms of the distinction between merely doing a wrong and there being someone in particular that you are wronging (on this distinction, see Thompson 2004; Kamm 2007: 230). Or, in terms less morally freighted, we might speak of there being someone in particular that one is *letting down*. Consider an individual who could easily increase general utility or well-being with no effort, but knowingly and needlessly does not. In neglecting to increase utility here, the individual acts wrongly but, arguably, there is no one (at least no one in particular) that is wronged by the action. Contrast the case of promising. We might speak generally of the obligation to keep one's promises, and when one fails to live up to this obligation by breaking a promise, one is acting wrongly. But in reneging on a promise one is, in addition, wronging someone in particular—namely, the individual to whom one has made the promise.

It should be noted that the possibility of wronging someone in particular is not sufficient for directed obligation holding between the individuals in question. Randomly assaulting a stranger is, one would think, to wrong someone. But in this case one does not have a preexisting substantive relationship with the victim, a relationship of the sort that we would expect given standard examples of directed obligation, such as those emerging from agreements or promises.[1]

Still, the possibility of wronging someone or letting them down might be a necessary condition of directed obligation. Applied to joint action, the thought is this. When one fails to do one's part, one is not merely at fault in failing to live up to a commitment or obligation; one is also wronging or at least letting down fellow participants. That is, if A has a directed obligation or contralateral commitment-to-B to do his share, then B is susceptible to being wronged or let down by A. A non-participant C is not necessarily let down when A fails to do his part—even if C would stand to benefit from the joint action much more than participants such as B would. (Imagine that the joint endeavor was to provide some assistance to C, assistance that it would be good but not obligatory, to provide.)

b. Another way one might characterize directedness is in terms of *accountability*. Accountability entails responsibility on the part of the agent. But it also involves a relationship with some other party to whom one is accountable. In the case of joint action, one is accountable to fellow participants. This is suggested by the fellow participant being in a *special position* to object when one doesn't do his part. Thus, accountability involves a kind of standing to complain, to demand explanation and conformity, and to protest. (See May 2015, citing Darwall 2006 and Feinberg 1970.)

If someone is to be a legitimate target of complaint for some φ-ing they did or failed to do, there is a presupposition that they are an agent of sufficient sophistication and in sufficiently favorable circumstances (e.g. not coerced or under duress). But the legitimacy of the complaint might also rest on the fact that the individual lodging the complaint has the standing to do so (Gilbert 2006: 133; Roth 2004: 384, especially note 14). The complaint of someone lacking this authority may be greeted with *it's not your business*. Rebuffing in this way is not available when the obligation being violated is a two place moral obligation. It is in this sense that, as far as doing one's part in joint activity is concerned, one is accountable to fellow participants and not necessarily to third parties.[2]

c. Strawson's (1962) influential approach to accountability and responsibility emphasizes, in the core case, 'the non-detached attitudes and reactions of people directly involved in transactions with each another, of the attitudes and reactions of offended parties and beneficiaries; of such things as gratitude, resentment, forgiveness, love and hurt feelings'.[3] Applying Strawson's picture to joint action, each participant is accountable to the other(s) in that failure to do one's part would amount to an expression of ill will (or a problematic indifference) toward other participants. One would be the legitimate object of the appropriate direct reactive attitude, e.g. of resentment. Thus, Strawson's picture of participant reactive attitudes offers one way to understand accountability, and thus one sense of the directedness of obligations to fellow participants. (Non-participants would only be in a position to adopt a vicarious or more impersonal attitude, such as that of indignation as opposed to resentment.)

But it's not clear that the emotional edge associated with reactive attitudes is always called for when holding a fellow participant accountable. On an alternative picture of accountability due to Scanlon (2008), if individuals are in a substantive relationship governed by normative expectations, and one party fails to meet expectations, the other might be in a position to modify the relationship or abandon it altogether in light of the judgment that the first has failed to meet the demands of the relationship. Applied to the case of joint action, if one person fails to do her part in the activity, it is up to the others to modify their relationship with the party at fault. In particular, they may be in a position to abandon the joint undertaking—which is, of course, something that no third party is in a position to do.[4]

I am not endorsing any particular theory of accountability here. The point is that on both Strawson's and Scanlon's views, accountability is understood relationally. So interpreted, accountability is a candidate for explicating the directedness of the obligation. In the three-place relation for directed obligation (or contralateral commitment), the third object-place would be reserved for one's fellow participants to whom one is accountable for doing one's part.

d. Gilbert recently has characterized the directedness in terms of claim or ownership rights. Thus, she articulates a sense in which an action of one participant can be owned by another, and that one can owe an action to another (Gilbert 2006: 35–9, 40, 157 (citing Hart 1955); Gilbert 2009: 175, pointing to Feinberg 1970).

> There is an important and closely linked family of concepts here . . . the linkage can be displayed as follows: one who has a right to someone's future action already owns that action in some intuitive sense of "own." Until the action is performed he is owed that action by the person concerned, thus being in a position to demand it of him prior to its being performed and to rebuke him if it is not performed. If it is performed, it has finally come into the possession of the right-holder, in the only way that it can.
>
> (Gilbert 2009: 176)

But some conceptions of ownership are not suitable for Gilbert's purposes. For example, ownership is often thought to involve the possibility of the transfer of property rights. It seems to be an unwelcome result that one might, when engaged in joint action with someone, somehow transfer one's "ownership" of a fellow participant's activity to some non-participant so that one's partner now owes it to the third party to do his share. There is, of course, the possibility that the ownership rights in this context are non-transferable. But whether some particular ownership right is transferable or not would seem to depend

(i) on moral considerations, or (ii) on the presence of some further social structure, such as some governing body. If (ii), then it seems that Gilbert's notion of joint action presupposes some larger collective form of agency as a backdrop. This is at odds with her approach in her 2006 work, which seeks to explain essential aspects of these larger structures in terms of the fundamental notion of joint commitment that we find in small-scale joint action. Thus, we are threatened with a regress if the larger structure is presupposed whenever we seek to account for the non-transferability of claim rights in the smaller structure. Turning to (i), the (non)transferability might depend on some moral constraints. Indeed, morality might be seen as imposing rather strict constraints on property rights and their transferability. But if that's the case, then Gilbert's appeal to ownership would be at odds with her conception, noted above, of the directed obligations as being non-moral.

   e. One element of the notion of ownership/property rights is particularly noteworthy in connection with understanding directed obligation. Ownership rights can be ceded. Thus, if I have something like this right over what a fellow participant does, then I would be in a position to cede my right to their contribution. This entails that one is able to exercise a kind of normative power: one would, by the expression of one's intention be able to make it the case that non-performance by a fellow participant would no longer violate an obligation or commitment. (On the possibility of exercising such a normative power in the context of promising, see Shiffrin (2008), Owens (2012)). Thus, in giving up my claim to your performance, it would no longer be the case that you would in some sense be at fault for non-performance. Moreover, some form of normative power was exercised in the first place in order to establish the obligations. Together we were able to make it the case that we would be at fault for not performing some relevant act. So, the exercise of a normative power to establish the obligations, and the ensuing normative control over maintaining or releasing them, offers a way of understanding the directedness of obligations that hold between participants. For it is only fellow participants and not third parties who have this sort of control over the normative status of certain kinds of acts for fellow participants.[5]

4. DIRECTEDNESS AND THE EXERCISE OF AGENCY

Finally, consider some approaches to directed obligations and contralateral commitments that invoke the idea of a distinctive form of agency being exercised by participants in joint activity. For example, Roth (2003, 2004) holds that the relevant intentions of fellow participants figure in one's practical reasoning much in the way that one's own prior intentions do. One acts directly on a prior intention without re-deliberating the matter. In this way, one's own prior intention settles the practical matter of what to do, and commits one to a course of action. The norms governing intention (means-end coherence, consistency, etc.) are elements of intention-based commitment, something that sets intention apart from other attitudes such as desire. Sometimes one decides and thus intends to φ, but later for no good reason one fails to act on it—e.g. out of laziness or weakness of will. In that case, one is *letting oneself down*. We might, in similar fashion, account for how one can let down (wrong) a fellow participant. Thus, in joint action, the intentions of *another* can settle what one is to do. And if for no good reason one fails to act on it, then one is letting down a fellow participant. Though not sufficient, the possibility of letting down or wronging someone is at least some sign of directedness/contralateral commitment. By imagining that the norms of intention-based commitment can sometimes span *across* people as well within a person over time, this approach aims to capture directedness and other normative aspects of the interrelatedness of participants in joint action.

This approach incorporates the three-place relation we saw in explicating the directedness of obligation (contralateral commitment) straight into the structure of intention. The notion of intention as a distinctive state associated with settling practical questions and a commitment to action is drawn from the literature on individual agency (e.g. Bratman 1987 and Harman 1986). Implicit in that literature is a conception of intention as a two-place relation holding between agent and prospective action. The current approach represents something of a departure by allowing for the possibility of acting directly not only on one's own intentions, but on intentions of others—in particular, those of fellow participants in joint action.

One challenge facing this view is understanding when another's intentions can figure in one's practical reasoning in this way; presumably most of the intentions of others do not. Until more is said about this, the explanation of the interrelatedness of participants is incomplete. Another concern is whether it is even coherent to speak of acting *directly* on another's intention. Admittedly, it seems that something like this can happen when, for example, one obeys the command of another. But if this addresses the worry about the intelligibility of the proposal, it raises another problem. How can acting directly on another's intention be understood in a way that is appropriate for an understanding of shared agency rather than one of domination over another? See Roth (2014) for discussion.

A somewhat different approach is taken by Gilbert, who understands directedness in terms of *joint commitment* (see Chapter 10). Though she regards this as a primitive, in more recent work, she, too, has invoked the notion of intention in order to give some characterization of (aspects of) joint commitment (2009: 179–80; see also 167, 168). The "key salient feature" of individual or personal commitment is that 'the one who formed or made the corresponding personal . . . intention is in a position unilaterally to expunge [the commitment] as a matter of personal choice'.[6] Thus, one *owns* the action conforming to the commitment associated with one's personal intention. Gilbert notes that joint commitment is akin to personal intention, except that it is made by more than one person, and only together can it be rescinded (2009: 182). A joint commitment also entails a sort of ownership, this time by all parties to the commitment. Gilbert (2009: 182–3) explains that 'in co-creating their joint commitment the parties together impose on each other a constraint such that, all else being equal, a given party will not act as he ought should he fail to respect it'. She continues,

> . . . a given party is in a position to demand conformity or rebuke for non-conformity as co-owner of the action in question . . . he might say "Give me that, it's mine—qua one of us!" . . . if A owns B's action in the intuitive sense now in question, that suffices to make it the case that prior to its performance B owes A the action.
>
> (Gilbert 2009: 183; see also 2006: 154–5)

That is, the relevant intention-based commitment to ϕ-ing entails ownership of ϕ-ing by the author of the commitment. In joint commitment, the author is all the individuals who, together, formed the commitment. One therefore owes one's part of the ϕ-ing to *all* those individuals. They, together, *own* one's action in the sense discussed in the previous section. For Gilbert, that suffices to account for the directedness. On Gilbert's recent view, then, ownership of the action mediates joint commitment and directed obligation.

Does this account for directed obligation? The creator of the joint commitment to ϕ is the entire group, hence *it* is the "owner" of the ϕ-ing. So it seems that a participant's directed obligation is to the group as a whole. How (or even whether) this translates to directedness to individuals within the group is not straightforward. Gilbert seems to acknowledge as much in saying that when there is a joint commitment,

> it is plausible to suppose that any one of the individuals . . . [who created it] . . . is in a position to demand conforming actions . . . in the name of this creator, by virtue of his constitutive relationship to it. Thus, he does not demand it in his own name, or as this particular person, but as co-creator of the joint commitment and co-owner of the actions in question.
>
> (Gilbert 2006: 154–5)

Another issue that arises for Gilbert is how to get joint action started. This requires that we secure *joint* commitment, rather than an aggregation of individual commitments. This matters because it's the "jointness" of the commitment that accounts for others having an ownership stake in your contribution. In getting joint action started, if all one is doing is expressing one's personal commitment to do one's part (even if it is conditional on the commitment of others to do their part), then no one else would own one's performance, and so on Gilbert's view there would be no directed obligation. Gilbert rightly rejects the proposal of interdependent conditional intentions that she seemed to endorse in earlier work.[7] Her view of getting joint action started now seems to involve various individuals expressing their personal readiness to be jointly committed (Gilbert 2009). Each individual expresses an individual or personal intention, albeit with some special sort of content: as a result of my own decision and intention, I am ready to walk up the hill *with you*, to *share* with you the intention of walking up the hill, etc. Suppose we all express such a readiness, and this is done in conditions of common knowledge, as required by Gilbert. Then the joint commitment, e.g. to walk to the top of the hill, is now in place. One wonders how exactly this happens. Everyone has expressed a *readiness* to share an intention. But just because we're ready to share an intention, it doesn't follow that we've already started to do so. What gets us going?

Gilbert might reply in the following way. Given that everyone has expressed his readiness in that sort of circumstance, it just is the case that certain types of obligations hold between individuals. (Compare how in some circumstances of promising, expressing one's willingness to ϕ creates the obligation.) And then we might say that the joint commitment just consists in the holding of these obligations. So we do not need to think that some special kind of group agency must be exercised in order to get things going. This comports with Gilbert's remarks that joint commitment doesn't entail anything like a mysterious group mind.

But having put it in this way, one wonders whether Gilbert would welcome this solution to the problem of getting started. The solution involves what we might call a "constitutivist" reading of joint commitment simply *as* the directed obligations spanning participants. Do we have here a theory invoking a kind of agency that's fundamentally distinct from individual agency, as Gilbert intends? I suspect not. On the suggested reading, individuals have formed their own intentions (of expressing readiness to share an intention) and, as a result, certain normative facts apply to their situation—in particular, a pattern of obligations holds between the individuals. Each is now subject to a sort of normative assessment in terms of those obligations, just as one might be judged in terms of whether one has lived up to some moral obligation, such as keeping a promise. One has put oneself into a situation where it is possible, if one does not act appropriately, to be charged with not being a team player.

Gilbert contrasts her view with those such as that of Bratman, who seeks to understand joint action in terms of personal intentions (Gilbert 2009: 168). Her project is described as asking the question, 'what does *our* intending amount to *at an individual level?*' (2009: 170). I take it that she thinks that whatever is going on at the individual level, it is quite different from what goes on in the exercise of ordinary individual agency. But if the constitutive reading of Gilbert mentioned in the previous paragraph is correct, then the only difference is that the individual is subject to a further kind of assessment having to do with the norms of teamwork and mutual obligation. And that, arguably, is not as fundamental a difference as we were led to expect.

Furthermore, Gilbert thinks of the notion of joint commitment as *explaining* these distinctive directed obligations. The obligations are not themselves supposed to be what it is to be jointly committed. So although the constitutive reading of joint commitment may go some distance toward dispelling any mystery about how individuals might be jointly committed rather than individually committed in shared activity, I am not sure whether this is, in the end, how Gilbert herself would like to see it.

RELATED TOPICS

Joint Commitment (Ch. 10), Proxy Agency in Collective Action (Ch. 5), Shared Values, Interests, and Desires (Ch. 8).

REFERENCES

Bratman, M. (1987) *Intention, Plans, and Practical Reason*, Cambridge, MA: Harvard University Press.
——— (1993) "Shared Intention," *Ethics* 104: 97–113.
——— (1997) "Shared Intention and Mutual Obligation," originally published as "Intention Partagée et Obligation Mutuelle," in J.-P. Dupuy and P. Livet (eds) *Les limites de la rationalité*, 1, Paris: Editions La Découverte, Joelle Proust, trans. Reprinted in Bratman (1999).
——— (1999) *Faces of Intention*, Cambridge: Cambridge University Press.
Darwall, S. (2006) *The Second-Person Standpoint: Respect, Morality, and Accountability*, Cambridge, MA: Harvard University Press.
Feinberg, J. (1970) "The Nature and Value of Rights," *Journal of Value Inquiry* 4 (4): 243–60.
Gilbert, M. (1990) "Walking Together: A Paradigmatic Social Phenomenon," *Midwest Studies in Philosophy* 15: 1–14.

——— (1996) *Living Together: Rationality, Sociality, and Obligation*, Lanham, MD: Rowman & Littlefield Publishers.

——— (1999) "Obligation and Joint Commitment," *Utilitas* 11: 143–63.

——— (2006) *A Theory of Political Obligation*, Oxford: Clarendon Press.

——— (2009) "Shared Intention and Personal Intentions," *Philosophical Studies* 144: 167–87.

Harman, G. (1986) *Change in View*, Cambridge, MA: MIT Press.

Hart, H.L.A. (1955) "Are There Any Natural Rights?" *Philosophical Review* 64 (2): 175–91.

Hohfeld, W. (1964) *Fundamental Legal Conceptions*, New Haven: Yale University Press.

Kamm, F. (2007) *Intricate Ethics: Rights, Responsibilities, and Permissible Harm*, New York: Oxford University Press.

May, S. (2015) "Directed Duties," *Philosophy Compass* 10 (8): 523–32.

Owens, D. (2012) *Shaping the Normative Landscape*, Oxford: Oxford University Press.

Roth, A.S. (2003) "Practical Intersubjectivity," in F. Schmitt (ed.) *Socializing Metaphysics: The Nature of Social Reality*, Lanham, MD: Rowman & Littlefield.

——— (2004) "Shared Agency and Contralateral Commitments," *Philosophical Review* 113 (3): 359–410.

——— (2014) "Prediction, Authority, and Entitlement in Shared Activity," *Noûs* 48 (4): 626–52.

Scanlon, T. (1990) "Promises and Practices," *Philosophy and Public Affairs* 19 (3): 199–226.

——— (1998) *What We Owe to Each Other*, Cambridge, MA: Harvard University Press.

——— (2008) *Moral Dimensions: Permissibility, Meaning, Blame*, Cambridge, MA: Harvard University Press.

Shiffrin, S. (2008) "Promising, Intimate Relationships, and Conventionalism," *Philosophical Review* 117 (4): 481–524.

Strawson, P. (1962) "Freedom and Resentment," *Proceedings of the British Academy* 48: 1–25.

Thompson, M. (2004) "What is it to Wrong Someone? A Puzzle about Justice," in R.J. Wallace, P. Pettit, S. Scheffler, and M. Smith (eds) *Reason and Value*, Oxford: Oxford University Press.

Velleman, J.D. (1997) "How to Share an Intention," *Philosophy and Phenomenological Research* 57: 29–50.

Wallace, J. (ms.) *The Moral Nexus: Towards a Relational Account*.

NOTES

1. As Shiffrin has pointed out in conversation, assaulting someone wouldn't be a way of establishing such a relationship.

2. This is not to deny that third parties may on some occasions be in a position to hold someone accountable for what they did or did not do. But this would be on grounds that are distinct from the special obligations of joint action. For example, suppose that joint action is being directed toward providing some sort of morally obligatory assistance, and suppose that a participant fails to do his part. This participant can, no doubt, be held accountable by third parties for their inaction not so much under the description of not doing his part in joint action, but simply for inaction that stymies morally overriding endeavors.

3. Strawson (1962); see also Darwall (2006), who emphasizes the relational element in Strawson's account. As is well known, Strawson extends his story beyond these cases of participant reactive attitudes involved in substantive relationships to handle blame and holding accountable in more impersonal cases. In the latter cases, one is not oneself a target of the ill will expressed by another individual B; instead, one adopts a reactive attitude of say indignation against B, on behalf of some distinct individual C who has been targeted by B.

4. Scanlon's view is meant as a general story about accountability, which would not be limited to participants in some substantive relationship such as friendship; Scanlon allows that any two rational beings are sufficiently related for the purposes of accountability. But his picture works most naturally for those who are in more substantive or intimate relationships, such as that of friendship.

5. Note that when I have normative control over what you do, this doesn't entail that I have control over what you actually do; my control is over the normative or moral status of what you do. (Compare how a promisee has control over whether the promisor is subject to promissory obligation, depending on whether or not the promisee exercises the power of release.)

6. Gilbert (2009: 180). She will want to take care to formulate this in a way that would not undermine the commitment that is essential to intending. The personal choice to expunge the commitment cannot be arbitrary; it would have to be backed by some considerations that are strong enough to override the intention-based commitment.

7. Velleman (1997) and Roth (2004) read her as subscribing to the interdependent conditional intentions as a way of establishing joint commitment.

5

Proxy Agency in Collective Action

Kirk Ludwig

1. INTRODUCTION

In proxy agency, what one person or group does, under appropriate conditions, counts as another agent or group having done something. Proxy agency is a common form through which institutional agency is expressed. For example, when an organization's spokesperson performs an utterance act in the right conditions, the organization is taken to have announced something. When a corporation's lawyers file bankruptcy papers, the corporation is said to file for bankruptcy. When the Senate ratifies a treaty, the United States is said to have entered into it. Proxy agency is not limited to groups. An individual may have a spokesperson, or assign a power of attorney to allow a proxy to close on a home sale. Even in these cases, proxy agency depends on a larger social context. How is proxy agency possible? What are its mechanisms? What does it show about institutional agency, in particular?

2. PRELIMINARY OBSERVATIONS

Not just anyone can be a proxy agent for a group. A proxy agent must be authorized to act for the group. This is why the proxy agent's acting licenses saying that the group thereby acts as well. Similarly, not just anything a proxy does counts as the authorizing group acting. Only certain things count, in certain circumstances, within certain constraints. For example, the group's spokesperson, in the simplest case, is given a message to deliver to an audience. Only the delivery of the authorized message counts as the group's announcing anything. Furthermore, success requires that the audience recognize the spokesperson to be acting in her role as spokesperson. Thus, there must be not only arrangements within the group about the spokesperson, but also between the group and its audience. This second arrangement between the group with its proxy, and those

58

with whom it interacts thereby, plays a crucial role in enabling what the proxy does to count as the group doing something. These observations guide the following discussion. Before we apply them, we must first introduce some additional concepts employed in the account.

3. ESSENTIALLY INTENTIONAL ACTION TYPES

The first concept is that of an essentially intentional action type. All actions by proxy agents qua proxy agents, and by the groups acting through them, are essentially intentional action types. Essentially intentional action types fall into two basic categories (which can be combined). The first subsumes action types being performed with an intention to achieve a certain end. Examples are searching for your lost keys and checking a calculation. These can't be unintentional because they are defined in terms of an intended goal. To search for your keys is to engage in behavior guided by the intention to find your keys. The second subsumes action types characterized in terms of a pattern of activity that is instantiated intentionally by its agent. Examples are walking and singing (for individuals), performing the Goldberg variations, having a conversation, shaking hands, playing chess, and dancing the tango. We focus on the latter category. I will call these action types essentially intentional pattern activities (IPAs). The key fact about IPAs is that they can be analyzed into at least two components. The first is a pattern of activity that can be instantiated unintentionally but need not be. The second is the requirement that the pattern be instantiated by the agent intentionally. When the activity pattern involves multiple agents, it requires the pattern be instantiated by the agents jointly intentionally, that is, by their executing a shared intention to instantiate the activity pattern.

4. CONSTITUTIVE RULES AND AGENCY

The second concept is that of a constitutive rule. Rules are often expressed using imperatives (drive on the left-hand side of the road) or statements of permission or constraint (a pawn may be advanced one or two squares the first time it is moved). Rules have descriptive content, e.g. drivers drive on the left in the United States, pawns are advanced one or two squares the first time they are moved. We turn descriptive statements about patterns of action into rules when we treat their content as guiding or constraining action for an agent or a group of agents, taken as their subjects. For convenience, I will call a description of an action pattern a descriptive rule.

A rule may merely regulate or also partly constitute the activity that it governs. Regulative rules govern a type of activity that can exist independently of the rules being followed. Robert's Rules of Order (RRO) for meetings are regulative rules because the type of activity they govern can occur independently of the rules being followed. Following RRO presupposes a meeting but does not constitute holding one, for if people following RRO stop, they may continue to conduct a meeting, and meetings would occur even if no one ever formulated RRO. In contrast, constitutive rules, as Searle put it in classic discussion, 'do not merely regulate, they create or define new forms of behavior' (1969: 33). Constitutive rules are rules the intentional following of which partially constitute the activity that they govern. The rules of chess are constitutive rules. If no one had formulated the rules, it would be impossible to play chess. Two people intentionally following the rules constitutes playing chess, and unless they are (largely) following the rules intentionally, they cannot be counted as playing chess at all.

What are constitutive rules? Constitutive rules govern IPAs. What makes the rules constitutive of them is that they are action types that can be analyzed into a pattern of activity plus the requirement that they be instantiated intentionally—often with other requirements, as in competitive games that the participants strive to win. Thus, constitutive rules are always constitutive relative to an action type. In essence, a descriptive rule (expressing a pattern of activity) yields a constitutive rule relative to an action type defined in part in terms of the activity pattern being instantiated intentionally. Every regulative rule is therefore a constitutive rule relative to a type of activity that requires those rules to be followed for its instantiation. If we define a *parliamentary meeting* as one that is held in accordance with RRO, they are constitutive rules for that action type. For constitutive rules governing joint action, the requirement is (inter alia) that the agents bring about the activity pattern by executing a shared intention to do so (see Chapters 3–4, this volume).

Constitutive rules provide a special mechanism for the expression of agency. In general, one is an agent of something if one brings it about by doing something else or one brings it about primitively, that is, not by doing anything else. There are various determinate ways of bringing one thing about by doing another (Ludwig 2007, 2010; Davidson 2001). For example, one is an agent of any event that something one does causes. A more determinate form of causal agency is doing something without the intervention of the agency of another. Many ordinary action verbs require this form of "direct causation" (as I will call it). For example, you cannot butter your bread by having someone else butter it for you. You are a causal agent of it but not in the way the verb requires. One may be a constitutive agent of an event if something one does contributes constitutively to bringing it about. One can color a wall by painting it blue. Painting it blue constitutes coloring it. One is likewise a constitutive agent of surrounding a house if one forms part of the group of people arranged around it. Similarly, when following a constitutive rule one is a constitutive as well as a causal agent of the action of that type. For one aims to realize an essentially intentional action type whose instantiation partially involves one's (largely) following the rules intentionally. Thus, the actions of two people playing chess do not merely cause but also constitute their playing a game of chess.

5. STATUS FUNCTIONS AND STATUS ROLES

The next concept we need is that of a status function (Searle 1995; Chapter 23, this volume). A status function is a function that an object, event, state, process, person or group has in a social transaction that it can serve only if the parties to the transaction collectively accept that it is to serve that function. Examples are being a $20 bill, a royal seal, a pawn or king in chess, a border between two states or counties, a driver's license, a professor, or policeman, or senator. The last three are status roles.

We can relate status functions to constitutive rules. The rules of chess introduce the term 'king' for a piece that plays a particular role in the game. The concept of a king is a role concept. The role is specified by the constitutive rules for chess. However, what counts as a white or black king for a particular game of chess depends upon the participants coordinating on the same things to play those roles. This coordination is a form of collective acceptance of the particular objects as playing the roles of the white and black kings. The coordination is required by the fact that the rules specify functional roles for objects in a social transaction in terms of how agents are to use them without specifying what things are to have those roles. That is why collective acceptance is required for those objects to serve the functions they are given.

Status functions can be attached to particular things, such as a royal seal, or the President of the United States. But they can also be attached to types of things, such as bills and coins in various denominations produced in accordance with an authorized pattern by an official mint. Types or particulars (for recurring use) to which status function have been attached have their status functions even when not being used in service of the function. They have them in virtue of the dispositions of members of the community to use them in accordance with their functions (their conditional we-intentions—see Ludwig 2014, 2015, 2016, 2017 and Chapters 3–4, this volume).

Status roles are a type of status function (see Ludwig 2014, 2017). A status role is a status function assigned to an agent whose function (ideally) requires the agent's intentional exercise of agency *in that role*. When the agent is a party to the collective acceptance that he have that role, we call it an *agent status role*. All roles involving agents exercising their agency in institutional roles are agent status roles: policeman, judge, lawyer, employee, professor, student, senator, governor, general, private, and so on. However, not every status role assigned to an agent need be accepted by the agent. POWs are expected by those who assign them that role to behave in accordance with rules connected with their status. Thus, they are assigned a type of status role. But it is not required that POWs be party to the collective acceptance that they be POWs and so follow the rules for that reason. The rules are rather enforced on those so designated under threat of sanction, and there are provisions for what to do if the POWs do not cooperate. We will be concerned in the following with agent status roles, and I will use "status role" henceforth to mean "agent status role."

6. PROXY AGENCY: THE CASE OF THE SPOKESPERSON

Proxy agency rests on the possibility of defining a status role whose function is (in part) to assign status functions to objects, or whose function is defined (in part) in terms of the products of agency in that role having certain status functions. Let me explain with the example of the group spokesperson.

The spokesperson functions in a transaction between a group and an audience. When the spokesperson performs an utterance act under the right conditions, the group thereby (formally) commits itself (to the audience) to act in accordance with the content of the utterance act, and the group is counted as having announced something. How is this possible? To get the clearest view of the mechanism, take the simplest case of a spokesperson appointed and given a message to deliver by group consensus.

Only in virtue of the group authorizing the spokesperson and her message (by appointing her and providing it) can what the spokesperson does count as the group saying something. In addition, for the mechanism to perform its function, the intended audience must be in on the arrangement. Thus, the spokesperson plays a role in a social transaction between group and audience. The concept of the spokesperson is therefore that of a status role whose function is expressed in the occupier performing utterance acts with authorized contents in circumstances in which the audience can recognize that she is performing in her role as spokesperson. When the group authorizes someone to be a spokesperson, the group assigns her the status role in accordance with an at least tacit agreement with the audience that they will coordinate in the relevant social transaction on the object so designated. The audience then is to attend to the spokesperson's utterance acts in her role as spokesperson. The spokesperson's utterance acts in that role count as the group's announcing something because the parties accept this mechanism for the purpose. This provides those utterance acts with a certain status function—the vehicle that conveys the content to which the group implementing the mechanism commits itself.

Authorization is the key to the mechanism. Without this, the group cannot announce via what anyone says any commitments. So the group's agency, contrary to initial appearances, is required for what the spokesperson does to count as their doing something. The members of the group are agents of the group announcement both causally and constitutively. In the case of the consensus choice, it is clear that each member of the group contributes to the authorization, and so each is constitutively an agent of the group announcement. We will look at more complicated cases in the next section. Importantly, the concept of a group announcement is different than that of an individual speech act. The same word is used but with a different significance. I return to this in Section 8.

7. PROXY AGENCY EXPANDED

There are at least three different dimensions along which we can construct forms of proxy agency more complicated than the simple case considered in the previous section.

(a) Proxy Agent Autonomy. In many cases, it is expedient to allow a proxy agent more autonomy in representing the group than the spokesperson above, who functions merely as a mouthpiece for the group. Typically a spokesperson is given considerable freedom in representing the position of a group and answering questions about policy. A proxy agent may also have the authority to formulate policy, or to make decisions, e.g. about the allocation of resources. These count as decisions made by the group (communicated as official decisions) in virtue of the person in the role being authorized to make them. Many of the official acts of organizations involve decisions by their agents exercising their authority with respect to the matters that lie within their range of responsibilities. For example, human resource departments have the authority to hire employees, determine benefits, adjudicate claims, and so on. These count as the organization as a whole hiring, determining benefits, and so on. Admissions committees for academic departments are authorized to make offers, which count as the department and the university making offers. President Truman's issuing executive order 9981 to desegregate the Armed Forces counted as the United States desegregating the Armed Forces.

Proxy agent autonomy entails that the group does not always act intentionally in the specific way that the proxy chooses in exercising her authority. In assigning a spokesperson and message by consensus, we can say that the members of the group shared an intention to announce the content of the message. If the group gives a proxy autonomy with respect to handling certain matters officially for the group, then while it is still an agent of what the proxy brings about insofar as that involves creating status functions that rely on the authorization, the group does not bring those things about intentionally under the specific descriptions given by the proxy's intentions. Take the case of a proxy for an individual agent, where this is clearest. If I assign a power of attorney to someone to handle my investments, giving her the freedom to invest my assets in accordance with her best judgment, I count as buying and selling stocks and bonds and the like, but I do not intentionally buy and sell the particular stocks and bonds my agent buys and sells in my name. I can be said to be intentionally handling my investments through my agent, but not intentionally undertaking the particular transactions that result. Similarly, if a club decides to hire office staff, and delegates to the club's president, when the president hires staff, the club does. But while the president intentionally hires the particular people the club hires, say, John Smith and Mary Jones, the club members do not share an intention to hire the John Smith and Mary Jones in particular. In this sense the club per se does not intentionally hire the particular people it hires. If we say that the club intentionally hired them, what we mean is that it intentionally hired staff, not the particular staff members hired, or that the appropriate agent of the club intentionally hired those particular people.

A corollary is that institutional groups can act without all members of the group knowing that it is doing so. What autonomous proxy agents bring about count as the group's bringing about particular events, but because their initiation and form is up to the proxy, other members of the group need not know what is being done by the group through authorized agents.

(b) Chains of Authorization. Second, proxies can be authorized to authorize others to act as proxies for the group. The same mechanism is at work. It requires recognition, by the group and its transaction partners, of the arrangements by which someone is to come to have the role of assigning further proxies for the group. For example, a legislature is a proxy agent for the citizens it represents, and it can in turn delegate authority to committees to decide, e.g. by majority vote, what legislation, in various areas, is to be voted on by the body as a whole. Virtually every organization of any complexity involves offices that have the power to assign to individuals or groups the power to act on behalf of the organization. The hiring and firing of employees by managers for positions in which they represent the firms is an instance of the pervasiveness the exercise of the power to assign (and revoke) proxy status. This is also an example of exercising decision-making autonomy with respect to who occupies further roles as proxy agents. Chains of authorization greatly extend the power and flexibility of proxy agency.

Chains of authorization are compatible with all members of a group being constitutive agents of what the group does through its proxies. Imagine an initial condition in which all members of the group participate in the assignment of the power to assign further proxy roles. Then as each is a constitutive agent of the first set of roles, and the possibility of the assignment of further proxies rests on this, they are likewise agents, partly causally and partly constitutive, of whatever those further proxies do in their official roles, and so of further assignments of proxy agents by them in turn, and so on. The members of the group become more distant causally from what the group's proxies do, and because of the autonomy of the proxies most of what the proxies do the group cannot be said to be doing intentionally under the descriptions under which the proxies intend them, but they are still both causally and constitutively agents of what the proxies bring about. This is not to say that the particular concepts under which we bring what the proxies do also apply to the group. While representatives are proxies for citizens, and so citizens are agents of what their representatives do in their names, when legislators vote on legislation, the citizens do not thereby vote on legislation. I return to this point below.

8. TWO PUZZLES ABOUT PROXY AGENCY

(a) Joining an ongoing institution. When new members are inducted into the group, prima facie they have not had any role in authorizing those already occupying such roles (and so no role in their authorizing of further proxies where they have the power to). Indeed, many organizations outlast their founders. In what way can late joiners be agents of what the proxies do in representing the group? If they are not, we must give up the idea that when groups act, all the members are agents in one way or another of what it does. In this case, we would get a form of autonomy of group agency from the agency of the totality of its members.

A first point to note is that even if this illustrates a mechanism by which a group may be said to act though not all its members contribute, it does not require a group level agent. It just requires a network of status roles in which some represent (in the sense above) the group in transactions with others. It is in virtue of there being arrangements for such representation, which are endorsed by the group and those with whom the group thereby interacts, that this is possible. But only individual agency is required at any stage in the creation and maintenance of these arrangements.

But a second, connected, point is that realization of these arrangements requires that they be accepted by those realizing them. The members of the group with proxies accept the arrangements by which they operate. In the most idealized case, upon joining an organization, someone accepts explicitly its organizational structure together with the powers invested in each role. Acceptance of membership in the group, marked overtly in some way, verbally, in writing, accepting an ID card, payment, etc., constitutes one's co-authorization with the other members of the group of the organizational structure and the powers of each role. Typically, someone joining a complex organization does not know the details of its organizational structure and the powers of various roles. But one can still accept the structure, just as one can accept a contract without reading the fine print. Since it is constitutive of there being an organization with various status roles that its members jointly accept them and operate in accordance with them, acceptance upon joining an organization is a form of constitutive authorization of the roles and their bearers. There is, then, still a sense in which every member of the group contributes constitutively to what the proxy agents bring about in the name of the group, even if they were not party to the original authorizations.

More needs to be said in connection with cases in which membership is coerced, or someone joins (or makes as if to join) an organization under false pretenses, or one or more members are going through the motions, but this must be set aside for space constraints in the present context. (See Ludwig 2014, 2017 for further discussion).

(b) Assignment of proxies by one group or agent for another. Sometimes a proxy may be assigned to a group or individual by a distinct group or individual. This can happen in at least two ways. First, as a group may assign to someone in the group the power to appoint proxy agents for it, so it may also assign the power to someone outside the group. In this case, the assignments of proxy agents for the group by the external agent is out of the group's hands. But since what the external agent does in acting on behalf of the group she does in virtue of the group's assignment of the power, the group members are still constitutive agents of the assignments and of the status functions assigned by the proxy agents assigned for them. As above, there can be institutional arrangements for this which one simply signs on to when joining a group. Second, a group may be a part of a larger institutional setting in which certain status roles are assigned by agents in the larger institutional setting. For example, the head of the US Office of Management and Budget, who has certain decision making powers for the Office, is nominated by the President and confirmed by the Senate, rather than chosen by members of the organization (though it may also be seen as a component of a larger organization of which it is a part). In this case, those who accept roles in the OMB sign onto the arrangements and so contribute constitutively to their operation.

There can also be institutional arrangements, in a legal system, for example, for the appointment of a legal representative of a person or group without their accepting the arrangement, for instance, when someone (a minor) or group (an insolvent bank) is thought not to be competent to perform certain functions. A guardian for a minor appointed by a court, charged with managing the minor's assets, provides an example of someone who acts *for* an individual but who is not chosen by the individual or subject to his direction, and need not be endorsed by him or her. In this case, the person represented does not determine even indirectly who the person who acts officially for her is. What makes this possible is the existence of an institutional setting in which other agents accept that what the person assigned does in her official capacity is done in the name of the person for whom she acts.

Is this proxy agency? Despite its sharing some of the infrastructure of proxy agency, the answer is "No." The core idea of proxy agency is that of one person or group acting through another who is authorized (directly or indirectly) by the group to perform actions that have a status function in social transactions with others. Authorization by the person represented is missing in the case of a court-appointed guardian. This distinction is recognized in the way we talk about these cases. When I assign a power of attorney to someone who buys or sells property in my name, we say that I buy or sell the property. But when a court-appointed guardian manages the assets of the person she represents, we say that she is acting for the person she represents, but we do not say that that person (the child, for example) buys and sells assets. Thus, we may distinguish between acting in someone's name and being a proxy agent for someone. Someone who is a proxy agent for an individual or group is acting in the individual or group's name, but not everyone acting in the name of an individual or a group is a proxy agent for that individual or group.

9. THE LANGUAGE OF PROXY AGENCY

We use terms both for what the proxies do and what groups (and individuals) do through their proxies. The President *negotiates* a treaty, the Senate *ratifies* it, and the United States *enters* into it. I give a power of attorney to someone to sign for me at closing. He *signs* the documents, but I *sell* the house. When we use distinct terms for the proxy's move and what the principal thereby does, we have a clearer view of the mechanism. The proxy agent plays her part in the whole, like someone making a move in chess. When there is special interest in the move a proxy agent makes, we have a term that isolates it. Police officers act as our proxies in making arrests, and we are agents of those arrests thereby, but the verb "arrest" takes as its subject the officer who places someone under arrest. Similarly, though citizens who vote for legislators are constitutive agents of the making of law, it is the legislature that passes laws and the legislators who vote on it. Sometimes, we use the same term for the move the proxy makes and what the group does through the proxy. We say that a company *announces a layoff* when its spokesperson does. We say that the United States declares war when the Congress does. I file bankruptcy papers when my attorney does (though I file for bankruptcy whereas my attorney does not). But even in the case where we use the same term, as we do for the spokesperson, it differs in significance when applied to the group and to the proxy. For what the group does, when the spokesperson acts, is to bring about a public utterance of a message in a way that confers on it the status of a group announcement. The spokesperson merely takes the last step. The spokesperson is not *the* agent of it. The spokesperson is the direct agent rather of the utterance act that has the relevant status. Part of the difficulty in seeing clearly the structure of proxy agency lies in the overlapping vocabulary we use to describe what is a moment in a group action and the group action as a whole.

10. SUMMARY

Proxy agency is a central mechanism by which organizations carry out transactions with other organizations and individuals. The group authorizes the proxy by assigning a status role to the proxy. This occurs against a background of conventions in the community providing for transactions involving agents with such roles. A status role is a special kind of status function. A status function is a function defined by constitutive rules for the use of an object, say, in an essentially intentional collective activity type, which is assigned, by a tacit agreement in the community using it, to a particular object or event, or type of object or event. A status *role* is a status function assigned to an agent who accepts the role and whose exercise of his or her own agency in the role is crucial to fulfilling the function assigned. In virtue of this, the proxy agent can represent a group in transactions with others when carrying out the functions of her role, typically by performing acts that themselves have or assign status functions or roles in turn. The members of the group, in virtue of the authorization, are constitutive as well as causal agents of what the proxy thereby does. Proxies may be authorized to act to a degree autonomously, and to assign other proxies to create chains of authorization. Co-authorization in ongoing groups consists in accepting one's role in the organization as it is constituted. The power to authorize can be ceded to another, or be located with another in a larger institution in which an organization is embedded. We often have terms for both what the group does, *enter into a treaty*, and what the proxy does as a part of that, *ratify a treaty*. We sometimes use the same vocabulary for both: when the Congress declares war the United States does. The dual use of the same vocabulary can obscure the mechanism of proxy agency.

RELATED TOPICS

Status Functions (Ch. 23), Institutional Responsibility (Ch. 26), Institutions and Collective Intentionality (Ch. 27), Collective Intentionality and Language (Ch. 28), Collective Intentionality in the Law (Ch. 29).

REFERENCES

Davidson, D. (2001) "Agency," in *Essays on Actions and Events*, New York: Clarendon Press.

Ludwig, K. (2007) "Collective Intentional Behavior from the Standpoint of Semantics," *Noûs* 41 (3): 355–93.

——— (2010) "Adverbs of Action," in T. O'Connor and C. Sandis (eds) *Blackwell Companion to the Philosophy of Action*, Oxford: Wiley-Blackwell.

——— (2014) "Proxy Agency in Collective Action," *Noûs* 48 (1): 75–105.

——— (2015) "What are Conditional Intentions?" *Methode: Analytic Perspectives* 4 (6): 30–60.

——— (2016) *From Individual to Plural Agency: Collective Action 1*, Oxford: Oxford University Press.

——— (2017) *From Plural to Institutional Agency: Collective Action 2*, Oxford: Oxford University Press.

Searle, J. (1969) *Speech Acts: An Essay in the Philosophy of Language*, London: Cambridge University Press.

——— (1995) *The Construction of Social Reality*, New York: Free Press.

6

Coordinating Joint Action

Stephen Butterfill

1. INTRODUCTION

It is often necessary that agents' actions are coordinated if they are to successfully exercise shared (or "collective") agency in acting together. An eloping couple clink plastic beakers of cheap wine together to toast their escape, sharing a smile of achievement; on the beach in front of them a small group of roadies are putting up a marquee outside for a concert later that evening while the musicians, having been made to wait while the audio technicians replace a cable, playfully improvise on stage. In cases like these, successfully exercising shared agency involves coordinating actions precisely in space and time. Such precise coordination is not, or not only, a matter of having intentions and knowledge, whether individual or collective. Intentions and knowledge states may play a role in long-term coordination—they may explain, for instance, why the couple's both being on the beach tonight is no accident. But they cannot explain how the precise coordination needed to clink beakers or to share a smile is achieved. Given that it is not only intention or knowledge, what does enable two or more agents' actions to be coordinated, and so enables exercises of shared agency such as these?

Much psychological and neuroscientific research bears directly on this question. This chapter introduces that research: it outlines some of the key findings and describes a minimal theoretical framework, identifying along the way issues likely to be of interest to researchers studying collective intentionality.

2. JOINT ACTION

Where philosophers tend to focus on notions such as intentional shared agency, scientific research on coordination mechanisms is usually interpreted in terms of a broader and simpler notion of joint action. This is standardly defined by appeal to Sebanz, Bekkering, et al.'s (2006) working definition as:

any form of social interaction whereby two or more individuals coordinate their actions in space and time to bring about a change in the environment.

(Sebanz, Bekkering, et al. 2006: 70)

Although widely used, this working definition has some drawbacks. It requires that joint actions should be "social interactions," thereby raising tricky issues about which interactions are social. The working definition also appears to require that coordinating their actions is something the individuals involved in joint action do, perhaps even requiring that this is done with the end of bringing about a change. As we will see, there are reasons to consider the possibility actions can be coordinated without both (or even either) requirements being met. We can avoid the drawbacks while remaining true to the implicit conception underlying scientific research with a simpler and extremely broad definition:

A *joint action* is an event grounded[1] by two or more agents' actions.

This definition of joint action, like Sebanz, Bekkering, et al.'s (2006) working definition, is neutral on representations and processes. So when two people swing their arms in synchrony, the event of them swinging their arms is a joint action. Likewise, if fish are agents then the movements of a shoal are joint actions.[2]

How does research on coordination in joint action bear on the question about shared agency? Not all joint actions involve exercising shared agency, but some or all exercises of shared agency are, or involve, joint actions. It is reasonable to conjecture that what enables the actions of agents exercising collective agency to be precisely coordinated are mechanisms of coordination common to many different forms of joint action. To illustrate, consider entrainment.

3. ENTRAINMENT

Entrainment, the process of synchronizing two or more rhythmic behaviors with respect to phase, is a feature of everyday life. People walking side by side may fall into the same walking patterns (Ulzen et al. 2008; Nessler & Gilliland 2009), conversation partners sometimes synchronize their body sway (Shockley et al. 2003) and gaze (D.C. Richardson et al. 2007), clusters of male fiddler crabs wave their claws synchronously to attract mates (Backwell et al. 1998; Merker et al. 2009), and an audience will sometimes briefly synchronize its clapping (Néda et al. 2000).

As these examples suggest, entrainment enables the coordination of a wide range of joint actions, not all of which involve shared agency. In fact, interpersonal entrainment is sometimes treated as a special case of a process by which sequences of actions can be synchronized with sequences of environmental stimuli such as a metronome (e.g. Repp & Su 2013; Konvalinka et al. 2010), and, more boldly, sometimes even as just one instance of what happens when oscillators are coupled (e.g. Shockley et al. 2009: 314).

Which exercises of shared agency might entrainment enable? Entrainment allows for extremely precise coordination of movements (Repp 2000) and is probably essential for joint actions involving rhythmic music, dance, drill, and some martial arts.

How is entrainment related to agents' intentions concerning coordination or the lack thereof? Entrainment of two or more agents' actions can occur without any intention concerning coordination (e.g. Varlet et al. 2015), and without the agents being aware of the coordination of their actions (Richardson et al. 2005). Further, although subjects can sometimes intentionally prevent entrainment, entrainment and related forms of coordination do sometimes occur even despite individuals attempting not to coordinate their actions (e.g. Ulzen et al. 2008; Issartel et al. 2007). So whether two agents' actions become entrained is not always, and perhaps not typically, something which they do or could control.

But entrainment is not always independent of agents' intentions (Miles et al. 2010; Nessler & Gilliland 2009). Because no one can perform two actions without introducing some tiny variation between them, entrainment of any kind depends on continuous monitoring and ongoing adjustments (Repp 2005: 976). One kind of adjustment is a phase shift, which occurs when one action in a sequence is delayed or brought forward in time. Another kind of adjustment is a period shift; that is, an increase or reduction in the speed with which all future actions are performed, or in the delay between all future adjacent pairs of actions. These two kinds of adjustment, phase shifts and period shifts, appear to be made by mechanisms acting independently, so that correcting errors involves a distinctive pattern of over-adjustment.[3] Repp (2005: 987) argues, further, that while adjustments involving phase shifts are largely automatic, adjustments involving changes in frequency are to some extent controlled. This may be key to understanding the influence of intention on entrainment. One way or another (contrast Fairhurst et al. (2013: 2599) with Repp & Keller's (2008) "coordinative strategies" proposal), intentions play a role in frequency adjustments and thereby influence how tightly agents synchronize their actions.

Entrainment is clearly necessary for coordination in many joint actions requiring precise synchronization such as those involving rhythmic music or dance. Entrainment may also be important in ways as yet barely understood for a much wider range of joint actions in which such precise synchronization initially appears unnecessary.[4] But there must be more to coordinating joint actions than entrainment. After all entrainment depends on repetition whereas many joint actions are one-off events, as when a couple clink plastic beakers. Which forms of coordination enable one-off joint actions?

4. MOTOR SIMULATION

Many one-off joint actions—those which do not depend on repetition or rhythm—require precise coordination. In clinking beakers, swinging a toddler between our arms, and executing a pass in football, the window for success may be fractions of a second in duration and but millimeters wide. One way—perhaps the only way—of achieving such precise coordination depends on the existence of a phenomenon often called "motor simulation" or "mirroring". What is this?

To understand motor simulation, it is necessary first to get a rough fix on the idea that motor processes and representations are involved in performing ordinary, individual actions. Preparing for, and performing, bodily actions involves not only intentions and practical reasoning but also motor representations and processes. To illustrate, consider a cook who has grasped an egg between her finger and thumb and is now lifting it from the egg box. She will typically grip the egg just tightly enough to secure it. But how tightly she needs to grip it depends in part, of course, on the forces to which she will subject the egg in lifting it. The fact that she grips eggs just tightly enough throughout such action sequences which vary in how she lifts the egg implies that how tightly she grips the egg depends on the path along which she will lift it. This in turn indicates (along with much other evidence) that information about her anticipated future hand and arm movements appropriately influences how tightly the cook initially grips the egg (Kawato 1999). This fine-grained, anticipatory control of grasp, like many other features of action perform-ance (see Rosenbaum (2010: ch. 1) for more examples), is not plausibly a consequence of mindless physiology, nor of intention and practical reasoning. The processes and repre-sentations it depends on are motoric.

Motor processes and representations lead a double life: they occur not only in performing actions but also observing them. For instance, in someone observing the cook gripping and lifting the egg, there may be motor processes and representations related to those which would occur in her if she, the observer, were performing this action herself. One dramatic piece of evidence for this claim comes from a study in which activity in an observer's motor cortex was artificially boosted with transcranial magnetic stimulation (TMS). This caused minute patterns of activation (specifically, motor-evoked potentials) to occur in a muscle of the observer at just the times the agent being observed used the corresponding muscle.[5] As this illustrates, motor processes in an observer can carry detailed information about the timing of components of actions. *Motor simulation* is the occurrence of motor processes and representations in an observer concerning an action which she is observing or imagining and which are driven by observing or imagining that action. Motor simulation enables observers to anticipate how others' actions will unfold and the likely outcomes the actions will achieve (Wolpert et al. 2003; Wilson & Knoblich 2005). Such anticipation is reflected both in explicit judgments (e.g. Aglioti et al. 2008) and in spontaneous eye movements (e.g. Flanagan & Johansson 2003; Rotman et al. 2006; Costantini et al. 2014; Ambrosini et al. 2011).

How does any of this bear on the coordination of joint action? If motor simulation is to play a role in coordinating joint actions, agents must be capable of using anticipation based on motor simulation in preparing and performing actions different from those simulated. Accordingly, Kourtis et al. (2013) used neural markers of motor activity to show that motor simulation can occur in joint action even where agents are performing different actions in close succession. To investigate, further, whether motor simulation in joint action can facilitate coordination, Vesper et al. (2013) instructed pairs of people to jump and land at the same time. They found evidence that in some subjects there was a motor simulation of her partner's jump which influences how she herself jumps and so enables precise coordination in landing together. This is one example of how motor simulation may enable coordination in joint action.[6]

Reflecting on entrainment and coordination driven by motor simulation, it is striking that one-off motor simulation allows greater flexibility at the cost of some precision. Is there a more general trade-off between flexibility and precision in mechanisms under-pinning coordination? If so, what might this tell us about the nature of mechanisms underpinning coordination for joint action and their relations to each other?

5. FLEXIBILITY VERSUS PRECISION

Consider two ways of partially ordering mechanisms underpinning coordination. The first is precision: How precise, in space and time, is the coordination they underpin in the best cases? For instance, mechanisms underpinning entrainment enable expert musicians to coordinate their actions to within tens of milliseconds, whereas one-off motor simulation permits coordination of actions to within larger fractions of a second. A second partial ordering is flexibility: How wide is the range of situations in which this mechanism can underpin coordination? For instance, motor simulation can underpin coordination whether or not repetition or rhythm is involved, unlike entrainment. Thinking just about motor simulation and mechanisms underpinning entrainment, there appears to be a trade-off between precision and flexibility. This appears to generalize to other forms of coordination too, such as forms of coordination driven by shared intention. Gains in flexibility seem to come at the cost of precision.

Why? Before attempting to answer this question, it is useful to fix terminology with some stipulations. A *goal* of an action or behavior is an outcome to which it is directed. Relative to a particular action or behavior, goals can be partially ordered by the means-end relation. In saying that one goal is more *abstract* than another relative to a behavior or action, I shall mean that the latter is linked to the former by a chain of outcomes ordered as means to ends. A *goal-state* is a mental state (or a structure of mental states) which represents, or otherwise specifies, an outcome and is the kind of thing in virtue of which some actions or behaviors can be directed to certain outcomes. Given that intentions are mental states, they are paradigmatic goal-states. But intentions are not the only goal-states: as we saw in Section 4, some motor representations are also goal-states.[7]

So why might flexibility in a mechanism underpinning coordination come at the cost of precision? One possibility involves two conjectures. First, achieving flexibility generally depends on representing goals, and the more abstract the goals that can be represented, the greater the flexibility. To illustrate, entrainment can occur without any representations of goals at all, whereas motor simulation involves motor representations which are goal-states. But relative to intentions or knowledge states, motor representations are limited with respect to how abstract the outcomes they can specify are. Motor representations can specify outcomes such as grasping or transporting a fragile object, and even sequences of such outcomes (see, e.g. Fogassi et al. 2005). But they cannot specify outcomes such as selecting an organic egg or testing for freshness: motor processes and representations are mostly blind to things so distantly related to bodily action. A further conjecture is that processes involving more abstract goal representations typically (but not necessarily always) place greater demands on cognitive resources, which typically (but not necessarily always) results in lower precision. This conjecture is suggested by an analogy with the physiological. Because physiological processes are a source of variability, coordinating with a given degree of precision should get harder as the duration and complexity of the actions to be coordinated increases. Given that cognitive processes, like physiological processes, are a source of variability, increasing cognitive demands by relying on representations of more abstract goals should likewise increase variability and so limit precision.

In short, flexibility may come at the cost of precision because increasing flexibility requires representations of more abstract goals, which impose greater cognitive demands and thereby increase variability, so reducing how precise the coordination underpinned by a mechanism can be in the best cases. This may be why forms of coordination such as entrainment and motor representation can occur independently of, and even contrary to, intentions concerning coordination: precision requires such independence.

Thinking about trading precision for flexibility suggests that there is a gap in the forms of coordination so far considered. To see why, consider the situation of a couple alone on a beach. Having filled plastic beakers with wine, they spontaneously and fluidly clink them together in a toast without spilling a drop of wine. To explain how they are able to coordinate so precisely we cannot appeal to motor simulation alone; but it would be no less plausible to appeal only to practical deliberation involving intentions or other propositional attitudes. We need something more flexible than motor simulation and more precise than practical deliberation.

6. TASK CO-REPRESENTATION

Consider individual agents acting alone for a moment. A *task representation* links an event to an outcome in such a way that, normally, the event's actual or expected occurrence would trigger motor preparation for actions that should realize the outcome. Why do we need task representations? Imagine yourself cycling up to a crossroad. Even if you are concentrating hard on dodging potholes without being hit by the rapidly approaching car behind you (will it slow down or should you risk going through this hole?), it is likely—hopefully—that the traffic light's turning red will cause you to brake. The connection between red light events and braking actions need not require intentional control, thanks to task representations.

How is task representation relevant to coordinating joint actions? Let us say that two individuals have a *task co-representation* if there is a task concerning which each has a task representation.[8] Sebanz, Bekkering, et al. (2006) argue that the agents of a joint action can have a task co-representation concerning a task which only one of them is actually supposed to perform. This, they suggest, would enable agents to exploit motor simulation prior to, and independently of, observing any actual actions. Thus, task co-representation could in principle greatly extend the range of situations in which motor simulation could underpin coordination in joint action. To illustrate, consider again the couple on the beach filling beakers with wine and then clinking them together. As noted earlier (in Section 5), their doing this spontaneously, fluidly and with precision could not be explained by motor simulation alone when neither of them plays the role of leader. But it could be explained by Sebanz et al's proposal about task co-representation. If the couple expect to clink beakers after the wine is poured and have task co-representations concerning the task of each in the clinking, then they will be able to use motor simulation to anticipate each other's actions in advance of starting to act. This is one illustration of how task co-representation might underpin coordination for one-off joint actions where agents have to respond to events in ways they have never done before.

The task co-representation hypothesis—agents involved in a joint action can have a task co-representation concerning a task that only one of them is supposed to perform—generates a variety of predictions. It predicts interference and facilitation effects: when acting together with another, your performance of your task will be affected by facts about which task the other is performing, and your performance will be impaired or enhanced in ways analogous to those in which it would be affected if you were performing both tasks alone. This prediction has been confirmed for a variety of tasks (Sebanz et al. 2005; Atmaca et al. 2011; Böckler et al. 2012; Wel & Fu 2015). The task co-representation hypothesis also predicts that, in some situations when you are acting with another, events linked to the other's task will trigger some preparation (but not necessarily full preparation) in you for a task which is actually supposed to be performed by the other. Evidence in support of this prediction includes signs that agents of a joint action sometimes inhibit tendencies to act when another, rather than them, is supposed act (Sebanz, Knoblich, et al. 2006; Tsai et al. 2008), as well as signs that agents of a joint action are sometimes preparing for, or even covertly performing, actions that another is supposed to perform (e.g. Kourtis et al. 2013; Baus et al. 2014).[9]

Task co-representation is valuable in coordinating joint actions at least in part because it is more flexible than bare motor simulation while also more precise than practical reasoning. But there is a limit to what can be explained with either motor simulation or task co-representation, at least as we have conceived of them so far. Suppose motor simulation (whether or not triggered by a task co-representation) enables agents of a joint action to anticipate each other's actions. How could these anticipations inform preparation for their own actions, and, in particular, how could they do so without requiring cognitive processes inimical to precision? To offer even a candidate answer to this question requires going beyond motor simulation and task co-representation as we have so far conceived them.

7. EMERGENT VS PLANNED COORDINATION

In thinking about coordination for joint action it is useful to have plural counterparts of the notions of goal and goal-state introduced earlier (in Section 5). To say of an outcome that it is a *collective goal* of some actions or behaviors is to say that they are collectively directed to this outcome—that is, they are directed to this outcome and their being so directed is not, or not only, a matter of each action or behavior being individually directed to that outcome. This is a broad notion: raising a brood can be a collective goal of some eusocial insects' behaviors,[10] and repairing a broken fence can be a collective goal of some neighbors' actions. A *collective goal-state* is a mental state or, more likely, a structure of mental states, which specifies an outcome and is the kind of thing in virtue of which some pluralities of actions or behaviors can be collectively directed to certain outcomes. Bratman's account of shared intention aims to describe one kind of collective goal-state (Bratman 1993).

Following Knoblich et al. (2011), we can distinguish between emergent and planned coordination. *Planned coordination* is coordination driven by a collective goal-state,[11] whereas *emergent coordination* is coordination not so driven. Planned coordination is familiar from philosophical discussions of shared intention, one of the functions of which is to coordinate agents' actions (Bratman 1993: 99). By contrast, all the forms of coordination discussed in this chapter so far—entrainment as well as coordination driven by action and task co-representations—are naturally thought of as forms of emergent coordination insofar as it seems they could occur independently of the agents having any collective goal-state.[12] But there is also a growing body of evidence about the existence of planned coordination for joint action.

8. COLLECTIVE GOAL-STATES

Two pianists are producing tones in the course of playing a duet. Consider one of the pianists. There is an outcome to which her action is directed, the production of a tone or melody; and there is an outcome to which her and her partner's actions are collectively directed, the production of a combination of pitches or harmony. Do dueting pianists represent collective goals, that is, outcomes to which their actions are collectively directed?

One way to investigate this question involves covertly introducing errors. Loehr et al. (2013) contrasted two kinds of error: those which were errors relative to the goal of an individual pianist's actions (the pitch) but not relative to the collective goal of the two pianists' actions (the harmony); and those which were errors relative to both. They found neural signatures for both kinds of errors in expert pianists. This is evidence that dueting pianists do indeed represent collective goals. A further study indicates that these collective goals are represented motorically (Loehr & Vesper 2015).[13]

How might motor representations of collective goals underpin coordination for joint action? One possible answer is suggested by Gallotti & Frith (2013) who propose that a "we-mode" is required. They explain:

> The central idea of the we-mode is that interacting agents share their minds by representing their contributions to the joint action as contributions to something that they are going to pursue together, as a "we". [. . .] To represent things in the we-mode is for interacting individuals to have the content of their individual actions specified by representing aspects of the interactive scene in a distinct psychological attitude of intending-together, believing-together, desiring-together, etc.
>
> (Gallotti & Frith 2013: 163)

An alternative possible answer is suggested by what Vesper et al. (2010) call a 'minimal architecture for joint action'. They propose to start by attempting to characterize joint action and its coordination without postulating distinct psychological attitudes and without invoking representations of interacting agents as comprising a "we." Instead their proposal is that some or all of the representations underpinning coordination for joint action are ordinary motor representations, task representations and other representations that are also involved in the coordination of ordinary, individual action. Relatedly, in at least some cases, coordination is driven by representations which are *agent-neutral*, that is, which do not specify any particular agent or agents. This proposal is consistent with theories about the roles of motor simulation and task co-representation in coordinating joint action (see Section 4 and Section 6): anticipating another's actions and their effects appears to involve much the same agent-neutral motor and task representations which would be involved if one were actually performing those actions oneself. Of course, motor and task representations concerning actions others will eventually perform must ultimately have effects different from those concerning actions the agent will perform;

but this is necessary for both observation and joint action and need not involve a novel kind of attitude.

But how, given Vesper et al.'s (2010) "minimal architecture" proposal, could motor representations of collective goals underpin coordination for joint action? In each agent of a joint action, the motor representations of collective goals trigger preparation for action in just the way any motor representations do. This has the effect that each agent is preparing to perform all of the actions comprising a joint action, although not necessarily in much detail (compare Loehr & Vesper 2015). Now this may appear wasteful given that each agent will only perform a subset of the actions prepared for. But it is not. One agent's preparing (to some extent) to perform all of the actions that will comprise a joint action ensures that the resulting motor plan for her actions will be constrained by her motor plan for the others' actions. And, given that she is sufficiently similar to the others and that the possibilities for action are sufficiently constrained in their situation, her motor plan for the others' actions will reliably match their motor plans for their actions. So one agent's preparing to perform all of the actions has the effect that her motor plan for her actions is indirectly constrained by the others' motor plans for their actions. In this way, motor representations of collective goals could in principle underpin coordination for joint action by enabling agents to meet relational constraints on their actions (see further Butterfill 2016).

The conjecture that motor representations of collective goals underpin coordination for joint action provides one response to a question raised at the end of Section 6. The question was how anticipations concerning another's actions arising from motor simulation (whether bare motor simulation or occurring as a consequence of task co-representation) feed into preparing and monitoring your own actions. When coordination depends on motor representations of collective goals, the presupposition this question makes is incorrect. There are not two processes but one. Anticipation of another's actions and preparation for your own are not two separate things. They are parts of a single process in the same sense that, in preparing to perform a bimanual action, preparation for the actions to be performed by the left hand and anticipation of the movements of the right hand are parts of a single process. So where motor simulation and task co-representation involve collective goals to which a joint action is directed, motor processes themselves can ensure the integration of anticipations concerning another's actions with preparation for your own.

This is not quite the end of the story about collective goals. Research on perceiving joint affordances points to a second way in which motor representations of collective goals may underpin coordination in joint action.

9. JOINT AFFORDANCES

A *joint affordance* is an affordance for the agents of a joint action collectively—that is, it is an affordance for these agents and this is not, or not only, a matter of its being an affordance for any of the individual agents. Perceiving (or otherwise detecting) joint affordances is critical for many mundane joint actions such as appropriately gripping objects and applying the right force in moving them together, and crossing a busy road while holding hands. It is possible that motor representations of collective goals enable the agents of some joint actions to perceive joint affordances, or so I will suggest in this section.[14] But first, what grounds are there for supposing that joint affordances even exist?

Doerrfeld et al. (2012: 474) argue that 'the joint action abilities of a group shape the individual perception of its members'. In their experiment, perceptual judgments of weight were affected by whether the perceiver was about to lift the box alone or with another. Others have investigated different situations in which performing actions independently or as part of a joint action can affect how you perceive affordances. For instance, consider two individuals walking through a doorway. How wide must the doorway be for them to walk though it without rotating their shoulders? Davis et al. (2010 Experiment 1) show that the answer cannot be obtained simply by adding the minimum widths for each individual, and (in Experiments 2–4) that people can perceive whether doorway-like openings will allow a particular pair of walkers to pass through comfortably.[15] Importantly, people can perceive joint affordances for walkers not only when they are one of those walking but also when they are merely observing others walking together (Davis et al. 2010 Experiment 4). This suggests that the perceptual capacity does not depend on the perceiver's own current possibilities for action. So what makes perception of joint affordances possible?

Consider the conjecture that joint affordances are perceived as a consequence of motor simulation (this is one of two possibilities discussed by Doerrfeld et al. (2012)). This conjecture is made plausible by independent evidence for two hypotheses. First, motor representations can modulate perceptual experience; for instance, how an event is represented motorically can affect how a pair of tones are perceived with respect to pitch (Repp & Knoblich 2007; Repp & Knoblich 2009; for discussion, see Sinigaglia & Butterfill 2015). Second, perceiving another's affordance involves motor activity (Cardellicchio et al. 2012). These two findings make it plausible that, in general, perceiving some affordances is facilitated or even enabled by motor simulation. The findings just discussed suggest that the same may be true for joint affordances, that is, affordances for agents involved in one or another kind of joint action. But of course this is possible only given that there are motor representations of collective goals. After all, perceiving joint affordances requires motor simulation concerning the joint action, which would be triggered by a motor representation of a collective goal of the actions grounding the joint action; merely having separate motor simulations of each agent's actions could not underpin the identification of a joint affordance. This is why motor representations of collective goals may facilitate coordination in joint actions not only by enabling the agents to meet relational constraints on their actions (see Section 8) but also by enabling them to perceive joint affordances.

10. CONCLUSION

What forms of coordination for joint action enable humans to exercise shared agency in doing things such as clinking beakers, sharing smiles, erecting marquees, or producing rhythmic music? We have seen that there is much diversity. Coordination for joint action includes not only emergent varieties such as entrainment (see Section 3) as well as the forms underpinned by motor simulation (see Section 4) and task co-representation (see Section 6), but also planned coordination underpinned by motor representations of collective goals (see Section 8).[16]

This diversity in forms of coordination may exist in part because of a trade-off between flexibility and precision for individual mechanisms underpinning coordination (see Section 5). Having multiple mechanisms is useful partly because each makes a different trade-off between flexibility and precision.

Many exercises of shared agency appear to require both flexibility and extremely precise coordination. Improvising musicians ideally achieve temporal synchrony without becoming enslaved to a rhythm. How is this possible? Exercises of shared agency can depend on multiple forms of coordination, of course. Individual mechanisms underpinning coordination may be constrained by the precision–flexibility trade-off, but this constraint does not apply to a diversity of mechanisms considered in aggregate. So there is no theoretical obstacle to relying on highly flexible mechanisms yet achieving extremely precise coordination. This requires only that diverse mechanisms can have synergistic effects on coordination.

Just here we encounter the *synergy challenge*. Achieving precise coordination in space and time probably demands that mechanisms underpinning different forms of coordination are to a significant degree independent of each other (see Section 5). Yet acting flexibility requires that the different mechanisms sometimes non-accidentally operate synergistically—the shared intention, the task co-representation, and the motor representation of the collective goal cannot all be pulling in different directions. The challenge is to understand how, in some situations, mechanisms underpinning different forms of coordination and which are driven by largely independent representational structures can nevertheless non-accidentally have synergistic effects. Meeting this challenge may require attention to differences between novices and experts, to why practice is sometimes necessary, to the effects of common knowledge on moment-by-moment coordination (see, for example, D.C. Richardson et al. 2007), and to phenomenal aspects of coordination (as Keller et al. (2014) hint), among other things. The synergy challenge is currently a significant obstacle to progress in understanding how high degrees of flexibility and precision can be combined in the coordination of joint actions.

Another issue likely to demand future research concerns which, if any, forms of coordination require postulating novel kinds of representations or processes specific to shared agency (see Section 8). Although scientists sometimes adopt terms from philosophical discussions of collective intentionality such as "shared" and "we"-representations, the discoveries about the representations and processes underpinning coordination reviewed in this chapter do not require representations to be shared other than in the sense in which barrel organ aficionados share a taste in music.

One theme in this chapter was that much coordination of joint action appears to involve not fully distinguishing others' actions from your own. Take motor simulation, task co-representation and motor representation of collective goals. In each case, coordination involves motor or task representations of actions, tasks or goals that relate primarily to another's part in the joint action. This is not a matter of representing another's goals or plans as an observer: it is a matter of preparing actions and representing tasks she will perform in ways that would also be appropriate if it were you, not her, who was about to perform them. To a limited but significant extent, then, coordination involves representing both another's actions and your own in ways that give them equal status as parts of a single activity. The existence of such a perspective on the actions grounding a joint action might just turn out to matter not only for coordination but also for other aspects of collective intentionality such as commitment and cooperation.

ACKNOWLEDGEMENTS

I have benefitted immeasurably from extended collaborations with Natalie Sebanz, Guenther Knoblich and Corrado Sinigaglia as well as from shorter (so far) collaborations with Cordula Vesper and Lincoln Colling. I am also indebted to many people for discussion. Thank you!

REFERENCES

Aglioti, S.M., Cesari, P., Romani, M. & Urgesi, C. (2008) "Action Anticipation and Motor Resonance in Elite Basketball Players," *Nature Neuroscience*, 11 (9): 1109–16.

Ambrosini, E., Costantini, M. & Sinigaglia, C. (2011) "Grasping With the Eyes," *Journal of Neurophysiology* 106 (3): 1437–42.

Ambrosini, E., Sinigaglia, C. & Costantini, M. (2012) "Tie My Hands, Tie My Eyes," *Journal of Experimental Psychology: Human Perception and Performance* 38 (2): 263–6.

Atmaca, S., Sebanz, N. & Knoblich, G. (2011) "The Joint Flanker Effect: Sharing Tasks With Real and Imagined Co-Actors," *Experimental Brain Research* 211 (3–4): 371–85.

Backwell, P., Jennions, M., Passmore, N. & Christy, J. (1998) "Synchronized Courtship in Fiddler Crabs," *Nature* 391 (6662): 31–2.

Baus, C., Sebanz, N., de la Fuente, V. & Branzi, F.M. (2014) "On Predicting Others' Words: Electrophysiological Evidence of Prediction in Speech Production," *Cognition* 133 (2): 395–407.

Böckler, A., Knoblich, G. & Sebanz, N. (2012) "Effects of a Coactor's Focus of Attention on Task Performance," *Journal of Experimental Psychology: Human Perception and Performance* 38 (6): 1404–15.

Bratman, M.E. (1993) "Shared Intention," *Ethics* 104: 97–113.

Butterfill, S.A. (2016) "Planning for Collective Agency," in C. Misselhorn (ed.) *Collective Agency and Cooperation in Natural and Artificial Systems, Philosophical Studies Series*, New York: Springer.

Butterfill, S.A. & Sinigaglia, C. (2014) "Intention and Motor Representation in Purposive Action," *Philosophy and Phenomenological Research* 88 (1): 119–45.

Cardellicchio, P., Sinigaglia, C. & Costantini, M. (2012) "Grasping Affordances With the Other's Hand: A TMS Study," *Social Cognitive and Affective Neuroscience* 8 (4): 455–9.

Costantini, M., Ambrosini, E., Cardellicchio, P. & Sinigaglia, C. (2014) "How Your Hand Drives My Eyes," *Social Cognitive and Affective Neuroscience* 9 (5): 705–11.

Davis, T.J., Riley, M.A., Shockley, K. & Cummins-Sebree, S. (2010) "Perceiving Affordances for Joint Actions," *Perception* 39 (12): 1624–44.

Doerrfeld, A., Sebanz, N. & Shiffrar, M. (2012) "Expecting to Lift a Box Together Makes the Load Look Lighter," *Psychological Research* 76 (4): 467–75.

Dolk, T., Hommel, B., Prinz, W. & Liepelt, R. (2014) "The Joint Flanker Effect: Less Social Than Previously Thought," *Psychonomic Bulletin & Review* 21 (5): 1224–30.

Dolk, T., Hommel, B., Colzato, L.S., Schütz-Bosbach, S., Prinz, W. & Liepelt, R. (2011) "How 'Social' Is the Social Simon Effect?" *Frontiers in Psychology* 2: 84.

Fadiga, L., Craighero, L. & Olivier, E. (2005) "Human Motor Cortex Excitability During the Perception of Others' Action," *Current Opinion in Neurobiology* 15 (2): 213–18.

Fairhurst, M.T., Janata, P. & Keller, P.E. (2013) "Being and Feeling in Sync With an Adaptive Virtual Partner: Brain Mechanisms Underlying Dynamic Cooperativity," *Cerebral Cortex* 23 (11): 2592–600.

Flanagan, J.R. & Johansson, R.S. (2003) "Action Plans Used in Action Observation," *Nature* 424 (6950): 769–71.

Fogassi, L., Ferrari, P.F., Gesierich, B., Rozzi, S., Chersi, F. & Rizzolatti, G. (2005) "Parietal Lobe: from Action Organization to Intention Understanding," *Science* 308 (5722): 662–7.

Gallotti, M. & Frith, C.D. (2013) "Social Cognition in the We-Mode," *Trends in Cognitive Sciences* 17 (4): 160–5.

Gangitano, M., Mottaghy, F.M. & Pascual-Leone, A. (2001) "Phase-Specific Modulation of Cortical Motor Output During Movement Observation," *Neuroreport* 12 (7): 1489–92.

Issartel, J., Marin, L. & Cadopi, M. (2007) "Unintended Interpersonal Co-ordination: 'Can We March to the Beat of Our Own Drum?'" *Neuroscience Letters* 411 (3): 174–9.

Kawato, M. (1999) "Internal Models for Motor Control and Trajectory Planning," *Current Opinion in Neurobiology* 9 (6): 718–27.

Keller, P.E., Knoblich, G. & Repp, B.H. (2007) "Pianists Duet Better When They Play With Themselves: on the Possible Role of Action Simulation in Synchronization," *Consciousness and Cognition* 16 (1): 102–11.

Keller, P.E., Novembre, G. & Hove, M.J. (2014) "Rhythm in Joint Action: Psychological and Neurophysiological Mechanisms for Real-Time Interpersonal Coordination," *Philosophical Transactions of the Royal Society of London B: Biological Sciences*, 369 (1658): 20130394.

Knoblich, G., Butterfill, S. & Sebanz, N. (2011) "Psychological Research on Joint Action: Theory and Data," in B. Ross (ed.) *Psychology of Learning and Motivation*, San Diego, CA: Academic Press.

Konvalinka, I., Vuust, P., Roepstor, A. & Frith, C.D. (2010) "Follow You, Follow Me: Continuous Mutual Prediction and Adaptation in Joint Tapping," *The Quarterly Journal of Experimental Psychology* 63 (11): 2220–30.

Kourtis, D., Sebanz, N. & Knoblich, G. (2013) "Predictive Representation of Other People's Actions in Joint Action Planning: An EEG study," *Social Neuroscience* 8 (1): 31–42.

Loehr, J.D. & Palmer, C. (2011) "Temporal Coordination Between Performing Musicians," *The Quarterly Journal of Experimental Psychology* 64 (11): 2153–67.

Loehr, J.D. & Vesper, C. (2015) "The Sound of You and Me: Novices Represent Shared Goals in Joint Action," *The Quarterly Journal of Experimental Psychology* 0 (ja): 1–30.

Loehr, J.D., Kourtis, D., Vesper, C., Sebanz, N. & Knoblich, G. (2013) "Monitoring Individual and Joint Action Outcomes in Duet Music Performance," *Journal of Cognitive Neuroscience* 25 (7): 1049–61.

Ménoret, M., Varnet, L., Fargier, R., Cheylus, A., Curie, A., des Portes, V., Nazir, T.A. & Paulignan, Y. (2014) "Neural Correlates of Non-Verbal Social Interactions: A dual-EEG study," *Neuropsychologia* 55: 75–97.

Merker, B.H., Madison, G.S. & Eckerdal, P. (2009) "On the Role and Origin of Isochrony in Human Rhythmic Entrainment," *Cortex* 45 (1): 4–17.

Meyer, M., Wel, R.P.R.D. van der & Hunnius, S. (2013) "Higher-Order Action Planning for Individual and Joint Object Manipulations," *Experimental Brain Research* 225 (4): 579–88.

Meyer, M., Hunnius, S., van Elk, M., van Ede, F. & Bekkering, H. (2011) "Joint Action Modulates Motor System Involvement During Action Observation in 3-Year-Olds," *Experimental Brain Research* 211 (3–4): 581–92.

Miles, L.K., Griffiths, J.L., Richardson, M.J. & Macrae, C.N. (2010) "Too Late to Coordinate: Contextual Influences on Behavioral Synchrony," *European Journal of Social Psychology* 40 (1): 52–60.

Néda, Z., Ravasz, E., Brechet, Y., Vicsek, T. & Barabási, A.-L. (2000) "Self-Organizing Processes: The Sound of Many Hands Clapping," *Nature* 403 (6772): 849–50.

Nessler, J.A. & Gilliland, S.J. (2009) "Interpersonal Synchronization During Side by Side Treadmill Walking Is Influenced by Leg Length Differential and Altered Sensory Feedback," *Human Movement Science* 28 (6): 772–85.

Novembre, G., Ticini, L.F., Schutz-Bosbach, S. & Keller, P.E. (2013) "Motor Simulation and the Coordination of Self and Other in Real-Time Joint Action," *Social Cognitive and Affective Neuroscience* 9 (8): 1062–8.

Pacherie, E. (2008) "The Phenomenology of Action: a Conceptual Framework," *Cognition* 107 (1): 179–217.

Pietroski, P.M. (1998) "Actions, Adjuncts, and Agency," *Mind* 107 (425): 73–111.

Prinz, W. (1997) "Perception and Action Planning," *European Journal of Cognitive Psychology* 9 (2): 129–54.

Ramenzoni, V.C., Sebanz, N. & Knoblich, G. (2014) "Scaling up Perception Action Links: Evidence from Synchronization With Individual and Joint Action," *Journal of Experimental Psychology: Human Perception and Performance* 40 (4): 1551–65.

Repp, B.H. (2000) "Compensation for Subliminal Timing Perturbations in Perceptual-Motor Synchronization," *Psychological Research* 63 (2): 106–28.

——— (2005) "Sensorimotor Synchronization: a Review of the Tapping Literature," *Psychonomic Bulletin & Review* 12 (6): 969–92.

Repp, B.H. & Keller, P.E. (2008) "Sensorimotor Synchronization With Adaptively Timed Sequences," *Human Movement Science* 27 (3): 423–56.

Repp, B.H. & Knoblich, G. (2007) "Action Can Affect Auditory Perception," *Psychological Science* 18 (1): 6–7.

——— (2009) "Performed or Observed Keyboard Actions Affect Pianists' Judgments of Relative Pitch," *The Quarterly Journal of Experimental Psychology* 62 (11): 2156–70.

Repp, B.H. & Su, Y.-H. (2013) "Sensorimotor Synchronization: A Review of Recent Research (2006–2012)," *Psychonomic Bulletin & Review* 20 (3): 403–52.

Richardson, D.C. & Dale, R. (2005) "Looking to Understand: the Coupling Between Speakers' and Listeners' Eye Movements and Its Relationship to Discourse Comprehension," *Cognitive Science* 29 (6): 1045–60.

Richardson, D.C., Dale, R. & Kirkham, N.Z. (2007) "The Art of Conversation Is Coordination Common Ground and the Coupling of Eye Movements During Dialogue," *Psychological Science* 18 (5): 407–13.

Richardson, D.C., Dale, R. & Schockley, K. (2008) "Synchrony and Swing in Conversation: Coordination, Temporal Dynamics and Communication," in I. Wachsmuth, M. Lenzen, & G. Knoblich (eds) *Embodied Communication in Humans and Machines*, Oxford: Oxford University Press.

Richardson, M.J., Marsh, K.L. & Schmidt, R.C. (2005) "Effects of Visual and Verbal Interaction on Unintentional Interpersonal Coordination," *Journal of Experimental Psychology: Human Perception and Performance* 31 (1): 62–79.

Richardson, M.J., Marsh, K.L. & Baron, R.M. (2007) "Judging and Actualizing Intrapersonal and Interpersonal Affordances," *Journal of Experimental Psychology: Human Perception and Performance* 33 (4): 845–59.

Rizzolatti, G. & Sinigaglia, C. (2010) "The Functional Role of the Parieto-Frontal Mirror Circuit: Interpretations and Misinterpretations," *Nature Reviews: Neuroscience* 11 (4): 264–74.

Rosenbaum, D.A. (2010) *Human Motor Control*, 2nd edition, San Diego, CA: Academic Press.

Rotman, G., Troje, N.F., Johansson, R.S. & Flanagan, J.R. (2006) "Eye Movements When Observing Predictable and Unpredictable Actions," *Journal of Neurophysiology* 96 (3): 1358–69.

Schulze, H.-H., Cordes, A. & Vorberg, D. (2005) "Keeping Synchrony While Tempo Changes: Accelerando and Ritardando," *Music Perception: An Interdisciplinary Journal* 22 (3): 461–77.

Sebanz, N., Knoblich, G. & Prinz, W. (2005) "How Two Share a Task: Corepresenting Stimulus-Response Mappings," *Journal of Experimental Psychology: Human Perception and Performance* 31 (6): 1234–46.

Sebanz, N., Bekkering, H. & Knoblich, G. (2006) "Joint Action: Bodies and Mind Moving Together," *Trends in Cognitive Sciences* 10 (2): 70–6.

Sebanz, N., Knoblich, G., Prinz, W. & Wascher, E. (2006) "Twin Peaks: An ERP Study of Action Planning and Control in Coacting Individuals," *Journal of Cognitive Neuroscience* 18 (5): 859–70.

Shockley, K., Richardson, D.C. & Dale, R. (2009) "Conversation and Coordinative Structures," *Topics in Cognitive Science* 1 (2): 305–19.

Shockley, K., Santana, M.-V. & Fowler, C.A. (2003) "Mutual Interpersonal Postural Constraints Are Involved in Cooperative Conversation," *Journal of Experimental Psychology: Human Perception and Performance* 29 (2): 326–32.

Sinigaglia, C. & Butterfill, S.A. (2015) "On a Puzzle About Relations Between Thought, Experience and the Motoric," *Synthese* 192 (6): 1923–36.

Tsai, C.-C., Kuo, W.-J., Hung, D.L. & Tzeng, O.J.L. (2008) "Action Co-Representation Is Tuned to Other Humans," *Journal of Cognitive Neuroscience* 20 (11): 2015–24.

Tsai, J.C.-C., Sebanz, N. & Knoblich, G. (2011) "The GROOP effect: Groups Mimic Group Actions," *Cognition* 118 (1): 135–40.

Ulzen, N.R. van, Lamoth, C.J.C., Daffertshofer, A., Semin, G.R. & Beek, P.J. (2008) "Characteristics of Instructed and Uninstructed Interpersonal Coordination While Walking Side-by-Side," *Neuroscience Letters* 432 (2): 88–93.

Varlet, M., Bucci, C., Richardson, M.J. & Schmidt, R.C. (2015) "Informational Constraints on Spontaneous Visuomotor Entrainment," *Human Movement Science* 41: 265–81.

Vesper, C., Butterfill, S., Knoblich, G. & Sebanz, N. (2010) "A Minimal Architecture for Joint Action," *Neural Networks* 23 (8–9): 998–1003.

Vesper, C., Wel, R.P.R.D. van der, Knoblich, G. & Sebanz, N. (2013) "Are You Ready to Jump? Predictive Mechanisms in Interpersonal Coordination," *Journal of Experimental Psychology: Human Perception and Performance* 39 (1): 48–61.

Wel, R.P.R.D. van der & Fu, E. (2015) "Entrainment and Task Co-Representation Effects for Discrete and Continuous Action Sequences," *Psychonomic Bulletin & Review* 22 (6): 1685–91.

Wenke, D., Atmaca, S., Holländer, A., Liepelt, R., Baess, P. & Prinz, W. (2011) "What Is Shared in Joint Action? Issues of Co-Representation, Response Conflict, and Agent Identification," *Review of Philosophy and Psychology* 2 (2): 147–72.

Wilson, M. & Knoblich, G. (2005) "The Case for Motor Involvement in Perceiving Conspecifics," *Psychological Bulletin* 131 (3): 460–73.

Wolpert, D.M., Doya, K. & Kawato, M. (2003) "A Unifying Computational Framework for Motor Control and Social Interaction," *Philosophical Transactions: Biological Sciences* 358 (1431): 593–602.

NOTES

1. Events $D_1, \ldots D_n$ *ground* E just if: $D_1, \ldots D_n$ and E occur; $D_1, \ldots D_n$ are each part of E; and every event that is a part of E but does not overlap $D_1, \ldots D_n$ is caused by some or all of $D_1, \ldots D_n$. (This is a generalization of the notion specified by Pietroski 1998.)

2. Note that what follows is neutral on whether joint actions are actions. As a terminological stipulation, I shall say that an individual is an *agent of a joint action* just if she is an agent of an action which, together with some other events, grounds this joint action. (Depending on your views about events, causation and agents, getting some edge cases right may require adding that for this individual to be an agent of this joint action, this particular plurality of grounding events—her action and the other events—must include actions with agents other than her.)

3. See Schulze et al. (2005: 474–6). Keller et al. (2014) suggest, further, that the two kinds of adjustment involve different brain networks. Note that this view is currently controversial: Loehr & Palmer (2011) could be interpreted as providing evidence for a different account of how entrainment is maintained.

4. See, for example, Richardson & Dale (2005). For relatively speculative discussions, see Richardson et al. (2008); Merker et al. (2009); Keller et al. (2014: section 4).

5. Gangitano et al. (2001); see further Fadiga et al. (2005); Ambrosini et al. (2012). For a review of evidence that, when observing an action, motor processes and representations occur in the observer like those which would occur if she were performing an action of the kind observed rather than merely observing it, see Rizzolatti & Sinigaglia (2010).

6. For evidence that motor simulation also enables coordination in musical performances, see Keller et al. (2007); Loehr & Palmer (2011); Novembre et al. (2013). For evidence on development, see Meyer et al.'s (2011) investigation of motor processes and coordination in 3-year-old children.

7. For more detailed arguments that some motor representations are goal-states, see Prinz (1997: 143–6), Pacherie (2008) and Butterfill & Sinigaglia (2014).

8. This definition needs refining in various ways not directly relevant to the present discussion.

9. Wenke et al. (2011) and Dolk et al. (2011); Dolk et al. (2014) have defended hypotheses which, if true, would enable some of the evidence for these predictions to be explained without accepting the task co-representation hypothesis.

10. The insects' behaviors cannot be regarded as directed to raising a brood just in virtue of each individual insect's behavior being so directed because there is (typically, at least) a division of labor.

11. Note that, despite the name, planned coordination does not by definition involve planning.

12. Some forms of entrainment are probably a hybrid of emergent and planned coordination since, as we saw in Section 3, the precision with which entrained actions are synchronized can be influenced by the agents' intentions concerning coordination and therefore probably also by collective goal-states.

13. Further evidence for motor representations of collective goals is provided by Tsai et al. (2011); Ramenzoni et al. (2014); Ménoret et al. (2014) and Meyer et al. (2013).

14. The notion of a collective goal was introduced in Section 7; evidence for the existence of motor representations of collective goals was discussed in Section 8.

15. See Michael J. Richardson et al. (2007) for a further study involving jointly lifting planks.

16. This is not a comprehensive list. Relevant reviews include Knoblich et al. (2011) and Keller et al. (2014).

II

Shared and Joint Attitudes

Introduction to Part II

Marija Jankovic and Kirk Ludwig

Beyond attributions of intentions and actions we find a wide range of additional attributions to groups that use psychological terms, such as *belief, desire, interest, value, anger, guilt, feeling*, and so on. Here are some examples drawn from ordinary news reports, headlines and company websites.

General Motors believes there's economic opportunity as well as a social imperative in lowering emissions and addressing climate change.

The Philippines wants the United States to provide aid without conditions.

Britain and Europe share an interest in an amicable split.

But if **Britain is dismayed, angry and divided**, so is the rest of the EU.

After Trump Rejects Pacific Trade Deal, **Japan Fears** Repeat of 1980s.

70 years later, **a tiny French village remembers** the Syracuse pilot who saved them from the Nazis.

It seems clear that these attributions are related to the actual and potential behavior of the groups that are their subjects, especially with respect to their potential for engaging in behavior toward realizing collective goals—but how exactly? What does it mean, or could it mean, to say that a group, as opposed to an individual, believes or accepts something? Does it entail that all the group's members believe it, or does it even require that any of them do? What is it for a group of people to want something, or to share values or interests? Does it require that they all individually want what they are said collectively to want? If Britain is angry and dismayed, are all the British angry and dismayed? Is there something it is like to be angry Britain? And what do we mean when we say that we or a community, or a couple, remember something? Can we remember more as a community or a collective than we do individually? Part II of the Handbook addresses these and related questions about psychological attitudes we attribute, at least at first blush, to groups as opposed to individuals, and their relation to our understanding of group behavior.

There are seven chapters in Part II on "Collective Belief and Acceptance," "Shared Values, Interests, and Desires," "Joint Attention," "Joint Commitment," "Collective Memory," "Collective Emotions," and "Collective Phenomenology."

The first two are concerned with the attribution of attitudes that are closely involved in the explanation of action, representations of how things are and representations of what is to be sought. In the individual case, intentions are the vector sum of an agent's beliefs and desires. But if the analysis of shared intention cashes out in terms of a distribution of we-intentions to members of the group, then either group attributions of beliefs and desires are not to groups per se, on analysis, or if they are, then their significance must be understood differently than in the individual case.

In Chapter 7, "Collective Belief and Acceptance," Frederick Schmitt reviews a range of proposals that have been made about the analysis of group belief and acceptance. There are three main approaches. The first is that attributions of group belief are summative: to ascribe to a group the belief that, e.g. the election was rigged, is to say that all or most or enough of the members believe that the election was rigged. The second, non-summative, approach rejects this in favor of the view that attributions of group belief have the group literally as its subject, though it allows that its significance might be different from the significance of belief attributions to individuals. The third approach rejects attributions of beliefs to groups per se but argues that we can instead speak of groups accepting a proposition, where this is, e.g. a matter of the group's having an action-oriented policy that takes it as a fixed point, and this may be true even though none of the members of the group accept the proposition.

Chapter 8, "Shared Values, Interests, and Desires," by Bryce Huebner and Marcus Hedahl, looks at the various senses in which values, and interests, and desires can be shared, and their significance for collective action. First, there are common values, interests, and desires that are shared in the sense that many people have them, for example, valuing hard work, or independence, or education. These values are common in the sense of being distributed across those who have them. They are normatively significant in that they can guide behavior in groups and be essential to understanding its social dynamics, but they don't require a group that acts together. Second, there are shared values, interests and desires that strengthen group bonds and facilitate collaborative activities, and so guide the behavior of individual group members qua group members. This can be conceived in two ways. First, group members may take up group values as part of their understanding of what it is to belong to the group. The values inform group activities and projects through the adoption of them by its members. Second, the values may be understood not merely to be values of the members qua members of the group but values that organizationally structure the group, robustly shared values, as Hedahl and Huebner put it. For example, a military organization, interested in coherent strategy, may put in place structures and procedures to ensure consistency across units at the same level and between levels of organization. These structure collective behavior in ways that allow behavioral generalizations that abstract from details about the members and provides a basis for adopting the intentional stance toward the group.

Chapter 9, "Joint Attention," by John Campbell, focuses on a capacity that forms part of the infrastructure for effective joint action. Campbell argues that joint (perceptual) attention is a primitive phenomenon that grounds (i) the possibility of mutual or common knowledge of perceptually distinguishable objects, and makes joint action with respect to them possible, (ii) the possibility of communication about them, and (iii) our knowledge of one another's conscious mental states. On the first point, Campbell sees appeal to a primitive co-consciousness of perceptual objects as the key to explaining why agents do not face rational paralysis when faced with situations in which communication is imperfect and failure to coordinate with others leads to disaster. On the second, he argues that joint attention enables a more primitive form of communication than the kind characterized by Gricean intention-based accounts, and one that underlies intentional communication. On the third, he argues that *de re* imagination of another's experience is necessary for knowledge of it, and that *de re* imagination rests on the possibility of joint attention, and he uses this to explain the ease of imagining the experiences of conspecifics as opposed to the experiences of members of other species.

Chapter 10, "Joint Commitment," by Margaret Gilbert, explains her account of joint commitment, as underlying social life. A joint commitment is a commitment by two or more wills. It may be basic or non-basic. A joint commitment is a joint commitment to intend/believe/act and so on as a body, where acting as a body is acting so as to emulate as far as possible a single body intending/believing/acting etc. In the basic case, joint commitments are formed by members of a group expressing their (actual) readiness to commit them as a group to something under conditions of common knowledge. In non-basic cases, the authority to commit the group may be delegated, by a prior basic joint commitment, to a member or subgroup. Joint commitments give rise to obligations (and rights with respect) to each party to the joint commitment which cannot be unilaterally rescinded. Gilbert argues understanding joint commitment as the basic social notion explains the features of joint action better than rivals, and requires rejection of singularism about social notions, the view that they can be analyzed in terms of personal intentions, beliefs, desires and so on.

In Chapter 11, "Collective Memory," Kourken Michaelian and John Sutton review work on collective memory both in philosophy and in psychology and the social sciences, and argue that greater interaction between these two traditions would yield important benefits for both. They distinguish between collective memory in small-scale and in large-scale groups. Small-scale collective memory has largely been the province of psychology, while large-scale memory has been the province of history and the social sciences. Large-scale collective memory seems to be limited to semantic memory (expressing knowledge-that) while small-scale collective memory may be semantic but also procedural (knowledge-how) and episodic (experiential). In psychology, memory is analyzed in stages: encoding, consolidation, storage, and retrieval. These stages may be fruitfully applied to the analysis of collective memory as well. Michaelian and Sutton focus on small-scale collective memory in discussing encoding and retrieval and large-scale collective memory in discussing consolidation and storage. Encoding and retrieval in groups may be parallel or interactive, yielding four cases for study. Parallel encoding and retrieval lies at one end of the spectrum of collective memory, being merely distributive. Parallel encoding and collective retrieval is individual in the first stage but involves collective processes when deployed. Interactive encoding and parallel retrieval involves interaction in encoding memories, e.g. of a joint trip, through conversation and other interactions, but then only individual retrieval when the group disperses. Finally, interactive encoding and retrieval involves collective interaction both at the first and last stages of collective memory. Michaelian and Sutton consider the limitations of accounts of shared activity that focus on shared intention as a model of the process by which collective encoding takes place, and suggest bottom-up processes are required as well as top-down processes. In the case of collective retrieval, they suggest that work on joint attention in the collective intentionality literature can shed light on how the process works and what is distinctively collective about it, and that the literature on collective belief, particularly non-summative accounts, can shed light on how collective memory may be realized at the group level, though there may be significant disanalogies as well. In discussing consolidation and storage they turn to large-scale groups. There is less scope for interaction in large-scale groups and so it is unclear that they support the strongest forms of shared memory. They discuss the analogies between consolidation and storage in individual memory and in large-scale collective memory, and the role of conflict about the past in consolidation and the role of artifacts in storage.

Chapter 12, "Collective Emotions," by Hans Bernhard Schmid, argues that emotions are ways of knowing what matters in relation to action that focus our attention on our aims and values and dispose us to act. They are a form of practical knowledge, on this account, and Schmid argues that this extends to the case of joint action, where we need to know what matters to us as a group and not just individually. In this case, we can speak of collective emotions in the sense of emotions that are those of a collective or group, where the subject is plural rather than singular. The chapter first discusses the account in relation to individual action and then in application to collective action, arguing that there is room for analogous states in groups, and against a strictly distributive understanding of such group emotions. This is not to say that there is an affective state at the group level but that the emotions are shared collectively rather than distributively.

Chapter 13, "Collective Phenomenology," by Elisabeth Pacherie, distinguishes three issues about collective phenomenology. The first is just whether there is group level phenomenology, whether there is something it is like for the group oriented toward joint action to be such a group. The second is whether there are collective phenomenal states, collective joy or grief, for example, which are to be conceived of as realized in the experiential states of individuals in a group, but which are shared in a way that makes them interestingly distinct from an aggregate of individual experiential states. The third is the question of the relation between individual subject experiences and experiences of individuals as members of a group collectively experiencing something. On the first issue, Pacherie considers the relation of three views about what makes us individually conscious. The first view is that it is the particular neural circuitry of the brain. The second is that it is a matter of there being a global workspace for integration and distribution of representations. The third is that consciousness is realized in a certain sort of information integration in a system. The latter two views, being substrate independent, are consistent with group consciousness, but it is unclear how they capture phenomenal consciousness in the first place, and in any case it is unclear whether any groups meet the relevant conditions. On the second issue, Pacherie distinguishes the relevant sense of collective experiencing something from mere distribution of the same state type across a group. Collective experiencing requires instead a sort of alignment of individual experiences, by two sorts of factors, bottom-up and top-down. Bottom-up mechanisms are perception-action matching, mimicry, emotional contagion, joint attention, entrainment, and the like. Top-down processes include social identification and adherence to the norms and standards of the group, a group ethos, and joint commitment. On the third issue, Pacherie distinguishes a minimalist view, which holds that collective experiences differ only in their intensity and strength from individual ones, from the view that there is something special either in their mode or their content that pertains to their "we-ness."

7

Collective Belief and Acceptance

Frederick Schmitt

1. SUMMATIVE ACCOUNTS OF GROUP BELIEF

In ordinary speech we frequently commit ourselves to statements that might be taken to attribute beliefs to social groups—e.g. "The Ford Corporation believes the Pinto is safe." Yet many have found it implausible to treat these statements as closely analogous to superficially similar statements attributing beliefs to individuals. It is natural to resist the suggestion that groups are single entities, unities, subjects, or agents possessing a mental attitude of belief, as individuals are regarded as subjects or agents possessing the attitude of belief. To preserve the truth of statements about group belief, we understand them as disguised statements about individual beliefs, rather than as attributing a state of belief to a single entity. Quinton adopts such a view and generalizes it to all statements about group mental attitudes: 'To ascribe mental predicates to a group is always an indirect way of ascribing such predicates to its members. With such mental states as beliefs . . . the ascriptions are of what I have called a summative kind' (Quinton 1975: 9; see also Gellner 1956). Cohen follows Quinton in treating attributions of group beliefs in this summative way, though he interprets an attribution of an acceptance to a group as non-summative, attributing a single attitude to the whole group understood as a unity (Cohen 1989: 383; for discussion of the distinction between belief and acceptance, see below). We may formulate the *simple summative account* of group belief proposed here in this way:

> A group G believes p just in case each member of G believes p (alternatively: most members, or enough members, of G believe p).

This account is offered by Quinton and Cohen as an analysis of the meaning of ordinary talk of group beliefs. It reduces such talk to talk of individual beliefs and avoids imputing an entailment between statements of group belief and the existence of a group entity or a single attitude belonging to the group (e.g. it may avoid this imputation by taking "G" to be a plural term—i.e. a term referring plurally to the members of G and not to a group entity).

The simple summative account of group belief may be defended from some counter-examples to its *sufficiency* by adding to the summative condition a *common knowledge* condition for group belief: it is common knowledge among the members of G that members of G believe p, in the sense that each member knows that members of G believe p, and each member knows that each member knows this, and so on (Gilbert 1989: 260–73). The addition of this condition to the account is innocent in the sense that it does not prevent the account from reducing talk of group beliefs to talk of individual beliefs and related individual attitudes (such as individual knowledge). However, the condition does not fend off all counterexamples to the sufficiency of the summative account of group belief.

There remain the following counterexamples to the sufficiency of the summative account. First, in any group, the members believe what all human beings believe—e.g. that the sky is blue. Moreover, it is common knowledge among the members of the group that members of the group believe this. But we would hesitate to say that a group believes that the sky is blue just because its members exhibit this common belief and have common knowledge that they do. There are sources and mechanisms of belief universally present in individuals that explain why the individuals invariably have these beliefs. But there are no sources or mechanisms of belief universally present in groups that invariably produce such beliefs in groups. So groups do not invariably have such beliefs. It is worth noting, too, that groups do not usually exhibit important earmarks of belief for the propositions commonly believed by their members: it is not usually true that the group has a disposition to affirm the propositions commonly believed by their members; nor does the group usually have a disposition to reason practically or theoretically from these propositions. These points may be enough to support the claim that groups do not invariably believe the propositions commonly believed by their members.

Gilbert poses the case of *coextensive* groups as a counterexample to the sufficiency of the simple summative account:

> It seems quite possible to say, without contradiction, that (a) most members of the Library Committee personally believe that college members have to consume too much starch . . . ; (b) the same goes . . . for the members of the Food Committee; (c) the Food Committee believes that college members have to consume too much starch, whereas the Library Committee has no opinion on the matter.
>
> (Gilbert 1987: 189; 1989: 273)

Claims (a) and (c) are not contradictory. But on the simple summative account, these claims are contradictory, since it cannot be both that most members of the Library Committee believe p (that college members have to consume too much starch) and that the Library Committee does not believe p. Gilbert's point is that on the simple summative account, the sufficiency of the beliefs of members for group belief entails that all coextensive groups believe p if any of them does; and this consequence of the account is implausible.

One might seek to rule out the counterexamples above to the sufficiency of the simple summative account by adding to the requirement that all members believe p the additional requirement that these individual beliefs are *caused* by the group. Gilbert considers a variant of this causal condition on which the members' individual beliefs that *p* are caused by group *G* in the sense that a practice 'within *G* provides one of the basic reasons for which most of the members of *G* set out to believe that *p*' (Gilbert 1989: 286). Gilbert argues that this condition too is not sufficient for group belief.

Gilbert proposes a counterexample to the *necessity* of the simple summative account:

> Joe meets Karen and, wanting to say something pleasant, comes out with "Lovely day!" Karen, wanting to be agreeable says "Yes, indeed!" Joe and Karen then come across Fred, who grumbles about the day's weather. Karen confidently responds, on behalf of Joe and herself "We think it's a lovely day!" Karen's statement seems to be on target, as a statement of collective belief, irrespective of any personal beliefs of the parties regarding the weather.
>
> (Gilbert and Pilchman 2014: 195)

Here we reach the conclusion that Joe and Karen jointly believe that it's a lovely day without considering whether either participant believes this proposition. From this it follows that these individual beliefs are not necessary for joint belief. Lackey resists the intuition that Joe and Karen jointly believe that it's a lovely day on the ground that such an intuition stands in the way of distinguishing sincere expression of group belief from group lies (Lackey 2014a: 34).

In the course of explaining "the discursive dilemma," List and Pettit offer examples that show that the simple summative account fitted with the principle of majority rule cannot be *both necessary and sufficient* for group belief if the individual and group beliefs are rational (List and Pettit 2011: 45; see Pettit, Chapter 19, this volume). Suppose a three-member panel of climate experts must issue a group judgment as to whether the global temperature will increase by at least 1.5 degrees Celsius over the next three decades ("*q*"). Panel member *A* believes *q*, but members *B* and *C* do not believe *q*. If a majority of members believing a proposition is necessary for the group to believe the proposition, then the group does not believe *q*. However, it happens that panel members *A* and *B* believe, and member *C* does not believe, that global carbon dioxide emissions from fossil fuels are above 6,500 million metric tons of carbon per annum ("*p*"). And it also happens that panel members *A* and *C* believe, and panel member *B* does not believe, that if *p* then *q*. The beliefs of *A*, *B*, and *C* regarding *p*, *q*, and if *p* then *q* are consistent with the conformity of these beliefs to *modus ponens*, so their individual beliefs are in this sense rational. If a majority of member beliefs is sufficient for group belief, then the group will believe *p* and believe if *p* then *q*. Rationality of the group belief requires conformity to *modus ponens*, hence that the group believes *q*. But as we have seen, the group does not believe *q*, given the individual beliefs with regard to *q* and the principle of majority rule. If the group beliefs are to be systematic and rational, then either the group must honor the majority in the premises, believing *p* and if *p* then *q*, and violate the principle of majority rule in the conclusion by believing *q*, or it must honor the principle of majority rule in the conclusion, not believing *q*, and violate the principle of majority rule in the premises by not believing both of the premises. In the former case, the principle of majority rule is not necessary for group belief, while in the latter case the principle of majority rule is not sufficient for group belief. This shows that the summative account fitted with the principle of majority rule cannot supply both necessary and sufficient conditions of group belief (assuming that the individual and group beliefs are rational). The discursive dilemma shows that the principle of majority rule (or any principle of rule less than unanimity) cannot consistently be applied to premises one at a time and also to the conclusion. However, Tuomela has pointed out that the discursive dilemma does not show that the principle of majority rule cannot be consistently applied to the *conjunction* of the premises and also to the conclusion, since B and C do not believe the *conjunction* of p and if p then q (Tuomela 2003b: 126, note 7). The discursive dilemma does not by itself rule out a revised summative account that derives group belief in component propositions from the majority belief in compound propositions in specified contexts of reasoning.

Mathiesen (2011) considers the claim, supported by Meijers (2002) and McMahon (2003), that in any case in which the group believes p but the members do not epistemically rationally believe p, the group belief must lack epistemic rationality, since the evidence regarding p possessed by or accessible to the group would be the same as that possessed by or accessible to the members, and this evidence fixes the epistemic rationality of the belief p. Mathiesen constructs a forceful case of epistemically rational group belief p in which, because of a difference between the epistemic risk settings of the group and the members, the members do not epistemically rationally believe p.

Many writers have regarded one or another of the foregoing counterexamples to the sufficiency or necessity of the simple summative account as decisive against the account, as well as against a fortified version of the view adding the requirement that the group causes the members' beliefs. Lackey has proposed a different version of summativism that, she claims, withstands genuine counterexamples to the simple summative view (Lackey 2014a: 34–9).

Does rejecting summative accounts rule out any successful reductive individualist account of group belief? It does not. Note that summative accounts define group belief only in terms of the *beliefs* of individual members, ignoring other attitudes of the members and their actions. There is little investigation in the literature of alternative reductive accounts on which group belief is characterized in terms of non-belief attitudes or actions of individual members (such as those exhibited in Gilbert's example of Joe and Karen, reported above). The failure of summative accounts does not preclude a successful reductive account of this kind (cf. Sylvan 2012: 276–81).

A non-reductive account of group belief parallel to the simple summative account might also be proposed. On this parallel account, group belief is not defined as a conjunction of individual beliefs but rather defined in a familiar way in functionalist terms, as a state playing a causal-functional role (i.e. causally related in the right way to other group attitudes, sensory stimuli, and behavioral responses); group beliefs are then said to be realized by composites of individual beliefs. This proposal would evade the common belief counterexample to the sufficiency of the simple summative account, since only composites of individual beliefs that realize the causal-functional role of group belief figure in group belief, and common beliefs do not generally realize this causal-functional role. It would similarly evade the coextensive groups counterexample to the sufficiency of the simple summative account, since the beliefs that belong to all the members of the coextensive groups may play a causal-functional role of belief for one group without playing any causal-functional role of belief for a coextensive group.

2. NON-SUMMATIVE ACCOUNTS OF GROUP BELIEF

The objections to the simple summative account encourage the thought that our apparent attributions of group beliefs are not attributions of attitudes or actions to the individual members; they are attributions of single beliefs to the group understood as an entity, as a subject and agent analogous to an individual subject or agent. The single belief attributed would be understood as analogous to a belief attributed to an individual. Gilbert, Tuomela, and Pettit have proposed such non-summative accounts.

Pettit's account of group belief aims to resolve the discursive dilemma (Pettit 2003; List and Pettit 2011). He proposes that a group's beliefs are determined by the principle of majority rule, but (to allow for rational group belief and resolve the discursive dilemma) the application of majority rule is governed by the group's employment of one or another procedure for aggregating members' beliefs (see also Roth 2014). A group may employ a premise-based or a conclusion-based procedure for fixing group beliefs by aggregating members' beliefs. On the premise-based aggregation procedure, the group first determines its beliefs in premises for purposes of group theoretical or practical reasoning. The group belief in the premises is determined by the principle of majority rule. Once these group premise beliefs are fixed, the group's belief in a conclusion is fixed by rational theoretical or practical reasoning from the premise beliefs, such inference conforming to modus ponens. The resulting group conclusion may well run counter to the majority of members' beliefs as to that conclusion. On the conclusion-based aggregation procedure, the group first determines its conclusion by the principle of majority rule. The group's premise beliefs are then constrained by conformity to rational theoretical or practical reasoning to that conclusion. The premise beliefs so constrained may also run counter to the majority of the members' beliefs as to those premises.

It is worth noting, however, that on Pettit's account, which beliefs a group holds must generally be fixed by the group's actual use of an aggregation procedure, rather than the mere availability of an aggregation procedure. For both premise-based and conclusion-based aggregation procedures are available in any case, and the discursive dilemma shows that the group beliefs that would be fixed or constrained by these different aggregation procedures may conflict. One question, then, is in virtue of what the group counts as using a premise-based rather than a conclusion-based procedure (or the reverse). The answer would appear to be that this depends on the group's thinking in employing the procedure. The group counts as using a premise-based procedure, for example, only if the group identifies certain propositions as premises (i.e. as potential premises in potential rational group inferences like *modus ponens*) and others as conclusions, and it aggregates by the principle of majority rule members' beliefs as to the premises rather than members' beliefs as to the conclusions. All this requires the group to have group beliefs about, e.g. potential premises and conclusions and about members' beliefs, prior to the use of the procedure. But these group beliefs cannot be fixed by aggregation procedures in accordance with Pettit's account of group belief, on pain of regress. So Pettit's account of group belief must presuppose a different and yet-to-be-specified account of group belief. Lackey makes another point also leading to the conclusion that Pettit's account of group belief is incomplete: whether a group that employs a premise-based aggregation procedure counts as believing a proposition will turn on whether it has the right (truth-directed) reasons for adopting this procedure (Lackey 2014c: 25–6). And that makes group belief dependent on attitudes prior to the adoption of the procedure. From these points it follows that Pettit's account of group belief is incomplete: it needs to be supplemented with an account of group beliefs that do not depend on a group aggregation procedure.

Gilbert has developed a non-summative account of collective belief as a joint commitment of its members to believe as a body (Gilbert 1987, 1989, 1994, 1996, 2000, 2002, 2004; Gilbert and Priest 2013; Gilbert and Pilchman 2014). On this account, the normative implications of such commitments are central to group belief. Tuomela has developed an account of "normative" group belief that bears some resemblance to Gilbert's: individuals are committed to accept the relevant propositions and bound by norms governing these acceptances (Tuomela 1992, 2003a, 2003b: 111–12, 2007: 134–9). But Tuomela's account differs from Gilbert's in tracing this commitment to the authority of operative group members in virtue of their special positions and tasks within the group. For limitations of space, we focus here on Gilbert's account. This account lends plausibility to the idea that the group amounts to a subject in virtue of there being a joint commitment among the members, and amounts to an agent if the group has other states, such as goals and intentions, that may also be treated as joint commitments parallel to the joint commitment involved in group belief.

On the joint commitment account,

> The members of a population, *P*, *collectively believe that p* if and only if they are jointly committed to believe that *p* as a body.
>
> (Gilbert and Pilchman 2014: 197)

A joint commitment is analogous to the sort of personal commitment entailed by an individual decision to perform an action such as going to the store. Such a personal commitment entails that 'all else equal, the committed person ought to conform to the commitment' (Gilbert and Pilchman 2014: 197). It is unilateral and may be rescinded by the individual. A joint commitment of individuals similarly entails that all else equal, those individuals ought to conform to the commitment. But the joint commitment differs from the personal commitment entailed by an individual decision in entailing that a party to the commitment has an obligation to other parties to the commitment to fulfill the commitment. These other parties accordingly have a right to rebuke an individual who falls short of conforming to the commitment. And unlike the personal commitment, the joint commitment cannot be unilaterally, only jointly, rescinded (Gilbert 1996). The joint commitment account of collective belief thus explains obligations, rights of rebuke, and burdens in rescission that we observe in the behavior of members of collectivities. These obligations, rights, and burdens are not explained by the summative account by itself. Gilbert leaves the relevant notion of joint commitment undefined but takes it to explain the associated obligations and rights. Mathiesen argues that we can explain some of the obligations and rights involved in collective belief by appealing, not to a joint commitment, but to general norms of individual communication and of conformity to others' expectations in light of one's assurances (Mathiesen 2006: 170–1). But an obstacle to this explanation is that when others lack an expectation that one will conform to a requirement, there is no obligation generated by any expectation; yet the obligations associated with collective belief seem to be present even when others lack any expectation of conformity.

The joint commitment account of collective belief refers to believing p "as a body." Given the inclusion of this reference, the joint commitment account entails that in collective belief 'the parties are jointly committed to emulate, in relevant contexts, a single believer—a single party who believes p—by virtue of the actions, including the verbal utterances, of each' (Gilbert and Pilchman 2014: 198). Evidently this account presupposes that there is a property of a single subject's believing that applies both to individuals and to collectivities. If the recognition of this property is to place a substantive constraint on what counts as a collective belief, then the account must presuppose that there is a substantial similarity between individual and collective belief. This presupposition makes it harder to resist objections to the joint commitment account on the ground that these objections cite features of beliefs that belong only to the beliefs of individuals and so are not pertinent to collective beliefs. The more similar individual and collective beliefs are, the more pertinent the features of individual beliefs to collective beliefs are likely to be.

For many propositions p, joint commitment to believing p as a body will commit the parties not merely to speaking but also to acting in certain ways. Members are committed to reasoning jointly from p as a premise where reasoning is called for and p is relevant to the reasoning. However, the joint commitment to believe p as a body is compatible with an individual member not *personally* believing p and even openly expressing the personal belief that not-p, so long as the member makes clear that this is merely a personal belief. There are qualifiers that can be used to express personal doubt or disbelief (e.g. "Personally, I doubt whether p") without running afoul of the requirements implied by the joint commitment to believe p as a body.

According to Mathiesen, on the joint commitment account of collective belief, 'group views will likely not be held in an epistemically rational way' (Mathiesen 2006: 169). For group belief-forming practices will not have the benefit of criticism by individual members, since 'Within the group one is obligated not to question the group view, even if one believes it is false' (Mathiesen 2006: 169). If the joint commitment account of collective belief makes it unlikely for a collective belief to be epistemically rational, this would indeed be a counterintuitive consequence of the account. But a proponent of the joint commitment account may reply that the account entails only that a member must acknowledge the truth of p in collective discussion and reasoning as long as the group maintains the belief that p. The account does not entail that a member cannot (or is not obligated to) request that the group reopen the question whether p, by saying for example, 'I know that we have settled that p, but I would ask us to reconsider whether p in light of counterevidence we have not adequately considered'. Presumably such reconsideration by the group is compatible with an ongoing obligation of members to continue to acknowledge p in group discussion and jointly to reason from p, until the members jointly rescind the collective belief that p.

3. COLLECTIVE BELIEF VERSUS COLLECTIVE ACCEPTANCE

Some philosophers allow that groups can hold cognitive attitudes in a way analogous to the way individuals do (as single entities or unities having a single attitude) but deny that groups can hold *beliefs* in this way. Cohen, for example, allows that a group can in this way *accept* a proposition, but denies that a group can in this way believe a proposition.

For believing p requires *feeling* that p is true, and groups lack such feelings (Cohen 1992: 4, 55). If groups are to count as believing p, they must do so in virtue of the fact that each member of the group believes p. A summative account of group belief is therefore correct. By contrast, accepting p does not require feeling that p. Rather, 'To accept that p, is to have or adopt a policy of deeming, positing, or postulating that p' (Cohen 1992: 4). Here Cohen means to deny an account of group acceptance as a sum of individual attitudes. So he must have in mind that for a group to accept is for the *group* to adopt a policy of the *group's* deeming that p. He cannot mean that group acceptance is a matter of each member adopting a policy of that individual's deeming that p, nor a matter of each member adopting a policy of several members deeming that p, or a policy of several members jointly deeming that p. For these would be accounts of group acceptance as a sum of individual attitudes, in particular adoptions of policies of deemings. Moreover, such summative accounts would rarely be satisfied by any group. For, except in circumstances in which an individual has an unusual degree of power or authority over others, an individual cannot adopt a policy of several individuals deeming that p or jointly deeming that p. Cohen's position is that groups can accept propositions in a manner analogous to the way individuals do, even though they cannot believe propositions in this way. Gilbert has called "rejectionists" those who maintain that groups can only accept, not believe, propositions (Meijers 1999, 2002; Wray 2001, 2003; Hakli 2006). Rejectionists generally allow that groups are capable of the joint commitments to believe as a body with which Gilbert identifies group belief, rejecting only this identity claim.

In considering whether groups believe or merely accept propositions, we must set aside several senses of "acceptance" that are not pertinent to rejectionism. (1) The term can be used synonymously with "belief" or "judgment"; but since rejectionists contrast belief and acceptance, that is not what they mean by "acceptance." (2) The term is sometimes used to mean *supposition*: we reason from a proposition to which we do not assent, in order to ascertain its consequences, often for the purpose of judging whether the proposition is true or probable. But this is not the sense of "acceptance" employed by rejectionists, which carries an entailment of assent. (3) The term "acceptance that p" may be defined in such a way that it entails a suitably related second-order *belief* (e.g. the belief that the proposition p is empirically adequate, (van Fraassen 1980); or the belief that the proposition p is worthy of belief (Lehrer 1997)); whereas "acceptance that p" in the rejectionists' sense does not obviously entail any belief. (4) Gilbert employs the terminology of collective acceptance to characterize what it is for there to be a *social convention* in a population: in the case of a social convention by fiat, a principle of action (that any member of population P is to perform action A if in circumstances C) is a social convention in P if and only if all members of P jointly accept the principle of action (and this is common knowledge in the population) (Gilbert 1989: 373–407). Gilbert explains collective acceptance in this special sense as akin to the notion of an agreement among members of the population. So joint acceptance in this sense would seem not to be joint acceptance in the sense of a joint cognition, as pertinent to the topic of collective belief, but in the sense of a joint agreement, a sort of willing. Similarly, Searle employs a notion of collective acceptance to characterize status functions (a sort of constitutive rule) and social institutions within which they obtain: X (this piece of paper) counts as Y (a dollar bill) in circumstances C because we collectively accept that individuals have the power to do certain things with X in C (e.g., exchange X for certain goods) (Searle 1995, 2010: 58–60, 84–122).

Although Searle uses "we collectively recognize" and "we collectively accept" inter-changeably (2010: 56–8, 102–3), suggesting that collective acceptance is a sort of cognition, the relevant notion of recognition seems not to be purely cognitive but akin to agreement and thus to Gilbert's notion of acceptance; this is indicated by Searle's treatment of these locutions as equivalent to 'we simply make it the case by fiat, by Declaration' (2010: 98). Tuomela employs a similar notion of collective acceptance to characterize social notions like that of a social institution (Tuomela 2002: 122–200). Tuomela is explicit that the language of "acceptance" in this sense is performative (2002: 123) and the attitude of acceptance has a world-to-mind direction of fit:

> Collective acceptance in the sense of the participants' actively holding—and being committed to hold—an idea for the use of the group is a disposition to collective social action in the we-mode. The actualization of this disposition is a collective social action with the purpose of realizing the accepted sentence, making it true (or correctly assertible), or acting on it, depending on the case.
>
> (Tuomela 2002: 129)

In later work Tuomela makes room for acceptances as commitments to seeing to it that a proposition is "permissible" for the group in a manner that has a mind-to-world direction of fit, and he uses this notion of acceptance to characterize group attitudes (Tuomela 2007: 125–7). Since this notion of acceptance gives acceptance a world-to-mind direction of fit, it is not the notion pertinent to rejectionism (Tuomela 2002: 127), which resembles belief in having a mind-to-world direction of fit (see Schmitt 2014).

Turning now to the cognitive notion of acceptance employed in the rejectionists' contrast between belief and acceptance, we may say that belief and acceptance are taken to contrast in one or more of the following ways (Bratman 1992). (a) Belief is *theoretical* and acceptance is merely *practical*: belief plays a role as a premise taken for granted in both theoretical reasoning (concluding in further beliefs) and practical reasoning (concluding in actions), whereas acceptance plays a role only as a premise taken for granted in practical reasoning. (b) Belief is *context-independent*, i.e. whether one believes (and whether it is proper to believe) does not vary with a context of reasoning, whereas acceptance is *context-dependent*, i.e. whether one accepts (and whether it is proper to accept) varies with context. (c) Belief (when reasonable) aims at (or functions to represent) the *truth* of what is believed—belief is, or is properly, produced or regulated so as to be true, or fulfills its natural function only if true—whereas acceptance only aims at what must be assumed in order to reason successfully in light of *practical* concerns. (d) Beliefs are ideally mutually *consistent* and subject to an ideal of integration with cognition that pertains to all contexts, whereas acceptances do *not* ideally have these features. (e) Belief is normally *involuntary*, whereas acceptance is *voluntary*. (f) Some beliefs are binary and others take on *degrees*, whereas acceptances are *only binary*. Rejectionists maintain that when beliefs and acceptances are distinguished along these lines, group views are more accurately characterized as acceptances than as beliefs. They similarly maintain that the joint commitments to believe as a body with which Gilbert identifies group beliefs are more accurately characterized as acceptances than as beliefs.

There are two main arguments for the rejectionist position that groups do not believe but merely accept propositions. One argument assumes that beliefs contrast with acceptances in essentially involving epistemic reasons (Meijers 1999, 2002; Wray 2001, 2003). According to this argument, beliefs are typically regulated (or, in an alternative version of the argument, properly regulated) by *epistemic* and not practical reasons, and they are held for epistemic, not practical reasons. It is only acceptances that are regulated by and held for practical reasons. But group views and joint commitments to believe *p* are typically regulated by *practical* reasons. Such views are held for practical reasons. So, the argument goes, group views and joint commitments to believe are not beliefs but only acceptances. For example, Wray argues:

> the scientists working in the laboratory together first set their goal of working together on a research project. This shared goal then leads them to adopt the view that whatever sub-field they choose to work in is a subject worthy of investigation.
> (Wray 2001: 325)

To reply to this argument for rejectionism, the proponent of group beliefs may ask whether the scientists described here adopt this view that their chosen sub-field is worthy of investigation by a discussion of its worth regulated by evidential reasons (reasons favoring the truth of this proposition), or instead adopt this view by a discussion not so regulated or by no discussion at all. There is no reason why scientists could not adopt the view by discussion regulated by evidential reasons. But if they do so, it is plausible enough to describe their view as a joint commitment to believe as a body and to describe it as a group belief; at any rate, it is not a view adopted merely for practical reasons. Then there is no argument that their view is a group acceptance rather than belief because it is adopted merely for practical rather than evidential reasons. If, by contrast, the view that their chosen sub-field is investigation-worthy is adopted without discussion regulated by evidential reasons, the view is not plausibly regarded as a group belief; in the right circumstances it might be regarded as a group acceptance. But then the case is not plausibly a counterexample to Gilbert's joint commitment account of group belief. It is not a case in which a joint commitment to believe as a body amounts merely to a group acceptance rather than a group belief. For it is not even a case of a joint commitment to *believe* as a body. Such a joint commitment would require commitment on the part of the members to do what is necessary for belief. But the members could not sensibly regard their formation of the group view as fulfilling such a commitment. What they do in forming the group view falls so far short of what is required by such a commitment as to be incompatible with the persistence of any commitment they might have made, and obviously the view the group actually forms can hardly be identical with a joint commitment that no longer even exists. Since in this case the group view is not a joint commitment to believe as a body, its being a mere group acceptance rather than a group belief, if that is what it is, can pose no threat to Gilbert's claim that a joint commitment to believe as a body is a genuine belief and not an acceptance.

The other argument for rejectionism turns on the *involuntariness* of belief. According to this argument, beliefs are involuntary; only acceptances are voluntary; yet group views are voluntary; so group views can be acceptances but not beliefs. Moreover, a joint commitment to believe as a body is also voluntary; so the item with which a group view is identified on Gilbert's joint commitment account of collective belief is voluntary; hence on Gilbert's account, a group view can be an acceptance but not a belief. To this argument

Gilbert responds that a group view, and a joint commitment to believe p as a body, can be involuntary for the group (Gilbert 2002: 59–64; Gilbert and Pilchman 2014: 202–5). The fact that *individual members* of a group must will actions or commitments in order to join a joint commitment to believe p as a body does not imply that the group itself must will anything to form a joint commitment to believe p as a body. Moreover, even if groups had to form a collective goal of a joint commitment to believe in order to form such a joint commitment, the group's formation of this collective goal does not by itself entail that the group wills the joint commitment to believe p as a body. The members of the group must join a new joint commitment to believe p distinct from the joint commitment that amounts to the collective goal of the group's believing p, and this new joint commitment need not be willed by the group. To these points, Hakli (2006) replies that the required new joint commitment to believe p may simply be willed by the group without the formation of a collective goal; in this case the new joint commitment is voluntary. But to respond, it does not follow from the fact that each member's joining this new commitment is subject to that *member's* will (conditional on a similar willing by each other member), that the *group* wills the new joint commitment itself.

4. RELATED ISSUES

Some writers have investigated the relation of group beliefs to communication within a group and to communication between a group and those outside the group. Gilbert and Priest have argued that '. . . in the course of a paradigmatic conversation, the parties are negotiating the establishment of one or more collective beliefs on the basis of proposals made by one or another participant'; in paradigmatic conversations, a goal of the conversation is the fixing of collective beliefs on the topic of discussion (Gilbert and Priest 2013: 2; see also Gilbert 1989: 294–8). Tollefsen (2007, 2009, 2011) and Lackey (2014a) have developed accounts of what is required for a group to give testimony to others. Such testimony normally involves the expression or avowal of group belief. Lackey (2014b, 2014c) has given accounts of what it is for a group to lie and to bullshit. She has appealed to the phenomena of group lies and group bullshit to cast doubt on Gilbert's and Pettit's non-summative accounts of group belief.

We may ask whether groups have knowledge, as individuals do. Just as individual knowledge requires more than individual belief, so group knowledge would require more than group belief. We may ask what more group knowledge requires than mere group belief. These and related questions about group knowledge and group justified belief have been addressed by Schmitt (1994), Goldman (2004), Tollefsen (2007, 2009), Tuomela (2004, 2011), List (2005), Mathiesen (2006, 2011), Wray (2010), Rolin (2010), Hakli (2011), List and Pettit (2011), Wright (2014); and see Lackey, Chapter 15, this volume.

Many organized religions are associated with and even partly defined by belief. Scientific enterprises are often regarded as aiming at knowledge. There is an initial plausibility to the position that the beliefs and knowledge relevant to the characterization of these cultural institutions include group beliefs and knowledge. Several writers have investigated the questions whether scientific knowledge belongs to particular individuals or to groups (Hardwig 1991; Kitcher 1994; Knorr Cetina 1999; Gilbert 2000; Giere 2002; Kusch 2002; Giere and Moffatt 2003; Wray 2006, 2007, 2010; Bird 2010, 2014; Fagan 2011, 2014).

ACKNOWLEDGEMENTS

I would like to thank Kirk Ludwig for comments that prompted substantial revision.

RELATED TOPICS

Common Knowledge (Ch. 14), Collective Epistemology (Ch. 15), Corporate Agency: The Lesson of the Discursive Dilemma (Ch. 19).

REFERENCES

Bird, A. (2010) "Social Knowing: The Social Sense of 'Scientific Knowledge,'" *Philosophical Perspectives* 24: 23–56.

——— (2014) "When Is There a Group that Knows? Distributed Cognition, Scientific Knowledge, and the Social Epistemic Subject," in J. Lackey (ed.) *Essays in Collective Epistemology*, Oxford: Oxford University Press.

Bratman, M. (1992) "Practical Reasoning and Acceptance in a Context," *Mind* 101: 1–15. Reprinted in *Faces of Intention: Selected Essays on Intention and Agency*, Cambridge: Cambridge University Press, 1999.

Cohen, L.J. (1989) "Belief and Acceptance," *Mind* 98: 367–89.

——— (1992) *An Essay on Belief and Acceptance*, Oxford: Clarendon Press.

Fagan, M.B. (2011) "Is There Collective Scientific Knowledge? Arguments from Explanation," *Philosophical Quarterly* 61: 247–69.

——— (2014) "Do Groups Have Scientific Knowledge?" in S. Chant, F. Hindriks, and G. Preyer, *From Individual to Collective Intentionality: New Essays*, Oxford: Oxford University Press.

Gellner, E. (1956) "Explanation in History," *Proceedings of the Aristotelian Society, Supplementary* v. 30: 157–76.

Giere, R. (2002) "Distributed Cognition in Epistemic Cultures," *Philosophy of Science* 69: 637–44.

Giere, R. and Moffatt, B. (2003) "Distributed Cognition: Where the Cognitive and the Social Merge," *Social Studies of Science* 33: 301–10.

Gilbert, M. (1987) "Modeling Collective Belief," *Synthese* Special Issue on Social Epistemology 73: 185–204.

——— (1989) *On Social Facts*, London: Routledge.

——— (1994) "Remarks on Collective Belief," in F.F. Schmitt (ed.) *Socializing Epistemology: The Social Dimensions of Knowledge*, Lanham, MD: Rowman and Littlefield: 235–55.

——— (1996) "More on Collective Belief," in *Living Together: Rationality, Sociality, and Obligation*, Lanham, MD: Rowman and Littlefield: 339–60.

——— (2000) "Collective Belief and Scientific Change," in *Sociality and Responsibility: New Essays in Plural Subject Theory*, Lanham, MD: Rowman and Littlefield.

——— (2002) "Belief and Acceptance as Features of Groups," *Protosociology* 16: 35–69. Reprinted in *Joint Commitment: How We Make the Social World*, Oxford: Oxford University Press, 2014.

——— (2004) "Collective Epistemology," *Episteme* 1: 95–107.

Gilbert, M. and Pilchman, D. (2014) "Belief, Acceptance, and What Happens in Groups: Some Methodological Considerations," in J. Lackey (ed.) *Essays in Collective Epistemology*, Oxford: Oxford University Press: 189–212.

Gilbert, M. and Priest, M. (2013) "Conversation and Collective Belief," in A. Capone, F. Lo Piparo, and M. Carapezza (eds) *Perspectives on Pragmatics, Philosophy, and Psychology* 1: 1–34.

Goldman, A.I. (2004) "Group Knowledge Versus Group Rationality: Two Approaches to Social Epistemology," *Episteme* 1: 1–22.

Hakli, R. (2006) "Group Beliefs and the Distinction between Belief and Acceptance," *Cognitive Systems Research* 7: 286–97.

——— (2011) "On Dialectical Justification of Group Beliefs," in H.B. Schmid, D. Sirtes, and M. Weber (eds) *Collective Epistemology*, Frankfurt: Ontos Verlag: 119–53.

Hardwig, J. (1991) "The Role of Trust in Knowledge," *Journal of Philosophy* 88: 693–708.

Kitcher, P. (1994) "Contrasting Conceptions of Social Epistemology," in F.F. Schmitt (ed.) *Socializing Epistemology: The Social Dimensions of Knowledge*, Lanham, MD: Rowman and Littlefield.

Knorr Cetina, K. (1999). *Epistemic Cultures: How the Sciences Make Knowledge*, Cambridge, MA: Harvard University Press.

Kusch, M. (2002) *Knowledge by Agreement: The Programme of Communitarian Epistemology*, Oxford: Oxford University Press.

Lackey, J. (2014a) "A Deflationary Account of Group Testimony," in J. Lackey (ed.) *Essays in Collective Epistemology*, Oxford: Oxford University Press.

——— (2014b) "Group Belief: Lessons from Lies and Bullshit," manuscript.

——— (2014c) "Group Lies," manuscript.

Lehrer, K. (1997) *Self-Trust: A Study of Reason, Knowledge, and Autonomy*, Oxford: Oxford University Press.

List, C. (2005) "Group Knowledge and Group Rationality: A Judgment Aggregation Perspective," *Episteme* 2: 25–38.

List, C. and Pettit, P. (2011) *Group Agency: The Possibility, Design and Status of Corporate Agents*, Oxford: Oxford University Press.

Mathiesen, K. (2006) "The Epistemic Features of Group Belief," *Episteme* 2: 161–75.

——— (2011) "Can Groups be Epistemic Agents?" in H.B. Schmid, D. Sirtes, and M. Weber (eds) *Collective Epistemology*, Frankfurt: Ontos Verlag.

McMahon, C. (2003) "Two Modes of Collective Belief," *Protosociology* 18/19: 347–62.

Meijers, A. (1999) "Believing and Accepting as a Group," in A. Meijers (ed.) *Belief, Cognition, and the Will*, Tilburg: Tilburg University Press.

——— (2002) "Collective Agents and Cognitive Attitudes," *Protosociology* 16: 70–86.

Pettit, P. (2003) "Groups with Minds of their Own," in F.F. Schmitt (ed.) *Socializing Metaphysics: The Nature of Social Reality*, Lanham, MD: Rowman and Littlefield: 167–93.

Quinton, A. (1975) "Social Objects," *Proceedings of the Aristotelian Society* 76: 1–27.

Rolin, K. (2010) "Group Justification in Science," *Episteme* 7: 215–31.

Roth, A.S. (2014) "Indispensability, the Discursive Dilemma, and Groups with Minds of Their Own," in S. Chant, F. Hindriks, and G. Preyer (eds) *From Individual to Collective Intentionality: New Essays*, Oxford: Oxford University Press: 137–62.

Schmitt, F.F. (1994) "The Justification of Group Beliefs," in F.F. Schmitt (ed.) *Socializing Epistemology*, Savage, MD: Rowman and Littlefield.

——— (2014) "Group Belief and Acceptance," in S. Chant, F. Hindriks, and G. Preyer (eds) *From Individual to Collective Intentionality: New Essays*, Oxford: Oxford University Press: 61–96.

Searle, J. (1995) *The Construction of Social Reality*, New York: The Free Press.

——— (2010) *Making the Social World: The Structure of Human Civilization*, Oxford: Oxford University Press.

Sylvan, K. (2012) "How to Be a Redundant Realist," *Episteme* 9: 271–82.

Tollefsen, D. (2007) "Group Testimony," *Social Epistemology* 21: 299–311.

——— (2009) "Wikipedia and the Epistemology of Testimony," *Episteme* Special Issue on the Epistemology of Mass Collaboration 6: 2009.

——— (2011) "Groups as Rational Sources," in H.B. Schmid, D. Sirtes, and M. Weber (eds) *Collective Epistemology*, Frankfurt: Ontos Verlag: 11–22.

Tuomela, R. (1992) "Group Beliefs," *Synthese* 91: 285–318.

——— (2002) *The Philosophy of Social Practices: A Collective Acceptance View*, Cambridge: Cambridge University Press.

——— (2003a) "Collective Acceptance, Social Institutions, and Group Beliefs," in W. Buschlinger and C. Lütge (eds) *Kaltblütig, Philosophie von einem rationale Standpunkt*. Stuttgart: Hirzel Verlag.

——— (2003b) "The We-Mode and the I-Mode," in F.F. Schmitt (ed.) *Socializing Metaphysics: The Nature of Social Reality*, Lanham, MD: Rowman and Littlefield: 93–127.

——— (2004) "Group Knowledge Analyzed," *Episteme* 1: 109–27.

——— (2007) *The Philosophy of Sociality: The Shared Point of View*, Oxford: Oxford University Press.

——— (2011) "An Account of Group Knowledge," in H.B. Schmid, D. Sirtes, and M. Weber (eds) *Collective Epistemology*, Frankfurt: Ontos Verlag: 75–117.

van Fraassen, B. (1980) *The Scientific Image*, Oxford: Clarendon.

Wray, K.B. (2001) "Collective Belief and Acceptance," *Synthese* 129: 319–33.

——— (2003) "What Really Divides Gilbert and the Rejectionists?" *Protosociology* 18–19: 367–77.

——— (2006) "Scientific Authorship in the Age of Collaborative Research," *Studies in History and Philosophy of Science* 37: 505–14.

——— (2007) "Who Has Scientific Knowledge?" *Social Epistemology* 21: 337–47.

——— ed. (2010) *Episteme* Special Issue: Collective Knowledge and Science 7: 182–283.

Wright, S. (2014) "The Stoic Epistemic Virtues of Groups," in J. Lackey (ed.) *Essays in Collective Epistemology*, Oxford: Oxford University Press: 122–41.

8

Shared Values, Interests, and Desires

Bryce Huebner and Marcus Hedahl

Marsella Effertz was born on an early February morning in 1908 in Sawyer, North Dakota (Population 318); Oscar Johnson was born near sunset on that same day, just a few hundred yards away. They were married 21 years later, and they moved onto the Johnson family homestead to raise cattle, hogs, poultry, and eventually, four children. With each passing year, they grew fonder of telling friends that they had shared a birthday, a doctor, a farm, a family, and a life. While Marsella and Oscar's story is distinctive in what they shared, it's less notable for the fact that they shared aspects of their lives with someone else. We humans are highly social animals, who share many significant (and less significant) aspects of our lives with others. Customers who have never met can share a desire for speedier service. Spouses can share more robust values that help them satisfy their interest in spending the remainder of their lives together. Across numerous domains, people share values, interests, and desires; and understanding this fact can yield insights regarding the thoughts and behaviors of group members.

Yet everyday claims about what people share are often ambiguous and imprecise. When someone notes that the US Army embodies the values of "Loyalty, Duty, Respect, Selfless Service, Honor, Integrity, and Personal Courage," they may be speaking of values that service members typically adopt, or of values possessed by the Army itself. Similarly, when someone claims that the Teamsters have an interest in maintaining craft seniority, this might be a claim about the interests of individual Teamsters, or about how these Teamsters understand the aims of their joint activities. Finally, when someone argues that the Zapatistas desire creating a world in which many worlds fit (*Un mundo en que quepan muchos mundo*), they might be speaking of a motivation that's essential to the shared activities of Zapatistas, or of desires that individuals typically form qua Zapatistas. The grammar of these claims does not reveal their ontological significance; and a close examination of patterns of group behavior is often necessary to understand what is shared, and how it is shared.

Our aim is to examine some of the ways in which values, interests, and desires are shared. We hold that a methodological individualist can account for many forms of sharing without revision to their theory, but we also aim to motivate reflection on the possibility that some kinds of joint activity complicate this ontological minimalism. Sometimes, joint activities do more than provide the social scaffolding that makes individual values, interests, and desires possible; sometimes, joint activities generate new loci for values and interests, and new ways of valuing.

Joint activities → new ways of valuing

1. COMMON VALUES, INTERESTS, AND DESIRES

Relatively passive forms of sharing can sustain a broad class of phenomena that we call *common values, interests, and desires.* Like many people who inhabit North Dakota, Marsella and Oscar valued wide-open spaces, hills, and buttes. Each cultivated these values early in life, and this fostered the desires that led them to take up farming; without these values, they would have been less likely to develop an interest in raising children and livestock together on the plains of North Dakota. The common value that people often place on the spaces they inhabit can impact choices about how to structure the world, especially when such values are prevalent within a population. Someone who lacks an understanding of these values will have difficulties accounting for anyone's decision to live in North Dakota (or New York City, or Austin, Texas); and understanding the prevalence of these values within a particular demographic is often necessary to develop viable public policies.

Many inhabitants of Washington DC, for example, value the European character of that city's classic row-houses, and desire the preservation of that character. Failing to take these values and desires into consideration has led to recent construction decisions that have evoked outrage and distress among many Washingtonians (Shapira 2015). Yet these values and desires only exist as attitudes of individual Washingtonians. They share much in common with the attitudes of strangers who are simultaneously running toward a rain shelter (Searle 1983: 3–4): each wants to stay dry, but these desires do not involve the desires of the others; each would continue to have the same desire even if they were running alone; and if one of them wanted to play in the rain, this would have little influence on the desires of the others. Understanding the importance of such desires requires attending to the attitudes of individuals, the contexts in which they guide individual action, and the prevalence of these attitudes within a particular population. But since these attitudes are not implicated in the production of intentionally organized collective behavior, they are best understood as commonly held, and not shared in any ontologically significant sense.

Still, where common values, interests, and desires are prevalent within a population, normatively significant effects can emerge as a result of their aggregation. Consider three recent disputes over land-use in Yellowstone National Park and the surrounding areas (*The Economist* 2015). People who desire to raise cattle have argued with people who desire to restore the ecological stability of Yellowstone by reintroducing gray wolves as an apex predator. Parallel disputes have developed because the interest of cattle ranchers in preventing the spread of brucellosis conflicts with the values environmentalists place on preserving the roaming rights of the surviving members of the once vast herds of American bison. Finally, snowmobilers have defended their interest and desire in using public roads against environmentalists who argue that these uses are at odds with environmental values—because of the effects of noise and exhaust pollution on wildlife.

Explaining the actions of ranchers, snowmobilers, and environmentalists requires understanding what the members of these groups typically value, what they are typically interested in, and what they typically desire. These disputes arise in part because different values are common within these three demographics (Farrell 2015). The environmentalists value ecological diversity and stability, and have an interest in fostering this value even when it conflicts with the economic interests of cattle ranchers, or the interest that snowmobilers have in access to public space. The ranchers and the snowmobilers tend to value liberty, property rights, and access to public lands; and they are often suspicious of interventions by the federal government and by environmentalists who are seen as outsiders trying to impose their desires from the outside. A more accurate understanding of these attitudes could foster increased empathy in political debates, and more successful political concessions from each demographic. But individual attitudes remain central to these explanations; and the attitudes of most individuals would be unaffected by the attitudes of an environmentalist rancher whose values, interests, and desires were at odds with their broader demographic. Put much too simply, the values, interests, and desires that are common within these demographics guide socially significant forms of action without requiring a group that acts together.

Similar effects can, however, arise in well-organized groups, so long as the relevant attitudes are not essential to the ongoing behavior of those groups. Consider a philosophy department whose members all value the subtle techniques required to produce excellent coffee. At different points during the day, each desires coffee, and each has an interest in being caffeinated. Each researches different beans and roasters; each discusses brewing techniques with local baristas; and each attends carefully whenever a new café opens. But no matter how central this value is to their life, a member of this department can regard their views about coffee as a private matter; and discussions in the hallway about coffee will have little impact on the department's ongoing activity, beyond cultivating a sense of collegiality and calibrating individual coffee preferences. Moreover, while the members of this department might find ambivalence about coffee perplexing, or even disturbing, it would be problematic to sanction a new colleague (in her role as a faculty member) for such ambivalence. Finally, a new faculty member who learned that everyone in her department happened to value excellent coffee would gain no more reason to desire drinking it than she would gain by learning that many of her friends happened to have a similar value.

Still, a visitor who didn't understand the value these faculty members placed on excellent coffee would miss a real pattern, and this could make some behaviors seem mysterious or even irrational. It might seem surprising when most of the faculty members are late to a departmental colloquium, because a new café has just opened near campus; and it might seem odd when every question is organized around facts about the farming, production, or distribution of coffee. But, even in these cases, the practical importance of this common value would derive from its role in guiding individual actions; and an adequate explanation of the resulting behaviors could appeal only to the values, interests, and desires of individual faculty members, as well as the prevalence of these attitudes within this group.

2. SHARED VALUES, INTERESTS, AND DESIRES

Values, interests, and desires are not always shared so passively. We often work to sustain shared values, interests, and desires because of their role in the formation and stability of our interpersonal connections. We often rely on them to strengthen mutual bonds and to further our pursuit of collaborative activities. And they often play a crucial role in structuring the values, interests, and desires we adopt as group members. When values, interests, and desires are intimately tied to ends that we seek together, they often become *shared* attitudes, and not just attitudes that are common among us.

Over the course of their lives together, Marsella and Oscar cultivated shared values that allowed them to successfully raise children and livestock on their North Dakota farm. They each valued hard work, cooperation, and companionship, among many other things, and they valued these things in the context of their relationship. Unlike the values they happened to hold in common, these were subjects of active avowal that played an important and ongoing role in their decisions about how to organize the division of labor on the farm, and in their ability to plan for the future. Marsella and Oscar also cultivated shared interests in successfully raising crops, livestock, and children. These values and interests fostered shared desires, directed upon shared ends, including a desire to keep their family happy. In all likelihood, their collaborative activities would have been less successful without these values, interests, and desires; and they would have faced far more substantial difficulties in coordinating their behavior as the world changed around them, were these attitudes not in place.

Similarly, the members of less intimate groups often rely on shared values, interests, and desires to organize their joint activities. Returning to our imagined philosophy department, suppose each faculty member values curricular diversity as much as they value excellent coffee. They research different cultural and philosophical traditions; they develop their own strategies to make their courses more inclusive and less colonialist; and they each discuss these strategies with people trained in other traditions. Valuing curricular diversity might ground individual practices of syllabus design and the development of novel teaching strategies. But this value could also influence, and be influenced by, department-relevant desires and interests. For example, these practices might underwrite a shared interest in hiring in particular areas, and shared desires to offer new kinds of courses; this in turn might heighten or enrich the value that each individual places on curricular diversity. The impact of this value could also stretch beyond the current members of the department. For example, a job candidate who learned of this shared value would need to evaluate her willingness to adopt such a value, to treat it as a reason for acting, and to give up conflicting values that she may have. More significantly, it would be reasonable for members of this department to sanction a new faculty member who failed to adopt this shared value, and who failed to act in ways that were consistent with this value. Simplifying, we might then say that shared values can play a significant role in guiding the behavior of individuals qua group members, and group members who deviate from these values can reasonably be criticized for acting in ways that are inconsistent with the values of the group.

But how should such cases be characterized from the perspective of social ontology? This is a difficult question, and in the remainder of this section we address two possibilities that vary in the robustness of their ontological commitments.

Sharing Values, Interests, and Desires Qua Group Members

The first possibility turns on the interplay between individual-level and group-level processes, and the resulting effects on the self-understanding of group members. In the cases we have just discussed, individuals have taken up shared values, desires, and interests as part of their understanding of what it means to be a group member or a partner. The internalization of shared attitudes plays an important role in increasing the likelihood of success in joint activities, as shared attitudes put pressure on individuals to preserve interpersonal consistency and to sustain forms of means-end coherence structured around shared interests and desires (cf. Bratman 2014; Pacherie 2012). Put differently, shared values, interests, and desires can become the normative standards against which individuals calibrate their behavior: they can shape individual desires and interests, bringing individuals into alignment with larger groups.

Shared values, interests, and desires can also organize collective decision-making by structuring the normative spaces within which group members make decisions. Recent research in the philosophy of science suggests that shared values play a variety of roles in guiding individual and collective decisions about which problems to address, which alternatives to explore, which criteria to use in evaluating these alternatives, and how much consensus is required to reach a decision (Biddle 2007; Douglas 2009; Wilholt 2009). Often, such values play a critical role in the moment-to-moment decisions of individual scientists, making it difficult to separate the role of these values from the scientific products they underwrite. In part, this is because an individual's understanding of what they are doing qua scientist is shaped by the values of her lab, her discipline, her funding sources, and her colleagues—as a result, their decisions are laden with shared values at every point in the scientific process, from hypothesis construction to hypothesis acceptance (Kukla 2012).

Research in psychology has converged on a similar conclusion, suggesting that shared values, interests, and desires can play an important role in guiding the strategies of self-regulation that people adopt qua group members (Sassenberg and Woltin 2009). Group members who identify strongly with a shared goal—because they value it, have an interest in achieving it, or desire to bring it about—can sometimes mitigate various types of failures that arise in attempting to carry out a joint activity. For example, the members of groups that distribute cognitive labor to pursue a desired end often have difficulties initiating group-relevant action, staying motivated in the face of obstacles, and budgeting sufficient cognitive resources to the pursuit of that end (Wieber et al. 2012). But when group members pre-commit to a determinate plan of action, at least where they strongly identify with a shared goal, this can help them recognize opportunities to act toward collective goals, and lead them to initiate the required actions in ways that are strategically appropriate and triggered automatically (Thürmer et al. 2014). Importantly, it doesn't matter whether these pre-commitments are framed in terms of what I will do, or what we do, the psychological effect is the same (Wieber et al. 2012: 285). And this suggests that individual action guidance is often driven by the attitudes that individuals have qua group members (either in the sense that these attitudes are tied to an individual's role in a group, are held in virtue of thinking of themselves as group members, or are otherwise conceptually tied to the activities that the group carries out).

We contend that shared values, interests, and desires often constitute a form of social scaffolding, which makes particular forms of valuing and desiring possible for individuals. Valuing the collective pursuit of truth, having an interest in preserving methodological transparency, and desiring the replication of significant results, for example, may be essential to membership in the modern scientific community (Anderson 2004; Kitcher 2001). Much as it is only possible to understand an action as a withdrawal given a background context of institutions such as banks (Mandelbaum 1955), it is only possible to value the collective pursuit of truth, the replication of significant results, and the preservation of methodological transparency given a background context of a scientific community that shares these values. Without such a community, an individual might be able to value the pursuit of truth; they might desire to bring about a world where they pursue the truth with others; and they might long for a time when they were collectively pursuing the truth with a community that no longer exists. But unless they are embedded in the relevant community, their value will lack the social scaffolding that is necessary to share a value. In such cases, a proper analysis of individual behavior must appeal to shared values, interests, and desires, the prevalence of these attitudes in a group, and the networks of social practice that make the relevant individual attitudes possible. Social ontology should thus strive to explain the values, interests, and desires that individuals have qua group members (cf. Phelan et al. 2013). This will be especially important where shared values foster forms of joint action-guidance in light of shared values or interests, and where the unique contours of individual attitudes depend on their role in a collective action.

Importantly, the values and desires we adopt qua group members can change the deontic status of the actions we engage in, either individually or collectively. While some of us might wish this weren't true, members of modern Western philosophy departments often suppose, without much criticism 'that philosophy will indefinitely revolve within the scope of the problems and systems that two thousand years of European history have bequeathed to us' (Dewey 1930: 27). However, if a member of our imagined department made this same supposition, her colleagues would be right to criticize her for deviating from the shared value of curricular diversity. Both because of the role this value plays in structuring departmental decisions, and because of the expectations people have regarding members of this department. For her, rejecting this value requires being able to justify this decision to other members of the department. Of course, the fact that something is valued by a group to which one belongs doesn't imply that the value is unrevisable, nor does it imply that challenges to it are off the table; but as a group member, challenges to shared values tend to be the exception rather than the rule (Graham 2002: 123ff). In part, this is because shared values, even when they are the values of individuals qua group members, are more than common expectations, and more than shared understandings of joint activities; they are the normative grounding that allows group members to treat particular activities, entities, and practices as worthwhile or as essential to what they do together.

There are cases where analogous claims might seem to be misguided. For example, a Klansman who becomes disaffected with white supremacy is making the right decision, all things considered, and deserves praise for abandoning bigotry (to the extent that he has). However, the disaffected racist can be criticized by his fellow Klansmen for deviating from shared values; and these criticisms will be intelligible, though misguided to the extent that they are directed at him qua Klansman, and to the extent that they are criticizing the disaffected racist for undermining his status qua participant in a shared endeavor. And this will be true even though they lack, all things considered, standing to criticize the abandonment of racist values.[1]

Robustly Sharing Values and Interests

The interests and values people share qua group members can sometimes conflict with the values and interests that guide joint activities. Often, individuals simply give way, adjusting their attitudes to conform with other group members. But when we act together to satisfy shared interests or to pursue shared values, we can also reflect upon our shared attitudes, consider how they relate to other individual, common, and shared attitudes, and change our mind about what we should do, and what we should care about. At times, we can privilege joint activities, yielding *robustly shared values and interests* that are grounded in our interpersonal relationships. And this can allow us to revise or reprioritize conflicting values and interests, organizing them to guide collective action in accordance with the values and interests of the groups to which we belong.

Suppose the members of our imagined philosophy faculty frequently meet to discuss projects that will foster curricular diversity. They agree to pursue projects that foster this value; they alter their course of action where their joint activities are unlikely to satisfy this value; and they revise their plans to improve their chances of fostering this value. These processes of updating and revising allow this robustly shared value to play a similar normative role in guiding collective action to the one that individual values play in guiding individual actions. It serves as an organizing principle for recruitment and hiring; it structures collective decisions about who to invite for the department speaker series; and it has a significant impact on the courses people are assigned to teach, as well as the courses people are not allowed to teach. More importantly, someone who understood the role of this value could provide reliable and voluminous predictions and explanations of the behavior of this department. Since such predictions would be counterfactually robust, and would allow for generalizations beyond the current and previous behavior of this department, understanding the role of this value in the department's behavior would allow for the adoption of an intentional stance toward this group (Clark 1994; Dennett 1989). Not only does this value structure individual behavior in collaboratively meaningful ways, it also influences collective behavior in ways that allow for behavioral generalizations about the department itself.

Philosophers with methodological individualist predilections might think it obvious that the values arising in philosophy departments are chosen and adopted by department members, but similar kinds of robustly shared values can also be instilled and managed from the top down. The US military values effective strategy, and this drives decisions about recruitment, retention, promotion, and training. This value also plays a critical role in shaping the decisions individuals make on a wide range of socially momentous issues. But it would not be sufficient for the individual members of the military to value good strategy—even if every member does so qua member of the military. Valuing good strategy requires that strategies adopted by different individuals mesh, both with one another, and with the ends of the military as such. If they didn't, the strategies of one commander, which could be appropriate if executed in isolation, could easily conflict with the strategies of another, which also would be appropriate if executed in isolation. This is not merely an academic point: current US military doctrine includes structural mechanisms to ensure that the strategies of individual commanders are effective both in isolation and in the aggregate (Joint Publication 1). Military practice relies on these mechanisms to integrate strategy at multiple levels of organizational hierarchy, not merely from the top down, but also across compartmentalized organizations. As a result, there are patterns of behavior that are best predicted and explained by appeal to the values of the US military, as such.

Likewise, robustly shared interests can guide collective deliberation and structure patterns of collective action that are stable and predictable from the intentional stance. Consider the Teamster's interest in maintaining craft seniority during the merger between US Airways and American Airlines. Many Teamsters may have had this interest qua Union members. But craft seniority is also a core Teamster value, and as an organization the Teamsters aim to 'honestly, fairly, and aggressively fight to protect craft seniority for every member' (The Teamsters 2013), in accordance with legislative, contractual, and rank-and-file constraints. Success in this regard requires mechanisms to integrate interests at multiple levels of organizational hierarchy, and from multiple kinds of groups. While satisfying these interests requires the cooperation of union members, the shared interest in craft seniority can conflict with the interests of individual employees. And where it does, the Teamsters may retain such an interest, even if it happens to contravene the interests of the individual members (cf. Gilbert 1996). Indeed, collective deliberation in accordance with robustly shared interests can, and often does proceed without direct recourse to the individual interests on which they depend; and doing so leads to patterns of collective behavior that are in accordance with broader institutional values. These kinds of patterns are neither rare nor surprising—they often stem from the needs and limitations of bureaucratic structures (Raz 1986). And this allows such interests to play a significant role in interpretation of group behavior, paralleling the role of interests in guiding individual deliberations and individual actions.

Nonetheless, we wish to remain agnostic about the ontological status of robustly shared values and interests. We have avoided calling these "collective values and interests" in hopes of sidestepping the debates commonly found in the literature on collective intentionality. Regardless of one's position with respect to those debates, we contend that the analysis above gives us reason to place robustly shared values and interests on the same ontological footing as collective actions. If the intentional actions attributable to groups are best explained by appeal to complex interactions of individuals-and-their-relations, then similar interactions should be posited to explain robustly shared values and interests. If, however, some collective behavior can only be explained by appeal to facts about collectives themselves, be they the intentions of plural subjects (Gilbert 1996), the decision-making of collective agents (List and Pettit 2013), or a group-level cognitive process (Huebner 2014; Tollefsen 2015), then robustly shared values and interests ought to receive a similar ontological treatment.

3. THE SIGNIFICANCE OF ROBUSTLY SHARED VALUES AND INTERESTS

We often care deeply about robustly shared values and interests, a fact that can take on a particular significance for groups of our own. As participants in joint activities, things happen to *us*; it's *our* interests that can be furthered or set back; and it's *our* values that can be fostered or diminished. While the significance of sharing a birthday or a doctor can be fully captured by appealing to its significance for each individual, explaining what it means to share a family or a life requires a deeper understanding of the relationships between the values and interests of individuals qua participants and the values and interests of the groups to which they belong. We contend that an individual's values and interests qua group member, and the values and interests of the groups to which they belong, can sometimes stand in a relationship of constitutive, bidirectional, counterfactual dependence. Where this happens, individual values and interests are not just furthered by collective action, the individual values and interests are partially constituted by these robustly shared values and interests. A committed methodological individualist might have a hard time accepting this possibility. But we contend that if values are robustly shared, then the dissolution of a group will entail the dissolution of any *shared* values that have emerged in the context of shared activities. An individual might still desire to reconstruct a network of shared values; and they might still strive to reconnect with a community that shares those values. But robustly shared values guide the unfolding of shared activities; so while such an individual might maintain a vestigial remnant of values that were once shared, the values will not continue to exist unless they are reconnected to shared activities.

Returning to our first example, Marsella and Oscar cultivated shared values and interests that fostered their desire to keep their family happy. Each of them had their own conception of what that meant in practice; and each had an interest in taking the necessary steps to make sure that the other's interests were furthered in that regard. But, as often happens with people who work together to achieve shared ends, the things Marsella cared about had a significant impact on the things Oscar cared about (and vice versa); over time this led them to cultivate meshing and overlapping values and interests, which were integrated with their shared desire to keep their family happy. Because of the structure of their relationship, Marsella's interests gave Oscar a reason to modify some of his interests to suit hers; and Oscar's interests gave Marsella reason to modify some of her interests. Partnerships often yield interests that have the ability to influence, both constitutively and causally, the interests of comrades. This integration of interest is part of what allows us to maintain our joint endeavors even as our individual interests evolve.

But individual values and interests cannot simply be subsumed under shared values and interests. People often continue to disagree even qua group members about what is best for the groups to which they belong. Yet when the interests of group members conflict, we do not look to outsider interests to resolve these conflicts. Even in these cases—perhaps even particularly in these cases—the shared values and interests that help to constitute a group's common identity offer the possibility to distinguish participants in joint activities from a mere conglomeration whose values and interests are aggregated mechanically. By integrating our interests with the interests of a group, we gain a further interest in the flourishing of that group; and this remains true even when the interests of a group conflict with our individual interests qua participants.

This integration of individual and group interests can have a significant effect on group behavior, as we see in the decision-making practices among the Zapatistas of Chiapas. These practices are facilitated by members who, qua Zapatistas, value listening to whatever others say, so joint activities have been designed to foster this value. All community-relevant decisions require consensus in community assemblies; and deliberative practices have been designed to foster egalitarian attitudes within these assemblies, and to provide alternatives to hierarchical systems with centralized power. Indeed, it is a core Zapatista value that everyone should take part in democratic decision-making as a way of demystifying the nature of politics. But in many cases, the forward-looking values of this group have outstripped the values of individual Zapatistas. And at many points, it has been necessary to create new forms of participatory dialogue to foster autonomy and dignity, as well as new forms of network-based organization to foster forms of cooperation that are locally salient, dynamic, and sensitive to everyone's needs and interests. There is an ongoing commitment to creating 'the power to solve their own problems and to do so democratically' (Starr et al. 2011: 102–3). And success in this regard requires more than individuals who value listening, and more than individuals who value democratic engagements. It requires a shared willingness to take responsibility for the structural mechanisms that organize joint activities, a shared willingness to adopt new values where they are revealed through these deliberative processes, and a shared willingness to reform those processes if they come into conflict with values that are revealed through further deliberation.

With these cases in mind, we would like to close by noting two points that warrant further consideration. First, we have not considered the possibility of robustly shared desires. Doing so would require explaining the possibility of shared connotative states— something that is not required for robustly shared interests or values. While such states could exist, it is not immediately evident how to establish that fact. Perhaps this limitation reveals a deep fact about connotative states, or perhaps it reveals little more than a failure of imagination. In either case, this limitation points towards another point that seems worthy of further reflection. While robustly shared values and interests may play an integral role in some of most normatively significant relationships that humans can achieve, it may prove difficult to create the structural mechanisms required to sustain the bi-directional feedback necessary for such values and interests. In other words, we believe that values and interests can become deeply integrated into patterns of ongoing collective activity. Borrowing a phrase from Rawls (1999: 452), we would even go so far as to say that it is only as partners, collaborators, and participants in collective practices governed by robustly shared values and interests that we 'cease to be mere fragments'. But the world we currently inhabit too often fosters atomization and separation. And that means, perhaps tragically, that our current social world may be poorly suited to fostering such values and interests. So while it is quite possible to create and maintain values and interests that are fully ours, rather than simply mine and thine, in our current fragmented and fractured world such robustly shared values and interests may prove to be quite rare.

RELATED TOPICS

Interpersonal Obligation in Joint Action (Ch. 4); Joint Commitment (Ch. 10); Collective Emotions (Ch. 12).

REFERENCES

Anderson, E. (2004) *Value in Ethics and Economics*, Cambridge, MA: Harvard University Press.
Biddle, J. (2007) "Lessons from the Vioxx Debacle: What the Privatization of Science Can Teach Us About Social Epistemology," *Social Epistemology* 21 (1): 21–39.
Bratman, M. (2014) *Shared Agency: A Planning Theory of Acting Together*, New York: Oxford University Press.
Clark, A. (1994) "Beliefs and Desires Incorporated," *Journal of Philosophy* 91 (8): 404–25.
Dennett, D.C. (1989) *The Intentional Stance*, Cambridge, MA: MIT Press.
Dewey, J. (1930) "From Absolutism to Experimentalism," *Contemporary American Philosophy*, 2: 13–27.
Douglas, H. (2009) *Science, Policy, and the Value-Free Ideal*, Pittsburgh: University of Pittsburgh Press.

Farrell, J. (2015) *The Battle for Yellowstone: Morality and the Sacred Roots of Environmental Conflict*, Princeton: Princeton University Press.

Gilbert, M. (1996) *Living Together: Rationality, Sociality, and Obligation*, Lanham, MD: Rowman and Littlefield.

——— (2014) *Joint Commitment*, New York: Oxford University Press.

Graham, K. (2002) *Practical Reasoning in a Social World*, Cambridge: Cambridge University Press.

Huebner, B. (2014) *Macrocognition: A Theory of Distributed Minds and Collective Intentionality*, New York: Oxford University Press.

Joint Publication 1 (2013) *Doctrine for the Armed Forces of the United States*, US Department of Defense, March 25.

Kitcher, P. (2001). *Science, Truth, and Democracy*, Oxford: Oxford University Press.

Kukla, R. (2012) "'Author TBD': Radical Collaboration in Contemporary Biomedical Research." *Philosophy of Science*, 79 (5): 845–58.

List, C. and Pettit, P. (2013) *Group Agents: The Possibility, Design, and Status of Corporate Agents*, Oxford: Oxford University Press.

Mandelbaum, M. (1955) "Societal Facts," *British Journal of Sociology* 6: 305–17.

Pacherie, E. (2012) "The Phenomenology of Joint Action," in A. Seemann (ed.). *Joint attention: New developments*, Cambridge, MA: MIT Press.

Phelan, M., Arico, A. and Nichols, S. (2013) "Thinking Things and Feeling Things: On an Alleged Discontinuity in Folk Metaphysics of Mind," *Phenomenology and The Cognitive Sciences* 12 (4): 703–25.

Rawls, J. (1999) *A Theory of Justice*, Revised Edition, Cambridge, MA: Harvard University Press.

Raz, J. (1986) *The Morality of Freedom*, Oxford: Oxford University Press.

Sassenberg, K. and Woltin, K.A. (2009) "A Self-Regulation Approach to Group Processes," in S. Otten, K. Sassenberg, and T. Kessler (eds) *Intergroup Relations: The Role of Motivation and Emotion*, New York: Psychology Press.

Searle, J. (1983) *Intentionality: An Essay in the Philosophy of Mind*, Cambridge: Cambridge University Press.

Shapira, I. (2015) "D.C. Residents Battle Over Future of High 'Pop-Up' Condos," Washington Post, http://goo.gl/KLZAk0 January 15, 2015; Retrieved May 31, 2015.

Starr, A., Martínez-Torres, M.E. and Rosset, P. (2011) "Participatory Democracy in Action Practices of the Zapatistas and the Movimento Sem Terra," *Latin American Perspectives*, 38 (1): 102–19.

The Economist (2015) "Ranchers vs Bison-Huggers," http://goo.gl/uJRRGT 3 January 2015; Retrieved May 31, 2015.

The Teamsters (2013) "Seniority Protection: A Core Value of the Teamsters," http://goo.gl/bcr9DX February 21, 2013; Retrieved May 31, 2015.

Thürmer, J., Wieber, F. and Gollwitzer, P. (2014) "When Unshared Information Is the Key," *Journal of Behavioral Decision Making* 28 (2): 101–13.

Tollefsen, D. (2015) *Groups as Agents*, Cambridge: Polity Press.

Wieber, F., Thürmer, J. and Gollwitzer, P. (2012) "Collective Action Control by Goals and Plans," *American Journal of Psychology* 125: 275–90.

Wilholt, T. (2009) "Bias and Values in Scientific Research," *Studies in History and Philosophy of Science* 40 (1): 92–101.

NOTE

1. Thanks to Kirk Ludwig for asking us to clarify this point; for a detailed discussion of such issues, see Gilbert (2014).

9

Joint Attention

John Campbell

In this paper I stake out the claim of joint attention to be what grounds (a) the common knowledge of perceived objects that underpins joint action with respect to them, (b) the possibility of referential communication about perceived objects, and (c) our knowledge of one another's conscious experiences. I don't aim for more than a preliminary mapping of what I take to be the main issues. I begin by stating these three topics a bit more fully, then look at each in a bit more detail.

1. THREE WAYS IN WHICH JOINT ATTENTION GROUNDS OTHER COGNITIVE ABILITIES

The term "joint attention" is usually used for cases in which two or more people share a focus of perceptual attention on a single thing or scene. It's possible, of course, for you and I to be having a discussion of, say, a presidential campaign, or the law of tort, and in such a case we could be said to be "attending to the same thing," even though for each of us the focus of our attention is being achieved not by perception but through the use of language. If we are having a discussion about Ur of the Chaldees, for example, we might be said to be jointly attending to the ancient city. But such non-perceptual cases will not concern us here. In the literature generally, "joint attention" is used for cases in which two or more people are jointly attending perceptually to one and the same object or scene. In this chapter, I'll focus on the case in which there are just two people attending.

Joint attention seems to play a significant role in the development of children. Children are of course usually intensely social from the moment of their birth. They will engage in one-one engagements with their caregiver that are compellingly interpreted as social, responding to mood and emotion on the part of the caregiver. But at around 1 year old, joint attention begins to emerge, and with it, an understanding of other people as having referential states, states that relate to external objects in the shared environment, about which child and caregiver can communicate. In one basic type of case, child and caregiver attend to a single object, exchanging glances between each other and that object (Reddy 2005). This seems to be a milestone on the way to a mature understanding of other minds, and children who do not achieve joint attention seem to be limited in their subsequent understanding of other minds (cf. e.g. Hobson 2005).

There are (at least) three reasons why the phenomenon of joint attention seems to be philosophically interesting:

(1) In cases of joint attention, it is "out in the open" between the two participants which thing they're attending to. Things being "out in the open" seems to be a distinctive mark of successful communication (Stalnaker 2002). Simple perceptual cases seem to be basic cases in which it's "out in the open" between two people which thing they're thinking about and perhaps acting on (Peacocke 2005; Campbell 2002, 2011).

(2) Joint attention has some claim to be considered the most basic type of referential communication. As I'll suggest below, it seems to be more basic than cases in which communication is a matter of having Gricean intentions recognized, or the communication of knowledge about an object. In ordinary childhood development, it marks the transition from the child's original intense focus on the psychological lives of people around it, to back-and-forth communication about an object or scene (Bruner 1983, 1995).

(3) Joint attention is arguably the foundation of our capacity for an imaginative understanding of others. In the most basic cases, your understanding of another person's perspective on the world is anchored by a prior knowledge of which thing or scene they are attending to. This anchor is provided by joint attention to the common thing or scene (Moll and Meltzoff, 2011).

In cases of joint attention, it is "out in the open" between the co-attenders which thing is in question. How should we characterize the sense in which it's "out in the open" what we're talking about? There are two notions that seem relevant here. One is the idea of mutual knowledge. We have level-1 mutual knowledge that p between two people just if they both know that p. We have level-2 mutual knowledge if they both know that they both know that p. We have level-3 mutual knowledge if they both know that they both know that they both know that. And so on. The other idea that seems relevant is common knowledge. We have common knowledge that p just if, for every n, there is level-n mutual knowledge that p (cf. Fagin et al. 1995). I'll argue that we should think of joint attention as a primitive phenomenon, the cognitive basis on which we can achieve arbitrarily high levels of mutual knowledge.

Joint attention scenarios can be thought of as the most basic types of referential communication. I'll argue that joint attention scenarios provide cases of communication that seem more basic than can be modeled in terms of Gricean intentions. One significant way in which this comes out is in how we think of the use of "you" in communication by one of the participants in a joint attention scenario. On a Gricean approach, this use of "you" is modeled by the speaker having an intention that the hearer form a first-person thought with the appropriate predicative content (Peacocke 2014: 149). In contrast to this, it's possible to argue that the coordination between you-thoughts and I-thoughts on the part of speaker and hearer happens at a more basic level: there is no need for Gricean intentions on the part of the speaker, since even to grasp the thought expressed by the speaker's use of "you," the hearer must think first-personally (cf. Eilan (in preparation); Longworth (2014); Salje (2016)).

You might, of course, immediately put pressure on this idea by noting that someone incapable of joint attention—say, an autistic child—might nonetheless graduate to being capable of back-and-forth talk with others about, for instance, Ur of the Chaldees. There is nonetheless, I'll suggest below, a sense in which the structure of this more advanced communication can be regarded as modeled on the structure of joint attention.

Although joint attention makes it out in the open which thing we're focusing on, it doesn't make it out in the open the *way* in which we're each perceiving the thing. Even though you and I are attending to the same thing, it may be that we have quite different ways of apprehending it—different "modes of presentation," to use Frege's term. How do we achieve knowledge of another person's mode of presentation of the object? Here I'll argue that joint attention actually provides the basis for knowledge of another person's way of thinking of an object; knowledge of their conscious experience of the thing, achieved by imaginative understanding of them.

2. OUT IN THE OPEN

In the most basic case of joint attention, in which child and caregiver are focused on a single object and exchanging looks and glances about it, there is something freewheeling about the interaction. They may have no predetermined task to engage in with regard to the thing. It may have nothing about it except that it is in some way salient. So there can be a very broad range of emotional or cognitive responses that are engaged in, as part of the joint attentional exercise. For example, is it scary, fun, how can it be explored? In these cases, though, which object the child and caregiver are focusing on is plainly in some sense "out in the open." As we'll see, there is something *de re* about what exactly is out in the open here. *Of that object*, it's out in the open between child and caregiver which thing they're focusing on and responding to. There is, of course, such a thing as the *way* in which the object is given to the child, and the *way* in which the object is given to the caregiver. But it may not be out in the open between them what the ways are in which they're being given the thing. All that is out in the open between them is which thing is in question, not how it's being given.

There's a basic puzzle about the notion of "being out in the open" here, which we can state by considering not the freewheeling case in which there is no predefined task, but cases in which there is a task determined for both parties in advance, with a specific payoff structure. Suppose we have two adults in a situation in which (a) if they both take action, they achieve a significant but limited payoff, but (b) if only one of them takes action, disaster ensues. Anything is better than this second outcome (Akkoyunlu et al. 1975). Ordinary joint attention scenarios seem to be replete with situations in which, faced with a coordination problem that has this payoff structure, it can be manifestly rational for people to do the thing: to act together against a single target, for example. Suppose what we have to do is fire together at the tiger. If only one of us fires, disaster ensues, if we both fire, it's a success. Here it comes; you point, I nod and we fire. In fact, we don't even need the point and the nod, if you and I are braced for it as it comes, with a terrifying unmistakeableness, charging through the grass, ready to pass us altogether if we don't fire. We just see it and shoot, each relying on the other. The whole thing seems like a straightforward exercise in basic rationality. In a joint attention case like this, where you and I are perceptually attending to the same thing, what we're attending to can be sufficiently "out in the open" for it to be perfectly straightforward what we ought to do.

The trouble with this kind of case is that on the face of it, for it to be rational for each of us to engage in the joint action, it seems as though our identification of the target must be "out in the open" in a very strong sense. It seems that we must have "common knowledge" of which thing is the target, in some sense like this: we both know which object is the target, we both know that we know this, we both know that we know that we know this, and so on, for every finite value level of iteration of "we know that." This seems like a very strong condition, and it's puzzling to know how ordinary people could be meeting it in practice, though it seems as though they must be if they are to be able rationally to engage in a coordinated attack. Notice too that this will feed back to what we say about the ordinary, "freewheeling" case of joint attention, where it will similarly be "out in the open" between child and caregiver which thing they're attending to.

One classic way to bring out why infinitary knowledge might be needed here is to consider cases in which the communication between the joint attenders is problematic, in this sense: each time one of the joint attenders sends a message to the other as to which thing is the target, there is only a 50 percent probability that the message gets through. You might get this effect by supposing, for example, that our agents are not hunters, but generals on a battlefield, each of whose messengers have to make their way to the other general through a hail of gunfire in which they stand only a 50 percent chance of survival. Or perhaps our agents are using electronic communications that only work 50 percent of the time. Suppose then that we have two agents in such a situation. If one fires but the other does not, the entire planet will be reduced to smoldering rubble. If they both fire at the same target, then they will capture a bight of no-man's land, a significant but limited victory. Suppose that A sends a message, "Let's attack the big one." It would clearly be irrational for A to attack at that point, without knowing whether the message has got through. Suppose B gets the message. Then B knows which one A has identified as the target. But that isn't enough for B to fire, since B knows that A doesn't know whether the message has got through. So B has to send a message back to A, confirming receipt of A's message. Until A gets the message, it would plainly be irrational for A to fire. But now, merely sending the message doesn't imply that B knows that A knows B got the original message. For all B knows, the message might not have got through. So B has to wait on receipt of confirmation from A. These points can obviously be iterated indefinitely. The implication seems to be that for every level of mutual knowledge, A and B must both know that they both know . . . that the big one is the target. That seems to imply both:

(a) infinitary common knowledge is required for the joint attack to be rational, and
(b) in the situation described, this infinitary common knowledge will not be available.

And this runs into the problem that it seems as though in fact, in practice, in ordinary joint attention scenarios, it could perfectly well be rational for our two subjects to engage in a coordinated attack, with the payoff structure described above. How can that be?

In some recent papers, Harvey Lederman has addressed this kind of problem (Lederman (2016); Lederman (in press)). Lederman remarks first that not only does it seem obvious to common sense that it could be rational for the joint attenders in this kind of situation to engage in a coordinated attack, but as a matter of empirical fact, people do perform the attack successfully in experimental situations. Lederman concludes that even in the situation I described above, with the messages getting through only 50 percent of the time, it could be rational for our joint attenders to attack, after some number, say 17, exchanges of messages. His proposal is that we give up the assumption, implicit in the reasoning I've outlined so far, that our joint attenders must have common knowledge of one another's rationality. Perhaps they are individually rational, but don't need, for rational attack, to have common knowledge of each other's rationality. (Incidentally, Lederman is not explicit about the assumption I have emphasized, that the messaging system is imperfect. But it is, of course, only on the assumption that the messaging system is imperfect that the method of giving receipts for messages can be used to calibrate which level of mutual knowledge has been achieved. If the messaging system is known by both parties to be "safe," in that messages sent are always received, then it would seem that arbitrarily high levels of mutual knowledge could be achieved without any need to send receipts for messages.)

I think that Lederman's diagnosis here is completely wrong, but it's a bold and ingenious attempt, and it's instructive to look at it. It seems to me that in the situation I described above, with the messages getting through only 50 percent of the time, and this being known with unshakeable certainty by the participants, it couldn't be rational for either participant to attack, no matter how many messages were exchanged: the reasoning I sketched above seems absolutely compelling. The puzzle is that in ordinary cases of joint attention, where we are aware of one another and the target, it's "out in the open" what the target is, in a way that transcends any mutual knowledge we can achieve through any number of uses of a 50 percent reliable messaging system. That's what seems to underpin the rationality of attack in the joint attention case, where rational attack is not possible in our messaging case. The puzzle is to explain this idea of it being "out in the open" what the target is in the joint attention case, if it can't be explained as a matter of achieving some n-level mutual knowledge of what the target is.

What about Lederman's point that, empirically, people do successfully attack after a certain amount of messaging back and forth? I think the point here is that, in practice, people do not regard it as an unshakeable certainty that the messaging system is only 50 percent reliable. If, after 17 shots, we find that our messages to one another have all got through, we are going to think that the 50 percent number needs revision: the messaging system is actually working fine. If you and I are in a phone conversation and keep getting dropouts, you might suggest that we switch to a landline. On the new phones, we try a couple of tests—"Is this better?," "Can you hear me now?"—and if they go OK then we take it that the system is working. The situation is somewhat analogous to the case in which a roulette wheel keeps coming up red. After say seventeen reds, it would be only the most resolute probability theorist who insists that on the next turn, black is just as likely as red. Anyone with a bit of common sense would be thinking that maybe the wheel isn't fair. Similarly, even on the battlefield, where the two generals can see the bullets whistling through the air and people being hit, if their messengers keep getting through to one another, the natural thought is that there is some dispensation saving the messengers between the generals specifically, and that in some mysterious way, their communications are not subject to the bullets. The point here is that if the messaging system is now thought by the two subjects to be safe, then there is a sense in which it's "out in the open" between them what the target is, that is similar to what's available in the joint attention case.

Lederman's positive proposal is that we drop the assumption of common knowledge of rationality between the two participants. But we need to distinguish between (a) merely dropping the assumption of rationality, and (b) assuming a quite specific form of madness. Merely dropping the assumption sounds reasonable enough—which of us really does manage to sustain rational performance uniformly throughout the day?—but doesn't make coordinated attack rational. After all, there's no saying in advance, so far, just what form the departure from rationality will take. We might be looking at a subject who simply forgets what the task was, or who gives way to a big attack of nerves. Lederman needs each of his subjects to assume, at some level, that the other person is, as we might say, "trigger happy." The simplest form would be to suppose that we have two subjects who're individually rational, but each supposes that the other is trigger happy, in the sense that the other will, merely on hearing the name of the target, blaze away at it, despite the payoff structure being as before—the destruction of the planet if only one attacks, the capture of a bight of no-man's land if they both attack. So we're dealing with subjects each of whom supposes the other to be like that: happy to risk the destruction of the planet, for the sake of the bight of no-man's land, by blazing away in the absence of any knowledge as to whether the other person will attack. Now this does allow the subjects to be individually rational while still engaging in coordinated attack. The trouble is that there seems to be absolutely no plausibility to the idea that, empirically, subjects routinely take one another to be trigger happy in this sense. So this can't be the explanation of why subjects do tend to engage in coordinated attack after a certain amount of messaging back and forth. And it can't explain why it seems so evident that it can be rational for subjects in a joint attention scenario to engage in coordinated attack.

I think that we ought to stay with the idea that I began with: that in ordinary joint attention cases, there's a sense in which it's "out in the open" between the two subjects which thing is the target of their attention. To put it another way, we should regard "X and Y are jointly attending to Z" as a primitive, not to be explained in terms of the knowledge or beliefs that each of X and Y have individually. We should regard joint attention as a fundamental type of conscious state that can explain other cognitive achievements of the subjects who are jointly attending, but that is not itself susceptible to explanation in terms of individualistic knowledge or beliefs of the two participants. This route is, I think, blocked to Lederman, who says, 'Two people are jointly attending to an object just in case they are engaged in a pattern of eye-movements between the object and one another's eyes, first looking at the object, and then checking that the other is also looking at the object' (Lederman (in press): 25–6). The trouble with this quasi-behavioristic conception of joint attention is that it's far too impoverished to explain the cognitive achievements that are possible on the basis of joint attention. Two subjects, each of whom took the other to be unaware of their presence, could meet Lederman's condition on joint attention. It's no surprise that Lederman has such difficulty in explaining what seems to be the evident possibility of rational coordinated attack on the part of subjects who are themselves rational. From this impoverished evidential base, they have to somehow, presumably through the use of auxiliary knowledge and further observation, work their ways up to knowledge that the other person is aware of their presence, is communicating about the target, and so on. Whether this can be done at all, on that evidential base, is by no means obvious. What I am proposing may seem to have the benefits of theft over honest toil: we start out with joint attention by both subjects to the target, a state that can epistemically ground mutual knowledge of the target, but that is not exhausted by this capacity for grounding mutual knowledge, and that can of itself rationalize coordinated attack (cf. Campbell 2011). But here as elsewhere in epistemology, it is important to recognize the richness of the starting points we have, and not generate spurious problems by supposing that our epistemic base is far thinner than it is in fact.

3. JOINT ATTENTION, NOT GRICEAN INTENTION, AS THE FOUNDATION OF REFERENTIAL COMMUNICATION

In his classic paper, "Meaning," Grice analyzed "X means that p" as "X intends to produce the belief that p, by means of recognition of the intention to produce that belief" (Grice 1957). A number of articles and books have been written about Grice's proposal (e.g. Moore 2017). For brevity and directness, I'll put my main point in this section in terms of Grice's original analysis.

It seems to me that joint attention, construed as a primitive three-place relation between the attenders and the target, provides a different picture to Grice's of the basis of referential communication. On the joint attention picture, we start out with child and caregiver in a three-place relation, jointly attending to the object, it thus being "out in the open" which thing is in question, and communicating about it, in a quite primitive way. Suppose, for example, the thing attended is frightening. I look at it, then at you. Looking at you, I show my fear. Perhaps you look back at me in perfect understanding, in a shared reaction. Or perhaps you look at me reassuringly. Whatever, there is communication between us about the object. Now applying Grice's analysis to this situation would say that when I look at you, I intend to produce some reaction in you, such as belief, or fear, by means of your recognition of that intention. But this is not a convincing analysis. I'm not intending to produce any particular reaction in you. I'm seeing your state, and I'm doing nothing to stop you seeing mine. This can initiate a "conversation," as when you put an arm round me to reassure me or grab my hand to run, confirming that I'm right to be frightened. But the basic communication here does not consist in our intentionally making changes to one another's mental states. It's rather that I am letting you see how I am, and observing how it is with you.

At this most basic level of communication, notice also that there isn't anything playing the role sometimes assigned to language, as an instrument by which we intentionally make our feelings plain to one another. That can happen if, for example, I make a face at you while we're jointly attending to something: here you do have to figure out what I was up to in pulling that face. But in an ordinary case, when I'm frightened as we both look at the object and exchange a glance with you, I'm not intentionally putting on any expression; on the contrary, I'm simply letting you see how it is with me, and looking to see how it is with you.

You might reasonably object that Grice's analysis was not intended to apply to these basic cases. In its own terms, that point is fair enough. The further point, though, is that basic cases of joint attention are fundamental cases of referential communication. Once we accept that Grice's style of analysis does not apply to these fundamental cases, we find that in these basic cases there is a style of communication that uses resources other than Gricean intentions. Later, more sophisticated communication, such as verbal communication, builds on what's available in this basic case. When Gricean intentions do come into play, they may be depending on the communicative structure available in this more basic case.

There's another, more structural, reason why a simple Gricean analysis is not convincing here in the most basic case. There are two quite separate parts to the communicative process in basic joint attention. There's the joint selection of a target. That can be achieved either because the thing draws both participants' attention to itself—as when an explosion goes off and you and I look in wonder, first at the thing itself, then at each other—or because one of us draws the other's attention to it. And then there are our open reactions to it, shared as we look at one another. A simple Gricean analysis which focuses only on our intentions to affect one another's propositional states does get the object in, as the referent of the affected propositional states, but it seems to lose that big structural division between the selection of the target and our freewheeling communication concerning it.

Moreover, as we discussed in the previous section, there seems to be a sense in which, in basic perceptual joint-attention cases, it's "out in the open" between the participants what the target is. I said that this being "out in the open" between the participants what the target is should be regarded as a primitive state, not analyzable in terms of the knowledge or beliefs that each participant has individually. It nonetheless should be regarded as capable of grounding mutual knowledge of what the target is. And it should be regarded as having something of the normative force of infinitary common knowledge in grounding rational action (Campbell 2011). We might put the idea by saying that in ordinary joint attention, X and Y are "co-conscious" of the target. However, if we regard joint attention as grounded in Gricean intentions and reactions to them, we seem incapable of getting anything like this effect. One participant points to the target, with the intention of getting the other to recognize it as the target, by means of the recognition of that intention. Use and iteration of this kind of procedure seems capable of getting us a series of finite pieces of individual knowledge of the (intended) target, not the full force of "co-consciousness" of what the target is.

Untutored common sense, as well as a flood of experimental data, points to a contrast between voluntary and involuntary guidance of attention (cf. for example Prinzmetal et al. 2009). The direction of attention can be endogenously driven, as when a detective monitors a doorway, or exogenously driven, as when an explosion captures your attention. A simple way to get away from the picture of joint attention as driven by the intentions of the participants is to consider cases in which joint attention seems to be largely driven exogenously. As you and I are independently walking down the street, there's an explosion about a block away. You and I stare open-mouthed at the site, then look at one another, both openly expressing surprise, concern and fear. Intention plainly doesn't enter the picture here, either in the securing of our joint focus of attention, or in the communication of our reactions to it. Neither of us was intentionally manipulating the other's direction of attention, or our own expressions of emotion. And in fact the same point can apply to cases in which joint attention to the object is endogenously driven, though here the point is just a little bit subtler. It's a little bit subtler, because it's often very natural to talk about cases in which attention is endogenously driven as cases in which attention is driven by the intentions of the subject. But the endogenous drives in this kind of case evidently cannot be read as Gricean intentions. One subject's primary goal may be to engage in joint attention with the other person, and so may cast around for an object to draw the other person's attention to. But the drive to engage in joint attention here may be at a quite primitive level. The initial pointing that draws the other person's attention to the object need not be conceived of as intentional at all; it may be a reflexive response to interest in the object combined with a context in which the other person is present, as a potential co-attender. The infant held by a carer who sees an engaging object and points or makes an interrogative noise need not be engaging in Gricean communication.

Now as I said, you would, of course, be quite right to point out that the basic joint attention case I am considering was not one that Grice was officially concerned to analyze. He was explicitly concerned with *meaning*—and part of my point about the basic joint attention case is that when we are simply sharing our emotions, for example, about the attended object or scene, there may be nothing by which we *mean* anything: we are simply observing one another and each letting the other see how it is with us. But this is nonetheless a basic case of referential communication. We are not simply staring into one another's eyes, we are communicating about the object. And once we accept that this basic type of referential communication lies outside the scope of Grice's analysis, it is natural to wonder about the uses of language that build on this basic capacity for joint attention. After all, isn't language originally learned and shared in the context of cases of joint attention? And could it not be that just as in the basic joint attention cases, we make ourselves open to the other and see how it is with the other, so too the most basic uses of language are to make ourselves open to the other and to allow the other to make themselves open to us? Simple uses of language such as "Truck," or "Ouch," or "Help" are after all not well modeled by the Gricean account; they seem better understood as relating to either (a) the selection of a target for joint attention, or (b) revealing one's own state to the other person (rather than intentionally affecting the other person's state).

Philosophers have often worked with myths about the origins of language. For example, one resilient idea is that it originated in the private thoughts of a number of animals, who eventually achieved the formulation of Gricean intentions about the way to have one's intentions recognized. Another is that warning signs animals give one another about the imminence of predators could eventually be manipulated, under intentional control. One way to explain what I'm suggesting here is to say that I'm proposing another creation myth. Perhaps the origin of language is in reflexive joint attention behaviors. These do not require linguistic or quasi-linguistic thought, merely the achieving of joint focus on an object, openness with the other in one's reactions to it, and observation of the other's reactions. But this reflexive joint attention may be the foundation on which communication is built.

In fact, something like this may be the literal truth about the origin of language. Over many years, Michael Tomasello has built the case that the cooperative social interaction is the key to our cognitive uniqueness (Tomasello 2014). There are quite simple coordination tasks that even 3- or 4-year-old children manage with ease, that can't be accomplished at all by non-human primates. Joint attention is one of the elements that make these coordinated behaviors possible. This distinctively human capacity for joint attention is, he argues, one of the elements that make possible the distinctively human capacity for language.

In an important recent book, Imogen Dickie (2015) argues that the normativity of reference must be understood in terms of "the mind's need to represent," suggesting that the mind has a basic need to represent objects outside itself. This is an arresting and engaging idea. She suggests that this "need" grounds the normativity of rational belief: that the procedures we use to justify our beliefs have their normative status in virtue of their being responses to our need to put together bodies of beliefs about the concrete particulars around us. But the status of this "need" is puzzling. Richard Heck writes:

> I suspect that the need to represent is, in effect, emergent from other, more basic needs, such as the needs for food and shelter. Suppose an organism has found shelter: a safe place to sleep, to raise its young, and so forth. To find food for said young, the organism will have to venture forth; to feed its young, it will then have to return home; finding food next time will be easier if the organism can remember where it has found food before. All of this points to the importance, to the organism, of having (at least) a "cognitive map" of its local environment, as we know many creatures do.
>
> (Heck, in press)

Tomasello's approach suggests another contextualization: that the "need to represent" should be thought of as existing in the context of a broader need humans have for cooperative social interaction, and specifically, for engagement in joint attention with others.

Robert Stalnaker (2002) proposed that we think in terms of the "common ground" between participants in a linguistic exchange, this being explained in terms of some notion of infinitary common knowledge. I've been proposing, in effect, that we should think of the perceptual identification of the target as providing a *de re* common ground between participants in basic communication. And we should think here in terms of a primitive notion of co-consciousness of the target. It seems possible that this approach should be extended to the kinds of presupposition that Stalnaker thought of as common ground in a conversation: that we should think of the "common ground" here too as matter of which the participants are co-conscious, rather than thinking in terms of infinitary common knowledge.

4. JOINT ATTENTION AS THE FOUNDATION OF IMAGINING *DE RE*

The final reason why joint attention is important is its role as the ground of our imaginative understanding of other people's conscious states. I'll first explain the role that imaginative understanding seems to have in our knowledge of conscious states, then suggest that the basic kind of imagination that matters here is imagination *de re*, then look at how that imagination *de re* is grounded in the capacity for joint attention.

On the role that imaginative understanding plays in our knowledge of conscious states, the point was made most sharply in Nagel's classic discussion: 'At present we are completely unequipped to think about the subjective character of experience without relying on imagination—without taking up the point of view of the experiential subject' (Nagel 1974). It's only imagination that provides knowledge of what another's conscious states are like.

We can distinguish between imagining *de re* and imagining *de dicto*. The canonical forms for an ascription of imagining *de re* would be:

(1) X imagines, *of* b, its being F; or
(2) X imagines *of* b, that it is F.

The corresponding forms, for ascriptions of imaginings *de re* of another's visual experience, would be:

(3) X imagines, *of* b, its being seen by Y; and
(4) X imagines, *of* b, that it is seen by Y.

For present purposes, the important point about the "*of* b" spot is that it's subject to existential generalization and substitutivity. For X to imagine of b, its being seen by Y, for example, there must be such a thing as b. And if b and c are one and the same, then X is thereby imagining, of c, its being seen by Y.

In contrast, canonical ascriptions of imaginings *de dicto* of another's visual experience would be:

(5) X imagines b being seen by Y; and
(6) X imagines that b is seen by Y.

Here the position occupied by "b" is subject to neither existential generalization nor substitutivity.

Philosophers of mind have generally not challenged Nagel's point that, currently, our only route to knowledge of other people's experiences is through the use of the imagination. They have, however, usually tacitly taken it for granted that the basic type of imagining required for knowledge of another's experience is imagining *de dicto*. The idea is that even in the most basic cases, imagining how things are from another person's perspective does not require presupposing the existence of anything external to that person. Engaging in the imaginative project is indifferent as to what is actually there in the surroundings of the other person. Imagination provides you with knowledge of what the other person's experiences are like, and what the other person's experiences are like has nothing (constitutively) to do with what's there in the environment.

Another perspective is suggested by the possibility that, just as belief *de re* is often now taken to be more fundamental than belief *de dicto*, imagination *de re* should be taken to be more basic than imagination *de dicto*. This idea has been pursued by the developmental psychologists Heinrike Moll and Andrew Meltzoff in a series of studies. They make two key points.

Their first point is that children at around 12 months will typically engage in joint attention. This is not simply a matter of gaze-following, for it will characteristically involve the types of primitive communication we discussed in the previous section (cf. Carpenter and Liebal 2011). But this joint attention does not involve imaginative understanding of the other (what Moll and Meltzoff call "perspective-taking"):

it would be mistaken to think that the earliest examples of infant joint attention imply a sophisticated understanding of another's mental states or perspectives.

The reason is that it does not involve any explicit determination of what the other sees, let alone how another perceives a given object from his or her viewpoint.

(Moll and Meltzoff 2011: 396)

Moll and Meltzoff's second point is that the development of imaginative understanding of others' perceptions depends on this primitive capacity for joint attention:

It seems that children start out with an understanding of "engagement" holistically conceived. They recognize whether a person is or was engaged with an object (one way or another), but they do not, at this early stage in their development, understand the specifics of seeing in contrast to hearing or other forms of perceptual engagement. Over the course of development, this holistic grasp of engagement becomes more differentiated and eventually includes knowledge about the "functioning" of, for example, visual versus auditory perception, the respective enabling and defeating conditions that go with the particular senses, and the role that they play in knowledge formation. This is in accordance with experimental findings on the development of visual perspective taking, the flowering of which lies well after the emergence of an ability to distinguish between what has and has not been shared—namely, between two and three years of age—. . . .

(Moll and Meltzoff 2011: 400–1)

Now the idea that joint attention is the ground of the capacity for imaginative understanding of other people's conscious states should not be pressed too hard. We can and do extensively analyze the workings of other minds in contexts in which joint attention is out of the question: a historian or biographer, for example, may be trying to understand the mind of someone who's been dead for thousands of years. And in everyday life, when you run across an acquaintance you haven't seen for some time, you may be keen to know how they are but it would be unusual for your inquiries to take the form of joint attention activities, such as going to a movie, rather than, for example, conversation over coffee. In all such cases, however, it still seems that imagination *de re* is functioning as the basic form of your knowledge of the other person. The first task facing the historian, biographer or friend is to establish the facts about the environment of the other person: the life they were leading. It's only within the context of that knowledge of the environment that you can imagine, of that environment, how the other person experienced it. And we can still argue that a capacity for joint attention is the epistemic basis for one's ability to engage in imagining *de re* how things are with other people.

This kind of approach suggests an analysis of Nagel's famous case of the bat. What we lack, in the case of the bat, is knowledge of the bat environment. We don't know which things or properties the bat is responding to. We may lack altogether, forever, any conception of the external properties of the environment that the bat is perceiving, just as the bat may lack, forever, any conception of the object colors that humans perceive. Because of that, we can't imagine *de re*, of the bat's environment, how the bat is experiencing it.

How is it that we have so readily, in the human case, knowledge of the kind of environment that one's conspecifics occupy, when it seems impossible to achieve in the case of the bat? It's because we have, from so early an age, a capacity for joint attention with our conspecifics. This capacity for joint attention seems to precede knowledge of what

Strawson called the "range and blocking" conditions on perception—that what I can see, for example, depends on how far away from it I am, and whether there is anything in the way (Moll et al. 2011). And joint attention precedes understanding of the fact that when you and I perceive the same thing, we may be nonetheless perceiving it in different ways. Rather, social engagement with another, in connection with an object that I perceive, seems to be what grounds my taking it to be an object that you can perceive.

5. JOINT ATTENTION AND KNOWING WHAT IT'S LIKE

In an instructive recent paper, Daniel Stoljar (2016) suggests an analysis of the phrase, "there's something it is like." This is valuable particularly because of the role the phrase plays in the flood of work on consciousness done in the past few decades; as Stoljar remarks, practically everyone who attempts to write on the subject of consciousness uses the phrase, "what it is like," in trying to explain what they are talking about. I want finally to remark on the relation between Stoljar's analysis and an approach to "knowing what it's like" that takes joint attention to be the epistemic basis of knowing what it's like.

According to Stoljar, a sentence such as, "There is something it is like to have a toothache" should be taken to have the logical form, "There is a way that x's toothache is to y" (2016: 1165, 1172). The need for two argument places, for x and y, is suggested by the availability of locutions such as "there is something it is like to Annie for Sally to have a toothache," in which the person to whom there's something it is like, and the person having the experience, are different; it looks as though the case in which they're the same is merely a special case (2016: 1167). And the need for a quantifier over "ways" is suggested by the difficulty of taking "like" to be a comparative: "What is Chicago like?," can be answered in a word, "Philadelphia," but it can also be answered by a direct description of the way Chicago is. And arguably the answer, "Philadelphia" only helps if one already knows the way Philadelphia is. Similarly, "What is it like to have a toothache?," might be interpreted comparatively, but it would more usually be regarded as answered by knowledge of the way toothache is (2016: 1171).

More centrally, Stoljar's proposal about the semantic interpretation of "there is something it is like to have a toothache" is in two parts:

> "There is something it is like to x for y to c" is true in a context c if and only if there is in c some way that y's c-ing affects x. . . . "Affect" means something like "influence" or "bring about a change or condition in".
>
> (Stoljar 2016: 1173)

> There are stereotypical contexts c such that "There is something it is like to x for y to c" is true in c if and only if there is in c some experiential way that y's c-ing affects x; in other words, there is in c some way that x experiences y's c-ing; in still other words, there is some way that x feels as a result of y's c-ing.
>
> (Stoljar 2016: 1176)

Now Stoljar's approach here seems to me to make possible a major reorganization of the way in which we usually think about the idea of imagining as providing knowledge of what an experience is like. The usual idea seems to be that for a state to be conscious is a matter of there being some "inner qualia" that it has, and imagining is thought of as some kind of picturing or mirroring of those qualia. But Stoljar's approach gives a way of finding a quite different role for the imagination in finding what another's experience is like.

Suppose you and I are jointly attending to the colors of the sunset. We are looking at the external spectacle as the colors bathe the valley. What does it come to, that I know what it's like for you to be seeing this? The usual answer is that it has to do with my knowledge of the color qualia you're having. But the alternative analysis is that my knowledge of the colors you're perceiving is already supplied by my own perception of them, in the context of our joint engagement with the scene. There is a kind of double counting involved in the idea that there are somehow both the colors "out there" and the colors "in here," and that I have to get on to the colors "in here." We don't need the colors "in here" to find the role of imaginative understanding. What imaginative understanding supplies, in addition to the knowledge I have of the external colors you're perceiving, is knowledge of the impact that those colors are having on you. Karl Jaspers, who is, with Nagel, the twentieth-century's great theorist of the imagination, said that the role of imaginative understanding has to do with appreciation of the dynamics of the other person's mind: 'We sink ourselves into the psychic situation and *understand genetically by empathy* how one psychic event emerges from another' (Jaspers 1913/1959: 301). On this picture, the role of imagination is not at all in providing some kind of picturing or mirroring of the other person's qualia. Rather, it has to do with grasping how one psychological state generates another: how your perception of the external colors of the sunset affects you. That's what "knowledge of what it's like" for you comes to.

To put this in terms of Stoljar's analysis, my knowledge of what it's like for you to see the red of the sunset is a matter of my knowing how seeing the red "affects," "influences," or "brings about changes" in you. Joint attention provides, in the most basic cases, my knowledge of which external property you're seeing. Imagination provides further my knowledge of what it's like for you to see that red, by providing knowledge of how that perception of red affects, influences, or brings about changes in you, particularly experiential changes, such as changes in mood or the eliciting of memories. Perception of the redness out there generates a range of further changes in you, and my imaginative understanding of you tracks those dynamics. A simple way to see the force of this picture is to consider the case in which perception of the redness of the sunset has a quite different experiential impact on you and me. Perhaps it produces in you a sense of energized tranquility, whereas it causes me to have fits. In that case, there doesn't seem to be any sense at all in which what it's like for you to see the sunset is the same as what it's like for me to see the sunset. Taken together, these points specify the way in which Bruner was right to take it that an analysis of the role of joint attention in understanding other people requires us to ascribe naïve realism, or something like, to the child (Bruner 1983: 122).

ACKNOWLEDGEMENTS

I have been helped a lot by discussion of these questions with Wes Holliday and Seth Yalcin.

REFERENCES

Akkoyunlu, E.A., Ekanadham, K. and Huber, R.V. (1975) "Some Constraints and Tradeoffs in the Design of Network Communications," Proceedings of the 5th ACM Symposium on Operating Systems Principles: 67–74.

Bruner, J. (1983) *Child's Talk: Learning to Use Language*, New York: W.W. Norton.

——— (1995) "From Joint Attention to the Meeting of Minds," in C. Moore and P.J. Dunham (eds) *Joint Attention: Its Origins and Role in Development*, Hillsdale, NJ: Erlbaum.

Campbell, J. (2002) *Reference and Consciousness*, Oxford: Oxford University Press.

——— (2011) "An Object-Dependent Perspective on Joint Attention," in A. Seeman (ed.), *Joint Attention: New Developments in Psychology, Philosophy of Mind and Social Neuroscience*, Cambridge, MA: MIT Press.

Carpenter, M. and Liebal, K. (2011) "Joint Attention and Knowing Together in Infancy," in A. Seeman (ed.) *Joint Attention: New Developments in Psychology, Philosophy of Mind and Social Neuroscience*, Cambridge, MA: MIT Press.

Dickie, I. (2015) *Fixing Reference*, Oxford: Oxford University Press.

Eilan, N. (ms.) "Joint Attention and the Second Person"

Fagin, R., Halpern, J.Y., Moses, Y. and Vardi, M.Y (1995) *Reasoning About Knowledge*, Cambridge, MA: MIT Press.

Grice, H.P. (1957) "Meaning," *Philosophical Review* 66: 377–88.

Heck, R. (in press) "Cognitive Hunger: Comments on Imogen Dickie's Fixing Reference," *Philosophy and Phenomenological Research*.

Hobson, P. (2005) "What Puts the Jointness into Joint Attention?" in N. Eilan, C. Hoerl, T. McCormack, and J. Roessler (eds) *Joint Attention: Communication and Other Minds. Issues in Philosophy and Psychology*, Oxford: Oxford University Press.

Jaspers, K. (1913/1959) *General Psychopathology*, Manchester: Manchester University Press.

Lederman, H. (2016) "Two Paradoxes of Common Knowledge: Coordinated Attack and Electronic Mail," *Noûs*, http://dx.doi.org/10.1111/nous.12186.

Lederman, H. (in press) "Uncommon Knowledge," *Mind*.

Longworth, G. (2014) "You and Me," *Philosophical Explorations*, 17: 289–303.

Moll, H. and Meltzoff, A. (2011) "Perspective-Taking and its Foundation in Joint Attention," in A. Seeman (ed.) *Joint Attention: New Developments in Psychology, Philosophy of Mind, and Social Neuroscience*, Cambridge, MA: MIT Press.

Moll, H., Carpenter, M. and Tomasello, M. (2011) "Social Engagement Leads 2-Year-Olds to Overestimate Others' Knowledge," *Infancy* 16: 248–65.

Moore, R. (2017) "Gricean Communication and Cognitive Development," *Philosophical Quarterly* 67 (267): 303–26.

Nagel, T. (1974) "What Is It Like to Be a Bat?" *Philosophical Review* 83: 435–50.

Peacocke, C. (2005) "Joint Attention: Its Nature, Reflexivity and Relation to Common Knowledge," in N. Eilan, C. Hoerl, T. McCormack, and J. Roessler (eds) *Joint Attention: Communication and Other Minds. Issues in Philosophy and Psychology*, Oxford: Oxford University Press.

——— (2014) *The Mirror of the World: Subjects, Consciousness, and Self-Consciousness*, Oxford: Oxford University Press.

Prinzmetal, W., Zvinyatskovskiy, A., Gutierrez, P. and Dilem, L. (2009) "Voluntary and Involuntary Attention have Different Consequences: The Effect of Perceptual Difficulty," *Quarterly Journal of Experimental Psychology* 62: 352–69.

Reddy, V. (2005) "Before the 'Third Element': Understanding Attention to Self," in N. Eilan, C. Hoerl, T. McCormack, and J. Roessler (eds) *Joint Attention: Communication and Other Minds: Issues in Philosophy and Psychology*, Oxford: Oxford University Press.

Salje, L. (2016) "Thinking About You," *Mind*, https://doi.org/10.1093/mind/fzw018.

Stalnaker, R. (2002) "Common Ground," *Linguistics and Philosophy* 25: 701–21.

Stoljar, D. (2016) "The Semantics of 'What It's Like' and the Nature of Consciousness," *Mind* 125: 1161–98.

Tomasello, M. (2014) *A Natural History of Human Thinking*, Cambridge, MA and London, England: Harvard University Press.

10

Joint Commitment

Margaret Gilbert

The present author has long argued that the concept of joint commitment at issue in this article is central to human life in society. More precisely I have argued that central everyday concepts of at least the following phenomena incorporate this concept: agreements, promises, social groups, group languages, social rules and conventions, doing something with another person, shared or collective plans, collective belief and other collective attitudes, collective emotions, and an important kind of mutual recognition (Gilbert 1989, 2006, 2014 and elsewhere).

The purpose of this article is to outline the pertinent concept of joint commitment, and offer some reasons for thinking that it plays a central role in human life. In some cases references are given to more detailed discussions of a given point.

1. COMMITMENTS OF THE WILL: PERSONAL COMMITMENTS

Among the most familiar occurrences in a human life are the forming of personal intentions and the making of personal decisions. In both cases it may be said that the person in question *commits* himself (or herself) to a certain course of action. One can break this down into a particular *process* and a particular *product*. The person's forming the intention or making of the decision is the process, which is psychological. The product is the commitment of the person.

In saying that the person is committed I mean that he is *normatively constrained* in a certain way. That is, there is now something that he ought to do, all else being equal. In other terms: if that person acts appropriately in light of all of the considerations to hand, he will act in accordance with his intention or decision, all else being equal. Naturally, if the decision or intention is rescinded, the associated normative constraint disappears. For further discussion of the normativity of personal decisions, see Gilbert (2013).

People can be normatively constrained by factors other than states or acts of their own will such as their personal intentions and decisions. For instance, if someone can easily prevent grave harm to another person, many would judge that he ought to do so, whether or not the imminent harm was in any way created by his own decisions or the like. I say therefore that the commitments engendered by personal decisions and intentions are *commitments of the will*.

More fully, they are, in my terminology, *personal* commitments of the will. The defining feature of such personal commitments is that the person in question is in a position unilaterally both to make and to rescind them.

2. COMMITMENTS OF THE WILL: JOINT COMMITMENTS

The notion of *joint commitment* at issue here involves, roughly, the commitment *of* two or more wills *by* two or more wills. Thus, like a personal commitment as sketched above, a joint commitment on this conception involves both a particular product—the commitment of the pertinent wills—and a particular process, a process involving those wills. In the following sections I expand on the above description.

There are both *basic* and *non-basic* joint commitments. The discussion that follows concerns basic joint commitments unless otherwise stated.

3. THE PROCESS OF JOINT COMMITMENT IN THE BASIC CASE

A basic joint commitment comes about as follows: each of two or more people openly expresses his readiness jointly to commit them all in a certain way, and their having made these expressions is common knowledge between the parties. By this I mean, roughly, that the expressions are entirely out in the open between them, and each knows this. (See Gilbert 1989: 188f.) The parties are now committed "as one"—something about which I say more when I turn to the product of joint commitment.

Note that what is at issue here is not simply behavioral *expressions* but something that is *expressed*: actual readiness on the part of each jointly to commit them all in a certain way. (See Gilbert 1989: 183–4.)

Further, as understood here, *readiness* for joint commitment can exist in circumstances that are more or less coercive. Thus, as a result of Ben's threats, Alice may be ready jointly to commit herself with him in a certain way, though she would prefer not to. (See e.g. Gilbert 2006: ch. 10.)

It is worth emphasizing that the expressions in question are not envisaged as conditional in form. Rather, as is understood by the parties, if and only if each openly expresses his or her readiness jointly with the other or others to commit them in some way, in conditions of common knowledge, the relevant joint commitment will be in place. There is, then, no "de-conditionalization problem," as there would be if what each party expressed was, for instance, "I am ready jointly to commit us, if you are ready to jointly commit us." Even in conditions of common knowledge such expressions would not yet lead to anything, on account of their conditional nature. This point is emphasized by Velleman (1997). For further references and discussion see Gilbert (2014: ch. 2).

The content of any joint commitment takes the following general form: the parties are jointly committed *to φ as a body*. Here "φ" represents a verb of action, in a broad sense, either transitive or intransitive, and "as a body" is shorthand for something longer which I now explain. To take just one example, two or more people may be jointly committed to believe as a body that it is raining. This means, roughly, that they are jointly committed to emulate, by virtue of their several actions and utterances, a single believer of the proposition that it is raining. Examples of such actions include saying "It's raining" if asked what the weather is like, objecting to someone who says "It's not raining," and so on. It should be clear from the foregoing explanation of "as a body" that other language would serve the same purpose. For instance, I might have written of the parties being jointly committed to φ *as one*.

It can be argued that one case of the formation of a joint commitment is the making of an everyday agreement, as when Cal says "Shall we meet at six?" and Dee says "Yes" (Gilbert 2014: ch. 13). It is important to emphasize, however, that a joint commitment can be formed by other means. Indeed, there are several ways in which the formation of a given joint commitment may differ from that of the typical everyday agreement.

First, in the case of an agreement the joint commitment in question is, by definition, created by particular, explicit process. That is, we would not have an agreement properly so-called without this process. The making of a joint commitment as such does not require this particular process. For example, Ed and Frank are rowing on a lake. Ed spots Gina who is calling for help from the middle of a lake and says, "Look, she may not make it!" Each of them bends to his oar and they begin rowing in the direction of Gina. Though they did not agree to try to save Gina, each expressed in other ways his readiness jointly to commit the two of them to espouse as a body the goal of saving her, in conditions of common knowledge, and hence jointly committed themselves in the relevant way.

Second, in the case of everyday agreements the parties generally relate to one another as particular individuals. For example, suppose that Hettie and Ivy agree to play tennis tomorrow. Neither one may know the other's name—each may know only that the other is a member of the local tennis club, for instance—but each knows she is making the agreement with the person in question. Knowledge that one is jointly committing with this particular individual or those particular individuals is not necessary to joint commitment formation as such. For instance, the members of a large crowd could jointly commit one another in some way without knowing that this or that particular person is a member of the crowd. Their expressions of readiness for joint commitment concern the members of the crowd as such, whoever they are, and it may be common knowledge among the members of the crowd that the relevant expressions have been made.

Third, as the last example illustrates, whereas the most familiar kinds of agreement are made between two parties or at most a few more, there can be many parties to a given joint commitment.

Fourth, the particular process required for an agreement is often quite limited in time and space, as when two people make an agreement when standing face-to-face. Neither aspect of these cases is necessary for joint commitment formation. Joint commitments can be formed by means of expressions of readiness for joint commitment that are made over an extended period of time and that involve people with great distances between them. For more on this and the previous two points see Gilbert (2006: ch. 8).

Fifth, the establishment of a given joint commitment may be delayed not by the number and geographical spread of the parties but by the need to disambiguate initially ambiguous expressions. An explicit, verbal agreement is liable to pin things down more quickly as far as each participant is concerned. When a joint commitment arises in other ways—and perhaps without words—there is more room for uncertainty and the need to wait things out before being sure of what the other party or parties have in mind.

In all cases the pertinent joint commitment is established once there is common knowledge in the relevant population that the pertinent expressions of readiness for that particular joint commitment have been made. This allows for the possibility that someone may "sign on" to a joint commitment established by others, a possibility that would explicitly be signaled if one of the parties to the established joint commitment says to an outsider something like "Want to join us?"

Rescission of a basic joint commitment requires the concurrence of the parties; no one party or proper subset of the parties is in a position unilaterally to rescind it. Thus the process of rescission parallels the process of creation.

Some parties could, of course, give their concurrence to rescission in advance, as when one person says to another "Just let me know if you want out. . . ." In this case if the other person later says "That's it!" without any concern for the concurrence of the first, it may look as if he is unilaterally rescinding when he is not.

In the next section I explain the difference between basic and non-basic joint commitments: this is a difference in the process of joint commitment, not the product.

4. FORMING NON-BASIC JOINT COMMITMENTS

The foundation of a *non-basic* or *derived* joint commitment is always a pertinent basic joint commitment. Here is an example of the formation of the relevant kind of *basic* joint commitment. Jo and Kit want to play a game some of whose rules they have forgotten. Jo says to Kit "Why don't you come up with some rules for us to play by," and he replies "Fine." They are now jointly committed to accepting as a body the rules Kit devises.

Suppose that Kit now says, "Well, one rule is that we'll throw a dice to decide who goes first." He and Jo are now jointly committed to accept that rule as a body. This commitment of theirs is a *non-basic* joint commitment.

Non-basic joint commitments differ from basic joint commitments in that in order to create a non-basic joint commitment to do a certain thing as a body, it is not necessary that the parties express their readiness *to do that thing* as a body. What is necessary is that there be an applicable background joint commitment from which the non-basic joint commitment in question can be derived in relevant circumstances.

A related feature of non-basic joint commitment is that *a given party may have no idea of its content*. The example just given can be altered so as to show this. After Jo and Kit agree that he will create some rules for them, Kit sits down some way from Jo and writes down a set of rules for their game, which he intends shortly to reveal to her. Given their basic joint commitment, he and Jo are already jointly committed to accept these rules as a body—though Jo has no idea what they are.

This kind of situation may be at issue when a member of a political society asks, of some proposed action, "Is that legal?" He may understand that he could be committed to conform to a certain law through a non-basic joint commitment of whose details he is unaware, a non-basic commitment that is grounded in a basic joint commitment through which he and the other members of his society have authorized a certain person or body of persons—"the government"—to make laws for them. For related discussion, see Gilbert (2006).

5. JOINT COMMITMENT AS PRODUCT

Two or more people who jointly commit themselves in some way thereby impose a normative constraint on those two or more people as one. In other words *they* are the subject of this constraint, the "one" who is constrained. This situation is the intended result of the process of joint commitment described above.

It is important to be clear that the resulting state of joint commitment is not comprised of a set of personal commitments of the will such as those entrained by a personal decision. An important difference between a set of such personal commitments and a joint commitment is that any personal commitment of the will is unilaterally rescindable. As noted earlier, a joint commitment is not unilaterally rescindable by a given party unless there are special background understandings in place. It is worth adding that no "part" of it is unilaterally rescindable either. A joint commitment does not have parts in any applicable sense.

That said, each of the parties is committed through the joint commitment, in the sense that once it is in place each is subject to an appropriate normative constraint. If Loren and Mike are jointly committed to, say, accept as a body the goal of saving up to buy a house as soon as possible, then each is normatively constrained to act as is appropriate to that commitment. Neither should give all of their current savings to charity, for instance, as far as their joint commitment is concerned.

Similarly, if Nell and Otto are jointly committed to accept as a body the goal of painting the house this afternoon, it is incumbent on each to be sure his or her actions are properly coordinated with those of the other. If Otto has painted one side of the house, Nell is not to paint that side herself, unless for some reason it needs re-painting.

To use a term that Michael Bratman has introduced into the literature on acting together: by virtue of their joint commitment, the pair need to develop sub-goals that *mesh*, where sub-goals are goals that are subsumed by the main goal of painting the house (Bratman 1993). The same goes for other joint commitments, with relevant changes.

We might call the normative constraint on a given party to a joint commitment his "individual" commitment, in order to distinguish it from a personal commitment, which is unilaterally brought into being and rescindable by the committed person. The individual commitments of the parties are *interdependent,* in the sense that there cannot be a single such commitment, pertaining to a given individual party to the commitment, that exists on its own.

Clearly the relevant normative constraints may have significant practical consequences, as when, say, a group of friends is jointly committed to believe as a body that someone outside the group should be shunned. Each of them is then normatively constrained to act in ways expressive of this belief, at least in the presence of other group members, so the person in question is likely to be shunned by members of the group.

A more positive example is a joint commitment to believe as a body that one should always help strangers in need. This normatively constrains the parties, up to a point, to act in a constructive fashion.

In every case, of course, there can be moral considerations such that all things considered the parties to a given joint commitment should not conform to it. These considerations may relate to the consequences of conformity or to the content of the joint commitment itself—it may require that some or all parties do something immoral. Though this is so, such countervailing moral considerations may not be salient: they may not come to the mind of the parties to the commitment. One reason for this could be the salience of the rights and obligations of joint commitment, to which I now turn.

6. RIGHTS AND OBLIGATIONS OF JOINT COMMITMENT

One can argue that the parties to a joint commitment have associated *obligations to one another* to conform to the commitment. Thus, if Quinn and Pam are jointly committed in some way, Quinn is obligated to Pam to conform and vice versa. Note that these obligations are relational or *directed*. Each party is obligated *to* or *toward* every other to conform to the commitment.

Each also has a right *against* every other to his conforming. This obligation and this right are not mere correlates. They are, as rights' theorist Wesley Hohfeld puts it, equivalent. Thus Quinn's obligation to Pam just is Pam's right against Quinn seen from Quinn's perspective (Hohfeld 1964).

According to a development of this idea that accords with the judgments of many rights theorists, correlative and equivalent to Quinn's obligation to Pam, and her right against Quinn, is her standing or authority to demand of him that he acts in the relevant way, along with the standing to rebuke him for not doing so when appropriate.

Such standing requires a ground, and one can argue that joint commitment provides such a ground (Gilbert 2012, and forthcoming).

Crucial here is the process of joint commitment. Suppose that Rex and Sally have jointly committed the two of them to believe as a body that it is raining. Sally ought now to act appropriately, all else being equal, given the normativity of any commitment of the will. Suppose now that she appears to be about to fail to do so. Perhaps she is going out for a walk without an umbrella. It seems that Rex is in a position to question her action on the basis of their joint commitment. Further he is in a position to *call her to order*. She could also call herself to order, on the same basis.

7. WHY INVOKE JOINT COMMITMENT?

Why think that joint commitment in the sense explained above plays a central role in human life in society?

The invocation of joint commitment is particularly plausible when one is dealing with people's sense of the appropriate reactions to certain actions of others as they conduct their lives. Among these reactions are the apparently authoritative *demands* and *rebukes* that are issued to others in a variety of contexts. These reactions could easily be considered "interference" were they not for some reason considered acceptable. I say more on this score shortly.

The invocation of joint commitment also offers a plausible explanation of the sense of unity that is often associated with social groups and related phenomena, and the appropriateness of the use of the collective "we"—the "we" that cannot be parsed as "we both" or "we all." For discussion of the collective "we" see Gilbert (1989: ch. 4).

8. DEMANDS AND REBUKES IN THE SOCIAL WORLD

I return briefly to authoritative demands and rebukes—and the rights and directed obligations that they imply. A familiar context for these is an everyday agreement, and it can be argued for this and other reasons that those who enter an agreement with one another create a joint commitment on the basis of a particular, particularly explicit, process (Gilbert 2014: ch. 13).

Agreements, however, are not the only context in which demands and rebukes are considered to be in place—even if we set aside promises, which are close cousins of agreements (Gilbert 2014: ch. 13).

It can be argued that all of the phenomena listed in the introduction to this article are such that the participants are authorized to issue demands and rebukes to other participants in relevant circumstances. Doing something with another person is just one example. Thus suppose that Tom and Una are going for a walk together, something whose proper course is understood to involve the parties walking along side by side for some period of time. Now suppose that Una starts drawing ahead. Absent special background understandings, Tom has the authority to call her back, should he so desire. Moreover, should he do nothing to bring things back on track, he too seems to be at fault, and open to rebuke from Una.

In the very common case of doing something with another person, the parties' joint commitment to accept as a body the relevant goal would explain these observed phenomena. It is by no means clear that anything else can give us as satisfactory an explanation. As I have argued elsewhere, a moral requirement relating, say, to expectations one has created in the other party, would not suffice to explain the parties' authority to issue demands and rebukes to one another. (See Gilbert 2014: ch. 12, and forthcoming: ch. 7).

Of course those who are acting together, or involved in any of the other phenomena mentioned at the outset, may choose not to exercise their standing to demand appropriate actions of one another. They may choose to use different means to keep things going. In the example, Tom could start running to catch up with Una.

A note on *helping* is also in order here. Though people are often glad to be helped when they are in difficulties, they can also feel that they are being intruded upon. In the case of acting together, for instance, such a feeling is unlikely to arise. An underlying joint commitment would explain that too, since the parties will sometimes need to help one another in order that their joint commitment is fulfilled.

9. PLURAL SUBJECTS

In my technical terminology two or more people constitute a "plural subject" if and only if they are jointly committed with one another in some way. The phrase "plural subject" is intended to indicate my belief that in order appositely to be referenced by the collective "we", two or more people must be thus committed.

The phrase should not be interpreted to imply that there is anything more "on the ground" in such situations than the people in question and their joint commitment, a normative condition that has been brought about by a particular process. Any metaphysical concerns about plural subjects are only apposite, then, if they are apposite in relation to a number of jointly committed persons. In particular, a joint commitment account of collective belief, say, does not bring with it a metaphysically suspect assumption of a "group mind" or "subject" of consciousness "over and above" the people in question.

10. THEORETICAL IMPLICATIONS FOR OUR UNDERSTANDING OF HUMAN SOCIAL PHENOMENA: SINGULARISM VERSUS NON-SINGULARISM

If even only one of the central everyday concepts of social phenomena listed at the outset were best articulated by reference to joint commitment one would have to reject what I have called *singularism* about such concepts. That is, one would have to reject the idea that they can all be analyzed in terms of one or more people's personal intentions, beliefs, desires, and so on.

Some may worry that going outside the conceptual framework of singularism violates the methodological tenet known as "Ockham's razor": roughly, do not multiply entities— including, let us assume, concepts—beyond necessity. After all, we clearly need the concepts of a person's personal intentions and so on: shouldn't we try to analyze our social concepts in these terms as well, rather than invoking the non-singularist concept of joint commitment? Perhaps that is a worthy endeavor. However, if what is otherwise the best account of one, let alone all, of these concepts invokes a joint commitment, we should not reject it out of deference to Ockham's razor.

11. SOME MORE OR LESS CLOSELY RELATED CONCEPTS OF JOINT COMMITMENT

In part to further clarify the concept of joint commitment that has been explored here, I now briefly outline two distinct but related concepts that could be given the label "joint commitment" with some aptness. In one there is the same process, but not the same product. In another there is the same product but not the same process.

First, it may seem that two or more people could in principle together commit just one of their number, or a proper subset of their number, in some way. Focusing on the first case, it appears that the committed person would then be obligated to them all to conform to the commitment, and they would all have rights against him to such conformity. It seems, however, that he would have no particular rights against them, and they would have no particular obligations to him, assuming that there is nothing for the rest to do by way of conforming to the commitment.

One might think that this concept of joint commitment could be useful in accounting for promissory obligation. However, it seems that a promisee does take on obligations to the promisor, including at least the obligation not to thwart the performance of the promise. That is one reason for preferring an account of promising that includes joint commitment in the sense on which this article has focused. See Gilbert (2014: ch. 13) for discussion of such an account. Nonetheless, there is room for further consideration of the process-focused notion of joint commitment just adumbrated.

Second, it seems that the same product—two or more people being jointly committed—might have a different source. Here I have in mind the possibility of our being jointly committed as a matter of morality. For instance, if only two of us working together can save a drowning man, it may be morally incumbent upon we two, as one, to act accordingly. (Compare Held 1970.) It is at best not clear that those who are jointly committed by an external source in this way would have *obligations towards* one another to conform or *rights against* each other to such conformity.

A more radically distinct notion of joint commitment is one in which the jointness is no more than a parallelism. Here a combination of personal commitments is such if everyone acts as he is committed to act, the result desired by each party will be obtained. Though Michael Bratman (Bratman 1993, 2014) does not use the phrase "joint commitment" in the statement of his singularist account of shared intention and agency, one could do so if intending to express this singularist notion of joint commitment. Bratman's account invokes concordant personal intentions and thus, according to the points made earlier here, concordant personal commitments. The notion of joint commitment invoked by psycholinguist Herbert Clark (1996) appears also to be a singularist one. Given these singularist notions there is no possibility of inferring directly a web of mutual obligations and rights of the kind implied by a joint commitment in the sense on which this article has focused. For theoretical purposes if one chooses to use the phrase "joint commitment" or similar phrases it is clearly best to be as explicit as possible as to which notion of joint commitment one has in mind.

12. APPLICATIONS OUTSIDE PHILOSOPHY

The arguments sketched in this chapter for the centrality of joint commitment, in the relevant sense, in human life are broadly speaking philosophical. On the basis of informal observations of the way people think, talk, write and otherwise conduct themselves in their lives in society, the hypothesis that they consistently operate with the concept of a joint commitment recommends itself.

A number of theorists and researchers in disciplines other than philosophy have found the concept of joint commitment adumbrated in this article to be helpful in understanding the phenomena with which they are concerned. These include communication theorists, developmental psychologists, political scientists, anthropologists, and many others. For examples from the first two fields just mentioned see Carassa and Colombetti (2009) and Tomasello (2016).

RELATED TOPICS

Collective Action and Agency (Ch. 1), Non-Reductive Views of Shared Intention (Ch. 2), Interpersonal Obligation in Joint Action (Ch. 4), Collective Belief and Acceptance (Ch. 7), Shared Values, Interests, and Desires (Ch. 8), Collective Emotions (Ch. 12), Collective Epistemology (Ch. 15), Social Groups (Ch. 21).

REFERENCES

Bratman, M.E. (1993) "Shared Intention," *Ethics* 105: 97–113.

——— (2014) *Shared Agency: A Planning Theory of Acting Together*, Oxford: Oxford University Press.

Carassa, A. and Colombetti, M. (2009) "Situated Communicative Acts: A Deontic Approach," *Proceedings of CogSci 2009*, Amsterdam, pp. 1382–7.

Clark, H. (1996) *Using Language*, Cambridge: Cambridge University Press.

Gilbert, M. (1989) *On Social Facts*, London: Routledge and Kegan Paul. Reprinted 1992, Princeton: Princeton University Press.

——— (2006) *A Theory of Political Obligation: Membership, Commitment, and the Bonds of Society*, Oxford: Oxford University Press.

——— (2012) "Giving Claim-Rights Their Due," in B. Bix and H. Spector (eds) *Rights: Concepts and Concepts*, Farnham, Surrey: Ashgate.

——— (2013) "Commitment," in H. LaFollette (ed.) *The International Encyclopedia of Ethics*, Hoboken, NJ: Wiley-Blackwell.

——— (2014) *Joint Commitment: How We Make the Social World*, New York: Oxford University Press.

——— (forthcoming) *Rights and Demands: A Foundational Inquiry*, Oxford: Oxford University Press.

Held, V. (1970) "Can a Random Collection of Individuals be Morally Responsible," *The Journal of Philosophy* 67: 471–81.

Hohfeld, W.H. (1964) *Fundamental Legal Conceptions, as Applied in Judicial Reasoning*, W.W. Cook (ed.), New Haven: Yale University Press.

Tomasello, M. (2016) *A Natural History of Human Morality*, Cambridge, MA: Harvard University Press.

Velleman, D. (1997) "How to Share an Intention," *Philosophy and Phenomenological Research* 57: 29–49.

11

Collective Memory

Kourken Michaelian and John Sutton

1. COLLECTIVE MEMORY AND COLLECTIVE INTENTIONALITY

There has been relatively little interaction between research on collective intentionality in philosophy and research on collective memory in psychology and the social sciences. Rather than being due to a lack of mutual relevance—as this chapter will demonstrate, the two traditions are very much relevant to each other—this lack of interaction is due largely to somewhat arbitrary disciplinary barriers. But disciplinary barriers, even when arbitrary, have real consequences, and one message of this chapter is that the lack of interaction has had negative consequences for both fields. Psychologists and social scientists have tended not to take advantage of philosophical resources that might sharpen their analyses of collective memory. Philosophers, meanwhile, have often presupposed overly simple models of the interactions among group members that are at work in the formation of collective memories and collective intentional states more broadly. There are thus important potential benefits to be realized for each field through increased interaction with the other.

Forms of Collective Memory

What sorts of *collectives* are at issue in collective memory? Collective remembering unfolds at a range of scales, and it is necessary to be alert to the possibility of real differences between *small-scale* collective memory and *large-scale* collective memory. It may turn out that the same process of collective remembering unfolds in both small-scale and large-scale groups, but it may be no coincidence that small-scale and large-scale collective memory have traditionally been investigated by different disciplines. The former, exemplified by remembering in married couples (Harris et al. 2014) or in parent-child dyads (Reese et al. 1993), has been studied primarily in psychology. The latter has been studied primarily in the social sciences and history. Indeed, reflecting what has been termed a "memory boom" (Blight 2009), an enormous amount of work on large-scale collective memory has appeared in recent years, building on older theories of remembering as a social process (Halbwachs 1994; see Wertsch 2009; Erll and Nünning 2010; Erll 2011; Olick et al. 2011). This disciplinary division of labor reflects an apparent difference between the kinds of remembering of which small-scale and large-scale groups are, respectively, capable.

In the standard taxonomy of kinds of memory (Michaelian, 2016), *episodic* memory refers to memory for experienced events. Episodic remembering is normally accompanied by a characteristic phenomenology, a sense of reliving the past (Tulving 1972). *Semantic* memory refers to memory for facts. Semantic remembering need not concern experienced events, and, when it does, it is not accompanied by a sense of reliving the past. Both episodic and semantic memory are declarative, in the sense that their contents can in principle be articulated; declarative memory aligns with what epistemologists refer to as "knowledge that." *Procedural* memory, in contrast, is non-declarative and aligns with what epistemologists refer to as "knowledge how"; the contents of procedural memory—e.g. acquired skills of various sorts—need not be articulable.

Memory in large-scale groups is typically memory for events which are of concern to the individuals who make up the group but in which those individuals did not necessarily take an active part and of which they often have only indirect knowledge. Extending the standard taxonomy to collective memory, large-scale collective memory thus appears often to be semantic. Consider the ways in which the citizens of a country might remember key events from its past: individual citizens may (episodically) remember personal experiences which are linked to the events in question, but, to the extent that remembering is concerned with large-scale, public events, it lacks the characteristic features of episodic memory.

Memory in small-scale groups—groups sufficiently small to allow their members to interact directly with each other—can likewise be semantic. Research employing the collaborative recall paradigm, which compares the information recalled by groups of individuals who remember alone to that recalled by groups of individuals who interact with each other, for example, normally concerns learned information of no particular personal significance (Weldon and Bellinger 1997). Small-scale collective memory can also sometimes be procedural. Research on transactive memory systems, for example, in some cases concerns group performance on a variety of practical tasks (Wegner 1987; Liang et al. 1995). The existence of procedural memory in small-scale groups may constitute an important difference between small-scale and large-scale collective memory, since there is no obvious sense in which large-scale groups are capable of remembering how to do something, but we will not pursue this here. Our focus, instead, will be on episodic memory. It appears that small-scale collective memory, unlike large-scale collective memory, may sometimes be episodic, in the sense that it is memory for events in which group members took an active part and hence of which they have direct knowledge.

Stages of Collective Remembering

What sorts of *remembering* are at issue in collective memory? In philosophy, remembering has sometimes been treated as a simple process in which a representation produced by a source other than memory is preserved over time. In psychology, in contrast, remembering is understood as a constructive, multi-stage process (Michaelian 2016). The initial stage of the process, leading from an experience to the production of a short-term memory representation, is *encoding*. Short-term representations are not mere copies of experience but result from processes of selection, abstraction, interpretation, and integration with existing knowledge (Alba and Hasher 1983). Encoding therefore often amounts to the production of a new representation. Following encoding, a process of *consolidation* is responsible for transforming the labile, short-term representation into a stable, long-term representation, with the representation remaining labile—subject to further transformation—throughout the extended consolidation process. Consolidation thus likewise amounts to the production of a new representation. Only when consolidation is complete can the representation be said to have achieved stable *storage*. Moreover, *retrieval*, like encoding and consolidation, is a constructive process in which a stored representation is recombined with other relevant information to produce another new representation.

The concepts of encoding, consolidation, storage, and retrieval are normally applied to remembering understood as an individual-level process, and the social dimension of remembering sometimes makes its appearance in the form of external factors affecting the accuracy of individual memory at the encoding, consolidation, or retrieval stages—often negatively, as in work on social contagion (Roediger et al. 2001) or the misinformation effect (Loftus 2005). Applying the concepts to remembering understood as a group-level process, however, may provide a useful means of distinguishing among different senses in which the memory process itself can be collective: rather than asking simply about "collective memory" in general, we can ask more precise questions about collective encoding, consolidation, storage, and retrieval.

2. ENCODING AND RETRIEVAL

Some stages of a given process of remembering might be best understood as occurring at the individual level, while others are best understood as group-level processes, giving rise to a range of more or less strongly collective forms of memory. Reflecting the emphases of the existing literature, we focus initially (in this section) on encoding and retrieval in small-scale collective memory and then (in Section 3) on consolidation and storage in large-scale collective memory. The wide range of views in the broader collective intentionality literature on what it takes for a phenomenon to be truly collective, and on the relations between individual and collective cognitive states and processes, will be reflected in discussions of memory as philosophers come to integrate these fields together more thoroughly. Here we aim to home in on stronger views, on which it is the small group itself that can in certain circumstances remember.

Memory in Small-Scale Groups

Both encoding and retrieval in groups might be either *parallel*, in the sense that each group member implements the process without significant interaction with the others, or *interactive*, in the sense that group members interact. Putting the interactive/parallel distinction together with the encoding/retrieval distinction, we can distinguish among four forms of collective memory.

In cases of *parallel encoding/parallel retrieval*, there is significant interaction among group members at neither stage of the process; each individual learns and recalls on his own. While it might seem odd to include such cases under the heading of collective memory at all, they do correspond to the small-scale "nominal groups" (groups of non-interacting individuals) used in collaborative recall experiments (Weldon and Bellinger 1997; Barnier et al. 2008). At the level of large-scale collective memory, they may correspond to what Olick (1999) has termed "collected memory"—in reference to the aggregated memories of a group, as opposed to properly "collective memory"—or to what Margalit (2002) has termed "common memory"—again, a purely aggregative notion, as opposed to "shared memory" (see Dessingué 2015). Collective memory in the parallel encoding/parallel retrieval sense is thus useful primarily for purposes of comparison with more robustly collective forms of memory.

In cases of *parallel encoding/interactive retrieval*, there is no interaction among group members at the time of encoding, but there is interaction at the time of retrieval; individuals learn on their own but recall together. Such cases, which represent a more robustly collective phenomenon, correspond to the "collaborative groups"—groups of individuals who study material on their own and later recall it together—used in collaborative recall experiments. Cases with a similar structure figure in eyewitness memory research, much of which focuses on the risks of contamination of individual memories by post-event information (Loftus 2005).

In cases of *interactive encoding/parallel retrieval*, there is interaction among group members at the time of encoding but none at the time of retrieval; individuals learn together but recall on their own. We might think here of a group of friends travelling together and interacting while they encode memories of the trip (Sutton 2008); perhaps the group later disintegrates, the friends going their separate ways, so that, when each remembers the trip, he does so individually.

But suppose that the group does not disintegrate; instead, it remains together, allowing its members to interact through conversation when they remember the trip. In such cases of *interactive encoding/interactive retrieval*, there is interaction among group members at both encoding and retrieval; individuals learn and recall together. Such cases correspond to the sorts of ongoing transactive memory systems—stable groups characterized by a division of cognitive labor, with group members responsible for remembering different aspects of events and playing different roles during encoding and retrieval (Wegner 1987)—that have increasingly been investigated through the lens of distributed cognition (Theiner 2013; Harris et al. 2014). Of the four forms of collective memory distinguished here, interactive/interactive cases—which we will refer to as cases of *strongly shared memory*—may have the best chance of representing a truly collective phenomenon, in the sense that we may legitimately treat the group itself as the remembering subject.

Joint Action and Collective Encoding

One concept from the collective intentionality literature that might help us to come to grips with the possibility of strongly shared memory is that of joint action. Joint *actions* are often understood as actions performed by groups as the result of joint *intentions* (though see Ludwig 2014). Different accounts of joint action are generated by different accounts of joint intention. Purely "summative" accounts—on which joint intentions are simply aggregations of group members' identical individual intentions—are available. But some theorists reject these in favor of accounts on which joint intentions cannot be reduced to mere aggregations of ordinary individual intentions. In an oft-referenced illustration, Searle (1990) contrasts a group of individuals spontaneously running for shelter with a group running for shelter as part of a prepared artistic performance. The latter scenario provides us with an instance of genuinely joint action; the former does not.

In Searle's view, the difference between the two scenarios lies in the nature of the group members' intentions. In the former, each individual's intention makes no reference to the other members of the group. In the latter, each individual intends to run to shelter as part of the group; his intention—a "we-intention," as opposed to an "I-intention" (Tuomela and Miller 1988)—essentially refers to the other members of the group. But on this approach joint action is still understood in terms of higher-level cognitive states. Hence it has difficulty recognizing joint action in cases where the participating individuals have not formed the relevant joint intention (Pacherie and Dokic 2006). Further, it is arguably not very robustly collective, in the sense that it only requires that group members share the contents of their intentions (Schmid 2009); by the same token, it does not explicitly require communication or interaction among group members during performance of the joint action.

One alternative approach that is somewhat more robustly collective is that developed by Bratman (2014). In Bratman's view, what is required for genuinely joint action is not just that each individual himself intends the action of the group. In addition, group members' intentions must "mesh"—they need not be identical, but they must be compatible, and may require some mutual responsiveness in interaction. This approach arguably requires that more be shared among group members. Importantly, however, it manages this only by viewing joint action primarily as a cooperative activity. This third limitation— a tendency to downplay cases in which group members act together in a non-cooperative or conflictual manner—along with the two just noted, are shared by most accounts of joint action in terms of joint intention. Together, they threaten to render such accounts inapplicable to collective encoding.

We return to the role of conflict below; here, we focus on the roles of intention and interaction. Consider again the case of strongly shared memory described above. When the members of the group encode short-term representations of their trip, their encoding is collective in the sense that their conversational interactions shape the representations that they end up encoding. They might—through the operation of mechanisms such as socially-shared retrieval-induced forgetting (Hirst and Echterhoff 2008), which can lead to convergent memories among group members—end up representing a common subset of the events that made up the trip as especially important, forgetting other events, endowing the remembered events with shared meanings in relation to the life of the group, and linking the remembered events in an overarching narrative structure. It is thus plausible to speak of encoding as a group-level process. Due to their lack of emphasis on interaction, accounts of joint action in terms of joint intention do not fully describe the way in which collective encoding might amount to a form of joint action.

Such accounts also fail to capture the dynamics of collective encoding due to their reliance on the notion of joint intention. The process of generating a shared representation of the past need not be and normally is not the result of a joint intention to form such a representation. Shared representations, instead, typically emerge spontaneously through the process of conversational interaction. It should be noted that this limitation of joint intention accounts is due not to a feature of collective encoding qua collective phenomenon but rather to a feature that collective encoding inherits from individual encoding: encoding is not, in general, the result of an individual intention to form a short-term memory representation; it is, rather, a largely spontaneous process. The relevant intentions are thus typically lacking both in individual and in collective encoding.

What is required, then, is an approach that captures both the fact that encoding is typically not the result of an intention to remember and the fact that it involves interaction among group members, through which they shape and reshape what each of them ends up remembering in such a way that it is legitimate to describe them as forming a shared memory. Tollefsen et al. (2013) provide the outlines of one approach that has these features. They argue for the existence of an "alignment system," an evolved set of interconnected processes designed to facilitate social interaction and joint action. While the alignment system is responsive to higher cognitive states operating at longer timescales, including intentions, it can also give rise to such states through bottom-up processes such as real-time coordination of bodily movements and use of common linguistic structures during conversation. Alignment refers to the dynamic matching of the behavior or cognitive states of group members over time, in a process of mutual adaptation, i.e. a mutually responsive coordination of behavior and cognition; it is thus well-suited to capture the interactive nature of collective encoding (see also Chapter 7, this volume). Critically, alignment can occur spontaneously; it is thus capable of respecting the fact that collective encoding can occur without the formation of joint intentions. Overall, an understanding of joint action which incorporates attention to the interactions of alignment systems at faster timescales might become central to a more adequate understanding of collective encoding as joint action (Bietti and Sutton 2015). Indeed, Tollefsen et al. suggest that the formation of transactive memory systems, in particular, might be seen as the outcome of iterated interaction among group members' alignment systems. During encoding, for example, coordination of eye gaze patterns might influence the types of information stored as well as the cues associated with stored information.

Joint Attention and Collective Retrieval

Strongly shared memory involves interaction not only during encoding but also during retrieval, and research conducted within the transactive memory framework has looked, for example, at how couples interact during retrieval to construct shared representations of their shared pasts (Harris et al. 2014). A concept from the collective intentionality literature that might help us come to grips with this aspect of strongly shared memory is that of *joint attention*. (See also Chapter 9, this volume.)

In order for two or more agents to count as jointly attending to the same object, it does not suffice for them simply to attend to the same object at the same time; each must, in addition, be aware that the other is attending to the same object. Much of the empirical work on joint attention has adopted a developmental perspective, focusing on the early emergence of the capacity for joint attention and its relation to capacities such as mindreading (e.g. Moore and Dunham 1995). Philosophical work, meanwhile, has been devoted primarily to the development of general theoretical accounts of joint attention; building on theories of mindreading, the main debates here have been between partisans of theory-theoretic approaches and partisans of simulation-theoretic approaches. While there are deep differences between these approaches, both understand joint attention as an interactive phenomenon emerging out of lower-level processes, and a view of collective retrieval as involving joint attention to the past thus has the potential to fit well with the understanding of collective encoding sketched above.

One view of this sort has been proposed by Hoerl and McCormack (2005), who combine philosophical and developmental approaches to argue that the very capacity to think about events as situated in time only develops in the context of learning to attend to past events together with others. In their view, it is through such joint attention to the past that the child comes to understand that later events in a causal sequence can alter the effects of earlier events, thus shaping the present, and it is through conversation about past events that children learn to construct temporally structured narratives that explain the influence of the past on the present. While Hoerl and McCormack provide a thorough exploration of the idea that the development of collective remembering can be understood in terms of joint attention, there is room for further work to develop an account of collective remembering as joint attention in mature subjects.

Assuming that such an account can be developed, there remains a question about how we are to understand the ultimate products of collective remembering—the collective memories produced by collective retrieval. Another concept from the collective intentionality literature, that of *collective belief*, has the potential to be of help here. Just as some theorists reject summative accounts of collective intention, some reject summative accounts of collective belief, which treat a group as believing a given proposition just in case all (or most) of its members believe it. (See also Chapter 7, this volume.) Non-summative accounts of collective belief, similar in spirit to the non-summative accounts of collective intention reviewed above, are motivated by apparent counterexamples to both the necessity and the sufficiency of shared individual belief for collective belief. Against the sufficiency of shared individual belief, Gilbert (1989) argues that two groups might count as having different beliefs despite having the same members (and thus the same shared individual beliefs). Against the necessity of shared individual belief, she argues that a group might count as having a given belief even if none of its members have that belief. This is not the place to attempt to identify analogous cases in the collective memory literature, but, to the extent that there are such cases, similar arguments would support viewing collective remembering as a group-level process. A distinct issue in the literature on collective belief is whether collective beliefs are states of the same kind as individual beliefs; on many accounts, collective beliefs do not behave much like individual beliefs, and this has led to debates over whether the notion of collective belief should be replaced with a notion of collective acceptance (e.g. Tuomela 2000). Future work might draw on analyses of differences between individual beliefs and group beliefs or acceptances to explore differences between individual memories and collective memories.

Pending such work, however, we should not take it for granted that analyses of collective belief or acceptance can be extended to collective memory in any straightforward way. An initial concern here is analogous to one that arises for attempts to understand individual memory in terms of individual belief. Just as individuals can in certain cases remember an event without believing that it occurred (Otgaar et al. 2014), a group might in principle remember an event without believing that it occurred. Individuals are capable of employing metacognitive monitoring which enables them to reject even sub-jectively compelling memories. Similarly, groups of individuals constituting transactive memory systems may be capable of employing group-level metacognitive monitoring which enables them to reject memories that they would otherwise accept (Michaelian and Arango-Munoz, forthcoming). The notion of collective belief or acceptance may thus simply fail to capture the nature of the states that are produced when we remember together.

A distinct concern is specific to collective memory; whereas analyses of collective belief focus on cases in which a group can be said to believe a single, determinate propo-sition, it is, in many cases of collective memory, implausible to ascribe a single, determi-nate memory to the group. The point is not merely that a group might be said to have a memory that diverges from the memories of its members. It is, rather, that, in many cases of collective memory, the group can be seen as remembering an event from its shared past despite the fact that we cannot ascribe a determinate narrative or representation even to the group as a whole. A group of friends remembering an event together might converge on a common representation of the event, but there is no guarantee that it will do so. If negotiation over the meaning of the shared past is perpetual and ongoing, it may make little sense to ascribe a determinate memory to the group, even while it remains meaningful to say that the group remembers the event. There is thus a need for work developing a notion of collective memory that would allow us to count a group as having a memory of an event despite a lack of internal consensus on the nature and significance of the represented event.

3. CONSOLIDATION AND STORAGE

The potential for lack of consensus should remind us that collective remembering is not always a purely cooperative process; indeed, as we will see in this section, conflict among group members is arguably at the very heart of collective remembering.

Memory in Large-Scale Groups

As our focus shifts from cooperation to conflict, it also shifts from small-scale to large-scale collective remembering. The latter shift raises a difficult question. The discussion so far has concentrated on strongly shared memory. We initially characterized strongly shared memory as involving interaction among group members during both encoding and retrieval, and this characterization can be extended to include interaction during consolidation (e.g. the role of a dominant narrator in shaping collective memory; Cuc et al. 2006) and storage (e.g. responsibilities of group members for remembering different components of an event; Wegner 1987). Due to their sheer scale, it is unclear whether large-scale groups are capable of anything like this form of strongly shared memory.

Even if forms of interaction analogous to those at work in small-scale memory can be identified, remembering in large-scale groups, since it is typically memory for events in which group members did not take an active part, is bound to lack the phenomenology characteristic of episodic memory. We return to the question of phenomenology below. Setting it aside for the moment, we consider a general model of large-scale collective memory developed recently by Anastasio et al. (2012). In addition to calling attention to the role, noted above, of *conflict* in collective consolidation, their model calls attention to the role of material *artifacts* in collective storage.

Conflict and Collective Consolidation

Anastasio et al.'s model explicitly builds both on social scientific research on large-scale collective memory and on psychological and neuroscientific research on individual memory. It thus aligns with our conception of collective remembering as involving processes of encoding, consolidation, storage, and retrieval analogous to those involved in individual remembering. In fact, Anastasio et al. take this analogy quite literally, arguing that the very same consolidation process that unfolds at the level of the individual also unfolds at the level of large-scale groups, including entire societies.

They argue, in particular, that both individual and collective consolidation depend on the workings of a selector/relator, which is responsible for selecting encoded short-term representations for consolidation into long-term representations and for determining how these are related to each other to produce a coherent whole. In the individual, the selector/relator is realized by the hippocampus. In a large-scale group, they argue, it is realized by groups of opinion leaders (e.g. intellectuals and journalists), who in effect constitute a "social hippocampus." Anastasio et al.'s overall claim is that, because the individual hippocampus and the social hippocampus play the same role in shaping long-term representations at their respective levels, we may speak of the same consolidation process unfolding at both levels.

While this claim is intriguing, there is reason to be skeptical of it. As Anastasio et al. themselves admit, there is, within a given society, not in fact a single social hippocampus but rather multiple, competing "social hippocampi." No one group of opinion leaders directs the overall process of collective consolidation. Instead, the course taken by collective consolidation—which events end up being represented in long-term collective memory and how they end up being represented—is determined by competitive and often outright conflictual interactions among different groups of opinion leaders. This amounts to a fundamental disanalogy between individual and collective consolidation.

This conclusion about Anastasio et al.'s model suggests a lesson both for research on small-scale collective memory and for research on collective intentionality. The former has tended to focus primarily on cooperative interactions, but there is room for additional work on ways in which memory in small-scale groups can be collective while being conflictual. The latter has tended to treat collective action as a basically cooperative phenomenon, but there is room for work, building on empirical studies of conflict in collective memory and social processes more broadly, on the ways in which conflictual interactions can underwrite collective action.

Artifacts and Collective Storage

In addition to this negative lesson, Anastasio et al.'s model suggests a positive lesson for research on small-scale collective memory and collective intentionality. Consolidation is the process responsible for transforming the short-term representations produced by encoding into long-term representations. At the level of the individual, such long-term representations can be understood as traces distributed across the brain (Sutton 1998). At the level of a large-scale collective, Anastasio et al. suggest, they are distributed across the society, in part in the form of material artifacts, such as museum collections and textbooks; short-term representations, on their approach, are likewise realized in part by a variety of material artifacts, such as articles in news media and scientific journals.

In line with this suggestion, we note that research on the role of material artifacts in remembering has implications for research both on small-scale collective memory and on collective intentionality. The former has tended to focus on purely social groups, ignoring the possibility that remembering might in many cases be best understood as a process executed by a distributed sociotechnical (as opposed to purely social) system (Michaelian and Arango-Munoz, forthcoming), and there is a need for additional work on ways in which remembering unfolds through interactions not only among human subjects but also among human subjects and technological resources. The latter has tended to treat collective intentionality and collective belief as purely social phenomena, ignoring the possible contributions of material memory traces and other material artifacts. It is, of course, highly counterintuitive to think of a system including not only agents but also artifacts as engaging in actions or holding beliefs. But if we are willing to think of groups of agents as doing so, there may be little reason to resist thinking of groups of agents and artifacts as doing so as well.

4. OPEN QUESTIONS: MEMORY, MENTALITY, AND PHENOMENOLOGY

Throughout this chapter, we have suggested that strongly-shared forms of collective memory may not be reducible to individual memory. Complementing older anti-reductionist arguments (tracing back to Halbwachs 1994), recent arguments (Huebner 2013; Theiner 2013) have sought to show more directly that certain forms of collective memory are irreducible. These recent arguments have focused on small-scale groups, such as transactive memory systems, and we might wonder whether they can be extended to large-scale groups. We will not attempt to determine this here. But we do note that any attempt to establish the existence of group-level episodic memory, in particular, will have to deal with a pair of important worries.

First, acknowledging group-level memory raises a worry about group-level mentality. Does acknowledging group-level memory require us to acknowledge group-level mentality? Group-level mentality seems implausible to many. However, though it is natural to suppose that, where there is memory, there must be mind (Rupert 2005), there may be space for views which divorce attributions of memory from attributions of mind (Sutton 2008).

Second, even if this worry about group-level mentality can in principle be overcome by driving a wedge between the notion of group-level memory and the notion of group-level mentality, there remains a worry about group-level phenomenology. Does acknowledging group-level memory require us to acknowledge group-level phenomenology? We noted above that episodic memory is characterized by a specific phenomenology: when one episodically remembers, one has a sense of reliving the past. If episodic memory implies episodic phenomenology, then, if groups—or perhaps even sociotechnical systems—are capable of episodic memory, they would have to be capable of episodic phenomenology. Group-level phenomenology is even less plausible than group-level mentality. We thus seem to face a choice between denying that episodic memory requires episodic phenomenology and thus leaving open the possibility that collective episodic memory and individual episodic memory are of the same kind and granting that individual episodic memory requires episodic phenomenology and hence admitting that collective "episodic" memory is different in kind from individual episodic memory. Given the centrality of episodic phenomenology to contemporary accounts of episodic memory, the latter option is likely to be preferable.

ACKNOWLEDGEMENTS

Supported by grant 16-UOO-016 to KM from the Marsden Fund, administered by the Royal Society of New Zealand.

RELATED TOPICS

Collective Action and Agency (Ch. 1), Non-Reductive Views of Shared Intention (Ch. 2), Reductive Views of Shared Intention (Ch. 3), Coordinating Joint Action (Ch. 6), Collective Belief and Acceptance (Ch. 7), Joint Attention (Ch. 9), Groups as Distributed Cognitive Systems (Ch. 18).

REFERENCES

Alba, J.W. and Hasher, L. (1983) "Is Memory Schematic?" *Psychological Bulletin* 93 (2): 203–31.
Anastasio, T.J., Ehrenberger, K.A., Watson, P. and Zhang, W. (2012) *Individual and Collective Memory Consolidation: Analogous Processes on Different Levels*, Cambridge, MA: MIT Press.
Barnier, A.J., Sutton, J., Harris, C.B. and Wilson, R.A. (2008) "A Conceptual and Empirical Framework for the Social Distribution of Cognition: The Case of Memory," *Cognitive Systems Research* 9 (1–2): 33–51.
Bietti, L.M. and Sutton, J. (2015) "Interacting to Remember at Multiple Timescales: Coordination, Collaboration, Cooperation and Culture in Joint Remembering," *Interaction Studies* 16 (3): 419–50.
Blight, D.W. (2009) "The Memory Boom: Why and Why Now?" in P. Boyer and J.V. Wertsch (eds) *Memory in Mind and Culture*, Cambridge: Cambridge University Press.
Bratman, M.E. (2014) *Shared Agency: A Planning Theory of Acting Together*, Oxford: Oxford University Press.
Cuc, A., Ozuru, Y., Manier, D. and Hirst, W. (2006) "On the Formation of Collective Memories: the Role of a Dominant Narrator," *Memory & Cognition* 34 (4): 752–62.
Dessingué, A. (2015) "From Collectivity to Collectiveness: Reflections (With Halbwachs and Bakhtin) on the Concept of Collective Memory," in S. Kattago (ed.) *Ashgate Research Companion to Memory Studies*, Burlington: Ashgate.
Erll, A. (2011) *Memory in Culture*, London: Palgrave Macmillan.
Erll, A. and Nünning, A. (eds) (2010) *A Companion to Cultural Memory Studies*, Berlin: De Gruyter.
Gilbert, M. (1989) *On Social Facts*, London: Routledge.
Halbwachs, M. (1994) *Les Cadres Sociaux De La Mémoire*, Albin Michel. Original publication 1925.
Harris, C.B., Barnier, A.J., Sutton, J. and Keil, P.G. (2014) "Couples as Socially Distributed Cognitive Systems: Remembering in Everyday Social and Material Contexts," *Memory Studies* 7 (3): 285–97.
Hirst, W. and Echterhoff, G. (2008) "Creating Shared Memories in Conversation: Toward a Psychology of Collective Memory," *Social Research: An International Quarterly* 75 (1): 183–216.
Hoerl, C. and McCormack, T. (2005) "Joint Reminiscing as Joint Attention to the Past," in N. Eilan, C. Hoerl, T. McCormack, and J. Roessler (eds) *Joint Attention: Communication and Other Minds*, Oxford: Oxford University Press.

Huebner, B. (2013) *Macrocognition: A Theory of Distributed Minds and Collective Intentionality*, Oxford: Oxford University Press.

Liang, D.W., Moreland, R. and Argote, L. (1995) "Group Versus Individual Training and Group Performance: The Mediating Role of Transactive Memory," *Personality and Social Psychology Bulletin* 21 (4): 384–93.

Loftus, E.F. (2005) "Planting Misinformation in the Human Mind: a 30-Year Investigation of the Malleability of Memory," *Learning & Memory*, 12 (4): 361–6.

Ludwig, K. (2014) "The Ontology of Collective Action," in S. Chant, F. Hindriks, and G. Preyer (eds) *From Individual to Collective Intentionality*, Oxford: Oxford University Press.

Margalit, A. (2002) *The Ethics of Memory*, Cambridge, MA: Harvard University Press.

Michaelian, K. (2016) *Mental Time Travel: Episodic Memory and Our Knowledge of the Personal Past*, Cambridge, MA: MIT Press.

Michaelian, K. and Arango-Munoz, S. (forthcoming) "Collaborative Memory Knowledge: a Distributed Reliabilist Perspective," in M. Meade, A. Barnier, P. van Bergen, C. Harris, and J. Sutton (eds) *Collaborative Remembering: How Remembering with Others Influences Memory*, Oxford: Oxford University Press.

Moore, C. and Dunham, P.J. (1995) *Joint Attention: Its Origins and Role in Development*, New York: Psychology Press.

Olick, J.K. (1999) "Collective Memory: The Two Cultures," *Sociological Theory* 17 (3): 333–48.

Olick, J.K., Vinitzky-Seroussi, V. and Levy, D. (eds) (2011) *The Collective Memory Reader*, Oxford: Oxford University Press.

Otgaar, H., Scoboria, A. and Mazzoni, G. (2014) "On the Existence and Implications of Nonbelieved Memories," *Current Directions in Psychological Science* 23 (5): 349–54.

Pacherie, E. and Dokic, J. (2006) "From Mirror Neurons to Joint Actions," *Cognitive Systems Research* 7 (2–3): 101–12.

Reese, E., Haden, C.A. and Fivush, R. (1993) "Mother-Child Conversations About the Past: Relationships of Style and Memory Over Time," *Cognitive Development* 8 (4): 403–30.

Roediger, H.L., Meade, M.L. and Bergman, E.T. (2001) "Social Contagion of Memory," *Psychonomic Bulletin & Review* 8 (2): 365–71.

Rupert, R. (2005) "Minding One's Cognitive Systems: When Does a Group of Minds Constitute a Single Cognitive Unit?" *Episteme* 1: 177–88.

Schmid, H.B. (2009) *Plural Action: Essays in Philosophy and Social Science*, New York: Springer.

Searle, J. (1990) "Collective Intentions and Actions," in P. Cohen, J. Morgan, and M. Pollack (eds) *Intentions in Communication*, Cambridge, MA: MIT Press.

Sutton, J. (1998) *Philosophy and Memory Traces: Descartes to Connectionism*, Cambridge: Cambridge University Press.

Sutton, J. (2008) "Between Individual and Collective Memory: Coordination, Interaction, Distribution," *Social Research*, 75 (1): 23–48.

Theiner, G. (2013) "Transactive Memory Systems: A Mechanistic Analysis of Emergent Group Memory," *Review of Philosophy and Psychology*, 4 (1): 65–89.

Tollefsen, D.P., Dale, R. and Paxton, A. (2013) "Alignment, Transactive Memory, and Collective Cognitive Systems," *Review of Philosophy and Psychology* 4 (1): 49–64.

Tulving, E. (1972) "Episodic and Semantic Memory," in E. Tulving and W. Donaldson (eds) *Organization of Memory*, New York: Academic Press.

Tuomela, R. (2000) *Cooperation: A Philosophical Study*, New York: Springer.

Tuomela, R. and Miller, K. (1988) "We-Intentions," *Philosophical Studies* 53 (3): 367–89.

Wegner, D.M. (1987) "Transactive Memory: a Contemporary Analysis of the Group Mind," in B. Mullen and G.R. Goethals (eds) *Theories of Group Behavior*, New York: Springer.

Weldon, M.S. and Bellinger, K.D. (1997) "Collective Memory: Collaborative and Individual Processes in Remembering," *Journal of Experimental Psychology: Learning, Memory, and Cognition* 23 (5): 1160–75.

Wertsch, J.V. (2009) "Collective Memory," in P. Boyer and J.V. Wertsch (eds) *Memory in Mind and Culture*, Cambridge: Cambridge University Press.

12

Collective Emotions

Hans Bernhard Schmid

Emotions are ways of *knowing what matters* in a situation that tightly connect cognition to evaluation and action. Emotions focus our attention on what's significant in the light of our aims and values, and they dispose us to act. Emotions are thus practical knowledge par excellence. As such, they are indispensable, at least for *our* kind of agency. To put all of this in a simple slogan: emotions are our way of getting our act together.

This chapter opens with a discussion of how this works in the individual case (1), and then proceeds to examining how this carries over to *joint* action (2). It is argued that in spite of some important differences between these cases, in order for *us* to get our *joint* act together, we need to know what matters to *us*. For such knowledge to be suitably related to action, it has to involve a single unified evaluative perspective (3). The way in which this perspective is unified is plural self-knowledge: a non-observational and non-inferential sense of our concerns *as ours*. Such emotion is *a collection's*, or *a group's*; its subject is plural rather than singular.

1. GETTING OUR ACT TOGETHER—DISTRIBUTIVELY

Let us first take a look at the role of emotion in individual action. The way in which the kind of knowledge that is emotion is indispensable for our kind of agency becomes particularly obvious if we consider the following (fictional) examples where agents fail to get their act together for lack of an emotional response. Daniel Dennett (1984) presents an artificial intelligence-empowered robot that receives the information that a bomb is going to explode in its hangar in a couple of minutes. The robot integrates this information in its database, and proceeds to processing. The bomb explodes while the robot has just figured out how exactly its leaving the hangar would influence the tea price in China. Another example is Little Red Riding Hood in the fairy tale. On her visit to the lonely house in the woods she registers all these remarkable new features of grandma's appearance, and she asks all these questions about why grandma has such a deep voice, furry skin, red glowing eyes, and clawed paws. While the Big Bad Wolf opens his mouth to swallow her up, she ponders the question of why grandma has those big yellow fangs.

The tragedy of Dennett's robot and Little Red Riding Hood is not that they fail to register relevant information; rather, it is that they fail to register it *in the right way,* and the right way to register that a bomb is going to explode nearby or that grandma has clawed paws and bared long fangs is *a pang of fear.* "Having fear"—being afraid—is to register that information in the right way because fear evaluates its target in the way in which it matters: as *danger.* The feature in virtue of which a pang of fear is the way of getting one's act together in such situations is that it is "fast thinking" (Kahneman 2011). And a pang of fear is thought of the sort that closes the gap between theory and practice, between cognition and volition, between thinking and acting (de Sousa 2013) because it is not only "mere knowledge" of danger, but knowledge of the *effective* kind. Fear—especially if it comes with a pang rather than creeping in slowly—typically induces readiness to leave, if not being on one's way out already (unless, of course, one happens to be among those unfortunate creatures whom fear tends to petrify). To say that fear is "motivationally charged" is an understatement. It is thus *practical* knowledge indeed. Similar cases could be made for other basic emotions such as anger and disgust (though admittedly, the argument works better for forward-looking emotions, and a more elaborate argument has to be made to include backward-looking emotions such as disappointment).

Parts of the history of philosophy have tended to be somewhat less enthusiastic about such emotional "fast thinking," and have not found emotion worthy of the title of practical knowledge. The most obvious reason is that for every case in which—like Little Red Riding Hood—we fail to get our act together for lack of an adequate emotional response, there are innumerable cases in which we fail to think and act appropriately *because* of an emotional episode. Instead of seeing emotions as evaluative judgments that constitute a form of intelligence (Nussbaum 2003), many authors have found emotional judgments to be too quick not to be dirty. Our fears are notoriously unreliable as indicators for real danger. Most of our pangs of fear yield false positives, targeting such harmless creatures as little spiders, howling owls, moving branches in windy parks at night, fictional characters in Hollywood horror movies, or perfectly friendly dogs. How are such emotions not a form of stupidity rather than intelligence, delusion rather than practical knowledge? Moreover, our fears tend to be recalcitrant against reason and persist in the face of solid better knowledge (Brady 2009). Conversely, many of the known very real dangers in our world fail to be registered by our emotions as what they are, such as in the case in which the smell of greasy fast food fills us with pleasure rather than fear. And even where fear happens to be right on target for a change, the kind of action tendency that is a pang of fear—panicking—is usually a way of getting oneself into deeper trouble rather than out of it.

This has often led to a conception of our true way of getting our act together as *reasoned choice* that is set in contradistinction to emotional action. In this view, Mr. Spock-like cool reason rather than emotion is the way of getting our act together properly. Yet recent philosophy has pointed out that emotion is not just a matter of quick affective reactions, but permeates the whole realm of reasoning. The basic intuition can be explained with a Humean insight. Not all emotions are passions of the "violent" sort, such as a pang of fear or a sudden surge of anger. Emotions can be passions of the "calm" sort, too.

Calm emotions are not a quick and dirty jump to a conclusion that bypasses careful consideration. Rather, they operate in a way that is compatible with—and indeed essential to—any form of practical reasoning. (Most emotion types include a spectrum between "calmer" and "more violent" cases—such as anger or fear—while other emotion types seem to be rather "calm" by nature, such as sadness.) To see how emotion operates in calm reasoning, consider Mr. Spock in the *Star Trek* series. Though he is not subject to such emotional episodes as sudden pangs of fear or fits of panic, and relies on "slow thinking" instead, he is by no means an unemotional automaton—indeed his case shows particularly well how "slow thinking," too, is imbued with emotion. Mr. Spock differs from Dennett's robot in that he knows exactly what's worth thinking about and what's not in a given situation. He does not engage in reasoning of the futile sort when he's confronted with imminent danger for his spaceship and its crew. He never panics, but he clearly knows danger in exactly the right way: as something that *matters* in a way that is connected to decided action. Knowing what matters in a way that is suitably action-related is *concern*, and this includes self-knowledge. Concern is not knowledge of what matters from an impersonal perspective, but knowledge of what matters *to the knower himself* in the light of what he or she *cares about*. His being worried is not just another thought that Mr. Spock needs to register in his reasoning. His knowledge is not of the sort that is in need of a transition from knowing that Mr. Spock is worried to knowing that *he* should act; the knowledge in question leaves no room for thoughts of the form "Mr. Spock seems to be worried, but why should *I* be bothered?" This is to say that Mr. Spock is non-observationally and non-inferentially *committed to act* by what he knows to be dangerous, and this is essential to his being such an impressive paragon of reasoned concern rather than a futile reasoner of Dennett's kind. Though he never lets his emotions get into the way of reasoning, his reasoning itself is focused and guided by emotion: He *cares* for the safety of his spaceship from a first-personal perspective that immediately translates into action-prompting concerns. Concerns are not judgments that underlie emotions; they are emotional judgments; without emotions—whether of the "violent" or "calm" sort—there is no way *for us* to be concerned. What matters in a situation impresses itself on us as concern in the kind of feeling that is emotion.

To be concerned in the light of what one cares about involves a whole system of emotions (Helm 2001). To care about something is to be *afraid* when it is in danger, to *hope* for its escape from danger, to be *relieved* when it is saved, to be *content* when it is well, to be *angry* when it is subject to wrong, and to be *joyful* at its thriving and success—and in virtue of their being self-knowledge, all of these attitudes are commitments to act. Care thus establishes an integrated system of emotional dispositions, and though the emotional nature of this system of dispositions may not become apparent in ordinary life very often, it structures the whole of our thinking and acting. Indeed, the point can be made that in this way, emotions are our way of getting our act together *over a lifetime* because what we care about makes us the agents we are; being emotionally disposed in a coherent and systematic way is having a specific character, as Aristotle argues. To put this insight in somewhat Heideggerian terms: our care is our being. Care is identity-conferring commitment (Frankfurt 1988). Caring is the way in which we live our lives as our own and in which living comes with a sense of meaning (de Sousa 2013). Thus the emotional "getting together" of our act not only extends to quick impulsive reactions and to reasoned choice, but indeed to the living of one's own life as the person one is.

2. GETTING OUR ACT TOGETHER—COLLECTIVELY

Assuming this is roughly what emotion is about, how does it relate to joint action? Obviously, getting our act together is not just something we do, or should do, *individually*—each of us by him- or herself. Very often, the getting together of action is something that we do, or should do, *jointly*—all of us *together*. Recent philosophical research has devoted increasing attention to the question of what exactly it means for a plurality of agents to be jointly engaged in, and jointly perform, one collective act, rather than just an aggregate of several individual acts. A widely shared agreement is that for you and me to do something *collectively,* the act has to be collectively intended. The disagreement is over what exactly this means, and what is collective about intentionality (Schweikard and Schmid 2013). Given the ways in which our individual agency is *emotional* throughout, an obvious question is: is the claim that emotion is our way of getting our act together plausible in a *distributive* sense only, or is it also true *collectively*? Is it only that it is in virtue of emotion that *each of us* gets *his or her own* act together, or is there a sense in which joint action, too, is emotionally integrated?

Turning first to the quick-and-dirty case of "violent" emotions, there seems to be reason to doubt that our joint actions can be integrated in this way. It is true that there are many dangers out there that cannot be avoided by individual acts of fear, but only by quick and decided joint action. In such cases, reacting *distributively* rather than *collectively* is a way of failing to get our act together. But the way our "quick" emotions work seems to be systematically geared towards failure at these tasks. If an aggregate of people suddenly confronted with the sort of danger that causes fear of the "violent" sort—say, a gruesome-looking monster—a pell-mell of individual reactions rather than a well-integrated and organized joint action is likely to ensue. Being in the grip of panic does not usually promote smooth cooperation. Affects tend to dispose us to act *individually* rather than jointly, it seems, and in many instances, strong affective reactions lead to a *breakdown* of team action ('all we like sheep have gone astray, each of us has turned to his own way', reports the King James Bible of a case in point). "Fast thinking," it seems, does not integrate joint action—knowing what to do *jointly* seems to be a matter of slow thinking, involving communication and joint deliberation.

There seems to be reason to think that this is not just a contingent fact about our psychology, but based in the very *nature* of emotion. Consider the way affects operate in establishing readiness to act. Fear works on us *bodily*; readiness to act is not just established in some mental disposition; in a pang of fear, it is realized "in flesh and blood," as it were. Teams, groups, or other collections of people do not have a body, only individuals have. Therefore, teams cannot experience fear in the way individuals can, and thus get their joint action together in the "quick and dirty" way of affective action. In the light of this and similar arguments, it has sometimes been argued that even if there are collective emotions, they do not extend to the "violent" kind (cf. for example Schmid 2014).

Yet in the light of recent research (e.g. Salmela and Nagatsu, forthcoming; Michael 2011), a case can be made for at least some forms of affect-driven and affectively integrated joint action. The basic insights are not new. Philosophers and psychologists have often noticed that there is something like an "automatic spread of affect through groups" that attunes and regulates the participant's emotions. This has traditionally been called "emotional contagion." Emotional contagion is clearly not sufficient for integrated joint action—dissolution of joint action and uncoordinated mass behavior is just as likely to ensue from a spread of fear than decided and well-integrated joint action. Some form of emotional contagion and mutual emotional attunement may be necessary, but emotional contagion does not yield the decisive feature of joint action that is its being coordinated. It has been argued in the recent literature that this feature exists (Kelly et al. 2014: 201). One of the candidates that is often invoked in accounts of shared emotional attitudes is (mutual) empathy, as widely studied in the phenomenological tradition (cf. for example Zahavi 2015). As emotional attitudes such as empathy and sympathy involve focusing one's attention on other people's emotions, it may be argued that they do not help in our cases. Engaging in mutual empathy and waiting for an "emotional we-experience" to "emerge" is hardly our way of getting our act together when we're faced with a gruesome monster. More likely candidates are some well-trained habitualized dispositions, which, once they are established will enable groups to engage in quick affect-driven joint action. If you're a member of a successful team of monster fighters, you don't react to the sudden appearance of a particularly frightening specimen in the way you would as an isolated individual. You react in the way you should as a member, and you do so spontaneously. There is often no need to proceed to "slow thinking" and communication. This may be interpreted as the effect of training routines, or some sort of conditioning. But as a member of the elite team of monster fighters, you may not just react "automatically" and blindly, but rather in the light of a spontaneous reaction in which what matters in a situation impresses itself on you as a *shared concern*; the affective reaction itself (rather than some blindly triggered routine) is the knowledge of what to do, and it often seems to work. Within his detailed layered account of the psychology of shared emotions, Mikko Salmela aims to accommodate such forms of shared affective fast thinking (Salmela 2012, 2015; for a rich early account that is somewhat skeptical concerning the possibility of impulsive, affect-driven team action cf. Stein 1922).

Insofar as such "quick and dirty" getting together of joint action ensues, it may seem plausible to say *of a team or group* that it has an experience of sudden fear of the affective sort, though certainly not in contradistinction to the individual level. The case at hand is not that of a collective entity that experiences fear at an emergent level that does not involve any such emotional experience at the individual level (for an attempt to make some sort of a case for this possibility using the case of a "panicking" ship with an apparently calm crew, see Huebner 2011). Rather, the case at hand is a *form of sharing* in which the participants seem to experience fear *collectively* rather than *distributively*. We may call this the *sharing* of emotion, where it is not the case that each party involved experiences an emotion of the same *type*, but where what is shared is the emotional state (or emotional episode, or evaluative judgment; see Schmid 2009; Krueger, forthcoming for further references).

A central intuitive challenge that is sometimes raised against this view in the literature is the claim that for a mental attitude such as a strong emotion to be genuinely collective, the attitude would have to be "lodged in a group body" (Connor 2013). In this view, our case of the monster fighters is just a case of suitably socially calibrated individual emotional dispositions, with nothing collective about the subject of the attitude. This argument can be countered with a phenomenological distinction that is inspired by Max Scheler's taxonomy of feeling types (Scheler [1912–16] 1973). There is a fundamental difference between bodily sensations of the sort of, say, a pain in one's finger, on the one hand, and bodily sensations of the sort involved in the feeling of sudden fear, on the other hand. The experience of pain in one's finger is an experience of one's finger, in which the finger is experienced as hurting. The experience of fear, too, involves bodily localized sensations—e.g. of one's hair standing on end on one's neck. But fear is not an experience of one's neck in the same way as pain is the experience of one's finger. The pain focuses our attention on the finger. The fear does not focus our attention on the neck— rather, the attention is focused on the target of the fear (e.g. the approaching monster). If you manage to focus your attention on your neck rather than on the monster, your attitude is not really one of fear anymore (but perhaps one of psychological curiosity, or some such). The phenomenological point to be made here is thus that feeling-sensations can be "bodily" in two very different ways; in pain, the body—or the affected part of it— is the focus of the experience. In fear, however, the body is not the object of the feeling (the feeling is a "feeling towards" whatever the fear is about; see Goldie (2000: 58ff); for an early detailed analysis of types of bodily feelings and of how they can be shared see Scheler [(1912–16) 1973]). In the latter case, the body plays an *adverbial role* rather than being the focus.

This opens up a perspective on how the above objection to the idea of collective feeling sensations works in the case of hurting fingers, but not in the case of the feeling-sensation involved in fear. There might be a sense in which the fact that a group does not have a single integrated group body over and above the bodies of the individual participants makes the idea of a collectively hurting finger absurd; the group does not have a finger that could be collectively experienced as hurting in a first-person plural perspective. Yet the same argument cannot be made in the case of fear, because the bodily feeling sensation involved in fear is not of each one's own neck, but rather of a danger (e.g. a monster). Though it is in different individual bodies that we are affected, the bodily experience is not of our different bodies, but of one and the same target. Though each one being bodily affected by the same target is clearly not *sufficient* for an emotion to be shared in the collective sense, this line of argument blocks the move from the inexistence of a collective body to the impossibility of bodily felt collective emotions.

If this line suggests that under the specified conditions, it may be possible that there are collective emotions in the sense of emotional evaluative judgments of the "quick" sort that integrate joint action in the same way that individual emotions usually enable the "getting together" of individual action, it remains true that in many cases, getting our joint act together does not work that way. Had we to rely on our "violent" emotions alone, we would be even more of a failure in getting our joint acts together then we already are. The way we usually cooperate involves planning and communication. Indeed, the getting together of our joint acts is even more in need of reasoning than the getting together of our individual acts; only in specific circumstances can we rely on our affective impulses in cooperation; joint action, it seems, is more often some form of reasoned choice rather than an impulsive spontaneous act. Yet we have argued above that it is a mistake to think of reasoned choice in contradistinction to emotion, because any reasoning, planning, and choosing is constituted by the concerns that establish a rational system of emotions. This, then, brings us to the second question: is there a sense in which planned joint intentional action is emotionally integrated in the same way as individual reasoned choice? Is there something like shared or collective evaluative perspective that plays a similar role for joint action as individual care plays in individual action?

Again, there is ample reason to think that the answer is likely to be in the negative. While it seems plausible that for any individual action, there has to be a meaningful way in which the agent's engagement relates to what *matters* to him or her, joint actions do not seem to be in need of any such collective care or concern. The participants may engage in joint action for reasons they do not share at all. If we are walking to the conference venue with each other, I might do so because there's something I'd like to ask you on the way, while you might do so because you don't know the way to the conference venue, and think that's where I'm headed. In such cases, there seems to be nothing like a single evaluative perspective in which we both participate, and in the light of which we share fears, hopes, and joys. A mere overlap of individual concerns does seem enough to get us going together. Whatever the feature may be in virtue of which our walking can be characterized as jointly intended, it seems obvious that it must allow for widely different individual evaluative perspectives (see Bratman 1999).

There are two responses to this challenge. The first is to point out that joint action that merely involves overlapping individual concerns, though perhaps possible, will not be modally robust in the way expected from "genuine" team action; in our case, we might split up if either I had my word with you, or if you learn the way to the conference venue.

The other reaction is more radical: it is to say that if in the given case, the *only* cares there are at play in the activity at hand is *my* caring for having my word with you, and your caring about finding your way, we're not really in this *together,* and whatever goes on between us cannot be a joint action after all (Helm 2008). For our intentional activity to be *joint* there has to be *some* way in which we actually *care* for it to succeed *as such.* To be engaged in a joint intentional activity is to care about the activity as joint in a way that involves some hope for success, fear of failure when it is in danger, and anger when the venture is wrongfully thwarted, and some such. In cases such as a joint walk, these emotions may be rather weak—we don't need to *care very much,* as it were, but not caring very much differs from not caring at all.

One way of analyzing joint action would be to say that for both of us to act together, each of us has to care about our joint venture, which implies a distribution of cares with a collective content. This is not a mere "overlap" of individual evaluative perspectives, as it implies a joint focus—but while it may be called a sort of unified perspective, it is not a single perspective either, but two perspectives that converge on one and the same target. This has consequences for how such evaluation carries over into action. The way in which our individual concerns commit us to act is *immediate* and *non-inferential* (recall Mr. Spock's concerns). If the concern involved in joint action is individual (*my* concern for our acting together and *your* concern, severally), the only action to which such concern commits in that way is individual: *my* concern commits *me* to do whatever is necessary to make it the case that we φ, and *your* concern commits *you* to do whatever is necessary to make it the case that we φ. While this seems to fit nicely to the analysis of shared cooperative activity Michael Bratman has proposed (Bratman 1999), it suggests a picture of joint action in which the participants are emotionally engaged in individually making it the case that they, together, act, rather than being emotionally engaged in acting intentionally together. This picture sets our concerns one step apart from our joint engagement, suggesting that whatever sense there is to "our" evaluative perspective can't stand to our act in the way my evaluative perspective stands to my act. The way in which our knowledge of what matters in a situation bears on our joint action, according to this picture, is not of the immediate sort, in which it is the form of knowledge itself, its being *self*-knowledge, that brings it to bear on action. Rather, on this view, joint activity is a matter of the *content* of what individuals non-inferentially know to matter. The absurdity of Bratman's picture of joint agency comes to the fore by comparison to the case of a highly weak-willed individual who knows that his present cares cannot, by themselves, commit his future self in any way, and therefore has to resort to self-commitment devices in trying to make it the case that he will φ. The way such trying to make himself φ is not, by itself, his intention to φ, let alone his intentional φ-ing, is the way in which my and your being committed to making it the case that we, together, φ is not our intention to φ, let alone our intentional φ-ing together. The care in the light of which each of us is individually engaged in making it the case that we φ, however much it might facilitate our φ-ing, is not, in itself, the getting together of our act. What gets us going is not that you care about our going and my caring about our going, but a unified evaluative perspective in the light of which it matters *to us—collectively—*that *we* go.

3. CARING TOGETHER

An account of such a plural first-personal perspective can build upon an intuition which Margaret Gilbert defended most fervently in the early decades on the debate on collective intentionality: the view that joint action involves a single agent perspective that is then, qua *joint* commitment, a *plural subject's*. Gilbert cashes this out in normativist terms, and while she was among the first to extend the analysis of collective intentional states to certain attitudes of the affective or emotional type (Gilbert 1997, 2002), she tended to treat these simply as special cases of joint commitments which do not involve feelings of any sort (Konzelmann Ziv 2007), rather than reconceiving of the system of commitments, entitlements, and obligations which she placed at the heart of plural subjecthood in terms of emotional dispositions. Allowing for the idea of a phenomenal plural subject that is constituted by plural pre-reflective self-awareness (Schmid, forthcoming) makes room for the possibility that *we,* together, may know what matters in a situation in a way that commits us to joint action in the same way in which what *I* know matters commits me to individual action. In this perspective, emotions that are shared in the collective sense are *our* (collective) knowledge of what matters in a situation that focuses our joint attention on what's significant in the light of our collective aims and shared values, and they dispose us to act *together* on our joint evaluations (Sánchez Guerrero 2014). Such knowledge of what matters is plural pre-reflective self-knowledge, that is, knowledge of the self-identifying and self-committing kind (Schmid 2015), and plural subjects are self-constituted in plural self-identification and self-commitment rather than being constructed by entering a joint commitment in the Gilbertian sense.

As plural subjects come into being and go out of existence with the teaming up and disbanding among people, the unified evaluative perspective that is a plural subject's may not appear to be particularly relevant to the role of emotion in living of one's life as the person one is. The "Western" way of life strongly favors a conception of the widest form of getting our act together that is strongly focused at the individual level. Yet getting their act together in a long-term perspective is not just something individuals do—some groups do that, too. It has sometimes been argued that collective emotions play a central role in the development and maintenance of social groups (Salmela 2014). From the perspective suggested here, it does not seem implausible to say that collective emotions qua cares of which the members are plurally self-aware as theirs, collectively, constitute us as groups in similar ways in which our individual identities as persons are determined by our individual concerns. While many of those plural evaluative perspectives are short-lived, some endure, and they are not limited by the birth and death of their members; our concern with those cares may be our only way of getting our act together that exceeds our short individual life-spans.

ACKNOWLEDGEMENTS

I'm greatly indebted to Bennett Helm, Mikko Salmela, Gerhard Thonhauser, and Kirk Ludwig for many helpful comments on earlier drafts of this paper.

REFERENCES

Brady, M.S. (2009) "The Irrationality of Recalcitrant Emotions," *Philosophical Studies* 145: 413–30.

Bratman, M.E. (1999) *Faces of Intention. Selected Essays on Intention and Agency*, Cambridge MA: Harvard University Press.

Connor, S. (2013) "Collective Emotions. Reasons to be Doubtful," The History of Emotions annual lecture given at Queen Mary, University of London, October 9, 2013. <http://stevenconnor.com/collective.html>

de Sousa, R. (2013) "Emotion," in E.N. Zalta (ed.) *The Stanford Encyclopedia of Philosophy* (Spring 2014 edition), http://plato.stanford.edu/archives/spr2014/entries/emotion/.

Dennett, D.C. (1984) "Cognitive Wheels: The Frame Problem in AI," in C. Hookway (ed.), *Minds, Machines, and Evolution: Philosophical Studies*, Cambridge: Cambridge University Press.

Frankfurt, H. (1988) *The Importance of What We Care About*, Cambridge: Cambridge University Press.

Gilbert, M. (1997) "Group Wrongs and Guilt Feelings," *The Journal of Ethics* 1: 65–84.

——— (2002) "Collective Guilt and Collective Guilt Feelings," *The Journal of Ethics* 6: 115–43.

Goldie, P. (2000) *The Emotions: A Philosophical Exploration*, Oxford: Clarendon Press.

Helm, B. (2001) *Emotional Reason. Deliberation, Motivation, and the Nature of Value*, Cambridge: Cambridge University Press.

——— (2008) "Plural Agents," *Noûs* 42: 17–49.

Huebner, B. (2011) "Genuinely Collective Emotions," *European Journal for Philosophy of Science* 1: 89–118.

Kahneman, D. (2011) *Thinking, Fast and Slow*, New York: Farrar, Strauss and Giroux.

Kelly, J.R., Iannone, N.E. and McCarty, M.K. (2014) "The Function of Shared Affect in Groups," in C. von Scheve and M. Salmela (eds) *Collective Emotions: Perspectives from Psychology, Philosophy, and Sociology*, Oxford: Oxford University Press.

Konzelmann Ziv, A. (2007) "Collective Guilt Feeling Revisited," *Dialectica*, 61 (3): 467–93.

Krueger, J. (forthcoming) "The Affective 'We': Self-Regulation and Shared Emotions," in T. Szanto and D. Moran (eds) *The Phenomenology of Sociality: Discovering the 'We'*. New York: Routledge.

Michael, J. (2011) "Shared Emotions and Joint Action," *Review of Philosophy and Psychology* 2: 355–73.

Nussbaum, M. (2003) *Upheavals of Thought. The Intelligence of Emotions*, Cambridge: Cambridge University Press.

Salmela, M. (2012) "Shared Emotions," *Philosophical Explorations* 15: 1–14.

——— (2014) "The Functions of Collective Emotions in Social Groups," in A. Konzelmann and H.B. Schmid (eds) *Institutions, Emotions, and Group Agents*, Dordrecht: Springer.

——— (2015) "Collective Emotions as 'the Glue' of Group Solidarity," in A. Laitinen and A.B. Pessi (eds) *Solidarity: Theory and Practice*, New York: Lexington Books.

Salmela, M. and Nagatsu, M. (forthcoming) "Collective Emotions and Joint Actions: Beyond Received Minimalist Approaches."

Sánchez Guerrero, H.A. (2014) "Feelings of Being-Together and Caring-With," in A. Konzelmann and H.B. Schmid (eds) *Institutions, Emotions, and Group Agents*, Dordrecht: Springer.

Scheler, M. ([1912–16] 1973) *Formalism in Ethics and Non-Formal Ethics of Values: A New Attempt toward the Foundation of an Ethical Personalism*, Evanston, IL: Northwestern University Press.

Schmid, H.B. (2009) "Shared Feelings. Towards a Phenomenology of Collective Affective Intentionality," in *Plural Action. Essays in Philosophy and Social Science*. Dordrecht: Springer.

——— (2014) "The Feeling of Being a Group: Corporate Emotions and Collective Consciousness," in: C. von Scheve and M. Salmela (eds) *Collective Emotions: Perspectives from Psychology, Philosophy, and Sociology*, Oxford: Oxford University Press.

——— (2015) "On Knowing What We're Doing Together: Groundless Group Self-Knowledge and Plural Self-Blindness," in M. Brady and M. Fricker (eds) *The Epistemic Life of Groups. Essays in the Epistemology of Collectives*, Oxford: Oxford University Press.

——— (forthcoming, 2017) "The Subject of 'We Intend'," *Phenomenology and Cognitive Science* 15.

Schweikard, D.P. and Schmid, H.B. (2013) "Collective Intentionality," in E.N. Zalta (ed.) *The Stanford Encyclopedia of Philosophy* (Summer 2013 edition), http://plato.stanford.edu/archives/sum2013/entries/collective-intentionality/.

Stein, E. (1922) "Beiträge zur Philosophischen Begründung der Psychologie und der Geisteswissenschaften. Zweite Abhandlung: Individuum und Gemeinschaft," in E. Husserl (ed.) *Jahrbuch für Philosophie und Phänomenologische Forschung*, 5: 116–284, Halle: Max Niemeyer.

Zahavi, D. (2015) "You, Me, and We: The Sharing of Emotional Experience," *Journal of Consciousness Studies* 22: 84–101.

13

Collective Phenomenology

Elisabeth Pacherie

1. INTRODUCTION

Phenomenology, understood as a field of enquiry rather than as a movement in the history of philosophy, is concerned with the study of subjective experience and investigates the structure and nature of various types of conscious experiences. But what is collective phenomenology about?

One might take collective phenomenology to be concerned with the study of group consciousness, of the subjective states of collectives qua collectives. This immediately raises the question whether such an object of study exists. Can a collective as such be a locus of subjective experience? Is there something it is like to be a group or a collective? Can collectives (e.g. the United States, Microsoft Corporation, Amnesty International) literally be said to experience perceptual states, emotions, a sense of agency, pleasure or pain or any other phenomenal states we readily ascribe to individuals?

One might be skeptical that collectives as such can have phenomenal states, but still be willing to countenance the existence of collective phenomenal states—e.g. collective joy, collective grief or a collective sense of agency for some achievement—conceived as experiential states had by individuals in a group and shared by them in some suitable way. On this understanding of "collective phenomenology," the main conceptual challenge is to elucidate in what sense experiences must be shared in order for them to constitute together a collective experience, and the main scientific challenge is to identify the mechanisms and processes that make this sharing possible.

A third issue we must confront concerns the subjective specificity of shared or collective experiences. How do they differ from individual subjective experiences? What specific subjective qualities, if any, characterize collective experiences? Are the elements of collectivity of these experiences reflected in their mode or their contents?

2. IS THERE SOMETHING IT IS LIKE TO BE A GROUP?

Business corporations, non-governmental organizations, political parties, supporter clubs, universities, and consumer associations are collective entities. Many have argued that intentional states can rightfully be ascribed to these collectives in their own right (Gilbert 1992; Rovane 2004; Pettit 2003; List and Pettit 2011; Tollefsen 2015; Tuomela 2013; see also Chapter 7, this volume). In particular, in taking groups or collectives to be genuine decision-makers or believers, one allows for the possibility that a group or collective sometimes make decisions or hold beliefs that the majority of members would not accept individually. But what about ascribing experiences to collectives or groups? Do groups have phenomenal consciousness? Can experiential states be had by a group in its own right, independently of the experiential states of the individuals that compose it?

Knobe and Prinz (2008) investigated people's intuitions about the ascriptions of intentional states (e.g. beliefs, intentions, and desires) and of phenomenal states (e.g. emotional experiences, feelings of depression, feelings of pain) to collectives. They presented the participants to their study with sentences that ascribed either intentional or phenomenal states to a fictional corporation, Acme Corp., and asked them to rate the acceptability of such sentences. Their participants found sentences ascribing intentional states to collectives perfectly acceptable, but sentences ascribing phenomenal states unacceptable. These results suggest that commonsense psychology draws a sharp distinction between phenomenal and non-phenomenal states. While our folk-psychological intuitions regarding the ascription of non-phenomenal states accord with a functionalist view of mental states, our intuitions regarding the ascription of phenomenal states appear to be sensitive to the physical make-up of an entity.

Several researchers, however, have offered reasons to think that the folk-psychological distinction between the ascription of phenomenal and non-phenomenal states may not be as sharp as this study suggests. First, as noted by Schmid (2014b), "Acme Corp." is the fictional corporation par excellence in American pop-culture and, moreover, corporate expressions of emotions are often prime examples of bullshit in Frankfurt's sense. They are used as tools for improving the corporation's public image and only the most naïve and credulous people would even think of taking them literally. The choice of "Acme Corp." as the ascribee in the sentences of the study may thus have contributed to the reluctance of the participants towards ascriptions of phenomenal states to collectives. Second, our willingness or unwillingness to ascribe psychological states to collectives may also be influenced by cultural factors, such as a more individualist outlook in Western cultures relative to the more collectivist perspective in East Asian cultures. Huebner et al. (2010) investigated this possibility with both American and East Asian participants, following the methodology used by Knobe and Prinz, but surveying a broader range of non-fictional collectives (e.g. the Ming Dynasty, Denmark, Sony Corporation). They found that while both groups of participants were more willing to ascribe phenomenal mental states to individuals than to collectives, the East Asian participants were far less reticent than their American counterparts to ascribe phenomenal states to groups.

One may question, however, whether we should abide by our folk-psychological intuitions in these matters and whether, moreover, these intuitions should be understood as metaphysical intuitions or merely as intuitions regarding the appropriateness of certain forms of figurative language. If these folk-psychological intuitions are simply linguistic intuitions, cultural differences should be expected. Talk of an ear of corn or the eye of a needle seems perfectly fine for English speakers, but their literal translations would sound weird to French speakers. Yet, this doesn't mean that English and French speakers have different biological intuitions: no one, whether English- or French-speaking, thinks that corn have ears or needles eyes in the same way we do. Another approach to the issue whether there is such a thing as group consciousness might be to use our best scientific theory of phenomenal consciousness as a guide. The idea is that we should consider what the theory says is needed for an agent to have phenomenal states and then investigate whether collective agents meet these requirements. While the general method makes sense, two difficulties immediately arise. First, there is as yet no generally agreed upon theory of phenomenal consciousness. Rather, it is a matter of intense debate in both philosophy and the cognitive sciences what it takes for an agent to enjoy phenomenal consciousness. Second, as pointed out by Schwitzgebel (2015), many existing theories either implicitly or explicitly limit themselves to human or at most vertebrate consciousness, and it is not obvious how properly to extend them to cases outside their original scope. Keeping in mind these difficulties and leaving aside classical dualist theories to concentrate on materialist views of consciousness, let us briefly consider here three influential options and tentatively assess the prospects of group consciousness from their respective perspectives.

According to materialism, our brains are what make us conscious. But what features of brains or of brain organization are responsible for phenomenal consciousness? On one family of views (e.g. Crick and Koch 1990; Melloni et al. 2007), phenomenal consciousness is tied to neural synchrony, and in particular to specific kinds of synchronous activation of neural populations at very fine temporal scales. Andy Clark (2009) has recently argued that if consciousness depends on such high-bandwidth synchrony, then consciousness may indeed require brains as the only physical structures with an architecture where this can be achieved. This conclusion may, however, be resisted. First, even from a biological standpoint, neural synchrony doesn't appear to be a sufficient condition for consciousness, since, for instance, seizure-induced loss of consciousness is associated with highly synchronous brain activity (Arthuis et al. 2009). Second, even if neural synchrony is what implements consciousness in the human brain, we lack, as Schwitzgebel (2015) and List (2016) point out, a principled motivation for excluding the possibility that consciousness may be implemented by a different architecture in other kinds of beings or entities.

Another family of views abstracts away from issues of neural implementation, focusing instead on information processing and attempting to characterize the forms of information processing that underlie consciousness and the kind of cognitive (rather than neural) architecture that could support these forms of processing. One very influential proposal is that consciousness requires integrated information processing and that this is made possible by cognitive architectures that involve a "global workspace" where information processed by various cognitive subsystems comes together, is made globally accessible, integrated and redistributed across subsystems (e.g. Baars 1988; Dehaene and Naccache 2001; Dennett 2005). The global workspace hypothesis can explain many important features of (human) consciousness, such as its role in handling novel situations, its limited capacity, its sequential nature, certain constraints on the nature of conscious contents, the flexible ways in which these contents can be manipulated and the subjective unity of consciousness.

As noted by Schwitzgebel, on this account of consciousness, group consciousness would appear to be largely unproblematic. All it would take for a group to be conscious is the existence of some "global workspace" that receives the information processed by cognitive subsystems (the individual members or sub-groups of the group), integrates it and redistributes it. For instance, one may think of the steering board of a business corporation, or of the bulletin board of your local sports club as playing the role of "global workspaces." While global workspace theory may be taken to offer a convincing account of access consciousness, it is much less clear, however, that it offers an account of phenomenal consciousness. As Chalmers (1995: 205) points out, 'nothing internal to the theory explains why the information within the global workspace is experienced. The best the theory can do is to say that the information is experienced because it is globally accessible'. Thus, their meeting the conditions laid out by the global workspace theories may provide sufficient justification for the attribution of access consciousness to groups or collectives. But unless one takes the conditions for access consciousness to be also sufficient conditions for phenomenal consciousness, the global workspace theory sheds no light on whether or not there is something it is like to be a group.

Let us conclude this brief survey with Integrated Information Theory (IIT), a much discussed "mathematical" theory of consciousness developed over the last decade by Giulio Tononi (2008, 2012). According to IIT, information integration of the relevant sort is both necessary and sufficient for consciousness regardless of the substrate (biological or not) in which is realized. The theory understands consciousness as a purely information-theoretic property of systems and proposes a mathematical measure φ that aims to measure a system's degree of informational integration. ITT conceives of consciousness as a graded property: a system with a higher φ value will be more conscious than a system with a lower φ value. In addition, it postulates that when a system is itself a complex integrating other systems, only the system in the complex with the highest φ value will be conscious (exclusion postulate). In other words, while a conscious system may have unconscious parts, or an unconscious system have conscious parts, a conscious system cannot have conscious parts.

It would seem to follow from ITT and its exclusion postulate that group consciousness does not exist, since the degree of informational integration (the value of φ) at the group level is quite low compared to the degree of information integration of some or most of its component parts (e.g. people and their brains). Schwitzgebel (2015) argues, however, that the exclusion principle on which this conclusion rests has no solid motivation and should be rejected. Indeed, Tononi defends the exclusion postulate on the grounds that it is intuitively absurd to suppose that group consciousness could emerge from two people talking. However, in the context of a discussion of group consciousness this defense of the postulate appears very much question-begging.

Yet, even if we set aside the exclusion postulate, it remains true, as List (2016) points out, that the degree of informational integration at the group level is quite low and indeed much lower than the degree of information integration found in the brain of a small mammal like a mouse. This, List points out, 'should suffice to cast doubt on the existence of any significant amount of group consciousness' (2016: 20).

So, is there something it is like to be a group? The jury is still out and a final decision might have to be postponed until we have achieved the Grail of a general theory of phenomenal consciousness. At present, however, the prospects of group phenomenal consciousness look rather dim. Even its more optimistic proponents would seem to agree that group consciousness, if it exists at all, is itself a rather dim affair and that there isn't much it is like to be a group.

3. COLLECTIVE EXPERIENCES AS SHARED EXPERIENCES

Many may be skeptical as to the existence of group consciousness, but few would doubt the existence of collective experiences understood as experiences had and shared by individuals as members of some group. Indeed, some of our most vivid experiences appear to be of that kind: the sense of awe experienced by humankind at large when Neil Armstrong stepped on the Moon on July 20, 1969, the joy experienced by the supporters of Manchester United when their team won the FIFA Club World Championship in 2008, or the mixture of grief, sadness, disgust and anger experienced by the French after the Charlie Hebdo shooting and the Jewish supermarket attack in Paris in January 2015 certainly count as very powerful collective experiences. However, the exact nature of such collective experiences remains difficult to pin down. In what sense must experiences be shared to qualify as collective experiences? What exactly are the elements of collectivity in such experiences?

On a minimalist sense of sharing, two individuals may be said to share a state if each happens to be in that state. Sharing in this sense is nothing more than aggregation. This notion of sharing appears too weak, however, to warrant talk of collective states, whether intentional or phenomenal. The vast majority of the French probably feel hungry around dinner time, but this doesn't seem sufficient ground for attributing to the French a collective feeling of hunger at dinner time. A slightly more demanding notion of sharing would require in addition that the states experienced by the individuals have a common target. The hungry French do not satisfy these further requirements, the feeling of hunger each experiences has a different target, the experiencer's own desire for food.

But even adding this requirement doesn't seem enough. Suppose after dinner, the French happen to all watch the film *The Texas Chainsaw Massacre* shown on French TV that night. At some point they may all feel scared and their fears have the same target, e.g. that Sally be caught by Leatherface. Yet, we would still be reticent to talk of a collective experience of fear.

Many would agree that collective experiences require some stronger form of alignment of individual experiences. With the exception of some recent work on experiences of collective agency, research on collective experiences has mainly focused on collective emotions, with a long tradition of investigation going back at least to the work of Gustave Le Bon (1895) on the psychology of crowds (see von Scheve and Salmela (2014) for a recent collection of papers exploring collective emotions from philosophical, psychological and sociological perspectives; see also Schmid, Chapter 12, this volume). This literature has explored various factors contributing to the alignment of individual experiences. These factors can be divided into two broad categories: bottom-up and top-down factors.

Important bottom-up alignment factors include interpersonal entrainment mechanisms, perception-action matching, mimicry, emotional contagion, and joint attention. Interpersonal entrainment is a process whereby two people interacting together automatically synchronize their movements and behavior, even in the absence of direct mechanical coupling (see also Butterfill, Chapter 6, this volume). Thus, two people sitting next to each other in rocking chairs will unconsciously synchronize their rocking frequency (Richardson et al. 2007), two people walking side by side will tend to fall in synchrony (van Ulzen et al. 2008) and, so will two individuals asked to tap at a comfortable tempo (Oullier et al. 2008). Another related process that can induce interpersonal alignment is perception-action matching. A number of recent theories—the common coding theory (Prinz 1997), the motor simulation theory (Jeannerod 1997, 2006), and the motor resonance theory (Rizzolatti and Sinigaglia 2008)—postulate an interface between perception and action such that the perception of an action leads to the activation of a corresponding action representation in the observer's action system. These alignment processes would not simply induce people who happen to be engaged in similar behaviors to synchronize them, they would also lead them to mimic the postures, mannerisms, voices, facial expressions, movements and actions of their interaction partners (for reviews, see van Baaren et al. 2009; Chartrand and van Baaren 2009).

Motor synchrony and mimicry have been shown to exert a number of effects on social interaction. Thus, they tend to increase rapport and promote positive relationships (Chartrand and Bargh, 1999; Miles et al. 2009), to increase affiliation (Lakin and Chartrand 2003; Hove and Risen 2009), and to lead to more pro-social behavior and cooperation (van Baaren et al. 2004; Wiltermuth and Heath 2009). In addition to these general effects, motor synchrony and mimicry appear to support the sharing of specific states, such as emotions or intentions. For instance it has been argued that automatic facial, vocal and postural mimicry allow people to catch one another's emotions and are important mechanisms in emotional contagion, which contributes in turn to the elicitation of collective emotions (Hatfield et al. 2014) and to what Durkheim (1912) called collective effervescence. Similarly, in the joint action domain, perception-action matching processes may help participants understand the actions of their partners and predict their outcomes, thereby facilitating mutual responsiveness in action. For instance, it has been shown that people tend to predict the sensory consequences not only of their own but also of other participants' actions (Wilson and Knoblich 2005) and that they tend to "co-represent" tasks that other people are performing next to them, even when it interferes with the performance of their own task (e.g. Atmaca et al. 2008).

Finally, joint attention provides a basic mechanism for sharing representations of objects and events and thus for creating a perceptual common ground (Tomasello and Carpenter 2007; Campbell, Chapter 9, this volume). Joint attention may thus play an important role in ensuring that agents acting together track the same objects and events in the environment, adjust what they do in response to relevant changes in the situation, including changes brought by their own actions, and be mutually aware that they do. Similarly, in tandem with emotional expressions, joint attention may allow information about the relevance of an event to be shared and contribute to aligning the appraisals of several agents, thus underlying the elicitation of collective emotions directed at the same target (Brosch 2014).

In addition to these bottom-up processes, top-down processes also contribute to the alignment of individual experiences. Social identification and adherence to the goals, values, norms, standards, beliefs, and practices of the group one identifies with—what Tuomela (2007; Chapter 2, this volume) calls the group ethos—may lead members to share emotions and other experiential states. Social psychologists characterize group-based emotions as emotional reactions that arise when people appraise events with respect to group concerns rather than their personal concerns (Kessler and Hollbach 2005; Smith et al. 2007). In particular, they have highlighted the important role of group-based emotions in intragroup and intergroup attitudes and behavior. But how exactly are social identification and group-based emotions arrived at? Margaret Gilbert proposes that collective emotions are arrived at in the same way as collective beliefs, intentions and attitudes are, namely through joint commitments (Gilbert 2002, 2014; Chapter 10, this volume). Just as a group has a collective intention in virtue of its members being jointly committed to intending as a body to perform a certain action, a group can have a collective emotion (e.g. collective guilt) in virtue of its members being jointly committed to being as a body in a certain emotional state. Two main worries can be raised against Gilbert's view. The first is an instance of the worry discussed in Section 2: emotions are phenomenal states and besides states in which bodily sensations play an important role and it is unclear that such phenomenal states can exist at the group level. The second worry is linked to the fact that commitments are, in Gilbert's phrase "creatures of the will." Emotions, however, do not seem to be states we can commit to having, since we cannot make ourselves feel an emotion at will (Salmela 2012). To defuse these worries, Gilbert is forced to adopt a strongly cognitive view of emotions, according to which emotions are essentially a matter of evaluative judgments and feelings play only a contingent role. Many, however, would see such a strong cognitivist view of emotions as implausible (e.g. Konzelmann Ziv 2007; Wilkins 2002).

Helm (2010) and Salmela (2012) defend another option and propose that we indirectly commit ourselves to emotions (and other phenomenal states) by collectively committing ourselves to the goals, values, norms and concerns that define our group's ethos, where the phenomenal states arrived at in this way are states of individuals rather than states of a group-entity. In addition, Salmela offers a typology of shared emotions inspired by Tuomela's analysis of shared attitudes of different degrees of collectivity. He distinguishes between weakly, moderately, and strongly shared emotions, according to whether these emotions have their sources in overlapping private concerns and attitudes of individuals (e.g. panic in the stock market), in shared, socially grounded private concerns and attitudes—i.e. concerns individuals commit to because they believe that other members of their group have them—or, finally, in concerns and attitudes group members are collectively committed to. Salmela also proposes that for emotions to be shared, it is furthermore required that their emotional responses be synchronized—via the bottom-up mechanisms described earlier—and that the group members must be mutually aware that others are feeling the same.

Thus, the emotions experienced by the French after the terrorist attacks in Paris in January 2015 would qualify as strongly shared emotions because these attacks were perceived by the French as attacks on fundamental values of the French society they were collectively committed to but also because the French responded with massive rallies where a whole range of lower-level synchronization processes were at work, inducing highly synchronized emotional reactions.

As Salmela's account of shared emotions suggests, both bottom-up and top-down processes are typically at work in sharing experiences. Importantly, they do not simply function in parallel. Rather, there are bi-directional connections between them. On the one hand, as we have seen already, low-level synchronization processes can increase group affiliation and promote pro-social behavior. On the other hand, social affiliation also appears to modulate bottom-up processes. For instance, there is evidence that actions are co-represented less when one's co-actor is an out-group member than when he or she is an in-group member (Müller et al. 2011) and that group membership modulates non-conscious behavioral mimicry (Yabar et al. 2006).

4. MODE AND CONTENT OF COLLECTIVE EXPERIENCES

The discussion in the previous section suggests that for experiences to count as shared or collective, it is not enough that individuals have experiences with the same or similar targets or causes. The individuals' experiences should also be interrelated in some tighter way via bottom-up causal processes of alignment and synchronization, via processes of social identification and commitments to certain attitudes, norms and concerns, or via both types of processes. In addition, there should be mutual awareness among the individuals concerned that they are feeling the same. Are these conditions on sharing somehow reflected in the mode or the content of shared experiences? Is the subjective feel of an experience of joy, for instance, different depending on whether the joy is individual or shared with others?

On a minimalist option, the content and mode of a singular and a collective experience would remain essentially the same. The only important way in which collective experiences might differ from their individual counterparts is in terms of their intensity or strength. Factors such as mimicry, contagion, joint attention and behavioral entrainment would contribute to the mutual reinforcement of the feelings experienced, as is typically the case in collective rituals, whether religious or not, where all these factors are typically present (Knottnerus 2014).

Many, however, would contend that there are more substantial qualitative differences between singular and collective experiences and argue that the shared character of the experience, its we-ness, is part of the subjective quality of collective experiences. This idea can be pursued in several ways.

Schmid (2014a; Chapter 12, this volume) defends the view that the "sense of us" present in collective experiences is best analyzed as involving a transformation in the mode of self-awareness constitutive of the experience. His view has close ties with self-presentational theories of consciousness, according to which pre-theoretical self-awareness is an intrinsic feature of conscious experiences: consciousness of something is always also necessarily consciousness for oneself. However, he proposes that the self-awareness feature of conscious experiences is not always singular and that there can be plural self-awareness as well. In other words, whereas singular self-awareness would be awareness of my experiences as my own, as experiences that are my own take or perspective on something, plural self-awareness of conscious experiences would be awareness of these experiences as ours, as our shared take or perspective on something. What Schmid proposes here is to distinguish between the ontological subject of an experience and its phenomenological subject (the subject as given in the mode of the experience). He does not deny that the ontological subject of an experience is the individual in whose brain the experience is realized, but he claims that ontological and phenomenological subject need not always coincide and that the phenomenological subject can be a "we," a plural subject rather than an "I." One might object to this view on several grounds. First, the view is premised on a conception of consciousness according to which self-awareness is constitutive of all conscious experiences and one might disagree with this conception of consciousness. Second, even if one accepts that consciousness implies self-awareness, one might disagree with the idea that the ontological and the phenomenological subject of experiences can really come apart, and argue that phenomenological we-ness is an illusion and that veridical self-awareness is always in the singular (Salmela 2012).

For those disinclined to accept the idea of a plural phenomenological subject or a plural mode of experience, but who still think that there are intrinsic differences between individual and collective experience, the avenue that remains open is to construe these differences as differences of contents. Several options are available. First, one might take as one's starting point a self-representational rather than, as Schmid does, a self-presentational theory of consciousness. Both theories claim that consciousness implies self-awareness, the key difference being that self-presentational theories capture self-awareness in terms of mode of awareness, whereas on self-representational theories, the self element is part of the content of the experience (e.g. Kriegel 2009). One could then make a move similar to Schmid's and argue that whereas in an individual experience, my experience represents something as so-and-so *for me*, in a collective experience my experience represents something as so-and-so *for us*. Again, one may not care for this approach either because one is skeptical about self-representational theories of consciousness or because one thinks that the self that is represented as having the experience cannot possibly be divorced from the ontological subject of the experience.

A second possibility would be to argue that when an experience is collective, the awareness we have that this feeling is shared has itself a phenomenal dimension and involves a feeling of its own—something akin to a sense of belonging or a feeling of social affiliation. On this proposal, collective experiences might be described as composite experiences, combining, or perhaps coalescing, a primary phenomenal experience (the experience that is shared) and a phenomenal experience of sharing.

Finally, a third possibility is that when an experience is shared, its primary contents might be modified or restructured in certain ways. There is, for instance, empirical evidence that attending to objects together from opposite perspectives makes people adopt an allocentric rather than the default egocentric frame of reference (Böckler et al. 2011), that the presence of another person makes an agent perceptually sensitive to affordances for joint action (Davis et al. 2010), and that social identifications affect bodily self-representations (Farmer and Tsakiris 2012). More generally, it has been proposed that, in social contexts, mechanisms for sensorimotor transformations and multisensory integration incorporate information relative to the other people's perceptual perspectives and motor capabilities to construct "shared action spaces," supporting key computations for social interactions and joint actions (Pezzulo et al. 2013).

5. PARTING REMARKS

With the exception perhaps of collective emotions, collective phenomenology remains to this day a largely uncharted territory. We still lack detailed conceptual analyses of what exactly collective experiences are, how they relate to individual experiences and what phenomenal properties they have. Likewise, empirical investigations of their psychological and neural underpinnings remain rare. While some of the central issues that need addressing have been briefly surveyed here, other issues are equally pressing. For instance, does the range of phenomenal properties that can be collectively experienced coincide with the range of properties that can be individually experienced? Existing work has concentrated on collective affective experiences and to some extent on collective agentive experiences, but what about collective perceptual or collective cognitive phenomenology? Similarly, we know little about the exact functions of collective phenomenal consciousness and their relations to the functions served by individual phenomenal consciousness. There are reasons to suspect, however, that this has broad societal relevance, and intrepid explorers are needed to further map this territory.

RELATED TOPICS

Shared Values, Interests, and Desires (Ch. 8), Joint Attention (Ch. 9), Joint Commitment (Ch. 10), Collective Emotions (Ch. 12).

REFERENCES

Arthuis, M., Valton, L., Régis, J., Chauvel, P., Wendling, F., Naccache, L., Bernard, C., & Bartolomei, F. (2009) "Impaired Consciousness During Temporal Lobe Seizures Is Related to Increased Long-Distance Cortical–Subcortical Synchronization," *Brain* 132 (8): 2091–101.

Atmaca, S., Sebanz, N., Prinz, W., & Knoblich, G. (2008) "Action Co-Representation: the Joint SNARC Effect," *Social Neuroscience* 3 (3–4): 410–20.

Baars, B.J. (1988) *A Cognitive Theory of Consciousness*, Cambridge: Cambridge University Press.

Böckler, A., Knoblich, G., & Sebanz, S. (2011) "Giving a Helping Hand: Effects of Joint Attention on Mental Rotation of Body Parts," *Experimental Brain Research* 211: 531–45.

Brosch, T. (2014) "Neurocognitive Mechanisms of Attentional Prioritization in Social Interaction," in C. van Scheve & M. Salmela (eds) *Collective Emotions*, Oxford: Oxford University Press.

Chalmers, D. (1995) "Facing up to the Problem of Consciousness," *Journal of Consciousness Studies* 2 (3): 200–19.

Chartrand, T.L., & Bargh, J.A. (1999) "The Chameleon Effect: The Perception-Behavior Link and Social Interaction," *Journal of Personality and Social Psychology* 76 (6): 893–910.

Chartrand, T.L., & van Baaren, R.B. (2009) "Human Mimicry," *Advances in Experimental Social Psychology*, 41: 219–74.

Clark, A. (2009) "Spreading the Joy? Why the Machinery of Consciousness Is (Probably) Still in the Head," *Mind* 118 (472): 963–93.

Crick, F., & Koch, C. (1990) "Towards a Neurobiological Theory of Consciousness," *Seminars in the Neurosciences* 2: 263–75, Saunders Scientific Publications.

Davis, T.J., Riley, M.A., Shockley, K., & Cummins-Sebree, S. (2010) "Perceiving Affordances for Joint Actions," *Perception* 39 (12): 1624–44.

Dehaene, S., & Naccache, L. (2001) "Towards a Cognitive Neuroscience of Consciousness: Basic Evidence and Workspace Framework," *Cognition* 79: 1–37.

Dennett, D.C. (2005) *Sweet Dreams*, Cambridge, MA: MIT.

Durkheim, E. (1912) *Les Formes Élémentaires de la Vie Religieuse*, Paris: Alcan.

Farmer, H., & Tsakiris, M. (2012) "The Bodily Social Self: A Link Between Phenomenal and Narrative Selfhood," *Review of Philosophy and Psychology* 3: 125–44.

Gilbert, M. (1992) *On Social Facts*, Princeton: Princeton University Press.

—— (2002) "Collective Guilt and Collective Guilt Feelings," *Journal of Ethics* 6: 115–43.

——— (2014) "How We Feel: Understanding Everyday Collective Emotion Ascription," in C. van Scheve & M. Salmela (eds) *Collective Emotions*, Oxford: Oxford University Press.

Hatfield, E., Carpenter, M., & Rapson, R.L. (2014) "Emotional Contagion as a Precursor to Collective Emotions," in C. van Scheve, & M. Salmela (eds) *Collective Emotion*, Oxford: Oxford University Press.

Helm, B. (2010) *Love, Friendship, and the Self*, Oxford: Oxford University Press.

Hove, M.J., & Risen, J.L. (2009) "It's All in the Timing: Interpersonal Synchrony Increases Affiliation," *Cognition* 27 (6): 949–60.

Huebner, B., Bruno, M., & Sarkissian, H. (2010) "What Does the Nation of China Think About Phenomenal States?" *Review of Philosophy and Psychology* 1 (2): 225–43.

Jeannerod, M. (1997) *The Cognitive Neuroscience of Action*, Oxford: Blackwell.

——— (2006) *Motor Cognition*, Oxford: Oxford University Press.

Kessler, T., & Hollbach, S. (2005) "Group-Based Emotions as Determinants of Ingroup Identification," *Journal of Experimental Social Psychology* 41: 677–85.

Knobe, J., & Prinz, J. (2008) "Intuitions About Consciousness: Experimental Studies," *Phenomenology and The Cognitive Sciences* 7 (1): 67–83.

Knottnerus, J.D. (2014) "Religion, Ritual and Collective Emotion," in C. van Scheve & M. Salmela (eds) *Collective Emotions*, Oxford: Oxford University Press.

Konzelmann Ziv, A. (2007) "Collective Guilt Revisited," *Dialectica* 61: 467–93.

Kriegel, U. (2009) *Subjective Consciousness: A Self-Representational Theory*, Oxford: Oxford University Press.

Lakin, J.L., & Chartrand, T.L. (2003) "Using Nonconscious Behavioral Mimicry to Create Affiliation and Rapport," *Psychological Science* 14 (4): 334–9.

Le Bon, G. (1895) *The Crowd. A Study of the Popular Mind*, London: Benn.

List, C. (2016) "What Is It Like to Be a Group Agent?" *Noûs*, doi:10.1111/nous.12162.

List, C., & Pettit, P. (2011) *Group Agency: The Possibility, Design, and Status of Corporate Agents*, Oxford: Oxford University Press.

Melloni, L., Molina, C., Pena, M., Torres, D., Singer, W., & Rodriguez, E. (2007) "Synchronization of Neural Activity Across Cortical Areas Correlates with Conscious Perception," *The Journal of Neuroscience* 27 (11): 2858–65.

Miles, L.K., Nind, L.K., & Macrae, C.N. (2009) "The Rhythm of Rapport: Interpersonal Synchrony and Social Perception," *Journal of Experimental Social Psychology* 45 (3): 585–9.

Müller, B.C.N., Kühn, S., van Baaren, R.B., Dotsch, R., Brass, M., & Dijksterhuis, A. (2011) "Perspective Taking Eliminates Differences in Co-Representation of Out-Group Members' Actions," *Experimental Brain Research* 211: 423–8.

Oullier, O., de Guzman, G.C., Jantzen, K.J., Lagarde, J., & Kelso, J.A.S. (2008) "Social Coordination Dynamics: Measuring Human Bonding," *Social Neuroscience* 3 (2): 178–92.

Pettit, P. (2003) "Groups with Minds of Their Own," in F. Schmitt (ed.), *Socializing Metaphysics*, New York: Rowman & Littlefield.

Pezzulo, G., Iodice, P., Ferraina, S., & Kessler, K. (2013) "Shared Action Spaces: A Basis Function Framework for Social Re-Calibration of Sensorimotor Representations Supporting Joint Action," *Frontiers in Human Neuroscience* 7: 800.

Prinz, W. (1997) "Perception and Action Planning," *European Journal of Cognitive Psychology*, 9: 129–54.

Richardson, M.J., Marsh, K.L., Isenhower, R.W., Goodman, J.R.L., & Schmidt, R.C. (2007) "Rocking Together: Dynamics of Unintentional and Intentional Interpersonal Coordination," *Human Movement Science* 26: 867–91.

Rizzolatti, G., & Sinigaglia, C. (2008) *Mirrors in the Brain: How Our Minds Share Actions and Emotions*, Oxford: Oxford University Press.

Rovane, C. (2004) "What Is an Agent?" *Synthese* 140 (1): 181–98.

Salmela, M. (2012) "Plural Emotions," *Philosophical Explorations* 15 (1): 1–14.

Schmid, H.B. (2014a) "Plural Self-Awareness," *Phenomenology and the Cognitive Sciences* 13 (1): 7–24.

——— (2014b) "The Feeling of Being a Group: Corporate Emotions and Collective Consciousness," in C. van Scheve & M. Salmela (eds) *Collective Emotions*, Oxford: Oxford University Press.

Schwitzgebel, E. (2015) "If Materialism Is True, the United States Is Probably Conscious," *Philosophical Studies* 172: 1697–1721.

Smith, E.R., Seger, C.R., & Mackie, D.M. (2007) "Can Emotions Be Truly Group Level? Evidence Regarding Four Conceptual Criteria," *Journal of Personality and Social Psychology* 93: 431–46.

Tollefsen, D.P. (2015) *Groups as Agents*, Cambridge: Polity Press.

Tomasello, M., & Carpenter, M. (2007) "Shared Intentionality," *Developmental Science*, 10: 121–5.

Tononi, G. (2008) "Consciousness as Integrated Information: A Provisional Manifesto," *Biological Bulletin* 215: 216–42.

—— (2012) "Integrated Information Theory of Consciousness: An Updated Account," *Archives Italiennes de Biologie* 150 (2–3): 56–90.

Tuomela, R. (2007) *The Philosophy of Sociality*, Oxford: Oxford University Press.

—— (2013) *Social Ontology: Collective Intentionality and Group Agents*, Oxford: Oxford University Press.

van Baaren, R.B., Holland, R.W., Kawakami, K., & Knippenberg, A.V. (2004) "Mimicry and Prosocial Behavior," *Psychological Science* 15 (1): 71–4.

van Baaren, R.B., Janssen, L., Chartrand, T.L., and Dijksterhuis, A. (2009) "Where Is the Love? the Social Aspects of Mimicry," *Philosophical Transactions of the Royal Society of London. Series B, Biological Sciences* 364 (1528): 2381–9.

van Ulzen, N.R., Lamoth, C.J., Daffertshofer, A., Semin, G.R., & Beek, P.J. (2008) "Characteristics of Instructed and Uninstructed Interpersonal Coordination While Walking Side-by-Side," *Neuroscience Letters* 432 (2): 88–93.

von Scheve, C. & Salmela, M. (eds) (2014) *Collective Emotions*, Oxford: Oxford University Press.

Wilkins, B. (2002) "Joint Commitments," *Journal of Ethics* 6: 145–55.

Wilson, M., & Knoblich, G. (2005) "The Case for Motor Involvement in Perceiving Conspecifics," *Psychological Bulletin* 131: 460–73

Wiltermuth, S.S., & Heath, C. (2009) "Synchrony and Cooperation," *Psychological Science* 20: 1–5.

Yabar, Y., Johnston, L., Miles, L., & Peace, V. (2006) "Implicit Behavioral Mimicry: Investigating the Impact of Group Membership," *Journal of Nonverbal Behavior* 30: 97–113.

FURTHER READING

Pacherie, E. (2013) "How Does It Feel to Act Together?" *Phenomenology and the Cognitive Sciences* 13, 1: 25–46. (An exploration of the sense of agency in joint action.)

Salmela, M. (2012) "Plural Emotions." *Philosophical Explorations* 15 (1): 1–14. (Proposes a typology of shared emotions according to their different degrees of collectivity.)

Schmid, H.B. (2014a) "Plural Self-Awareness." *Phenomenology and the Cognitive Sciences* 13 (1): 7–24. (A defense of the view that self-awareness can take a plural form).

Schwitzgebel, E. (2015) "If Materialism Is True, the United States Is Probably Conscious." *Philosophical Studies* 172: 1697–1721. (A discussion of the possibility of group consciousness.)

von Scheve, C. & Salmela, M. (eds) (2014) *Collective Emotions*, Oxford: Oxford University Press. (A collection of papers exploring collective emotions from philosophical, psychological and sociological perspectives.)

III

Epistemology and Rationality in the Social Context

Introduction to Part III

Marija Jankovic and Kirk Ludwig

The epistemology and rationality of groups, and their implications for our understanding of group agency, are an important focus of research on collective intentionality. Questions about the epistemology and rationality of groups come in both at the level of individual agents participating in joint action, and at the level of groups. At the level of individuals, for example, common knowledge among participating agents of their intentions and corresponding beliefs in success of joint action is often (though not always) cited as a precondition for shared intention, and so for joint intentional action. At the group level, we say that, for example, "The tobacco companies knew and for most part accepted the evidence that cigarette smoking was a cause of cancer by the late 1950s." Scientific knowledge raises questions about both levels. It is the result of a massive coordinated effort by many people, often as members of large research teams or organizations, in an institutional environment designed for sharing information, duplicating experiments, and critically evaluating hypothesis and proposals. Arguably the knowledge that results cannot be analyzed exhaustively in terms of the aggregate knowledge of individual scientists.

Similarly, groups as well as individuals are evaluated as behaving rationally. A group may act irrationally, in the sense of acting in ways that are obviously incoherent given its goals, even though each of its members considered independently appears to be acting entirely rationally. Reasoning by participants in group action may also take an importantly different form, team reasoning, where individuals reason about what to do in relation to the team's goals or utility rather than purely individualistically. It has been argued that team reasoning is the key to resolving certain collective action dilemmas that classically characterized individualistic strategic reasoning cannot (such as the Hi-Lo game and the Prisoner's Dilemma—see Chapters 16–17), as well as to understanding what distinguishes shared intentions from an aggregate of individual intentions.

Notably, groups can solve problems or carry out tasks that their members cannot by way of a decomposition of the problem and a distribution of labor, frequently drawing on different skills from different members. These are cases of distributed cognitive systems that engage in complementary problem solving. It has been suggested that in these cases there are cognitive processes that take place not in individual heads but in the group as a whole, and sometimes this has been seen as a ground for claiming that something like a group mind is realized in the activities of individual agents coordinating their efforts in a way that is not merely aggregative.

Finally, judgment aggregation procedures in organizations often face problems when they must make a decision on a variety of different propositions that jointly bear on a decision the organization must make. This can give rise to what has been called the Discursive Dilemma. A three-member committee, for example, may be charged with making a recommendation on a merger with another corporation, where the merger is to be approved if it is low cost, synergistic, and profitable. Each member may believe that it meets a different pair of the criteria but not all three. So though a majority is in favor of each, none individually are in favor of all. They are faced with a question of how to aggregate their judgments, and one way, a premise first approach, results in a decision by the group that none of the individuals endorse. In this case, the organization appears procedurally to have some autonomy from the decisions of individuals. What are the implications for its status as an autonomous agent?

There are six chapters in Part III, "Common Knowledge," "Collective Epistemology," "Rationality and Cooperation," "Team Reasoning: Controversies and Open Research Questions," "Groups as Distributed Cognitive Systems," and "Corporate Agency: The Lesson of the Discursive Dilemma."

In Chapter 14, "Common Knowledge," Harvey Lederman distinguishes an informal notion of public information, information intuitively shared openly by everyone in a community, e.g. everyone knowing that Trump is President, from a formal notion of common knowledge, in which everyone knows that Trump is President, and everyone knows that everyone knows that everyone knows that Trump is President, and so on. Public information has been thought to play an important role in social interactions. Lederman focuses on a common assumption that public information and common knowledge coincide, that is, that the informal notion is correctly characterized as common knowledge, and surveys arguments on both sides of this debate.

Chapter 15, "Collective Epistemology," by Jennifer Lackey, focuses on the question how we should understand a group's justifiably believing something. Lackey reviews four approaches to justified group belief: an inflationary approach, a deflationary approach, a Condorcet-inspired approach, and a group epistemic agent approach. Inflationary approaches treat groups as full-fledged epistemic agents. The main argument is that it appears that what individual members and a group are justified in believing come apart, e.g. a jury may be justified in believing a defendant innocent, because of rules of evidence, while its members are not. Deflationary approaches seek to understand talk of justified group belief in terms of the epistemic states and relations among their members. Summative accounts are in this sense deflationary: a group is justified in believing something just in case some (e.g. a majority) or all of its members do. Lackey develops problems for both approaches, and then turns to a Condorcet-inspired account on which group aggregation of judgments which are more reliable than individual judgments are identified with group justified beliefs. However, this would allow group justified beliefs even when no member of the group had any justification for her beliefs. The final approach seeks to respect two principles, first, that the justification of group beliefs depends on the justifications its members have, and, second, that it should pay attention to the evidential relations that exist among members' beliefs and their bases.

In Chapter 16, "Rationality and Cooperation," Paul Weirich develops accounts of collective rationality (acting in accord with members acting rationally) and of cooperation (working together for a common benefit) and then on their basis an account of the collective rationality of cooperation, that is, the conditions under which it is rational for a group to cooperate. Weirich argues that when conditions are ideal for joint action, cooperation is rationally required, and responds to objections to the account of collective rationality he introduces. He also considers its relation to team reasoning and circumstances in which there is the possibility of shifting coalitions.

Chapter 17, "Team Reasoning," by Natalie Gold, looks at the theory of team reasoning introduced separately by Robert Sugden and Michael Bacharach. The theory of team reasoning is motivated by problems in orthodox game theory. The problem is that orthodox game theory appears to give the wrong result for certain game-theoretic situations that people face frequently in everyday life. People seem to be able to rationally solve these problems by cooperating when orthodox game theory predicts either that there is no rational solution or that the rational solution excludes cooperation. Two prominent examples are the Hi-Lo game and the Prisoner's Dilemma. In the Hi-Lo game, two agents can coordinate behaviors in two ways for some benefit (and otherwise none), though one way of coordinating is better (for both) than the other. Orthodox game theory does not distinguish the better from the less good way of coordinating. In the Prisoner's Dilemma, two agents can choose to cooperate or defect. If they cooperate, they get off. If they both defect, they get some jail time. If one cooperates and the other defects, the cooperator gets a lot of jail time and the other gets off and, say, a small favor. Orthodox game theory says they should each defect. In orthodox game theory, agents reason from the standpoint of what they should each do, conditional on what others do. Team reasoning allows agents to consider what the group facing the problem should do. Team reasoning occurs when members of a group identify with the group. Gold discusses theoretical options for how to think about identifying with a group, and whether rational group identification is possible, and whether in particular it could be instrumentally rational. Gold also discusses the question of what the team's goals should be facing different sorts of problems. Different options have different results. A further issue is the relation between team reasoning and collective or shared intentions. Gold and Sugden (see the chapter for references) propose that shared intentions are formed when members of a group team-reason. Gold discusses the virtues of the proposal as well as criticisms, and explores what is required for the sort of reasoning involved to take place. Gold discusses the state of empirical testing of the hypothesis that team reasoning explains how people often solve collective action problems optimally. Finally, Gold notes that one could conceptualize the problem of taking into account future benefits and costs in considering present behavior as a matter of a present time slice deciding whether to identify with, and so team reason with, future time slices of the same series of selves.

In Chapter 18, "Groups as Distributed Cognitive Systems," Georg Theiner takes up the topic of distributed cognition in relation to collective intentionality. Distributed cognition, understood neutrally, is a matter of a group of cognitive agents working together to solve some cognitive problem, especially when they make complementary contributions. One of the central questions about distributed cognition is whether (or when) it amounts to genuine group level cognition or collective intelligence. Theiner's chapter aims to map out the conceptual terrain against which this debate is taking place. What are the various levels of organization of cognitive activity in a group? How do they arise? What are the similarities in the kinds of processes going on at various scales? How do they depend on the components, at a given level of scale, and their relations? Does socially distributed cognition amount to, in some cases, group level cognition? Theiner begins with an analysis of the notion of socially distributed cognition into joint, distributive, and shared aspects. Next he considers central properties—organization-dependence, novelty, autonomy— associated with emergent properties of socially distributed cognition. Finally, he considers five theoretical stances that have been adopted to identify group level cognitive organiz- ation: the Intentional Stance, the Information Processing Stance, the Computational Stance, the Ecological Stance, and the Dynamical Systems Stance.

The final chapter in Part III, Chapter 19, by Philip Pettit is on "Corporate Agency: The Lesson of the Discursive Dilemma." Pettit distinguishes between the effects of the actions of many agents (unintentional collective action), their bringing about shared a goal (shared intentional action), and groups that themselves constitute an agent (the corporate agent). Pettit argues that the discursive dilemma illustrates the conditions under which a group of the third kind can arise. The discursive dilemma is a kind of decision problem facing groups that requires that they adopt explicitly a decision procedure for aggregating judgments to avoid the possibility of incoherence. In the simplest case, a three-member committee may vote on three propositions p, q and r, which if jointly accepted support a fourth, s, and on the proposition s itself that p, q, and r are relevant to. In this case, it is possible for aggregating judgments by a majority vote to lead to an inconsistent set of group judgments. Two may support each of p, q, and r, but a different two in each case, and so all reject s. But a group that accepts p, q, r, should not also reject s. When the group adopts, e.g. a premise-based approach, voting on basic assumptions and adopting what they support, they resolve the difficulty. This illustrates in a simple case how a group may institute decision-making procedures that aim to develop a consistent and coherent group view, one which is flexible and reflective, and may draw on a variety of mechanisms for checking results and procedures. Pettit argues that this amounts to the members of the group constructing a corporate mind that has an identity of its own.

14

Common Knowledge

Harvey Lederman

1. TWO NOTIONS OF COMMON KNOWLEDGE

Common knowledge is widely used in economic theory, theoretical computer science, linguistics, and philosophy. It has been invoked in explanations of rational coordination, in characterizations of joint attention and shared intention, in theories of communication, speaker meaning, innuendo, and conversational context as well as in analyses of conventions, social norms, and social groups.[1]

The expression "common knowledge" in fact has two, distinct, technical uses.[2] Jane Heal introduces the "informal" notion of common knowledge by way of the following case:

> Suppose that you and I are dining together. At the next table, clearly audible to both of us, another diner begins a loud quarrel with his companion. You catch my eye and make a grimace of distaste. Contrast this with another situation. You and I are again dining together. I messily drop a piece of potato on the table. I attempt to field it inconspicuously and hope you have not noticed. In fact you have noticed, but out of regard for my feelings you pretend that you have not.
>
> There is a clear difference between the two situations. In the first the beginning of the quarrel is completely open, public, or, as I shall say, it is *common knowledge* between us that a quarrel has broken out. In the second case my bungling is not similarly open.
>
> (Heal 1978: 116)

A second, "formal" notion of common knowledge is defined as follows. Some people *commonly know* that p if and only if they all know that p, they all know that they all know that p, they all know that they all know that they all know that p, and so on. Related notions can be defined using "believe" and "is certain that," as well as other propositional attitudes. For example, some people commonly believe that p if and only if they all believe that p, they all believe that they all believe that p, and so on. Often, especially in economic theory (and almost without exception in economic theory from the 1980s and 1990s), the expression "common knowledge" is used generically to mean "common knowledge, common belief, or common certainty" (where someone is certain that p just in case they assign p probability 1). Thus authors speak of "common knowledge assumptions" where the assumptions may not require knowledge at all. I will sometimes use "common knowledge" in this more general way to simplify the presentation, but where it is important I will mark distinctions between common knowledge, common belief, and common certainty.

To avoid confusion, I will use the expression "public information" for the first, "informal" notion of common knowledge introduced by the example from Heal.[3] From here on, I will use the term "common knowledge" only for the second, formal notion. The reader should be aware, however, that what I call "public information" is often called "common knowledge" by other authors.

These two different notions give rise to different questions. It is reasonable to ask (as Heal does) whether one can give a clear psychological characterization of public information, and if so, what that characterization is. These questions do not arise for (the formal notion of) common knowledge. But common knowledge comes with its own set of questions. Do people ever have it? And if they do, does it play an important role in human social interactions?

While the two notions of common knowledge are conceptually distinct, the default position in the literature has been that they coincide. According to this *Default Position*, some people have public information that p just in case they have common knowledge that p.

This chapter focuses on conceptual issues related to the Default Position. In Section 2, I consider an influential argument in favor of the position. In Section 3, I consider an influential argument against it. In Section 4, I discuss how one might use a famous formal example, the electronic mail game, to argue for or against the position.

I will not discuss the mathematics of common knowledge, or its uses in game theory and computer science in any detail. Excellent surveys of these issues can be found in other places. Geanakoplos (1994) is accessible and highly recommended. Vanderschraaf and Sillari (2014) touches on many issues which I cannot discuss here. For those wishing to delve deeper into the logic of common knowledge, the excellent textbook Fagin et al. (1995) remains the best starting point; for those specifically interested in game theory, Dekel and Siniscalchi (2015) is a useful recent survey. I have not made any attempt to give comprehensive references in this chapter.

2. AN ARGUMENT FOR THE DEFAULT POSITION

An influential argument for the Default Position proceeds by way of a series of examples; I'll use those from the recent paper of Greco (2015):[4]

> PUBLIC ANNOUNCEMENT: A professor tells her class that they will play the follow-ing game. Without communicating to one another in any way, each student in the class will write down the name of a US state on a piece of a paper. If all students

write the same state name, with the exception of the name of the state the class is taking place in, the students will each receive $10. If any two students write down different state names, or if they all write down the name of the state the class is taking place in, no prize money will be awarded. Before handing out the pieces of paper, the professor tells the class that she grew up in Maine (which is not the state the class is taking place in), and that it is lovely in the fall.

(Greco 2015: 755)

Contrast this case with the following:

PRIVATE INFORMATION: Just like the previous case, except instead of publicly announcing that she grew up in Maine, the professor whispers the following to each student privately as she hands out the pieces of paper: "while I'm not telling anybody else this, I'd like you to know that I grew up in Maine, and it is lovely in the fall."

(Greco 2015: 756)

In the first case, the fact that the professor grew up in Maine has the "openness" or "publicity" that Heal describes in her example; the students have public information that the professor grew up in Maine. In the second case, the fact that the professor grew up in Maine is not "open" in the same way; the students do not have public information of this fact.

A theory of public information should explain this contrast. Prior to reading the above examples one might have been attracted to the simple view that some people have public information that *p* just in case they all know that *p*. But PRIVATE INFORMATION is a counterexample to this simple theory. In PRIVATE INFORMATION, the students all know that the professor is from Maine. But intuitively this fact is not out in the open for them as a class.

In response to this counterexample, one might propose adding a second "layer" of knowledge: some people have public information that *p* just in case they all know that they all know (two occurrences of "know") that *p*. But the following elaboration of PRIVATE INFORMATION appears to be a counterexample to this new proposal, as well:

MORE PRIVATE INFORMATION: Just like the previous case, except this is what the professor whispers: "I'm privately telling everybody in the class that I grew up in Maine and that it's lovely in the fall. However, you're the only one who I'm telling that I'm telling everyone. Each other student thinks that she's the only one who knows that I grew up in Maine."

(Greco 2015: 756)

Here, the students presumably all know that they all know that the professor is from Maine. But nevertheless there is a felt difference between MORE PRIVATE INFORMATION and PUBLIC ANNOUNCEMENT: in the former, the students do not seem to have public information that the professor is from Maine; it is not out in the open in the relevant way.

To consider generalizations of this style of argument, it will be useful to have some terminology. Some people *mutually know* (or: mutually know[1]) that *p* just in case they all know that *p*. Since everyone in my department knows that the department office is on the tenth floor, the members of my department mutually know[1] that the department office is on the tenth floor. Progressing further, some people mutually know[2] that p just in case they all know that they all know that p. Since everyone in my department knows that everyone in my department knows that the department office is on the tenth floor, the members of my department mutually know[2] that the department office is on the tenth floor. And we can continue: some people mutually know[3] that p just in case they all know that they all know that they all know that p. Since everyone in my department knows that everyone in my department knows that everyone in my department knows that the department office is on the tenth floor, the members of my department mutually know[3] that the department office is on the tenth floor.

Extending this pattern, in general for n > 1 some people mutually know[n] that p just in case they mutually know that they mutually know[n-1] it.[5] We can use these definitions to give a compact characterization of common knowledge: some people commonly know that p just in case for all n, they mutually know[n] that p.

The examples given so far seem to show that people may have mutual knowledge[2] that p, although they do not have public information that p. But many authors have agreed that the examples can be extended to show in general that for any n, mutual knowledge[n] does not suffice for public information. To give a sense of how the generalization proceeds, we can give a related example for mutual knowledge[3] by altering the teacher's announcement:

EVEN MORE PRIVATE INFORMATION: Just like the previous case, except this is what the professor whispers: "I'm privately telling everybody in the class that I grew up in Maine and that it's lovely in the fall and that I have told everyone this. However, you're the only one who I'm telling that I'm telling everyone that I've told everyone. Each other student thinks that she's the only one who knows that everyone knows that I grew up in Maine."

The basic recipe should now be clear. For each n, one can alter the professor's secret so that it seems the students would be able to achieve mutual knowledge[n] that the professor is from Maine, although they would not intuitively have public information that the professor is from Maine. The argument based on these cases is thus in the first instance a negative one. A natural analysis of public information states that (for some fixed k) some people have public information that p just in case they have mutual knowledge[k] that p. The argument casts doubt on analyses of this form: it appears to show that for any n, no matter how great, mutual knowledge[n] is insufficient for public information.[6]

This negative argument can be resisted. The technical notion of public information was introduced on the basis of examples such as Heal's; the notion does not come with hard and fast rules for how it is to be extended to cases such as EVEN MORE PRIVATE INFORMATION. It does not make sense to appeal to "intuitions" about the application of this technical notion. Rather, in thinking about how to extend the notion we must consider which way of extending it fits best with the theoretical work we want the notion to do. It is at least possible that the most theoretically fruitful extension of this concept gives the result that the people in EVEN MORE PUBLIC INFORMATION (or some later case in the sequence) do have public information, at least if all goes well.

Still, there might seem to be strong reasons for not extending the concept in this way. For if we did so extend it, we might seem to be left without a way of explaining the undeniable felt contrast between PUBLIC ANNOUNCEMENT and the subsequent cases.

This concern, however, is not as powerful as it might seem. To see this, consider a proponent of MK[4], the view that people have public information that p just in case they have mutual knowledge[4] that p. In response to an elaboration of EVEN MORE PRIVATE INFORMATION intended to be a counterexample to MK[4], the proponent of this view might argue as follows: "The students will have mutual knowledge[4] if, and (let us suppose) only if, they (a) understand the secret told to them, (b) believe what the teacher says, (c) know that everyone else will understand the secret, and (d) know that everyone else will believe it. Let us set aside (b) and (d): for present purposes we may grant that if the students understood the speeches they would believe them and that this is known by all. Still, (a) and (c) may present difficulties. People in the students' shoes will not always understand complex statements they are told about others' epistemic states (e.g. 'I told the others I was telling everyone that I was telling everyone that I'm from Maine'). This would result in a failure of (a). More often, a person in the students' position may be uncertain whether on hearing 'I told everyone that I told everyone that I am from Maine,' the *others* will understand that all the students know that all the students know that the teacher is from Maine (a failure of (c)). The difficulty of understanding statements of this form has been documented in the empirical literature.[7] Readers of these cases typically believe that the students do not satisfy (a) or (c), and thus they typically judge that the students do not have mutual knowledge[4] that the professor is from Maine. It is for this reason that they judge the students not to have public information of this fact. The example is thus not a counterexample at all; the judgments readers report are exactly in line with my theory." This proponent of MK[4] might further claim that if one focuses on cases where the students do satisfy (a)–(d), the felt contrast disappears. Or she might propose a kind of error theory, stating that the difficulty of satisfying (a)–(d) makes it natural to judge incorrectly that the students fail to have public information in the case so described.

This style of response to the argument in fact has considerable appeal. But it has not been much discussed in the literature, so from now on we will set it aside.[8] In the remainder of this essay, then, we will suppose that the negative argument based on these cases succeeds. How can this negative argument be extended to a positive argument for the claim that public information requires common knowledge? The most obvious way of extending it uses a further premise: that public information in this case is to be analyzed solely in terms of what the students know about where the professor comes from, and what they know about what others know about where the professor comes from, and so on. Given this additional premise, if we can rule out all finite levels of mutual knowledge, we will have shown that common knowledge is required for public information.

One might, however, reject the new premise of this extended, positive argument. The sense of openness or publicity in the examples might derive from features of the situation other than how many levels of mutual knowledge are present. For example, situations might fail to produce a sense of openness simply when they are confusing, unusual or unfamiliar to the participants. The above cases involve very unusual statements on the part of the professor; according to the suggested criterion, that is why they do not produce the relevant kind of openness. A full development of this approach would require a more systematic explanation of what these other factors are; "unusual" is hardly an informative characterization. But the general strategy for rejecting this new premise again seems at least prima facie appealing, and again has not received much discussion.[9]

3. PROBLEMS WITH THE DEFAULT POSITION?

Although these arguments have been taken by many authors to motivate the idea that common knowledge is at least importantly related to public information, some of the same authors have also been suspicious of the idea that public information requires common knowledge itself. The most common concern has been that because common knowledge requires knowledge of an infinite collection of claims it is impossible for finite creatures to have common knowledge. Heal (1978) and Clark and Marshall (1981) are good examples of early skepticism on these grounds; in a later book, Clark for example writes: 'CG-iterated [that is, common belief] obviously cannot represent people's mental states because it requires an infinitely large mental capacity . . .' (1996: 95–6).

In this passage, Clark is concerned with how we should "represent common ground". In context, it is clear that by "represent" he means "give a theory of," and that "common ground" is used here loosely for public information. The objection is not particularly powerful. People often believe every member of an infinite collection of claims. For every natural number $n > 0$, I believe that no one has ever seen Santa Claus exactly n times. This belief about how many times Santa Claus has been seen is clearly possible, in spite of the fact that it involves believing an infinite set of claims. So observing that common knowledge or belief is somehow infinite does not seem to be an interesting objection to the possibility of common knowledge or belief.

Nevertheless, in response to this and related objections, there has been a great deal of discussion of alternative analyses of public information which do not require that people know an infinite collection of claims. Although these analyses do not require that people in fact have common knowledge, they do imply that ideal agents would have common knowledge were they to have public information. In other words, they imply:

> IDEAL COMMON KNOWLEDGE: Necessarily, if some agents have common knowledge that they are ideal reasoners, then if they have public information that p, they commonly know that p.[10]

The Default Position is the benchmark position in the literature; it is almost invariably the starting point of discussions about common knowledge and public information. But few people accept the Default Position as it stands. By contrast, almost every author who has discussed public information at any length accepts IDEAL COMMON KNOWLEDGE (or a related thesis about common belief).

An important example of such a theory can be motivated using a notion of "the scene." In the opening example from Heal, there is some sense in which the diners both know the scene which is unfolding around them. The obvious features of what they can see and hear—the color of the tablecloth, the location of the bar in the restaurant, whether there is music playing or not—are all part of the scene. Not every detail, of course, must be part of the scene: details on the ornamentation of the ceiling or the color of the waiters' shoes may not be part of the scene in this sense. But it is supposed to be part of the scene that both diners are normal perceivers attentive to the world around them. In other words, it is part of the scene that they each know the scene.

What does it mean for something to be "part of the scene"? One explication of this abstract idea states that for something to be part of the scene is for the scene to entail it. Thus we have:

> SHARED ENVIRONMENT: Some people have public information that p just in case there is an E ("environment") such that it is the case that E, E entails that p, and E entails that everyone knows that E.[11]

Under plausible assumptions about entailment, and assuming that ideal knowledge is closed under entailment, this definition will satisfy IDEAL COMMON KNOWLEDGE. Informally, the basic idea is as follows. The scene entails that there is a quarrel happening beside the diners. The scene also entails that both diners know the scene. Thus the scene entails that both diners know something which entails that both diners know that there is a quarrel beside them. But since the scene also entails that both know the scene, it further entails that both know something which entails that both know something which entails that both know that there is a quarrel. And we can continue to add iterations of "know something which entails" ad infinitum. If ideal agents' knowledge is closed under entailment, in the case of ideal agents we can replace each occurrence of "know something which entails" with "know." The formal details of an argument to this effect are sketched in a footnote.[12]

Earlier I suggested that at least one motivation for these alternatives to common knowledge itself is not as strong as it has been taken to be. But there other ways of using these alternative analyses of public information. My infinite collection of beliefs about Santa Claus is plausibly in some sense explained by my having a more basic belief, namely, that no one has ever seen Santa Claus. What is the corresponding "basic belief" in the case of common belief? If this talk of "basic beliefs" is cashed out in terms of how beliefs are cognitively represented, answering this question would mean offering a theory of how common knowledge and common belief are cognitively represented. Perhaps SHARED ENVIRONMENT could be suitably modified to provide such an account.

While, as we have seen, some have worried that common belief would be too hard to achieve, others have argued that in fact common belief is easier to achieve than mutual belief^k for only finite k. Robert Stalnaker, for example, writes:

> Instead of thinking of beliefs and presuppositions in terms of sentences that express them, in the language of thought, stored in the belief or presupposition box of the mind, think of them negatively: it is the live options—the space of possibilities one allows for—that need to be represented. One's beliefs or presuppositions are the propositions that are true in all of those possibilities. What would put an unrealistic computational load on the mind would be a situation in which one believed, up to six iterations, that one believed that, but failed to believe the seventh iteration. That would require representing a possible situation (and a representation of the complex relational structure of possibilities compatible with possibilities that are compatible with possibilities compatible with . . . etc.) in which this mind-bogglingly subtle distinction is made. Infinitely iterated beliefs and presuppositions are much simpler for the subject to represent, and to understand.
>
> (Stalnaker 2009: 402–3)

Stalnaker's own notion of representation is somewhat obscure. It is not clear in what sense if any including "more" possibilities requires some "computational load." For every n greater than or equal to zero, it is consistent with what I believe that there are exactly n creatures living in the universe now on planets other than earth: an infinite set of live possibilities which differ with regard to the numbers of extraterrestrial creatures are consistent with my beliefs. Thus making these possibilities live cannot have imposed an "unrealistic" computational load on my mind.

4. COMMON KNOWLEDGE AND COORDINATION

In Section 2, we saw an argument that mutual knowledge[n] is not sufficient for public information. There, we were focused on the sense of openness that was supposed to be the hallmark of public information. But one might also see the examples as the basis for a different argument, about rational action. In PUBLIC ANNOUNCEMENT, it is rational—perhaps rationally required—for the students to write down "Maine," and it is likely the students would coordinate to win the prize money. In PRIVATE INFORMATION (and also in at least some of the subsequent cases), this behavior does not seem rationally required, and, moreover, it is unlikely that the students would be able to coordinate on writing down "Maine." One theoretical role for public information might be to explain rational social behavior. For example, one might think that in a range of situations it is rational for people to coordinate if and only if they have public information of relevant facts about their situation. If the examples show that finite levels of mutual knowledge are insufficient to justify coordination, this might give us a second, independent argument for the Default Position.

But one might wonder: is it really true that the students would still fail to coordinate in the four-hundredth case in this series? It might seem that, whatever one's views about the "openness" of the professor's birthplace in these examples, the students would eventually be able to coordinate. It is quite difficult to reason about rational behavior in such alien examples, so it is natural to turn to formal, mathematical theories of rationality for help. The famous "electronic mail game" (Rubinstein 1989) is a formal example in which it is irrational for players to coordinate if they have only finite levels of mutual knowledge, although it would be rational for them to coordinate in the presence of common knowledge. At least in this example, rational students would not coordinate even in the analogue of the four-hundredth case in the series. I'll present the example in very crude outline; readers who want to understand the details should consult the original, highly accessible paper.[13]

In the electronic mail game, Row and Column are uncertain which of two smaller games, G_A or G_B, they are playing (see Figure 14.1).

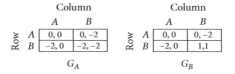

Figure 14.1 The Electronic Mail Game

In the first, the action A ensures the best payoff of 0 to each player, regardless of what the other player does. In the second, there is no such simple choice: the players each receive a payoff of 1 if they both play B, and a payoff of 0 if they both play A. If their actions don't match, however, then the player who plays B alone pays a penalty of 2.[14]

The games are to be selected by the toss of a fair coin: with probability $\frac{1}{2}$, the game is G_A, and with probability $\frac{1}{2}$ the game is G_B. But the players' information about the outcome of the toss is asymmetric. Row will observe the outcome of the toss. Column will not, but will learn about the outcome by receiving messages from Row. If the game is selected to be G_B, Row will automatically send an email message to Column. If either Column or Row receives an email message from the other, his or her computer automatically sends a new message in reply. At each stage of this process, however, there is a positive, equal and independent rate of the message failing; with probability 1 the process will be cut off at some point. And when it has ended, each player will be told only the tally of the messages he or she sent.

A *strategy* for a player is a function from the natural numbers (the number of messages the player has sent) to the set of probability distributions over actions (i.e. $\{A, B\}$). A strategy is *rationalizable* if and only if it is consistent with the players' having common certainty of one another's rationality (in the sense of maximizing expected utility). We then have the following result:

Theorem (Rubinstein 1989). For each player, the unique rationalizable strategy is the constant function which takes every number of messages sent to A.

In the example, then, rational coordination is impossible if the players have only finite levels of mutual certainty. Many have found this result highly counterintuitive. After one message has been sent, each of the players is certain that the game is G_B—that is, they are certain that if they both played B, that would be the best outcome for each of them. But, because they are not certain that they are certain that the game is G_B, they are certain that the other player will *not* play B. The point carries over to higher message counts, too. If they each send two messages, they are certain that the game is G_B, and in fact certain that the other is certain of this. But even so they remain certain that neither will play B.

In philosophy, perhaps the most common lesson that has been drawn from this surprising result is that common knowledge (or at least, common certainty) is important for successful coordination. If the players had common knowledge that the game is G_B, it would clearly be rationally permitted for them to coordinate on B. But if common knowledge fails in the way described in the electronic mail game, they cannot rationally coordinate on B. So, some have concluded, common knowledge must be important for coordination in general.

There are, however, a number of ways of resisting this argument. Although people cannot coordinate on the better outcome *in the above situation* it does not follow that common knowledge is important for rational coordination in other situations. This point can be sharpened once we see that the argument is sensitive to a number of highly unrealistic features of the setup. For example, Rubinstein already recognized that if it is guaranteed that communication will stop at some pre-ordained number of messages, it becomes possible for players to coordinate rationally on B (Rubinstein 1989: 388, Remark 1). Since in everyday life, communication is always truncated in this way, the example is crucially different from any situation people would ordinarily encounter. A detailed study of consequences of this important observation can be found in the elegant paper of Binmore and Samuelson (2001).

In fact, on reflection, one might take the example to tell against the importance of common knowledge, rather than in favor of it. The background assumptions for the above result (including common knowledge of rationality) imply that in the standard technical sense of "rational" the only rational action is to coordinate on A in this situation. But there is a powerful intuition that this is not the only rational action. Instead of taking this case to show that rational agents cannot coordinate, we might instead conclude that the assumptions used in proving the result make the wrong predictions about the case, so that these background assumptions should be rejected. On this interpretation, the case yields an argument against the assumptions of common certainty used to prove the result, not an argument for the role of common certainty in everyday coordination (Lederman 2017).

One might take this last point to suggest that rational coordination must not require any doxastic state resembling common knowledge. But this would be too quick. A person p-believes that q just in case the person assigns q probability greater than or equal to p. It can be shown that for particular choices of p, agents may have common p-belief about the setup of the electronic mail game and common p-belief that they are rational but nevertheless coordinate after finite numbers of messages have been sent (Monderer and Samet 1989). Thus one might take the argument to show merely that the important notion for theories of behavior is common p-belief, as opposed to common certainty (or common knowledge, or common belief).[15]

We have seen arguments both for and against the prevalence of common knowledge based on the electronic mail game. Other arguments related to this issue are based on the use of common knowledge assumptions in the social sciences more generally. Common knowledge assumptions can be seen as part of simple, strong theories of human behavior. On the grounds that one should generally put confidence in simple, strong hypotheses, one might hold that there is at least a presumption in favor of the claim that people often have a great deal of common knowledge. In reply to this argument, however, one might respond that any such presumption is defeated by apparent counterexamples to the truth of common knowledge assumptions, such as the false predictions these hypotheses seem to generate in examples such as the electronic mail game itself.

A different argument begins from the claim that the prevalence of models which impose common knowledge assumptions in mathematical game theory shows these assumptions to be part of our best social-scientific theory of human behavior. If one holds that what a person believes and knows is what he or she believes and knows according to the best theory of his or her behavior, then it would follow that people have a great deal of common knowledge and belief.[16] One could resist this argument by rejecting the theory of belief it is based on, or (as above) by rejecting the premise that theories which include common knowledge assumptions are in fact good theories of human behavior.

5. CONCLUSION

This brief survey has left untouched a vast range of issues related to common knowledge. Even among the issues it has touched on, many questions remain unsettled. There has not been enough philosophical work on the underpinnings of social behavior to determine whether common knowledge or even public information plays the roles it has been claimed to play. The orthodoxy that common knowledge is importantly connected to public information has not been subjected to sustained scrutiny. As a result there have been few arguments for or against this orthodoxy. A start has been made in some recent work arguing against IDEAL COMMON KNOWLEDGE (Lederman, forthcoming), but this remains only a first step.

A good example of the uncertain state of play concerns one of the most important applications of common knowledge and public information in philosophy, in theories of the common ground of a conversation. In linguistics and the philosophy of language, it is typically assumed that there is a body of shared information among the participants in a conversation which plays an important role in determining what sentences will mean in context, and how extra-semantic inferences will be drawn by conversational participants. It is standardly assumed that this body of shared information is determined roughly by what the participants commonly know (Stalnaker 2002, 2014; cf. for example Pinker 2007; Pinker et al. 2008). There have been few arguments offered in favor of this position, however. It is unclear whether the linguistic data require the assumption, or whether we can make do with something weaker. If we can make do with something weaker, it is unclear what shape this weaker characterization will take. There is a great deal of work to be done.

ACKNOWLEDGEMENTS

Thanks to Marija Jankovic, Kirk Ludwig, Cédric Patternotte and especially Dan Greco for comments on this article. Thanks also to Peter Fritz for discussion of an earlier version of some of this material.

RELATED TOPICS

Collective Action and Agency (Ch. 1), Reductive Views of Shared Intention (Ch. 3), Coordinating Joint Action (Ch. 6), Joint Attention (Ch. 9), Joint Commitment (Ch. 10), Social Groups (Ch. 21), Collective Intentionality and Language (Ch. 28).

REFERENCES

Barwise, J. (1988) "Three Views of Common Knowledge," in *Proceedings of the 2nd Conference on Theoretical Aspects of Reasoning About Knowledge*, Los Altos, CA: Morgan Kaufmann Publishers Inc.
Bicchieri, C. and Muldoon, R. (2014) "Social Norms," in E.N. Zalta (ed.) *The Stanford Encyclopedia of Philosophy* (Spring 2014), https://plato.stanford.edu/archives/spr2014/entries/social-norms/; Metaphysics Research Lab, Stanford University.
Binmore, K. and Samuelson, L. (2001) "Coordinated Action in the Electronic Mail Game," *Games and Economic Behavior* 35 (1): 6–30.
Bratman, M.E. (1992) "Shared Cooperative Activity," *The Philosophical Review* 101 (2): 327–41.
——— (1993) "Shared Intention," *Ethics* 104 (1): 97–113.
——— (2014) *Shared Agency: A Planning Theory of Acting Together*, Oxford: Oxford University Press.
Campbell, J. (2002) *Reference and Consciousness*, Oxford: Oxford University Press.
Chant, S.R. and Ernst, Z. (2008) "Epistemic Conditions for Collective Action," *Mind* 117 (467): 549–73.
Chwe, M.S-Y. (2001) *Rational Ritual: Culture, Coordination, and Common Knowledge*, Princeton: Princeton University Press.
Clark, H.H. (1979) "Responding to Indirect Speech Acts," *Cognitive Psychology* 11 (4): 430–77.

——— (1996) *Using Language*, Cambridge: Cambridge University Press.

Clark, H.H. and Marshall, C.R. (1981) "Definite Reference and Mutual Knowledge," in A.K. Joshi, B. Webber, and I. Sag (eds) *Elements of Discourse Understanding*, Cambridge: Cambridge University Press.

Clark, H.H. and Carlson, T.B. (1982) "Speech Acts and Hearer's Beliefs," in N.V. Smith (ed.) *Mutual Knowledge*, Cambridge, MA: Academic Press.

Cubitt, R.P. and Sugden, R. (2003) "Common Knowledge, Salience and Convention: A Reconstruction of David Lewis' Game Theory," *Economics and Philosophy* 19 (2): 175–210.

Dekel, E. and Siniscalchi, M. (2015) "Epistemic Game Theory," in H.P. Young and S. Zamir (eds) *Handbook of Game Theory with Economic Applications, Volume 4*, Amsterdam: North Holland.

Fagin, R., Halpern, J.Y., Moses, Y. and Vardi, M.Y. (1995) *Reasoning About Knowledge*, Cambridge, MA: MIT Press.

——— (1999) "Common Knowledge Revisited," *Annals of Pure and Applied Logic* 96 (1–3): 89–105.

Fine, K. (2012) "The Structure of Joint Intention," *Collective Intentionality VIII*, Manchester, UK: University of Manchester.

Friedell, M.F. (1969) "On the Structure of Shared Awareness," *Behavioral Science* 14 (1): 28–39.

Geanakoplos, J. (1994) "Common Knowledge," in R.J. Aumann and S. Hart (eds) *Handbook of Game Theory with Economic Applications Volume 1*, Amsterdam: North Holland.

Gilbert, M. (1989) *On Social Facts*, Princeton: Princeton University Press.

——— (1990) "Walking Together: A Paradigmatic Social Phenomenon," *Midwest Studies in Philosophy* 15 (1): 1–14.

——— (2008) "Social Convention Revisited," *Topoi* 27 (1–2): 5–16.

Greco, D. (2014a) "Could KK be OK?" *Journal of Philosophy* 111 (4): L169–97.

——— (2014b) "Iteration and Fragmentation," *Philosophy and Phenomenological Research* 88 (1): 656–73.

——— (2015) "Iteration Principles in Epistemology I: Arguments For," *Philosophy Compass* 10 (11): 754–64.

Grice, H.P. (1969) "Utterer's Meaning and Intention," *The Philosophical Review* 78 (2): 147–77.

Halpern, J.Y. and Moses, Y. (1990) "Knowledge and Common Knowledge in a Distributed Environment," *Journal of the ACM (JACM)* 37 (3): 549–87.

Harman, G. (1974) "Review of *Meaning* by S. Schiffer," *Journal of Philosophy* 71: 224–9.

——— (1977) "Review of Jonathan Bennett's Linguistic Behaviour," *Language* 53 (2): 417–24.

Heal, J. (1978) "Common Knowledge," *The Philosophical Quarterly* 28 (111): 116–31.

Heinemann, F., Nagel, R. and Ockenfels, P. (2004) "The Theory of Global Games on Test: Experimental Analysis of Coordination Games with Public and Private Information," *Econometrica* 72 (5): 1583–99.

Jankovic, M. (2014) "Communication and Shared Information," *Philosophical Studies* 169 (3): 489–508.

Kinderman, P., Dunbar, R. and Bentall, R.P. (1998) "Theory-of-Mind Deficits and Causal Attributions," *British Journal of Psychology*. 89 (2): 191–204.

Kölbel, M. (2011) "What Is Assertion?" in J. Brown and H. Cappelen (eds) *Assertion: New Philosophical Essays*, Oxford: Oxford University Press.

Lederman, H. (2017) "Two Paradoxes of Common Knowledge: Coordinated Attack and the Electronic Mail Game," *Noûs*, doi:10.1111/nous.12186.

——— (forthcoming) "Uncommon Knowledge," *Mind*.

Lee, J.J. and Pinker, S. (2010) "Rationales for Indirect Speech: The Theory of the Strategic Speaker," *Psychological Review* 117 (3): 785–807.

Lewis, D. (1975) "Languages and Language," *Minnesota Studies in the Philosophy of Science* 7: 3–35.

——— (1969) *Convention: A Philosophical Study*, Cambridge, MA: Harvard University Press.

Lismont, L. and Mongin, P. (2003) "Strong Completeness Theorems for Weak Logics of Common Belief," *Journal of Philosophical Logic* 32 (2): 115–37.

Mertens, J.-F. and Zamir, S. (1985) "Formulation of Bayesian Analysis for Games with Incomplete Information," *International Journal of Game Theory* 14 (1): 1–29.

Milgrom, P. (1981) "An Axiomatic Characterization of Common Knowledge," *Econometrica: Journal of the Econometric Society* 49: 219–22.

Monderer, D. and Samet, D. (1989) "Approximating Common Knowledge with Common Beliefs," *Games and Economic Behavior* 1 (2): 170–90.

Morris, S. (1999) "Approximate Common Knowledge Revisited," *International Journal of Game Theory* 28 (3): 385–408.

——— (2002) "Coordination, Communication, and Common Knowledge: A Retrospective on the Electronic-Mail Game," *Oxford Review of Economic Policy* 18 (4): 433–45.

——— (2014) "Coordination, Timing and Common Knowledge," *Research in Economics* 68 (4): 306–14.

Moses, Y.O. (1986) "Knowledge in a Distributed Environment," Ph.D. thesis, Stanford University.

Paternotte, C. (2011) "Being Realistic About Common Knowledge: A Lewisian Approach," *Synthese* 183 (2) Springer: 249–76.

——— (2016) "The Fragility of Common Knowledge," *Erkenntnis?* 1–22.

Peacocke, C. (2005) "Joint Attention: Its Nature, Reflexivity, and Relation to Common Knowledge," in N. Eilan, C. Hoerl, T. McCormack, and J. Roessler (eds) *Joint Attention: Communication and Other Minds*, Oxford: Oxford University Press.

Pinker, S. (2007) "The Evolutionary Social Psychology of Off-Record Indirect Speech Acts," *Intercultural Pragmatics* 4 (4): 437–61.

Pinker, S., Nowak, M.A. and Lee, J.J. (2008) "The Logic of Indirect Speech," *Proceedings of the National Academy of Sciences* 105 (3): 833–8.

Radford, C. (1969) "Knowing and Telling," *The Philosophical Review* 78 (3): 326–36.

Rubinstein, A. (1989) "The Electronic Mail Game: Strategic Behavior Under 'Almost Common Knowledge'," *The American Economic Review* 79 (3): 385–91.

Schiffer, S.R. (1972) *Meaning*, Oxford: Oxford University Press.

Sperber, D. and Wilson, D. (1986) *Relevance: Communication and Cognition*, Oxford: Blackwell.

Stalnaker, R. (1998) "On the Representation of Context," *Journal of Logic, Language and Information* 7 (1): 3–19.

——— (2002) "Common Ground," *Linguistics and Philosophy* 25 (5): 701–21.

Stalnaker, R.C. (1978) "Assertion," in P. Cole (ed.) *Syntax and Semantics*, 9, New York: Academic Press.

——— (2009) "On Hawthorne and Magidor on Assertion, Context, and Epistemic Accessibility," *Mind* 118 (470): 399–409.

——— (2014) *Context*, Oxford: Oxford University Press.

Stiller, J. and Dunbar, R.I.M. (2007) "Perspective-Taking and Memory Capacity Predict Social Network Size," *Social Networks* 29 (1): 93–104.

Strawson, P.F. (1964) "Intention and Convention in Speech Acts," *The Philosophical Review* 73 (4): 439–60.

Thomas, K.A., DeScioli, P., Haque, O.S. and Pinker, S. (2014) "The Psychology of Coordination and Common Knowledge," *Journal of Personality and Social Psychology* 107 (4): 657.

Tuomela, R. and Miller, K. (1988) "We-Intentions," *Philosophical Studies* 53 (3): 367–89.

Vanderschraaf, P. and Sillari, G. (2014) "Common Knowledge," in E.N. Zalta (ed.) *The Stanford Encyclopedia of Philosophy* (Spring 2014), http://plato.stanford.edu/archives/spr2014/entries/common-knowledge/.

NOTES

1. For coordination, see Lewis (1969), Heal (1978), Moses (1986), Halpern and Moses (1990), Fagin et al. (1995: ch. 6, ch. 11), Fagin et al. (1999), Morris (2002), Morris (2014), Heinemann, Nagel, and Ockenfels (2004), Thomas et al. (2014). For joint attention, see Peacocke (2005) (although cf. Campbell (2002: ch. 8)). For shared intention, see Tuomela and Miller (1988: 375), Bratman (1992: 335 with note 15), Bratman (1993 passim, with note 8), Bratman (2014: 5 with note 9), Fine (2012), cf. Gilbert (1990: 3). For communication and speaker meaning, see Strawson (1964), Grice (1969), Schiffer (1972), Sperber et al. (1986), and Jankovic (2014). For innuendo, see Clark (1979), Pinker (2007), Pinker, Nowak, and Lee (2008), Lee and Pinker (2010). For conversational context, see Radford (1969), Stalnaker (1978, 1998, 2002, 2014), Clark (1996) (although cf. Kölbel (2011)). For conventions, see Lewis (1969, 1975). For social norms, see Bicchieri and Muldoon (2014) and references therein. For social groups, see Gilbert (1989). A number of concrete examples of social practices are discussed in Chwe (2001) (see also Friedell 1969).

2. Neither of these technical senses is supposed to explicate the ordinary language uses of the expression "common knowledge," for example, the sense in which facts in an encyclopedia are common knowledge.

3. This is also intended as a technical term. For example, I take it that "public information" as it is used to describe corporate disclosures is not synonymous with "public information" in my sense.

4. I will present the argument using the notion of public information, although Greco himself does not. Early versions of this argument can be found in Heal (1978) and Clark and Marshall (1981). Throughout this section I focus on common knowledge, but all of the considerations I describe could also be applied, *mutatis mutandis* to common belief or common certainty.

5. In older work, e.g. Schiffer (1972), "mutual knowledge" is sometimes used synonymously with "common knowledge." But the terminology in the main text has now become standard; see, e.g. Fagin et al. (1995).

6. In the cases I have taken from Greco, if the students have mutual knowledge^n that the professor is from Maine, they also falsely believe that they do not have mutual knowledge^n that the professor is from Maine. Having the announcement generate this additional false belief simplifies the presentation (and strengthens the intuition), but it is inessential. We could alter this aspect of the teacher's announcement, while preserving the intuitive difference between PUBLIC ANNOUNCEMENT and the other cases.

7. In Kinderman et al. (1998) and Stiller and Dunbar (2007), people were found to be essentially at chance in remembering reports involving six nested attitudes. So even if the reader is unhappy with this response to this case, it becomes even more plausible, for example, for mutual knowledge^7.

8. For a different kind of argument against the view that people have public information that p just in case they have mutual knowledge^k that p, see Heal (1978: 125).

9. This alternative strategy might be supported by the suggestion that the examples above prove too much: one can construct an elaboration of them that might suggest that even common knowledge would be insufficient for public information:

> SUPERTASK SECRETS: As in EVEN MORE PRIVATE INFORMATION, but the teacher programs a computer to broadcast the message to the students, and the computer and students are all capable of supertasks. At first the students receive a message which simply says that the teacher is from Maine. After this, at intervals of $\frac{1}{2^n}$ seconds each student's screen displays a new line, saying: 'the others know that together you have mutual knowledge^n that the teacher is from Maine, but do not know that you know this'.

This case is hard to think about it. But some may be inclined to claim that, although the super-students have common knowledge that the professor is from Maine, they do not have public information of this fact.

10. Margaret Gilbert comes closest to advocating this thesis in so many words; Gilbert (1989: 186–97); cf. Gilbert (2008).

11. This approach is most closely associated with the work of Barwise (1988); cf. Mertens and Zamir (1985). Further definitions of a related kind may be found in: Lewis (1969) (cf. Cubitt and Sugden (2003) and Paternotte (2011)); Harman (1977: 422) (cf. Harman (1974: 225), Peacocke (2005: 307–8)); Heal (1978); Milgrom (1981); Clark and Marshall (1981); and Clark and Carlson (1982). Lismont and Mongin (2003) give a clear, simple presentation of some definitions in this family.

12. For simplicity, I use a language that allows quantification into sentence position, and take "entails that" (somewhat unnaturally) to be a binary sentential operator. The argument is not particularly delicate and could be conducted in many other settings, for example, using only first-order quantification, a notion of propositional truth, and entailment understood as a relation between propositions.

First some definitions: q is *mutually entailed by what some agents know* if there is a p such that they mutually know that p, and p entails that q; q is mutually^n entailed by what some agents know if there is a p such that they mutually know p, and p entails that q is mutually^{n-1} entailed by what they know. Finally q is commonly entailed by what some agents know just in case for all n, q is mutually^n entailed by what they know.

We can show that if some people satisfy SHARED ENVIRONMENT with regard to p, then p is commonly entailed by what they know, using four additional assumptions about entailment. The first assumption relies on the idea that propositions are closed under a countable conjunction operation: ENTAILMENT CONJUNCTION-IN: if p entails that q_a for every $q_a \in \{q_a\}_{a \in A}$ where A is countable, then p entails that $\wedge_{a \in A} q_a$. Second, DETACHMENT: if it is the case that q and q entails that p, then p. Third, ENTAILMENT OF ENTAILMENT: if p entails that q, then r entails that $[p$ entails that $q]$. Fourth, EXISTENTIAL INTRODUCTION: if p entails that $\varphi(q)$, where q is a sentence variable, then p entails that $\exists r \varphi(r)$, where $\exists$ is a quantifier for the type of sentences, and r is a variable of the corresponding type. This fourth principle allows quantifying in, in sentence position: if p entails that S knows q, then p entails that there is something S knows.

Given the above laws, we first prove a lemma: if p entails that everyone knows that q, and if q entails that s, then p entails that there is an r such that [everyone knows that r, and r entails that s]. The proof first uses ENTAILMENT OF ENTAILMENT, then ENTAILMENT CONJUNCTION-IN, and finally EXISTENTIAL INTRODUCTION.

Now, given SHARED ENVIRONMENT, and supposing that some agents have public information that p, there is an E such that E entails that everyone knows E and such that E entails that p. So, by the lemma, E entails that there is an r such that everyone knows that r and such that r entails that p. That's the base case of an induction: E entails that p is mutually[1] entailed by what everyone knows. Now for the induction hypothesis, we suppose that E entails that p is mutually^n entailed by what all know, and show that E entails that p is mutually^{n+1} entailed by what all know. Since E entails that all know that E, and by hypothesis E entails that p is mutually^n entailed by what they know, then again by the lemma, E entails that there is some r such that they all know r and r entails that p is mutually^n entailed by what all know. So, by definition E entails that p is mutually^{n+1} entailed by what everyone knows. This induction shows that for all n, E entails that p is mutually^n entailed by what all know, so by ENTAILMENT CONJUNCTION-IN, E entails that p is commonly entailed by what they know. Given that the agents in fact have public information that p, it is the case that E, so by DETACHMENT p is commonly entailed by what they know.

If the agents in question are ideal, and ideal knowledge is closed under entailment (in the sense that if p entails that q and the agent knows that p then the agent knows that q), the same argument can be used to show that they have common knowledge that p, and not merely that p is commonly entailed by what they know. Perhaps a more plausible assumption, that ideal knowledge is closed only under known entailments, would require different background assumptions; the point here has just been to give a worked example of how this kind of view implies IDEAL COMMON KNOWLEDGE.

13. Chant and Ernst (2008) and Lederman (2017) give further discussion of the philosophical import of arguments about the relationship between common knowledge and coordination.

14. I present a variant of the original electronic mail game, which appeared in Morris (2002). Rubinstein used a slightly different game and obtained a slightly weaker result.

15. Note that the standard technical notion of "common p-belief" is in fact defined by analogy to SHARED ENVIRONMENT, and not by analogy to the "iterated" definition given at the start of this article. These definitions coincide if $p = 1$, but they come apart if $p < 1$. For discussion of these differences see Morris (1999). Paternotte (2016) is a recent discussion of differences between common belief and common p-belief, given one popular way of relating belief and p-belief.

16. For an argument of this kind, see Greco (2014a, 2014b).

15

Collective Epistemology

Jennifer Lackey

Groups[1] are often described as having beliefs. We talk about police departments believing that their officers acted reasonably, universities believing that academic freedom ought to be upheld, and governments believing that their citizens have the right to carry concealed weapons. Some of these beliefs amount to knowledge while others do not, with epistemic justification being one of the central features distinguishing these two categories. But how should we understand a *group's justifiedly believing* that *p*?[2]

1. AN INFLATIONARY APPROACH

This question is at the center of work in collective epistemology, and much of the work that has been done on justified group belief can be broadly divided into two different camps. On the one hand, there are those who favor an *inflationary* approach, where groups are treated as entities with "minds of their own." Groups on this model are something more than the mere collection of their members, and group states are distinct from the states of individuals. Such an inflationary approach is typically supported through divergence arguments, which purport to show that a phenomenon can be had at the group level despite the complete absence of it at the individual level. In particular, it is claimed that a group can justifiedly believe that *p*, even though not a single one of its members justifiedly believes that *p*.[3] Consider the following:

DIFFERENT EVIDENCE: A jury is deliberating about whether the defendant in a murder trial is innocent or guilty. Each member of the jury is privy to evidence that the defendant was seen fleeing the scene of the crime with blood spatter on his clothes, but it is grounded in hearsay that, though reliable, was ruled as inadmissible by the judge. Given only the admissible evidence, the jury as a group justifiedly believes that the defendant is innocent, but not a single juror justifiedly

196

believes this proposition because it is defeated for each of them as individuals by the relevant reliable hearsay evidence.

Cases of this sort are prevalent in the collective epistemology literature, but Schmitt (1994) provides the most developed and detailed version.[4] According to Schmitt, different evidence cases successfully function as divergence arguments only when they involve chartered groups, where '[a] chartered group is one founded to perform a particular action or actions of a certain kind', and 'has no life apart from its office' (1994: 272–3). In other words, chartered groups must function only in their offices or risk ceasing to exist. The US Congress, the Sierra Club, and juries are all groups of this sort. Moreover, given the particular charter of a group, it may be governed by special epistemic standards, such as the exclusion of hearsay in a court of law. Since the jury in DIFFERENT EVIDENCE is a chartered group, Schmitt argues that its charter prohibits it from considering the hearsay evidence about the defendant fleeing the scene of the crime with blood spatter on his clothes. Without this crucial testimony, the jury justifiedly believes that the defendant is innocent of the murder in question. But since the jurors qua individuals are not governed by these special standards of available reasons, they each have a defeater provided by the hearsay evidence for believing in the defendant's innocence. Thus, the jury justifiedly believes that the defendant is innocent despite the fact that not a single individual member justifiedly holds this belief.

This purported divergence between what happens at the group level and at the level of the individual members leads most philosophers to endorse an inflationary view of group justification, with the most widely accepted being a version of the joint acceptance account. On this view, whether something counts as a reason possessed by a group is determined by its members jointly accepting it, or being such that the group would jointly accept it, as the group's reason. While acceptance does not require belief, it brings with it a commitment to act as if the accepted proposition is true. The epistemic goodness or badness of the group's reason is then fleshed out in terms of traditional justification-conferring features, such as being produced by a reliable process, being grounded in adequate evidence, and so on.[5]

One of the central virtues of the joint acceptance account is its ability to account for how groups can justifiedly hold beliefs that no single member justifiedly believes. For instance, in DIFFERENT EVIDENCE, we can easily explain how the jury justifiedly believes the defendant is innocent without a single juror justifiedly believing this: as a group, the members of the jury accept only the admissible evidence, and thus justifiedly believe the defendant is innocent. However, the individual members not only don't believe that the defendant is innocent, they also don't have justification for believing it, as the hearsay evidence provides them with counterevidence.

There is, however, a problem with the joint acceptance account that cuts to the heart of the view.[6] Consider the following:

IGNORING EVIDENCE: Philip Morris is one of the largest tobacco companies in the world, and each of its members is individually aware of the massive amounts of scientific evidence revealing the links it has with lung cancer. Moreover, each individual member believes that the dangers of smoking give the company a reason to believe that warning labels should be placed on cigarette boxes.

However, because of what is at stake financially and legally, none of these members would accept that the dangers of smoking give Philip Morris a reason to believe that it should put warning labels on cigarette boxes.

Does Philip Morris have a reason to believe that it should put warning labels on cigarette boxes? Clearly, yes. Every member of this group is aware of the scientific evidence showing the dangers of smoking and believes that warning labels should be put on cigarette boxes. The mere fact that the company illegitimately ignores relevant evidence through dogmatically refusing to jointly accept what is not to its liking should not result in its not having this reason, too. This conclusion is supported by noticing that we would surely hold Philip Morris responsible for the ill effects caused by smoking precisely because we take it to have a good reason to warn people about the dangers of cigarettes. Yet, according to the joint acceptance account, Philip Morris does not have a reason to put warning labels on cigarette boxes. Indeed, were the company to do so, it would be acting without a reason.

It is just a small step from here to show that the joint acceptance account also leads to problematic results regarding the epistemic justification of group beliefs. Consider IGNORING EVIDENCE, again: given that all of the evidence showing that smoking is dangerous is not available to the group because of the members' refusal to jointly accept it, none of it is part of the justificatory basis of the group's belief. It is, then, not at all difficult to imagine scenarios in which the remaining evidence leaves the group justifiedly believing that smoking does not pose any health hazards. For instance, the group might have access to some studies that, though reliably conducted, had a very limited sample of subjects, none of whom happened to develop lung cancer despite years of smoking. In this case, Philip Morris's "belief" that smoking is not unhealthy would be reliably formed and, given the total evidence available, well-grounded, thereby being epistemically justified. But this result is absurd.

The upshot of these considerations is that joint acceptance cannot ground the justification of group beliefs. In particular, IGNORING EVIDENCE makes clear that group justification cannot be wholly determined *by factors over which the members of the group have direct voluntary control*. For it is this voluntary control that enables the members of Philip Morris to simply decide to not jointly accept what they should. Because of this, joint acceptance can be guided by factors that are *utterly disconnected from the truth*, such as the economic and legal goals of a company. Thus, any account of group justification that relies entirely on joint acceptance succumbs to what might be called the *Illegitimate Manipulation of Evidence Problem*:

> If the justification of group beliefs can be achieved through wholly voluntary means, then the evidence available to the group can be illegitimately manipulated, thereby severing the connection between group epistemic justification and truth-conduciveness.

Given that the joint acceptance account clearly faces this problem, we need to look elsewhere for an account of the justification of group beliefs.

Returning to DIFFERENT EVIDENCE, recall that the standard interpretation of this sort of case is that, while the jury as a group justifiedly believes that the defendant is innocent, none of the jurors justifiedly believe this proposition because their justification is defeated by the relevant reliable hearsay evidence. But why, it might be asked, should we think that the notion of justification is epistemic in both evaluations? The reason that there might be the inclination to say that the jury justifiedly believes that the defendant is innocent is because hearsay evidence is deemed inadmissible by the court. However, being inadmissible is clearly not the same as being unreliable or otherwise non-truth-conducive. Consider, for instance, that 'hearsay evidence is generally not admissible because it may place crucial evidence before the court without allowing the other side to confront the person who is being quoted to challenge the accuracy of the statement or the credibility of the person who made it'.[7] The problem with hearsay evidence mentioned here is not that it is more likely to be unreliable or lacking in evidential value, but rather that the opposing side is denied the possibility of confronting the source of the information. This is a practical or procedural concern, but not necessarily an epistemic one. This is made clear by the fact that we can imagine a piece of hearsay evidence that has been produced by a far more reliable process and is better grounded in evidence than a piece of first-hand evidence. Nevertheless, the former would be inadmissible in a court of law, while the latter would not be. Given this, the mere fact that something is ruled inadmissible does not necessarily reveal anything about its epistemic status.

Applying these considerations to DIFFERENT EVIDENCE, the reliable hearsay evidence that the defendant was seen fleeing the scene of the crime with blood spatter on his clothes is highly epistemically relevant to the jury's beliefs, even if the rules of the court prohibit it from being factored into their verdict. This shows that while both the jury and the individual jurors justifiedly believe that the defendant is guilty in an *epistemic sense*, the jury is *legally justified* in believing that the defendant is innocent. This is because, as was mentioned above, the law's exclusion of hearsay evidence can be radically disconnected from truth-conduciveness, which is precisely what we find in DIFFERENT EVIDENCE. Thus, this case fails to establish what divergence arguments purport to show: namely, that the epistemic justification of a group's beliefs can diverge from the epistemic justification of the beliefs of its individual members.

2. A DEFLATIONARY APPROACH

In light of the problems facing an inflationary approach to understanding the justification of group beliefs, a natural response is to move toward a *deflationary* one, according to which groups do not have minds of their own and group states are nothing more than collections of individual states. The most widely accepted deflationary view is what has come to be known as summativism, according to which the justification of a group's belief is understood simply in terms of the justification of the individual members' beliefs. More precisely, a group's justifiedly believing a proposition is understood in terms of some or all of the group's members justifiedly believing that proposition.

Deflationary summativism draws inspiration from a judgment aggregation framework.[8] 'Aggregation procedures are mechanisms a multimember group can use to combine ("aggregate") the individual beliefs or judgments held by the group members into collective beliefs or judgments endorsed by the group as a whole' (List 2005: 25).[9] For instance, a majority procedure understands group belief in terms of the beliefs of a majority of its individual members. This framework for aggregating member judgments into collective ones can easily be extended to justified beliefs. Indeed, in recent work,[10] Alvin Goldman does just this and, in so doing, provides the most detailed deflationary summativist view to date. According to Goldman, there are two different conceptions of group justification within an aggregative framework—what he calls *horizontal* and *vertical* justifiedness. The best way to understand these notions is to consider the following case:

> DIFFERENT BASES: G is a group whose members consist of 100 guards at the British Museum, M_1-M_{100}. Each of the first 20 guards, M_1-M_{20}, justifiedly believes that guard Albert is planning an inside theft of a famous painting (= A). By deduction from A, each of them infers the (existential) proposition that there is a guard who is planning such a theft (= T). The remaining 80 guards do not believe and are not justified in believing A. Each of the second 20 guards, M_{21}-M_{40}, justifiedly believes that Bernard is planning an inside theft (= B), and deductively infers T from B. The other 80 members do not believe B and are not justified in believing B. Each of a third group of 20 members, M_{41}-M_{60}, justifiedly believes that guard Cecil is planning an inside theft (= C) and deductively infers T from C. The 80 others do not believe and are not justified in believing C. Thus, 60 members of G (justifiedly) believe T by deduction from some premise he/she justifiedly believes.
>
> (Goldman 2014: 16)

Most of the leading aggregation procedures—e.g. supermajoritarian and majoritarian—have the result that G believes T. But does G justifiedly believe this proposition? Goldman writes:

> . . . G's belief in T may be considered from two perspectives: the *horizontal* perspective and the *vertical* perspective. The horizontal perspective addresses the question of the J-status of G's belief in T solely in terms of other beliefs of G, i.e., *group-level* beliefs. . . . G's belief in T is unjustified in terms of horizontal J-dependence. This is because, although G believes T, G does not infer T from any justified group-level belief of its own. The situation is different, however, when we consider G's belief in T by reference to *vertical J-dependence*. Consider all of the members' beliefs in T and the proportion of them that are justified. . . . given . . . [the] vertical criterion of J-dependence, G's belief in T *is* justified (because 60% of G's members justifiedly believe T).
>
> (Goldman 2014: 18)

On Goldman's view, then, G justifiedly believes that someone is planning an inside theft at the museum when vertical justifiedness is considered, that is, when the justificational status of the group's belief is determined, not by the group's beliefs, but by all of the members' relevant beliefs and the proportion of them that are justified. In particular, because the individual members have different bases for their beliefs that someone is planning a theft, there is no group-level basis from which the group's belief to this effect can be justifiedly inferred. Hence, there is no horizontal justification. But if the group's belief that someone is planning a theft is viewed independently of a group-level basis, then the proportion of the members' relevant beliefs that are justified render it vertically justified. Indeed, it is precisely this vertical perspective that Goldman adopts when offering his positive account of the justification of group beliefs.

Moreover, Goldman claims that it is preferable to think of justifiedness as a matter of degree, and thus to regard it as a gradable notion instead of a categorical one. Rather than sketch a full-blown theory of justificational gradability for collective entities, however, he offers a few sample principles so as to give a sense of the results such a theory will deliver. Assuming that members' doxastic attitudes have categorical justificational status, a central principle is the following:

(GJ) If a group belief that p is aggregated based on a profile of member attitudes toward that p, then (*ceteris paribus*) the greater the proportion of members who justifiedly *believe* that p and the smaller the proportion of members who justifiedly *reject* that p, the greater the group's level, or grade, of justifiedness in believing that p.

(Goldman 2014: 28)

On Goldman's view, the justificational statuses of members' doxastic attitudes depend on the processes by which they severally arrived at their respective attitudes and, as (GJ) makes clear, the justificational status of the group belief depends on the justificational statuses of the members' attitudes. Put succinctly, group justifiedness increases with a greater percentage of individual member justifiedness.

Despite the intuitive plausibility of this deflationary approach to understanding group justification, there is a significant problem, which I call the *Group Justification Paradox*. Consider the following:

CONFLICTING BASES: G is a group whose members consist of 100 guards at the British Museum, M_1-M_{100}, each of whom justifiedly believes that an inside theft of a famous painting is being planned by only one of a total of five possible guards—Albert, Bernard, Cecil, David, and Edmund. Each of the first 20 guards, M_1-M_{20}, justifiedly believes that only guard Albert is planning the inside theft (= A). By deduction from A, each of them infers the (existential) proposition that there is a guard who is planning such a theft (= T). The remaining 80 guards do not believe and are not justified in believing A. Each of the second 20 guards, M_{21}-M_{40}, justifiedly believes that only Bernard is planning the inside theft (= B), and deductively infers T from B. The other 80 guards do not believe and are not justified in believing B. Each of a third group of 20 members, M_{41}-M_{60}, justifiedly believes that only guard Cecil is planning the inside theft (= C) and deductively infers T from C. The 80 others do not believe and are not justified in believing C. Each of a fourth group of 20 members, M_{61}-M_{80}, justifiedly believes that only guard David is planning the inside theft (= D) and deductively infers T from D. The remaining 80 guards do not believe and are not justified in believing D. The final group of 20 members, M_{81}-M_{100}, justifiedly believes that only guard Edmund is planning the inside theft (= E) and deductively infers T from E. The 80 others do not believe and are not justified in believing E. Thus, 100 members of G justifiedly believe T by deduction from some premise he/she justifiedly believes.[11]

In the original DIFFERENT BASES, 60 out of 100 members of G justifiedly believe that there is a guard who is planning an inside theft of a famous painting at the museum and, thus, the group itself justifiedly believes this proposition. In CONFLICTING BASES, 100 out of 100 members of G justifiedly believe that there is a guard who is planning an inside theft of a famous painting at the museum and, thus, the group again justifiedly believes this proposition. According to (GJ), then, the group's level of justifiedness is greater in CONFLICTING BASES than it is in DIFFERENT BASES since the proportion of members who justifiedly hold the relevant proposition in the former is greater than in the latter.

But let us take a closer look at CONFLICTING BASES. Each of the first 20 guards, M_1-M_{20}, justifiedly believes that only guard Albert is planning the inside theft. Given this, combined with the fact that all of the guards are aware that Albert, Bernard, Cecil, David, and Edmund are the only possible thieves, each of these 20 guards also justifiedly believes that Bernard, Cecil, David, and Edmund are not planning the theft. Each of the second 20 guards, M_{21}-M_{40}, justifiedly believes that only Bernard is planning the inside theft and, given their other background beliefs, also justifiedly believes that Albert, Cecil, David, and Edmund are not planning the theft. Similar considerations apply with respect to the other three subgroups: each believes that one, and only one, guard is planning the theft, and believes that the other four possible guards are not so planning.[12]

We are now in a position to see the Group Justification Paradox unfold; for each of the five possible candidates of the theft in question, 80 out of 100 guards justifiedly believe that he is not planning it. According to nearly every judgment aggregation function, it follows from this that the group, G, also justifiedly believes that each of the five possible candidates is not planning the theft. Since the group justifiedly recognizes that Albert, Bernard, Cecil, David, and Edmund are the only possible candidates for planning the theft, the group justifiedly believing that none of them is planning the theft amounts to the group justifiedly believing that no one is planning the theft. But, according to the vertical perspective, G also justifiedly believes that someone is planning an inside theft of a famous painting at the British Museum since 100 members justifiedly believe this. (GJ) thus leads to what we might call the Group Justification Paradox: G ends up justifiedly believing both that no one is planning the theft and that someone is planning the theft.[13]

3. A CONDORCET-INSPIRED ACCOUNT OF JUSTIFIED GROUP BELIEF

There is another approach to characterizing justified group belief that should be considered, one that is inspired by the Condorcet jury theorem and developed in the work of Christian List.[14] Though List presents his account specifically as one of group knowledge, it can be adapted for our purposes here. In particular, on this view, (1) the theory of judgment aggregation is followed in holding that a group's belief *simpliciter* is a function of the members' individual beliefs, but (2) *being justified* is understood as a collective property that a group's belief may or may not have, depending on whether it satisfies certain "truth-tracking" or "reliability" conditions at the group level. For instance, it has been shown that each of a committee members' individual beliefs might be only very slightly better than random at "tracking the truth," thereby meeting only the very minimal Condorcetian "greater than 1/2" probability-of-correctness condition, but, nevertheless, a sufficiently large committee of independent individuals could be very close to perfect in its collective reliability.[15] On a truth-tracking or reliabilist conception of justification, then, the group belief that p might be regarded as justified, even though each of the underlying individual beliefs falls short of the threshold required for counting as such.

Unlike Goldman's deflationary summativist view, then, justified group belief on this Condorcet-inspired picture is *not* merely an aggregate of justified individual beliefs. Rather, a justified group belief may be an aggregate of individual beliefs, all of which are unjustified, yet where the group belief meets the relevant truth-tracking or reliability conditions at the collective level. And unlike inflationary non-summativism, justified group belief *is* constructed out of the epistemic features of the individual beliefs of the group's members. It is just that the level of justification at the collective level outstrips what is possessed by any single belief. This presents a view of justified group belief that does not fit neatly into either the inflationary non-summativist or the deflationary summativist camp, and also seems to tell against requiring justified belief at the level of individual members. For if this view is correct, then individually justified beliefs—of any sort or quantity—are not necessary for justified group belief.[16]

It is undeniable that this Condorcet-inspired approach shows that there can be epistemic value at the level of the group's belief that is not present at the level of any of the individual beliefs. But the question that I want to focus on is whether this value is plausibly regarded as *epistemic justification*.

The first point to emphasize is that this view counts as justified group beliefs that have an inappropriate epistemic grounding, both at the individual and at the collective level. Let's begin with the former; notice that in order for there to be justified group belief on this picture, the central requirements are (i) that the group have a large enough number of independent members who (ii) satisfy the "greater than 1/2" probability-of-correctness condition. But then a group could go about achieving epistemic justifiedness simply by extending membership to more and more people, with no regard whatsoever to the grounds of the individual beliefs beyond independence. Suppose, for instance, that we are talking about a scientific research group: it wouldn't matter whether the members believe that p on the basis of experimental results or some biased testimony, via methodical research or wishful thinking. So long as (i) and (ii) are met, group justifiedness can be, too. Indeed, rather than checking the CVs of potential members and evaluating the epistemic quality of the relevant individual beliefs, a research group could achieve justified group belief by simply surveying the beliefs of individuals and recruiting a large enough number of members who satisfy (i) and (ii). There's no need for any members to go to the expense of actually conducting experiments.

This leads to a related, though slightly different, concern: the grounds of the individual beliefs of members *surely matter* to the justifiedness of the group, yet this Condorcet-inspired view cannot account for this. A group with members all of whom performed excellent scientific experiments would clearly be better justified in its resulting scientific belief that p than one where they all held the same belief because of independent idiosyncratic websites. The former group would, for instance, be quite likely to have a great deal of p-related beliefs that are justified, to be able to draw appropriate inferences regarding that p, to have the capacity to explain why that p is the case, and so on, while the latter group would not. Even if none of these features is necessary for group justifiedness, they surely have the capacity to affect the level or grade of epistemic justification present.

But if the truth-tracking or reliability at the collective level of the two groups is equivalent, then the Condorcet-inspired view counts them as equally justified in their respective beliefs. In fact, if the group's belief grounded in idiosyncratic websites is slightly more reliable than the one based on excellent scientific experiments, then it would have a greater level of justifiedness, despite the fact that its basis is wildly inappropriate from a scientific point of view.

So far, the focus has been on the bases of the individual members, but there are also similar concerns that could be raised at the level of the group and its structure. A group that luckily stumbles into reliability at the collective level through having a large enough group of members who believe that p and satisfy (i) and (ii) could end up more justified than one that sets up a structure where, for instance, evidence is vigilantly gathered, shared among members, and checked multiple times over. Or a group that isolates members and forces them to obtain information from epistemically questionable sources could end up more justified than one that engages in collective deliberation and forms beliefs on the basis of pooled evidence that has been scrutinized. In this way, the Condorcet-inspired approach lacks the resources for allowing group justifiedness to be affected by the way in which truth-tracking or reliability is achieved at the collective level.

There are also considerations involving group action that tell against this approach. At a minimum, there is a close connection between a group believing that p and its being epistemically permissible for such a group to act as if p.[17] Without making any commitments here about this connection being one of either necessity or sufficiency, we can surely say that if one justifiedly believes that p, then it is *generally* the case that it is epistemically permissible for one to act as if p. It is also the case that groups cannot offer assertions, engage in negotiations, sign contracts, break the law, or perform any of the other sorts of actions typically attributed to groups without there being action on the part of some of its members. Of course, this does not mean that for every group, G, and act, a, G performs a only if at least one member of G performs a. It may be that one member performs action b, and another performs action c, and still another performs action d, which, when taken together, involves G performing a. But it is the case that for every group, G, and act, a, G performs a only if at least one member of G performs some act or other that causally contributes to a. Moreover, for many groups, particular members are granted the authority to serve as proxy agents, where this means that the actions performed by such individuals count as actions of the group.[18] For instance, a spokesperson might be given the authority to testify on behalf of a corporation, a CEO the authority to purchase property for a company, and an administrator the authority to deny a colleague tenure for the college. Notice, however, that in each of these cases, justified belief at the level of the individuals serving as proxy agents is crucial for rendering the group actions in question epistemically permissible. If, for instance, the administrator believes that the colleague should be denied tenure merely because, say, a department member with a grudge told him so, then the denial of tenure is clearly epistemically improper. In particular, the administrator is not properly epistemically positioned to deny the colleague tenure, given such a poor basis. This is even clearer if we assume that there is no member of the College who has a basis that is epistemically better than the administrator's. But if justified group belief is entirely severed from the justified beliefs of members, as the Condorcet-inspired approach does, then such a denial of tenure could turn out to be entirely permissible.[19]

For all of these reasons, the Condorcet-inspired view might point to features of groups that are undoubtedly epistemically valuable, but it is doubtful whether they track justified group belief.

4. A GROUP EPISTEMIC AGENT ACCOUNT

The paradigmatic versions of both inflationary and deflationary views of justification suffer from debilitating objections. The joint acceptance account treats groups as epistemic entities that can float freely of the evidential profiles of their individual members. For instance, as IGNORING EVIDENCE reveals, even if every member of Philip Morris possesses massive amounts of scientific evidence revealing the links between smoking and lung cancer, such a view permits groups to choose not to accept this evidence and thereby end up justifiedly believing that smoking does not pose a health hazard. But groups cannot pick and choose what evidence is available to them—they are constrained by the evidence possessed by their individual members. This is the central lesson of the Illegitimate Manipulation of Evidence Problem.

In contrast, the aggregative account altogether avoids concerns associated with this problem by securing a close dependence of group justifiedness on member justifiedness. But this is done at the cost of failing to appreciate the distinctive epistemic issues that arise at the group level. For the proponent of the aggregative account, group justifiedness is a simple "justified belief in/justified belief out" matter. Yet we have seen that this model ignores the complexity of justified belief at the group level, particularly the evidential relations that exist between members' beliefs and the bases, or grounds, for such beliefs.

Thus, the justified beliefs of groups should be treated neither as states that can float freely of the evidence possessed by their individual members, nor as nothing more than the aggregation of the justified beliefs of their members. Instead, groups should be understood as *epistemic agents in their own right*, though ones whose justified beliefs are constrained by the epistemic statuses of their individual members.

As a start, group justification should be grounded in the justification that at least some of the group's members have for the proposition in question—perhaps a significant percentage of those members who have decision-making authority in the domain in question. A group's belief, then, will inherit a strong, positive epistemic status from the members' justified beliefs in which it is based. These member beliefs will, in turn, be justified by whatever features are required at the individual level, such as that they are produced by reliable processes or grounded in adequate evidence.

In addition, group justification should depend, not only on the justification of the individual members' beliefs, but also on the bases for those beliefs. This is what was learned from CONFLICTING BASES: member justifiedness does not necessarily transmit smoothly to group justifiedness, since the bases of the members' beliefs might be wildly conflicting. When this happens, such a view faces the Group Justification Paradox. To avoid this problem, it is clear that group justification is possible only when the members' bases for their individual beliefs can be combined in a coherent belief set.

It should be clear that the inclusion of the first requirement altogether avoids the Illegitimate Manipulation of Evidence Problem afflicting inflationary views. One of the features that make the joint acceptance account susceptible to this objection is that the evidence available to the group can end up being a matter of choice. But if the justification of group beliefs is necessarily a matter of the justification of the beliefs of individual members, and the evidence that is available to individual subjects is not a matter of choice, then there is no worry that epistemic justification for group beliefs can be achieved through the illegitimate manipulation of evidence.

At the same time, it should also be apparent that including the second requirement denies justified group belief in CONFLICTING BASES and so avoids the Group Justification Paradox. In particular, adding together the bases of the museum guards' beliefs yields an incoherent set of beliefs. This results in the group failing to justifiedly believe that someone is planning a theft, despite the fact that all 100 members of the group justifiedly believe this. Since it was the attribution of justified belief to the group that generated the problem stemming from CONFLICTING BASES in the first place, it simply doesn't arise once this requirement is in place.

This, of course, is just a start to understanding group justification and, more broadly, when groups have knowledge.[20] But it is an important start. For including these two requirements—individual justification and the coherence of individual bases for belief—handles the problems facing the two dominant approaches to the justification of group beliefs. While inflationary theorists focus entirely on what a group *does*—i.e. whether its members engage in joint acceptance or not—deflationary ones focus exclusively on what a group *has*—i.e. whether its members' beliefs are individually justified. What is needed, however, is a view that incorporates both components. Groups should be understood as epistemic agents in their own right, ones that have evidential constraints that arise only at the group level, but group justifiedness should still significantly depend on member justifiedness. Walking this middle ground between inflating and deflating group epistemology promises to carve out space for both groups, and the individual members that make them up, to shoulder the responsibility of group actions.

REFERENCES

Bird, A. (2010) "Social Knowing: The Social Sense of 'Scientific Knowledge'," *Philosophical Perspectives* 24: 23–56.

Cariani, F. (2011) "Judgment Aggregation," *Philosophy Compass* 6: 22–32.

——— (2013) "Aggregating with Reasons," *Synthese* 190: 3123–47.

Dietrich, F. (2005) "Judgment Aggregation: (Im)possibility Theorems," *Journal of Economic Theory* 126: 286–98.

Fantl, J. and McGrath, M. (2002) "Evidence, Pragmatics, and Justification," *The Philosophical Review* 111: 67–94.

——— (2009) *Knowledge in an Uncertain World*, Oxford: Oxford University Press.

Gilbert, M. (1989) *On Social Facts*, New York: Routledge.

——— (2004) "Collective Epistemology," *Episteme* 1: 95–107.

Goldman, A.I. (2014) "Social Process Reliabilism: Solving Justification Problems in Collective Epistemology," in J. Lackey (ed.), *Essays in Collective Epistemology*, Oxford: Oxford University Press.

Hakli, R. (2011) "On Dialectical Justification of Group Beliefs," in H.B. Schmid, D. Sirtes and M. Weber (eds), *Collective Epistemology*, Frankfurt: Ontos Verlag.

Hawthorne, J. and Stanley, J. (2008) "Knowledge and Action," *The Journal of Philosophy* 105: 571–90.

Lackey, J. (2014) "Socially Extended Knowledge," *Philosophical Issues* 24: 282–98.

——— (forthcoming) "Group Lies," in E. Michaelson and A. Stokke (eds), *Lying: Language, Knowledge, Ethics, and Politics*, Oxford: Oxford University Press.

——— (2016) "What Is Justified Group Belief?" *The Philosophical Review* 125: 341–96.

——— (Unpublished) "Group Belief: Lessons from Lies and Bullshit."

List, C. (2005) "Group Knowledge and Group Rationality: A Judgment Aggregation Perspective," *Episteme* 2: 25–38.

List, C. and Pettit, P. (2002) "Aggregating Sets of Judgments: An Impossibility Result," *Economics and Philosophy* 18: 89–110.

——— (2004) "Aggregating Sets of Judgments: Two Impossibility Results Compared," *Synthese* 140: 207–35.

——— (2011) *Group Agency: The Possibility, Design, and Status of Corporate Agents*, Oxford: Oxford University Press.

Ludwig, K. (2014) "Proxy Agency in Collective Action," *Nôus* 48: 75–105.

Mathiesen, K. (2011) "Can Groups Be Epistemic Agents?" in H.B. Schmid, D. Sirtes and M. Weber (eds), *Collective Epistemology*, Frankfurt: Ontos Verlag.

Pauly, M. and van Heese, M. (2006) "Logical Constraints on Judgement Aggregation," *Journal of Philosophical Logic* 35: 569–85.

Pettit, P. (2003) "Groups with Minds of Their Own," in F. Schmitt (ed.), *Socializing Metaphysics*, New York: Rowman and Littlefield, 167–93.

Schmitt, F.F. (1994) "The Justification of Group Beliefs," in F.F. Schmitt (ed.), *Socializing Epistemology: The Social Dimensions of Knowledge*, Lanham, MD: Rowman & Littlefield.

Stanley, J. (2005) *Knowledge and Practical Interests*, Oxford: Oxford University Press.

Tuomela, R. (2004) "Group Knowledge Analyzed," *Episteme* 1: 109–27.

Williamson, T. (2005) "Contextualism, Subject-Sensitive Invariantism and Knowledge of Knowledge," *The Philosophical Quarterly* 55: 213–35.

NOTES

1. A discussion of what distinguishes a group from a mere collection of individuals lies beyond the scope of this paper, but see Gilbert (1989, 2004), Bird (2010), List and Pettit (2011), and Lackey (unpublished) for a treatment of this issue.

2. I will frequently speak simply of a "group justifiedly believing" a proposition, "group justification," or "group justifiedness." All of these locutions should be understood as involving group *epistemic* justification.

3. See, for instance, Schmitt (1994), Tuomela (2004), and Hakli (2011).

4. See, also, Gilbert (1989) and Mathiesen (2011).

5. See, for instance, Schmitt (1994) and Hakli (2011).

6. This is developed in detail in Lackey (2016).

7. Quoted from the Ohio State Bar Association at www.ohiobar.org/ForPublic/Resources/LawYouCanUse/Pages/LawYouCanUse-90.aspx.

8. While one can appeal to the resources of the judgment aggregation framework to support a deflationary summativist view of justified group belief (as Alvin Goldman does below), it is important to note that not all aggregation procedures support this approach. For instance, Pettit (2003) discusses what he calls the "Doctrinal Paradox" by considering a case involving the employees of a company deciding whether to forgo a pay-raise in order to spend the saved money on implementing a set of workplace safety measures. The employees are supposed to make their decision on the basis of considering three separable issues:

> first, how serious the danger is; second, how effective the safety measures that a pay-sacrifice would buy is likely to be; and third, whether the pay-sacrifice is bearable for members individually. If an employee thinks that the danger is sufficiently serious, the safety measure sufficiently effective, and the pay-sacrifice sufficiently bearable, he or she will vote for the sacrifice; otherwise he or she will vote against.

> (Pettit 2003: 171)

Imagine now that the company's three employees vote in the following way:

	Serious danger?	Effective measure?	Bearable loss?	Pay sacrifice?
A.	Yes	No	Yes	No
B.	No	Yes	Yes	No
C.	Yes	Yes	No	No

If the group judgment is determined via a premise-based aggregation procedure, then the group conclusion is to accept the pay sacrifice since there are more "Yes"s than "No"s in each of the premise columns. In such a case,

> the group will form a judgment on the question of the pay-sacrifice that is directly in conflict with the unanimous vote of its members. It will form a judgment that is in the starkest possible discontinuity with the corresponding judgments of its members.
>
> (Pettit 2003: 183)

This is the Doctrinal Paradox.

9. For more on the theory of judgment aggregation, see List and Pettit (2002, 2004), Dietrich (2005), List (2005), Pauly and van Hees (2006), and Cariani (2011).
10. See Goldman (2014).
11. I discuss a similar case, though in relation to group belief, in Lackey (unpublished).
12. For further discussion of some of the issues surrounding groups with conflicting bases, see Cariani (2013).
13. It should be noted that the Group Justification Paradox is analogous to the general result in judgment aggregation theory that no supermajority rule short of unanimity will always secure a deductively closed and consistent set of collective attitudes. (I am grateful to an anonymous referee for this point.)
14. See List (2005).
15. For an extended discussion of this, see List (2005).
16. I am grateful to an anonymous referee for a presentation of this alternative account of justified group belief.
17. See, for instance, Fantl and McGrath (2002 and 2009), Stanley (2005), Williamson (2005), and Hawthorne and Stanley (2008).
18. For a detailed discussion of proxy agency, see Ludwig (2014) and Lackey (forthcoming).
19. I develop this line of argument in far more detail, and in response to a broader range of theories than just the Condorcet-inspired one discussed here, in Lackey (2014).
20. This account is developed in more detail in Lackey (2016).

16

Rationality and Cooperation

Paul Weirich

People cooperate to form societies that benefit their members. The value of cooperation is evident in everyday life, as when drivers regulate their behavior to keep traffic flowing smoothly. When some cut corners, exploiting the cooperativeness of others, cooperation may break down, hurting all. Are the prospects of gains from cooperation enough to win the participation of rational people? An answer needs an account of rationality and an account of cooperation. After formulating these accounts, I advance a position about the rationality of cooperation.

1. RATIONALITY

Some disciplines use technical definitions of rationality to facilitate proofs about rationality as technically defined. However, the ordinary sense of rationality has a prominent place in normative principles directing behavior, so I adopt it when exploring rationality's implications for cooperation.

According to one usage, rationality is a capacity for cognitive activity, and according to another related usage, it is a standard of evaluation for acts, beliefs, and desires that issue from the capacity. I treat only rationality as a standard of evaluation, and consider only evaluation of acts. According to a representative principle of evaluation, an agent's act is rational only if it has prospects at least as attractive as any alternative's prospects, or, more specifically, only if for the agent the act's utility is at least as great as the utility of any act that the agent may have performed instead.

The principle of utility maximization assumes an agent who is cognitively ideal and in ideal circumstances for maximizing utility. The idealizations are crucial because rationality's demands are sensitive to an agent's abilities and circumstances. Rationality demands more of an adult than of a child, and demands more of an adult with time for reflection

209

than of an adult harried by adverse circumstances. Cognitive limits and unfavorable circumstances provide excuses for failing to meet rationality's goals for an agent's behavior. Only unexcused shortcomings count as irrational.

Ignorance of an unsuccessful act's consequences commonly excuses the act. A choice that is unsuccessful because insufficiently informed need not be irrational and thus blameworthy. Although rationality advances the goal of informed choices, it recognizes that an agent without blame may make a choice not informed by the choice's consequences. It obliges an agent to gather information about options before reaching a decision when circumstances are favorable for gathering information and when the importance of the decision warrants the effort. However, it recognizes that despite reasonable efforts to gather information, an agent in a decision problem may not know all the relevant consequences of all options. In these cases, rationality's requirement is not a choice that maximizes utility informed by the facts, but a choice that maximizes expected utility, that is, utility considering the probabilities and utilities of an option's possible outcomes, assuming as an idealization that these probabilities and utilities are available.

An act that is not rational is irrational. Because an irrational act is blameworthy, all agents in all circumstances have available some act that is rational and escapes blame. Blame is not justified unless an agent has a way of escaping it. Decision problems in which no option is rational do not arise if rationality has its ordinary, normative meaning. If an agent has an infinite number of options that are better and better without end, then some option good enough is rational, even if another option is better. Rationality does not require maximizing utility when no option has maximum utility.

Individuals have unified minds, and rationality evaluates an individual's beliefs and desires along with the acts they issue. Groups of individuals do not have minds, much less unified minds, and so lack beliefs and desires that rationality can evaluate. However, groups perform acts, as when a committee passes a resolution. If free acts of members of a group constitute the group's act, then the group's act is free and evaluable for rationality. A committee's resolution, produced by free acts of the committee's members, is evaluable for rationality.

Collective rationality is rationality's extension from individuals to groups. It shares many features with rationality for individuals. In particular, collective rationality is sensitive to a group's abilities and circumstances. A group may have a good excuse for failing to attain a goal of collective rationality and thereby escape blame for the failure so that its act is not collectively irrational. For example, a committee out of ignorance, and without irrationality, may pass a resolution with ruinous consequences.

Rationality lacks practical, action-guiding value if it is impossible to follow all its directives. For practicality, rationality's requirements for a group are consistent with its requirements for the group's members. If rationality requires that a committee pass a resolution, it does not permit each committee member to vote against the resolution. If all the members of a group act rationally, then the collective act the group thereby performs is rational.

The rationality of the acts of all members of a group yields a sufficient condition of collective rationality but not a necessary condition. A group may act rationally despite the irrational acts of some members. For example, a committee following majority rule may rationally pass a resolution despite a minority's irrational votes against the resolution. A necessary condition of the collective rationality of a group's act is the possibility of its arising from rational acts by all members. A committee's passing a resolution is rational only if passage would result from all members voting rationally. In general, in a collective action problem for a group, a collective act is rational if and only if it is compatible with an act that the group performs by all members contributing rationally.

A theory of collective rationality, to extend its evaluation of collective acts, may adopt a technical definition of collective acts. It may count as a group's act any combination of acts of the members with exactly one act for each member; a group performs such combinations of acts. This broad definition does not require that a group's act result from a collective intention to perform the act, defined in a technical sense, as, perhaps, a shared intention to perform the act. For example, the pedestrians at a street corner waiting for a red light to change before crossing a street, cross the street together when the light turns green, even if none intends that they cross the street together and they do not have a collective intention to cross together. Collective rationality evaluates a collective act in the broad sense, such as a group of drivers' creating a traffic jam, even if the act does not spring from a collective intention. Although acts that are products of collective intentions form an interesting class of collective acts, collective rationality evaluates additional collective acts.

Strict standards of collective rationality apply to groups that are in ideal conditions for joint action. In ideal cases, groups may organize so that they act as if they were individuals with unified minds. Useful technical definitions of collective beliefs, desires, preferences, and intentions identify features of a group that justify applying common principles of rational action that assume mental states. For instance, if all a committee's members prefer passing a resolution to not passing it, then their common preference may count as a collective preference, and the committee's passing the resolution may count as an expression of a collective intention to pass the resolution.

2. COOPERATION

Cooperation is a type of collective act, namely, a working together for a common benefit. Sobel (2009: 279–89) distinguishes cooperation from coordination, which is also a working together for a common benefit, by noting that in cases of coordination, agents have common interests, whereas in cases of cooperation, agents have partly conflicting interests so that working together requires compromise. Two students sharing a dormitory room may coordinate to walk to class together and also cooperate to clean the room. Barriers to coordination, such as inability to communicate, differ from barriers to cooperation, such temptations to exploit cooperative parties. However, the reasons for coordination and cooperation alike are common benefits. An account of reasons for cooperation may therefore put aside the distinction between cooperation and coordination, and take cooperation broadly to be no more than working together for a common benefit.

For generality, this definition counts as a benefit attaining an altruistic goal. Hence, lifeguards may cooperate to save a swimmer in danger of drowning. Although they serve the swimmer's interests rather than their own, attaining their common goal of saving the swimmer counts as a common benefit. Also, for generality, the definition assumes that a common benefit may be an outcome that cooperators want for different reasons. If two students cooperate to clean their dormitory room, their cleaning brings a common benefit even if one student wants a clean room for aesthetic satisfaction, whereas the other student wants a clean room for compliance with dormitory regulations.

Cooperators, despite working together, may fail to obtain the benefit they seek, perhaps because of insufficient skill. For simplicity in stating the reasons for cooperation, I treat only cases in which a group's working together for a common benefit brings the benefit because the members can at will perform their parts in a cooperative act that succeeds. Also, I treat just cases in which the common benefit successful cooperators gain is a net benefit with respect to their not working together. Thus, I put aside cases in which the costs of cooperation outweigh the benefits.

For generality, the definition of cooperation assumes that agents may work together for a common benefit without being aware of each other's acts. Hence, donors to a cause may cooperate to fund it without each being aware of the others' contributions. Furthermore, the definition assumes that agents may work together for a common benefit without being aware of their own contributions. Hence, bacteria in a colony may cooperate for survival without any awareness of what they are doing.

Although my definition of cooperation covers non-human agents, this essay investigates the reasons people have for cooperation. The definition's features anticipate, in particular, an investigation that uses idealizations to control for some factors in the explanation of rational collective action and thereby display more clearly the operation of other factors in the explanation. For example, ideal conditions for joint action do not include common interests, which characterize coordination problems. The assumption of common interests removes no barrier to joint action if conditions are otherwise ideal for joint action. Conditions may be ideal for joint action even if agents have some conflicting interests, and they must compromise to achieve a common benefit. Hence, the assumption of common interests does not aid identification of significant factors in the explanation of rational collective action. It is a restriction that a general theory of rational collective action forgoes.

The members of a group cooperate when they work together to realize an outcome better for all than an alternative outcome that they might have realized. If one outcome is better for all than an alternative outcome, the first is *strictly Pareto superior* to the second. A *weakly Pareto optimal* outcome is such that no alternative outcome is strictly Pareto superior to it. To simplify terminology, I say *superior* instead of strictly Pareto superior and say *optimal* instead of weakly Pareto optimal. Thus, a group's members cooperate if they work together to achieve an outcome superior to an alternative outcome, and they cooperate optimally if their cooperation achieves an optimal outcome. Although non-optimal cooperation is possible, I examine only the case for optimal cooperation, the culmination of reasons to cooperate. The general reasons that motivate people to work together in ways that benefit all also motivate them to work together in ways that benefit all as much as possible.

3. THE PRISONER'S DILEMMA

A *game* presents a group of agents with decision problems in which the consequences of an agent's choice depend on the other agents' choices. The foregoing accounts of collective rationality and cooperation yield an analysis of a famous game, the Prisoner's

	Cooperate	Don't
Cooperate	2, 2	0, 3
Don't	3, 0	1, 1

Figure 16.1 The Prisoner's Dilemma

Dilemma. In this two-person game, each player may act either cooperatively or else uncooperatively. If each player acts cooperatively, each player does better than if each player acts uncooperatively. However, each player does better by acting uncooperatively than by acting cooperatively no matter how the other player acts; acting uncooperatively *strictly dominates* acting cooperatively. The players cannot communicate and so cannot make binding agreements to act cooperatively. Figure 16.1 displays in a matrix the payoffs for the players from combinations of their acts. Each cell lists the utilities for the players of a combination's outcome, with the row chooser's utility listed first and the column chooser's utility listed second.

In the Dilemma, the outcome of cooperative acts by each player is superior to the outcome of uncooperative acts by each player; in fact, the outcome of cooperative acts by each player is optimal. However, because for each player acting uncooperatively strictly dominates acting cooperatively, acting uncooperatively is rational for each player. Moreover, the combination of their rational acts is rational for the pair of players. Hence, the Dilemma shows that in some cases collective rationality does not require optimal cooperation. In fact, it shows that in some cases collective rationality does not require any form of cooperation; the outcome of each player's acting uncooperatively, not being superior to any other possible outcome of the game, does not qualify as any sort of cooperation.

Some theorists, such as Sen (2002: 212), state that individual and collective rationality conflict in the Dilemma. They have in mind collective rationality taken as optimality and observe that in the Dilemma the rationality of each player prevents the players from achieving optimality. However, Section 1 eliminates conflict between individual and collective rationality to make its account of rationality consistent. It holds that rational players achieve collective rationality, but also holds that the demands of collective rationality adjust to the players' circumstances. In the Dilemma, non-ideal conditions for joint action excuse the pair of players' failure to achieve optimality.

Achieving cooperation often calls for preliminary creation of conditions that are favorable to cooperation. In a revision of the Prisoner's Dilemma that gives the players opportunities to make binding agreements, the players make a binding agreement to act cooperatively, adhere to the agreement, and reap the benefits of cooperation. Besides introducing a means of making binding agreements, people can prevent the Dilemma from arising by attaching rewards to cooperative acts or penalties to uncooperative acts. For example, suppose that encouraging an interest in the welfare of others produces agents who want benefits for others as well as for themselves and seek to cooperate with others to achieve benefits for all. The value such agents find in advancing the welfare of others serves as a reward that enhances the utility for a player of acting cooperatively and thereby alters the Dilemma's payoff matrix so that acting uncooperatively does not strictly dominate acting cooperatively and acting cooperatively is rational for each player. Also, some reasons against acting cooperatively disappear when for the same two players the

Dilemma, with payoffs in amounts of money, recurs indefinitely, and a player's acting cooperatively in a round of the Dilemma maximizes utility for the player because it promotes cooperative action from the other player in a later round.

Opportunities for cooperation arise in many situations besides the Dilemma. A complete theory of cooperation identifies generally the circumstances that promote and the circumstances that impede cooperation. Being cooperative may impose a cost on an agent, so an institution of compensation for losses arising from cooperation is a means of promoting cooperation. Also, an agent with an aversion to risk thinks twice about acting cooperatively because of the risk that others will not reciprocate. Any reduction in the risk or the agent's aversion to risk promotes the agent's cooperative action. Learning that others have acted cooperatively in the past reduces the risk that they will act uncooperatively now. Past cooperative behavior builds trust in current cooperative behavior. The agent's risk of unreciprocated cooperative action need not vanish before his acting cooperatively is rational because rationality requires agents to take risks justified by prospects of benefits, and because a substantive, non-instrumental principle of rationality prohibits excessive aversion to risk.

4. EPISTEMIC GAME THEORY

Section 1's account of collective rationality suits epistemic game theory, which Perea (2012) presents. This branch of game theory evaluates combinations of strategies the players in a game may realize by evaluating the rationality of each player's strategy in the combination considering the player's information about the game and the other players. In this branch of game theory, a solution is a *profile of strategies*, that is, an assignment of exactly one strategy to each player, such that each player's strategy is rational. Given idealizations about the players, including their having information that enables each player to foresee the responses of other players to his strategies, a solution is a profile of strategies that are rational given the profile and in this sense form an equilibrium.

Section 1's broad definition of a collective act accommodates a profile of strategies that the players in a game realize by each adopting a strategy, a type of act. A strategy profile counts as a collective act, being a combination of players' acts, even if it is not a product of a collective intention. Collective rationality evaluates as a collective act the profile of strategies that two chess players follow, although the two players do not have a collective intention to produce the profile. Because a solution is a profile of rational strategies, it is a rational collective act according to Section 1's account of collective rationality. The rational strategies of the players that constitute it make it collectively rational.

Some games create for a player a decision problem in which each option carries information about the consequences of options that makes another option a better prospect. In the game Matching Pennies two players display pennies simultaneously with one player winning both pennies if the pennies match and with the other player winning both pennies if the pennies do not match, as the payoff matrix in Figure 16.2 indicates, assuming that the row chooser wins when the pennies match.

Imagine an agent playing Matching Pennies against another agent that he knows is a perfect predicator of his choice. For each of his choices, either to display Heads or else to display Tails, his choice provides evidence that the other choice would have been

	Heads	Tails
Heads	2, 0	0, 2
Tails	0, 2	2, 0

Figure 16.2 Matching Pennies

better. If mixed strategies are not available, no equilibrium of players' strategies exists. Because rationality is always possible, the agent acts rationally by displaying Heads despite thereby acquiring evidence that Tails would have been better, and similarly for displaying Tails. Rationality does not require a player's strategy to be a best response to the other player's strategy in this special situation. Although another strategy is better given the other player's strategy, the alternative strategy carries information that the other player adopts a different strategy, to which the alternative strategy is not a best response. Given the information the agent's strategies carry, he has no strategy that maximizes utility on the assumption that it is adopted. Hence appropriate standards of rationality in the ordinary, normative sense do not require such a strategy. The game still has a solution, a profile of rational strategies, because both players can simultaneously adopt a rational strategy even if some player's rational strategy does not maximize utility given the information it carries about the other player's strategy. The two players can achieve a solution without achieving an equilibrium with respect to utility maximization.

5. RATIONALITY'S REQUIREMENTS

Let us return to our original question. Does rationality require cooperation? More specifically, does collective rationality, taken as ordinary rationality extended to groups, require cooperation, taken as collective action superior in outcome to some alternative, whenever cooperation is possible? In particular, does collective rationality require optimal cooperation whenever cooperation is possible? The answer for a group of agents depends on the agents' abilities and circumstances. Suppose that cooperation is possible. When conditions create obstacles to joint action, as in the Prisoner's Dilemma, rationality does not require cooperation. However, when conditions are ideal for joint action, rationality requires optimal cooperation. Consider a game with opportunities for cooperation. In ideal conditions for joint action, agents are cognitively unlimited, can without cost communicate and enter binding agreements, and know their game and each other well enough to predict their responses to each other and to predict their game's resolution. In these ideal conditions, rationality requires an optimal outcome and so optimal cooperation.

The argument from rationality to cooperation, which Weirich (2010) elaborates, shows that rational agents head off realization of a non-optimal outcome because some agent proposes a contract binding all to joint action that realizes an optimal outcome instead. The optimal outcome is better for the agent and so motivates the contract's proposal. The optimal outcome is also better for the other agents and so motivates their accepting the contract. Because the agents prevent every non-optimal outcome, they realize an optimal outcome.

6. DISTRIBUTED KNOWLEDGE

Lackey (2014) presents an objection to Section 1's account of collective rationality. She claims that rationality by individuals does not guarantee collective rationality. To support her claim, she constructs an example along these lines. A nursing home has three nurses that care for a patient. Each nurse is responsible for administering one medicine to the patient. The patient benefits from receiving any medicine by itself and needs any two medicines to survive, but given two medicines, does not benefit from a third medicine, as each nurse knows. Each nurse withholds the medicine she is responsible for administering, incorrectly assuming that the other two nurses administer their medicines. Because the patient receives no medicines, he dies. Lackey holds that although each nurse acts rationally, the nurses' collective act of withholding all medicines is irrational.

An elaboration of this example maintains that although no nurse knew the nurses were withholding all medicines, the group of nurses knew that the nurses were withholding all medicines and, because it also knew that withholding all medicines would cause the patient's death, irrationally acted contrary to its goal of keeping the patient alive. This elaboration applies to a group a principle of rationality that prohibits acting to frustrate a dominant goal knowingly. Because the group of nurses does not have a mind and so does not literally have knowledge or goals, the principle's application requires a technical definition of a group's knowledge and also its goals. However, if the definitions ground a sound principle of collective action, then according to the definition of collective knowledge, knowledge of a set of propositions distributed through a group, with each proposition known by just one member of the group, is insufficient for collective knowledge of the set of propositions; such distributed knowledge, without irrationality, fails to direct collective action toward collective goals. Rationality demands less of an agent without a unified mind than it demands of an agent with a unified mind. Standards of rationality are lower for groups than they are for individuals. Individuals must ground their acts in their knowledge, whereas groups often have excuses for not grounding their collective acts in knowledge distributed among their members.

In the example, the group of nurses did not know that they were withholding all medicines. Although each nurse knew about the withholding of the medicine for which she was responsible, she did not share her knowledge. Because the group did not knowingly kill the patient, the principle against frustrating a dominant goal knowingly does not entail given the circumstances that the group's collective act was irrational.

Let us put aside the foregoing principle of collective action and consider independent evaluations of each nurse's act and the nurses' collective act. The evaluations of these acts depend on the nurses' circumstances. Suppose that the nurses can communicate and keep track of the care each gives to the patient, but they fail to stay informed. Then although each nurse acts rationally given her information, she fails to act rationally. A non-conditionally rational act not only maximizes utility given current information but also rests on relevant information reasonably gathered prior to the act. Each nurse unreasonably fails to gather relevant information prior to withholding a medicine, and thus her act is not rational non-conditionally. Although the nurses' collective act is irrational because of the nurses' negligence, its components are not rational acts of the individual nurses. Hence, the example does not refute the sufficiency of individual rationality for collective rationality.

Suppose, in contrast, that the nurses cannot communicate about their steps to care for the patient. Although they make reasonable efforts to learn about the medicines the patient receives and form beliefs rationally using their limited information, each mistakenly thinks the others have administered medicines to the patient. Then each nurse acts rationally, and the combination of the nurses' acts is rational despite causing the patient's death. Because of ignorance, in some cases individuals rationally perform acts with tragic consequences, and groups do the same. Given the barriers to communication, the example does not refute the sufficiency of individual rationality for collective rationality.

7. EQUILIBRIUM WITHOUT OPTIMALITY

Bacharach (2006: ch. 1) maintains that agents who are rational according to standards for individuals may nonetheless perform an act that is not collectively rational. His argument uses the two-person game Hi-Lo, in which each player at the same time as the other player chooses either High or else Low, with the payoffs for the players' combinations of choices as in Figure 16.3.

The players have common interests, and although they cannot communicate, may coordinate by each adopting the strategy High, or by each adopting the strategy Low. In both combinations, each strategy maximizes utility given the other strategy, so both combinations create a type of equilibrium. However, the combination of High by each is superior to the combination of Low by each.

Suppose that in Hi-Lo the players are rational, cognitively unlimited, and informed about their game and each other. Bacharach contends that nonetheless standards of rationality for individuals give neither player a reason to adopt High. A player lacks a reason to choose High unless the other player has a reason to choose High, and the other player lacks a reason to choose High unless the first player has a reason to choose High. Consequently, neither player has a reason to choose High. If by chance they coordinate on Low, Bacharach claims that they are rational according to standards for individuals despite not achieving an optimal outcome, as collective rationality requires. People coordinate on High because, he maintains, they adopt the perspective of the team they form and do their parts in the collective act best for the team; they engage in team reasoning (see Gold, Chapter 17, this volume).

Blocking communication in Hi-Lo removes a means of coordination, and non-ideal conditions for joint action may excuse a failure to achieve optimality. However, rationality promotes coordination on High without communication because its principles consider not only an act's utility but also the act's utility given the act's realization. As Section 4 explains, an act may carry information about its consequences, and an evaluation of an act for rationality considers the information it carries. Imagine a version of Hi-Lo without communication but with rational, cognitively ideal players informed well enough about

	High	Low
High	2, 2	0, 0
Low	0, 0	1, 1

Figure 16.3 Hi-Lo

their game and each other for each player to predict his counterpart's responses to his choices. A player may perform High, even if before performing the act he does not have a reason to think that his counterpart will perform High, because when he performs High, he thereby acquires such a reason. His act supplies a reason for its performance because it carries information that the other player, predicting his act, will choose High in response; his performing High is self-supporting. Moreover, although both High and Low are self-supporting acts, High has greater self-conditional utility than does Low. A rational, cognitively ideal player prepares for the game by acquiring a disposition to adopt High that his counterpart infers and bolsters. When collective rationality demands optimality, individual rationality yields it.

8. COALITIONAL GAMES

Section 1's account of collective rationality assumes that a group always has available an act that is collectively rational. Some coalitional games, as reviewed by Binmore (2007: ch.18), challenge the assumption of collective rationality's attainability. In a coalitional game, players have opportunities to propose and form coalitions that constitute agents. A coalitional game supervenes on a sequential game in which each player may make and respond to proposals to form coalitions. A coalition that forms and acts optimally achieves a gain, called the coalition's *value*, which it divides among its members according to an agreement forming the coalition. A coalition receives the sum of the gains its members receive. Each player counts as a coalition of one, so all agents in the game are coalitions.

To illustrate, suppose that three musicians may play either each alone, or one alone and two in a pair, or all three together. A musician playing solo earns $100, a duo earns $400, and a trio earns $900. If coalitions that form divide earnings equally, a coalition of two yields $200 for each member, and a coalition of three yields $300 for each member. If amounts of money equal amounts of utility, then the amounts coalitions earn equal the coalitions' values.

If an outcome gives each coalition at least its value, it is in the game's *core* and realizes a *core allocation* of gains to players. In the example, an allocation giving each musician $300 is a core allocation and is in the game's core. No coalition can do better than it does given this allocation. Every coalition of one fares worse because on its own it receives only $100, and every coalition of two fares worse because on its own it receives only $400 rather than the $600 it has when each musician has $300.

The players achieve a type of equilibrium if they produce a core allocation because then no coalition gains by forming and acting on its own to produce another allocation. A rational resolution of the game seems to require an outcome in the game's core, that is, an outcome in which each coalition does at least as well as it could have done by forming and acting on its own.

A coalitional game may, however, have an empty core because no allocation the players can achieve is in the game's core. For every possible allocation of gains, some coalition profits from forming and achieving an allocation that increases each member's gain; for every possible outcome, some coalition profits from blocking it. Suppose that a group of three players have six dollars to divide any way a majority favors. Any two players form a majority and can divide the whole six dollars between themselves. However, for any division of the six dollars, some majority of two players can obtain an alternative division that improves the lot of both players. For instance, if two players form a majority that gives three dollars to each member, then one of its members and the player it excludes can form another majority that gives four dollars to the former player and two dollars to the latter player.

The coalitional game described, despite not having an outcome that gives each coalition at least its value, has a solution consisting of rational acts by each player, granting that rationality's requirements consider the players' circumstances. Suppose that each player knows the game and the other players well enough to know for any proposal the other players' response. Also, suppose that the game ends with a particular allocation of the six dollars among the three players. For some pair of players, another allocation the pair can in theory achieve gives more money to each member of the pair. However, the pair foresees that allocation's being blocked. Although the alternative allocation appeals to the pair, it is not a realistic alternative. The allocation the players achieve is a solution if no coalition gains from a realistic alternative.

9. CONCLUSION

Rationality requires gathering information relevant to assessment of options in a decision problem and requires taking account of information that an act carries about its consequences. These requirements explicate rationality's relation to cooperation. Does rationality require cooperation? No, not in all cases, but, yes, when conditions are ideal for joint action. In non-ideal cases, rationality requires cooperation among the members of a group when for each member acting cooperatively has beneficial prospects that justify so acting despite the risk that other members will not reciprocate. In many but not all circumstances, rationality requires cooperation because of its benefits.

RELATED TOPIC

Team Reasoning (Ch. 17).

REFERENCES

Bacharach, M. (2006) *Beyond Individual Choice: Teams and Frames in Game Theory*, N. Gold and R. Sugden (eds), Princeton: Princeton University Press.

Binmore, K. (2007) *Playing for Real: A Text on Game Theory*, New York: Oxford University Press.

Lackey, J. (2014) "Review of S. Chant, F. Hindriks, and G. Preyer, *From Individual to Collective Intentionality: New Essays*," *Notre Dame Philosophical Reviews*, https://ndpr.nd.edu/news/50020-from-individual-to-collective-intentionality-new-essays/

Perea, A. (2012) *Epistemic Game Theory: Reasoning and Choice*, Cambridge: Cambridge University Press.

Sen, A. (2002) *Rationality and Freedom*, Cambridge, MA: Harvard University Press.

Sobel, J.H. (2009) *Walls and Vaults: A Natural Science of Morals (Virtue Ethics According to David Hume)*, Hoboken, NJ: Wiley.

Weirich, P. (2010) *Collective Rationality: Equilibrium in Cooperative Games*, New York: Oxford University Press.

FURTHER READING

Arrow, K. (1951) *Social Choice and Individual Values*, New Haven, CT: Yale University Press. (A classic treatment of collective preferences.)

Broome, J. (2013) *Rationality Through Reasoning*, Chichester, UK: Wiley-Blackwell. (An account of the motivation for doing as one ought.)

List, C. and Pettit, P. (2013) *Group Agency: The Possibility, Design, and Status of Corporate Agents*, Oxford: Oxford University Press. (An extension of Arrow's ideas to collective judgment.)

Peterson, M. (ed.) (2015) *Essays on the Prisoner's Dilemma*, Cambridge: Cambridge University Press. (Recent perspectives on the Prisoner's Dilemma.)

Skyrms, B. (1996) *Evolution of the Social Contract*, Cambridge: Cambridge University Press. (An account of the evolution of cooperation using game-theoretic models.)

Skyrms, B. (2004) *The Stag Hunt and the Evolution of Social Structure*, Cambridge: Cambridge University Press. (An application of evolutionary game theory to cooperation.)

Sugden, R. (2005) *The Economics of Rights, Co-operation and Welfare*, Second edition, Houndmills, UK: Palgrave Macmillan. (A game-theoretical account of cooperation.)

Weirich, P. (2007) "Initiating Coordination," *Philosophy of Science* 74: 790–801. (An account of the reasons individuals have for coordinating.)

17

Team Reasoning: Controversies and Open Research Questions

Natalie Gold

1. TEAM REASONING

The theory of team reasoning was developed separately by Robert Sugden (1993, 2000, 2003) and Michael Bacharach (1999, 2006). Its development was motivated by games that are puzzling for orthodox game theory because they have an arguably rational solution, which a substantial number of people play in real life, whose play game theory cannot explain or predict.

One of these games is Hi-Lo, a version of which is shown in Figure 17.1. There are two pure-strategy Nash equilibria, (*high, high*) and (*low, low*), and (*high, high*) is strictly better than (*low, low*) for both players. It seems clear that the two players should each play *high*. However, standard game theory cannot recommend that. A Nash equilibrium involves a player maximizing her payoff given what the other player is doing. Thus it can only recommend that, if a player expects the other player to play *high*, then it is rational for her to play *high*. However, if she expects the other player to play *low*, then it is rational for her to play *low*. What it is rational for Player 1 to do is conditional on what Player 2 does, and standard game theory gives her no reason to expect Player 2 to play *high* rather than *low*. (For fuller statements of this argument, see Hodgson (1967), Sugden (1993), or Bacharach (2006).)

The other game is the Prisoner's Dilemma, a version of which is shown in Figure 17.2. The only Nash equilibrium in this game is (*defect, defect*); indeed *defect* is a dominant strategy, a player is better off playing it whatever the other player does, so standard game theory recommends to each player that she play it regardless of her expectations about the other player. However, (*defect, defect*) leaves both players worse off than if they had played (*cooperate, cooperate*).

In standard game theoretic reasoning, an individual player asks "what do *I* want to achieve and what should *I* do to achieve it (given my beliefs about what other players will do)?" The answer is a complete strategy, roughly speaking a contingency plan, which she

		Player 2	
		high	*low*
Player 1	*high*	2, 2	0, 0
	low	0, 0	1, 1

Figure 17.1 Hi-Lo

		Player 2	
		cooperate	*defect*
Player 1	*cooperate*	3, 3	0, 4
	defect	4, 0	1, 1

Figure 17.2 The Prisoner's Dilemma

then carries out. Team reasoning extends the syntax of game theory, to allow players to ask "what do *we* want to achieve and what should I do to play my part in achieving it?" This allows each player to choose the best profile of actions for the team and reach the conclusion that she should choose her component of that profile. Team reasoning de-conditionalizes players' choices, allowing profile selection.

A player team reasons when she *group identifies,* conceiving of herself as part of a team, where the group is a unit of agency, acting as a single entity in pursuit of some single objective. Then, provided that there is common knowledge that each member group-identifies, and common knowledge of the best team profile, she will choose her part of the best profile for the group. (For discussion of what happens when we relax the common knowledge conditions and when the team of actors is smaller than the whole group, and how different theorists deal with it, see Gold and Sugden (2007b); Gold (2012).) In the Hi-Lo game it is clear that (*high, high*) would be the best profile of actions for the team so, in the simplest case, if there is common knowledge that each member group-identifies and common knowledge that each member aims to choose the best team profile, then each can reason that she should play *high,* as a part of playing (*high, high*). In a similar manner, if the best team profile in the prisoner's dilemma is (*cooperate, cooperate*) and the common knowledge conditions are fulfilled, then team reasoning can predict that players will choose *cooperate* (Gold and Sugden 2007b).

This is the common core of the theory of team reasoning. It leaves open questions about what exactly it is to group identify, whether it can be rational to group identify, and what the team should take as its goal. These are answered in different ways by Sugden, Bacharach, and others who have written about team reasoning. Other open research questions include how to test the theory, the relation of team reasoning to collective intentions, what is the role of reasoning, and the application of team reasoning to other levels of agency. Each of these is the subject of a section below.

2. GROUP IDENTIFICATION

An individual is said to *group identify* if she conceives of herself as part of a team, where the group is a unit of agency, acting as a single entity in pursuit of some single objective.

(Strictly speaking, we should separate "entification," where an individual conceives of a group as a unity of agency, or team, from "identification," where she identifies herself as a part of that group agent. But we will simplify and just speak of identification here.) A team reasoner must first come to frame a decision as a problem for "us" and then do team reasoning. But theorists disagree about how group identification happens and what exactly it entails. In order to better understand these differences, I will locate them in a more general framework of decision-making.

We can distinguish three steps involved in framing and decision-making: noticing, noticing as choice-relevant, and deciding to act on a reason (Gold 2012). Standard decision theory only recognizes individual agents, but the setting up of those agents' decision-problems still involves the three steps. There are an infinite number of ways of describing a situation. As finite individuals, we cannot see them all at once. The way that a situation is described or "framed" conveys information about the situation. For a fact to become the basis of an agent's reason for action (her "motivating reason"), first she must notice it. The agent can only reason from premises about the world that are accessible to her, so frames set the parameters of reasoning. But noticing alone is not enough. For the fact to influence an agent's decision, she must also recognize that it is relevant to her choice and is a potential reason for action. Finally, the agent must act on the reason, it must have a "motivational grip."

We can apply this framework to team reasoning. Standard decision theory only recognizes individual agents. Once we allow that there can be different levels of agency, it matters whether the individual frames herself and her co-players only as individuals, using an "*I*-frame," or as a team, using a "*we*-frame." First the agent must see the possibility of cooperation and notice the potential for team reasoning, then she must group identify and see team reasoning as choice-relevant; third she must decide to act on team reasoning. So, once the agent notices the possibility of acting as a team, there are two more steps to becoming a team reasoner. We might think of the second of these steps, noticing as choice-relevant, as group identification.

There is disagreement about whether these steps are filled by psychological processes or choices. In Bacharach's theory of team reasoning, group identification is simply a psychological process. Salient features of the situation may promote group identification via *affiliation*, 'a psychological process in which a person who does think about a certain group, defined by some shared property, comes to think about it as "us"' (Bacharach 1997: 2). Among those salient features are the payoffs of the game. A feature's *effectiveness* is its tendency to stimulate group identity. Both Hi-Lo and the Prisoner's Dilemma have a feature that Bacharach called *strong independence,* roughly speaking a Nash equilibrium that is worse than some other outcome in the game from every player's individual point of view. Bacharach speculated that seeing the possibility of cooperating to achieve (*high, high*) instead of (*low, low*), or (*cooperate, cooperate*) instead of (*defect, defect*), would promote group identification. However, in the Prisoner's Dilemma, the player may also see the *double-crossing feature*, whereby an individual can benefit if she unilaterally deviates from the team reasoning solution, which inhibits group identification.

For Bacharach, group identification then primes team reasoning: another psychological process. In most of *Beyond Individual Choice,* Bacharach assumes that once an individual group- identifies, then she will always team reason (although he recognizes in a footnote that this is a simplification (Bacharach 2006: 152)). Individuals either frame the decision as a problem for "me," in which case they use individual reasoning, or they frame it as a problem for "us" and use team reasoning. (Hence, Bacharach's theory has been referred to as producing team reasoning as a result of framing, see Gold and Sugden (2007a, 2007b).) In other work, he allows that both the *I*-frame and the *we*-frame come to mind at the same time (Bacharach 1997). Nevertheless, reasoning about whether or not to team reason does not enter the picture.

For Sugden, in contrast, both the step from noticing to group identification and the step from group identification to team reasoning are opportunities for choices. *Assurance* is necessary for group identification: 'to construe oneself as a member of a team, one must have some confidence that the other members of that team construe themselves as members too' (Sugden 2000: 194). Such assurance could be created by public acts of commitment or induced by repeated experience of regularities of behavior in a population. But, even once an individual group identifies, she would still have to decide whether team reasoning was a mode of reasoning that she wanted to endorse. Assurance enters the picture again, as endorsing Sugden's "mutually assured team reasoning" is to make a uni-lateral commitment to a certain form of practical reasoning, but that reasoning does not generate any implications for action unless one has assurance that others have made the same commitment.

This difference between Sugden and Bacharach, between their views of how group identification occurs, also manifests in different ways of conceptualizing the relationship between a team reasoner and the group goal. For Bacharach, a team reasoner who iden-tifies with the group takes on the goals of the group and will aim to do her part in what is best for the group, even when not all of the group are team reasoners. We might say in this situation that the "team" is smaller than the "group" whose interests are promoted by the team. In contrast, for Sugden, a team reasoner who identifies with a group stands ready to do her part in joint actions in pursuit of the group's objective; but she does not necessarily take this objective as *hers* in the stronger sense of wanting to pursue it even if other members of the group do not reciprocate.

3. THE POSSIBILITY OF RATIONAL GROUP IDENTIFICATION

The theory of team reasoning allows that groups, as well as individuals, can be agents; and it shows how it can be rational to play *high* in Hi-Lo and *cooperate* in the Prisoner's Dilemma, given that a player group-identifies. According to Hurley (1989: 145) 'an ade-quate theory of rational choice should address the question of what the unit of agency among those possible should be'. But neither Bacharach nor Sugden thinks that we can make an instrumentally rational choice to team reason.

For Bacharach, group identification is a psychological process that leads to team reason-ing. Further, the evaluation of outcomes is always done by an agent within the perspective of one of the two frames, the *I*-frame or the *we*-frame (Bacharach 1997). The standards of evaluation and goals are co-determined with the unit of agency; there is no agent-neutral perspective from which we can assess the rationality of team reasoning. All Bacharach can say is: given that an individual group-identifies, then it is rational for her to team reason.

Even though, for Sugden, team reasoning is a matter of choice, he also does not think that it is a matter of instrumentally rational choice. Sugden does not acknowledge an agent-neutral concept of "rationality," or even of the "validity" of reasoning. For Sugden, both individual reasoning and team reasoning are simply modes of reasoning that a person might endorse. As with Bacharach, all goals are the goals of agents, so there is no instrumentally rational way to make assessments prior to determining the unit of agency.

Hurley differs, suggesting that a person should choose the unit of agency that best realizes her goals, where these are chosen 'according to one's substantive goals and ethical views' (1989: 147): 'As an individual I can recognize that a collective unit of which I am merely a part can bring about outcomes that I prefer to any that I could bring about by acting as an individual unit' (Hurley 2005a: 203). Thus she makes team reasoning a matter of instrumental rationality.

There are two ways that Hurley's position could be construed and they are both problematic. Hurley might mean that we should privilege individual level "substantive goals"; or she might mean that morality specifies agent-neutral goals, which ought to be pursued regardless of the unit of agency, but, since thinking usually occurs at the individual level, these will be determined by the individual's "ethical views." However, once we acknowledge that there are multiple levels of agency, it is not clear why one should privilege the individual level over the group level for the purpose of making evaluations (Bardsley 2001).

Elizabeth Anderson and David Gauthier have also expressed the opinion that group identification (Anderson) or cooperation (Gauthier) is rational, but both admit to lacking an argument for this position.

Anderson maintains that morality requires us to transcend our various identities and harmonize their demands, by identifying with a community that comprehends them all, the Kantian Kingdom of Ends. However, she admits to having no argument that this is rationally required (Anderson 2001: 37).

Gauthier also argues that something like team reasoning could be instrumentally rational. Gauthier has long held that it can be instrumentally rational to cooperate in the Prisoner's Dilemma game (Gauthier 1986). In a recent reworking of his theory, Gauthier (2013) claims that *Pareto-optimization* is a necessary condition for rationality in multi-player games, where a Pareto-optimizing theory 'provides only a single set of directives to all the interacting agents, with the directive to each premised on the acceptance by the others of the directives to them' (Gauthier 2013: 607). The outcome selected must be both efficient and fair in how it distributes the expected gains of cooperation. Although he does not explicitly use the term "team reasoning," it is clear that Gauthier's theory is similar to ideas of team reasoning for mutual gain. His goal is to show that 'social morality is part of rational choice, or at least, integral to rational cooperation' (Gauthier 2013: 624). However, he does not provide a connection to practical rationality—his moral justification for team reasoning is that it would pass a contractarian test whereby it is 'eligible for inclusion in an actual society that constitutes a cooperative venture for mutual fulfilment' (Gauthier 2013: 618)—and he concedes that he has not yet been successful in bridging social morality and rational choice.

If team reasoning is rational, it looks like it is not instrumentally rational. Anderson (2001) expresses the hope that we can discover principles of rational self-identification. If we do, for the reasons given above, in the discussion of Hurley, then they will have to be thicker principles of rationality than instrumental ones.

4. THE TEAM'S OBJECTIVE

In the Hi-Lo and Prisoner's Dilemma games above, it is fairly obvious which outcome a team should aim at. In other situations, things may not be so clear. In particular, there may be a question of how the team should treat its members' different interests and priorities. There are two main approaches to specifying the objectives of the team: to assume that a team, like an individual, has a utility function and to specify how individual team members' interests should be traded off against each other; or to treat team reasoning as a form of mutual cooperation or bargaining and to describe what team outcomes the individual members would agree to.

Bacharach (2006) sees the team goal as being captured in a team payoff function and asks how the team function should relate to the payoff functions of the individual members (ch. 2, section 4.3). He argues that, at a minimum, the team function will be Paretian with respect to the payoffs of the players, i.e. if every individual agent gets at least as much utility in outcome x than outcome y, and at least one agent does strictly better, then the group function will rank outcome x above outcome y. This will be enough to identify a preferred team outcome in coordination games, where players' interests are aligned, but in mixed-motive games, where there is some conflict of interest—maybe because there are multiple possible cooperative solutions and different individuals do better in each one—we will need to supplement it with an account of how the team function adjudicates between the interests of different members. Bacharach (2006: 88) puts forward as a "testable hypothesis" that

> in circumstances in which nothing is perceived by individual members about other individual members beyond the facts recorded in a bare game representation, principles of fairness such as those of Nash's axiomatic bargaining theory will be embedded in U [the team function].

One function that is Paretian is the utilitarian function. Many papers on team reasoning talk about maximizing the average of the players' payoffs, which is equivalent to the utilitarian function (Bacharach 1999, 2006; Colman et al. 2008, 2014; Smerilli 2012). Allowing this sort of trade-off between individual members' interests enables team reasoning to explain cases where one member sacrifices themselves for the rest of the team, for instance the martyrdom of one member for the good of the group. Maybe unsurprisingly, discussions of team reasoning that favor something like the utilitarian function are either psychological theories, such as Bacharach (2006), or moral ones, such as Regan (1980), who assumes that we should aim for a utilitarian outcome and asks what level of reasoning utilitarians should use.

An alternative way of conceptualizing team reasoning is as cooperation for mutual advantage (Sugden, 2011). In this interpretation of the theory, an individual would not team reason if it would leave her individually worse off. Sugden (2015) proposes that we measure mutual advantage relative to the payoff that each player can guarantee herself in a game. A strategy profile where each player receives a payoff that is greater than this threshold and where each player's participation is needed to attain these higher payoffs is said to be mutually beneficial. (There are similarities to Gauthier (2013). See Karpus and Gold (2016) for more discussion.) Karpus and Radzvilas (2015) formalize these ideas of mutual advantage and mutual benefit, together with a Pareto efficiency criterion. Misyak and co-authors argue in a similar vein that we-thinking should be construed as *virtual bargaining*, where people reason about what they would agree on, if they were able to bargain. If it is obvious which outcome they would agree on, then they can choose it directly without doing any actual bargaining (Misyak and Chater 2014; Misyak et al. 2014; Chater et al. 2016).

The utilitarian function allows the sacrifice of some members for the good of others: as John Rawls (1999: 164) put it, utilitarianism neglects the separateness of persons. In contrast, theories of team reasoning as mutual advantage will not allow this. They privilege the individual level of agency, in that the acceptable team outcomes are defined in terms of what would be acceptable to the individual members.

5. COLLECTIVE INTENTIONS AND REASONING

The intentions that we have when we act together are collective intentions. If we decide to go to New York together, that you will buy the tickets and I will book the hotel, then there is a sense in which "we intend to go to New York," as well as a sense in which "I" intend my part in our joint action. Most analyses of collective intentions focus on the properties of collective intentions as mental states, so anything that is distinctive to cooperative activity has to be represented as a distinctive feature of the corresponding intentions. However, Gold and Sugden (2007a) argue that collective intentions are distinguished from individual intentions by reference to the unit of agency in the reasoning that led to the formation of the intention; that collective intentions are the sort of intentions that are formed when people team reason.[1]

Pacherie (2011) argues that leading accounts of collective intentions, such as those of Bratman (2009a, 2009b) and Gilbert (1997, 2009), require too much sophistication on the part of agents and therefore cannot explain the intentions behind the cooperative actions of children, who do not have a sophisticated theory of the mental states of others. She argues that Bacharach's theory of team reasoning gives an account of collective intentions that is less cognitively demanding and therefore to be preferred.

The team reasoning account of collective intentions is consistent with evidence from cognitive linguistics, which shows that *we* is composed of notions of *I* and grouphood (Gold and Harbour 2012). These cognitive requirements would be satisfied by someone who has the individual concept *I* and the notion of grouped implicit in team reasoning.

The idea that collective intentions are the result of team reasoning has been criticized on the grounds that there are spontaneous collective intentions (Tuomela 2009; Schweikard and Schmid 2013). There are a variety of things that could be meant by this criticism. One of them is that there are spontaneous collective intentions, which are not formed as the result of conscious reasoning. This raises the question of what is meant by "reasoning" in team reasoning.

Philosophers often take reasoning to mean conscious deliberation (e.g. Pettit 2007). However, this is not normally how decision theorists think of reasoning. Among economists, patterns of consistent behavior provide evidence of rationality and of the agent's mental states which caused the behavior; or, for more philosophical theories of rational choice, which relate it to practical reasoning, given people's beliefs and desires one can identify what behavior would be rational. In both cases the "reasoning" that is imputed to agents is a rational reconstruction based on their mental states and the standard of rationality is an "external" one applied to behavior, not an "internal" one applied to decision processes.

This is compatible with the way that "reasoning" is used in cognitive science and AI. Cognitive science has abandoned classical logic, as logical inference mechanisms are too slow to model the "automatic" information processing that is antecedent to decision. While manipulation of propositions may be a suitable model at Marr's (1982) *computational* level, where the goal of the system and the logic behind its output are specified, it is a less good model at the *algorithmic* level, representing and implementing the computational theory, and at the level of *implementation*, or how the algorithm is realized in the brain. Instead we have the idea that people can implicitly reason according to some rule without explicitly being able to articulate the content of their reasoning (Polanyi 1962).

In the literature on team reasoning, Hurley (2005b) has explicitly taken this line. She investigates local procedures and heuristics from which collective units of agency can emerge, and she argues that the processes in an agent that actually generate his or her rational behavior need not be isomorphic with the theoretical account of why the behavior counts as rational. Bacharach also denies conscious access to reasoning processes, saying, 'We should not expect people to be able to identify the reasoning principles that govern their conclusions even when these principles are sound' (Bacharach 2006: 45). Team reasoning models the computational level: the goal of the system and the logic behind the output. Therefore the claim that team reasoning leads to collective intentions should be understood as the idea that the team goal and logic of team reasoning underpin behavior resulting from collective intentions.

6. TESTING TEAM REASONING

Tests of team reasoning have been tests of behavior (as would be expected from the discussion in Section 5), testing hypotheses about how team reasoners will behave in various games, usually pitted against a leading alternative theory. In order to predict behavior, some assumptions must be made about team goals and group identification, as discussed in Sections 2 and 4. It must also be possible to make predictions from the financial payoffs that are observable in the lab.

We would expect that team reasoners would be more likely to cooperate in mixed-motive games, like the Prisoner's Dilemma, than the individual reasoners of rational choice theory. However, it is difficult to isolate the effect of team reasoning in such games. The predictable effects of group identification include increased interpersonal affect amongst group members and an increased expectation of cooperation by other group members (both of which might also "transform" the financial payoffs, so that the effective payoffs that motivate a player's behavior are different from the observed financial outcomes). Each of these, altruism and expectations, is the basis of alternative theories of cooperation. It's not clear how we can measure which proposed correlates of group identification—team reasoning, in-group altruism, or expectation that others will cooperate—is causal.[2]

Luckily, coordination may be more fundamental than cooperation. Theories of cooperation in the Prisoner's Dilemma that invoke payoff transformations or expectations and social norms turn (*cooperate, cooperate*) into an equilibrium but do not change the status of (*defect, defect*), which remains an equilibrium. (For more detailed explanation of this, see Gold and Sugden (2007b), or Gold (2012).) In other words, coordination is still necessary; often the game becomes a Hi-Lo. Coordination games are also attractive for other reasons. There is no problem with identifying the observed laboratory payoffs with the utility payoffs that motivate people because the players' payoffs are equal in all outcomes, so it is safe to assume that all players have the same preference ordering over the outcomes. This also means that the team's objective is not controversial in coordination games.

However, we're remarkably good at coordination, especially Hi-Lo![3] If the hypothesis is that team reasoning causes coordination on (*high, high*), then the experimenter needs to get a low baseline level of coordination on that outcome in order to see an effect of team reasoning. Hence, in order to test team reasoning, people have tried to make coordination harder. They have done this in three different ways.

Bacharach and Guerra (reported in ch. 4 of Bacharach 2006) made coordination harder by making one of the low paying options salient. Bacharach took the main competitor theory to be the idea of Harsanyi and Selten (1988) that people play *high* because the high payoff makes it salient, call this *payoff salience*. In that case, it should be possible to induce people to choose *low* by labeling *low* in a manner that makes it more salient. Call this *label salience*. For instance, one could give the two strategies flower names, calling the low paying strategy "rose" and informing people that in previous experiments, "rose" was the most common choice. If that produced a significant amount of *low* choice, then it would be possible to test whether group identity manipulations make *high* choice more likely. Using a design like this, Bacharach and Guerra ran a small pilot that provided modest support for team reasoning.

A second way to make coordination harder is to increase the number of options, as done by Bardsley et al. (2010) and Bardsley and Ule (2014). A third possibility is to make the payoffs asymmetric, as done in two experiments by Faillo et al. (2013, 2015). Both sets of experimenters pitted team reasoning against *cognitive hierarchy theory*, where players are individualistic reasoners and where coordination is supposed to be the result of beliefs about the other players. The theory assumes that there is some very basic strategy, such as choosing at random or choosing according to label salience or choosing according to payoff salience—which one depends on the version—that is done by level-zero players. Then level-one players assume all other players are level-zero and play a best response against that strategy; level-two players play a best response to level-one players; and in theory so on ad infinitum, although in practice no one has found anything higher than level-two reasoners. These four experiments have mixed results, which are hard to explain within a unified theory. For more detailed examination and discussion see Karpus and Gold (2016). But it is hard to conclude anything on the basis of so few experiments. More research is needed.

7. OTHER LEVELS OF AGENCY: THE PERSON OVER TIME

In decision theory, problems of intertemporal choice are often analyzed as if, at each time *t* at which the person has to make a decision, that decision is made by a distinct transient agent or *timeslice*, the person at time *t*. Each timeslice is treated as an independent rational decision-maker, so that 'the individual over time is an infinity of individuals' (Strotz 1955: 179). This does not imply any metaphysical commitments, in particular it is not an endorsement of perdurantism, the view that things really do consist of temporal parts. Rather, it is a natural way of modeling people because the self at a particular time is the locus of choices, experiences, and perceptions.

This generates a neat model of giving in to temptations and procrastination (O'Donoghue and Rabin 1999): A timeslice makes a choice that benefits itself (going out, eating dessert) but imposes costs on future selves (failing the exam, not getting into that dress); even if the timeslice cares about future selves, that may not be enough to get her to make a sacrifice for them. This way of thinking about the self is not alien to philosophers. It is the view put forward in Parfit (1984), who argues that it is only rational for the current self to take into account her future outcomes to the extent that she is "connected" to the future self.

The decision theoretic picture does not include intentions (and, in this, it differs from Parfit (1984)). Agency is vested in timeslices, who each act on their own preferences, and it is considered naive to think that an earlier timeslice could motivate her later self to do something just by forming a plan. And even agents who are sophisticated enough to recognize their own self-control problems can end up procrastinating (O'Donoghue and Rabin 1999).

These self-control problems have a similar structure to the puzzles that motivated the development of interpersonal team reasoning. So we can give a similar solution: intrapersonal team reasoning, or the idea that the timeslices can see themselves as constituting a "team over time" and act on team reasoning (Gold 2013). Being a part of a team over time can give an earlier self a reason to take into account the outcomes of future selves even if she does not feel connected to her future self (Gold 2015). The plan made by the earlier self is the intention and, when a timeslice identifies with the team over time, she has a reason to carry out her part of the plan, or to act on her prior intention.

8. CONCLUSION

I have related the motivation for the theory of team reasoning and explained a basic version. I have detailed some controversies within the theory of team reasoning about group identification, the rationality of team reasoning, and the team's objective. I have sketched some open research questions and the attempts that people have made in answering them, covering collective intentions and reasoning, testing team reasoning, and the application of other levels of agency. Once we admit into the theory the possibility that individuals have more than two levels of agency, or are members of many different groups, then the question of which team someone identifies with and the interplay of different memberships becomes important. However, there is little or nothing on this question, which is an obvious direction for future research.

RELATED TOPICS

Collective Action and Agency (Ch. 1), Non-Reductive Views of Shared Intention (Ch. 2), Reductive Views of Shared Intention (Ch. 3), Interpersonal Obligation in Joint Action (Ch. 4), Shared Values, Interests, and Desires (Ch. 8), Joint Commitment (Ch. 10), Rationality and Cooperation (Ch. 16), Social Groups (Ch. 21).

REFERENCES

Anderson, E. (2001) "Unstrapping the Straitjacket of 'Preference': A Comment on Amartya Sen's Contributions to Philosophy and Economics," *Economics and Philosophy* 17 (1): 21–38.

Bacharach, M. (1997) "'We' Equilibria: A Variable Frame Theory of Cooperation," Oxford: Institute of Economics and Statistics, University of Oxford, 30.

——— (1999) "Interactive Team Reasoning: A Contribution to the Theory of Co-operation," *Research in Economics* 53: 117–47.

Bacharach, M. (2006) *Beyond Individual Choice: Teams and Frames in Game Theory*, Princeton: Princeton University Press.

Bardsley, N. (2001) "Collective Reasoning," *Critical Review of International Social and Political Philosophy* 4 (4): 171–92.

Bardsley, N. and Ule, A. (2014) "Focal Points Revisited: Team Reasoning, the Principle of Insufficient Reason and Cognitive Hierarchy Theory," Munich Personal RePEc Archive Paper No. 58256.

Bardsley, N., Mehta, J., Starmer, C. and Sugden, R. (2010) "Explaining Focal Points: Cognitive Hierarchy Theory versus Team Reasoning," *The Economic Journal* 120: 40–79.

Bratman, M. (2009a) "Shared Agency," in C. Mantzavinos (ed.) *Philosophy of the Social Sciences: Philosophical Theory and Scientific Practice*, New York: Cambridge University Press.

——— (2009b) "Modest Sociality and the Distinctiveness of Intention," *Philosophical Studies* 144 (1): 149–65.

Chater, N., Misyak, J.B., Melkonyan, T. and Zeitoun, H. (2016) "Virtual Bargaining: Building the Foundations for a Theory of Social Interaction," in J. Kiverstein (ed.) *Handbook of the Social Mind*, London: Routledge.

Colman, A.M., Pulford, B.D. and Rose, J. (2008) "Collective Rationality in Interactive Decisions: Evidence for Team Reasoning," *Acta Psychologica* 128: 387–97.

Colman, A.M., Pulford, B.D. and Lawrence, C.L. (2014) "Explaining Strategic Cooperation: Cognitive Hierarchy Theory, Strong Stackelberg Reasoning, and Team Reasoning," *Decision* 1: 35–58.

Faillo, M., Smerilli, A. and Sugden, R. (2013) "The Roles of Level-k and Team Reasoning in Solving Coordination Games," Cognitive and Experimental Economics Laboratory Working Paper (No. 6–13), Department of Economics, University of Trento, Italy.

——— (2015) "Identifying the Roles of Level-K and Team Reasoning in Coordination Games," (unpublished ms).

Gauthier, D. (1986) *Morals by Agreement*, Oxford: Oxford University Press.

——— (2013) "Twenty-Five On," *Ethics* 123: 601–24.

Gilbert, M. (1997) "What Is It for Us to Intend? in G. Holmström Hintikka and R. Tuomela (eds) *Contemporary Action Theory, Vol. 2: Social Action*, Dordrecht: Kluwer.

——— (2009) "Shared Intention and Personal Intentions," *Philosophical Studies* 144 (1): 167–87.

Gold, N. (2012) "Team Reasoning, Framing and Cooperation," in S. Okasha and K. Binmore (eds) *Evolution and Rationality: Decisions, Co-operation and Strategic Behaviour*, Cambridge: Cambridge University Press, ch. 9, 185–212.

——— (2013) "Team Reasoning, Framing, and Self-Control: An Aristotelian Account," in N. Levy (ed.) *Addiction and Self-Control: Perspectives from Philosophy, Psychology, and Neuroscience*, Oxford: Oxford University Press

——— (2015) "Guarding Against Temptation: Rational Intentions and Intra-personal Team Reasoning," (unpublished manuscript).

Gold, N. and Sugden, R. (2007a) "Collective Intentions and Team Agency," *Journal of Philosophy* 104: 109–37.

——— (2007b) "Theories of Team Agency," in F. Peter and H.B. Schmid (eds) *Rationality and Commitment*, Oxford: Oxford University Press.

Gold, N. and Harbour, D. (2012) "Cognitive Primitives of Collective Intentions: Linguistic Evidence of Our Mental Ontology," *Mind & Language* 27 (2): 109–34.

Hakli, R., Miller, K. and Tuomela, R. (2010) "Two Kinds of We-Reasoning," *Economics and Philosophy* 26 (3): 291–320.

Harsanyi, J. and Selten, R. (1988) *A General Theory of Equilibrium Selection in Games*, Cambridge MA: MIT Press.

Hodgson, D. (1967) *Consequences of Utilitarianism*, Oxford: Clarendon Press.

Hurley, S.L. (1989) *Natural Reasons: Personality and Polity*, Oxford: Oxford University Press.

——— (2005a) "Rational Agency, Cooperation and Mind-Reading," in N. Gold (ed.), *Teamwork: Multi-Disciplinary Perspectives*, London: Palgrave Macmillan.

——— (2005b) "Social Heuristics that Make Us Smarter," *Philosophical Psychology* 18: 585–612.

Karpus, J. and Gold, N. (2016) "Team Reasoning: Theory and Experiment," in J. Kiverstein (ed.) *Handbook of the Social Mind*, London: Routledge.

Karpus, J. and Radzvilas, M. (2015) "Team Reasoning and a Rank-Based Function of Team's Interests," (manuscript under review).

Marr, D. (1982) *Vision: A Computational Approach*, London: W.H. Freeman and Company.

Misyak, J.B. and Chater, N. (2014) "Virtual Bargaining: A Theory of Social Decision-Making," *Philosophical Transactions of the Royal Society B: Biological Sciences* 369 (1655): 20130487.

Misyak, J.B., Melkonyan, T., Zeitoun, H. and Chater, N. (2014) "Unwritten Rules: Virtual Bargaining Underpins Social Interaction, Culture, and Society," *Trends in Cognitive Sciences* 18 (10): 512–19.

O'Donoghue, T. and Rabin, M. (1999) "Doing It Now or Later," *American Economic Review* 89: 103–24.

Pacherie, E. (2011) "Framing Joint Action," *Review of Philosophy and Psychology* 2 (2): 173–92.

Parfit, D. (1984) *Reasons and Persons*, Oxford: Oxford University Press.

Pettit, P. (2007) "Rationality, Reasoning and Group Agency," *Dialectica* 61 (4): 495–519.

Polanyi, M. (1962) "Tacit Knowing: Its Bearing on Some Problems of Philosophy," *Reviews of Modern Physics* 34 (4): 601–15.

Rawls, J. (1999) *A Theory of Justice*, revised edition, Cambridge MA: Harvard University Press.

Regan, D. (1980) *Utilitarianism and Co-operation*, Oxford: Clarendon Press.

Schweikard, D.P. and Schmid, H.B. (2013) "Collective Intentionality," in E.N. Zalta (ed.) *The Stanford Encyclopedia of Philosophy* (Summer 2013 edition), http://plato.stanford.edu/archives/sum2013/entries/collective-intentionality/.

Smerilli, A. (2012) "We-Thinking and Vacillation Between Frames: Filling a Gap in Bacharach's Theory," *Theory and Decision* 73: 539–60.

Strotz, R.H. (1955) "Myopia and Inconsistency in Dynamic Utility Maximization," *The Review of Economic Studies* 23: 165–80.

Sugden, R. (1993) "Thinking as a Team: Towards an Explanation of Nonselfish Behavior," *Social Philosophy and Policy* 10: 69–89.

——— (2000) "Team Preferences," *Economics and Philosophy* 16: 175–204.

——— (2003) "The Logic of Team Reasoning," *Philosophical Explorations: An International Journal for the Philosophy of Mind and Action* 6: 165–81.

——— (2008) "Nash Equilibrium, Team Reasoning and Cognitive Hierarchy Theory," *Acta Psychologica* 128: 402–4.

——— (2011) "Mutual Advantage, Conventions and Team Reasoning," *International Review of Economics* 58: 9–20.

——— (2015) "Team Reasoning and Intentional Cooperation for Mutual Benefit," *Journal of Social Ontology* 1: 143–66.

Tuomela, R. (2006) "Joint Intention, We-Mode and I-Mode," *Midwest Studies in Philosophy* 30: 35–58.

——— (2009) "Collective Intentions and Game Theory," *Journal of Philosophy* 106: 292–300.

NOTES

1. The idea that collective intentions result from team reasoning may be related to Tuomela's (2006) idea of reasoning in the *we*-mode, where agents must function as group members and intend for a group reason (see also Hakli et al. 2010).
2. Colman et al. (2008, 2014) use prisoner's dilemma type games to pit team reasoning against individual reasoning. As well as the confounds identified above, Sugden (2008) has pointed out that subjects' behavior in the experiments would also be predicted by another theory of coordination, cognitive hierarchy theory. See Karpus and Gold (2016) for more discussion.
3. See tasks NA6 and NA8 in Bardsley et al. (2010), where 54 out of 56 subjects (96 percent) chose *Hi*.

18

Groups as Distributed Cognitive Systems

Georg Theiner

1. INTRODUCTION AND OVERVIEW

The concept of *distributed cognition* (DC) figures prominently in contemporary discussions of the idea that the social, cultural, and technological distribution of cognitive labor in groups can give rise to "group cognition" or "collective intelligence." Since there are different ways of understanding the notion of DC, there is much debate about what "ontological heft" we should attach to the thesis that groups are distributed cognitive systems. The goal of this chapter is to map out the conceptual terrain on which this debate is taking place. My approach is grounded in the framework of DC which has been developed, since the mid-1980s, notably by Edwin Hutchins, Donald Norman, and David Kirsh. In particular, I borrow here as my starting point their suggestion that taking up the DC perspective is not itself an empirical thesis about a certain *kind* of cognition; rather, it is a methodological decision to select scales of investigation from which *all* of cognition can be analyzed as distributed. As Hutchins (2014: 236) recently put this point,

> the interesting question then is not "is cognition distributed or is it not?" or even "is cognition sometimes distributed and sometimes not distributed?" Rather, the interesting questions concern the elements of the cognitive system, the relations among the elements, and how cognitive processes arise from interactions among those elements.

Let me begin by outlining two key methodological principles of the DC framework (cf. Hutchins 1995: 2014).

First, we cannot tell ahead of empirical investigation how to draw the boundaries for the units of DC analysis, or even identify what those units are, because they depend on the scale of the cognitive system under investigation. The DC perspective can be taken up with respect to cognitive systems at multiple spatial scales, ranging from neural circuits inside the brain, to systems that are distributed across areas of the brain and parts of one's body, material artifacts and cultural practices, or entire social groups. Groups that have been analyzed as socially distributed cognitive systems include couples, families, work teams, social networks, communities, crowds, organizations, markets, cultures, or entire ecosystems. Furthermore, within a particular scale of DC, what constitutes the relevant *unit* of cognitive analysis is not fixed but can change dynamically within the context or development of a cognitive activity.

Second, the choice of a scale and unit of DC analysis depends on the phenomena one wishes to study, and the questions one seeks to answer. Many phenomena of cognitive interest, such as memory, language, problem-solving, or decision-making, can be studied at multiple, interacting scales of cognitive analysis, including processes that unfold both within and across people (Goldstone and Theiner 2017). By taking up the DC perspective, researchers aim to discover principles and regularities applying at multiple scales of analysis, and across different kinds of cognitive systems. In the eyes of DC proponents, the suggested flexibility of drawing the boundaries of cognitive systems in ways that cut across biological boundaries is of great explanatory value; in the eyes of its critics, playing "fast and loose" with the concept of cognition is a vice which depletes its explanatory value (Adams and Aizawa 2010; Rupert 2011; Ludwig 2015).

The focus of the present chapter rests on the more specific issue of whether *socially distributed* cognition (SDC) amounts to *group level* cognition. By "group (level) cognition," I mean the thesis that the group as a whole, embedded in the right sociocultural and material environment, can have cognitive states, processes, activities, properties, or capacities[1] that are not possessed by any of its members. Without further argument, and some conceptual housekeeping, we cannot assume that SDC supports the thesis of group cognition. The intended inference can go awry in two critical respects.

First, it could deliver a group-level product that fails to be recognizably *cognitive*. Being able to diagnose this failure presupposes that we have a principled criterion for demarcating cognitive from non-cognitive patterns, a so-called "mark" of the cognitive. There is much debate over whether there is such a generic criterion, and to what extent we need to have it fully articulated before we can meaningfully identify groups as units of cognitive analysis (Rupert 2005, 2011, forthcoming). Contemporary proponents of group cognition typically restrict their claims to particular kinds of psychological attributes which they take to be shareable by individuals and groups. Such attributes can be drawn from folk psychology (e.g. belief, intention, or rational agency), refer to classical mental faculties (e.g. memory, decision-making, or problem-solving), or involve more theoretically driven notions (e.g. computation, network theory, or coordination dynamics).

Second, the inference could deliver a cognitive product that fails to be a distinctively *group*-level phenomenon. It is by no means necessary that the social distribution of property X within a group G entails that G itself must also have X. For example, the social distribution of illness or crime rates in the US does not turn the US as a whole into a sick patient or a criminal. We would rightfully dismiss the above entailment as the "category mistake" of supposing that what is true of parts must be true of the whole. However, just because it is not simply a matter of logical consequence, this does not mean that it can *never* be true that whatever is distributed among the parts of a system cannot also be rightfully ascribed to the system as a whole. But the onus here rests on the proponent of group cognition to show that "cognition" is of the latter type.

In summary, it is incumbent upon proponents of group cognition to secure the desired conclusion by doing several things. First, they must clarify what exactly it means to say that cognition is "socially distributed" in groups, and why this supports their claim that group cognition is not reducible to individual cognition. Second, even if we bracket the question of whether there is a generic "mark" of the mental, we need an account of how to identify cognitive attributes at the group level. The structure of my chapter adheres to this scheme: first, I break down the multifaceted notion of SDC into a *joint*, a *distributive*, and a *shared* aspect; next, I highlight organization-dependence, novelty, and autonomy as central features associated with the *emergent* qualities of SDC. Finally, I survey five theoretical "stances" that have been invoked to identify the presence of *cognitive* organization at the group level, and thus bridge the suggested inferential gap between SDC and group cognition.

2. WHAT DOES IT MEAN TO SAY THAT COGNITION IS "SOCIALLY DISTRIBUTED"?

If we treat as an open, substantial question whether SDC implies group cognition, we ought to conceptualize the "social distribution" of cognitive labor that is carried out by a plurality of individual cognitive agents in a metaphysically neutral manner with respect to our answer to that question. Intuitively, we must leave room for the fact that the cognitive contributions of individual agents, even when considered as members of the same group, can be combined or aggregated in ways that are insufficiently integrated, or "wrapped up into one" (Bennett 2011), for the group as a whole to be truthfully considered as a bearer of cognitive attributes. Group cognition does not come cheap. In what follows, I offer a two-dimensional taxonomy of the modes in which cognition can be said to be "socially distributed." The first dimension concerns different conceptions of what it means to "share" or "distribute" something; the second dimension speaks to the conditions under which we individuate a set of interconnected parts as elements of a single system, often with collective properties that are irreducible to the properties of its parts. I take it as a virtue of my taxonomy that it doesn't prejudge the issue of whether the suggested analysis of SDC implies that groups are *cognitive* systems. At the same time, as we shall see more clearly in the next section, it helps to explain why certain modes of SDC are more apt than others to give rise to cognition at the group level.

a. "Shared" vs "Distributive" vs "Joint" Aspects of SDC

Discussions of SDC often equivocate between three different conceptions of what it means to "distribute" or "share" a cognitive attribute. One sense of distribution ("sharing-with") refers to the fact of having some cognitive attribute in common, such as when people have the same (or similar) memories, beliefs, or values. A different sense of distribution ("sharing-out") refers to different ways of apportioning a cognitive task by divvying the workload, and combining individual contributions to get the job done. A third sense of distribution ("sharing-in") refers to the way in which people can jointly participate in a cognitive activity as a group. This last sense of "sharing-in" arguably requires the capacity for distinctive forms of joint (or collective) intentionality—an awareness of intentionally doing something together (this volume). For the sake of disambiguation, let us refer to the above three interpretations as the *shared*, *distributive*, and *joint* aspects of SDC.

What more can we say about them, how are they related, and how are they relevant for understanding groups as distributed cognitive systems?

We can pin down the *joint* aspect of SDC by reflecting on what it takes for people to engage in a "shared cooperative activity" (Bratman 1992) such as carrying a sofa or painting a house together. The performance of a shared cooperative activity (in this sense) requires having the corresponding joint intention to do so (this volume). This notion has been analyzed in several ways. But abstracting from important differences that need not concern us here, we can extract four conditions that are typically met if two or more people jointly intend to do something (Pettit and Schweikard 2006; cf. Ludwig 2007 for discussion):

J1. Shared goal: They each intend that all members perform in ways that promote a common goal.

J2. Individual contributions: They each intend to do their work as part of a more or less specified plan for achieving that goal.

J3. Interdependence: They each form these intentions at least in part because of believing that the others (have or will) form similar intentions.

J4. Common awareness: Conditions J1–J3 are satisfied in conditions of common knowledge.

The role of "joint intentions" is to support the social coordination of individual actions, the formation of shared plans, and to provide a framework for relevant bargaining (Bratman 1992, 2014). It has been argued on empirical grounds that the "Bratman conditions" are too cognitively and conceptually demanding to be satisfied in all instances of joint action, and several counterproposals have been offered (cf. Pacherie 2013; Tomasello 2014). My goal here is not to adjudicate this ongoing debate, but rather to point out that any such analysis of joint intentions is ontologically neutral with respect to the type or nature of activity that is to be carried out jointly. In particular, it does not discriminate against the joint (intentional) performance of *cognitive* or *epistemic* activities such as solving a LEGO puzzle, making a medical diagnosis, or solving a math problem *together*. Thus, we can let a suitably modified version of the Bratman conditions do double duty to elucidate the "joint" aspect of SDC. How do the other two aspects fit into this picture?

The *distributive* aspect of SDC, which subcategorizes (subcategorizes) the above Bratman condition J2, highlights specific forms of mutual interdependence in a group that results from the social organization of cognitive labor. It is widely recognized that ascriptions of agency or mentality to collectivities are ambiguous between a collective ("Greece rejected the bailout offer") and a distributive reading ("Greek citizens rejected the bailout offer") (cf. Ludwig 2007). However, this dichotomy has precious little to say about importantly different ways in which individual contributions can be combined to yield a group outcome. Progress can be made by appealing to a taxonomy of group tasks, developed by Steiner (1966)(cf. Laughlin 2011), which recognizes five elementary modes of social combination:

D1. Additive tasks: The group outcome is the sum of individual contributions. For example, it has been estimated that the German men's soccer team ran an average of 75.12 miles per game during the 2014 World Cup.

D2. Compensatory tasks: The group outcome is a function of individual contributions, such as when the formation of a group judgment is the outcome of adopting averaging, plurality, or unanimity decision schemes.

D3. Disjunctive tasks: Each member works independently on a problem, but the group must select a single solution as the outcome. For example, a trivia quiz group has to decide on a single response among conflicting solutions suggested by its members.

D4. Conjunctive tasks: The group outcome consists of a series of (more or less) identical tasks which each member has to perform in order for the group to succeed. An example would be a 4×400 m relay race.

D5. Complementary tasks: The group outcome stems from a division of labor which assigns distinct but complementary subtasks to different members which are then pooled together. Since individuals can bring their different abilities, skills, and knowledge to the table, complementary task distributions make effective use of parallelization and specialization. They often result in group activities that greatly exceed what any individual could have achieved in isolation, such as an orchestra performing a symphony or a football team running a pass play.

The literature on SDC has focused mostly on the non-summative aspects of compensatory and complementary task distributions when cognitive tasks are performed at the group level.

A striking demonstration of *compensatory* problem-solving is the "wisdom of crowds" effect (Surowiecki 2004). Under certain conditions, the social aggregation of individual decisions can lead to superior collective outcomes than either group deliberation or individual expert judgment. Unlike traditional methods for group decision-making (e.g. consensus formation), which rely on the power of interactive dialogue, the wisdom of crowds is unleashed through decentralized aggregation mechanisms (such as market pricing, as used in prediction markets, or Delphi methods) designed to preserve a greater diversity of opinions[2]. By incentivizing independently acting decision-makers to draw on local, specialized sources of information, minimally collaborative groups are more resistant to the pressures of conformism, "groupthink," and negative effects of information cascades. Bettencourt (2009) discusses under which conditions the aggregation of information in social collectives can provide more (surplus) or less (redundancy) information than is contained in the sum of its parts (see also condition E1 below).

At the other end of the SDC spectrum are maximally collaborative instances of *complementary* problem-solving, which include maritime navigation (Hutchins 1995), scientific research (Giere 2002), early modern theatric performances (Tribble 2005), bioengineering labs (Nersessian 2006), and crime scene investigation (Baber et al. 2006). In each of those cases, the complementarity of problem-solving is not only spread across people but includes the functional integration of material and sociocultural resources made available by the environment in which they take place, which is often deliberately designed to "scaffold" the performance of work-related activities (Sutton et al. 2010; Palermos 2015).

Comparing these two types of group tasks reveals a "double dissociation" between the distributive and joint aspects of what constitutes—albeit in importantly different senses—a socially "distributed" activity. On the one hand, the statistical mechanism of aggregating individual judgments in a crowd is not a "jointly intended" activity (*sensu* Bratman). Individual decision-makers may, but need not, form a joint intention to figure out the correct answer together, and the corresponding *lack* of interpersonal dependence and social influence is precisely what accounts for the greater accuracy of group judgments in a compensatory task. On the other hand, four people who jointly recite a Latin poem on stage, in perfect synchrony, engage in a conjunctive task with a role distribution that does not amount to a "complementary" activity (*sensu* Steiner).

The sense in which people belonging to the same group, community, or culture tend to "share-with" each other, in a non-accidental manner, a salient "mentality" of beliefs or values was historically an important facet of the "group mind" thesis in the late nineteenth and early twentieth century (Wegner 1986). All by itself, this sense of "sharing-with" is perhaps best understood as a form of socially manifested individual cognition (Wilson 2005), rather than SDC. For example, group-induced cognitive similarities that were attributed to the manifestation of a "crowd" mind (Le Bon 1895), such as emotional contagion or group polarization, are likely to be explainable in terms of context-dependent individual-cognitive mechanisms triggered by specific types of social interactions. However, the act of "sharing-with" cognitive attributes combines and interacts with the other two aspects to form the larger complex of psychological mechanisms that enable and causally underlie SDC. For example, the formation of "team mental models" (Mohammed et al. 2010), understood as a set of shared mental representations of "teamwork" and "taskwork" related categories, has been invoked to explain why teams perform better when their members interpret information in a similar manner, share expectations concerning future events, and develop similar causal accounts of their situation. From a different, dynamical systems perspective, the fluid performance of joint actions in real time has been shown to depend on multiple systems of "alignment" or dynamic matching between the cognitive and behavioral states of the participant actors, such as bodily posture, visual attention, or patterns of speech (Dale et al. 2013; Cooke et al. 2013).

The formulation of a unified framework for analyzing the complex interactions among the shared, distributive, and joint aspects of socially distributed cognitive systems remains a distant goal. An important desideratum would be to show how the development of the largely species-specific capacity for SDC draws on the psychological infrastructure of a multi-level "alignment" system which has evolved in human beings to scaffold the performance of joint activities (Gallotti et al. 2017).

b. "Emergent" Aspects of SDC

The second dimension of SDC concerns the processes by which the cognitive contributions of individual agents are combined and integrated into a group level outcome, and the related question of how the nature of these processes affects the quality, quantity, and type of outcome that it produces. Often, the term "emergence" is used to denote certain types of socially distributed cognitive processes that are heavily structured by the interactions among individual contributors whose cognitive and behavioral activities are strongly interdependent ("coupled"). This stands in contrast to "aggregative" combination schemes in which individuals work more or less independently from each other, such that the combined outcome of their interactions amounts to nothing more than a function of the individual contributions taken in isolation. Upon closer inspection, we find that that the term "emergence" is used—often in an ambiguous fashion—to denote three distinct (albeit related) aspects of this basic idea (cf. Theiner and O'Connor 2010).

E1. Organization-dependence: SDC is "emergent" in this sense if it involves cognitive processes whose realization depends on the structure and organization of the interactions by which the actions, ideas, and resources of individuals are combined and integrated in the production of a group-level outcome. From a complex systems perspective, this form of organization-dependence illustrates a more general phenomenon: first, the joint outcome of two or more interacting parts of a system differs from the aggregated outcome of the parts operating independently ("emergence"); second, the behavior of mutually interacting parts is different from the behavior of those parts in isolation ("synergy"). Wimsatt (1986) defined emergence as the failure of "aggregativity" in complex systems, determined by the degree in which system-level properties are affected by (i) the substitution of parts, (ii) the addition or subtraction of parts, (iii) the rearrangements of parts, and (iv) the prevalence of cooperative or inhibitory interactions among parts. Following Wimsatt's conception, many instances of SDC can be shown to involve emergent group-level phenomena (Theiner et al. 2010; Theiner 2013). The impact of organizational structure underpins the reality of groups as causal units that are capable of interacting with individuals, other groups, and their environment.

It must be emphasized that E1 concerns purely *organizational* aspects of complexity. Hence, it ought to be distinguished from *performance* measures that compare group-level outcomes (e.g. quality of decision-making) to outcomes produced by individuals working independently (relative to some benchmark criterion, such as "better than best" or "better than average"). For example, Collins and Guetzkow (1964) coined the phrase "assembly effect bonus" to denote outcomes where the group performance 'exceeds the potential of the most capable members and also exceeds the sum of the efforts of the group members working separately' (1964: 58). There has been a tendency in the literature to conflate those two notions, but they are not the same. The failure of aggregativity (i.e. emergence) in collaborative groups is, in fact, a *precondition* for performance gains or losses due to interactivity. The conditions under which interactivity does lead to *superior* group outcomes are surprisingly fragile, and dependent on skillful coordinative practices (Larson 2010; Bahrami et al. 2012).

E2. Novelty: SDC can have unexpected consequences at the group level that were not intended (either individually or jointly) or purposefully designed by any of the individuals (or some central planning agency). More precisely, we also need to distinguish between effects that were not intended but anticipated, and effects that individuals not only failed to anticipate but may not even notice when they occur. The feature of novelty is related to the epistemic incompleteness of individual-level explanations, because it suggests that there can be qualitatively novel group-level regularities which cannot be predicted from the standpoint of individual cognitive behavior (Sawyer 2003).

E3. Autonomy: SDC gives rise to group-level patterns that have a certain autonomy which makes them, in some important sense, not reducible to the cognitive behavior of individuals, their social aggregation, and the material environment in which they are embedded. A common theme underlying various arguments for autonomy is that one and the same collective pattern can be observed in many different configurations that may otherwise have little or nothing in common. Within the literature on SDC, this theme has been developed in two main variations. Drawing on the "hardware/software" distinction within functionalist philosophy of mind, one reason offered for the irreducibility of socially distributed cognitive patterns is that they are similarly "multiply realizable," insofar as they can in principle be realized by different kinds of individual-cognitive contributions, combined by different types of social interactions (Theiner and O'Connor 2010). In the study of complex systems, the notion of "universality" refers to scale-invariant principles that hold for a large class of physically diverse systems, independent of the dynamical details of those systems. Examples of universality include phenomena such as "self-organized criticality" or "diffusion-limited aggregation." Goldstone and Theiner (2017) offer a network-theoretic perspective on cognitive principles and mechanisms that can be found at multiple levels, including within and across people.

3. A "MACROSCOPE" FOR VIEWING GROUP COGNITION

Thus far, we have discussed various dimensions and aspects of SDC, and how it can give rise to emergent group level properties. However, this does not necessarily allow us to infer the occurrence of group level cognition. In order to establish this conclusion, one needs to identify the presence of a recognizably *cognitive* organization at the group level, and show how it plays a causal-explanatory role with respect to the behavior of the group (and, derivatively, its members). In what follows, I review five theoretical "stances" that have been invoked to bridge the suggested inferential gap. Each stance starts from a different set of assumptions, and uses different concepts, methods, and tools for studying cognition[3]. We can conceive of each stance as a "macroscope" (Rosnay 1979) for rendering intelligible the idea that cognition can be socially distributed among people in ways that constitute group level cognitive systems, instantiating group level cognitive attributes.

GC1. The Intentional Stance:

> Our practice of interpreting the actions of organizations is just an extension of our practice of making sense of individuals, and it is governed by the same constitutive rules. Our attempt to make sense of the actions of organizations would fail unless we assumed that the organization itself is rational. This involves assuming that the organization has a rational point of view from which members engage in the same sorts of cognitive activities individuals engage in and that the organization is governed by the same norms of rationality.
>
> (Tollefsen 2002: 402)

In common parlance as well as social scientific research, we often talk about what a company intends to do, what a court of law judges illegal, or what a church holds sacred. In doing that, we attribute inferentially connected intentional mental states ("propositional attitudes") such as beliefs, desires, and intentions to groups, organizations, and other collectivities. GC1 seeks to elucidate the nature of mental states by reflecting on the intelligibility of our social practice of understanding each other as rational agents. Based on "intentional systems theory"—a view of commonsensical psychological explanations developed most notably by Daniel Dennett—if we can "usefully and voluminously" predict, explain, and interpret the behavior of a collectivity by adopting the intentional stance, then that collectivity *is* an intentional agent (Tollefsen 2002, 2004; Clark 1994).

To see how this works, consider an application of the intentional stance to organizations (Tollefsen 2002). First, we presuppose that the structure of the organization synthesizes the diverse perspectives of its members to yield a collectively rational point of view that forms the locus of deliberation, agency, and responsibility. We need not suppose that this collective point of view, and the epistemic demands of rationality which it implies, are always jointly intended, or indeed grasped, by each individual member. More plausibly, the organizational rationality required to coordinate complex collaborative efforts is made possible, and mediated, through subordination to rules and policies, routines and "truces," authority relations, complex member-tool-task networks, control systems, and "sense-making" practices (Gordon and Theiner 2015). Second, we then determine what intentional states the organization ought to have in order to accomplish its goals in a rational manner. This includes the ability to monitor and adjust its own goals, but also to recalibrate the norms and standards by which the organization evaluates its agency.

List and Pettit (2011) adeptly draw on formal results in social choice theory to justify taking the intentional stance towards organized collectivities. Their main argument for the irreducibility of group agency is based on the generalization of a logical paradox ("discursive dilemma") that arises when a multi-member group has to aggregate conflicting sets of individual intentional attitudes, with respect to sets of interconnected propositions, into a single system of collective attitudes. As List and Pettit show, groups are able to display the rationally unified perspective that agency requires only if their collective attitudes are not determined by a majoritarian (or other equally "summative") function of its member attitudes. One strategy is to "collectivize" reason at the expense of individual rationality, e.g. by letting the majority views on certain judgments ("premises") dictate the group's view on other judgments ("conclusion"), even when this contradicts what the majority individually believe about the conclusion. Another strategy is to adopt distributed decision-making procedures where different subgroups are authorized to "fix" the group's attitudes on specific judgments. This allows a group to take advantage of special expertise in some members, but curtails other members' input on the issue at hand. By detailing a plethora of situations in which individual and group attitudes can come apart, often in surprising ways, List and Pettit offer an epistemological argument for the autonomous character of group agency (for a criticism, see Szigeti 2015).

GC2. The Information Processing Stance:

> We suggest that the term "social cognition" can be usefully applied at the group level of analysis to refer to those social processes [. . .] that relate to the acquisition, storage, transmission, manipulation and use of information for the purpose of creating a group-level intellective product.
>
> (Larson and Christensen 1993: 6)

There has been a growing trend in small-group research to consider collaborative groups as cognitive units in their own right (Wittenbaum et al. 2004). GC2 combines a functional analysis of the steps or processes that groups follow in the course of producing group-level cognitive outcomes with the use of information-processing models to compare and contrast how individuals and groups perform those functions as they engage in the same types of cognitive tasks. I refer to this broadly "functionalist" approach as the collective "information processing" stance (Larson and Christensen 1993; Hinsz et al. 1997).

Consider, by way of example, a group decision-making sequence that goes through an *orientation* phase, a *discussion* phase, a *decision* phase, and an *implementation* phase (cf. Forsyth 2006: 316). Associated with each step are several tasks; for example, during the orientation phase, a group has to define the problem, set goals, and develop a strategy. Next, we associate each task with one or more components of a generic information processing model. For example, the information a group *acquires* during the discussion phase is embedded in a context that provides a *processing objective*; information must be selectively *attended*; it must get *encoded* in representations that can be *stored, manipulated,* and *retrieved.* In the *processing work space* of the group, information integration and schematic processing occur on the basis of various rules, strategies, and procedures. Eventually, the group issues a *response* or output that creates *feedback* about situational changes (Hinsz et al. 1997: 44). Depending on the nature of the cognitive task (e.g. collective decision-making, memory, induction, evaluation), those information-processing components are "realized" by different types of interpersonal and intrapersonal processes and interactions.

For example, the ability of small groups to cooperatively allocate the tasks of encoding, storing, modifying, and recalling task-relevant information among members with specialized abilities or knowledge, has been studied as *transactive memory systems* (TMSs; Wegner 1986). The effective functioning of a differentiated TMS requires that its members develop a shared set of higher-order ("transactive") memories for keeping track of who knows what, so that they can confidently rely on but also challenge each other's perspectives. For example, transactive memories can be used for determining where, and in what format, incoming information ought to be stored in a group, and for cueing the recognized experts whenever an interactive information search is executed (Sutton et al. 2010). Using TMSs as a specimen, Theiner (2013) argues that adopting the collective information-processing stance to explain group-level cognitive capacities is akin to mechanistic explanations in individual psychology, albeit with an added (social) level of hierarchical organization.

GC3. The Computational Stance: '[. . .] the computation observed in the activity [ship navigation] of the larger system [crew] can be described in the way cognition has been traditionally described—that is, as computation realized through the creation, transformation, and propagation of representational states' (Hutchins 1995: 48). 'The system formed by the navigation team can be thought of as a computational machine in which social organization is computational architecture' (1995: 228).

Within DC, the theory of "computation" has been used as a "lingua franca" to analyze the cognitive functions and processes of both individuals and groups. Computations can be performed by physically diverse mechanisms and procedures that operate across a wide range of representational media. For DC, those media include representations formed inside a person's head, but also external representations such as verbal exchanges, bodily gestures, social transactions, maps, charts, and displays. In Hutchins (1995), the inference from SDC to group cognition is justified by uplifting Marr's (1982) tri-level scheme for analyzing mind and cognition as information-processing systems (1. computational task analysis; 2. algorithmic design; 3. physical implementation) from an individual to a collective unit of cognitive analysis. This results in a nested hierarchy of computational systems; what qualifies as "implementational" (level 3) for the crew as a whole sets task constraints (level 1) for the cognitive performances of individual members. As Hutchins shows, the differences between individual and collective computations, each carried out in tandem to perform a variety of navigational (sub-) tasks, arise from the combined effects of the social distribution of labor, mediated by people's interactions with technology.

Huebner (2013) defends group cognition with a sophisticated blend of GC1 and GC3. He argues that even if the behavior of groups is expediently predictable from the intentional stance, this has no real causal-explanatory purchase unless those predictions are firmly grounded in a mechanistic understanding of the cognitive architecture giving rise to those intentional states. Drawing on extant work in cognitive science, Huebner sketches an account of cognitive systems as "kludges" of interfaced networks of parallel distributed subsystems that work relatively independently of one another on specialized computational tasks. Each of the subsystems ("modules") processes only a narrow range of information, their operation is (largely) informationally "encapsulated" from the rest of the system, and they produce relatively domain-specific representations. The outputs of those subsystems must be integrated through local interfaces to yield meaningful system-level behavior. In human collectivities, those interfaces often involve the use of "trading languages" (Galison 1997) where people draw on local skills and strategies to negotiate the exchange of information across disparate domains. Group cognition 'only occurs where no subsystem is capable of producing an authoritative representation and where the representations of multiple subsystems can be coordinated and integrated to yield flexible, goal-directed system-level behavior' (Huebner 2013: 14).

Huebner's articulation of GC3 puts substantial architectural constraints on what types of groups are capable of robustly cognitive modes of organization. Many socially distributed cognitive systems fall short of his mark, because they do not eventuate in the production (and consumption) of genuinely collective mental representations. To distinguish the latter from mere collective "recordings" of individual mental activity, a group must collectively occupy content-bearing states and processes that are part of a larger representation scheme which allows a group to foresee and skillfully cope with changes in its environment, in systematic ways that can be decoupled from immediately present stimuli, and amenable to standards of correctness (Huebner 2013: ch. 7.4). Huebner's proposal is maximally geared towards "representation-hungry" knowledge-creating endeavors that are carried out, in a radically collaborative manner, by specialized workforces operating in abstract, technologically highly instrumented task environments (e.g. research communities in high-energy physics). But even among those collectivities, Huebner cautiously suggests that only very few are poised to exhibit the right kind of collective computational architecture to underwrite the norm-abiding "censoriousness" and "authentic" intentionality which some regard as the pinnacle of the intentional stance (cf. Haugeland 1998).

GC4. The Ecological Stance:

> To speak of cognitive ecology is to employ an obvious metaphor, that cognitive systems are in some specific way like biological systems. In particular, it points to the web of mutual dependence among the elements of an ecosystem. [. . .] just as a full understanding of biological organisms must include their relations to other organisms and physical conditions in their environments; so, an understanding of cognitive phenomena must include a consideration of the environments in which cognitive processes develop and operate.
>
> (Hutchins 2010: 706)

Hutchins (2010) formulates the ecological stance, with explicit reference to the cybernetic approach of Bateson (1972), as an alternative to GC2 and GC3. This may seem surprising, since all three evidently accord the notion of "information" an important role for under-standing mind and cognition. However, when Bateson applied cybernetics to ecological anthropology, he sought to emphasize that the information loops which constitute "mind" promiscuously criss-cross the boundaries of brain, body, and world. This orien-tation allowed him to identify dynamic patterns of correlation and social interdepen-dence that were profoundly shaped by culture, context, and history. In contrast, the classical computational approach focused on the representational role of static, inner symbolic structures. Hence, the individual brain seemed like the privileged unit of cognitive analysis, whereas the contributions of body, culture, and society could be sealed off as mere "inputs" or "stimuli" for the mind.

Choosing the right boundaries for a "unit" of analysis is a central problem in all of science, and depends on the ratio between the density of connections among the elements of a chosen unit vis-à-vis those between the elements inside and outside of the unit. But how this ratio is perceived is in part dependent on our stance: 'What looks like low connectivity under one theory may look like a region of high connectivity to another theory' (Hutchins 2010: 706). For the computational stance, points of contact between organism and environment look like rigid "barriers" to be surmounted; for the ecological stance, they are permeable "membranes" through which structural couplings and world-involving informational circuits can be built.

The "ecological" argument for group cognition, which advocates the suggested perspec-tival shift, involves two key steps. Step 1 is to show that by choosing the brain (or biological individual) as our unit of cognitive analysis, we arrive at an incomplete and distorted picture that leaves important cognitive phenomena unexplained. Thus, individualists are guilty of committing a "frame of reference" error (Clancey 1997). Step 2 is to show that certain cognitive phenomena which can be fully characterized only if we adopt a wider frame of reference should in fact be attributed to the group as a whole, understood as a "dynamic unit" (Mandelblit and Zachar 1998) embedded in its material and cultural surround. The second step rests on the identification of emergent cognitive properties that are found only at the collective unit level, but not present in the elements from which the unit is composed.

We should note here the logical gap between these two steps. Even if it is granted that step 1 is sufficient to break the individualist mold, it does not always fund a defense of group cognition unless we also have reason for assenting to step 2. There are cognitive phe-nomena that we attribute to individuals, although explaining them requires that we take into consideration the larger context in which the phenomenon unfolds. For example, the continuous availability of search engines for memory retrieval increases a person's transac-tive reliance on remembering where to find the information rather than the content itself. Proponents of SDC will argue (step 1) that the "Google" effect on memory shows how a person's technological environment can play an "enabling" or perhaps even "constitutive" role in the explanation of individual memory. However, this does not automatically imply that the collection of all Google users forms a mutually co-adapting and jointly collabora-tive network that is necessary for groups to develop and sustain a TMS (Huebner 2016).

GC5. The Dynamical Stance:

The array of mechanisms [of human interaction] must have interdependencies operating in a coherent fashion that organizes the system into a lower dimensional functional unit, and possibly a much smaller number of stable higher level behaviors, expectedly lower than what would be anticipated from the complexity of the system's composition. For example, [. . .] one could see stable modes in the form of *arguing* [. . .] or *flirting* [. . .] or *joint decision making* [. . .] or *giving directions.*

(Dale et al. 2013: 55)

Dynamical systems theory is increasingly embraced not only in those areas of cognitive science studying the minds of individuals, but as a foundation for research on SDC (Arrow et al. 2000; Dale et al. 2013). With its emphasis on time-evolving properties of complex systems, it offers a powerful suite of concepts and tools to analyze how members of dynamically "coupled" social systems (such as dyads or groups) continually interact and mutually constrain each other in the performance of socially coordinated activities. The dynamical stance approaches human interaction from the general perspective of 'self-organization into functional synergies[4]' (Dale et al. 2013), which in the case of groups can be achieved through multiple channels of interpersonal coordination that range from perception-action links, joint attention, emotional affiliation, joint intentionality, dialogical interaction, to shared norms and conventions. Dale et al. distinguish three kinds of self-organizing mechanisms structuring human interactions: i) behavioral *synchrony* (e.g. mimicking each other's postures or gestures) and interactive *alignment* (e.g. imitating each other's choice of words or speech rates); ii) behavioral *complementarity*, such as conversational turn-taking or compensatory "helping" behaviors that require a role reversal; iii) *interactional patterns* and *coordinative routines* that emerge from a shared history of interactions, and subsequently scaffold and constrain the interaction space (e.g. narratives that frame situation awareness).

Utilizing the apparatus of dynamical systems theory, Palermos (2016) offers a succinct statement of the "dynamicist" argument for group cognition from SDC, based on three key premises: the first implicitly refers to a pre-theoretical understanding of cognitive processes; the other two concern the conditions under which groups of two or more interacting individuals are rightfully considered as proper *systems* ("subjects") of the relevant (cognitive or non-cognitive) processes. Concerning the first premise, dynamicists will point out that psychologists generally individuate cognitive systems in terms of their ability to carry out processes or tasks they intuitively consider as cognitive, mostly because they are implicated in the production of intelligent (e.g. flexible, adaptive, goal-directed) behavior. This characterization leaves open whether group cognition involves cognitive processes that are also carried out by individuals (e.g. *learning, reasoning, decision-making*), or refer to cognitive processes that are more explicitly interactive by nature (e.g. *arguing* or *flirting* in the quote above).

Second, the mutual interactions among people—understood as dynamically coupled (non-autonomous) systems—give rise to emergent systemic properties and regularities ("collective variables") that cannot be meaningfully attributed to any of the individuals in isolation. Those might include (say) recurring patterns of dialogical interaction, or changes to the temporal dynamics or outcomes of transactive remembering processes. The presence of irreducibly group level collective variables does not establish, nor does it require, their status as *cognitive* properties; still, it disarms the objection that positing groups as distributed cognitive *systems* has no explanatory value, because the instantiation of collective variables would otherwise be unaccounted for.

Third, the special role of continuous reciprocal feedback loops explains how the cognitive contributions of individual members can constitute a unified group level system. Intuitively, if two non-autonomous systems are dynamically coupled, the way in which each system is causally affected by the other is itself partly determined by its own behavior ("endogenously"), rather than triggered by external causal determinants ("exogenously"). The non-linear dependence of "dynamic couplings" enmeshes the cognitive processes of individual contributors into a causally integrated functional unit, making it mathematically impossible to decompose the behavior of the overall system into separate subsystems interacting via discrete "inputs" and "outputs." In other words, the presence of "ongoing feedback loops" yields an empirical criterion for distinguishing genuinely *distributed*, two-way cognitive processes from regular, one-way causal interactions (e.g. asking a stranger for directions). For example, in a study of joint perceptual decision-making, Bahrami et al. (2010) found that dyads who were more adept at sharing, combining, and integrating task-relevant information showed an improved cognitive performance, and their degree of success can be associated with dynamic measures of dialogical interactivity (cf. Fusaroli and Tylén 2016).

4. CONCLUDING REMARK

The multifaceted phenomenon of group cognition forces us to reconsider, and possibly overhaul, traditional assumptions about the bounds of cognition, and the privilege of individuals as the sole bearers of cognitive states and processes. The main ingredients for a unified framework for studying group cognition are available but, like scattered pieces of a puzzle, they must be retrieved from different corners of the intellectual landscape. In this chapter, I have provided a prolegomenon that I hope will help to advance this important project.

REFERENCES

Adams, F., & Aizawa, K. (2010) *The Bounds of Cognition*, Malden, MA: Wiley.

Arrow, H., McGrath, J.E., & Berdahl, J.L. (2000) *Small Groups as Complex Systems: Formation, Coordination, Development, and Adaptation*, Thousand Oaks: Sage Publications.

Baber, C., Smith, P.A., Cross, J., Hunter, J., & McMaster, R. (2006) "Crime Scene Investigation as Distributed Cognition," *Pragmatics and Cognition* 14: 357–85.

Bahrami, B., Olsen, K., Bang, D., Roepstorff, A., Rees, G., & Frith, C. (2012) "What Failure in Collective Decision-Making Tells Us About Metacognition," *Philosophical Transactions of the Royal Society of London B: Biological Sciences* 367 (1594): 1350–65.

——— (2010) "Optimally Interacting Minds," *Science* 329 (5995): 1081–5.

Bateson, G. (1972) *Steps to an Ecology of Mind*, Chicago: University of Chicago Press.

Bennett, K. (2011) "Construction Area (No Hard Hat Required)," *Philosophical Studies* 154 (1): 79–104.

Bettencourt, L.M.A. (2009) "The Rules of Information Aggregation and Emergence of Collective Intelligent Behavior," *Topics in Cognitive Science* 1: 598–620.

Bratman, M. (1992) "Shared Cooperative Activity," *Philosophical Review* 101 (2): 327–41.

——— (2014) *Shared Agency*, New York: Oxford University Press.

Clancey, W.J. (1997) *Situated Cognition*, Cambridge, UK: Cambridge University Press.

Clark, A.G. (1994) "Beliefs and Desires Incorporated," *Journal of Philosophy* 91: 404–25.

Collins, B.E., & Guetzkow, H. (1964) *A Social Psychology of Group Processes for Decision-Making*, New York: Wiley.

Cooke, N.J., Gorman, J.C., Myers, C.W., & Duran, J.L. (2013) "Interactive Team Cognition," *Cognitive Science* 37 (2): 255–85.

Dale, R., Fusaroli, R., Duran, N.D., & Richardson, D.C. (2013) "The Self-Organization of Human Interaction," in B.H. Ross (ed.) *Psychology of Learning and Motivation*, Waltham, MA: Academic Press.

Forsyth, D. (2006) *Group Dynamics* (5th edition), Belmont, CA: Wadsworth.

Fusaroli, R., & Tylén, K. (2016) "Investigating Conversational Dynamics: Interactive Alignment, Interpersonal Synergy, and Collective Task Performance," *Cognitive Science* 40 (1): 145–71.

Galison, P. (1997) *Image and Logic*, Chicago: University of Chicago Press.

Gallotti, M., Fairhurst, M., & Frith, C.D. (2017) "Alignment in Social Interactions," *Consciousness and Cognition* 48: 253–61.

Giere, R. (2002) "Scientific Cognition as Distributed Cognition," in P. Carruthers, S.P. Stich, & M. Siegal (eds), *The Cognitive Basis of Science*, Cambridge: Cambridge University Press.

Goldstone, R., & Theiner, G. (2017) "The Multiple, Interacting Levels of Cognitive Systems (MILCS) Perspective on Group Cognition," *Philosophical Psychology*: 1–35.

Gordon, B., & Theiner, G. (2015) "Scaffolded Joint Action as a Micro–Foundation of Organizational Learning," in C.B. Stone & L.M. Bietti (eds), *Contextualizing Human Memory*, London: Psychology Press.

Haugeland, J. (1998) *Having Thought*, Cambridge, MA: Harvard University Press.

Hinsz, V.B., Tindale, R.S., & Vollrath, D.A. (1997) "The Emerging Conceptualization of Groups as Information Processors," *Psychological Bulletin* 121: 43–64.

Huebner, B. (2013) *Macrocognition*, New York: Oxford University Press.

––– (2016) "Transactive Memory Reconstructed: Rethinking Wegner's Research Program," *The Southern Journal of Philosophy* 54 (1): 48–69.

Hutchins, E. (1995) *Cognition in the Wild*, Cambridge, MA: MIT Press.

––– (2010) "Cognitive Ecology," *Topics in Cognitive Science* 2 (4): 705–15.

––– (2014) "The Cultural Ecosystem of Human Cognition," *Philosophical Psychology* 27 (1): 34–49.

Larson, J.R. (2010) *In Search of Synergy in Small Group Performance*, New York: Psychology Press.

Larson, J.R., & Christensen, C. (1993) "Groups as Problem-Solving Units: Toward a New Meaning of Social Cognition," *British Journal of Social Psychology* 32: 5–30.

Laughlin, P.R. (2011) *Group Problem Solving*, Princeton: Princeton University Press.

Le Bon, G. (1895) *The Crowd*, New York: Viking Press.

List, C., & Pettit, P. (2011) *Group Agency*, Oxford: Oxford University Press.

Ludwig, K. (2007) "Collective Intentional Behavior from the Standpoint of Semantics," *Noûs* 41 (3): 355–93.

––– (2015) "Is Distributed Cognition Group Level Cognition?" *Journal of Social Ontology* 1 (2): 189–224.

Mandelblit, N., & Zachar, O. (1998) "The Notion of Dynamic Unit: Conceptual Developments In Cognitive Science," *Cognitive Science* 22 (2): 229–68.

Marr, D. (1982) *Vision*, Cambridge, MA: MIT Press.

Mohammed, S., Ferzandi, L., & Hamilton, K. (2010) "Metaphor No More: a 15-Year Review of the Team Mental Model Construct," *Journal of Management* 36 (4): 876–910.

Nersessian, N.J. (2006) "The Cognitive-Cultural Systems of the Research Laboratory," *Organization Studies* 27: 125–45.

Pacherie, E. (2013) "Intentional Joint Agency: Shared Intention Lite," *Synthese* 190 (10): 1817–39.

Palermos, S.O. (2015) "Active Externalism, Virtue Reliabilism and Scientific Knowledge," *Synthese* 192 (9): 2955–86.

––– (2016) "The Dynamics of Group Cognition," *Minds and Machines* 26 (4): 409–40.

Pettit, P., & Schweikard, D. (2006) "Joint Actions and Group Agents," *Philosophy of the Social Sciences* 36 (1): 18–39.

Rosnay, J. de (1979) *The Macroscope*, New York: Harper & Row.

Rupert, R. (2005) "Minding One's Cognitive Systems: When Does a Group of Minds Constitute a Single Cognitive Unit?" *Episteme* 1: 177–88.

––– (2011) "Empirical Arguments for Group Minds: A Critical Appraisal," *Philosophy Compass* 6: 630–9.

––– (forthcoming) "Individual Minds as Groups, Group Minds as Individuals," in B. Kaldis (ed.) *Mind and Society: Cognitive Science Meets the Philosophy of the Social Sciences*, Synthese Library Special Volume.

Sawyer, R.K. (2003) *Group Creativity*, Mahwah, NJ: Erlbaum.

Steiner, I.D. (1966) "Models for Inferring Relationships Between Group Size and Potential Group Productivity," *Behavioral Science* 11: 273–83.

Surowiecki, J. (2004) *The Wisdom of Crowds*, New York: Little, Brown.

Sutton, J., Harris, C.B., Keil, P.G., & Barnier, A.J. (2010) "The Psychology of Memory, Extended Cognition, and Socially Distributed Remembering," *Phenomenology and the Cognitive Sciences* 9: 521–60.

Szigeti, A. (2015) "Why Change the Subject? on Collective Epistemic Agency," *Review of Philosophy and Psychology* 6: 1–22.

Theiner, G. (2013) "Transactive Memory Systems: A Mechanistic Analysis of Emergent Group Memory," *Review of Philosophy and Psychology* 4: 65–89.

Theiner, G., & O'Connor, T. (2010) "The Emergence of Group Cognition," in A. Corradini & T. O'Connor (eds), *Emergence in Science and Philosophy*, New York: Routledge.

Theiner, G., Allen, C., & Goldstone, R. (2010) "Recognizing Group Cognition," *Cognitive Systems Research* 11: 378–95.

Tollefsen, D. (2002) "Organizations as True Believers," *Journal of Social Philosophy* 33 (3): 395-410.

Tollefsen, D. (2004) "Collective Epistemic Agency," *Southwest Philosophy Review* 20: 55–66.

Tomasello, M. (2014) *A Natural History of Human Thinking*, Cambridge MA: Harvard University Press.

Tribble, E.B. (2005) "Distributing Cognition in the Globe," *Shakespeare Quarterly* 56: 135–55.

Wegner, D.M. (1986) "Transactive Memory: A Contemporary Analysis of the Group Mind," in B. Mullen, & G.R. Goethals (eds) *Theories of Group Behavior*, New York: Springer.

Wilson, R. (2005) "Collective Memory, Group Minds, and the Extended Mind Thesis," *Cognitive Processes* 6 (4): 227–36.

Wimsatt, W.C. (1986) "Forms of Aggregativity," in M.G. Grene, A. Donagan, A.N. Perovich, & M.V. Wedin (eds) *Human Nature and Natural Knowledge*, Dordrecht: Reidel.

Wittenbaum, G.M., Hollingshead, A.B., Paulus, P.B., Hirokawa, R.Y., Ancona, D.G., Peterson, R.S., Jehn, K., & Yoon, K. (2004) "The Functional Perspective as a Lens for Understanding Groups," *Small Group Research* 35 (1): 17–43.

NOTES

1. Henceforth, I shall use the term "attribute" when I wish to speak generically of these categories.
2. The famous "Condorcet jury theorem" is another example of this effect.
3. I will stop short of claiming that each stance puts forth its own "mark of the cognitive." Also, my list is not meant to be exhaustive, and the different stances are not (all) mutually exclusive.
4. Here, "synergy" refers to the functionally driven reduction of the range of possible behaviors (or informational states) in dynamically interdependent components of a system (see E1 above); and absent a central controller, this reduction must occur solely through reciprocal interactions among locally coupled elements.

19

Corporate Agency: The Lesson of the Discursive Dilemma

Philip Pettit

There are different types of combined agency, as there are different theories that seek to make sense of any particular type. This paper begins with a distinction between aggregate agency, shared agency, and corporate agency. Treating aggregate agency as a residual category, not a genuinely interesting form of collective action, it draws attention to a recognized way of explaining shared agency that can claim to make the phenomenon intelligible without reducing its fascination: 'to improve intelligibility', in Donald Davidson's (1984: 183) phrase, 'while retaining the excitement'. And then it explores the question of whether that desideratum can be satisfied in the case of corporate agency. The thesis is that this is possible and that the discursive dilemma represents an important step in understanding why.

1. THREE VARIETIES OF COMBINED AGENCY

It is useful to distinguish between three levels at which the agency of individuals may combine (Pettit and Schweikard 2006). At a first level the combination involves a single effect of many actions on the part of many individuals; at a second, a single action performed by many individuals; and at a third, a single agent constituted by those many individuals. When there is just a single effect of many actions, there is aggregate agency. When there is a single action performed by many individuals, then there is shared or joint agency. And when there is a single agent, there is corporate agency.

At the first level many individuals combine to bring about a single effect but do not perform a single action or constitute a single agent. Here a standard example is the way in which the buyers and sellers in a competitive market can bring about the effect of pushing the prices of goods and services towards the competitive level: the lowest level, roughly, at which it remains in the interest of sellers to continue in business. The participants in the market bring about a generally welcome result by means of a not necessarily visible hand.

In this first case the different individuals each pursue their own goals—say, the goal on the part of each of buying low and selling high—in a doubly robust way, and their doing so occasions the single effect, whether or not they foresee this. They each register the best means of pursuing their goal, more or less regardless of differences in the circumstances they confront, and they act so as to realize their goal, more or less regardless of what the means identified involves. In other words, they register the best means to adopt, robustly over various differences in the circumstances they face, and they act in implementation of the means they identify as best, robustly over differences in what it requires. Or at least they do this when things go normally or well, with no independently plausible obstacles getting in the way of how they function on those fronts.

At the second level there is a single goal that many individuals pursue—presumably, because they can only realize it together—not just a single effect that they bring about. An example might be the case where the sunbathers on a beach pursue the goal of saving a child who is in difficulty in the water. Those individuals share that goal as a matter of common awareness, or something approaching common awareness: they each target it, they each believe that they each target it, they each believe that they each believe this, and so on in the usual hierarchy (Lewis 1969).[1] And sharing that goal in this way, they pursue it together, acting to a common purpose according to a common plan.

More specifically, they pursue it together in the doubly robust fashion characteristic of agency. They register the best means by which they can pursue it as a body, robustly over certain differences in the circumstances they face, presumably sharing that perception as a matter of more or less common awareness. In the actual circumstances, where there is a rip tide, they take the best means to require a chain into the water but in circumstances where the main danger comes from rocks they might have taken it to require a circle of adult swimmers. And they act in implementation of the means or plan they identify as best, robustly over certain differences in what it requires. Or at least they do this under conditions where no independently plausible obstacles get in the way of their processing or performance.

At the third level distinguished, there is a single group agent, not just a group of individuals in joint pursuit of a single goal.[2] As an example, consider the voluntary association that seeks to advance a variety of environmental goals, the political party that pursues government, or the corporation that seeks to maximize the returns to its shareholders. Here as at the second level there may be a single goal—this is salient in the case of the power-seeking party or the profit-seeking corporation—but the goal is so abstract that it breaks down into a variety of different sub-goals. And what characterizes the group is that it is designed so that for the goals or sub-goals in the domain of its concern, which presumably are a matter of common awareness, the members—or at least those relevant in any instance—are disposed to pursue them robustly.

The goal of each individual in the first case, as well as the goal of the collectivity in the second, is taken as given, so that all that is required is the selection and implementation of means. In this third case the collectivity has to identify the goal, if any, to be furthered in one or another context and so the members have to pursue their goals in a triply robust fashion. First, they must have a way of registering the relevant goal or set of goals to address in any context, robustly over differences in what if anything that context requires. In any context, second, they must have a way of registering the best means by which to pursue the relevant goal, robustly over circumstantial differences that bear on its pursuit.

And, third, they must have a way of acting so as to realize the means identified as best, robustly over certain differences in what it requires. Or at least this is so in the absence of plausible obstacles to their performance on any of these fronts.

2. MAKING SHARED AGENCY INTELLIGIBLE AND EXCITING

We may assume that there is no problem about how individual agency is possible, including the individual agency involved in aggregate action. But, given this assumption, it is natural to ask whether we can make shared and corporate agency intelligible, and do so without diminishing the excitement that attaches intuitively to each. The idea of shared agency is exciting insofar as it suggests that it is a mistake to focus, as we generally do within our folk psychology, on individual-level competence. The idea of corporate agency is exciting insofar as it suggests that the agents in the social world are not restricted, as they may seem to be within our folk ways of thinking, to individual people.

One way of making shared agency intelligible would be to follow H.P. Grice's (1975) creature-constructive methodology, as Michael Bratman (2014: 151) does. This explicitly claims to show that shared agency could in principle have emerged on the basis of an individually intelligible, intentional kind of interaction among the parties. And it implicitly assumes, I would say, that once we see this we can envisage other, psychologically more plausible, processes that might have the same effect.

By Bratman's account, shared agency could emerge from an interaction in which the parties recognize, as a matter of common awareness, a shared goal, a shared plan for realizing the goal, the sub-plans they can individually follow in order to implement that plan, the need for coordinating their sub-plans, and so on. This is not the place to rule on the differences between Bratman and his competitors in this area (Miller 2001; Ludwig 2007; Tuomela 2007; Searle 2010; Ludwig 2014; Gilbert 2015), but it is surely clear that if his sort of story shows how intentionally controlled interactions could have given rise to shared agency, then it will make sense of it in terms of individual psychology, thereby demystifying the phenomenon. It will demystify it, at any rate, insofar as it is plausible to assume that the effect of such intentional planning can be mimicked by other sub-intentional processes and that shared agency need not depend on the very sophisticated planning that Bratman's model invokes.

Bratman contrasts his conservative approach, as he describes it, with approaches like those of Searle and Gilbert that introduce elements not countenanced independently in our folk psychology of individual agents. 'In Searle's view . . . what is needed is a new attitude of "we-intention." In Gilbert's view . . . what is needed is a new relation of "joint commitment" between the participants, a relation that necessitates distinctive mutual obligations' (Bratman 2014: 9; see also 155). His attempt, as formulated above, is to show how there is nothing inherently mysterious, from the point of view of individual folk psychology, in the phenomenon of shared agency.[3]

Would Bratman's account of shared agency preserve the excitement that the phenomenon is likely to elicit, while claiming to make it intelligible in this way? As suggested, the excitement derives from the idea that shared agency is easily overlooked in our standard focus on individuals and, contrary to what that perspective suggests, that it plays a central role in our psychology. Michael Tomasello (2009, 2014, 2016) bears witness to the central role of shared agency in arguing that it is distinctive of our species, not of primates in general, and that it comes on stream in early development. Human toddlers achieve a level of joint attention and shared agency before they can even speak, according to Tomasello, and so presumably before they can interact in the intentional manner envisaged in Bratman's model.

Bratman's account preserves the excitement of shared agency insofar as it allows us to recognize the central role of shared agency in human life. The intentional, sophisticated interactions he postulates may not be very common. But once we see that shared agency could arise on that basis, there is no problem in assuming that it can be brought about by sub-intentional adjustments—presumably the adjustments displayed by Tomasello's toddlers—that parallel the intentional interactions he describes.

Sub-intentional adjustments of the kind required are not confined, of course, to toddlers. Think of how we act as partners in a tango, when each of us may be able to conceptualize what we do only as part of what we do together. We may be as unaware of the individual responses that the tango requires of us as I am unaware of how my right and left hands have to move in order to tie my shoelaces. Tying my laces is a basic action I perform, intentionally pursuing it without intentionally pursuing anything more basic: say, moving my right hand this way, my left hand that way (Hornsby 1980). And tangoing may be a basic action that you and I perform together, each of us intentionally pursuing that joint activity without intentionally pursuing anything more individualistic and basic. Bratman can allow us to marvel at the role of shared agency in our tangoing psychology, despite the fact that his intentional model does not strictly apply there. His claim is that there is nothing individualistically mysterious about the fact that we can align ourselves with one another in this spontaneously social manner, not that we always do so in the manner he describes.

On this account, what Bratman claims to do is comparable with Donald Davidson's (1984) claim to make sense of how finite subjects like you and me can grasp an indefinite range of meaningful sentences. Davidson claims to do this by showing that we could develop unlimited semantic competence on the basis of learning the finite axioms, basic and recursive, of a Tarskian truth-theory. But he does not suggest, of course, that we have semantic competence on the basis of actually mastering such axioms; he assumes, I take it, that that mastery can derive from sub-intentional processes that play a parallel role. What he offers, essentially, is a creature-constructive account of semantic competence. In the same way Bratman can claim to make sense of how individually intelligible subjects like you and me can practice shared agency, without suggesting that we do so on the basis of operating according to his model. And so, operating with a creature-constructive methodology, he can claim to make shared agency suitably intelligible without diminishing the excitement of the idea.

3. HOBBES'S THEORY OF CORPORATE AGENCY

Is it possible to make corporate agency intelligible and exciting in terms of individual-level psychology and indeed the psychology of shared agency? I believe that it is, but in order to mount that argument, we must begin with the classic view of corporate agency elaborated in the seventeenth century by Thomas Hobbes (Pettit 2008; Skinner 2010).

Hobbes certainly thought that it was possible to make corporate agency intelligible in individualistic terms, thereby vindicating its reality; in doing this he wrung some changes on existing themes in the legal theory of group agency, which derived from the Middle Ages. But while corporate agency is real by this account, it relates to individual agency as a fiction relates to the real thing; the account makes the phenomenon intelligible in a way that reduces the excitement attaching to the idea.[4]

Hobbes (1994: ch. 16) begins from the observation that we individual human beings not only act, as other animals do, on the basis of the goals we embrace and the representations we form; we also avow corresponding attitudes of belief or desire or promise to act on corresponding intentions. We are distinctively personal agents, in other words: we represent or "personate" ourselves to others, authorizing them to rely on us to live up to our words. Hobbes argues that any group of individuals can mimic personal agency of this kind, relying on resources of individual psychology and shared agency. The members can authorize one individual to speak for them, for example; they can invite others to rely on them as a group to live up to the words of that "representer"; and they can plan and prove to be faithful to those words.

Hobbes (1994: ch. 16) thinks that in such a case the members of the group "own" everything that the spokesperson does in their name, whether unconditionally—"without stint"—as in the case of a political sovereign; or conditionally, as in the case of a private organization such as a company. The individual provides a voice that the individuals authorize as a source of avowals and promises, living up to it in the domain where "they gave him commission to act." By hitching themselves to that pre-existing voice— and that pre-existing mind—they make themselves into a single agent, collectively acting in accord with that voice in the way in which a natural person acts in accord with his or her own voice. Let that voice avow a belief or intention and the members will act collectively in the way that that attitude requires; let it promise an action, say within the context of a contract, and they will act collectively in a way that ensures performance.

On this picture, the existence of a corporate agent becomes intelligible in individual-level terms. It comes about as a result of individually intelligible arrangements that members make among themselves in establishing a common spokesperson and in binding themselves to his or her authority. We can easily see how they would be able, under those arrangements, to satisfy the three robustness requirements mentioned earlier. Recognizing a range of goals on the basis of the spokesperson's general brief, they would be able to rely on specific dictates to identify the goal that is relevant for them in any context; to select the means that is best suited for pursuing it; and to implement whatever means is selected. They would exist as a corporate agent by virtue of co-opting the voice of the spokesperson and giving it the role in relationship to themselves as a whole that the voice of an individual plays in relationship to that natural person.

But this is only to make intelligible the unusual sort of corporate agent that operates via a single spokesperson. In order to be able to make corporate agency more generally intelligible, Hobbes has to show that the device of the authorized voice is still available in the standard case where there is no single individual designated as spokesperson.

In response to this challenge, Hobbes argues that not only can an individual provide the voice that the members of a group co-opt and authorize in forming a corporate agent, so can a committee provide such a voice, whether that be a committee of a few or a committee of the whole. A committee can serve this function, on his view, insofar as majority voting is capable of generating a suitably unambiguous voice, at least when provision is made to cover ties.[5] 'And if the representative consist of many men', he says, 'the voice of the greater number must be considered as the voice of them all'. By following the voice of the majority the committee can serve, as an individual spokesperson might serve, to rule on what goal among recognized candidates to prioritize in any context; on what means to adopt in pursuit of that goal; and on how to implement the plan or means selected.

Hobbes does not suggest that actual corporate agents, in particular commonwealths, form in this way. But he holds that how they actually form need not be a mystery, so long as we can see the formation as a process that mimics the explicit contractual mode that he describes. Thus he maintains that even if a commonwealth is formed by conquest or acquisition rather than by contract or institution, essentially the same sort of body is established, so that the 'rights and consequences', as he calls them, 'are the same in both' (Hobbes 1994: ch. 20).

Before raising questions about the success of Hobbes's way of making corporate agency intelligible, it is worth noticing that it does so in a way that consciously diminishes the excitement that might have attached to the idea. Corporate agency is likely to be exciting, as suggested earlier, insofar as it means that incorporated groups can count, in the same way as individual human beings, as bona fide agents. And Hobbes's account, by his own admission, does not do this. He holds that unlike their natural counterparts, corporate agents borrow a voice and a mind from elsewhere—from a spokesperson or a spokes-majority—and exist as agents only by virtue of this "feigned or artificial" device.

Assuming 'the consent of every one', Hobbes agrees that 'a multitude of men are made one person when they are by one man, or one person, represented' or when they are represented in that way by a committee. But 'it is the unity of the representer', he insists, 'not the unity of the represented, that maketh the person one. . .and unity cannot otherwise be understood in multitude'. He wants to emphasize that the group agent that exists on the basis of representation by an individual or majority is a parasitic entity. It may count as a unified agent or person—a "personatee", if not a "personator" (Pettit 2008)—but it does so only parasitically on the unity of the individual or the committee that gives it a voice and a mind. In comparison with individuals, it constitutes a pretend agent.

This means, by Hobbes's light, that while corporate agents certainly exist, they do not exist in the same way as individual agents. Describing them as agents or persons underlines the undoubted fact that the members of any such body are committed to acting like a single agent, living up to the words uttered in their name.[6] But, unlike natural persons, corporate agents materialize only insofar as members coopt the pre-existing voice of an individual or the algorithmic voice of a majority. They treat that voice as if it were their own, seeking to manifest the mind that it expresses. But the voice is not actually their own: it is only theirs "by fiction."

4. THE DISCURSIVE DILEMMA

Ingenious though it is, Hobbes's theory of corporate agency fails, as we must now see, to make the phenomenon intelligible. Still the failure carries an important lesson. There is an obvious way to revise it, as we shall see later, and that revised version has the extra bonus of retaining the excitement attaching to the idea of corporate agency.

The Hobbesian theory fails in the case of the group represented by a majoritarian committee. And that is a serious flaw, as the dictatorially led group is a marginal, even a degenerate case of corporate agency; it exemplifies the empowerment of the individual dictator, we might say, rather than the incorporation of those represented into group agency. The problem with the non-dictatorial group is that the voice provided by majority voting—we can assume that there are no problems with tied votes—is not recruitable in the service of the group in the way in which the voice of an individual spokesperson might be recruitable to that purpose. It is just not fitted to serve in the directive role required for corporate agency.

In order for a voice to serve in that directive role, it must not avow inconsistent beliefs or intentions or promise inconsistent actions. At the very least, the members of the group must generally be able to adjust the voice they follow in response to evidence of such failures; they must not be locked into inconsistency by the way it is generated. If the voice they follow did flout consistency in that manner, then it would lead them as a group into behavioral stalemates, pointing in different directions at once. And it would ensure that others could not give the group the credence or trust they might give a personated agent: it is impossible to do business with an entity that fails to display a sense of what consistency requires.

The problem with the majoritarian voice that Hobbes takes to be capable of guiding a group is that it is liable to lock members into precisely this sort of inconsistency. That is the core lesson of the discursive dilemma (Pettit 2001a, 2001b; List 2006).[7]

Suppose that a group of just three people, A, B and C, wish to operate as a group, committing themselves to act on the basis of majority voting. Imagine that the group confronts three logically connected issues at a particular time or over a particular period: say, issues such as whether p, whether q, and whether $p\&q$; or whether p, whether if p, q, and whether q. In any case of this kind, perfectly consistent individuals may vote in such a pattern that the group gets to be committed to an inconsistent set of judgments or representations.

Thus, to take the first case, A and B might vote for "p," with C against; B and C might vote for "q," with A against; and so A and B would vote against "$p\&q$," with only B supporting it. This would leave the group with an inconsistent set of judgments to endorse and follow: p, q, and not-$p\&q$. The following matrix in Table 19.1 displays the problem.

The dilemma that the members of the majoritarian group face, then, is this: be responsive to majority opinion, thereby making it impossible to act as a corporate agent; or make it possible to act rationally as a corporate agent—say, by endorsing p, q, and $p\&q$—thereby rejecting one or another majority opinion. The group can be individually responsive to the votes of its members. Or it can be collectively rational: that is, sensitive to the demands of collective rationality. But it cannot be both.

Table 19.1 The Problem with the Majoritarian Voice

	Question 1: p?	Question 2: q?	Question 3: $p\&q$?
Person A	p	Not q	Not $p\&q$
Person B	p	q	$p\&q$
Person C	Not p	q	Not $p\&q$
The majority	p	q	Not $p\&q$

5. MAKING CORPORATE AGENCY INTELLIGIBLE AND EXCITING

How might a group of individuals constitute a corporate agent, authorizing a voice they can follow, without resorting to majority voting and, of course, without endorsing a single spokesperson? For all the discursive dilemma shows, we might think that they could rely on some non-majoritarian voting or aggregation procedure, ensuring both the individual responsiveness it would support and their collective rationality. But it turns out that the dilemma illustrates a wider difficulty, registered in the surge of impossibility theorems that have recently appeared in the domain of judgment-aggregation (List and Pettit 2002; List and Polak 2010). What these theorems combine to suggest is that there is no possibility of generating a consistent group voice on a set of connected propositions such as "p," "q" and "$p\&q$" by practically any procedure involving these two steps: first, aggregating the individual votes on each proposition in a bottom-up way, majoritarian or not; and, second, letting the group view of that proposition be fixed by the result of the aggregation. More broadly, there is no way of squaring individual responsiveness, majoritarian or otherwise, with collective consistency or rationality.

But this is not to say, of course, that there is no way whatsoever for a group of individuals to find a directive voice that would enable them, rallying behind it, to constitute a reliable corporate agent. The individuals A, B and C might identify a voice recruitable to this effect by following, for example, a simple, straw-vote procedure, relying on the usual resources of individual psychology and shared agency (List and Pettit 2011). This would prescribe these steps for members of the group:

- take a majority vote on each issue as it comes up;
- check whether there is an inconsistency with any existing view;
- if there is not, endorse the vote; and
- if there is, isolate the minimal inconsistent set and
- decide as a group on which proposition to reject.

Following this procedure in our example, the group might come to endorse p, q, and $p\&q$, or indeed any consistent set of answers: say, not-p, q, and not-$p\&q$; or p, not-q, and not-$p\&q$; or not-p, not-q, and not-$p\&q$. The benefit is that they would thereby generate a consistent voice behind which they could rally as a corporate agent. But the cost, of course, is that they would have to be prepared to adopt a collective view on some issue—say, on whether $p\&q$—that is not responsive in a majoritarian way to the views of the members on that issue.

Why does the straw-vote procedure promise to work? In a word, because it allows the members of the group to get top-down feedback on the corporate voice that their individual votes generate in a bottom-up way—this, by contrast with purely bottom-up procedures such as majority voting—and to amend the output of those votes in order to ensure the consistency of the voice they follow. But this means that the straw-vote story not only shows how a corporate agent might emerge; it also indicates quite different ways in which incorporation might materialize. This is because there are any number of procedures that can allow for top-down feedback as well as bottom-up generation and construct thereby a consistent, recruitable voice for members of a group to authorize.

The procedures that allow top-down feedback may operate on the outputs, not of voting by members of the group as a whole, majoritarian or otherwise, but on the outputs of different committees of members on different issues, or indeed on outputs that require the support of independent committees in order to be considered. And of course the top-down adjustment itself may be conducted in different ways: by the membership as a whole, or by a particular committee, or by different committees in different areas. The possibilities are legion and include the sort of mixed constitution— "mixarchy," as he called it—that Hobbes himself was anxious, for anti-republican reasons, to resist in the case of the state (Pettit 2008). As exemplified in the United States, for example, this would require laws to be supported by two houses of Congress as well as the President and would allow the Supreme Court to strike any law down on grounds of being inconsistent with constitutional and other commitments; in that way, it would seek to ensure the consistency of the law—the voice of the community—as a whole.

These observations direct us to an approach that does better than Hobbes in making corporate agency intelligible, in particular the sort of corporate agency that avoids a single dictator. It shows how a corporate agent could emerge on a purely individualistic, intentional basis under a straw-vote procedure. And it directs us at the same time to other ways in which groups might incorporate, structuring their decisions around a set of procedures designed also to generate a coherent, recruitable voice for members to follow (French 1984). But the approach also does better than Hobbes in a second respect. It makes corporate agency intelligible in a way that retains the excitement attaching to the idea that there are bona fide agents in social life apart from individuals.

The corporate agents that Hobbes envisages are all parasitic in the following sense: the members satisfy the conditions of group agency *because* they co-opt an existing, agential voice as the voice behind which to rally; this voice may be provided by an individual dictator or by a majoritarian algorithm. But the direction of dependence is reversed in the case of a group that operates with any procedure involving top-down feedback and adjustment. What holds here is rather this: that the members construct a suitable agential voice *because* they seek to satisfy the conditions of group agency.

This reversal of direction means that the mind of the corporate agent is not expressed in a voice that is borrowed from elsewhere—from a pre-existing individual or algorithm—in a way that would mark a contrast with individual agents. On the contrary it is expressed in a voice that the members have to construct as they go along, establishing their identity as a functioning agent with which others can do business. And in constructing that voice, and forming that mind, the members will often have to put aside their own individual attitudes, recognizing that corporate coherence may require them to support positions that they individually reject.

The corporate agent they create will not channel an independently determinable mind, then, whether it be that of a dictator or majority or whatever. In response to the problems they face, members will have to construct a mind that has an identity of its own. This mind will characterize the group, and only the group; it will be a corporate mind that is distinct from the individual minds of the members (Pettit 2003).

In this respect, the corporate agent is going to be of a kind with individual agents; it will be an agent by right, not just by courtesy. Every corporate agent will be an artificial entity, of course, and will lack many of the features that distinguish natural persons. But qua agent it will be the real thing, and not merely an agent of the pretend or fictional kind envisaged by Hobbes.

REFERENCES

Austin, J. (1869) *Lectures on Jurisprudence, or the Philosophy of Positive Law*, London: J. Murray.

Bratman, M. (2014) *Shared Agency: A Planning Theory of Acting Together*, Oxford: Oxford University Press.

Davidson, D. (1984) *Inquiries into Truth and Interpretation*, Oxford: Oxford University Press.

French, P.A. (1984) *Collective and Corporate Responsibility*, New York: Columbia University Press.

Gilbert, M. (2015) *Joint Commitment: How We Make the Social World*, Oxford: Oxford University Press.

Grice, H.P. (1975) "Method in Philosophical Psychology," *Proceedings and Addresses of the American Philosophical Association* 68: 23–53.

Hobbes, T. (1994) *Leviathan*, (ed.) E. Curley, Indianapolis: Hackett.

Hornsby, J. (1980) *Actions*, London: Routledge.

Kornhauser, L.A. and Sager, L.G. (1993) "The One and the Many: Adjudication in Collegial Courts," *California Law Review* 81: 1–59.

——— (2004) "The Many as One: Integrity and Group Choice in Paradoxical Cases," *Philosophy and Public Affairs* 32: 249–76.

Lewis, D. (1969) *Convention*, Cambridge, MA: Harvard University Press.

List, C. (2006) "The Discursive Dilemma and Public Reason," *Ethics* 116: 362–402.

List, C. and Pettit, P. (2002) "Aggregating Sets of Judgments: An Impossibility Result," *Economics and Philosophy* 18: 89–110.

——— (2011) *Group Agency: The Possibility, Design and Status of Corporate Agents*, Oxford: Oxford University Press.

List, C. and Polak, B. (2010) "Symposium on Judgment Aggregation," *Journal of Economic Theory* 145 (2).

Ludwig, K. (2007) "Collective Intentional Behavior from the Standpoint of Semantics," *Noûs* 41: 355–93.

——— (2014) "Proxy Agency in Collective Action," *Noûs* 48: 75–105.

Miller, S. (2001) *Social Action: A Teleological Account*, Cambridge: Cambridge University Press.

Pettit, P. (2001a) "Deliberative Democracy and the Discursive Dilemma," *Philosophical Issues* 11: 268–99.

——— (2001b) *A Theory of Freedom: From the Psychology to the Politics of Agency*, Cambridge and New York: Polity and Oxford University Press.

——— (2003) "Groups with Minds of their Own," in F. Schmitt, *Socializing Metaphysics*, New York: Rowman and Littlefield.

——— (2008) *Made with Words: Hobbes on Language, Mind and Politics*, Princeton: Princeton University Press.

——— (2014) "Group Agents are not Expressive, Pragmatic or Theoretical Fictions," *Erkenntnis* 79 (9): 1641–62.

Pettit, P. and Schweikard, D. (2006) "Joint Action and Group Agency," *Philosophy of the Social Sciences* 36: 18–39.

Searle, J. (2010) *Making the Social World: The Structure of Human Civilization*, Oxford: Oxford University Press.

Skinner, Q. (2010) *A Genealogy of the Modern State*, London: British Academy.

Tomasello, M. (2009) *Why We Cooperate*, Cambridge, MA: MIT Press.

——— (2014) *A Natural History of Human Thinking*, Cambridge, MA: Harvard University Press.

——— (2016) *A Natural History of Human Morality*, Cambridge, MA: Harvard University Press.

Tuomela, R. (2007) *The Philosophy of Sociality: The Shared Point of View*, Oxford: Oxford University Press.

NOTES

1. They cannot actively register the appropriate lesson at each level, which would require an infinite hierarchy. But what may be the case is that for more or less any level, they are disposed to accept the appropriate lesson, should the question arise as to whether it holds there.

2. Shared agency involves a single agent in the sense of a single causal source of the action but there is not a single agent in the sense in which agency requires unity and interconnection in a web of attitudes. (See Bratman 2014: 126). Unity and interconnection emerge only with corporate agency, as we shall see.

3. Bratman (2014: 194) also suggests that his approach is more conservative than Tuomela's (2007), who introduces "we-mode mental states."

4. Thus Hobbes's fictionalism contrasts with an eliminativist theory of the sort maintained by John Austin (1869: 364) when he holds that we speak of corporate agents 'only by figment, and for the sake of brevity of discussion'. Such eliminativism continues to survive in many economic treatments of the topic. For a fuller discussion see Pettit (2014).

5. He acknowledges that a committee that is even in number will not generally work well, being 'oftentimes mute and incapable of action', and that special measures are required to cover that sort of case.

6. Margaret Gilbert (2015) takes the view that since even joint action requires a commitment on the part of members not to let others down, the members constitute a plural subject. In that respect her view parallels that attributed here to Hobbes.

7. The discursive dilemma is a generalized version of the doctrinal paradox in legal theory; see Kornhauser and Sager (1993, 2004).

IV
Social Ontology

Introduction to Part IV

Marija Jankovic and Kirk Ludwig

Social ontology studies the nature of the elements of the social world, things such as universities, university presidents, artifacts, checks, and opera performances. Collective intentionality has seemed to many to be central to this project. For what these seemingly very different types of entities have in common is that they are roughly a product of people acting or deciding together. But describing the way in which the social world is *constructed* or built out of individuals and their attitudes is not straightforward. It is also not clear that there is a unique sense in which the vast diversity of social entities is constructed.

In Chapter 20, "Social Construction and Social Facts," Brian Epstein distinguishes several senses of the construction of a social fact. The most important distinction for us is the one between the *grounds* or building blocks of a fact, and its *anchors*, factors that set up the conditions for its obtaining. To use Epstein's example, the grounds of the fact that *John is married* are facts such as John's having uttered certain words in an appropriate context. Its anchors are the facts that make it the case that conditions of marriage are as they are, for example, the collective acceptance that uttering certain words in an appropriate context counts as marriage. Using the distinction between grounds and anchors, Epstein classifies theories of social construction into four categories: (a) theories that take attitudes to be grounds of social facts, (b) theories that take attitudes to be anchors of social facts, (c) theories that take non-mental facts as grounds for social facts, and (d) theories that take non-mental facts to be anchors of social facts. While theories in the first and especially the second category have been prevalent, Epstein cautions against assuming that there is a single type of ground or anchor for the rich diversity of social facts and, more specifically, against assuming that this single ground or anchor is collective intentionality.

Philosophers have indeed appealed to collective intentionality in accounts of virtually all aspects of social reality: social groups, social kinds, and status functions. Chapters 21–3 discuss the main philosophical debates concerning these categories.

In Chapter 21, "Social Groups," Paul Sheehy describes the debate between individualism and holism concerning the ontological status of groups. Individualist views hold that "individuals and their relations enjoy ontological and explanatory priority." Holist views deny this, maintaining that social groups cannot be identified or reductively analyzed into sets of individuals and their relations. Sheehy outlines difficult problems facing the individualist. Continuing a theme set by Epstein, he argues that collective intentionality is not necessary for a group of individuals to constitute a social group. As with social construction in general, we ought to be open to the possibility that there isn't a unified explanation of conditions of group-constitution.

In Chapter 22, "Social Kinds," Ásta describes the main debates concerning social kinds. In philosophical usage, *kinds* are understood as collections or structures of entities that somehow reveal the structure of the world, as opposed to arbitrary collections that reveal only the interests of the classifier. In a familiar slogan, kinds are said to be those collections that "carve the nature at its joints," though for our discussion "nature" should be understood quite broadly, so as to include kinds that might be revealed by social sciences. There is little concerning social kinds that is uncontroversial, and Ásta guides the reader through the debates over (a) what makes a social kind *social*, (b) what makes it a *kind*, (c) whether social kinds are real and objective and (d) whether they are compatible with naturalism.

In Chapter 23, "Status Functions," John Searle describes a central tool in the construction of social reality, the notion of a status function. Searle first introduced the notion in *The Construction of Social Reality* in the following passage.

> The radical movement that gets us from such simple social facts as that we are sitting on a bench together or having a fistfight to such institutional facts as money, property, and marriage is the collective imposition of function on entities, which—unlike levers, benches, and cars—cannot perform the functions solely by virtue of their physical structure. . . . The key element in the move from the collective imposition of function to the creation of institutional facts is the imposition of a collectively recognized *status* to which a function is attached. Since this is a special category of agentive functions, I will label these *status functions*.
>
> (*The Construction of Social Reality*, 1995, Free Press, p. 41)

On Searle's current account, outlined in this chapter, we create status functions through speech acts of declaration. By declaring something, *p*, we make *p* the case by representing it as being so. For example, in saying "the meeting is adjourned," I make it the case that the meeting is adjourned simply by representing it as being so. All status functions are created through representations (which are not necessarily explicit utterances) that have this feature of declarations. Unlike some other contributors to this section, Searle thinks that the fundamental structure of social reality is simple. He writes that "all of the things we think of as distinctly features of human civilization, features by which we differ from other animals, are Status Functions."

20

Social Construction and Social Facts

Brian Epstein

1. INTRODUCTION

There is more to the social world than groups and their intentional states. Work on collective intentionality, by and large, involves the analysis of groups of people—their actions and attitudes, reasoning and mental states. Groups, however, are only one sort of social entity. Corporations, restaurants, contracts, musical performances, works of art, technical artifacts, money, bank accounts, mortgages: all of these are elements of the social world. These do not appear to be collectives or groups. Nor do they seem to be attitudes.

Yet on the other hand, things like these do seem to be a *product* of people in at least some sense. The actions and attitudes of individuals seem to play a role in making or constructing these things. What is the connection, if any, between collective intentionality and the construction of the social world in general?

This chapter has two goals. The first is to present some prominent approaches to the construction of the social world, paying particular attention to intentionality and collective intentionality in them. This presentation is far from a comprehensive taxonomy; rather it can only gesture toward the diverse views and approaches to the topic.

The second goal—perhaps the more important one—is to issue a caution. With the enormous recent attention paid to collective intentionality, there is a growing temptation to suppose that collective intentionality is the key to the construction of the social world in general. But this is almost surely not the case. And even if it should eventually turn out to be correct, at this stage it is little more than one hypothesis among many. Most of the interesting and promising research avenues in social construction barely touch on collective intentionality at all. In some cases, that may be because researchers are unaware of the collective intentionality literature. But in many cases it is because for well-considered reasons they regard intentionality as playing only a peripheral role.

The inquiry into the nature and construction of the social world is a natural one for researchers interested in collective intentionality. But it is crucial that we be aware of—and humble about—the role that intentionality, collective and otherwise, may play in social construction.

2. TERMINOLOGY AND BACKGROUND

a. Social Construction

The construction of the social world is a topic with ancient roots, and has appeared in so many theories and guises that the terminology is confusing and fraught. This confusion was exacerbated by the fashion, in the 1980s and 1990s, to declare commonplace objects and concepts socially constructed, without being terribly clear about what that declaration was supposed to amount to. To be sure, claims about the social construction of categories such as genders, races, and disabilities are plausible and important. But even much of the work on these categories has left it unclear just what social construction is.

For example, a common approach for advocating the social construction of some category is to tell its history. Foucault (1977), for instance, lays out a history of Western penal systems. Foucault describes both the contingency and the political influences behind the contours of our contemporary categories surrounding imprisonment and other forms of punishment. A history like this one can be quite effective at what Ricoeur (1970) has called "the hermeneutics of suspicion": providing evidence that categories we naively employ may have darker (or at least richer) underpinnings than we realize. It can suggest, for instance, that categories we regard as natural are not so natural after all, but instead are fairly arbitrary and gerrymandered. However, there is only so much a history can do. Telling a narrative of a category's development, however twisted, cannot demonstrate that the category itself is contingent or unnatural at all: after all, *every* category, natural and unnatural alike, has a history of discovery and development. Does the claim that a category is socially constructed amount to nothing more than that it was discovered or shaped over time? Surely Foucault is demonstrating more than this. But what, exactly? To make clear sense of social construction, we need an analysis of what our objects and categories are. We need an ontology or metaphysics of the social world, and a history on its own cannot provide this.

Another issue that social construction theorists need to be sensitive to is the breadth of their focus. Despite the ubiquity of claims about social construction, a typical aim is to highlight surprising or counterintuitive examples, to demonstrate that some category that appeared natural was in fact a hidden or covert construction. This strategy has a good deal of merit, but it also risks leaving out the many categories whose sociality is not covert at all. Much of the social world—institutions, governments, money, and so on—is obviously social. If the aim is to figure out which parts of the social world are constructed, and how they are, it may be an error to overlook the obvious cases.

For certain social categories, it remains fruitful to think about social construction as revealing hidden or covert construction. This is particularly so in some politically salient cases, such as gender, race, and disability. But even for these cases, it can be helpful to see work on social construction as either subsumed under, or the same as, work on social ontology more generally. In this chapter, I regard questions of social construction as questions about the making or building of the social world overall.

b. Social Facts

The term "social fact" predates Durkheim's *The Rules of Sociological Method* of 1895 (see for instance, Guizot 1837: 9; Mill 1843: 586), but it was with Durkheim that the term gained currency. Durkheim noted that nearly everything about us is social, so he defined social facts as a special category he held to be of interest to social theory. Social facts, according to Durkheim, exist external to individuals and 'are invested with coercive powers' over the individual. Examples of social facts, according to Durkheim, are legal and moral rules, religious dogmas, financial systems, and the institution of marriage. Among Durkheim's interpreters, there is debate about the extent to which social facts are autonomous of individuals, or rather emerge from the thoughts and actions of individuals in communities. But in either case, social facts on his conception exert powers over individuals, and the explanation of individual action should often be given in terms of these facts.

To a contemporary ear, it is a little odd to use the term "fact" to refer to rules and institutions. We say "It is a fact that John is married": a fact is usually understood nowadays to be a state of affairs that obtains, or instead to be the exemplification of a property or relation by one or more objects. Some philosophers, such as Searle (1995, 2010) and Armstrong (1997) speak of objects as facts, but it tends to be clearer to think of social facts as states of affairs or property-exemplifications that are social in some way, and to distinguish them from social objects, social properties, social kinds, and social events.

Among all the facts, which are the *social* ones? It is probably best to specify them in a way that does not commit us to one particular theory or another. If, for instance, we find that social facts are not autonomous of individuals, or non-coercive, then there are no social facts in Durkheim's sense. By coupling the description of social facts with a particular analysis of it, Durkheim does not leave enough room to theorize about what social facts might be.

Instead, it is better to indicate more generically what facts are the social ones. If we think of facts as property exemplifications by objects, then we might regard the social facts as including exemplifications of social properties by any object or objects, and exemplifications of any property by a social object. That, of course, only advances the metaphysical analysis a smidgen: it does not give an answer to which objects and properties are themselves social. But it does allow us to distinguish the social fact *John is married* from the non-social fact *John is cold*. (In the following I use italicized sentences to name facts.) We might also want to include in the social facts ones that are "set up" in social ways, a topic I will discuss just below.

It is far from clear that there is a clean line between the social and non-social facts altogether. Some projects in analyzing social facts depend on trying to establish a distinction between social and non-social facts, especially those that attempt to "naturalize" the social. But many projects do not rely on making this distinction. Indeed, the social construction literature has largely been concerned with showing that what seems to be non-social actually is social: that is, with taking facts that seem biological or otherwise natural, and arguing that they are actually social products in one way or other.

c. Four Senses of the "Construction" of a Social Fact

What is it to analyze the building or construction of a fact such as *John is married*? Or, to take a less metaphorical example of building, of a fact such as *There is a house at 100 Main Street*? We need to distinguish four different inquiries:

1. *The grounds for that fact*: First is the inquiry into what other facts about the world are metaphysically sufficient and explanatory of a fact such as *John is married*. These would be facts such as John's having uttered the appropriate words in the appropriate context, and his partner having done the same thing, or the minister's having uttered certain words. Likewise, the fact *There is a house at 100 Main Street* is grounded or metaphysically explained by facts about wood, bricks, drywall, and shingles arranged in an appropriate way. An inquiry into the grounds of a social fact investigates the metaphysical reason or explanation of that fact.

2. *The causes for those grounds to obtain*: Houses have builders, or construction workers. The process of constructing a house is the *causing* of the materials to be arranged, that is, the causing of the grounds of the fact to obtain. The house, though, is not built *of* the builders; it is merely built *by* the builders. The facts that cause the grounds to obtain, that is, are not the metaphysical building blocks of the house. They are the causal building blocks. Similarly for John's marriage. A sequence of events, starting from that evening at the bar and leading up to the diamond ring, are the causal building blocks of the fact John is married. These are distinct from the metaphysical building blocks.

3. *The inquiry into why that fact is grounded the way it is*: Suppose that, in our society, one needs to utter certain words in order to be married. The fact that those words were uttered are the grounds for John being married. However, what sets up the category of marriage that way, making *those* the words one needs to utter? What is the metaphysical explanation for the grounds of a social fact being what they are? That explanation is given by a different set of facts. (In Epstein 2015a, I call these the "anchors.") These other facts are the metaphysical reason for why a social fact of some kind is grounded the way it is. It may be, for instance, that we all signed an explicit agreement about what the conditions for being married are. And that that signing is the explanation of those conditions. When we analyze the construction of the fact *John is married,* it is often our intent to analyze the anchors—why is it that *John is married* gets grounded the way it does?—not to analyze the grounds themselves. As I will discuss below, many current theories of social construction are theories of how social facts are anchored.

4. *The causes for those "anchors" to obtain*: Just as the grounding facts have causes, so do the anchoring facts. Supposing that we have an explicit agreement about the conditions to be married—that agreement has a causal history.

Among these four questions are two about the causal construction of the social world (i.e. questions 2 and 4), and two about the metaphysics of the social world (questions 1 and 3). And the two metaphysical questions address different topics: questions 1 and 3 address two distinct senses of the metaphysical building of the social world. It is helpful to keep these separate.

The inquiry of this chapter is limited to questions 1 and 3—metaphysical construction, not causal construction (see Haslanger (2003) for more on the distinction between these kinds of construction). In the next section, I discuss theories that put intentionality at the center of the construction of social facts. Some theories regard intentionality to be the key to grounding social facts, and some regard intentionality as the key to anchoring social facts. Then in the following section, I turn to theories where intentionality plays less of a role.

3. THEORIES PUTTING INTENTIONALITY AT THE CENTER OF SOCIAL CONSTRUCTION

Many theories of social facts, both historical and contemporary, regard them as built largely or exclusively out of attitudes and other mental states. In this section, I discuss variants of these theories: in subsection (a), theories that take attitudes and mental states to be the *grounds* of social facts—some of which take individual attitudes as grounds, and some of which take collective attitudes as grounds. Then in subsection (b), I discuss theories that take attitudes and mental states to *set up* or *"anchor"* social categories.

a. Attitudes as the Grounds of Social Facts

A clear example of the grounding of social facts in attitudes is Michael Bratman's treatment of shared intention. According to Bratman, the shared intentions of certain kinds of social groups can be grounded by the possession of certain interlocking attitudes by members of the group (see Bratman 1993, 1997, 2014; also Chapter 3, this volume).

The idea behind Bratman's view is that if a collection of individuals has certain individual attitudes in place, including attitudes toward the attitudes of one another, then that is sufficient to ground a certain kind of social fact. The social fact in question is the shared intention of that kind of group. In Bratman's account, there is a clear separation between the grounding facts, consisting of attitudes at the individual level, and the social facts that are thereby grounded.

Bratman is careful to limit the scope of his claim: his analysis gives one sufficient set of conditions for the grounding of a shared intention by a particular kind of small and structured group. His analysis does not preclude other ways shared intentions can be grounded, nor does it address more structured groups, nor does it make any claims about social facts other than shared intentions of such groups. However, there is a long history of views that take attitudes more generally to be the grounds of social facts.

J.S. Mill, for instance, asserts in his *System of Logic* that social phenomena in general are built exclusively out of the psychologies of individual people. The laws of sociology, according to Mill, are derivable from the laws of human nature, which, in turn, come from the study of psychology. 'The laws of the phenomena of society', says Mill,

> are, and can be, nothing but the laws of the actions and passions of human beings united together in the social state . . . Human beings in society have no properties but those which are derived from, and may be resolved into, the laws of the nature of individual man.
>
> (Mill 1843: 550)

Sociology as the science of society, on Mill's conception, is an analogue to the science of man's nature: sociology is the study of laws of the mind of the group or society. (See also Comte (1830–42) on sociology as founded in "cerebral physiology.")

In Mill's discussion, we can distinguish two different claims, both of which have been highly influential. One is a claim about the existence of causal laws of society and their derivation from laws about human nature. The other is an ontological claim about social facts: that they are built out of the psychological states of individual people. It took many years for theorists to realize that these claims really are distinct from one another. There may or may not be laws of society, and there may or may not be laws of human nature. And even if there are both, the social laws may or may not be derivable from those of human nature. But the ontological claim does not involve laws at all. That claim is about what grounds the social facts, not about how social facts are causally related to one another.

Nowadays Mill's claim about ontology is more widely endorsed than his claim about laws and explanations. Many theorists are skeptical about social laws and explanations being performable in terms of laws of individual human nature. The ontological claim, however, is weaker and regarded as more plausible. Still, the scope of his ontological claim is broad. Mill does not give a clear characterization of what the social facts are, but whatever they are, he holds them to be *exhaustively* determined by facts of individual psychology. In fact, Mill—following Comte and followed by many subsequent social theorists—seems to regard sociology as the study of the "mind of society," so it is natural to regard social facts as themselves psychological.

Bratman's strategy is similar in one way, and more limited in another. The particular social fact Bratman addresses is carefully specified: it is only facts of the form *group G intends to J*. And the sorts of groups to which the analysis applies are also carefully delimited. Still, the relation between the social fact and individual psychology is the same. Like Mill, Bratman takes the relevant social fact to be a fact about the "mind of the group," i.e. its intention. He does so in a way that is meant to demystify group psychology, and in this sense, he is also like Mill. He and Mill share a reductive goal: he does not only say that such shared intentions are exhaustively determined by the attitudes of the group members, but specifies exactly what those member attitudes are that determine the group intention. Still, the accounts are vastly different in scope. Bratman makes no claim about social facts in general. A view that takes individual attitudes to be the grounds of all social facts, like Mill's, is more sweeping.

A different sort of account, involving collective intentions and grounds, asks a further question about collective intentions: in addition to the question of how collective intentions are themselves grounded, it is also concerned with what collective intentions themselves are the grounds for. Margaret Gilbert, for instance, gives a theory of sociality and of the existence of social groups (Gilbert 1989, 2014). According to Gilbert, the sphere of the social and the creation of social groups as independent ontological entities are grounded by joint commitment. Joint commitment, that is, is the thing that metaphysically explains the existence of sociality and social groups. In Gilbert's theory, one topic is how joint commitments are grounded. That is a question like Bratman's: what facts about individuals, their histories, their utterances, etc. determine that the individuals share a joint commitment. A separate topic in her theory, however, is what joint commitments themselves are the grounds for. This is perhaps the more distinctive aspect of her view. One might disagree with her account of how joint commitment is grounded, while endorsing her claims about the social phenomena that joint commitments ground.

We can thus identify two different roles collective intentions may play in the grounds of social facts. Collective intentions may be the social facts whose grounding we investigate. A distinctive role is if certain sorts of collective intentions or attitudes are themselves the grounds of distinctive social facts. This latter role, however, tends to be a small part of the inquiry even into collective intentionality, to say nothing of the grounding of social facts in general. The study of collective intentions tends, for the most part, to be inquiry of how they are grounded, or else, as I discuss in the next section, their role in setting up or anchoring other social kinds.

b. Attitudes as "Setting Up" or "Anchoring" the Social World

Many approaches to social facts take them to be a product of attitudes in a different sense: they take social facts to be set up, carved out, or "*anchored*" by people's attitudes. On these approaches, attitudes are not the building blocks of the social world in the same way that bricks are the building blocks of houses. Instead, it is our beliefs, perspectives, and conceptual machinery that *set up the conditions* for being a corporation, contract, artifact, or house.

In certain theories, it is unclear whether social kinds are put in place by individual attitudes, by collective attitudes, or by factors other than attitudes. Ian Hacking (1995, 2000), for instance, gives a theory of the construction of "human kinds" in which they are interactively generated over time. Hacking discusses the kind *refugee,* for instance. Members of the community begin with a certain theory about the conditions for applying the label "refugee" to people. Based on that theory, they apply the label to certain people, but then that labeling itself has an effect on the behavior and characteristics of the people so-labeled. Those changes falsify the prior theory of "refugee" by the people doing the labeling (which may include the labeled people themselves), so the theory must be revised, changing the application conditions of the label, which in turn affects the people so-labeled; and so on in a feedback loop.

An interesting feature of Hacking's account is that the conditions for being a member of the kind *refugee* changes over time. Indeed, Hacking regards this as a defining characteristic of human kinds: he holds them to be not only interactive, but essentially unstable. Still, it is not fully specified in Hacking's theory what exactly does the work of setting up the conditions for being a member of the kind.

Perhaps the simplest interpretation is that it is *the community's theory, at a given time*, that sets up the conditions for being a refugee at that time. As the theory changes, the conditions we associate with *refugee* change, and so the kind changes. These are the anchors at time t for *x is a refugee*: the attitudes of the labelers at t.

This may not be the best interpretation of Hacking's theory. Putting it this way may underestimate the role of the people labeled refugees in anchoring the conditions for the membership in the kind. It may also underestimate the role of the instability and the feedback loop. Hacking seems to hold that the feedback loop is essential in some way to the kind *refugee*. But if so, we need to clarify what role the feedback loop and other factors play. One option is that the feedback loop is merely a restriction on what sorts of kinds count as human kinds, properly speaking. That is, the membership conditions for *refugee* might still be anchored at time t by the community's theory at time t, and an "interactive kind" is just a particular species of kind: it is one whose community-theory anchors are affected according to that causal pattern. A different option regards the feedback loop as playing a more central role in anchoring the kind: the fact of having a certain causal looping history prior to time t may play some role in determining the membership conditions of *refugee* at time t. But in that case, we need more clarity on how the causal history adds to setting up the membership conditions of *refugee* at t, above and beyond the community's theory at t.

A number of prominent theories introduce a clearer role for collective attitudes in setting up social kinds. Traditions stretching back to the ancient world debate whether certain features of the social world are or are not a product of agreement. Plato's *Cratylus* debates whether objects have natural names, or whether names arise from agreement. Aristotle considers in *De Interpretatione* whether the law is a matter of agreement or nature. In the seventeenth century, it became clear that agreement was too impoverished a category to account for the generation of language and law, since much of both arise with no explicit agreements at all. Pufendorf ([1673] 2007) thus argued that we need to consider tacit as well as explicit agreement as the basis for these, and introduced the notion of convention to accommodate these more generally.

Subsequent theories of convention extend this analysis and apply it to a broader range of cases. Hume presented patterns of attitudes as being at the heart of convention, and argued that a number of social entities, including property, promises, money, and government, are generated by convention. According to a conventionalist theory of property, we have a structured set of attitudes about certain types of practices. These are individual attitudes that fit a particular pattern; typically, they are understood as involving beliefs about one another's beliefs and preferences, with accommodations made for tacit beliefs. It is these beliefs that set up the conditions for something to count as a piece of property. One person's beliefs are inadequate for making something property; rather, it is a structure of attitudes in a community.

A contemporary variant on conventionalism is Searle's theory of "institutional facts." Searle (1995, 2010) puts collective attitudes at the heart of the construction of certain social facts. According to Searle, institutional facts are created by the *collective acceptance or recognition* of a *constitutive rule*. A constitutive rule is a formula that assigns to a physical object, like a piece of paper, a normative status, such as serving various monetary functions. A community's collective acceptance of such a rule essentially means that that community accepts that such objects count as performing those functions. This collective acceptance anchors the conditions for the existence of dollars and for the powers that dollars have. Searle also proposes a theory of collective attitudes, such as acceptance; this part of this theory fits into the theories discussed in previous subsections, on the grounding of collective attitudes.

Searle's view is the most explicit one putting collective attitudes at the center of the creation of the social world. All institutional facts, according to Searle, are put in place by a community having collective attitudes toward a constitutive rule. There is one way, on this view, that all social facts are anchored, i.e. by collective intentionality.

4. DEMOTING INTENTIONALITY IN SOCIAL CONSTRUCTION

The above theories regard the social world as being entirely or largely a product of human intentionality. Different theories take it to be a "product" in one of two different senses—either as constituents or grounds of social facts, or else as anchors of social facts. The views vary in terms of how social or collective the intentionality is that does the grounding or anchoring work.

More significant than the divide between individual and collective intentionality, however, is whether intentionality of either kind is adequate either to ground or anchor social facts. A number of approaches take a broader view of the building of social facts, in both senses.

a. Non-Mental Facts as the Grounds for Social Facts

In Section 3 I discussed the view that social facts are facts about the psychology or mind of society. Understanding social facts in this way, it may be reasonable to think of the grounds of social facts to be the attitudes and mental states of individual people. This, however, is a limited conception of social facts. The sorts of examples we began with—facts about corporations, universities, dances, money, artifacts, and so on—are at least in part material facts about the world and human behavior in it. They are not merely psychological. This is obvious to everyone, of course. The "psychology of society" approaches address this in one of two ways. Either they restrict the social facts to facts to the subset that pertains to psychological facts alone, or else they implicitly take the psychological component to be separable from the material component. For instance, if a group of people are dancing, these views may implicitly take the social fact to be the group mental state, and regard the physical aspect of it to be either non-social or effectively governed by the mental states. In this way, it may be possible to regard the social facts to be grounded strictly by the mental.

Many theorists have worried that any such treatment of the social is overly mentalistic. Some anti-mentalistic theories have their roots in Marx, who regarded technologies and material relations among people to be more fundamental building blocks of the social than their beliefs or mental states. Other versions of anti-mentalism came out of twentieth-century empiricism: behaviorism was a radical form of anti-mentalism, going so far as to deny the coherence of talk of mental states altogether. Social sciences working in the behaviorist tradition regarded themselves as systematizing the observable behaviors of people, and thought of social facts as patterns of behavior alone.

Another anti-mentalistic approach is "textualism" in anthropology, most prominently represented by Geertz (1973). Geertz builds on the work of Wittgenstein to argue that cultures are publically accessible "texts," whose meanings we interpret much as we interpret literary texts. Unlike a written text, cultures are dynamic rather than static. Still, just as the words on a page are publically accessible, so what is interpretable about a culture—and hence what a culture is, on his view—is publically accessible speech acts and actions.

A more balanced set of theories has emerged in recent years, with the advent of "theories of practice" (Bourdieu 1977; Giddens 1984). Theories of practice take the social world to be a product of human practices, where practices are broadly understood to be routines involving both individual mental activity and also the external world with which we engage. Dance practices, for instance, include conscious and unconscious routines of thinking, and also bodily movements and physical resources with which dancers interact. The practice is a type of which particular tokens will involve instantiation of all these components.

Theories of practice seek to allow for the role of both mental states and the non-mental in composing the social world, but do so by taking practices essentially to consist of hybrids of all these elements. It makes little sense, on these views, to discuss the contribution of the mental or the material independently of one another. Correspondingly, it is also not particularly sensible to ask what part of the social world is grounded by the mental.

b. Non-Mental Facts as Setting Up or Anchoring Social Categories

To many theorists, it is intuitive that social facts are not limited to the "minds of groups," and therefore that the grounds for social facts are not merely psychological. When it comes to setting up or anchoring social categories, however, prevailing theories still put attitudes—nowadays, typically collective attitudes—at the center. Theories involving collective acceptance, in particular, are a popular approach to how social categories are put in place.

It is not always easy to distinguish when a theory is best understood as proposing how social facts are grounded, and when as proposing how categories are anchored. For instance, theories of practice may be regarded as doing both: as giving a theory of the parts of the world that are the "bricks" of social facts, and as also arguing that patterns of practices explain how social categories are carved up. Other non-mentalistic theories, however, are more straightforwardly understood as theories of anchoring. The most prominent of these are the functionalist theories of mid-twentieth century sociology, and more contemporary versions of functionalism, such as "teleofunctionalism."

Functionalist theories take the social world to be a set of connected and interacting functional systems. Individuals play roles in the systems, but are often unaware of the functions of the systems they operate in, and of their contributions to those systems. Parsons (1954), for instance, takes a common function of social behaviors to be the maintenance of the stability of an institution. For instance, it may be traditional for members of a country club to have elaborate members selection procedures, or to criticize certain sorts of nonconformity. The members might have rationalizations for their behaviors, or just appeal to tradition. But the behaviors are actually realizers of a functional kind; that is, of a kind having the function of maintaining the persistence of the country club within the larger social system in which it is embedded.

According to such a theory, the intentional states of individuals play only a minor role in the anchoring of such kinds. For one thing, individuals can be radically mistaken about their own social systems. And they need not only be mistaken at a conscious level: on this theory, they do not need to have even tacit or background knowledge of the functions of their social entities. The members of the country club may have a range of explanations for why they have the selection procedures they do. If they have read enough sociology, they may have a correct theory of these reasons, or their self-understanding may be completely misguided. But even if the members of the society are aware of the nature and roles of the functional systems in which they participate, their intentional states are not the anchors for their social categories.

Contemporary teleofunctional theories, stemming from work on biological kinds by Ruth Millikan and others, cash out in more detail the facts that put a functional kind in place. Millikan (1984) proposes an approach to kinds, social as well as biological, in which the functions they have are the explanations for their reproductive histories. In the case of the behaviors at the country club, for instance, it is not an unanalyzed stabilizing drive that anchors the fact that they have a stabilizing function. Instead, when the behavior is reproduced from person to person and generation to generation, that reproduction has an explanation, typically in terms of what that behavior accomplishes. On Millikan's view, kinds—both social and biological—are present when there are families of reproduced tokens which, as a family, have characteristics which persist because those characteristics contribute to the reproduction in a common way. (Millikan does not separate the facts which anchor or set up the kind from the grounds for membership in the kind, so the present characterization is a slight modification of her view. See Epstein (2015b) for defense of this separation.)

A significant feature of the teleofunctional view is the role for actual historical tokens in setting up kinds. What matters is not our attitudes or beliefs about how tokens are unified in their reproductive histories, but the actual properties of the tokens and how they are actually reproduced. It is their real features, not any attitudes at all, that play the central role in setting up the kinds. The basis for reproduction could involve individual attitudes. The beliefs of the individuals about the contribution of the practice, for instance, may be part of the explanation of the practice's reproduction. So there is room for individual intentionality in the account. But individual intentions may only be a part of the explanation, and frequently the explanation will not involve intentionality at all.

Other theories of kinds also include actual tokens at the center of their explanations as well. Boyd (1999) gives an account of kinds—natural and social—in which they are formed by clusters of properties for which there is a "homeostatic" causal mechanism maintaining the properties in a cluster. The properties that are actually instantiated, together with the homeostatic causes, are the things that explain what sets up the kind with the tokens as members. (Boyd, like Millikan, also does not separate the anchors from the membership grounds, but here too it is advantageous to distinguish them.)

All of these views are alternatives to mentalistic theories of anchoring such as the "collective acceptance" theories. Mentalistic theories of anchoring take attitudes—individual or collective—to set up the grounding conditions for social facts. That is, to set up the social categories and kinds in a community to be what they are. Non-mentalistic theories draw on broader resources to accomplish this task.

5. CONCLUSION

We are still in early days in analyzing how the social world is constructed. None of our contemporary theories provides anything close to an account of the construction of the mundane social entities I mentioned at the outset—corporations, restaurants, contracts, musical performances, works of art, technical artifacts, money, bank accounts, or mortgages. One question we might reasonably ask is whether there should be a single answer that applies to all of them—a single answer to the question of how facts about them are grounded, or a single answer to the question of how the grounding conditions for facts about them are set up. Collective intentions may play an important role in grounding certain social facts, and also in anchoring certain social facts. And surely it is important to clarify how facts about collective intentions are themselves grounded. However, it may be advisable for theorists in the field to take a broader look, before assigning a comprehensive role to collective intention in the construction of social facts.

RELATED TOPICS

Reductive Views of Shared Intention (Ch. 3), Social Kinds (Ch. 22), Status Functions (Ch. 23), Collective Intentionality and the Methodology in the Social Sciences (Ch. 30).

REFERENCES

Armstrong, D.M. (1997) *A World of States of Affairs*, Cambridge: Cambridge University Press.

Bourdieu, P. (1977) *Outline of a Theory of Practice*, Cambridge: Cambridge University Press.

Boyd, R. (1999) "Homeostasis, Species, and Higher Taxa," in R. Wilson (ed.) *Species: New Interdisciplinary Essays*, Cambridge: MIT Press.

Bratman, M. (1993) "Shared Intention," *Ethics* 104 (1): 97–113.

——— (1997) "I Intend That We J," in R. Tuomela and G. Holmstrom-Hintikka (eds) *Contemporary Action Theory, Vol. 2: Social Action*, Dordrecht: Kluwer.

——— (2014) *Shared Agency*, Oxford: Oxford University Press.

Comte, A. (1830–42) *Cours de Philosophie Positive*, Paris: Bachelier.

Durkheim, E. ([1895] 1982) *The Rules of Sociological Method*, London: Macmillan.

Epstein, B. (2015a) *The Ant Trap: Rebuilding the Foundations of the Social Sciences*, New York: Oxford University Press.

——— (2015b) "How Many Kinds of Glue Hold the Social World Together?" in M. Galloti and J. Michael (eds) *Perspectives on Social Ontology and Social Cognition*, Dordrecht: Springer.

Foucault, M. (1977) *Discipline and Punish: The Birth of the Prison*, New York: Pantheon Books.

Geertz, C. (1973) *The Interpretation of Cultures: Selected Essays*, New York: Basic Books.

Giddens, A. (1984) *The Constitution of Society: Outline of the Theory of Structuration*, Cambridge: Polity Press.

Gilbert, M. (1989) *On Social Facts*, Princeton: Princeton University Press.

——— (2014) *Joint Commitment*, Oxford: Oxford University Press.

Guizot, F. (1837) *Lectures on European Civilization*, London: John Macrone.

Hacking, I. (1995) "The Looping Effects of Human Kinds," in D. Sperber and A.J. Premack (eds) *Causal Cognition*, Oxford: Oxford University Press.

Hacking, I. (2000) *The Social Construction of What*, Cambridge, MA: Harvard University Press.

Haslanger, S. (2003) "Social Construction: 'The Debunking' Project," in F. Schmitt (ed.) *Socializing Metaphysics*, Lanham, MD: Rowman and Littlefield.

Mill, J.S. (1843) *A System of Logic, Ratiocinative and Inductive*, London: John W. Parker.

Millikan, R.G. (1984) *Language, Thought, and Other Biological Categories: New Foundations for Realism*, Cambridge: MIT Press.

Parsons, T. (1954) *Essays in Sociological Theory*, Glencoe: Free Press.

Pufendorf, S. ([1673] 2007) *On the Duty of Man and Citizen According to Natural Law*, Cambridge: Cambridge University Press.

Ricoeur, P. (1970) *Freud and Philosophy: An Essay on Interpretation*, New Haven: Yale University Press.

Searle, J.R. (1995) *The Construction of Social Reality*, New York: Free Press.

——— (2010) *Making the Social World: The Structure of Human Civilization*, Oxford: Oxford University Press.

21

Social Groups

Paul Sheehy

1. INTRODUCTION

In this chapter, I outline rival positions on the ontology of social groups, ontological individualism and realism (or holism).[1] Ontological individualism maintains that ultimately we need only refer to individual persons and their relations when describing the social world (i.e. the domain of human interaction), offering explanations of social phenomena, forming judgments or developing theories. Realism or holism by contrast is the thesis that reference to social groups is ineliminable from such discourse and that they are entities in their own right. A social group is a type of object over which we quantify in our folk and formal social scientific discourses.

Next I explain two key points of dispute between individualism and holism. First, can groups be identified with sets of individuals? Second, can talk of social groups be wholly analyzed in terms of reference to individuals and their relations? If the answer to either of these questions is "yes," then it is possible for individuals (in relations) to enjoy the kind of explanatory priority which eviscerates holism of substance or interest. I sketch reasons why the answer to each is "no" and propose there is at least a prima facie case to prefer holism.

Third, I consider whether shared or collective intentions are necessary for individuals to constitute a social group and present reasons to show that they are not.

2. THE OLD QUESTION

It is an old question. What kind of thing is a social group? Indeed it might now be regarded as one that is superannuated, coming to be superseded by, inter alia, interests in social properties, collective intentional states, systemic and model theoretic approaches to society.[2] Notwithstanding the interest and importance of such issues the old question has

277

never gone away, for it is at the core of an understanding of the nature of our everyday talk and of the formal discourse of the social sciences. In each our forms of explanation and description, laden with reference to groups, carry with them ontological commitments that ought to be rendered transparent.[3]

The truth conditions of many propositions about the social world depend upon the existence of groups such as nations, peoples, classes, communities, teams, tribes and families and the referential status of the terms we use to talk about them. A proper understanding of what is said by sentences containing such terms—of what we mean—turns on how we are to treat references to social groups. The justification of moral evaluations, the articulation of practical judgments and action, and the formation of policies depend upon the object of such judgments or actions being an appropriate one. In particular, it must be the kind of thing capable of bearing such judgments and of being responsive to particular policies and actions. To the extent, then, that certain kinds of judgment depend upon the object of our judgment having intentional states—as seems central in moral evaluation—the question of whether social groups can be the bearers of intentional states and act on the basis of their intentions is central to understanding both the meaning and aptness of assigning moral praise or blame (and directing certain actions) to groups such as gangs or nations.

3. ANSWERING THE OLD QUESTION

The majority view among philosophers is that the question can be answered in a straight-forward fashion. Groups can (at least in principle) be excluded from folk and formal social scientific discourse. Labeling a diverse set of views as "individualism," this position maintains that individuals and their relations enjoy ontological and explanatory priority. Depending on its form, individualism holds groups to be identical to sets (or mereological sums of individuals or person-stages), mere fictions or reductively analyzed out of social scientific discourse. See e.g. Copp (1984), Effingham (2010), May (1987), Tuomela (1995), Watkins (1955, 1957).

Roughly, reductionism maintains that the truths about groups are expressible, without loss, as truths about individuals. The reductionist view about groups accepts that there are groups, but that the science or body of generalizations in which facts about groups are explained can be reduced—typically they have in mind the reduction of the social sciences to psychology (plus certain aspects of other relevant bodies of knowledge such as biology and ecology). Through this procedure one domain is said to be reduced to the other. Examples of reductionist programs include the reduction of numbers to sets, chemical properties (e.g. solubility) to the properties of molecules and atoms, mental properties to physical properties, and the laws of "special" sciences to those of physics. Similarly, it has been proposed that social groups, properties and the laws of the social sciences can be analyzed in reductive terms. Indeed, Pettit (1996: 145) has noted that recent individualism takes the regularities of social science to be reducible to intentional regularities, with the social-structural properties involved in social regularities being defined in terms of intentional psychology. The appeal of reduction is held to be its onto-logical economy and conceptual unity in promoting explanations and descriptions couched in unifactorial terms. It may appear, moreover, to touch deep epistemological and ontological truths in revealing to us the gap between our ways of talking and the structure of the world.

Fictionalism denies that there are groups to be reduced. Instead there are only persons and the relations in which they stand. However, the concept of a group plays a significant role in explaining the actions of and relations between individuals. For example, Raimo Tuomela (e.g. Tuomela 1995) holds that groups possess only an intentional existence (e.g. as psychological constructs, concepts or posits) and Larry May (1987: 23) takes himself to be an ontological fictionalist about groups in explaining that:

> relations among individuals do have a reality, a distinct ontological status which is different from the individuals who are so related. However the reality of these relations is not sufficient to ensure that the groups, which are composed of individuals in relationships, have reality independently of the individuals who compose these groups.

The truths about groups are held to be expressible (at least in principle) without loss as truths about individuals. Individualism holds that there is no need to quantify over a social group composed of those individuals in our best description or explanation of the social world.

Others have argued that social groups cannot be identified with sets or aggregates nor reductively analyzed out of our social scientific descriptions, explanations and predictions. One realist thesis holds groups to be composite material particulars standing in causal and explanatory relations. See e.g. Hirsch (1982), Gilbert (1989, 1996), Sheehy (2006a). A realist who disavows the materiality of social groups is Ruben (1985). He takes social substances, examples of which he suggests are France, Ealing (a borough in London) and the Red Cross, to be spatio-temporally locatable but non-material entities. He observes that such entities are puzzling.

For (materialist) realism, then, at a high level of taxonomic categorization, groups feature alongside kinds such as organisms and artifacts. This entitlement to individuate groups as material objects relies on three interconnected claims. First, that the strategies of identification or reduction fail. Second, that reference to groups in social scientific and everyday discourse is ineliminable. Third, that ineliminability from our best theoretical model is the hallmark of realism in general. Granted these claims, realism cashes out as a thesis for the individuation of a type of entity. [4] It is now—the realist may insist—the job of the social sciences to elucidate why particular groups have certain features, to trace the ways in which different types of groups are treated and the impact of such treatment on their members.

How then are we to decide between individualism and holism? Intuition seems to point in both directions. While our employment of group or collective terms is woven into our folk and formal discourses about the social world, the idea of collective entities or agents carries the whiff of metaphysical weirdness. (The reader should consult the bibliography and the suggestions for further reading).

I shall examine claims that we can dispense with reference to social groups because (1) a group is identical to a set of individuals or (2) reference to a social group can be reduced to reference to individuals and their relations. If either (1) or (2) is successful, then a form of individualism seems to be the right answer to the old question.

4. GROUPS, SETS AND IDENTITY

We can dispense with an ontological commitment to groups if groups turn out to be identical to some familiar type of entity. On the view that the social sciences pick out just individuals standing in relations one tempting analysis of our group talk is to identify a social group with the set of its (diachronically specified) individual members.[5] Such a strategy of identification fails, though.

> A set can be specified as a list. The set of prime numbers less than 10 is given by the list:[6]

> {2,3,5,7}.

Or a set can be specified as an extension of a property:

> {x: x is a prime number less than 10}.

Taking the Welsh people as an example of a social group, the Welsh would then be identical to the set of individuals {i^1, i^2 . . . i^n} which represents its membership. Alternatively, the Welsh could be identified as the set, S, of all i such that i is φ, where φ is a property(s) sufficient for Welshness; that is the property or family of properties that is "Welsh-making." On its face this identification is attractive to the individualist because there is now no obvious commitment to any social objects save individuals and artifacts. The Welsh could be identified as the set, S, of persons (i^1 . . . i^n) who were, are or will be Welsh—that is, possess the relevant "Welsh-making" properties.

However, now problems arise with counterfactual claims such as "Maradona might have been English"[7] or "Magwa might have been a Mohican." The difficulty arises because sets are extensional and preserve their membership across possible worlds. The identity of sets conforms to a principle of extensionality. A set *is* its members. Set A is identical to set B if and only if its constituents are the same. The set A exists at the actual world and at a possible world if its members are present in both.[8] If the group of English people is identified by the set S, and that set cannot survive a change in its membership, then it cannot be the case that Maradona might have been English. Maradona is not in the set S, although there is of course a set, the members of which are S and Maradona. Yet, it appears that the group of English people has the capacity to sustain such counterfactual claims, whereas sets do not. One member more or less makes no difference to the English, but is absolutely vital to set identity. A key problem with identifying a group with a set is that some other set than the actual set S could have been the group (e.g. of English people), but no other set could have been S. We can conceive of worlds in which a group is wholly composed of individuals other than those who are its members in the actual world while the set of individuals who are its members in the actual world is also present. In such a world there would be e.g. two English peoples.

Let us turn to the French. It is possible that there may never have been a French people, or it could have been the case that at some point in time the French ceased to exist as a culture or people.[9] In a Frenchless world those biological individuals could also exist who are actually members of the French people.[10] By the principle of extensionality we are compelled to say that the French would exist as a group in such a world—set A is identical to set B if and only if they share exactly the same members. Worlds with and without the French could have just the same individuals, some of whom in the former scenario constitute the French through time. The same set of persons exists in both cases, and so if the French People is identical with a set, the French People is present at both worlds. Yet, one of the ways in which we have distinguished these worlds is in terms of the survival or existence of the French. The individualist is faced with the following set of propositions:

P1 In the actual world W the French People is identical with the set S of individuals $\{i^1 \ldots i^n\}$.

P2 There is a possible world W^* in which there is no French People

P3 In W^* there is set S.[11]

By P1 and P3, P2 must be false if groups are identical to sets. The identification of a group with a set of individuals requires us to accept that a group can exist at a world when we have no reason to suppose that it does given the nature of that world. In W^* there would, it seems, both be and not be a French People.

The identification of a group with the set of its members leads to some deeply counter-intuitive conclusions, forcing a massively revisionary account of what we mean when we talk counterfactually of groups. The roots of the difficulty are first my assumption of the necessity of identity, so that if a set of individuals is identical to a group then that relation holds across counterfactual contexts. The necessity of identity is open to challenge,[12] and the individualist can try to argue that at least the identification of groups with sets is a contingent one. Even if we accept this (mistaken) move there is a second source of trouble. While the composition of a group by a particular set of individuals is a contingent matter, constitution is not identity. To point to the things of which an entity consists is not yet to explain what kind of thing it is nor does it furnish us with its identity criteria.

5. GROUPS AND EXPLANATION: REDUCTION-IN-PRINCIPLE

According to the ontological individualist social phenomena such as the impact of mobs, the transmission and development of cultural norms, values and practices, and the significance of some sanctions can be explained in terms of individuals linked in sometimes extremely complex relations. The individualist sees no need to go beyond an understanding of, say, a people as a network of individuals linked through time by a series of practices and attitudes, which they both determine and by which they are in turn partly shaped. To talk literally of groups is just to indulge in the reification of these relations; to mistakenly assume that a description of often complex relations between individuals as a "web" or "network" warrants a commitment to some *object* existing. Beware, the individualist will urge, of seduction by the surface form of our language: reference to the mob is merely a feature of the grammatical structure of language. The individualist criticism takes the holist not to have heeded the warning sufficiently, because the predication of a property or causal power to the group can itself be analyzed in terms of the individuals-in-relations.

As I shall explain, this reductive analysis is to be rejected because the plural predication of a property to individuals-in-relations supposes that they together possess just the kind of unity underwriting the objecthood of groups. Moreover, the individualist commitment to the availability (in principle) of a reductive explanation means that she must sometimes offer an "ultimate" or best explanation from which the (explanatorily) salient information has been lost.

To explain the fear of the police officer by reference to the charging mob approaching his post, the individualist can say that the individuals of the mob together instantiated certain properties, which induced the officer's fear. Some properties such as size and volume are simply additive. A lot of small people may form an aggregate that occupies a large area. Other properties such as the fearsomeness or fury of a mob may only arise when individuals are interacting in certain ways: a bunch of frightening people may not add up to a frightening group. Indeed, together they may appear comical or merely strange. For them to be frightening they must interrelate in a way that brings it about that together they instill fear in others.

The ontological individualist can hold that, for example, the fearsomeness of the mob is a property predicated collectively of a certain number of individuals. Together they have a certain property. Likewise, artistic endeavor may be encouraged within the culture of a certain people; or, a people may be said to be tolerant. In these cases, ontological individualism will maintain that there is no need to introduce a group. Rather, it is a property or propensity of the individuals collectively that they encourage the arts or are tolerant. The property of being tolerant need not be one that is possessed by each person, but it is instantiated through their interactions, which can take place in a complex network of cultural, political and economic relations.

A property or power is then being attributed to individuals considered together. The property is not held by any one individual, but is instantiated through individuals standing in certain relations. This kind of collective or plural predication seems, however, to be committed to an irreducible "them." They (the mob, the people and so on) are furious or tolerant. Rather than explaining away the introduction of a group qua object, this individualist strategy has in effect identified an equivalent in the form of a plural entity. Furthermore, the notion that a property is held by persons standing in certain forms of relations suggests that the property disappears from view if the relations undergo sufficient change. That is, it is the units held together (as a whole) which possess or instantiate or give rise to the property.

It might be helpful here to draw an analogy with the constitutive parts of artifacts and organisms. Consider the parts of a house or table or cat. When these parts stand in object-constituting relations, properties and causal powers are evident and attributed (at the level of everyday objects and experience) to the house, table or cat. The house may cast a shadow on my garden and its red wall annoy me; the family may sit around the table each night to eat a meal, because the table can act as a load-bearing device; the cat is a living organism. Alter the relations of the parts in certain ways and certain of the properties fall from view (alter the relations between the parts enough and the thing itself will drop out of the picture too). Therefore, to offer an explanation in terms of individuals-in-relations carries with it a commitment to regarding those individuals as united, for it is the unity of those parts that bears the relevant property. Taking the individuals severally, one by one as it were, ignores the way in which they are related, and it is just in virtue of being so related that they together possess the property.

Individualism promises that the reduction to individuals and their relations is in principle always an explanatory option. This is not, though, the case. At least sometimes the identification of the *relevant* individuals must refer to the group, thereby leaving the group within the explanation rather than reductively analyzing it away; or, the individualist must assume that *all* individuals are the ones relevant to a particular explanation. Let me explain.

An explanation must be informative. An individualist explanation of the fact that a group encourages, say, civic duty or artistic endeavor takes the form of a list of individuals, their properties and the relations in which they stand, which bring it about that individuals will be encouraged or disposed to encourage, for example, joining the police or engaging in art. The problem of plural predication is assumed to be addressed by the aggregation of the individual properties and relations bringing about the relevant state of affairs. However, for the explanation to be informative it must go beyond a claim that the encouraging of civic duty or art can be explained in principle by reference to properties and relations of individuals (considered singularly). It must be demonstrated that civic duty (or artistic endeavor or toleration and so on) is encouraged *because* of the aggregation of individual properties. Importantly, the claim must not be the trivial one that any social phenomenon depends on the possession by individuals of certain (explanatory) properties. The individualist needs to provide an explanation in which the salient properties of the individuals are not dependent upon the impact of groups. In the absence of actual explanations of this kind we have little reason to suppose that they are in principle always possible. An appeal to an "in-principle" individualist analysis just presupposes the point at hand.

Of course, such a presupposition does not rule out the possibility that given enough time and energy reductive explanations could always be found, allowing groups to drop without loss from our view. For all that needs to be said can be expressed in the language of individuals, their properties and relations.

In response to both reductionist and fictionalist approaches the holist may object that in order to pick out the relevant individuals we must look first to the groups of which they are members. This presents no special problem for ontological holism, since it individuates a group through its causal impact and properties: a group is picked out at a certain level of enquiry. As material objects, the boundaries and composition of a group may be vague—in at least the epistemic sense of underdetermination. But, so are many other material objects at a sufficiently fine-grained or "micro" level of investigation. The individualist by contrast owes an account of the principled basis for restricting the range of individuals and relations that might feature ("in principle") in an explanation.

The individualist program is then the reduction of a group to its members analyzed in terms of their relations or an account of the group-fiction in terms of individuals and their relations. The question for the individualist is which individuals and relations are the right ones. Imagine a town set ablaze by a rampaging mob. The individualist cannot (ultimately) explain the burning town in terms of the rioting mob, but must offer an account referring only to individuals and their relations. The obvious set of individuals is the mob's membership, but each member may have his own set of relationships, distinct from those he has with his "co-mobees." A reductive explanation cannot exclude these other relations on the basis that they are not constitutive of the mob, because they may in part explain why that individual participated in the rioting. Indeed, all the facts about each individual will contribute to the fullest possible specification of why he participated in bringing about the burning of the town. Yet not all the facts are salient in an explanation of the burning. The individualist needs a criterion in order to exclude those facts that are in practice irrelevant.

The obvious way of identifying the relevant individuals and relations is to appeal to membership of the mob, or to those relations that brought about the burning of the town. The first move is not available to the individualist because it suggests that the group is on an explanatory par with the individuals. The second is precisely what needs to be established. Individualism is driven to the position of holding that in principle a particular social fact may be explained by the totality of individual facts.

Imagine that a person, P, becomes a police officer because her society encourages active citizenship. According to the individualist the fact that P became a police officer is explained only in a shorthand way by reference to the nature of her group. In principle, though, it is explained by the totality of facts about individuals. This is not an informative explanation, but reflects what both sides accept: groups and social facts in general, depend (constitutively) upon the existence of individuals.

There is much more to be said for both individualism and holism.[13] That there is a prima facie case for holism emerges once the demands of identifying groups with sets or furnishing a reductive analysis of group facts are recognized.

6. THE PRICE TO PAY

Each position faces challenges internal to its central claim. There is a price to pay for one's ontological commitments. If individualism is true, then it seems we are systematically in error when talking about the social domain. For we appear to take the existential status of groups at face value. That the surface of our language can mislead is a familiar danger and individualism can embrace the virtue of acting as a corrective or therapy for our misleading ways of talking.

Realism has the burden of addressing two challenges. First, the possibility of synchronic co-extensive memberships of groups (e.g. the philosophy department and the wine appreciation society) suggests that two material particulars of the same kind can be in the same place at once. This appears to fly in the face of our common-sense understanding of material particulars. Second, the realist owes an account of the survival conditions of a group. A group can undergo change through time, while remaining the same group, most obviously through changes in its membership. For most objects the very same thing survives change in its parts, provided its parts continue to be organized through time in the form characteristic of that kind of object. Groups, though, by being composed of intention-forming persons seem more prone to mergers, divisions and changes in their defining characteristics (e.g. the prevalent attitudes and values) than artifacts or organisms.[14]

7. SOCIAL GROUPS AND COLLECTIVE INTENTIONS

Grant the prima facie case for realism and the question follows of what kind of relations between individuals are group-constituting. An influential answer is that it is necessary for individuals to share certain mental states to interrelate in a group-constituting form. Typically, they share a conception of themselves as members together of a group and have intentions to act collectively. Prominent among realists in arguing for this intentionalism is Margaret Gilbert (e.g. Gilbert, 1989, 1996, 2000; see also Chapter 10, this volume). In developing her plural subject theory, she characterizes intentionalism as

> the view that according to our everyday collectivity concepts, individual human beings must see themselves in a particular way to constitute a collectivity. In other words, intentions (broadly construed) are logically prior to collectivities.
>
> (Gilbert 1989: 12)[15]

A member of a group conceives of herself as linked in some relevant fashion with the others. Individuals must share certain goals, commitments or psychological states in order to constitute a group. Individuals can constitute a social group only when each believes or understands himself to be linked in some salient way with the others, or when each conceives of himself as a member of the group. Now, the claim here is not just that our (or their) sharing salient beliefs or attitudes is sufficient for us (or them) to constitute a group, but that it is necessary that we (or they) do so.

Intentionalism is a thesis about what has to be true of individuals for it to be true that they constitute a group. In holding that individuals must share certain psychological states, intentionalism requires that group-making individuals have a certain mental content in the process of its formation and ongoing maintenance. There is, though, scope for a distinction to be made between the psychological facts about individuals and the explanatory concepts used in elucidating social facts. The beliefs individuals have about their own actions and relations may not report the true or full nature of those actions and relations in not revealing to the individual the fact that he along with relevant others constitutes a group.

Let us imagine four egoists, each of whom has escaped independently from a prison. By chance they arrive at the same river bank where a large oared boat is moored.[16] The boat is the only means of escape. Its size means that it is evident to each of them that no individual rower would be able to propel it. Now, whether they leap into the boat and just start rowing, or begin rowing after exchanging significant looks or after each has affirmed his commitment to share in the rowing, none of the escapees considers himself to be part of a collectivity or group, even though each recognizes the necessary contribution of the others.[17] They all share the belief that "I am escaping" and, in the circumstances its entailment, "we are escaping." There is no basis, though, to suppose that they have as a goal their ("our") escape, but only each one's ("my") successful flight.

If captured and questioned what he thought he was doing, each escapee could answer: "we were escaping," taking the extension to be an aggregate of individuals. An interrogator may take "we" to refer to either an aggregate of individuals considered severally or to a body or group of individuals considered jointly or united. The belief expressed depends significantly on the sense in which "we" is understood. Even if each prisoner has the belief "we were escaping," the object of the belief varies depending on the referent of "we."[18]

It seems to me that they do constitute a group, even though each may sincerely deny that he is linked or united or constitutes a group with the others. It is not the individuals' beliefs about themselves and their peers that are essential to their "grouphood," but the relations in which they stand. It may often be the case that our relations with others are bound up with our shared beliefs, including those beliefs about the beliefs of others with respect to oneself. However, a group is formed through the ways in which individuals interrelate and interact, and group-constituting patterns of relations are not necessarily those in which the kinds of beliefs essential to the intentionalist thesis will feature.

The fugitive prisoners come to form a group in the rowing of the boat and, as far as the story goes, the group is maintained by their ongoing rowing of it. Motivated by the purely selfish desire for flight, the processes and interrelatedness of the rowing unites the individuals into a unit, independently of their beliefs and attitudes about the others. The extension of "we" is the group as a collectivity or whole, while it also remains the case that each prisoner is indifferent to the fate of the others, and is possessed only of singular goals. Nonetheless, the rowing of the boat is effected by a body, formed through the interrelations of the prisoners, which constrains and influences the rowing of each individual. If the collective action can only arise because of the way in which individuals are interrelating, then the extension of "we" or "they" is a social group.

Consider a market consisting of selfishly motivated individuals who do not regard themselves as being members of a group—the market.[19] The performance of the market is the outcome of the complex array of interactions between the traders. The totality of these interactions both constitute the market at any time, and are in part made possible or constrained by the state of the market. Furthermore, the market has an influence on the wider economy, determining to a greater or lesser degree price behavior and levels of activity elsewhere—but particularly in those sectors utilizing the commodities traded on the market, or influenced by the pricing of financial assets traded. It may be that the London Metal Exchange and the Chicago Mercantile Exchange are best understood as individual entities constituted by the complex interactions of those who trade in them, and individuated within the social world by tracing their impact upon, for example, individuals, companies and governments. Like the escaping prisoners there is no need for traders to think of themselves as members of a group, or as united with fellow traders. Indeed, it may be more likely that they conceive of themselves qua traders in specifically atomistic and adversarial terms.

If there is a non-intentionalist mode of group-constitution, then it may still be true that a social group is only capable of formation by creatures with a certain cognitive capacity. However, the forms of interrelations from which a group is established and sustained need not be restricted to those characterized by shared beliefs, attitudes and so on. There is more to be said here and more needs to be done in order to demonstrate that the intentionalist thesis does set the barriers of entry to grouphood too high, but intentionalism cannot be merely assumed as an obvious truth about groups (see Sheehy (2002) and chapter 2 of Sheehy (2006a) for an extended discussion of Gilbert and intentionalism). Non-intentionalism allows for the possibility of non-human groups. See e.g. Sheehy (2006a: 129–30) and Chapter 33, this volume.

8. CONCLUDING REMARKS

This entry focuses on the old question of what kind of thing a social group is. A wider discussion embraces three issues. First, there is the ontological issue addressed here of whether we should be realists about social groups. Second, there is the question of whether collective intentions are to be regarded as states possessed by a collective entity (a social group) or whether our talk of collective intentions is reducible (analyzable fully) in terms of the intentions of individual agents. Third is the question of what we are doing when we attribute intentional states to something. On one view, we are describing a system with intrinsic features in virtue of which it has representational states responsible in part for certain internal changes and (external) actions (see, e.g. Searle 1983). A rival view (see, e.g. Dennett 1987) maintains that in assigning intentional states we are adopting an explanatory stance. Here intentionality is "as-if" rather than intrinsic and we talk in such terms because of its explanatory and predictive value.

Realism about groups as an answer to the first question need not entail a non-reductive answer to the second question. It need not presuppose that there is anything more to collective intentionality than the possession by individuals of individually analyzable mental states. However, realism does create the conceptual scope for recognition of genuinely collective intentional states possessed by a group (or the instrumentalist/fictionalist attribution of such states). For, it maintains that groups qua material objects exist and, given the right kind of constitutive interrelations and structure, such an object may be capable of possessing intentional states in its own right. Investigating this will take us to a fuller answer to the old question.

REFERENCES

Bratman, M. (1992) "Shared Cooperative Activity," *Philosophical-Review* 101 (2): 327–41.
Clark, A. (1984) "Beliefs and Desires Incorporated," *Journal of Philosophy* 91: 404–25.
Copp, D. (1984) "What Collectives Are: Agency, Individualism and Legal Theory," *Dialogue* XXIII: 249–69.
Dennett, D. (1987) *The Intentional Stance*, Cambridge, MA: MIT Press.
Effingham, N. (2010) "The Metaphysics of Groups," *Philosophical Studies* 149: 251–67.
Gibbard, A. (1975) "Contingent Identity," *Journal of Philosophical Logic* 4: 187–221.
Gilbert, M. (1987) "Modelling Collective Belief," *Synthese* 73:185–204.
——— (1989) *On Social Facts*, Princeton: Princeton University Press.
——— (1996) *Living Together*, Lanham, MD: Rowman & Littlefield.
——— (1997) "What Is It for Us to Intend?" in J. Holmstrom-Hintikka and R. Tuomela (eds) *The Philosophy and Logic of Social Action*, Dordrecht: Kluwer Academic.
——— (2000) *Sociality and Responsibility: New Essays in Plural Subject Theory*, Lanham, MD: Rowman & Littlefield.
Hirsch, E. (1982) *The Concept of Identity*, New York: Oxford University Press.
Lewis, D. (1986) *On the Plurality of Worlds*, Oxford: Blackwell.
May, L. (1987) *The Morality of Groups*, Notre Dame: University of Notre Dame.
Perry, J. (1979) "The Problem of The Essential Indexical," *Nôus* 13: 3–21.
Pettit, P. (1996) *The Common Mind (With Postscript)*, New York: Oxford University Press.
Quine, W. (1980) "On What There Is" reprinted in *From a Logical Point of View*, Cambridge: Harvard University Press.
Ruben, D.-H. (1985) *The Metaphysics of The Social World*, London: Routledge & Kegan Paul.
Searle, J. (1983) *Intentionality*, Cambridge: Cambridge University Press.
——— (1995) *The Construction of Social Reality*, London: Penguin Books.
Sheehy, P. (2002) "On Plural Subject Theory," *Journal of Social Philosophy* 33: 377–94.
—— (2006a) *The Reality of Social Groups*, Aldershot: Ashgate Publishing.
—— (2006b) "Sharing Space: The Synchronic Identity of Social Groups," *Philosophy of the Social Sciences* 36 (2): 1–18.
Swindler, J.K. (1996) "Social Intentions. Aggregate, Collective and General," *Philosophy of the Social Sciences* 26: 61–76.

Tuomela, R. (1995) *The Importance of Us*, Stanford: Stanford University Press.

Tuomela, R. and Miller, K. (1988) "We Intentions," *Philosophical Studies* 53: 367–89.

Watkins, J. (1955) "Methodological Individualism: A Reply," *Philosophy of Science* 22: 58–62.

——— (1957) "Historical Explanation in the Social Sciences," *The British Journal for the Philosophy of Science* 8: 104–17.

Weber, M. (1978/1922) *Economy and Society*, Berkeley: University of California Press.

NOTES

1. One could also adopt an eliminativist strategy to groups, holding the concept "group" to be part of a radically false theory. I shall not explore here how elimination can be progressed within the social sciences and philosophical consideration thereof. Perhaps following a completed neuroscience, folk social science will undergo radical abandonment along with our folk psychology.

2. Much recent work has focused on the nature and role of group, collective or "we" intentions. See for example Bratman (1992), Clark (1984), Gilbert (1987, 1997), Searle (1995), Tuomela and Miller (1988), Tuomela (1995). Swindler (1996: 61) goes so far as to claim that '(T)he issue between individualists and holists is no longer, as it once was, what kinds of entities are involved in sociality so much as what kinds of intentional contents constitute social and therefore moral relations'.

3. It is important to note that the issue of the ontological status of groups runs through the question of whether a proper understanding of the social sciences is naturalistic, interpretive, critical or post-modern. No position on the nature of the social sciences can ignore the question.

4. See Quine (1948, reprinted 1980) for a defense of this approach. Quine is, of course, discussing the ontological commitments entailed by our best set of natural scientific theories. He would not agree that groups are ineliminable.

5. If a group is identical to the set of its members at a specified time, t, then a group could only be identical with a set of individuals if one is prepared to accept that identity is extremely ephemeral. This fragility worry is defused if set membership is defined diachronically to include individuals who were, are and will possess the relevant properties.

6. I do not include 1, as contemporary mathematical opinion is that 1 is not obviously prime. Thanks to Dr. Mike Ward for this point.

7. Compare with Ruben (1985).

8. Those who endorse the modal realism and counterpart theory of David Lewis might put this point in terms of the counterparts—see, e.g. Lewis (1986).

9. For the purposes of this discussion we need not consider the extent of the other changes that would be necessary to make such a world possible.

10. Modal realists will put the point in terms of the counterparts of the actual French individuals existing at a possible world in which there is no French People. The criticisms of the identification of groups with sets do not depend on one's position with regard to modal realism.

11. Or the set of the counterparts of $\{i^1 \ldots i^n\}$.

12. See especially Gibbard (1975).

13. See e.g. Sheehy (2006a: ch. 1) for a detailed discussion of a range of individualist strategies.

14. For further discussion see, e.g. Sheehy (2006a, 2006b).

15. The way in which individuals must see themselves is as being committed together to a belief, goal, intention and so on, and for such a commitment to be common knowledge. Gilbert's 'pro-intentionalist stance finds its positive basis (in the argument) that people must perceive themselves as members of a plural subject' (1989: 13).

16. Unlike, say, the passengers on a plane, which is hijacked, the prisoners have no shared history as elements in an aggregate prior to a change in circumstances, which may encourage a group-forming pattern of relations.

17. The escapees' actions are social in Weber's sense, according to whom an action is social when 'by virtue of the subjective meaning attached to it by the acting individual(s) it takes account of the behavior of others and is thereby oriented in its course' (Weber 1978/1922: 88).

18. Compare with Perry's (1979) discussion of the "essential indexical."

19. Of course, traders frequently must be formally members of an exchange in order to trade in a market. However, the formal and institutional requirements regulating access should not be confused with the ontological status of the market itself.

FURTHER READING

For book-length discussions of the ontological debate see Gilbert (1996), Ruben (1985), Sheehy (2006a) and Tuomela (1995).

22

Social Kinds

Ásta

1. WHAT IS A SOCIAL KIND?

When we want to characterize a theoretical notion such as that of a *social kind*, we do well to ask what that notion is for: who uses it and for what purpose? In our case, the answer is social scientists on the one hand and social theorists on the other, which includes theorists of race, gender, disability, sexual orientation and the like, but also historians and archeologists, to name a couple of fields that may not fit squarely under the rubric of "social science." But what is the notion of a social kind and the various social kinds for? Social kinds get used in forms of explanation of phenomena. These phenomena to be explained are often social phenomena, but can also be natural phenomena, when there is interaction between the natural and the social.

What are social kinds? That is one of the questions we will be addressing in this chapter, so I will offer you a minimal preliminary definition to stake out our territory. On the minimal definition a social kind is a collection of phenomena defined by a property or feature that is a *social* property or feature. For instance, it includes *money*, with the defining feature *being money, waiters* (*being a waiter*), *refugees* (*being a refugee*), and *recessions* (*being a recession*). It is a further question whether some other requirements must hold for the collection to have the status of a *kind*, and we will return to that question in due course. I use the term "collection" deliberately here, instead of "set," because what is in the collection need not be countable entities, such as refugees, but may include mass phenomena, such as money.

In this chapter I will introduce the reader to some of the main controversies over social kinds. They are:

1. What makes a social kind a *kind*?
2. What makes a social kind *social*?
3. Are social kinds real and objective?
4. Are social kinds compatible with naturalism?

2. WHAT MAKES A SOCIAL KIND A *KIND*?

Traditionally, philosophers influenced by Aristotle maintain that for a collection of entities or stuffs to be a kind, the members of the kind have to share an essence that is explanatory of the behavior of the members across a range of contexts. An essence is a set of properties such that if a member were to lose it, it would not only cease to be a member of said kind, but cease to be *simpliciter*. This essentialist conception involves two claims: a) a kind has an essence such that nothing is a member of that kind without sharing that essence; and b) an individual member of a kind has an essence (derived from the kind essence) such that it would cease to be what it is were it to lose it. This conception of a kind has been part of the revival of Aristotelian essentialist metaphysics, coupled with scientific realism, that we see in Kripke (1980), Putnam (1975), Wiggins (1980), and other philosophers of the late twentieth century. Their work on natural kind terms involves a commitment to this notion of a kind. But as most contemporary theorists of social kinds are skeptical of the existence of social kinds with an essence, I will not assume the essentialist conception of kind in my use of the term "kind."[1]

Even if we reject the essentialist conception of a social kind, we may want the notion of a social kind to involve something more than merely be a collection of entities or stuffs sharing a social property. For instance, we may think that the collection of popular kids at Mission High does not qualify for being a true social kind, like genders or races, on pain of allowing any arbitrary collection to be a social kind. In the absence of the essentialist conception of kinds, what else can we appeal to, to distinguish social kinds from mere arbitrary collections?

There are three types of feature that we can appeal to, to draw such a distinction: a structural, a pragmatic, and a causal one. For instance, we can appeal to the *stability* of kinds across contexts (spatial or temporal) and say that the existence or membership of kinds are stable across contexts, whereas that isn't the case for arbitrary collections. We can also say that kinds play a *useful* role in explanation, whereas the arbitrary collections do not. And then, we can insist that kinds play a *causal* role in the world, whereas arbitrary collections do not. Given the interest in social kinds in the first place, i.e. that we are interested in them because they feature in social explanation, the last two ways of distinguishing social kinds from arbitrary collections are most helpful for our purposes and help us distinguish between two different conceptions of kinds at work among social scientists and theorists:

1. A deflationary, pragmatic, conception of a kind: a social kind is a collection of phenomena that features in social explanation.
2. A robust, causal, conception of a kind: a social kind is a collection of phenomena that plays a causal role in social explanation.

3. WHAT MAKES A SOCIAL KIND A SOCIAL KIND?

All answers to the question what makes a kind a social kind appeal to something about subjects, but what that "something" is varies. I will explore the views that claim that: a) social kinds are description-dependent; b) social kinds are dependent on subjective attitudes; and c) social kinds are dependent on attitudes and/or behavior of subjects.

a. The Social as Description-Dependent

Ian Hacking (1999) makes use of Elizabeth Anscombe's (1957) idea that intending something is acting under a description when he gives his account of kinds of people, or *human kinds*. The examples of human kinds that he is particularly concerned with involve ones that have been used in social or psychological analysis, such as child molesters, homosexuals, hysterics, and manic-depressives, but also ones that exemplify a particular culturally specific way of being, such as the Parisian *garçons de café*. His contention is, first, that one cannot be a member of such human kinds unless the concept of being such a person is available and, second, unless one intentionally acts in a certain way, which, following Anscombe, is to act under a particular description. This is part of his deeply historicist conception of human kinds, which means that kinds exist in their historical contexts but are not to be found also in other historical times and places that lack that historical specificity and the accompanying conceptual resources. Both his claims are controversial and in my view not sustainable without some further work. Can there have been homosexuals in Ancient Greece, for example, before the nineteenth-century concept was available? If not, how do we make sense of the intuition that there have always been homosexuals and on what basis do we base our solidarity with people across spatial and temporal locations? Here one might want to distinguish between two kinds of groupings of humans: a thin one that requires only that the individuals fit a certain description; and a thick one where it is a necessary condition of belonging to that kind that one think of oneself as belonging to that kind and act out one's conception of oneself as such. The *garçon de café* may be just such a latter kind, as well as other ones that involve specific historically situated ways of being in the world, as mentioned above. The other type of cases that involve psychosocial analysis may fall into the thin category, where what is at work is classification of individuals by a third party, be it the state, doctors, or social scientists.

I have suggested that the cases Hacking discusses should be separated into two categories: those that involve a classification by a third party and those that involve self-identification. Following Foucault and Hegel, Hacking believes that the classification of human individuals always has causal effect on those classified and that they have to respond to how they are classified. They don't have to embrace how they are classified, they can try to resist the classification or negotiate it, but have to respond in some way. And often the response is at least a partial embrace of the classification. Why? Because often those classified are marginalized within society and especially marginalized when it comes to conceptual resources to make sense of their own experiences, or what get called "hermeneutical resources," and the promise of a conceptual framework to make sense of those experiences is very tempting. For this reason, what was initially just a third-party classification of individuals, may develop into a culturally specific way of being in the world that people can identify with and aspire to. Thus a "thin" kind can become a "thick" one.

So, on Hacking's conception, for a kind to be a social kind requires the availability of a concept of that kind, with an associated description. Can we extract a conception of the social here? Yes, a social kind is a *description-dependent* kind. Some kinds require that the description be something the members are acting under, others simply require that the description be available. If we generalize this conception to all social kinds, then on this account phenomena such as recessions do not exist until the conceptual and linguistic resources exist to describe them. That may strike some as overly restrictive. Don't we want to allow, for example, that historians of antiquity be able to offer as an explanation of a certain famine and population migration that there was a recession, even though the concept of a recession was not available at the time?

As the reader can see, there are some issues involved in fleshing out Hacking's idea that social kinds are description-dependent, even if we restrict ourselves to human kinds only. I will not settle the question here how well the theory can hold up to scrutiny, but move on to another conception of the social, according to which what makes a social kind social is its dependency on subjective attitudes.

b. The Social as Dependent upon Subjective Attitudes

When characterizing what makes a kind social, the main question in the social ontology literature in recent years has not been that of description-dependency but to what extent social kinds are dependent upon subjective attitudes.[2]

John Searle draws a distinction between two kinds of subjectivity: what he calls "ontological" and "epistemic" (Searle 1997). A phenomenon is ontologically subjective if the existence of the phenomenon depends on subjects in some way, including their beliefs, thoughts, and practices. A phenomenon is epistemically subjective if the truth value of statements about those phenomena depends on subjects in some way, including their beliefs, tastes, and opinions. Searle argues that the social world is ontologically subjective but epistemically objective. For instance, the existence of money depends on people's collective beliefs and commitments, but then it is an epistemically objective question whether a piece of paper is money and whether there is such a thing as money at all. In his earlier work (Searle 1997: 32), Searle is committed to the view that what it is for something to be a social kind is for it to be believed to be and regarded so, e.g. for something to be money is for it to be regarded as or believed to be money. Although generally in agreement, Amie Thomasson (2003a, 2003b) has rightly objected that not only can there be social phenomena that are of the kind they are even though no one has beliefs about them, there can exist social kinds no one believes there are. For instance, we can be in a recession, even though no one has beliefs about it, including beliefs to the effect that it is a recession, or even that there are such things as recessions. In response to such criticism, Searle is in his later work committed to kind existence being dependent on collective acceptance, but kind membership generally not (Searle 2010). As for phenomena such as recessions, he thinks they do, at base, depend on some sort of collective acceptance, because they are "systematic fallouts" or consequences of the attitudes we have to other social phenomena.

Recently, Mohammad Ali Khalidi (2013) has argued for a tripartite distinction among social kinds. While he thinks that social kinds are attitude-dependent, what kinds of attitudes are at work can help distinguish among three kinds of social kinds.

1. Neither kind existence nor kind membership depend on attitudes of subjects towards the kind itself or its members, although these kinds depend on subjective attitudes about other things. For example, whether there are such things as recessions does not depend on whether anyone thinks there are and whether something is a recession does not depend on the attitude of subjects towards the phenomenon in question.

2. Kind existence depends on attitudes of subjects towards the kind itself but not kind membership. For example, on Searle's account, whether the kind money exists depends on the attitudes of subjects, but whether a particular piece of paper is a member of the kind money does not depend on anyone's attitude towards it.
3. Both kind existence and kind membership depend on attitudes of subjects. For example, on Searle's account, whether there are such things as cocktail parties depends on subjective attitudes and whether a particular gathering is a cocktail party or not also depends on what people think about it.

Searle is chiefly concerned with institutional phenomena so his commitment to thesis 2 on the Khalidi scale fits such phenomena well. It does not fit well with phenomena such as recessions, or what I call "communal" phenomena such as races and genders.

I have argued elsewhere that what makes a social human kind social is that what its members share is a social property and I offer a conferralist framework to make sense of social properties (Ásta Sveinsdóttir 2011, 2012, ND). I make a distinction between two types of social property: institutional and communal. The key difference between institutional and communal properties is that an institutional property is conferred by someone or something in authority, whereas a communal property is conferred by people or entities who have non-authorized standing. The source of the authority can vary. In some cases it has been conferred on the person in authority at an earlier date (think of judges and umpires); in others it is produced by means of individual or collective acceptance or consent at the time. Likewise, the source of the standing can vary. The conferred property amounts to a social status that is constituted by the constraints and enablements on the bearer's behavior in the context. For example, being married is an institutional property conferred upon a couple by a one-time act and being popular is a communal property conferred on a person by the sentiments others bear towards them.

This account of social properties fits best for the social properties that humans and other subjects bear, and can also be extended for things that acquire new powers such as money (a piece of paper acquires a status or power), but it isn't obviously applicable to things such as recessions. This theory deals best with social phenomena that are the results of things acquiring social meaning. This social meaning can be institutional or communal. In the examples above, there is a grounding property that the conferrers are attempting to track in the conferral and that property is the property that acquires a social meaning. Acquiring a social meaning is then fleshed out as constraints and enablements on the person or entity that gets the property conferred onto them. But things like recessions aren't that type of thing. Recessions are defined mathematically. A recession is something that meets certain mathematical conditions. It is a mathematical pattern that fits social phenomena. There cannot be recessions without people and their practices, but it isn't the attitude of people towards a phenomenon that makes it a recession; nor is it the attitude of people that makes there be such things as recessions. To be a recession is simply to fit a certain mathematical description that contains many variables such as economic growth and the like. This is so even though nothing can be a recession in the absence of social practices, and there can be no social practices in the absence of subjects engaging with each other.

It might now seem that Khalidi's useful tripartite distinction is exhaustive and that any social kind is going to fall into one of his three types. If so, then the various philosophers of social kinds would simply disagree about which kind falls into which category. But things are not so simple. On Sally Haslanger's view (2012), there are social kinds that need not be dependent on subjective attitudes at all, but rather merely unconscious behavior of people.

c. Social Kinds as Places in Hierarchical Structures

In Haslanger (2012), her chief focus is on the construction of gender and race and other communal and institutional kinds of people. In her view, when one argues that a kind is not a natural kind, but a social kind, one is arguing that membership in the kind does not consist in the presence of some natural features, but in the members' occupying some social position in a hierarchy. In other words, on Haslanger's view a social property is a social status. While this is in line with other authors discussed above, Haslanger is less intellectualist than those authors in her view of how such statuses come into being and how one acquires that status, in that, on her view, subjects need not have attitudes towards the kind or the membership for social statuses to get constructed and for people to acquire them. These statuses, and the corresponding social kinds, are sometimes dependent upon subjective attitudes, but sometimes constructed by the unconscious behavior of people (Haslanger 2012: 128). The social kinds Haslanger has in mind are not just the kinds that satisfy a certain description, such as recession, but can even be human kinds that don't have a special name yet but are what she calls "thick" social positions that are due to 'the unintended and unconceptualized impact of practices'. For example, in a context in which being a widow carries with it huge social consequences, being a child of a widow may also be a "thick" social position, with particular behavioral constraints and enablements, even though no one has, as of yet, conceptualized it as such or named the particular social position. It then is a consciousness-raising project to identify that social position and the corresponding social kind.

It might be tempting to fold Haslanger's position into the views discussed directly above and say that what Haslanger's example brings out is that the kinds of subjective attitudes involved need not be conscious. That would then be in line with my conferralist position that allows that the attitudes or states of subjects that do the conferring need not be conscious. But bringing Haslanger into the fold would be a mistake. On her view, there can be social kinds, even human kinds, that are created by the systematic behavior of people. No attitude need accompany that behavior. The larger point here is simply that on Haslanger's view the key to our understanding the social is not to locate the social in subject dependency, but to look at social practices and phenomena that play some role in those practices. With that reorientation, we get a completely general and different account of what makes social kinds social. Social kinds are kinds of social relationship; they are places on a map of hierarchical social structures.

4. ARE SOCIAL KINDS OBJECTIVE AND REAL?

We have seen that most writers on social kinds take social kinds to be existentially dependent on attitudes or behavior of subjects. What does that say about their objectivity? They are clearly existentially subjective, but, as Searle pointed out, that does not mean that there are no facts of the matter pertaining to them. Social kinds are objective objects of knowledge, or as Searle calls it "epistemically objective." We can do empirical research on social kinds and find out facts about them. Truths about social kinds are not subjective in the way in which whether an apple tastes good or not is subjective and depends on the particular person taking a bite. We give social kinds existence with our attitudes and behaviors but then they take off and lead a life of their own.

This conception of the objectivity of social kinds is shared by other writers who work specifically on the metaphysics of social kinds, such as Hacking, Haslanger, and me, but in the race literature, and to some extent the literature on gender, it is common to see the view that if something is social or socially constructed then it is altogether subjective (see James 2017 and Mikkola 2017), but I think that view rests on a confusion.

Questions about whether a phenomenon is real or not are notoriously hairy partly because the meaning of "real" varies wildly. For instance, sometimes, the word "real" is used to designate that it can be an objective object of knowledge, in the sense we discussed directly above. I have sided with the consensus among metaphysicians of the social above and argued that it is. Sometimes the word "real" is used to capture existential objectivity of the kind also discussed: is its existence independent of subjects and their attitudes, behavior, or practices? The answer to that question is clearly NO. But the sense of "real" that yields disagreement among theorists of social kinds pertains to ontological commitment: do we have to allow social kinds into our ontology? Here the old medieval debate between realists and nominalists about universals gets a modern frock: do we have to be committed to the existence of social kinds as well as their members? Are the properties the members share part of our ontology?

Hacking has advocated what he calls "dynamic nominalism" about human kinds. On this view, the kind comes into being hand in hand with its members and with the availability of the name or description of the kind. This is why it is a *nominalism*. It is a *dynamic* nominalism because kinds come into being and then go out of existence with their membership, as opposed to existing independently of the existence of members. Hacking's dynamic nominalism has been influential and some theorists who work on race have followed Hacking and argued for a dynamic nominalism of race (e.g. Sundstrom 2002) or been otherwise influenced by him (Appiah 1996). Other theorists have argued for a different form of nominalism about specific kinds. For example, Natalie Stoljar (2011) argues for resemblance nominalism about genders on the grounds that there is no one property that all and only women (or men or some other gender) share. Instead someone is a woman, say, if they resemble the paradigm case of a woman sufficiently closely[3].

Haslanger explicitly argues for realism about social kinds. Her *critical realism* about social kinds has it that social kinds, while socially constructed, are real types. For Haslanger, saying that a type is "real" means that talk about that type is truth-apt (in contrast to the error-theorist or the eliminativist). But her commitment to realism about social kinds is not limited to the claim that talk of social kinds is truth-apt, because she thinks that a social kind can exist in the absence of conceptual and linguistic resources to identify it, as we saw above. We thus have a clear difference between her view and Hacking's on the relationship of language and conceptual resources to the social kinds they access. Hacking thinks the kinds are dependent on those resources, Haslanger does not.

5. ARE SOCIAL KINDS COMPATIBLE WITH NATURALISM?

The debate over whether social kinds are real or not is a debate fueled by desires not to allow "spooky" entities and stuffs into one's ontology and disagreements over what is spooky or spooky enough. The debate over whether social kinds are compatible with naturalism is similarly about such qualms. What is a commitment to naturalism? That is a notoriously hard question to answer. While many naturalist philosophers were influenced by Quine's conception of naturalism (Quine 1969), most contemporary self-avowed naturalists seem to have departed considerably from Quine's conception (see, e.g. Kim 1988 and Rooney 1998). Quine's conception of naturalized epistemology consisted of two methodological theses:

1. Normative epistemology should be given up: there is no such thing as a justification for a belief; there is only an explanation for it.
2. Epistemology is properly a branch of empirical psychology and its methods thus empirical.

Let me consider the question whether a Quinean naturalist who finds normativity spooky can embrace social kinds. I distinguish between a hard core and a soft core version.

The hard core naturalist who rejects normativity altogether will have a hard time with social kinds not because an investigation into social kinds is inherently normative, but because the analysis of the creation and maintenance of some social kinds, in particular human kinds, involves positing norms for behavior. If one thinks there are no such things as norms, such explanations will not be palatable.

A soft core naturalist will allow for normativity but maintain that all normativity is constituted by the behavior or attitudes of subjects. There are no subject-transcendent norms, no subject-independent moral facts, and the like. Social kinds do not pose a problem for this kind of naturalist. They can do empirical studies on how social kinds are created and maintained and it is an empirical question which norms are at work there and how those norms come into being.

It is thus only the hard core Quinean naturalist who has a problem with social kinds. While most contemporary naturalists aren't hard core Quineans (a number of them are soft core) we haven't thereby settled the question of naturalism yet, because there are other commitments that naturalism can bring besides the one inherited from Quine. The most important one is not methodological, like the Quinean one above, but metaphysical. Are social kinds compatible with a picture of the world where the explanatory framework for all that is allowed into our ontology is that of natural science? Can the study of social kinds be reduced to the study of phenomena belonging to a branch of natural science?

When a commitment to philosophical naturalism involves the metaphysical commitment that only phenomena posited by theories of natural science are allowed into the ontology, social kinds pose a problem. Unless we can reduce talk of social kinds into talk of observable behavior and measurable brain activity, social kinds won't belong to the "fabric of the world" of this sort of naturalist. And while metaphysical naturalism is a prevalent commitment in the academy, as evidenced by the number of research programs that attempt to link mental states of various kinds with brain states, despite the failure of identity theory in the philosophy of mind of a few decades ago, theorists who are concerned with the social put any such questions of reduction to the side. If the social cannot be reduced to the physical, that just shows the shortcomings of a worldview that insists everything there is has to be describable by natural science. Meanwhile, there are serious social problems to attend to calling for both serious conceptual work and serious empirical work.

There is a weak sort of naturalism prevalent in much work on gender, race, and other such social kinds. This weak sort of naturalism involves a methodological commitment to having the theorizing informed by the empirical facts. But it isn't a one-way street: just as the theorizing is informed by the empirical facts, so can the empirical facts be interpreted in a new light with new theoretical concepts. This ongoing process of attempting to gain a deeper understanding of the social world is one form of the method of reflective equilibrium, where the aim is to reach a reflective equilibrium between what we count as the empirical data and the theoretical framework we devise to interpret and explain that data (cf. Goodman 1955).

To sum up, a commitment to social kinds is compatible with all but the most extreme naturalist positions, those involving a rejection of normativity and those involving a metaphysical commitment to a physicalist ontology.

6. CONCLUSION

In this chapter I have introduced the reader to the main controversies over social kinds. They are: what makes a social kind a kind? What makes it social? and, Are social kinds real, objective, and compatible with naturalism?

ACKNOWLEDGEMENTS

I thank Eyja Margrét Brynjarsdóttir and the editors of this volume for reading over an earlier draft of this chapter. Naturally, I am solely responsible for the views herein and all remaining errors.

RELATED TOPICS

Social Construction and Social Facts (Ch. 20), Social Groups (Ch. 21), Status Functions (Ch. 23).

REFERENCES

Anscombe, G.E.M. (1957) *Intention*, Oxford: Basil Blackwell,(2nd edition, 1963).
Appiah, K.A. (1996) "Race, Culture, Identity: Misunderstood Connections," in K.A. Appiah and A. Gutmann (eds) *Color Conscious: The Political Morality of Race*, Princeton: Princeton University Press.
Ásta Sveinsdóttir (2011) "The Metaphysics of Sex and Gender," in C. Witt (ed.) *Feminist Metaphysics*, Berlin: Springer.
——— (2012) "The Social Construction of Human Kinds," *Hypatia* 28 (4).
——— (ND) *Categories We Live By*, (ms. under contract with Oxford University Press).
Goodman, N. (1955) *Fact, Fiction, and Forecast*, Cambridge, MA: Harvard University Press.
Guala, F. (2014) "On the Nature of Social Kinds," in M. Gallotti and J. Michaels (eds) *Perspectives on Social Ontology and Social Cognition*, Berlin: Springer.
Hacking, I. (1999) *The Social Construction of What?* Cambridge, MA: Harvard University Press.
Haslanger, S. (2012) *Resisting Reality: Social Construction and Social Critique*, Oxford: Oxford University Press.

James, M. (2017) "Race," in E.N. Zalta (ed.) *The Stanford Encyclopedia of Philosophy* (Spring 2017 edition), https://plato.stanford.edu/archives/spr2017/entries/race/.

Khalidi, M.A. (2013) "Three Kinds of Social Kinds," *Philosophy and Phenomenological Research* 90 (1): 96–112.

Kim, J. (1988) "What is Naturalized Epistemology?" in J.E. Tomberlin (ed.), *Philosophical Perspectives* 2: 381–406.

Kripke, S. (1980) *Naming and Necessity*, Cambridge, MA: Harvard University Press.

Mikkola, M. (2017) "Feminist Perspectives on Sex and Gender," in E.N. Zalta (ed.) *The Stanford Encyclopedia of Philosophy* (Summer 2017 edition), https://plato.stanford.edu/archives/sum2017/entries/feminism-gender/.

Putnam, H. (1975) "The Meaning of 'Meaning'," *Minnesota Studies in the Philosophy of Science* 7: 215–71.

Quine, W.V.O. (1969) "Epistemology Naturalized," in: W.V.O. Quine, *Ontological Relativity and Other Essays*, New York: Columbia University Press.

Rooney, P. (1998) "Putting Naturalized Epistemology to Work," in L.M. Alcoff (ed.) *Epistemology: The Big Questions*, Oxford: Blackwell.

Searle, J.R. (1997) *The Construction of Social Reality*, New York: Free Press.

——— (2010) *Making the Social World: The Structure of Human Civilization*, Oxford: Oxford University Press.

Stoljar, N. (2011) "Different Women. Gender and the Realism-Nominalism Debate," in C. Witt (ed.) *Feminist Metaphysics*, Berlin: Springer.

Sundstrom, R. (2002) "Racial Nominalism," *Journal of Social Philosophy* 33 (2): 193–210.

Thomasson, A. (2003a) "Foundations for a Social Ontology," *Protosociology* 18–19: 269–90.

——— (2003b) "Realism and Human Kinds," *Philosophy and Phenomenological Research* 67: 580–609.

Wiggins, D. (1980) *Sameness and Substance*, Cambridge, MA: Harvard University Press.

NOTES

1. Essentialist conceptions of kinds such as races and genders have been popular in the past, and been an integral part of racist, sexist and other oppressive ideologies, but that has been coupled with the claim that these kinds were natural kinds, not social. See Mikkola (2017) and James (2017).
2. In addition to the authors discussed below, see also, e.g. Guala (2014).
3. See also discussion in Mikkola (2017).

23

Status Functions

John Searle

The whole subject of collective intentionality has become a booming area in contemporary philosophy. This is to be welcomed. Traditionally, most of the analyses of intentionality had a very narrow range; they typically focused on beliefs, sometimes belief and desire, and almost always on individuals' beliefs and desires. I think a natural extension of the philosophy of intentionality to cover perception, and of course intentional action, as well as all of the emotions, is clearly necessary. Indeed I have worked on all of these issues (Searle 1983, 2015). Furthermore, we need to examine not only intrinsic intentionality, but also derived intentionality, as, for example, when we treat a mark as a symbol standing for something else or a sentence as having truth conditions. The sentence, as a syntactical object, has no intrinsic intentionality. The intentionality of sentences, symbols, pictures, marks, etc. is all derived from the intentionality of human beings.

When we consider the derived intentionality of language and linguistic expressions in general, we immediately encounter the problem of *collective intentionality*. The derived intentionality of a sentence has to be derived from the collectivity of the intrinsic intentionality of the speakers of the language of which the sentence is a part. What is going on in the collectivities? Well, let us slow down and consider different sorts of cases. It is clear that groups of people or animals can share intentionality. This is most obvious in cases where there is animal cooperation, where for example, you see animals cooperating in building a beaver dam, or hunting for prey. But it's important that collective intentionality be recognized as existing not just in collective action, but in collective desires and collective beliefs. When a church congregation recites a prayer together, it is not a question of single individuals expressing their faith, but the congregation as a collectivity expressing its common faith. Common forms of cooperative behavior, such as playing in a symphony orchestra or engaging in a baseball game, or cooperating in a political movement, are cases of collective intentionality.

In what follows, I am going to take for granted the general account of intentionality that I have developed elsewhere (Searle 1983), which makes a clear distinction between intrinsic and derived intentionality, and within the intentional state between the type of state that it is (belief, desire, fear, or hope) and the content that it has (fear of rain, desire for an improvement in the economic situation, hope for a cure for diseases). I am going to also assume an apparatus that includes the causal self-reflexivity of certain sorts of intentional states, so an intention-in-action to raise my arm is satisfied only if the intention-in-action itself causes the arm to go up. And furthermore, we will take for granted that there are different directions of fit. The intentional states of belief and visual perception are supposed to fit how things are in the world; they have the mind-to-world direction of fit. And desires and intentions are not supposed to represent how things are in fact, but how we hope they will be in the case of desires and how we intend to make them in the case of intentions; they have the world-to-mind direction of fit.

When we focus our attention on intentional actions, we discover at least two important theoretical points that we need to make. First, there is the distinction between the intention that I have *prior* to the initiation of the action, and the actual *intention-in-action* that I have when carrying out the action. It is absolutely central to see these because they have different conditions of satisfaction. My prior intention to raise my arm has as its condition of satisfaction that I should perform the action of raising my arm, and that that action should be caused by that very prior intention. The intention-in-action in raising my arm is simply that my arm should go up and that its going up is caused by the intention-in-action. The action consists of the two components of the intention-in-action and the bodily movement caused by the intention-in-action. So the prior intention represents the whole action, and the whole action has two components—the intention-in-action and the bodily movement. There is thus a causal sequence: the prior intention causes the intention-in-action, which causes the bodily movement.

The intentions of an intentional action can be separated into those that are simple, where you simply intend to do something without intending to do anything else by way of which or by means of which you do it. So when I raise my arm, I just do it, I do not do something else first which enables me to do it. Such actions as this have been baptized "basic actions," but in addition to basic actions there are complex actions where you do something by-way-of or by-means-of doing something else (Danto 1965). So for example, raising my arm is a basic action; I just do it. But if I vote for the motion by raising my arm, then I do one thing (vote for the motion) by-way-of doing something else (raising my arm). There is only one action, not two. The relation of raising my arm to voting in such an action is a constitutive *by-way-of* relation because raising my arm in that context constitutes voting for the motion. In addition, there is a causal by-means-of relation. For example, I might turn on the light switch by pushing it with my finger. That is, I turn on the switch *by means of* pushing it with my finger, and the by-means-of relation is a causal relation. Pushing the finger causes the switch to be turned on. It is not a constitutive by-way-of relation. In the example of the causal by-means-of relation there is only one action performed, not two. I perform the single action of turning on the switch by-means-of pushing it with my finger. The complexity of the intentional structure of actions divides into these two kinds, the constitutive by-way-of relations and the causal by-means-of relations. It turns out that the by-way-of relations are much more important for human beings than they are for animals, because humans have institutional structures and these enable them to do one thing by way of doing something else. You buy something by exchanging money, you vote by making a mark on a ballot paper, you pay a bill by signing your name to a document—all of those are examples of the constitutive by-way-of relation.

In what follows, I am going to assume all of this apparatus as given. I realize that a lot of this could be debated, and I am happy to debate it, but I do not really have any doubts about it. But let me turn to collective intentions-in-actions. We discover some interesting complexities. Typically in cooperative action, different people have to do different things in order to achieve a collective goal. In the performance of the symphony, I have to play the violin while somebody else plays the French horn, yet the symphony requires both the horn part and the violin part and together with the other members of the orchestra, we do something that constitutes playing the symphony. What exactly is the relationship between the individual and the collective intentionality? That is not a trivial question. Many people write about the relation of the individual and the collective as if it did not need further discussion. So for example, Michael Bratman talks of what he calls "meshing subplans" (Bratman 2014). But what one needs to know is what exactly is involved in the subplan's meshing. That is, when two people are cooperating, and they have a collective goal G and a subplan S1 and S2, how exactly do the conditions of satisfaction of S1 and S2 relate to each other? And how do they relate to G? It is no help to be told that they "mesh." What exactly are the constitutive principles of the meshing as it relates to how the conditions of satisfaction of both the individual and the collective relate to each other? I have actually written about that (Searle 1990); it gave me a lot of headaches and I am not sure that I have the right answer to it, but I think this cannot be taken for granted. We are going to have to assume that we have a solution to the relationship between the individual and the collective intentionality.

Before turning to the main aim of this paper, the explanation of the notion of Status Functions, I make two more fundamental distinctions.

1. OBJECTIVITY AND SUBJECTIVITY

The famous distinction between the objective and the subjective is ambiguous between the epistemic and the ontological or metaphysical sense. In the epistemic sense, it is a difference between types of claims. If I say that the Democrats won the last presidential election, that is a matter of fact that can be settled. It is a definite matter of fact; it is epistemically objective. If I say, on balance, Democratic presidents have been better than Republican presidents, well that is a matter of subjective opinion; it is epistemically subjective. The ontological sense is a difference between modes of existence. Most of the things studied by the natural sciences such as atoms and molecules and tectonic plates have a mode of existence which does not depend on being experienced, so we can say they are *ontologically objective*. Pains, tickles, and itches on the other hand, are *ontologically subjective*. They exist only insofar as they are experienced by human or animal subjects.

2. THE DISTINCTION BETWEEN THE OBSERVER RELATIVE AND THE OBSERVER INDEPENDENT

Human beings, as already remarked, have the capacity to impose intentionality on phenomena that are not intrinsically intentional. So, the photograph on my driver's license is considered as a physical object—just a collection of chemical stains in a piece of plastic. But we have imposed an intentionality on this; we treat it as a picture of me. It has a derived or observer relative intentionality. The fact, however, that the driver's license has the chemical structure that it does, is not observer relative, it is an intrinsic fact.

We can say, as a general point, that all observer relative phenomena such as money, property, government, marriage, universities, cocktail parties, and summer vacations, are created by the conscious intentionality of human agents. Because all unconscious mental phenomena are at least potentially conscious, they are the sort of thing that in principle can be brought to consciousness, we can say that all observer-relative phenomena are created by human consciousness. But the conscious intentionality that creates them is not itself observer relative. The conscious intentionality that creates money, property, government, and marriage is intrinsic or observer-independent. These two distinctions are actually important for what follows because we are going to be discovering a class of institutional facts about money and universities etc., and these facts are epistemically objective though they are all observer relative and thus are created by a set of psychological processes that create them as observer-relative phenomena. It is observer-relative that Barack Obama is the president of the United States, but the fact that he is president is itself epistemically objective. All observer-relative phenomena contain an element of ontological subjectivity, but that does not prevent us from having, in principle, an epistemically objective account of these phenomena.

3. STATUS FUNCTIONS AS THE ESSENCE OF HUMAN CIVILIZATION

Now let us build human civilization from the bottom up, starting with conscious animals. Well the first thing we have to notice is that conscious animals have a capacity to impose functions on objects where the functions are not intrinsic to the object. Functions are always observer-relative. So, for example, chimpanzees can use a stick as a digging device, as a tool to dig ants with. The fact that the stick is a tool is observer-relative; the fact that it is made of carbon-based molecules is observer-independent.

We can say, in general, all functions are observer-relative. It is only relative to attitudes of humans and other animals that objects have the functions they do. So this object functions as a house because we have imposed that function on it. We are blinded to the observer-relativity of all functions by the fact that we often *discover* functions in the biological sciences. We discover that the function of the heart is to pump blood. But it should be emphasized that when we say that the function of the heart is to pump blood, we are doing more than describing the fact that the heart does pump blood. To describe it as having a function is to impose a set of evaluative categories. It now makes sense to talk of good hearts and bad hearts and diseased hearts and malfunctioning hearts, and all of that comes only because the notion of function is observer-relative. We could put the point crudely by saying a function is a cause that serves a purpose, and the purpose has to come from conscious human beings, and that is what makes functions observer-relative. So far, then, we have humans and animals imposing functions on objects. Now we imagine that they do this collectively, that by collective intentionality they agree that a certain log is a bench, or that they carve a certain log into a canoe, which they can then use collectively. Many functions are created by collective intentionality.

But now we come to a peculiar class of functions that, as far as I know, no other animal can create. The beavers impose the functions of a beaver dam, and humans impose the function of a house on objects that do not have these functions intrinsically. But humans have a capacity that, as far as I know, is unique to humans. (It does not matter if it is unique to humans; if it turns out that chimpanzees can do it, well, I welcome them to the club. It is just that so far the only cases we know of are cases involving humans.) Humans have the ability to impose functions on objects or people, where the function is imposed on an object or person or collection of persons, not in virtue of its physical structure, or not solely in virtue of its physical structure, but in virtue of the fact that the humans have assigned a status to that person or object. And it is in virtue of the collective recognition or acceptance of the object or person as having that status, that the object or person can perform that function that has been assigned to it. Examples are everywhere. Think, for example, of the piece of paper you have in your hand which is a $20 bill, or think of the fact that Barack Obama is president of the United States. Both of these are cases of functions—the function of money or the function of presidency—assigned, where the assignment confers a status and in virtue of the collective acceptance of the status that he is the president or that this is money, the function can be performed. Now I want to make a strong claim, which is the simple claim that all of the things we think of as distinctly features of human civilization, features by which we differ from other animals, are Status Functions. Humans create money, property, government, marriage, universities, lawyers and doctors, cocktail parties, summer vacations, and world wars, all by assigning Status Functions to phenomena that do not have those functions intrinsically.

I said that Status Functions are functions imposed on objects where the objects cannot perform the function without the imposition of the status. This point has to be stated carefully because often, the object is *physically* capable of performing the function. I, for example, can physically drive a car regardless of what any status has assigned to me. However, for many things, such as driving a car, we do not *permit* the person to drive the car without authorization, without the *status* of a licensed driver. Status Functions can be imposed on objects which are capable of performing the function without the imposition of that status, but we do not allow or permit the object to be used for that function without the authorization of an assigned status.

4. THE CREATION OF STATUS FUNCTIONS

As soon as we understand that Status Functions are the essential trait of human civilization, a whole slew of questions immediately confronts us. How exactly are these Status Functions created? It seems to be an objective fact that this piece of paper is money or that I am a citizen and yet, in some sense, these are all created by subjective human attitudes. So what is the point of doing this? Why do we do it? How, once created, are they maintained in existence? And how is that the existence of many of these Status Functions is so powerful? Think of a nation-state such as the United States of America, or the Republic of China. Such Status Functions have enormous power. Why do we create such powerful structures?

We are going to answer all of those questions in what follows, but let us start with the first question. That is, what exactly is the nature of the creation of the Status Function?

Many years ago, I found it useful to distinguish between rules which regulate antecedently existing forms of behavior, what I called "regulative rules," and rules that constitute new forms of behavior, the very behavior they regulate, and these I called "constitutive rules" (Searle 1969). An example of a regulative rule is the rule of the road in the United States to drive on the right-hand side of the road. Driving exists independently of any such rules. The rules regulate a pre-existing activity. But the rules of game, such as the rules of chess, are not like that. The rules of chess do not regulate a pre-existing activity. Rather, the rules of chess constitute the activity in the sense that playing chess *consists in* acting in accordance with at least a large enough subset of these rules. What exactly are these constitutive rules? Well I argued that the rules typically have the form "X counts as Y," or more precisely, "X counts as Y in context C." So such and such a move counts as a legal Knight move in chess. Such a position in chess counts as White being in check. Such and such a form of check counts as checkmate. In every case, you get an application of the form "X counts as Y in context C," and I think this applies to Status Functions generally. So getting a majority of votes in the Electoral College counts as being president-elect in the United States. And being president-elect and being sworn in by the Chief Justice of the Supreme Court counts as becoming president of the United States. So getting married, becoming a professor, getting a degree from a university, buying a house—all of these seem to be an application of the "X counts as Y in C" principle. So our first hypothesis—we will have to make it more precise later on—is that all Status Functions are created by the application of the principle that "X counts as Y in context C." They are founded by the application of constitutive rules.

A couple of other further reflections are appropriate here. First, what we create with this X counts as Y principle are institutional facts, and it looks like we have a co-extension between Status Functions and institutional facts. Roughly speaking, all Status Functions are institutional facts, and all institutional facts are Status Functions. They are all created by these constitutive rules and we can say that an institution, such as the University of California or the institution of money, consists in a set of constitutive rules, rules of the form "X counts as Y."

So far, so good. But now we have a number of questions that I want to consider in order. It looks like the principle "X counts as Y in context C" is too feeble an apparatus to construct all of human civilization. But it has two formal features that give it a great deal of logical power. First, it iterates upward indefinitely. So making such and such noises counts as uttering an English sentence. Uttering certain English sentences counts as making a promise. Making a certain sort of promise counts as undertaking a legally binding contract, and so on upward. Now notice what we have in each case. Initially, X_1 counts as Y_1, but Y_1 equals X_2 and X_2 counts as Y_2. This procedure can be iterated upward indefinitely. There seems to be no upward limit on how we can count something as something else. How we can build institutional facts on institutional facts and Status Functions on Status Functions. And indeed, this is how real life works. As a professor in Berkeley, I am eligible to become chairman of my department or I am liable to be made a member of a certain committee. Both of these, the chairmanship and the committee membership, are Status Functions imposed on other Status Functions.

Furthermore, not only does the principle "X counts as Y in context C" iterate upward indefinitely, it spreads out laterally. So the Y Status Functions in general do not exist in isolation but only in relation to a complex of other Status Functions. So I do not just have money but I have money, for example, in my bank account, and I can use the money in my bank account in relation to other Status Functions such as paying my income tax or paying my utility bills. So there are two principles of the application of the form of the constitutive rule that give it more power: it iterates upward and its application spreads out laterally.

So far, this gives us a simple application of the principle by which Status Functions are created, but it raises some interesting questions. How about those Status Functions where you do not actually have a pre-existing rule? If a group of children just vote for somebody to be the captain of their softball team, there was no pre-existing institution. It was an ad hoc case where they just did it on the spot. There is no institution of electing captains of the softball team. Should we say that this is an institutional fact? What is going on in these cases? Furthermore, there even seem to be cases when you do not need an X term. You just create the Status Function out of thin air. A good example of that is the rule for creating corporations in the state of California. It does not say a pre-existing object has to be made into a corporation. It just says a corporation is created as soon as people perform a certain sort of speech act, called "filing articles of incorporation."

So, we have to modify our earlier account of the creation of institutional facts by constitutive rules in at least two respects. First, you do not need an antecedently existing rule. You can informally create a Status Function even though there was no previously existing institution. And second, you do not always need an X term. You can simply create an institutional fact such as a corporation or money out of, so to speak, thin air. You simply declare it to be the case that there is a corporation or that such and such money exists.

5. THE POWER OF STATUS FUNCTIONS

So far, we seem to have a rather simple set of equivalences. All Status Functions are institutional facts and all institutional facts are Status Functions. Furthermore, at least tentatively, we can say they are all created by the same operation, which is a form of collective intentionality by which the collective members of a community count some entity X as having the Status Function Y. Before answering the questions that I just posed, I want to discuss why we do this and why it is such a powerful mechanism.

The first question is, why do we create Status Functions? And of course, the answer would have to be extremely complex to discuss the many different sorts of institutional facts there are. The reason that people create corporations is quite different from the reasons for which they create softball teams, and those are quite different from the reasons for which they create religions or military armies. There are so many varieties of institutional facts that there can be no general objective, except the purely formal objective, which I am now going to state. All institutional facts create power. All of these Status Functions that we have been describing are collectively created power relations. As a citizen of the United States, as a possessor of a $20 bill, and as a professor in my department, I have a series of positive and negative powers. My positive powers are that I have certain *rights*. I have a right to use an office and to use the university computer system. But also I have certain *obligations*. I have an obligation to teach my courses at the assigned time and to hold office hours to consult with my students. Rights and obligations are characteristic of institutional facts. Indeed, I want to say that in general all institutional facts create such powers, and the names are not just rights and obligations, but duties, requirements, authorizations, permissions, etc. Just to have a general term, I will call all of these "deontic powers," after the Greek word for "duty." And we can now say that all institutional facts create deontic powers.

6. STATUS FUNCTION DECLARATIONS

So far, I have been assuming that there is nothing problematic about the formula "X counts as Y in context C." But what does that mean, to say that something counts as something else? What kind of an activity is the activity of counting something as something else? Furthermore, I have been talking as if language were just one institution among others, and that seems to me wrong—it is the fundamental institution in that all the others presuppose language, and language does not presuppose the others. So we now need to explore everything we have said so far to a much deeper level.

In performing speech acts, we have different ways of relating words to reality. The Assertive class of speech acts, which famously include statements and descriptions, are supposed to represent reality, how reality is. They have the word-to-world direction of fit. A good clue to this direction of fit is that they can literally be said to be true or false. Orders and commands are in a different class of speech acts; they are what I call Directives, and they have the world-to-word direction of fit. The world, in the form of the person who receives the order, is supposed to change reality to match the content of the order. Such speech acts are not true or false, but obeyed or disobeyed. A third class is Commissives, by which the speaker commits himself to some course of action. The philosopher's favorite Commissive is promising, but other cases are vows, threats, and pledges. In these cases, as in Directives, there is a world-to-word direction of fit, and promises are not said to be true or false in the sense in which statements are, but they are said to be kept or broken. A fourth class is Expressives, where we just express our feelings and attitudes. Apologizing, thanking, and congratulating are all classes of Expressives, and in general, not always but at least in general, in these cases we presuppose that the fit already exists. If I say, "I apologize for stepping on your foot," I am not trying to get your foot stepped on and I am not trying to claim that it has been stepped on, I simply *presuppose* that it has been stepped on. But now we come to a very interesting class where we change reality simply by declaring it to be so changed. Favorite examples of these are Austin's performative utterances, so you can adjourn the meeting by saying "I adjourn the meeting," or you can pronounce two people husband and wife by saying "I pronounce you husband and wife." All of the performative utterances are in this class, which I call Declarations.

Declarations are remarkable in that they have both directions of fit simultaneously. When I adjourn the meeting by saying, "The meeting is adjourned," I make it the case that the meeting is adjourned, and thus achieve the world-to-word direction of fit. But I do it by representing the meeting as being adjourned, by the word-to-world direction of fit. And notice that it is not two speech acts but one speech act with both directions of fit simultaneously.

Now, if we use this apparatus and go back and ask the question, "What sort of a speech act is counting X as Y?" or "What is the speech act type which is articulated in the form,

'X counts as Y in C'?", it seems to me obvious that it is a Declaration. We make it the case that you are the captain of the club, or that this is a $20 bill, or that Barack Obama is president by *declaring* it to be the case. I now want to put forward the next major hypothesis of this chapter, and that is, all Status Functions are created by representations that have the form of Declarations, and I will call them Status Function Declarations. It need not always be an explicit speech act. You can perform a Declaration by repeated representations, which have the effect of changing reality so that reality matches the representation. So, for example, somebody might become the boss of the group just by being repeatedly treated and referred to and described as the boss. "We cannot make the decision until the boss gets here"—such utterances, if frequent and repeated, have the same effect as us all getting together and saying, "We hereby vote you as the boss of the group." But the general point remains—all Status Functions are created by a certain type of representation that has the double direction of fit characteristic of Declarations. And we can say, allowing for these inexplicit cases, that all Status Functions are created by Status Function Declarations.

7. CONCLUSION

So far, we have considered how Status Functions are created, and we now must discuss the questions of what exactly is their power in society, and how are they maintained. Status Functions, as I have said, always provide deontic powers, and these are rights, duties, obligations, requirements, permissions, authorizations, etc. I have also said that these are the glue that hold human civilization together. Why? To the extent that a conscious agent recognizes the validity of a Deontic Power, he recognizes that he has desire-independent reasons for performing a certain course of action. For example, I recognize the validity of a promise I made to write this article, and that gives me a reason for writing the article which is independent of my other inclinations.

So we have a rather simple set of equivalences and implications. Here is how it goes: all Status Functions are institutional facts. All Status Functions are created by the same type of logico-linguistic operation—the Status Function Declaration. This need not be an explicit speech act, but there must be a representation or set of representations that add up to the creation of a Status Function by Declaration. All Status Functions create Deontic Powers, and Deontic Powers provide desire-independent reasons for action.

How are Status Functions maintained in their existence? The answer is that the continued use of the Status Function and its continued representation reinforce its continued existence. One way to see this is to see how revolutionary movements try to get control of the vocabulary. In the Soviet Union, the traditional Russian forms of address with their elaborate status differences were replaced by a single expression, "Comrade," which was supposed to apply to everybody, generally to mark the equality that they supposedly had in a Bolshevik state. Reformist movements such as feminism in the United States were anxious to get rid of the traditional vocabulary of "ladies" and "gentlemen," because this marked a set of Status Functions that they wished to reject. And sometimes a Status Function will simply fall out of power because it is no longer represented. The expression, "spinster," is a traditional term in the United States, and it is even used in legal contexts. But when I asked my class, "How many of you are spinsters?" only one middle-aged lady had the courage to raise her hand. I think, for most people, this term has simply become obsolete. The Status Function that went with being a spinster has ceased to exist.

The test for whether or not something is a Status Function is, does it have a deontic power? Thus there are lots of informal Status Functions; think of a love affair or friendship. There are *obligations* of friendship and these are the sure mark of a Status Function. Similarly, lovers have rights, duties, and obligations to each other; once again, the mark of a Status Function. Notice that because the Status Function exists only insofar as it is represented as existing, it is always possible to codify it, to make it explicit, to give some terms for describing it, some explicit statement of a constitutive rule. Though this is possible, it would destroy the flexibility of a lot of Status Functions. If there were officially recognized obligations of friends and lovers, much of the flexibility of the present informality would be lost, but the lack of codification does lead to a lot of misunderstanding. It turns out that friendship in one country might not mean the same thing as friendship in another country.

In spite of the incredible complexity of human societies, it seems to me that the underlying structure of civilization has a rather simple form. We create Status Functions by a certain type of linguistic representation, and these Status Functions serve to organize society along institutional lines. They organize hierarchical and power relations. I do not think that we as a species are clever enough to do this with a whole lot of differing complex formulae, so we use the same device over and over. We create the same institutional reality by representing it as existing, and that is another way of saying that we create Status Functions by Status Function Declarations.

RELATED TOPICS

Non-Reductive Views of Shared Intention (Ch. 2), Proxy Agency in Collective Action (Ch. 5), Social Construction and Social Facts (Ch. 20), Social Kinds (Ch. 22), Institutions and Collective Intentionality (Ch. 27), Collective Intentionality and Language (Ch. 28).

REFERENCES

Bratman, M. (2014) *Shared Agency: A Planning Theory of Acting Together*, Oxford: Oxford University Press.
Danto, A. (1965) "Basic Actions," *American Philosophical Quarterly* 2: 141–8.
Searle, J. (1969) *Speech Acts: An Essay in the Philosophy of Language*, London: Cambridge University Press.
——— (1983) *Intentionality: An Essay in the Philosophy of Mind*, Cambridge: Cambridge University Press.
——— (1990) "Collective Intentions and Actions," in P.R. Cohen, J. Morgan and M.E. Pollack (eds) *Intentions in Communication*, Cambridge, MA: MIT Press.
Searle, J.R. (2015) *Seeing Things as They Are: A Theory of Perception*, Oxford: Oxford University Press.

Collectives and Responsibility

Introduction to Part V

Marija Jankovic and Kirk Ludwig

The Deepwater Horizon oil spill, which began on April 20, 2010, with an explosion on the drilling rig that killed 11 workers, was the largest accidental marine oil spill in history. The well was finally capped on July 15, 2010, after several failed efforts, discharging in total an estimated 4.9 million barrels. The spill eventually covered 68,000 square miles of the ocean's surface. By early June oil was washing up on the coasts of Louisiana, Mississippi, Florida and Alabama. By July roughly 500 miles of coast were contaminated with oil. The final tally was that approximately 2,100 miles of coastline were affected to some degree. The spill resulted in extensive damage to wildlife, fishing stocks, and gulf and coastal ecologies. The environmental disaster spawned a massive clean-up effort. Estimates of lost tourism dollars to Gulf Coast communities were up to 22.7 billion by 2013.

Who was responsible, and in what sense? No single individual was responsible for the spill. Hence, we have a case in which a judgment about collective responsibility is called for, a case where the locus of responsibility is not a particular individual but a group or groups, or individuals as members of one or another group. As a matter of fact, British Petroleum LLP (BP) was widely blamed, as well as Transocean Ltd., the owner and operator of the oil rig, and the contractor for the seal on the oil well, Halliburton Energy Systems. At trial, BP was found to be grossly negligent and to bear the majority of the responsibility, 67 percent, among the companies involved in the spill, with Transocean Ltd. bearing 30 percent, and Halliburton 3 percent. By 2016, BP had paid (pre-tax) fines amounting to $61.6 billon. In addition, two BP executives were indicted on manslaughter charges connected with the eleven deaths in the initial explosion—though the charges were later dropped.

These are legal judgments. They establish at least some form of institutional responsibility, and perhaps also for the executives it is ultimately institutional responsibility that is at issue. Questions of institutional responsibility are determined by the nature and structure of the institutions. We can ask about the institutional responsibilities of individuals in virtue of their institutional roles, as well as of larger groups of which they are members, in virtue of those groups' roles in larger institutional settings, and so on. But beyond the legal question there is also the question who is morally responsible, as distinct from institutionally and legally. While institutional responsibilities can be expected to have some bearing on moral responsibilities, they need not always align, as in the case of someone assigned the institutional role of torturing prisoners for information.

When we turn to the question of moral responsibility, there are broadly speaking three sorts of answers we might give to the question who is morally to blame in cases of collective responsibility. First, we can say that only individuals who were playing one or another sort of role in the various companies involved bear moral responsibility for what happened. Second, we can say that only the companies themselves, and as such, bear moral responsibility, in which case we treat the companies as liable per se and hence as moral agents. Third, we can say that both individuals and the companies involved bear moral responsibility. These questions generalize to attributions of responsibility in the context of group action in general. Do attributions of responsibility to groups cash out ultimately to attributions to their members? If so, how is responsibility to be distributed across the members, and what is the relevance of organizational structure and role responsibility in this? Do attributions of responsibility to groups, at least sometimes and in some cases, stop at the group level, so that the members of the group are insulated from blame (or praise) themselves? Or is it a mix of group level and individual responsibility? How is this related to our understanding of the structure of collective action and intention?

Part V of the Handbook addresses three aspects of these questions about collective responsibility.

In Chapter 24, "Collective Intentions and Collective Moral Responsibility," Marion Smiley considers what sort of collective intention is required for collective moral responsibility. Smiley argues against one standard picture on which collective moral responsibility is grounded in the group being an agent causally responsible for something which makes it liable to moral blameworthiness. Collective intentions enter this picture as a condition on moral *blameworthiness* attaching to the group agent *causally responsible* for some outcome. Smiley argues that the usual accounts of shared intention, from Bratman to Gilbert to Tuomela, do not give us a notion of shared intention appropriate for collective responsibility on the model above. She traces this failure to a Kantian model of moral responsibility that requires moral agents to have inner moral lives, moral consciousness, and free choice, which groups, even if we construct a notion of a group level intention, simply lack. Smiley suggests reconceiving the nature of collective moral responsibility in a more Aristotelian vein, on which we think of how the agent's behavior fits into our practices of praise and blame rather than focus on the nature of the agent. There will still be some agent-side requirements. It requires purposeful action, a capacity to represent the environment, though in the case of groups the purpose may be expressed in its policies, laws, codes of conduct, and general statement purpose. In this way, we can locate the purpose with the group itself rather than its (changing) members.

In Chapter 25, "Complicity," Saba Bazargan-Forward analyzes the concept of complicity. One is complicit when one is liable to some extent for the actions of another or the actions of others. The general question is how one's actions must be bound up with the others for one to be complicit, and whether one must be in some sense part of the group that acts or not, and if not, then how one is bound up with what is done. Bazargan-Forward distinguishes juristic concepts, joint action concepts, and group agent concepts of complicity, focusing on the juristic concept of complicity as the most developed so far. He describes the role of complicity in the law, which allows someone who is not counted as having committed a crime to be as liable for it as the principal. He then argues that the motivations offered for treating complicity as having a basis distinct from criminal liability are flawed. Finally, he argues that, despite this, there is a place for complicity as distinct from criminal liability, whose ground lies not in our causal, but in our agency relations with others, and, specifically, in our authorization of others to act for us. Thus, for example, if we pool our money to hire an assassin to kill someone, though it turns out not all the money was necessary, we are all still complicit in the killing, though none of us did it, and none made a necessary contribution, because the assassin acts as our agent. Similarly, if we intentionally cooperate to further an end, we may all be liable for (complicit in) what any of us do in its pursuit, on the grounds that we have all mutually authorized the others to act at our behest.

In Chapter 26, the final chapter in this part, Seumas Miller discusses "Institutional Responsibility," distinguishing it from moral responsibility, from being blameworthy or praiseworthy, and from accountability. Institutions are constituted in part by a system of interrelated roles structured by relations of authority. Specification of role responsibilities, and their assignment, is done in the light of the institutions' overall purpose or function, for they are to serve that function or purpose, and so may be criticized to the extent they do not. Given this, Miller distinguishes three sorts of responsibility in connection with institutions: responsibility to institutions; responsibility of institutions; responsibility of institutional role occupants. Miller focuses on the third. Miller argues for an account of collective responsibility in which responsibility is assigned only to individual human beings, but jointly, so that in the case of collective responsibility the individual responsibility is understood in relation to the responsibility of all of them for what the group does or is to do together. Miller distinguishes between joint institutional actions and joint institutional mechanisms (a special case), such as voting. What mechanism is involved depends on more than the inputs. In voting, the significance of the votes depends on how they are related to the outcome (majority or supermajority, proportional or first past the post). The same sort mechanism extends to what Miller calls chains of institutional responsibility, illustrated in the division of responsibility between the police and the jury in the work of the justice system. They have different complementary roles in a larger process with the end of finding the factually guilty to be legally guilty (and no one else). The segregation of roles (investigator, prosecutor, judge, jury) is itself a part of the institutional design, to ensure a more just system, and gives rise to chains of institutional responsibility. Miller finally turns to the interrelation between institutional and moral responsibility. Do they come apart? Can institutional arrangements make a difference to whether one bears full or only partial moral responsibility for something the institution does? Can assignment of institutional roles give one moral responsibilities that one did not previously have? Miller argues that the answers to each of these questions is "Yes."

24

Collective Intentions and Collective Moral Responsibility

Marion Smiley

The kinds of collective intentions that are required by the prevailing notion of collective moral responsibility are notoriously difficult to locate. Hence, we are frequently reluctant to pursue collective moral responsibility in either theory or practice. But, I argue below, such reluctance is not necessary. For, contrary to conventional wisdom, we do not have to accept the prevailing notion of collective moral responsibility or the standards of intentionality associated with it. Instead, we can develop an alternative (and hopefully better) notion of collective moral responsibility and associate it with standards of intentionality that at least some groups can meet.

I set out to develop such a notion in this essay. In Section 1, I underscore the difficulties that arise when we try to employ even the most compelling notions of collective intentions to make sense of collective moral responsibility as we now understand it. In Section 2, I suggest that we are held back in this context by our assumption that collective moral responsibility has to be akin to its individualist, Kantian, counterpart. I develop an alternative, non-Kantian, notion of collective moral responsibility in Section 3 on the basis of what I take to be the nature of group moral blameworthiness and sketch the kind of collective intentions that it requires.

1. THE ETHICAL CONTEXT OF COLLECTIVE INTENTIONS

While the term *collective intention* always refers to an intention that is collective in some respect, it does not always refer to the same kind of intention or bring intentions and collectives together in the same way. Indeed, it can—and often does—formulate its subject matter, including what is collective about the intentions that it refers to, according to the particular context in play, e.g. collective consciousness, collective action, collective blame. Likewise, it can—and often does—pick up on those aspects of the subject matter that speak to what collective intentions are supposed to be doing for us in this particular context.

As we might expect, not all contexts are the same with respect to these matters. Hence, when pursuing our own projects, we cannot simply borrow a notion of collective intentions from other contexts without asking whether it is appropriate to our own. Instead, we have to make sure that the notion of collective intentions that we use accords with the place that such intentions have in our own projects. What place do collective intentions have in ethical projects? How do we formulate collective intentions in these projects and is our formulation of them appropriate? If it is not appropriate, what other formulation might work better for us?

While legal theorists pursue the possibility of collective intentions out of a concern for group punishment and philosophers of action do so for the sake of making sense of collective action, contemporary moral philosophers make clear that what is at stake for them in this context is the possibility of groups being morally blameworthy for harm in the world. In other words, they make clear that their concern is with the possibility of collective moral responsibility. Hence, they focus on those kinds of collective intentions that they assume are required by collective moral blameworthiness rather than by, say, group punishment or collective action.

But of course they might not have focused on the right kind of collective intentions for their context or have gotten straight what is required of collective moral responsibility in general. Hence, we cannot, as we might be tempted to do, jump right into a conversation about whether collective intentions of this kind can be located in the world. Instead, we have to make sure that we are looking for the right kind of collective intentions for our context. In other words, we have to ask: What kind of collective intentions, if any, are required by collective moral responsibility?

Not surprisingly, our answers to these questions will depend largely on the nature of collective moral responsibility itself. I explore the range of possibilities elsewhere[1] and suggest below that we should choose carefully among them before thinking about collective intentions. Suffice it to point out here that those who now argue about the possibility of collective moral responsibility do not generally explore the nature of collective moral responsibility itself in detail. Instead, they move directly to the question of whether collective intentions are possible.

But they do make three basic assumptions about collective moral responsibility that turn out to be important here. The first is that, unlike individual moral responsibility, collective moral responsibility is associated with a collective moral agent of some kind, e.g. a corporation, a nation state, or a club. The second is that, like all other kinds of moral responsibility, it has causal responsibility as one of its key components. (How else could we hold collectives morally responsible for harm in the world?) The third is that, unlike purely causal (or legal) responsibility, it has moral blameworthiness built into it.

Where do collective intentions enter the picture? Since a group's having been causally responsible for harm precedes our even asking if the group intended to cause the harm, collective intentions cannot be necessary to ascribing causal responsibility to groups. Nor do we generally think that they are. Instead, we think that they are necessary to ascribing moral blameworthiness to groups. Moreover, we do so because we assume that, in the absence of such intentions, groups would not be able to muster the kind of moral agency necessary to moral blameworthiness. What kind of moral agency is this? What kind of moral blameworthiness?

Interestingly enough, those writing on collective moral responsibility do not generally address the possibility that collective moral blameworthiness might be different from its individualistic counterpart. Nor do they address the possibility that it might bring with it different requirements than those of individual moral blameworthiness. Instead, they assume that we can simply transfer over the requirements of individual moral blame-worthiness to its collective counterpart. Hence, in talking about collective moral respon-sibility, they feel comfortable referring to the collective intentions in play as a source of moral guilt.

What kinds of intentions could these possibly be? Critics of collective moral responsi-bility (see below) make clear that these intentions have to be associated with a collective moral agent capable of free willing if they are going to support a notion of moral guilt (a condition that they think cannot be met in the case of collective entities). But we should keep an open mind here and ask whether any of the prominent notions of collec-tive intentions that we have before us—notions that do not insist that collectives can freely will—might be able to make sense of group moral guilt. Take, for starters, those notions of collective intentions that begin by positing a collective mind and then show how it is manifested in individual intentions.

In some cases, the collective intentions put forward here are a matter of collective consciousness, that is, a collective mind that captures the imaginations of individuals who then think similar thoughts. In other cases, they are a matter of shared intentions, i.e. intentions that are the same across group members. In still other cases, they are inten-tions to pursue a collective project or to be part of a conjoint activity that is organized around a collective goal. In all of these cases, the collective aspect of collective intentions has to do with *what* is being intended rather than with *how* it is being intended or with *whom* the intending is being done.

Emile Durkheim famously chose to pursue what has come to be known as collective consciousness in his efforts to show how a collective mind can be—and frequently is—registered in the intentions of group members. Wilfrid Sellars argued that we-intentions, which are always formulated in contexts where individuals act together, are *shared among individuals*. According to Sellars, while such intentions are collective with respect to content, they take place in individuals' own minds. Likewise, when two individuals we-intend to do something together, e.g. pursue a goal that requires both individuals' cooperation, the content of their we-intentions is collective by virtue of the project that they share. 'But the intendings are two in number' (Sellars 1968: 217).

Michael Bratman, like many others now writing on the subject matter, chooses to place collective intentions in the context of conjoint activity. According to Bratman, when we say that we have a collective intention, we say that

> [w]e *intend to do J* if and only if: (1) (a) I intend that we J and (b) you intend that we J and (2) I intend that we J in accordance with and because of (1) (a), (1) (b) and meshing sub-plans of (1) (a), (1) (b), and you intend likewise. (3): (1) and (2) are common knowledge between us.
>
> (Bratman 1999: 121)

Collective intentions are here not a shared state of intending but intentions shared among group members directed to conjoint activity. In other words, they are collective, not with reference to a collective moral agent, but by virtue of the fact that they involve a resolve on the part of group members to pursue a collective activity together.

All of these formulations of collective intentions are very helpful in particular contexts. Durkheim's helps us to understand how groups cohere and even take on group identities, as well as come to believe the same things. Sellars' shows how intentions that are collective with respect to content can resolve into individual states of intending. Bratman's provides us with a way of understanding how, among other things, we can intend together as part of conjoint activity. I suspect that—regardless of their authors' own interests in the matter—these formulations could also help us to understand the logic of conjoint activity more generally.

But when they are invoked in the context of collective moral responsibility, they fall short. For, even though they are attached to something genuinely collective, e.g. a shared set of beliefs or a conjoint activity or a shared resolve to pursue the latter, and even though they are potentially locatable in the world, they do not speak to a collective moral agent that is capable of being morally blameworthy qua collective agent. Instead, they speak to individuals who share an intention with others which is collective by virtue of content (and who perhaps even intend together within conjoint activity) but who nevertheless intend as discrete individuals.

How might we think about groups themselves as intending in the sense required of collective moral guilt? Margaret Gilbert puts forward what she calls a "plural subject" account of shared intentions and does so in large part, like Bratman and others, by zeroing in on joint commitments. But she goes further than these others do in positing a collective moral subject attached to these commitments. According to Gilbert, groups have intentions qua groups when two or more persons constitute the plural subject of an intention to carry out a particular action, or, in other words, when 'they are jointly committed to intending as a body to do A' (Gilbert 2000: 22).

All of this makes sense both linguistically and logically. But we still have to know what it means to say that two or more persons constitute a plural subject. *How*, we have to ask, do they constitute such a subject? David Velleman takes us part of the way by arguing that '[a] truly plural subject involves two or more subjects who combine in such a way as to make one subject' (Velleman 1997: 29). But we still need to know what that one subject is and how the two or more individuals who make it up come together. Do they simply share commitments or do their minds come together into one collective mind? If the latter, how do their minds come together? Do they meld or do they merely overlap?

Gilbert suggests here that we treat the plural subject as constituted by members of a group having the right sort of commitments. 'A and B . . . constitute a plural subject (by definition) if and only if they are jointly committed to do something as a body—in a broad sense of "do"'(Gilbert 2006: 145). Velleman for his part argues that we can locate something like a collective intention in cases where A says that he will do something if B does, where B agrees to do it, where they carry through, and where, in carrying through, they are in a state that represents them as doing something together and which is causally sufficient to bring about a state of affairs C.[2]

Both models may help us to grasp the nature of joint commitments and acting together. But they do not tell us how plural subjects come together to make one collective subject. Nor do they make their collective subject out to be the kind of moral agent capable of being held morally blameworthy for acting badly. Hence, while their notions of a collective self and a collective intention might satisfy the requirements of some other kinds of projects, they do not satisfy the requirements of the project of collective moral responsibility as we now understand it.

Three things are important to keep in mind here. First, if plural subjects are to constitute the kind of beings capable of being held morally responsible for harm in the world, they cannot simply be subjects. Instead, they have to be moral agents. Second, if they are to be moral agents, they have to have one mind, rather than a plurality of minds. Third, if they are to be the kinds of agents capable of being morally responsible for harm in the world, they have to be able to formulate intentions of the kind that render them morally blameworthy.

Raimo Tuomela comes close to showing how this might be possible by revamping the notion of we-intentions associated with collective moral responsibility. Tuomela, like Gilbert, constructs the collective subject on the basis of joint commitments and then applies it to the notion of collective moral responsibility. However, he does not, like Gilbert, stress plurality in his construction of the collective subject. Instead, he stresses unity and argues for it by claiming collective intentional agency *supervenes* on individual moral agency in ways that allow us both to posit a genuine collective self and to associate it with a genuinely collective mind (Tuomela 1989, 2005).

In order for Tuomela's notion of supervention to provide us with what we need here it would have to support the possibility of a genuine collective moral agent. Does it? What does Tuomela have in mind by *supervention* and how is it supposed to work? According to Tuomela, actions by collectives supervene on the actions of the operative members of the collective in such a way that the properties of particular collectives, such as their intentions, beliefs, and desires, are "embedded in" and "determined by" the perspectives of individual members (Tuomela 1989: 494).

In general, Tuomela is obliged to show how collectives, as distinct from their operative members, can have intentions, beliefs, and desires, and how they can, as collective entities distinct from their members and capable of supervening on them, be construed as agents. Likewise, he is obliged to show how a collective's intentions, beliefs, and desires can be both "embedded in" *and* "determined by" the perspective of its individual members. (Why, if these things are determined by individual members, do they need to be embedded in them?)

Moreover, if Tuomela's notion of supervention is going to help us in this context, it will have to show how the collectives in question can be construed, not just as agents, but as the kind of agents capable of being morally blameworthy. Can it do these things? Two problems arise here. First, once we concede that a collective's beliefs, intentions, and desires are determined by group members, we lose a sense of their being moral agents, even if we can posit a kind of collective consciousness. What, we have to ask, does the collective *do* in this context? Is supervention a kind of moral agency? If so, how does the supervener function as the moral agent?

Second, we cannot use the fact that those group members who are determining the collective's beliefs, intentions, and desires have moral agency to say that the collective has moral agency. Nor can we suggest that the collective takes on the moral agency of group members in the process of supervening on them. For, moral agency is not the kind of thing that can be transferred to others. Nor is it, like, say, the content of an intention, the kind of thing that can be detached from the moral agent doing the intending and placed elsewhere. Instead, it is part of the act of intending itself and hence has to be located in the collective itself.

2. MORAL BLAMEWORTHINESS AND THE REQUIREMENTS OF COLLECTIVE INTENTIONALITY

Three points of importance emerge from the above. The first is that the kinds of collective intentions required of collective moral responsibility are not the kinds that are collective by virtue of either their content or their association with conjoint activity (or a collective goal). Nor are they the kinds of collective intentions that are collective by virtue of the fact that they are shared across all group members. Instead, they are the kinds of collective intentions that are collective by virtue of the fact that the agent doing the intending is itself a collective. In other words, they are the kinds of collective intentions that have a collective agent.

Second, if the collective agents are going to be considered morally responsible for harm in the world, they have to be able to intend such harm—or anything else—in ways that render them morally blameworthy. In other words, they have to be moral agents that can be morally blameworthy by virtue of what they have intentionally done in the world. Likewise, the collective intentions that we associate with them cannot simply be possible. Instead, they have to be the kinds of collective intentions that can be the source of moral blameworthiness.

Third, groups, construed as collective entities, do not appear capable of meeting these requirements. For, while they might be understood to act as collectives and even to form intentions as collectives, they do not appear to be the kinds of moral agents that are called for here or capable of the kind of intending required of moral blameworthiness. Nor do they appear to have the kinds of minds or inner moral lives—soul equivalents—that could serve as sources of moral guilt and/or render an agent's intentions morally salient in the sense required.

The apparent lack of such capacities has led many to dismiss the possibility of collective moral responsibility altogether. R.S. Downie's early concerns here are typical. According to Downie,

> [c]ollectives do not have moral faults, since they don't make choices, and hence they cannot be properly ascribed moral responsibility. . . . For there to be moral responsibility there must be moral blameworthiness involving a morally faulty decision, and this can take place only on the individual level.
>
> (Downie 1969: 67)

Jan Narveson goes as far as to argue that the bearers of moral blameworthiness *have* to be individuals because only individuals can have moral agency. 'Nothing else can literally be the source of full responsibility' (Narveson 2002: 179).

All of this might suggest that we should give up talking about collective moral responsibility altogether. But we need to be careful here. For, collective moral responsibility is defeated only if the kind of moral blameworthiness—and hence the kind of collective intentions—that we are talking about here are necessary or are the only ones available to us. Presumably, if we could posit another kind of collective moral responsibility that requires another kind of collective intention, we might be able to render collective moral responsibility possible while still requiring collective intentions of groups. How might we do so?

As things now stand, we do not generally ask what distinguishes the moral blameworthiness of groups from that of individuals. Nor do we generally explore the notion of moral blameworthiness associated with moral responsibility. Instead, we simply assume that group moral blameworthiness is akin to the moral blameworthiness of individuals and that the moral blameworthiness of individuals is such that we need to be able to posit the kind of intentionality associated with free will. But, we need to ask, why does the moral blameworthiness of groups have to be akin to the moral blameworthiness of individuals and why does the moral blameworthiness of individuals have to be what we now assume it is?

I suggest below that we can—and should—rethink moral blameworthiness for groups and only then ask what kinds of collective intentions collective moral responsibility requires. Suffice it to suggest here that the notion of moral blameworthiness that we now frequently fall back on in this context is not moral blameworthiness per se. Instead, it is a distinctly Kantian notion of moral blameworthiness that even non-Kantians appropriate in their own arguments.

Joel Feinberg captured this notion when he wrote of moral responsibility:

> [a] stubborn feeling persists even after legal responsibility has been decided that there is still a problem—albeit not a legal one—left over: namely, is the defendant *really* responsible (as opposed to "responsible in law")—for the harm? This conception of a "real" theoretical responsibility as distinct from a practical responsibility relative to the purposes and values of a particular legal system is expressed very commonly in the terminology of "morality"—*moral* obligation, *moral* guilt, *moral* responsibility.
>
> (Feinberg 1970: 30)

Moral responsibility is from this perspective a purely factual matter and as such not relative to worldly practice: 'Like all matters of "record", moral responsibility must be read off of the facts or deduced from them; there can be no irreducible element of discretion' (Feinberg 1970: 31). Likewise, it must be construed as independent not only of any purposes, policies, or goals that we may embrace, but of our own opinions about whether or not a particular individual is blameworthy. For, unlike its worldly counterparts, it is

> liability to charges on some ideal record, liability to credit or blame (in the sense that implies no action). Just as it is "forever to the credit" of a hero or a saint that he performed some noble act, so a man can be "forever to blame" for his faults.
>
> (Feinberg 1970: 31)

Three things about moral blameworthiness as so understood are worth underscoring here. The first is that moral agents, who are traditionally individuals, are morally blameworthy, not in virtue of worldly practices of blame, but in virtue of their having themselves caused—freely willed—harm. The second is that moral blameworthiness as so understood is not relative to external purposes but is instead an aspect of moral agency itself: 'an absolute responsibility within the power of the agent' (Feinberg 1970: 30).

The third is the only kind of intending strong enough for such a notion of moral agency—and for moral blameworthiness itself—is that akin to freely willing.

Moral blameworthiness as so understood is hard enough to fathom in cases involving individuals, but it is especially difficult to fathom in cases where the moral agents are collectives, since even if collectives can have minds of their own, they do not appear capable of exercising the kind of moral agency required of moral blameworthiness here. Nor do they appear capable of formulating the required kinds of intentions or having the kind of self that is rendered morally blameworthy solely by virtue of its having freely willed/intended a bad action. How, then, are we to proceed? Are there alternative notions of moral responsibility that might help us here?

3. AN ALTERNATIVE VIEW OF COLLECTIVE MORAL RESPONSIBILITY

The Aristotelian notion of moral responsibility is, like its Kantian counterpart, associated with individual moral agents. But, unlike its Kantian counterpart, it associates moral blameworthiness with communal practices of blame. Hence, while it, too, requires intentionality, it does not construe intentionality as a source of moral blameworthiness or require intentions akin to freely willing. Instead, it views intentionality as a condition of communal blame and blameworthiness as relative to social practice. Likewise, it makes both intentionality and blameworthiness out to be both potentially applicable to groups and locatable in the world.

The utilitarian notion of moral responsibility does not distinguish between moral and social blameworthiness. Nor does it associate moral blameworthiness with moral agency itself. Instead, it associates moral blameworthiness with both the social practice of blame and a utilitarian calculation concerning when blaming individuals will lead to an increase in overall happiness. Not surprisingly, in doing so, it underplays the importance of both agent causation and intentionality—leading critics to reject it for opening up the floodgates to unfair blaming.

While neither of these notions of moral blameworthiness apply directly to groups, they do suggest the possibility of both viewing the notion of moral blameworthiness associated with collective moral responsibility as part of a relationship between groups and those in the position to blame them and construing this notion of moral blameworthiness as a judgment on the part of the community that a group deserves to be blamed. In other words, they do suggest the possibility of looking to communal standards of blame, rather than to moral agency per se, for the requirements of both moral blameworthiness and the kind of intentionality that it requires.

How, though, could groups, as distinct from their members, be considered morally blameworthy? What would such blameworthiness look like? While we could not go as far as to talk about moral blameworthiness here as, in Michael Zimmerman's terms, a 'black mark on one's soul' (Zimmerman 1988: 38), we could talk about groups as worthy of our moral condemnation, i.e. as selfish, negligent, unfair, in violation of others' rights, etc. Likewise, we could talk about them as morally responsible for harm in the world by virtue of their having knowingly caused it.

Not all groups would be appropriate objects of this kind of moral condemnation. Indeed, in order for a group to qualify, it would have to be well organized enough for us to talk about it as both taking purposeful action—see below—and having a particular identity as moral agent. Groups such as mobs, which have a general group identity ("mob") but not a particular identity (mob X, Y, or Z) would not do here (even if they were organized). Presumably, though, there would be many other groups—corporations, clubs, and nation states—that would.

How might we ground such a notion of collective moral blameworthiness? Since we cannot locate a conscious mind capable of willing in this context, we might want to jettison both agent causation and intentionality altogether and invoke a purely utilitarian notion of collective moral blameworthiness. But to do so would be a mistake. For, once we jettison agent causation and intentionality, we cannot talk about collective moral responsibility—which, unlike moral blameworthiness per se, requires causal responsibility for harm. Nor, for that matter, could we ensure that our practice of blaming is fair.

What, then, might agent causation and intentionality be in this context? Since we do not have to ground moral blameworthiness in moral agency per se, we do not, in our efforts to locate agent causation here, have to insist that a group have freely willed harm in the world. Instead, we can speak more loosely of the group as having either *produced* or *created* harm. In other words, we can invoke a notion of agent causation—that associated with producing or creating—that, while looser than others, is both locatable and appropriate to group moral blameworthiness.

Not surprisingly, not just any kind of *producing* or *creating* will do here. Instead, it will have to be a kind that is attached to the collective itself, whether by virtue of the latter's structure, laws, authority, or ethos, and involve a requisite level of control—even in cases where it is group members who performed the bad actions that resulted in harm. Likewise, it will have to be both necessary to the harm's having come about—individuals could not have produced or created it on their own—and a condition under which these individuals were able to act badly.

While *producing* and *creating* of this kind may not be strong enough for a Kantian notion of moral blameworthiness, it is strong enough for a notion of moral blameworthiness that relies on communal standards of moral blameworthiness. For, as long as moral blameworthiness does not have its source in moral agency per se, we do not have to infuse agent causation itself with moral blameworthiness. Instead, we have to show only that the group was causally responsible for the harm to the extent required of communal standards of collective blame.

Causal responsibility of course does not get us all the way to moral blameworthiness on its own, for it does not tell us anything about the moral agent itself—and only moral agents can be morally blameworthy in the context of moral responsibility. Hence, we will have to go one step further and show that a group which caused harm did so *intentionally*. In other words, we will have to show that the group in question brought about harm either by design or by virtue of its ideology, its laws, its official code of conduct, or its general statement of purpose.[3]

The notion of intentionality that emerges here is that of *purposiveness*. Purposiveness is easiest to show in cases where a group does something as a result of a decision or deliberative process, since in these cases we can say very easily that the group "did x, y, or z on purpose." But it is also present in (some) cases where a group's purposes—which are written into its laws, ideology, ethos, codes of conduct, etc.—lead it to produce harm in the world. In these cases, we can say that a group has, by virtue of the norms that govern it, purposively brought about harm.

Three points are worth underscoring here. First, while this notion of intentionality may be associated with the efforts of group members—or their predecessors—to develop the particular laws, ideologies, codes of conduct, statements of purpose, etc. that now constitute the group's governing norms, it still has to be associated with the group itself rather than with group members. So, too, does the notion of control inherent in it. For, otherwise, the group itself, as distinct from its members, could not be held morally responsible for the harm in question.

Second, intentionality as purposiveness is not being put forward here as a *source of moral guilt as traditionally understood*. Instead, it is being put forward as a *condition of communal moral blame*. ("According to our communal moral standards, group A must have exercised x, y, or z level of purposiveness to qualify for collective moral responsibility.") Hence, while it may not be strong enough for a Kantian notion of collective moral responsibility, it is strong enough for a notion of collective moral responsibility that both grounds moral blameworthiness in worldly practices and requires intentionality for the sake of retaining a notion of moral agency.

Third, while we may have made things easier for ourselves empirically by introducing a notion of collective moral responsibility whose requirements for agent causation and intentionality are less stringent than those of other notions, we have made things more difficult—and more interesting—for ourselves normatively. For, once we ground collective moral responsibility in worldly standards of moral blameworthiness, rather than in moral agency per se, we are obliged to ask: What kinds of collective intentions *should* we associate with group moral blameworthiness? What level of purposiveness *should* we deem appropriate to collective moral responsibility?

I have not addressed these (very important) normative questions here. Instead, I have provided a basis for pursuing them by making two more general claims. The first is that even if our most sophisticated notions of collective intentions are not sufficient to sustain collective moral responsibility as we now know it, and even if we cannot come up with any other notions of collective intentions that will suffice, we do not have to give up on collective moral responsibility itself. Instead, we can develop an alternative notion of it that requires different kinds of collective intentions. The second is that, by doing so, we might be able to render collective moral responsibility, as well as the kinds of collective intentions associated with it, both coherent and discoverable in the world.

RELATED TOPICS

Collective Action and Agency (Ch. 1), Non-Reductive Views of Shared Intention (Ch. 2), Reductive Views of Shared Intention (Ch. 3), Proxy Agency in Collective Action (Ch. 5), Joint Commitment (Ch. 10), Social Groups (Ch. 21), Complicity (Ch. 25), Institutional Responsibility (Ch. 26), Collective Intentionality in the Law (Ch. 29).

REFERENCES

Bratman, M. (1999) *Faces of Intention: Selected Essays on Intention and Agency*, Cambridge, UK: Cambridge University Press.
Downie, R.S. (1969) "Collective Responsibility," *Philosophy* 44: 66–9.

Feinberg, J. (1970) *Doing and Deserving*, Princeton: Princeton University Press.

Gilbert, M. (2000) *Sociality and Responsibility, New Essays in Plural Subject Theory*, New York: Rowman and Littlefield.

——— (2006) *A Theory of Political Obligation*, Oxford: Oxford University Press.

Narveson, J. (2002) "Collective Responsibility," *Journal of Ethics* 6: 179–98.

Sellars, W. (1968) *Science and Metaphysics*, New York: Humanities Press.

Tuomela, R. (1989) "Actions by Collectives," *Philosophical Perspectives* 3: 491–4.

——— (2005) "We-Intentions Revisited," *Philosophical Studies* 125: 327–49.

Velleman, D. (1997) "How to Share an Intention," *Philosophy and Phenomenological Research* 57: 29–50.

Zimmerman, M. (1988) *An Essay on Moral Responsibility*, Totowa, NJ: Rowman and Littlefield.

NOTES

1. I explore different ways of formulating moral responsibility in general in *Moral Responsibility and the Boundaries of Community* (University of Chicago Press: 1992) and different ways of formulating collective moral responsibility in particular in "Collective Responsibility," *Stanford Encyclopedia of Philosophy* (2017).

2. Velleman (1997: 30) makes clear here that he is 'filling in a gap in Gilbert's view' by using an interpretation of Sellars to show 'how distinct intentions held by different people can add up to a single token of collective intention, jointly held'.

3. Here again it is important to recall that what we are talking about is collective moral responsibility rather than, say, legal responsibility. In the case of legal claims of negligence, for example, we do not always have to show intentionality, since we can fall back on various legal standards. In the case of moral responsibility, though, we need to be able to talk about intentions, since they are the source of the kind of blameworthiness in play.

25

Complicity

Saba Bazargan-Forward

1. INTRODUCTION

Complicity marks out a way that one person can be liable to sanctions for the wrongful conduct of another. There are at least three approaches to an analysis of complicity. The first is a juristic; it adverts to the theoretical grounds for complicity in the law. The second is a joint-action approach which grounds complicity in the shared actions and intentions of individuals engaged in a cooperative project. The third is a group-agency approach which locates complicity in the individuals who together compose a group agent. A comprehensive analysis of complicity would incorporate the insights of all three approaches into a univocal account. But that project is beyond the scope of this essay. Instead, I will focus mostly on the juristic approach, as it provides the most developed account of complicity. After describing the role of complicity in the law, I will argue that much of the motivation for presenting complicity as a separate basis of criminal liability is misplaced; paradigmatic cases of complicity can be assimilated into standard causation-based accounts of criminal liability. But unlike others who make this sort of claim (Moore 2007) I will also argue that there is still room for genuine complicity in the law and in morality. In defending this claim, I sketch an approach to complicity which grounds our liability for what others do not in our causal relation to their actions but in our "agency-relations" with others.

2. WHAT COMPLICITY IS

In Anglo-American criminal law an individual can become liable for a crime by committing it herself. Doing so requires both performing the prohibited act (the *actus reus*) and harboring a culpable state of mind (the *mens rea*). However, the doctrine of complicity (also known as the law of aiding and abetting, or accessorial liability) states that an

327

individual (known as the secondary actor, the accomplice, or the accessory) can be liable for the crimes of someone else: the individual (known as the primary actor, or the principal) who actually committed the crime. In such cases the secondary becomes complicit by intentionally aiding or encouraging the primary to perform the prohibited act.[1] Complicity, then, is not a crime in its own right. One cannot be guilty of "complicity" (unlike the crime of "conspiracy"). Rather, complicity is a way to become liable for a crime committed by another. Once the complicity of the secondary is proved, then unless she is an accessory after the fact, she is as treated as if she had fulfilled the *actus reus* and *mens rea* conditions of the crime itself. In that respect she is treated like the primary.

Crucially, however, the secondary's liability is derivative rather than vicarious vis-à-vis the primary. In cases of vicarious liability, the defendant has committed no wrong; she is still (vicariously) liable for what the primary does in virtue of the defendant's formal relationship with the primary (such as the relationship between a parent and child or between a commanding officer and her subordinates). This relationship permits attributing to the defendant responsibility for the wrongful actions the primary commits. When, alternatively, an individual is *derivatively* liable, her liability is parasitic off the primary's liability in virtue of her own intentional actions—specifically actions aimed at contributing to the primary's wrongful conduct. It is in virtue of so culpably contributing that she shares in the primary's liability.

3. REQUISITES OF COMPLICITY

Under the law, for an individual to be complicit in the criminal wrongdoing of another, the secondary must not only contribute to the wrongful conduct of the primary, but do so with some *mens rea* directed towards the primary's crime. It is generally acknowledged that accomplices need not have an intention with the same content as the primary. That would rule out the possibility of complicity altogether since a secondary intentionally performs acts of assistance or encouragement, not the prohibited act itself. But there is no further consensus over what the requisite mental state is. Some have argued that the secondary must provide aid with the purpose that the crime in question succeed (Judge Learned Hand in *United States v. Peoni*, 100 F.2d 401, 402 (2d Cir. 1938)). This is despite the fact that many crimes do not require the mental state of purpose on the part of the primary. Others argue that mere knowledge of the fact that acting will enable the primary to commit the crime in question suffices for satisfying the *mens rea* (Weiss 2002: 1396–1409). Still others abandon the notion that there is a single *mens rea* that the secondary must possess, in favor of the more flexible view that the requisite *mens rea* for complicity varies with the *mens rea* required for the crime in question (Weiss 2002: 1410–14).

It might seem useful to repair to the literature on joint action since it tends to meticulously detail the mental states that cooperators must have in order to qualify as joint actors. Since cooperative action in furtherance of wrongdoing seems to imply complicity, the mental states partly definitive of joint action might help resolve the requisite *mens rea* for complicity in the law. But this strategy cannot ground the existing law of complicity. This is because in the law, the secondary can be complicitously liable for having provided assistance in furtherance of the primary's criminal act, even if the primary was unaware that she had been aided, as in this case:

Guardian Devil

J witnesses, without being noticed, a bank robbery in progress. J sees a patrol car approaching the scene. She wants the robbery to succeed (since she has a grudge against the bank). So J pretends to require assistance, thereby preventing the police from discovering the robbery. The robbery consequently succeeds.

Under the doctrine of liability in Anglo-American law, the conditions for complicitous liability are satisfied so long as influence succeeds as intended in contributing to the decision of the principal to commit the crime. Accordingly, J is complicit in the robbers' wrongdoing in that she can be charged as an accessory. But even on the most minimalist account of joint action (see for example Ludwig (2007)) the robber does not count as acting jointly with J since the robber has no intentions directed toward an action by a group that includes himself and J. Complicity in the law overflows joint action, in that it is possible to be complicit for a crime without partaking in a jointly intentional conduct. We cannot, then, simply turn to the literature on joint-action in an effort to ground complicity (though, as I will argue, the philosophy of joint action will have an important role to play in making sense of the agency-relation approach to liability).

In what follows I focus on an issue that will inform the remainder of the discussion. If satisfying the *actus reus* of complicity requires a causal contribution to the wrong in question, what need is there for an account of complicity at all?

4. SUPERFLUITY OF COMPLICITY

In standard cases of liability where the wrongdoer acts on her own and without assistance from others, she is liable in virtue of culpably causing the wrongful event in question (liability for omissions and inchoate crimes notwithstanding). In such cases, the liability is "direct" or "non-derivative" in that we need only appeal to the fact that the wrongdoer has culpably caused the wrongful event in order to explain her liability. But it is alleged—famously by Sanford Kadish, (1985) following Hart and Honoré (1958)—that we cannot appeal to direct liability in cases where one party contributes to a wrong via another's voluntary acts. Where the primary's actions are fully voluntary, the secondary cannot be characterized as having caused the primary's actions. On this agent-causal view of human agency, the voluntary actions of agents are literally uncaused events. Accordingly, the secondary cannot be held liable for the crime on the basis that she caused it. The role of complicity, then, is to provide separate grounds for liability in such cases.

A doctrine ruling out interpersonal causation seems to render otiose contributory action—a requisite for the *actus reus* in complicity. But Kadish, again following Hart and Honoré, distinguishes between causation properly construed and mere causal influence. A "causal influence" simply raises the probability of an event's occurrence, whereas a "cause" necessitates that event's occurrence. Thus, Kadish writes that voluntary human actions can only be causally influenced, rather than outright caused: 'Since an individual could always have chosen to act without the influence, it is always possible that he might have' (Kadish 1985: 360).

The disjunctive structure of liability—derivative versus direct—is necessary, then, to accommodate the liability of aiders and abettors given an agent-causal view of autonomous agency. But agent-causation is an untenable view of metaphysics, at odds with a naturalistic view of the world. It claims that the will when operating freely does so in a realm distinct from that of ordinary natural events and laws, thereby insulating autonomous agents from the causal effects. It is hard to square this with a view that identifies willing with mental states that supervene on the neurological structure of our brains. While it might be true that we ineluctably tend to regard the voluntary actions of others as uncaused events, any account of morality ought to be based not on our debunked pretheoretic intuitions about metaphysics, but on the most plausibly developed account of how things actually are.[2]

Once we jettison the metaphysical baggage of agent-causation, we are in a position to see that the criminal law is not as dependent on a distinct doctrine of complicity as it might otherwise seem. Consider the following pair of examples.

Uncertain Murder 1

I want my innocent enemy dead. I have a friend—you—who might aid me in my goal. I ask you to kill him. I calculate that there is a 60 percent chance that you'll do so. You subsequently commit the murder.

Uncertain Murder 2

I want my innocent enemy dead. I constructed a machine which, if it functions correctly, will kill my enemy. The machine is not perfectly reliable though; it works only 60 percent of the time. The machine nonetheless successfully kills my enemy.

The basis of liability in the two versions of the example should be exactly the same. The fact that my contribution to the innocent's death in *Uncertain Murder 1* is mediated by an agent, whereas in *Uncertain Murder 2* it is not, makes no difference to my liability. In both cases, the basis of my liability is *direct* (or, alternatively put, non-derivative) in that I culpably act in a way that causes the innocent's death. It just so happens that in the first case my causal relation to the death is mediated by an autonomous agent whereas in the second case it is not.

The basis of an individual's liability for a harm is the same regardless of whether she causes the harm by a) committing it, or b) aiding and abetting a voluntary accomplice. In both cases the individual is directly/non-derivatively liable in that it is her causal relation *to the wrong* (rather than merely to the agent who commits it) that grounds her liability. The notion of complicity does no work in undergirding her liability.

One might raise the following objection. For some acts, what the agent brings about precludes certain kinds of mediating agency. That is, some acts cannot "go through" the agency of others—at least not in certain ways. Sanford Kadish famously called these actions "nonproxyable" (Kadish 1985: 372–85). A paradigm example of a nonproxyable act is rape. It is possible to contribute to the commission of a rape (by, for example, providing the perpetrator with access to the victim) but the contributor does not thereby *commit* the rape, regardless of how integral the contribution was. 'In such cases', John Gardner writes, 'whoever acts through a principal must be an accomplice' (Gardner 2007: 135). The upshot is that any attempt to subsume complicity under causation by recasting accomplices as non-derivatively liable for what the principal does must fail—at least for nonproxyable wrongs.

But this objection fails. It is true that if, for example, P1 pays P2 to lie, which P2 consequently does, it is a semantic fact that only P2 committed the lie—not P1. But our interest is not in whether P2 can be felicitously described as having lied. Rather, our concern is with morality. What P1 does, by intentionally contributing to the act of lying, is morally tantamount to what P2 does, precisely because P1 acted in a way to bring about *a lie*. The point can be put differently: there is no substantial *moral* difference between intentionally committing a nonproxyable wrong and intentionally causing that wrong to be brought about.[3] It is thus a mistake to think that the only way to ground the liability of contributors of nonproxyable acts is by introducing derivative forms of liability.

We might deny that causal contributors act *as* wrongly as proximate wrongdoers. But there are ways to accommodate this view without having to deny that the contributor is non-derivatively liable. For instance, when P1 commits his act—i.e. when he pays P2 to lie—the probability that this will result in a lie is less than when P2 commits her act—i.e., when she utters the lie. If the probability that an act will result in a wrongdoing is relevant to the assessment of the wrongfulness of that act, then *ceteris paribus* P1 acts less wrongfully than P2. In addition, if the nonproxyable wrong is something particularly gruesome or heinous such as torture or rape, we might be inclined to think that the proximate wrongdoer is a morally worse person than an upstream contributor. But this is because performing these heinous crimes while actually facing the victim requires vicious character traits which the proximate wrongdoer, by virtue of committing the act, reveals himself to possess, whereas we cannot safely attribute these traits to the upstream contributor.

So again, in the sorts of cases described so far, the contributor's causal relation *to the wrong* (rather than merely to the agent who commits it) grounds her liability. We do not need to invoke the notion of complicity *as a form of derivative liability* to ground a causal contributor's liability.

If what I have argued is correct, many paradigmatic instances of complicity, construed as derivative liability, will fall under the rubric of causal liability. Suppose P2 wants to commit an armed robbery, but she lacks a firearm. P2 asks P1 for a weapon; she agrees to give him a quarter of the loot in compensation. P1 agrees. On the orthodox account of complicity, P1 is liable for armed robbery even though she didn't commit it; her liability in this case is derivative, where derivative liability is grounded in an attempt to enable the wrongdoer to commit a wrong. It is also the case, on the account I have presented, that P1 is liable for armed robbery even though she didn't commit it—but her liability on my view is non-derivative. Like the protagonist in *Uncertain Murder 1* and *2*, she bears it wholly in virtue of the fact that she culpably acted in a way that risked causing an armed robbery. The fact that it was mediated by the agency of another does not itself change the basis of her liability.

If the liability in such cases is non-derivative is there any room for complicity construed as a form of genuinely derivative liability? I will argue that there is.

5. COMPLICITY REVIVED

On both the orthodox account of complicity and the revised account, which dispenses with derivative liability, an individual is complicit in the wrongdoing of another only if she causally contributes to that wrongdoing or causally influences the wrongdoer. The problem, though, is that it's possible to causally contribute to a wrongdoing without making a morally relevant difference to that wrongdoing. To see why, it's necessary to look closer at what it means to causally contribute to an event.

The two dominant theories of causation today are *regularity* and *counterfactual* accounts. Regularity accounts explicate the notion of causal necessity undergirding accounts according to which one event is a cause of another event when the first event is an insufficient but necessary element of a set of conditions actually sufficient but not necessary for the occurrence of the second event.[4] On counterfactual accounts, the first event is a cause of the second other if the two can be related to each other, either directly or by a chain of mediating events, such that if the first had not occurred, the second would not have occurred.[5] There are, of course, numerous problems plaguing both accounts. But the problem of preemptive overdetermination in particular reveals the role that complicity plays in morality.[6] Here is a typical example.

Assassination Fund

A villain wishes to assassinate a political figure meddlesome to local criminal elements. With the expressed purpose of doing so, the villain solicits financial donations from various criminals in furtherance of hiring a hitman. Hundreds of small donations pour in. The donations she receives are far more than what is necessary to hire a hitman, which she subsequently does. No one donation was necessary or sufficient for hiring the hitman.

This sort of case is troublesome for any account of liability grounding an accomplice's liability in her contribution to the wrongful act. Though each donor contributed to the fund, no particular contribution was a necessary element of a set of funds sufficient for hiring the assassin. We have difficulty, then, explaining why any donor is liable *for a murder* when no single donor caused that murder. An appeal to the supposedly "derivative" character of complicity is of no help, since we still need to explain why a contributor can be derivatively liable for a wrong that she did not empower the principal to commit. For any particular donor, she alone makes literally no difference to whether the murder occurs. It might be argued that she slightly raised the antecedent probability of the murder's occurrence by donating, but it is unclear why this should make her liable for the murder when it turns out that her donation made no actual difference to the murder's occurrence. We can imagine her donation lying at the bottom of the barrel, unused—yet she is liable for murder.

Some have attempted to circumvent this problem by foregoing causal accounts of derivative liability altogether. For example, Christopher Kutz denies that a causal contribution is necessary for complicity; the "participatory intentions" of the accomplice are what grounds liability (Kutz 2000). Michael S. Moore defends a singularist account of causation, which purports to solve problematic cases of overdetermination (2009: 496–512). (He also argues that subjective chance-raising can be a determiner of culpability). Sanford Kadish suggests that by 'extending our wills' to the actions of others we come to be complicit in what they do (1985: 355). Daniel Yeager, taking a different approach, argues that there is a morally relevant distinction between *helping* and *doing*; complicitous individuals, by merely helping, incur a risk-based rather than a harm-based form of liability (Yeager 1996).

I believe Kutz and Kadish are on the right track. When we intentionally cooperate in furtherance of some collectively caused event, each cooperator can become liable for what any other cooperator does, in virtue of making herself the principal's *agent*. That is, when someone agrees to act at your behest in furtherance of some goal you specify, you can become liable for what that person foreseeably does in furtherance of that goal *independent of whether you caused (or even causally influenced) your agent to so act.* Consider this case:

Yard Cleaning

P1, who is physically disabled, asks P2 for a favor: that P2 clean P1's front yard. While on an errand, P2 happens to be driving by P1's house—though she doesn't know that this house is P1's. Detesting the sight of an unsightly front yard, P2 takes it upon herself to clean it, not knowing that she is cleaning P1's yard. In the process of doing so, P2 recklessly damages prized orchids belonging to P1's neighbors.

P1 bears remedial liability for the damages that P2 causes even though P1's agreement with P2 in no sense contributed to P2's conduct. Of course, if it weren't for P1, P2 wouldn't have caused the damage since P2 was, after all, cleaning P1's yard. But this alone does not ground P1's liability—after all, if P2's assistance were unsolicited, then P1 would not be remedially liable even though she is a *sine qua non* of the damage P2 causes. What grounds P1's remedial liability, then, is not her causal or counterfactual relation to what P2 does, but the fact that she intentionally made P2 her agent. It is the normative rather than the causal relationship P1 bears to P2 that makes P1 liable for what P2 foreseeably does in furtherance of the ends specified in that relationship. P1 vests in P2 the fiduciary power to act on P1's behalf; this fiduciary power is insensitive to the causal route by which P2 comes to subsequently act, so long as those actions fall within the rubric of the proffered agreement.

Successful uptake of the agency-relation requires that P2 see herself as having accepted P1's request to act as an agent. But the satisfaction-conditions for acting as someone's agent are extensional in the sense that P2 needn't occurrently regard herself as P1's (or anyone's) agent when P2 is fulfilling her duties to P1. Rather, she need only act in a way that achieves what is required of her. This might seem to problematically ambiguate liability in cases where multiple principals establish agency-relations with one and the same individual who ultimately acts in ways that extensionally fulfills several of the roles she agreed to adopt.[7] If in the course of doing so she acts recklessly, it might seem unclear which if any of the principals bears liability if we cannot repair to the agent's intentions—specifically, those occurrent intentions specifying for whom she saw herself as acting. But there is another option: the intentions the agent *would* have possessed upon careful, informed reflection specify the principal for whom she is acting in cases where there are multiple principals. If there is no mere single principal she settles on, this suggests that they share liability among them.

So though in *Yard Cleaning* it is not the agreement that causes P2 to damage the orchids but rather a deviant causal chain, and though P2 did not take herself to be acting under the aegis of P1's authority when the former was cleaning the latter's yard, P1 is nonetheless liable. This is a non-causal, derivative basis of liability. It is not vicarious liability, since it is grounded in an agreement made between P1 and P2—an agreement establishing what is called an "agency-relationship."

We have, then, a way to ground complicity in cases where the accomplice does not causally contribute to what the primary wrongdoer does. Recall that in *Assassination Fund* each donator, by virtue of donating with the intention of enabling the villain to fund the assassination thereby makes the villain his or her agent; this, in turn, makes each donator liable for what the villain does in foreseeable furtherance of carrying out the assassination. Because the villain hires the hitman in furtherance of the assassination, and because this was the expressed purpose of the fund, the donors are liable for the assassination.

To better understand the nature of the agency-relation between the donors and the villain, it is helpful to strip the example of its inessential elements. Suppose the villain simply announces to the criminal underworld that if she receives enough donations, she will hire an assassin. That is the extent of the relationship between the villain and the donors. It seems, then, that the villain is not acting at the behest of the donors in that she does not seem to be acting as their representative or under their authority. In short, there seems to be no "agency-relation" between the villain and the donors. But this is illusory. If the villain presented her conditional intention to hire an assassin *as a promise* to the donors—a promise to hire an assassin should she receive enough funds—and, if the donors donated to the fund on the understanding that doing so is tantamount to accepting that promise, then the villain is thereby in an agency-relation with the donors. On this view, simply offering and accepting a promise establishes an agency-relation since the promisee now has a special authority over the promisor that the promisor act in accordance with the terms of the mutually agreed-upon promise. This authority is asymmetrical: the promisee but not the promisor can at any time unilaterally free the promisor of the obligation the latter bears to the former.

Some might balk at the suggestion that merely accepting a promise can be enough to establish an agency-relation. There is a high bar for entering into an agency-relation with others. It is typically thought to require an explicit agreement to that effect, and for good reason: because entering into an agency-relation with another has such sweeping effects on liability, the provisions for entering into such a relationship should be accordingly hard to satisfy. It might therefore seem that I am using the agency-relation (and with it, its normative upshots) over-inclusively.

This is a potent objection, but I believe it can be defused. The agency-relation is typically thought of as bivalent—you are either in such a relation or you are not. I propose that this is the wrong way to think about the agency-relation. It is best construed as a scalar relation in that there are degrees to which one is in an agency-relation with another. The stronger the agency-relation, the greater the deprivations to which the principal (P1) is liable for what the agent (P2) does, and the greater the range of actions committed by P2 for which P1 can be held liable. Put differently, the strength of the agency-relation affects the degree to which P1 is liable for any given harm, and the harms for which P1 can be held liable. These factors can be respectively called the *depth* and the *breadth* of liability.

I cannot here provide all the criteria determining the strength of the agency-relation. But I will present a few viable candidates: 1) how each party characterizes their relationship to each other, 2) what is at stake in establishing the agency relation, and 3) the stringency of the agreement, all play a role in determining the strength of the agency-relation. I will briefly discuss these in order.

In cases where the agency-relation is at its strongest, P2 not only agrees to be P1's agent, but in addition, P1 is disposed to characterize herself as vesting a fiduciary power in P2; P2 likewise is disposed to characterize herself as acting on P1's behalf. But it is possible to establish an agency-relation without either party thinking of her relation to the other in such terms. It is enough if P2 agrees to assist P1 in furthering some end that P1 has. In such a case, P2 acts at the behest of P1, as P1's agent; after all, if P2 subsequently fails to act in accordance with the agreement absent good reason, P1 has a claim against P2. And only P1 can release P2 of the obligation that P2 has. It is not infelicitous, then, to describe P2 when she acts in accordance with that agreement (regardless of whether the agreement is what is *motivating* her to so act) as acting under P1's authority. But the strength of the agency-relation established in such a case is weaker than in a case where each is disposed to characterize herself as in an agency-relation with the other.

Another factor determining the strength of the agency-relation is this: the more at stake in establishing the agency-relation, the greater its strength. For example, agreeing to act as someone's bodyguard will, simply by virtue of what is at stake in such a role, constitute a stronger agency-relation than agreeing to act as someone's gardener. This suggests, in *Yard Cleaning*, that the strength of the agency-relation between P1 and P2 is relatively low.

A final factor (in an incomplete list of factors) determining the strength of the agency-relation is the strength of the agreement between P1 and P2. Some agreements are stronger than others, where the strength determines among other things the stringency of the presumptive duty to follow through with the agreement. The strength of the agreement is determined by the reasonableness of the view that each party has a second-personal duty to follow through with the agreement. One factor determining the reasonableness of such a belief is whether and the extent to which the agreement is formalized. An agreement put in writing, assessed by a lawyer, and signed in the presence of a notary, will *ceteris paribus* be stronger than an agreement sealed by a wink and a nudge. Note, though, that as I indicated above, the agreement in question need not be one in which P2 agrees to act as P1's agent—an agreement in which P2 agrees to aid P1 in furtherance of some end will suffice to establish an agency-relationship, albeit a weaker one.

With this preliminary and incomplete investigation of the factors influencing the strength of the agency-relation, we are now in a better position to assess the grounds for complicity in cases like *Assassin Fund* and *Yard Cleaning*. In the former case, it might seem that the donors made no agreement with the villain. But in soliciting financial assistance the villain is understood as having agreed to use those funds in furtherance of hiring a hitman. Indeed, if he used it for completely different purposes the donors would have a claim against the villain precisely because the villain has broken his promise. This shows that we can interpret donating money under those circumstances as establishing a weak agency-relation between the villain and each donor. That the content of the agreement is largely implicit and informal, and that the villain might not see himself as an agent of the donors, weakens the agency-relation established between them. But the fact that what is at stake is morally important—a matter of life or death—is a factor strengthening the agreement. (Determining how to weigh these against each other is a task for another time).

Contrast this with *Yard Cleaning*. Again, the agreement between P1 and P2 is not one in which P2 is expressly characterized as P1's agent—this weakens the strength of the resulting agency-relation. But such a relation nonetheless exists in virtue of the agreement P2 makes to aid P1 in furtherance of cleaning P1's yard. Since this end is morally trivial, the strength of the relation is accordingly diminished, which weakens the depth and breadth of P1's liability for what P2 foreseeably does in furtherance of the ends specified in the agreement. Suppose, for example, that P2, instead of recklessly damaging the prized orchids belonging to P1's neighbor, somehow ends up recklessly killing the neighbor's child. P1 will bear little or no liability for what P2 does, not just because that eventuality was not relevantly foreseeable, but because the weak nature of the agency-relation accordingly narrows the breadth of P1's liability—i.e. the range of acts committed by P2 for which P1 is liable.

6. IMPLICATIONS

Regardless of how an agency-account of complicity is developed, it will not do the work that complicity does in Anglo-American criminal or tort law; this is because in the law an individual can be complicit in a wrongdoing by contributing to it without the wrongdoer's knowledge. Consider again *Guardian Devil*, where J aids robbers unbeknown to them. Since J assists without their knowledge, clearly there is no agency-relation between J and them. Yet in Anglo-American criminal law, J is legally complicit in their wrongdoing. J can be charged as an accessory to robbery. But I argued that this is a straightforward case of *non-derivative* liability—it is J's causal relation to the wrongdoing (in combination with satisfying the requisite culpable mental states) that grounds her liability. So, although this sort of case will not be covered by an account of complicity based in the agency-relation, it does not need to do so. It is no limitation of the agency-relation account that it does not impute complicity in cases like *Guardian Devil*.

There are many issues pertaining to derivative and non-derivative complicity which need much more discussion, such as the possibility of *reckless* derivative liability (whereby the agency-relation makes us complicit for wrongdoing we do not intend but are in a position to foresee); whether we can bear non-derivative liability for the unsuccessful attempts of wrongdoers we enable; whether an unsuccessful attempt to enable a wrongdoer who nonetheless succeeds can make the attempted enabler liable; whether we should treat non-derivative liability for the harm we enable another to commit differently from the non-derivative liability of innocent agency (i.e. cases where we use unwitting or cognitively impaired individuals in furtherance of wrongful ends), and so on. In addition, there is obviously much more to say about the determinants of the agency-relationship and its application, in a broader range of cases. But my goal here is more modest: to show that insofar as there is room for genuinely non-causal derivate liability— which seems necessary to implicate wrongdoers in cases of concurrent and preemptive overdetermination—we should take more seriously the possibility that the agency-relation can serve as grounds for complicity in such cases.

RELATED TOPICS

Collective Action and Agency (Ch. 1), Proxy Agency in Collective Action (Ch. 5), Joint Commitment (Ch. 10), Collective Intentions and Collective Moral Responsibility (Ch. 24), Institutional Responsibility (Ch. 26), Collective Intentionality in the Law (Ch. 29).

REFERENCES

Gardner, J. (2007) "Moore on Complicity and Causality," *University of Pennsylvania Law Review* 156: 432–43.

Hart, H.L.A. and Honoré, T. (1958) *Causation in the Law*, 2nd edition, Oxford: Clarendon Press.

Kadish, S. (1985) "Causation and Complicity: A Study in the Interpretation of Doctrine," *California Law Review* 73: 323–410.

Kutz, C. (2000) *Complicity: Ethics and Law for a Collective Age*, Cambridge: Cambridge University Press.

Lewis, D. (1973) "Causation," *Journal of Philosophy* 70: 556–67.

Ludwig, K. (2007) "Collective Intentional Behavior from the Standpoint of Semantics," *Noûs* 41 (3): 355–93.

Mackie, J.L. (1974) *The Cement of the Universe*, Oxford: Clarendon Press.

Moore, M.S. (2000) "The Metaphysics of Causal Intervention," *California Law Review* 88: 827–78.

——— (2007) "Causing, Aiding, and the Superfluity of Accomplice Liability," *University of Pennsylvania Law Review* 156 (2): 395–452.

——— (2009) *Casuation and Responsiblity*, New York: Oxford University Press.

Weiss, B. (2002) "What Were They Thinking?: The Mental States of the Aider and Abettor and the Causer Under Federal Law," *Fordham Law Review* 70 (4): 1341–81.

Wright, R. (2001) "Once More Into the Bramble Bush: Duty, Causal Contribution, and the Extent of Legal Responsibility," *Vanderbilt Law Review* 54 (3): 1092–6.

Yaffe, G. (2012) "Moore on Causing, Acting, and Complicity," *Legal Theory* 18 (4): 437–58.

Yeager, D. (1996) "Helping, Doing, and the Grammar of Complicity," *Criminal Justice Ethics* 15: 25–35.

NOTES

1. In the UK, this doctrine is stated in the "Accessories and Abettors Act of 1861" (amended by the Criminal Law Act of 1977): 'Whosoever shall aid, abet, counsel, or procure the commission of any indictable offence . . . shall be liable to be tried, indicted and punished as a principal offender'. In the US the doctrine is stated in the Model Penal Code §2.06, and in the federal aiding and abetting statute: '[w]hoever commits an offense against the United States or aids, abets, counsels, commands, induces or procures its commission, is punishable as a principal' 18 U.S.C. § 2(a) (1982).

2. For a compelling series of arguments in support of this view, see Moore (2000).

3. For a far more thoroughgoing analysis of nonproxyability friendly to the sort of suggestion I'm making here, see Moore (2007) and Moore (2009). But see Yaffe (2012).

4. For variations of this account, see Hart and Honoré (1958), Mackie (1974), Wright (2001).

5. The modern progenitor of such accounts is David Lewis. See Lewis (1973).

6. For a detailed analysis, see Moore (2009).

7. I thank a referee for challenging me on this point.

26

Institutional Responsibility

Seumas Miller

1. INTRODUCTION

Institutional responsibility is a species of responsibility and contrasts, perhaps most obviously, with moral responsibility (Fischer 1999). Jones might be morally responsible for failing to assist an old woman to cross the road without being institutionally responsible for his failing. Equally, Smith might be institutionally responsible for seeing to it that her desk is tidy but we might baulk at regarding this as a moral responsibility. Moreover, responsibility can be used in a backward or a forward looking sense. An example of the former sense is: "Jones is responsible for the car crash since he failed to stop at the red traffic light." An example of the latter sense is "The mechanic is responsible for seeing to it that the brakes in my car are fixed."

Responsibility needs to be distinguished from blameworthiness/praiseworthiness (Strawson 1962), on the one hand, and accountability (Bovens 2007), on the other. If a cleaner does his job of cleaning the office to an acceptable standard, but not to a high standard, then he is responsible for having cleaned the office; but he is presumably neither praiseworthy nor blameworthy. Evidently, therefore, praiseworthiness and blameworthiness presuppose responsibility, but should not be equated with it. Again, responsibility should not be confused with accountability. The cleaner is responsible for cleaning the office, but accountable for his performance as a cleaner to (say) his supervisor. That is, the supervisor might be tasked with monitoring and assessing the cleaner's performance and, if necessary, intervening in the case of poor performance by retraining, disciplining or perhaps even firing him.

The notion of institutional responsibility (Ladd 1982), including but not restricted to legal responsibility (Duff 2007), presupposes some notion of an institution (Searle 2011; Miller 2010). Sometimes the term "institution" (see Chapter 27, this volume) is used to refer to simple social phenomena such as conventions (Lewis 1969), e.g. handshakes, and sometimes to complex social forms that are not organizations such as human languages or kinship systems (Giddens 1984). However, the concern in this entry is only with institutions that are also organizations and/or systems of organizations.

Such organizations (or systems thereof) are complex social forms that reproduce themselves and include governments, police organizations, universities, hospitals, business corporations, markets, and legal systems. Moreover, social institutions in this sense are among the most important of collective human phenomena; they enable us to feed ourselves (markets and agribusinesses), to protect ourselves (police and military services), to educate ourselves (schools and universities), and to govern ourselves (governments and legal systems). In short, institutions have purposes or functions.

Institutions consist in part of institutional roles defined in terms of tasks and these roles are structured in terms of relationships of authority. Institutional role structures vary greatly. Compare, for example, the hierarchical top-down structure of military organizations with the flat democratic structures typical of amateur sporting clubs.

The third main dimension of institutions is culture (Harre 1993): the "spirit" or informal set of attitudes that pervades an organization and which might reinforce or negate the more formal requirements of the organization. An example of the latter is the culture in certain police organizations which protects those engaged in corruption rather than exposing them.

Among other things a normative theory of institutions specifies what the purpose or function of particular types of institution *ought to be*, as opposed to what in fact it is. Enron, for example, apparently had the de facto institutional purpose of enriching its CEO and other senior officers; but this was surely not what its institutional purpose ought to have been.

One normative theory of social institutions is based on an individualist theory of joint action (Miller 2010). Put simply, on this account the organizations or systems of organizations are ones that provide collective goods by means of joint activity. The collective goods in question include the fulfillment of aggregated moral rights, such as needs-based rights for security (police organizations), material well-being (businesses operating in markets), education (universities), governance (governments) and so on.[1]

Whether one accepts this normative theory or some other, establishing, maintaining or redesigning the institutional responsibilities of institutional role occupants ought to be done in the context of some normative account of the institutional function or purpose of the institution in question. For to some extent this purpose or function will determine what is an appropriate structure and culture and, therefore, what the tasks to be performed by the institutional role occupants ought to be and the manner in which they ought to be performed. That is, institutional role structure and associated culture ought to facilitate institutional purpose. This is most obvious in relation to the tasks definitive of a role; mechanics ought to know how to fix brakes, adjust steering and so on. It is less obvious in relation to authority relationships. Perhaps a hierarchical structure is necessary if military organizations are to realize their institutional purposes of successfully waging war. On the other hand, top-down hierarchical structures may not be conducive to academic work and, therefore, ought not to be imposed on universities.

In the light of the above, we can distinguish three possible ways of understanding institutional responsibility. First, there is the responsibility *to institutions*. This is the responsibility (possibly moral responsibility) that an individual or, more likely, group might have to establish, maintain or redesign an institution. Here the property "institutional" does not qualify the notion of responsibility; rather it is part of the content of the responsibility. This sense of institutional responsibility is not our direct or principal concern in this entry.[2] Second, there is the responsibility *of institutions*. For example, corporations are ascribed *legal* responsibilities (in some weak sense of that term) (Moore 2009). However, some theorists have wanted to ascribe *moral* responsibility to institutions. This is the notional possibility that institutional *and* moral responsibility might attach to collective entities (specifically, institutions) per se. This possibility could only obtain if institutions (and like collective entities) were *minded* agents: agents possessed of mental states, such as desires, intentions, and beliefs (French 1979; Erskine 2001). For only minded agents perform actions in the appropriate sense of action, and only minded agents can sensibly be held morally responsible for their actions. However, the idea that institutions per se, as opposed to their human members (institutional role occupants), have minds is problematic or, at the very least, controversial (Copp 2007; Miller 2007a). At any rate, in this entry I set aside any further consideration of this way of understanding institutional responsibility. I do so while acknowledging that for heuristic reasons institutional responsibility (in some weak sense) can be ascribed to institutions per se. Third, there is the responsibility *of institutional role occupants*. This is the institutional responsibility of the human beings who occupy institutional roles: responsibility qua institutional role occupant. It is this third sense of institutional responsibility that is our principal concern in this entry

2. INDIVIDUAL AND COLLECTIVE (INSTITUTIONAL) RESPONSIBILITY

Evidently individual role occupants are *individually* institutionally responsible for at least some of their actions and omissions. For example, an office cleaner might be individually institutionally responsible for seeing to it that a given office is cleaned (responsibility in the forward-looking sense). Moreover, if the cleaner fails to clean the office in question to the required standard then he is individually responsible for not having cleaned it properly (backward-looking sense) and this failure attaches to him qua institutional role occupant.

Again, an institutional role occupant in a position of authority over another (e.g. the supervisor in relation to the cleaner) might have an *individual* institutional responsibility (forward-looking sense) to see to it that her subordinate performs the tasks definitive of the subordinate's role. Moreover, if the subordinate (the cleaner) consistently fails to perform the tasks in question, and his superior (the supervisor) fails to intervene, then the supervisor is individually responsible (backward-looking sense) for seeing to it that the cleaner does his job and this failure attaches to the supervisor qua institutional role occupant.

On the other hand, a number of institutional role occupants might be *collectively* institutionally responsible for some outcome (Thompson 1980; May 1992; Zimmermann 1985). The paradigmatic cases here are ones of joint action; actions involving cooperation between institutional actors to achieve some outcome.

Roughly speaking, a joint action (Bratman 2014; Miller 1992; Miller and Tuomela 1988) can be understood thus: two or more individuals perform a joint action if each of them intentionally performs an individual action (or omission), but does so with the (true) belief that in so doing they will jointly realize an end which each of them has. So joint actions are interdependent actions directed toward a common goal or end. But what is such an end?

This is a controversial issue (Schweikard and Schmid 2013). However, in order to simplify matters, I shall assume that this notion of a common goal or, as I shall refer to it, a collective end, is a construction out of the prior notion of an individual end (see also Chapter 3, this volume). Roughly speaking, a collective end is an individual end more than one agent has, and which is such that, if it is realized, it is realized by all, or most, of the actions of the agents involved; the individual action of any given agent is only part of the means by which the end is realized. The realization of the collective end is the bringing into existence of a state of affairs. Each agent has this state of affairs as an individual end. So a collective end is a species of individual end (Miller 2007b). Moreover, it is an end that each has interdependently with the others. So in joint action there is interdependence of action and interdependence of ends. Consider two walkers whose pathway is blocked by a heavy log. Neither can push the log aside acting on her own, but if they combine their efforts they can remove it. Again, consider a team of firefighters putting out a raging bush-fire. None could do it acting on his or her own. Nevertheless, if they combine their efforts they can succeed in putting out the fire. What of collective responsibility?

Collective responsibility of the kind in question here is the responsibility that attaches to the participants of a joint action for the performance of joint action and, in particular, for the realization of the collective end of the joint action. (See also Chapter 24.) There are different accounts of collective responsibility, some of which pertain to the responsibility of groups and organizations per se for their group or "corporate" (so to speak) actions. Here our concern is only with collective responsibility for joint actions of human beings in their capacity as institutional role occupants. One such salient account conceptualizes collective moral responsibility for joint action as *joint responsibility* (Mellema 2006; Miller 2006).

On this view of collective responsibility as joint responsibility, collective responsibility is ascribed to individual human beings only, albeit jointly.[3] Moreover, institutional actors can be ascribed collective institutional responsibility when they act jointly in accordance with their institutional roles. Consider the firefighting team. Each member of the group is individually institutionally responsible for their contributory action and also for the aimed at outcome (the collective end) of the set of actions. However, each fire officer is individually responsible for that outcome, *jointly with the others*; so the conception is relational in character. Thus in this firefighting example, each member of the team is institutionally responsible jointly with the others for extinguishing the fire because each performs his or her contributory action in the service of that collective end (putting out the fire). So the members of the firefighting team are collectively institutionally responsible for extinguishing the fire (in both the forward-looking and the backward-looking senses of responsibility).

Collective institutional responsibility is involved not only in joint (institutional) actions but also in the related phenomena of *joint institutional mechanisms*. An example of the use of a joint mechanism is two friends tossing a coin to resolve a dispute as a one-off action. Some such mechanisms are institutionalized, e.g. the practice of tossing a coin to decide who is to bat first in an international game of cricket between England and Australia. Let us refer to these as joint *institutional* mechanisms.

I now offer an analysis of joint institutional mechanisms taking the institutional practice of voting in a democracy as our example (Miller 2015, 2016; Estlund 2007). Joint institutional mechanisms consist of: (a) a complex of differentiated, but interlocking, intentional actions (the input to the mechanism); (b) the result of the performance of those actions (the output of the mechanism), and; (c) the mechanism itself. Here the mechanism itself is to be understood as consisting of an operation on the inputs that yields an output; so strictly speaking inputs and outputs are constituents of the mechanism only in the sense of being placeholders or variables. Thus, the notion of a joint mechanism does not collapse into the notion of a joint action. For in the case of a joint action, as we saw above, the individual actions are not inputs upon which an operation is performed; rather they are simply actions directed at a collective end and, as such, are constitutive of the joint action. Accordingly, while joint actions are individuated in part by their constitutive individual actions,[4] joint mechanisms are individuated in part by their various operations. Thus it would be a different joint action (albeit one realizing the same collective end) if the participants had lifted the log blocking the pathway rather than pushing it aside. However, it would have been the same joint mechanism if voters x, y etc. had voted for Smith rather than Jones. On the other hand, if the voters voted for exactly the same candidates, but the voting mechanism had been proportional rather than first past the post, then it would have been a different joint mechanism. Importantly, unlike mere joint actions, joint mechanisms enable the production of outputs that qua results are not necessarily aimed at, as we will see below.

Consider the joint institutional mechanism of voting. Citizen A exercises her institutional right (if not duty) by casting her vote in an election and A does so only if others, B, C, D etc. also vote, and only if there is someone to vote for. So in addition to the actions of voting there are the actions of the candidates, X, Y, Z etc., in standing for political office. That they stand as candidates is (in part) constitutive of the input to the voting mechanism; after all, voters vote *for candidates*. So there are interlocking and differentiated actions (the inputs). Further there is some result of the operation of the mechanism: some candidate, says Smith, is voted in by virtue of having secured the most votes (the output). What of the mechanism itself? A key constitutive feature of this voting mechanism is as follows: to receive the most number of votes *is* to win the election.[5] Importantly, that Smith, in particular, is voted in is not something aimed at by all of the participants; specifically, those who voted for Jones were (obviously) not aiming at getting Smith elected!

How does joint action figure in this, given that voters who voted for Jones were not participants in the joint action to vote in Smith? Each voter, of course, performs an intentional individual action of voting and believes others are doing likewise. However, being a species of joint action there must be, on our analysis, a collective end which *all* the voters have. Here we need to be careful. Naturally, it is not an end of *all* the voters (and, therefore, not a *collective* end of all the voters) that Smith is voted in; for a number of voters voted for other candidates, such as Jones. Rather it is only a collective end of those who vote for Smith that he be voted in; each member of this sub-group of voters votes for Smith in the belief (or, at least, hope) that others will also vote for Smith. Since we are assuming Smith did in fact receive the most votes it follows that those who voted for him have realized the collective end of their joint action. Likewise it is a collective end of those who voted for Jones that she be voted in. However, since Jones did not receive sufficient votes to win the election theirs is an unsuccessful joint action. So at the level of sub-groups of voters there may be multiple joint actions, only one of which is successful.

Importantly, there is also a collective end of *all* the voters and *all* the candidates (or at least all those voting and standing for election in good faith). This is the collective end that the one who gets the most votes—whoever that happens to be—is the winner. This is a collective end of all bona fide participants in the joint institutional mechanism and reflects the commitment of the participants to the above-mentioned key constitutive feature of the institutional mechanism, i.e. that the candidate with the most votes wins the election. Accordingly, participants in this joint institutional mechanism perform the individual actions of casting a vote and/or standing as a candidate having as a collective end that the one who gets the most votes—whoever that is—wins the election. So voting is a species of joint action and, more specifically, a joint institutional mechanism.

Collective institutional responsibility is also involved in an institutional phenomenon that is an extension of joint institutional mechanisms in the above sense, namely, in what I refer to as *chains of institutional responsibility* (Miller 2014). Let me explain.

Consider a team of detectives investigating a major crime. Let us assume that the team is engaging in a joint institutional action, namely, that of determining who is the Yorkshire Ripper. So members of the team gather physical evidence, interview witnesses and, in particular, the main suspect, Peter Sutcliffe. Moreover, they do so having as a collective end to determine the *factual* guilt or innocence of this and other suspects. At some point the detectives complete this process and provide a brief of evidence to the prosecutors according to which, and based on all the evidence, Sutcliffe is the Yorkshire Ripper. So far so good, but the criminal justice processes do not terminate in the work of the detectives. For there is now the matter of the trial; that is, the determining by the members of a jury of the *legal* guilt or innocence of Sutcliffe. Let us assume that the members of the jury perform the joint action of deliberating on *legal* guilt or innocence of Sutcliffe, and jointly reach the verdict of guilty (as in fact happened). The question that now arises concerns the institutional relationship between the joint institutional action of the detectives and the joint institutional action of the members of the jury. It is here that the notion of a chain of institutional responsibility is illuminating.

Let us assume in what follows that the collective end of the criminal justice process comprising both the investigating detectives *and* the members of the jury (as well as others, but here I simplify), is that the factually guilty be found legally guilty (and the factually innocent not be found legally guilty). Note that from the perspective of this larger institutional process the collective end of the detectives (that of determining the factual guilt or innocence of a suspect) is merely *proximate* whereas that of the members of the jury is *ultimate*. (It is, of course, only penultimate from the perspective of the criminal justice system more broadly conceived, given the need for sentencing and incarceration).

Moreover, in all this there is an institutional division of labor and segregation of roles which involves each type of institutional actor, e.g. investigator, prosecutor, judge, jury, etc. making a contribution to the further (collective) end of identifying and appropriately punishing the guilty and exonerating the innocent. However, unlike many institutional arrangements, the criminal justice process is predicated on strict adherence on the part of institutional actors to the segregation of roles on pain of compromising this further end. I emphasize that this segregation of roles is consistent with all of these actors, each with their own different and segregated role, having a common further aim; agents can have a common aim and yet it be a requirement that each is to make a different and distinct contribution to that aim, and not perform the tasks assigned to the others, and do all this in the service of that common aim.

In respect of this segregation of roles, the relationship between the institutional actors, including investigators, in the criminal justice process is *unlike* that which holds between (say) a manager, a waiter and a barman in a small pub. There is no reason why, for example, the manager and the waiter might not assist the barman in doing his job of pouring beers during a rush period or even stand in his place when he is called away. But there is a good reason why the prosecutor should not also be the judge and the investigator should not also be the jury; in an adversarial system, any such conflation of roles would constitute a structural conflict of interest and, as such, would be likely to undermine the administration of justice.

Institutional arrangements, such as this, in which there is a segregation of roles (and associated responsibilities) but, nevertheless, a common further end involve a chain of institutional responsibility.

In chains of institutional responsibility all the participants aim (or should be aiming) at the further end in addition to undertaking their own roles (and, therefore, aiming at the end definitive of their own particular role). Moreover, all the participants (at least, in principle) share in the *collective responsibility* for achieving that further end (or for failing to do so). Let us work with our example of Peter Sutcliffe, the Yorkshire Ripper, who was ultimately convicted of 13 counts of murder (the victims being prostitutes working in Yorkshire in the UK).

The detectives involved were (collectively in the sense of jointly) institutionally responsible for gathering and analyzing the evidence which identified Peter Sutcliffe as the Yorkshire Ripper; they acquired the required knowledge of Sutcliffe's *factual* guilt and, thereby, realized the collective end of their institutional role as detectives. On the other hand, members of the court and, in particular, the members of the jury were (collectively) institutionally responsible for finding Sutcliffe *legally* guilty and, thereby, realized the (collective) end of their institutional roles as jury members. So far so good; but what was the ultimate end that was realized by the detectives *and* the members of the jury (as well as the other actors involved in the institutional process, e.g. the judge)?

Presumably the end in question is for the factually guilty to be found legally guilty (and the factually innocent not to be found legally guilty[6]) and this is an end (a collective end) that is realized by the detectives working jointly with the members of the jury (and the other relevant institutional actors). It is not an end that the detectives could achieve on their own; they can only arrive at knowledge of factual guilt. But equally it is not an end that the members of the jury could realize on their own; for they rely on the knowledge provided by the detectives.[7]

Notwithstanding this above-described mandatory segregation of roles (in the context of a chain of institutional responsibility), detectives have been known to try to pre-empt the outcome of the criminal justice process, e.g. by "loading up" suspects they believe are guilty and deserving of severe punishment, rather than remaining within the confines of their designated role of evidence-gathering in the service of truth and being content to rely on prosecutors, judges and juries to undertake their different (albeit, ultimately interlocking) roles in relation to assessing the case against suspects, determining guilt, passing sentence, and so on.

3. INSTITUTIONAL AND MORAL RESPONSIBILITY

The relationship between institutional responsibility and moral responsibility is a difficult one to unravel, not least because the notion of moral responsibility is itself theoretically complex and a matter of controversy. Moreover, I cannot in this short entry elaborate on these complexities and controversies. However, there are some general points that can be raised. In raising them I assume that (roughly speaking) an agent, A, is morally responsible for an action (or omission), x, or the foreseeable and avoidable outcome of x, if x is morally significant (and A is aware, or should be aware, of this moral significance), A intentionally performs x, A's intention to x causes x, and A's intention to x is under A's control.

We saw above that some institutional actions—actions performed by the human occupants of institutional roles in their capacity as institutional actors—are not morally significant and some morally significant actions are not institutional. On the other hand, many institutional actions are morally significant.

Let us henceforth consider only institutional actions that are morally significant and known to be so by the relevant institutional actor—or, at least, the institutional actor should know the actions in question to be morally significant. A question now arises as to whether or not with respect to these actions at least, moral responsibility tracks institutional responsibility. If so, then an institutional actor who is institutionally responsible for performing a (morally significant) institutional action, or for failing to perform one, is necessarily morally responsible for the performance of that action or omission. However, this appears not to be case. Consider, for example, a senior government official, such as a cabinet minister, a number of whose subordinates engage in serious and ongoing acts of fraud. Such acts are morally significant and the subordinates are morally responsibility for perpetrating them. What of the senior government official? Under some institutional arrangements, the senior official might be held institutionally responsible for failing to ensure that such fraud as this did not take place and, consequently, might be forced to resign. Nevertheless, the senior official might not be morally responsible for failing to prevent this fraud. Let us assume that the senior official could have prevented these frauds, if he knew about them and he could have known about them if he had spent a good deal of his time focused on fraud prevention. However, he did not; he had other legitimate and more pressing priorities. Perhaps the senior official took all the steps that might reasonably be expected of him to prevent these frauds but his job is an onerous one, the fraudsters were exceptionally clever, and so on. In short, whereas he is institutionally responsible for failing to prevent these frauds he is, arguably, not morally responsible. So apparently institutional responsibility does not necessarily track moral responsibility. Nor is it obvious that such an institutional arrangement, supposing it exists, is necessarily deficient qua institutional arrangement. I note that Schauer, for example, has argued in detail (Schauer 2003) that institutional arrangements, including laws, are necessarily blunt instruments and, as such, cannot be sensitive to all the requirements of morality.

A second claim concerning the relationships between moral responsibility and institutional responsibility is that institutional arrangements can sometimes make a difference with respect to whether moral responsibility is full or partial (Miller 2015). Thus, as a consequence of institutional arrangements put in place to deal with some collective action problem, each agent might, it is claimed, have full moral responsibility (jointly with others) for some adverse outcome O, notwithstanding the fact that each only made a very small causal contribution to the outcome. Suppose the impoverished members of sailing ships' crews in the eighteenth century are informed of a law to the effect that anyone stealing one or more of the (somewhat expensive) screws inserted into their ship's woodwork to hold its wooden planks together will be flogged and, further, if the ship sinks as a consequence of multiple screws being removed in this manner, then anyone who has removed at least one of these screws will be held to be *fully* legally responsible for any deaths resulting from the ship sinking and to be legally liable to the death penalty. Let us assume that this admittedly harsh criminal law is morally justified in the circumstances in large part because of its significant deterrence effect. Indeed, let us assume that this apparently harsh law is the only means to prevent these wooden ships frequently sinking and, therefore, the only means to prevent great loss of life. In that case it might be thought to be morally justified for each screw-thief who contributed to causing a ship to sink to be held *fully legally responsible* for the loss of life, notwithstanding that his causal contribution to the sinking might be relatively small. This being so, it might be further argued that each such screw-thief is also *fully morally responsible* for any loss of life. If so, then the establishment of institutional arrangements can evidently transform prior *partial* moral responsibility for an adverse outcome (e.g. prior to the existence of a relevant law) into *full* moral responsibility (post the enactment of the law). Moreover, it can do so notwithstanding that the underlying causal responsibility is unchanged and is only *partial causal* responsibility for the adverse outcome.

A final claim concerning the relationships between moral responsibility and institutional responsibility is that institutional arrangements assign moral responsibilities to agents that those agents did not previously have and, indeed, in some cases that no agent previously had (Miller 2010).[8] In the case of the institutional role of police officer, for example, the moral basis appears to be aggregate human security. Each member of a community has an individual human right to, say, some minimum level of security, if he or she needs it. It is only when a certain threshold of aggregate need exists, however, that the establishment of an institution takes place. For example, a police organization with its constitutive institutional role occupants—police officers—is not established merely because a single person's right to security is not being realized. When such a threshold of aggregate need exists, what is required is collective or joint action on the part of many persons. Accordingly, a cooperative enterprise or institution is established that has as a collective end the provision of security to the needy many by means of the joint activity of the police officer members of the police institution.

The (collective) duty to assist may, then, in certain cases, imply the duty to establish and support institutions to achieve the object of the duty. Once such institutions with their specialized role occupants are in place it may be that we generally have no further duty to assist within the area of the institutions' operations. Indeed, it may be that generally we should not even *try* to assist, given our relative lack of expertise and the likelihood that we will get in the way of the role occupants. Moreover, these specialized role occupants have duties that they did not have before and, indeed, that no one had before the establishment of the institutional role with its specific duties. For example, police officers may have an institutional and, indeed now, *moral* duty to put themselves in harm's way in a manner and to an extent that is not morally required of ordinary citizens and, indeed, that was never morally required of anyone prior to the establishment of police organizations.

Once institutions and their constitutive roles have been established on some adequate moral basis, such as the duty to aid, then those who undertake these roles necessarily put themselves under obligations of various kinds—obligations that attach to, and are in part constitutive of, those roles. To understand the specific content of institutional role morality, then, we need to examine the purposes—to meet aggregate security needs, in the case of police officers—which the various institutions and their constitutive roles have been formed to serve, and the way in which roles must be constructed in order to achieve those purposes. Of course, one only comes to have an institutional role through voluntary action, but the morality that comes with that role is not itself ultimately grounded in the individual's choice but rather in the larger purposes (collective ends) of the role, or so the argument goes.

RELATED TOPICS

Proxy Agency in Collective Action (Ch. 5), Corporate Agency: The Lesson of the Discursive Dilemma (Ch. 19), Status Functions (Ch. 23), Collective Intentions and Collective Moral Responsibility (Ch. 24), Complicity (Ch. 25), Institutions and Collective Intentionality (Ch. 27), Collective Intentionality in the Law (Ch. 29).

REFERENCES

Bovens, M. (2007) "Analysing and Assessing Accountability," *European Law Journal* 13 (4): 447–68.
Bratman, M. (2014) *Shared Agency: A Planning Theory for Acting Together*, Oxford: Oxford University Press.
Copp, D. (2007) "Collective Moral Autonomy Thesis," *Journal of Social Philosophy* 38 (3): 369–88.
Duff, R.A. (2007) *Answering for Crime: Responsibility and Liability in the Criminal Law*, Oxford: Hart Publishing.
Erskine, T. (2001) "Assigning Responsibilities to Institutional Moral Agents," *Ethics and International Affairs* 15 (2): 67–85.
Estlund, D. (2007) *Democratic Authority: A Philosophical Framework*, Princeton, NJ: Princeton University Press.
Fischer, J.M. (1999) "Recent Work on Moral Responsibility," *Ethics* 110 (1): 93–139.
French, P. (1979) "The Corporation as a Moral Person," *American Philosophical Quarterly* 16 (3): 207–15.
Gert, B. (2007) *Common Morality*, Oxford: Oxford University Press.
Giddens, A. (1984) *The Constitution of Society: Outline of the Theory of Structuration*, Cambridge: Polity.
Gilbert, M. (1989) *On Social Facts*, Princeton, NJ: Princeton University Press.
Harre, R. (1993) *Social Being: A Theory for Social Psychology*, (2nd edition), Oxford: Blackwell.
Ladd, J. (1982) "Philosophical Remarks on Professional Responsibility in Organizations," *International Journal of Applied Philosophy* 1 (2): 58–70.
Lewis, D. (1969) *Convention: A Philosophical Study*, Cambridge, MA: Harvard University Press.
List, C. & Pettit, P. (2011) *Group Agency*, Oxford: Oxford University Press.
May, L. (1992) *Sharing Responsibility*, Chicago: University of Chicago Press.
Mellema, G. (2006) "Collective Responsibility and Qualifying Actions," in P. French (ed.) *Midwest Studies in Philosophy* 30: 168–75.
Miller, K. & Tuomela, R. (1988) "We-intentions," *Philosophical Studies* 53 (3): 367–89.
Miller, S. (1992) "Joint Action," *Philosophical Papers* 21 (3): 275–99.
——— (2006) "Collective Moral Responsibility: An Individualist Account," in P. French (ed.) *Midwest Studies in Philosophy* 30: 176–93.
——— (2007a) "Against the Moral Autonomy Thesis," *Journal of Social Philosophy* 38 (3): 389–409.
——— (2007b) "Joint Action: The Individual Strikes Back," in S.L. Tsohatzidis (ed.) *Intentional Acts and Institutional Facts: Essays on John Searle's Social Ontology*, Dordrecht: Springer Press.

——— (2010) *The Moral Foundations of Social Institutions*, New York: Cambridge University Press.

——— (2014) "Police Detectives, Criminal Investigations and Collective Moral Responsibility," *Criminal Justice Ethics* 33 (1): 21–39.

——— (2015) "Joint Epistemic Action and Collective Moral Responsibility," *Social Epistemology* 29 (3): 280–302.

——— (2016) "Joint Epistemic Action: Some Applications," *Journal of Applied Philosophy* (online edition, 22 February).

Miller, S. & Makela, P. (2005) "The Collectivist Approach to Collective Moral Responsibility," *Metaphilosophy* 36 (5): 634–51.

Moore, M.S. (2009) *Causation and Responsibility: An Essay in Law, Morals and Metaphysics*, Oxford: Oxford University Press.

Schauer, F. (2003) *Profiles, Probabilities and Stereotypes*, Cambridge, MA: Harvard University Press.

Schweikard, D. & Schmid, B. (2013) "Collective Intentionality," in E.N. Zalta (ed.), *The Stanford Encyclopedia of Philosophy* (Summer 2013 edition), http://plato.stanford.edu/archives/sum2013/entries/collective-intentionality/.

Searle, J.R. (2011) *Making the Social World: The Structure of Human Civilization*, Oxford: Oxford University Press.

Strawson, P.F. (1962) "Freedom and Resentment," *Proceedings of the British Academy* 48: 187–211.

Szigeti, A. (2014) "Are Individualist Accounts of Collective Moral Responsibility Morally Deficient?" in A. Konzelmann-Ziv and H.B. Schmid (eds) *Institutions, Emotions and Group Agents: Contribution to Social Ontology*, Dordrecht: Springer.

Thompson, D.F. (1980) "Moral Responsibility and Public Officials: The Problem of Many Hands," *American Political Science Review* 74 (4): 259–73.

Zimmermann, M. (1985) "Sharing Responsibility," *American Philosophical Quarterly* 22 (2): 115–22.

NOTES

1. So collective goods in this sense are not public goods in the economists' sense of public goods, i.e. non-excludable, non-rival goods.
2. Although it is indirectly relevant. See final point in Section 3 below.
3. Accordingly, there is no need to hold that collective responsibility attaches to collective entities per se, as collectivist theorists such as Margaret Gilbert (1989) and (in a somewhat different vein) Christian List and Philip Pettit (2011) have done. For criticisms of these collectivist accounts see Seumas Miller and Pekka Makela (2005) and Andras Szigeti (2014).
4. And in part by their collective ends.
5. There are, of course, any number of alternative voting systems in democracies. However, this does not materially affect the analysis on offer here.
6. Assuming there are only two possible verdicts, guilty and not guilty; which is not the case in some juris-dictions, e.g. Scotland.
7. Chains of institutional and moral responsibility consist of a process in which the completion of one stage institutionally triggers the commencement of the next stage, e.g. arrest is followed either by the suspect being charged or released within a specified time frame.
8. For a contrary view see Gert (2007).

VI

Collective Intentionality and Social Institutions

Introduction to Part VI

Marija Jankovic and Kirk Ludwig

Institutions—governments, families, languages, legal systems, corporations—are among the elements of the social world that have the most profound impact on our lives. Some of them, like governments, wield substantial power over us, and we are naturally interested in developing theories about the appropriate scope of that power. Others, like families or languages, are so intertwined with our conception of ourselves, that investigating how they become so embedded in our lives promises important insights into ourselves as social agents. The chapters in this part describe several ways in which the philosophical theory of social institutions intersects with the theory of collective intentionality.

In the concluding paragraphs of the chapter on status functions, Searle presents a temptingly simple picture of institutions. They are all created through a single procedure—assigning a status function to an object by way of a status function declaration. The assignment of status function is intrinsically tied up with collective intentionality since, according to Searle, an object can have the status only in virtue of the collective recognition or acceptance that it has that status. In Chapter 27, "Institutions and Collective Intentionality," Frank Hindriks questions the view that institutions necessarily depend on collective intentionality. Collective attitudes are typically invoked to explain the normativity of institutions, their construction out of individual attitudes, and their function in solving collective action problems. Hindriks argues that these features of institutions can all be explained in other ways, and that the more plausible thesis is that institutions are based on collective intentionality as a matter of contingent fact.

Regardless of whether collective intentionality is necessarily involved in the creation of institutional reality, it remains a (perhaps contingent) fact that attitudes of collective intentionality are at the center of most of our actual institutions. We should expect that the philosophical theory of social institutions and the theory of collective intentionality can be put into a fruitful conversation. The following two chapters, Chapters 28 and 29, can be read as contributions to this conversation. And they indeed show that it is one in which each side can learn from the other.

In one direction of influence, insights from the theory of collective intentionality can bring to the fore new perspectives in the debates about the nature of a particular social institution. In Chapter 28, "Collective Intentionality and Language," Marija Jankovic describes several important but overlooked ways in which understanding language use as a collective intentional activity can illuminate issues in philosophy of language. Two of the central arenas of language use—conversation and communication—are collective intentional action types. Thus, progress in our understanding of collective intentionality is bound to have consequences for a number of long-standing issues in the philosophy of language, such as the nature of linguistic and speaker meaning, the principles of pragmatic inference, and so on.

In the other direction of influence, careful study of social institutions can help us make progress on the issues in the theory of collective intentionality. In Chapter 29, "Collective Intentionality in the Law," Gideon Yaffe argues that criminal law embeds a theory of necessary and sufficient conditions for collective intention and action. He describes three ways in which an agent can be justifiably punished for a crime of a certain type even though what the agent did does not constitute a crime of that type—complicity, joint perpetration, and vicarious liability. For example, A can be guilty of arson as an accomplice if she hands B a jug of gasoline that B then uses to set someone's house on fire. He argues that this can be explained given the principle that an agent can be justifiably punished for a crime of a certain type if the agent is a member of a collective that is justifiably attributed with a crime of that type. If so, then the doctrines of complicity, joint perpetration, and vicarious liability embed a theory of three kinds of relations that tie people strongly enough to constitute a collective that is responsible for a certain action.

Finally, in Chapter 30, "Collective Intentionality and Methodology in the Social Sciences," Deborah Perron Tollefsen describes the methodological debates encountered in the study of the social world. The first is the old debate between methodological individualism and holism, which is historically a debate about the methodology of social sciences, but is also relevant in thinking about the proper method of the philosophical research of collective intentionality. Tollefsen refines the terms of the debate, distinguishing, for example, between approaches that require that social phenomena be explained only in terms of individual intentional states (including, e.g. we-intentions) and those that require that they be explained in terms of concepts drawn from the conceptual scheme used to understand individual agency (which would exclude we-intentions, at least as *sui generis* attitudes). She calls the latter approaches, following Gilbert, *singularist*. Both deserve the name of individualism, yet have very different methodological commitments. Tollefsen argues that the philosophical theories of collective intentionality widely adopt individualism while rejecting singularism. Finally, she argues that the philosophical study of collective intentionality benefits from expanding its methodology to incorporate the insights of empirical research.

27

Institutions and Collective Intentionality

Frank Hindriks

Institutions shape many of the things people do. Think of waiting in line in a store, giving way to a car coming from the right (or left, depending on where you are), ordering a meal in a restaurant, buying a house, getting married, chairing a meeting, and running a multi-billion corporation. There are two perspectives on what examples such as these have in common in both philosophy and the social sciences. According to the first, each is an instance of a particular kind of behavioral regularity or recurring activity. According to the second, each is an instance of a certain kind of rule-based behavior. These two perspectives are sometimes combined (Aoki 2011; Greif and Kingston 2011; Hindriks and Guala 2015). In this vein, Raimo Tuomela (2013) argues that institutions are norm-governed social practices. As social practices are recurring activities and as norms are rules, this definition—on which I will rely in this chapter—captures both perspectives.

Institutional actions are caused by intentional attitudes. Often those attitudes are taken to be individual beliefs and desires—or, in the language of rational choice theory, expectations and preferences. I might, for instance, have a preference to drive on the right hand side of the road given that everybody else drives on this side. My decision to drive on this side of the road, on this type of analysis, is based in part on what I take your beliefs and desires to be, as well as on mutual beliefs about such attitudes. Your attitudes feature as parameters in my decision process and vice versa. In light of each other's attitudes, we mutually adjust our behavior to each other. This form of interdependence is commonly referred to as "strategic interaction."

Alternatively, institutional actions might involve a stronger form of interdependence in that they are based on collective attitudes instead. Collective intentional states involve a "we" as their subject instead of merely two or more I's. As a consequence, a collective attitude such as a belief or intention will be conceived of as "our" attitude, our belief or intention. Parties to a collective attitude take each other's agency more seriously than agents whose attitudes are regarded merely as parameters in strategic interaction. As I discuss in Section 1, different theories of collective intentionality spell this out in different terms.

The core thesis that I consider in this chapter is that institutional actions necessarily depend on collective attitudes. I refer to this as "the Necessity Thesis" (NT).

After introducing the notion of collective intentionality in Section 1, I discuss three arguments in favor of the Necessity Thesis in Sections 2–4. Section 2 zooms in on the normative dimension of institutions and evaluates the claim that institutional normativity can only be adequately explicated in terms of collective attitudes. Section 3 addresses the idea that institutions are social constructions, and assesses the claim that social construction is to be understood in terms of collective attitudes. Section 4 introduces the thesis that institutions solve problems of interaction—more specifically, coordination problems and collective action problems—and considers the claim that collective attitudes are required for successfully doing so. None of these claims survive careful scrutiny, or so I argue. It is much more plausible to maintain instead that collective attitudes contribute to institutions as a matter of contingent fact.

1. DOING SOMETHING TOGETHER: THE I-MODE AND THE WE-MODE

Theories of collective intentionality are first and foremost theories of doing something together. Prominent examples in the literature include going for a walk together, painting a house together, carrying a piano upstairs, and dancing the tango (note that only this last example concerns an institutional action as dancing the tango is a rule-governed recurring activity). Note that you and I might paint a house without doing it together. You might intend to paint it red, while I intend to paint it blue. When I learn of your plan, I might set out to frustrate your endeavor, as it conflicts with mine. Michael Bratman (1992, 1993, 2014) argues that in order for us to paint the house together we must have a common objective and conceive of it in terms of "we." More specifically, each of us must have an intention of the form "I intend that we J" (where "J" is an action specified in cooperatively neutral terms). Furthermore, these intentions interlock among others in that mine depends causally on yours and yours on mine. In addition to this, the perhaps provisional and incomplete subplans we each have are intended by each of us to mesh, that is, to be capable of co-realization. This is part of what it means for us to work with each other rather than against or parallel to each other. Bratman says that a group of agents who have interlocking intentions to J that meet these conditions share an intention to J or have a shared intention to J.

Bratman's goal in developing a theory of collective intentionality is to identify a set of attitudes that can play the same functional role at the social level as individual intentions play at the individual level. The core idea is that they form a reliable and predictable guide for thought and action. Individual intentions, Bratman (1987) argues, are governed by norms of rationality including, for instance, consistency, means-end coherence, and stability. Intentions should be consistent with one another, an intention to do something comes with a demand to settle on appropriate means to satisfy it, and, even though an agent can reconsider an intention, rampant and arbitrary reconsideration invites a charge of irrationality. These norms also apply to shared intentions, or so Bratman argues. In this context, they typically give rise to shared action that is both reliable and predictable, and in this sense shared intentions play the same functional role as individual intentions. A central feature of Bratman's analysis is that, as shared attitudes are interlocking individual attitudes, the commitments involved in shared intentions are individual commitments.

Margaret Gilbert's (1989, 1996, 2006) theory of collective intentionality differs particularly in this last respect. Gilbert argues that, in contrast to individual commitments, collective intentions come with joint commitments. Such joint commitments entail reasons for action that are typically sufficient for performing the relevant action. Gilbert holds that those involved in a joint commitment, for instance to go for a walk together, have a social obligation to act accordingly. As a consequence, none of the relevant individuals can unilaterally rescind from it. This means that, if one of us departs from what we intend—say you start walking faster and faster and make it difficult for me to keep up—the other can appropriately rebuke him or her. The upshot is that, as Gilbert conceives of them, collective intentions have a normative dimension. The obligations they entail are social rather than moral. A collective intention can have an immoral content, as when two people intend to kill an innocent person for no good reason. Gilbert argues that, even if the moral reasons not to do this are weightier, they do not annul the social reasons implicated by the collective intention. Gilbert says that when a group of agents have a joint commitment to, for example, take a walk together, they have a joint intention to do so.

These two theories are often seen as rivals. And they do indeed involve conflicting claims. In particular, whereas Gilbert maintains that social obligations are inherent to doing something together, Bratman denies this (see Section 3). At the same time, however, it seems possible to treat the core of these theories instead as complementary. This is in effect what Tuomela (2003, 2013) is on to when he argues that collective attitudes can be held in the I-mode or the we-mode. A key difference between attitudes held in the we-mode versus attitudes held in the I-mode is that only the former involve collective commitment that gives rise to *sui generis* social obligations (see Section 3 for more on the we-mode). I will refer to collective attitudes that involve collective commitment as "joint attitudes," and to those that do not as "shared attitudes." In light of this, I will treat Bratman's and Gilbert's theories as respective proposals for analyses of shared and joint intentions (see Tuomela 2003 and 2013 for alternatives). The functional and normative dimensions highlighted in the discussion of their views will play an important role in the arguments for and against conceiving of institutional action as social interaction.

Bratman (2014) maintains that his analysis of shared intentions captures a form of modest sociality. More demanding analyses of collective attitudes can be taken to capture stronger forms of sociality. In light of this, I use the term "social interaction" to refer to forms of interdependence that are stronger than those involved in strategic interaction. I will refer to the individual attitudes involved in strategic interaction as "common attitudes" (List 2014).[1] Whereas strategic interaction involves common attitudes, social interaction involves either shared or joint attitudes (or both). Recall the Necessity Thesis formulated in the introduction: institutional actions necessarily depend on collective attitudes. In terms of forms of interaction, a proper defense of the Necessity Thesis consists of an answer to why institutional action should be conceived of in terms of social interaction—shared or joint—rather than strategic interaction.

2. INSTITUTIONS AS NORMS

Institutions are governed by social norms. In order for an institution to exist, relevant social norms have to be in force in the context at issue. The first argument for collective intentionality as a necessary component of institutions (NT) is that in order for an institutional norm to be in force it must be the object of collective attitudes. The idea is that a norm must provide the relevant agents with reasons for acting accordingly in order for it to be in force in the context at issue. Gilbert (1989, 1996, 2008) presents a version of this argument in her work on joint intentions and conventions (see also Tuomela 2013). She maintains that 'an adequate account of convention . . . will explain the normativity of convention' (Gilbert 2008: 9). Social norms such as those involved in conventions, she argues, provide people with reasons for action due to the fact that they are the objects of a joint attitude. Joint attitudes come with joint commitments, and such commitments provide people with reasons to act accordingly.

According to Gilbert (2008: 12), a regularity in behavior is a convention when those who are party to it are jointly committed to the claim that it ought to be conformed to.[2] Gilbert formulates three conditions of adequacy for the analysis of conventions: the collectivity criterion, the appropriate-ought criterion, and the offense criterion. According to the collectivity criterion, those who are party to a convention form a social group. Her analysis meets this criterion given that she analyzes the notion of a social group in terms of joint commitment. According to the appropriate-ought criterion, 'the normativity of convention, at its core, is the normativity of joint commitment' (2008: 14). This means that 'each party owes every other this conformity to the commitment'. Gilbert holds that it is a matter of rationality that joint commitments entail reasons. According to the offense criterion, 'the account must explain how, for any convention, the non-conforming action of any party offends against the other parties, as such, who are for this reason in a position to rebuke him, their having the convention being a complete justification for the rebuke' (2008: 7). This criterion is closely related to the appropriate-ought criterion, as the fact that participants owe each other conformity to the convention entails that they are in a position to rationally criticize each other for failing to conform to it. These criteria are met because of the role that joint commitment plays in Gilbert's analysis.

It may well be that joint attitudes do indeed involve joint commitments that offer those who are party to them reasons for action. If that is indeed the case, then joint attitudes can account for the normativity of conventions in particular and of institutions more generally. This does not imply, however, that joint attitudes are necessary. There may be alternative ways of accounting for the fact that institutions involve norms that govern behavior. There are two alternatives that the argument fails to rule out. First, the normativity involved in institutions might be moral. Second, institutions might involve norms that do not provide people with reasons for action. If either of these alternatives works, a joint commitment account of institutions does not provide for an adequate argument in the favor of NT.[3]

A moral conception of the normativity of institutions will deny that collective attitudes as such can provide reasons. Instead, that normativity is based on moral norms. Note that attitudes can play a role in such an account. It leaves open that attitudes provide people with reasons when combined with moral norms. Consider a simplified version of Scanlon's (1990) principle of fidelity: If A provides B assurance that she will do x, in the absence of special justification, A must do x unless B consents to x's not being done. It seems plausible that someone can provide someone else assurance by having certain attitudes and communicating them to the other person. This may in turn require an institutional context that provides for a socially accepted and recognized way of doing this. The key point is that the principle of fidelity entails a moral obligation if certain empirical conditions are satisfied including in particular the instantiation of certain attitudes. This moral conception of institutional normativity differs from the joint commitment conception in that the ultimate basis for institutional obligations is a moral principle rather than a set of attitudes per se (see Hindriks 2013).

The assumption that these two conceptions have in common is that institutions are genuinely normative in the sense that institutions as such provide people with reasons for action. Whereas this view might appeal to philosophers, it is rare if non-existent among social scientists. Practices can be governed by social norms without those norms as such providing people with reasons. Presumably, a social practice is governed by a norm only if that norm features in the attitudes of at least some participants. However, when these are common or shared attitudes, they do not entail normative reasons. It is important to realize at this point that a norm can affect the reasons people have without that norm as such providing those reasons. For instance, people might tend to disapprove of norm-violating behavior and they might dislike to be disapproved of. Alternatively, there might be sanctions for norm-violating behavior, and people might be motivated to avoid incurring those sanctions. The upshot is that norms can be in force without being genuinely normative in either the rational or moral sense.

3. SOCIAL CONSTRUCTION

Institutions are social constructions. This means that they are man-made. Houses are man-made as well, but they are not social constructions in the intended sense. Institutions are social constructions in that they depend on the attitudes of a number of agents. The second argument for collective intentionality as a necessary component of institutions (NT) is that those attitudes must be collective attitudes. Full-blown social construction consists of two features: performativity and reflexivity. Performativity is a matter of intentional states making a difference to the way the world is. Pieces of paper are money, for instance, because people have certain attitudes towards those pieces of money. Reflexivity is a matter of collective attitudes being conceptually entailed by true claims about institutions. The very fact that a piece of paper is money entails that people have attitudes towards that piece of paper (or pieces of paper of that kind). Both performativity and reflexivity are captured by what I have elsewhere called "the Collective Acceptance Principle" (CAP), with "CA" for collective acceptance and "p" for an institution-expressing proposition such as "pieces of paper of this particular kind are money" (Hindriks 2012):[4]

$$[CAP] \; CA(p) \leftrightarrow p$$

The right-to-left implication represents performativity; the left-to-right implication represents reflexivity. Collective acceptance is a matter of collective belief or intention. If CAP is correct, social construction involves collective attitudes (and necessarily so, as CAP is meant to express a necessary truth). As social institutions are socially constructed, CAP entails NT.

Searle's (1995) claim that institutions are systems of constitutive rules suggests he subscribes to CAP. The structure of a constitutive rule is "X counts as Y in C". The Y-term refers to an institutional status—what Searle calls "a status function"—such as money. The X-term refers to an entity on which the status is imposed, such as a piece of paper. And the C-term specifies a context, for instance a country. An entity counts as another entity exactly if this is collectively accepted to be the case. Searle (2010: 68–9) explicitly addresses the two core features of social construction, performativity and reflexivity. All this suggests that he subscribes to CAP.

Searle's main argument as to why institutions depend on collective acceptance is that they involve status functions that can only be performed due to their being collectively accepted. He contrasts status functions to the functions of technical artifacts such as screwdrivers and hammers. The physical features of such artifacts (typically) enable the performance of certain actions such as driving screws or hammering nails. Status functions are different in that the physical features of the entities that have them are more or less arbitrarily related to those functions. Collective acceptance is required in order for those entities to perform them. It is not very clear what Searle takes a status function to be (see Hindriks 2013). It seems to mean nothing more than that having a status enables people to perform certain actions, or to use the relevant entity for designated purposes (which involve deontic powers). The Y-term of a constitutive rule designates the concept of the status function.

Even if social construction is best explicated in terms of performativity and reflexivity, Searle fails to establish that the relevant attitudes must be collective attitudes. It will not help to point out that statuses are normative. As discussed in Section 2, individual attitudes can support socially existing norms. The striking thing is that Searle (2010) has come to the same conclusion. He has come to adopt a rather permissive use of the term "collective acceptance" (as well as "collective recognition") that encompasses situations in which all attitudes are ordinary individual attitudes (to which he adds a requirement of mutual belief; 2010: 58). Collective attitudes are not needed, he argues, because institutions do not require cooperation (2010:58). I return to this claim in Section 4.

Tuomela (2002, 2007, 2013) develops a similar argument in more detail. He argues that the attitudes required for social construction are joint attitudes. Institutions may involve shared attitudes as well, but in contrast to joint attitudes they will not be constitutive of those institutions (Tuomela 2007: 195).[5] Furthermore, entities will have institutional statuses only if people act on the basis of the relevant attitudes (2007: 186). None of this implies, however, that those actions have to be generated by collective attitudes, let alone by joint attitudes. Sometimes Tuomela (2007: 185) restricts his claim to full-blown institutions. Now it may well be that certain institutions depend on joint attitudes rather than common attitudes or even shared attitudes. It is not very clear, however, what it adds to call those "full-blown." Perhaps they best fit the folk concept of institutions, or perhaps they are a particularly rich or in some sense ideal form of institutions. Be that as it may, none of Tuomela's arguments establish NT.

The upshot is that neither Searle nor Tuomela provide valid arguments in favor of the constructive version of NT. One might think that collective attitudes make institutions more successful as social constructions. This could mean that they are more inclined to perform the relevant institutional actions. There might be more to it, however. Perhaps an institution is (more) successful when it (better) serves its function. I explore this idea in the next section.

4. THE FUNCTION OF INSTITUTIONS

Institutions can be seen as norm-governed social practices that serve a function. The function is that of solving problems of interaction, more specifically of coordination problems and collective action problems. In coordination problems, there are several courses of action that serve the interests of the agents more or less equally well. For instance, each of us has an interest in driving on the same side of the road as the others do. In principle, it does not matter much which side this is. Collective action problems involve substantial conflicts of interests. When you and I go hunting, for instance, our combined efforts make a difference to our success, but each of us has an incentive to do less than the other. Solving problems of these two kinds is a matter of settling on a common course of action that is beneficial for all. According to the functionality argument for NT, collective attitudes are necessary for institutions to serve their function. Recall Searle's claim that institutions need not be supported by collective attitudes because they do not require cooperation (Section 3). The functionality argument turns this claim on its head. The key idea is that, as institutions are cooperative devices, they do require collective attitudes.[6]

Tuomela provides the most developed defense of this functionality argument. He argues that institutions serve to satisfy basic human needs in the face of scarcity (Tuomela 2007: 192, 195). They create collective order in the process, and provide individuals with guidance as to what to do. Institutions are "meant to" or "purport to" solve interaction problems of the two kinds mentioned (2002: 167–8, 171; 2007: 196).[7] Hence, a social institution 'is *functionally successful* if it solves a collective action dilemma' (2002: 171). The function of money is 'usability of exchange and storage of value' (2013: 239). At the same time, Tuomela maintains that the function of an institution 'can be represented by the outcomes that they lead to because of collective action', adding that those outcomes usually are equilibria (2013:239). Tuomela takes this to require collective attitudes in the we-mode. He maintains: 'cooperative solutions cannot rationally be arrived at without a substantial amount of we-mode action towards shared collective goals' (2002: 182; cf. 159 and 175–6). He also claims that 'we-mode we-attitudes are required by institutional action' (2002: 175–6; see also 2007: 182–3 and 195).

Tuomela maintains that joint attitudes are 'functionally the best' (2013: 239). Furthermore, he argues that the degree to which an institution can perform its function depends on the extent to which the attitudes it involves are joint attitudes. More specifically, 'the better the group succeeds in acting as a group [i.e. on the basis of joint attitudes] the more functional it and its institutions will be in the long run'. (Tuomela 2002: 181) This is a contingent explanatory claim that can be reformulated as what I call "the Tendency Thesis": institutions tend to function better when they are supported by collective attitudes rather than individual attitudes especially when they are joint attitudes. How well an institution functions is a matter of how large its cooperative benefits are.

How exactly do, according to Tuomela, joint attitudes contribute to the functionality of institutions? When they face a situation that calls for a decision, people who have adopted joint attitudes engage in group reasoning. Such reasoning enables people to settle on a particular course of action in a coordination problem. When faced with a conflict of interest, group reasoning leads to the (possibly implicit) formulation of a group utility function. Such a group utility function ranks highest what is collectively best. As it is formulated from a group perspective, it does not reflect any of the individual differences in interests there might be when the situation is conceived of in strategic terms. A group simply does not conceive of any situation involving only its members as a collective action problem (Tuomela 2013: 205–11). People are collectively committed to this preference ordering, and they have a group reason to perform the action that maximizes it. Tuomela assumes that this normative reason will typically have a substantial motivational force. In this way, joint attitudes are conducive to cooperation not only in the case of coordination problems but also in the case of collective action problems.

The functionality argument for NT faces the challenge that there are numerous rival explanations that account for the cooperative dimension of institutions that depend exclusively on individual attitudes. David Lewis's (1969) game-theoretic analysis of conventions is perhaps the most famous one. The only attitudes that he invokes are individual beliefs and desires (expectations and preferences). The agents involved in an interaction problem conceptualize it in strategic terms and do not think in terms of "we" as agents engaged in social interaction do. Rather than relying on group reasoning, the relevant individuals can use a salient feature or a correlation device, perhaps some meaningful feature in the immediate environment, in order to coordinate their behavior. Conventions are solutions to coordination problems. Also for collective action problems, however, numerous solutions are available that do not invoke collective attitudes, irrespective of whether they are joint or shared. I mentioned two at the end of Section 2: the approval-seeking motive and sanctions. Tuomela does not have a convincing argument that these alternatives are conceptually inadequate. The explanatory Tendency Thesis fares better in this respect. Tuomela (2013) discusses empirical evidence for why joint attitudes are more conducive to cooperation than other attitudes. It may well be, then, that joint attitudes enable institutions to serve their function better than other attitudes.

5. CONCLUSION

The Necessity Thesis, according to which collective attitudes are necessary for institutions, has turned out to be implausible in that none of the three arguments offered in favor of it are particularly convincing. The normative, constructive, and functional dimensions of institutions can each be accounted for in other ways. At the same time, however, collective attitudes account for these dimensions in potentially powerful ways. Institutions can involve norms that are merely socially believed to exist and do not have any genuine normative force. It might be, however, that when people are collectively committed to a norm, the relevant institution has normative power of its own, independently of morality. Furthermore, institutions constructed out of collective attitudes might be particularly solid. Collective attitudes serve well to explain the symbolic significance involved in institutions. Finally, institutions supported by collective attitudes, particularly those in the we-mode, might be especially successful in generating cooperative benefits. In other words, collective attitudes enable institutions to fulfill their function.

RELATED TOPICS

Collective Action and Agency (Ch. 1), Non-Reductive Views of Shared Intention (Ch. 2), Reductive Views of Shared Intention (Ch. 3), Proxy Agency in Collective Action (Ch. 5), Collective Belief and Acceptance (Ch. 7), Corporate Agency: The Lesson of the Discursive Dilemma (Ch. 19), Status Functions (Ch. 23), Institutional Responsibility (Ch. 26).

REFERENCES

Aoki, M. (2011) "Institutions as Cognitive Media Between Strategic Interactions and Individual Beliefs," *Journal of Economic Behavior and Organization* 79: 20–34.

Bratman, M. (1987) *Intention, Plans, and Practical Reason*, Cambridge, MA: Harvard University Press.

——— (1992) "Shared Cooperative Activity," *Philosophical Review* 101 (2): 327–41.

——— (1993) "Shared Intention," *Ethics* 104: 97–113.

——— (2014) *Shared Agency: A Planning Theory of Acting Together*, Oxford: Oxford University Press.

Gilbert, M. (1989) *On Social Facts*, London: Routledge.

——— (1996) *Living Together: Rationality, Sociality, and Obligation*, New York: Rowman & Littlefield.

——— (2006) *A Theory of Political Obligation: Membership, Commitment, and the Bonds of Society*, Oxford: Oxford University Press.

——— (2008) "Social Convention Revisited." *Topoi* (1–2): 5–16.

Greif, A. and Kingston, C. (2011) "Institutions: Rules or Equilibria?" in N. Schofield and G. Caballero (eds), *Political Economy of Institutions, Democracy and Voting*, Berlin: Springer.

Hindriks, F. (2012) "But Where Is the University?" *Dialectica* 66 (1): 93–113.

——— (2013) "Collective Acceptance and the Is-Ought Argument," *Ethical Theory and Moral Practice* 16 (3): 465–80.

Hindriks, F. and Guala, F. (2015) "Institutions, Rules and Equilibria: A Unified Theory," *Journal of Institutional Economics* 11 (3): 459–80.

Lewis, D. (1969) *Convention: A Philosophical Study*, Cambridge, MA: Harvard University Press.

List, C. (2014) "Three Kinds of Collective Attitudes," *Erkenntnis* 79: 1601–22.

Scanlon, T. (1990) "Promises and Practices," *Philosophy and Public Affairs* 19: 199–226.

Searle, J.R. (1995) *The Construction of Social Reality*, New York: The Free Press.

——— (2010) *Making the Social World: The Structure of Human Civilization*, Oxford: Oxford University Press.

Tuomela, R. (2002) *The Philosophy of Social Practices: A Collective Acceptance View*, Cambridge: Cambridge University Press.

——— (2003) "The We-Mode and the I-Mode," in F. Schmitt (ed.), *Socializing Metaphysics: The Nature of Social Reality*, Lanham, MD: Rowman and Littlefield.

——— (2007) *The Philosophy of Sociality: The Shared Point of View*, Oxford: Oxford University Press.

——— (2013) *Social Ontology: Collective Intentionality and Group Agents*, Oxford: Oxford University Press.

NOTES

1. An attitude is a common attitude if within a population everybody has the attitude, and this is a matter of common awareness, which requires that everybody believes that every other member has the attitude and that this is a matter of mutual belief (List 2014).

2. Tuomela defends a rather similar view of group norms more generally when he argues that 'the very notion of a group norm is a we-mode notion' (2007: 205).

3. Gilbert takes herself to analyze a central everyday sense of the term "convention." She acknowledges that there is another sense of "convention" that is captured by Lewis's (1969) analysis of the term, although she doubts that this is a prevalent folk concept (Gilbert 2008: 16). Lewisian conventions, however, are not intrinsically normative. In light of this, Gilbert's acknowledgement that there can be other senses of the

term leaves open that she holds that the normativity of conventions—of those conventions that do involve norms—has to be explicated in terms of joint commitment.

4. This is a simplified version of Tuomela's (2002) Collective Acceptance Thesis.

5. According to Tuomela (2013: 34–46), joint attitudes not only involve collective commitment, they also require a collective for which the relevant attitude is satisfied only if it is satisfied for all members. Furthermore, they constitute group reasons.

6. Recall from Section 1 Bratman's argument that shared attitudes are needed for reliable and predictable shared action, that this is their functional role. The claim considered in this section is that joint attitudes are needed for reliably and predictably reaping cooperative benefits in institutional settings.

7. Tuomela also claims that institutions '*tend to* offer cooperative solutions to collective action dilemmas' (2007: 183, emphasis added).

28

Collective Intentionality and Language

Marija Jankovic

Concepts from the study of collective action have been used in explanations of a wide range of phenomena related to language and communication. For example, *common knowledge* has been used in accounts of common ground (e.g., Stalnaker 2002), speaker meaning (Schiffer 1972), speaker reference (Clark and Marshall 1981), linguistic conventions (Lewis 1969), and insinuation (Pinker 2009); *joint attention* has been used to explain the evolution of language (Tomasello 2008) and infant word learning (Sabbagh and Baldwin 2005); and *joint commitment* has been used in accounts of conversational context (Gilbert and Priest 2013) and joint meaning (Carassa and Colombetti 2009). As this list shows, it would be difficult to do justice in the space allotted to all the ways in which research into collective intentionality promises to advance our understanding of language. In this chapter, I focus on a core element of the theory of collective intentionality, the theory of collective intentional action, and its relation to the study of language.

Two kinds of collective—and, I will argue, collective *intentional*—action are central to our use of language: conversation and communication. A virtual consensus in the theory of collective intentional action holds that it is not a mere aggregation of individually intentional actions. According to one kind of view, the explanation of collective intentional action needs to appeal to the distinctive content of the *intentions* of the participants.[1] For example, my intention to run a lap around the field alone and my intention to do it as a part of a four-person relay are states with distinct contents. I will call intentions of *individuals* to participate in a collective intentional action *participatory* or *we-intentions*.[2] We act together intentionally when we act on the basis of interlocking we-intentions.

If this is correct, then we cannot hope to theorize about our use of language without appealing to our distinctive capacity for collective intentionality, and specifically, the capacity to form and act on we-intentions. In this chapter, I examine several ways in which the theory of collective intentional action provides a basis for reconceiving traditional debates in the philosophy of language. Section 1 describes resources that become available for pragmatic explanation when conversations are understood as rule-governed collective intentional activities. Section 2 argues that minimal communication is a collective intentional action type and explores the consequences for accounts of speaker meaning. Section 3 tentatively proposes an account of linguistic meaning that employs irreducibly collectivist concepts.

1. CONVERSATION

Conversations are understood as cooperative enterprises by Gricean pragmatics, the most influential account of conversational implicature (the ability of speakers to mean something different from what they literally say). According to Paul Grice, participants in a typical conversation act, and expect each other to act, in accordance with the Cooperative Principle, which requires each party to a conversation to make her move "such as is required, at the stage at which it occurs, by the accepted purpose or direction of the talk exchange in which [she is] engaged" (Grice 1989: 26).

The accepted purpose of the talk exchange can involve the interlocutors' domain (i.e. non-linguistic) goals. If so, the cooperativeness required by the Cooperative Principle can be understood as helpfulness in fulfilling the domain goals of our interlocutors.[3] To see how the presumption of this sort of helpfulness can generate implicatures, consider a speaker who says "There's a gas station around the corner" to the frustrated driver repeatedly turning the ignition key. The speaker implicates that the gas station is open because of the expectation that she is helpfully proposing a way to reach a mechanic, a goal the driver clearly has.

But certain types of implicature can be made in adversarial conversations. (See Davis 1998; Pinker 2009.) Consider this example from Davis (1998: 116).

> Karen: Were you with Jennifer last night?
> George: I was out drinking with the guys.

George implicates that he was not with Jennifer last night, even if Karen knows that he is lying.

This is sometimes cited as a problem for accounts of conversational implicature that invoke the presumption of cooperativeness (e.g., in Davis 1998). But we can admit that there is a good sense in which courtroom cross-examinations or price negotiations can be described as adversarial, while at the same time maintaining that there is a sense in which any conversation must be cooperative to be possible at all. Richmond Thomason makes this suggestion.[4]

> [I]t helps us to get a better grip on the relevant sort of cooperation if we think not so much of shared *domain goals* as of a shared sense of where the conversation has been and where it is heading: the common plan of the conversation. Sharing a plan of the conversation may involve shared goals, but these have to do with discourse rather than with the subject at hand, and such goals, along with a common sense of the conversational record, can be shared even though the participants have few domain goals in common.
>
> (Thomason 1990: 356)

It is tempting to think that an elucidation of a common plan for the conversation will appeal to the notions from the theory of collective intentional action. A good place to start is the observation that conversation is a *collective intentional action type*, a type of action—like playing chess or dancing the waltz—that can only be performed by several agents acting together intentionally.[5] It's certainly possible for agents who have conflicting goals to engage in collective intentional action. For example, two agents playing chess may have few goals in common besides that of playing chess. And even when the game might be described as adversarial, the shared goal of playing chess entitles the participants to certain expectations about each other's behavior. Here is how.

Let's say that a goal is *shared* between us only if each of us has a we-intention in favor of us bringing it about.[6] Tuomela and Miller (1988) and Michael Bratman (e.g., in 1999) have suggested that participatory intentions of this kind are (or include) intentions of individuals in favor of the *joint activity*. For example, if we intend to play chess, each of us intends that *we* play chess.

What is it to intend *our* activity? Bratman's (1987) planning theory of intention enables us to think of these intentions as exactly analogous to intentions directed at individual actions, i.e. as states of commitment to a plan governed by norms such as consistency and means-end coherence. If I intend to perform some individual action at some future time, I am rationally required not to adopt intentions incompatible with my performing that action at that time. For example, if I intend to go to New York on Wednesday, I cannot at the same time plan to be in London on Wednesday. I am also rationally required to eventually settle on means—for example, buying a plane ticket and driving to the airport. Similarly, if I intend that we perform some collective action *J-ing*, I am committed to filtering out intentions incompatible with *both of our J-ing*. So I cannot rationally plan to interfere with your doing your part. For example, I cannot plan to steal your chess pieces when I intend that we play chess. Our intention incorporates a more or less specific plan for how to perform our joint action, and I am committed to doing my part in accordance with that plan. And—provided that the cost of help does not cause me to abandon my intention in favor of *J-ing*—I will intend to help you do your part if needed, for example, to help you look for a misplaced piece.[7] Finally, when I believe that we both have these participatory intentions, I will expect you to act and intend accordingly—i.e., to not do things incompatible with both of our *J-ing*, to act in accordance with our plan, as well as, in some circumstances, help me perform my part of the collective action.

Some collective actions, like going to New York together, require agents to devise a joint plan. Some, like playing chess, are governed by rules constitutive of the action type. The rules play the role of a *pre-made* partial plan—our further planning is restricted by the rules.[8] So, if I intend that we play chess and believe that you do as well, I expect you to conform to the rules. The rules of chess do not have the form of a description of a specific action-sequence that counts as chess (as, for example, rules for waltzing do), but allow us to generate many acceptable sequences. So, when we intend to play chess, our intention is not that we perform a particular sequence of actions, but that we act in accordance with the rules and perform one of the acceptable sequences.

Let us apply this to conversations. Like a game of chess, a conversation is a collective intentional action type—one cannot have a conversation alone or with someone else but without intending to. Agents may share an intention to have a conversation without sharing non-discourse goals. Conversations described as adversarial are those in which parties who have a shared intention to have a conversation have conflicting domain goals.[9] Insofar as they share this intention, each is committed to not doing anything that would hinder the other's performance of her part. Typically, each will come to intend to do what is required to help the other perform her part, and each will expect this of the other.

This framework gives us a general mechanism behind presupposition accommodation (in line with the proposal by Thomason (1990)). Presupposition accommodation can be seen as an instance of a general tendency of participants in a collective intentional action to help the others do their part. Call our interlocutors A and B. Suppose that A recognizes the sub-plan associated with B's intention to contribute to the conversation and sees that certain assumptions need to be added to the conversational record if B's sub-plan is to succeed. Insofar as A intends that *they* have a conversation, she intends for B to do her part in accordance with the plan B associates with her participatory intention. A therefore intends to help B by adding the assumption in question to the conversational record, i.e. by accommodating. If B knows that A shares with her the intention that they have a conversation, she will expect A to accommodate and plan her utterance accordingly.

Like games of chess, conversations are governed by rules. But unlike rules of chess, rules of conversation are not explicitly recorded. Nevertheless, the fact that some conversational moves are considered appropriate and others not is a mark of their existence.[10] Research on discourse coherence relations (e.g., Hobbs 1985; Asher and Lascarides 2003; Ginzburg 2012) and work in artificial intelligence on discourse structure in the design of dialogue systems (e.g., Grosz and Sidner 1990; Grosz and Kraus 1996; Traum and Hinkelman 1992; Traum and Allen 1994; Poesio and Traum 1997) can be seen as aimed at describing these rules. When two people intend to have a conversation, they intend to engage in an activity governed by these rules. This does not mean that they have the same idea of where the conversation is going, as the rules do not determine a uniquely appropriate sequence of speech acts. As Ginzburg puts it,

> [a]s in most games the beginning and end are reasonably constrained [. . .] What will happen in the middle is typically less predictable [. . .] once an initial move is made, what happens subsequently (or rather what is expected to happen) is constrained by certain conventions but this still leaves things quite open-ended.
>
> (Ginzburg 2012: 61)[11]

Still, insofar as they intend to have a conversation, they intend and expect each other to act in accord with these rules.

For an example of how implicatures may be generated by such conversational rules, consider the following from Solan and Tiersma.

> John and Mary have recently started going together. Valentino is Mary's ex-boyfriend. One evening, John asks Mary, "Have you seen Valentino this week?" [a] Mary answers, "Valentino's been sick with mononucleosis for the past two weeks." [b] Valentino has in fact been sick with mononucleosis for the past two weeks, but it is also the case that Mary had a date with Valentino the night before.
>
> (Solan and Tiersma 2005: 231)

This is an antagonistic conversation insofar as the parties have conflicting goals with respect to disclosing some information. Mary still seems to implicate that she did not see Valentino. Most people would likely say that her answer to John was misleading. A plausible conversational rule might be that an utterance that follows an interrogative is either a direct or an indirect answer to the question (provided that the question can be answered). If it is, then when I ask you a question, I expect your utterance to be a direct or indirect answer to my question, and you make your utterance expecting me to expect that. Thus, John expects (and Mary expects him to expect) that Mary's utterance (b) is an indirect answer to his question (a). (b) conveys that the answer to the question is "no," given the assumption (that John believes is shared) that Valentino's sickness prevented him from meeting people.[12]

2. COMMUNICATION

An important task for philosophy of language is to explain the nature of linguistic meaning. On one type of view, any explanation has to start from the fact that language is fundamentally a tool for communication.[13] This starting point naturally leads to the view that words mean what they do in virtue of their function in communication, that is, in virtue of the fact that they are (conventionally) used to mean a certain thing. To mean something is to perform a certain kind of action, i.e. to act with a certain intention. Putting this together yields the view that words mean what they do in virtue of intentions of language users regarding their use in communication. This is the basic thesis of theories of meaning that take linguistic meaning to be a function of mental attitudes of language users, which have dominated discussions of meaning since at least the middle of the last century. (See, e.g., the classic papers in Grice 1989; Schiffer 1972; Lewis 1975.) If the theory of collective intentional action reshapes our understanding of intentions of participants in communication, it will also reshape our understanding of linguistic meaning.

Specifically, if the basic action by which speakers mean something is an action by which they participate in a collective intentional action (conversation or communication), then speaker meaning is a matter of having an appropriate sort of we-intention, and so the psychological states that form the basis of linguistic meaning are we-intentions. But most accounts of speaker and linguistic meaning fail to recognize this, taking, on the one hand, conversations to be cooperative enterprises, while embracing a thoroughgoing individualism concerning speaker meaning and communicative action, on the other.[14] Prominent examples are Grice and David Lewis.

It was Grice's powerful idea that once we describe communicative acts as intentional activities of a certain type, we will be able to explain puzzling linguistic phenomena as applications of general principles of rational action to the case of communicative action (rather than *sui generis* principles of language use). But—despite the implication of the Cooperative Principle—Grice ultimately views conversation as a sequence of individually intentional actions of utterers. This is apparent in Grice's (1957) analysis of an act by which an utterer contributes to a conversation—a *meaning* act. According to Grice, a meaning act is an act performed with an intention to *produce* or *induce* a response in an audience by way of the audience's recognition of that very intention. The terms "produce" and "induce" frame communication as something done *to* rather than *with* an audience.

For even if the inducement of a response requires the audience to do something, she need not intend to do it as her part in a collective intentional action with the utterer.[15]

Lewis is even more explicit in taking a communicative act to be an individual act of the utterer. Communicative use of language involves coordination between "the *action* of the truthful speaker and the responsive *believing* of his trusting hearer" (Lewis 1975: 11; emphasis added). The audience's part, believing—which is "not ordinarily an action" (1975:11)—is contrasted with the speaker's part, an action.[16]

But the audience's *believing*, while itself not an action, may be a culmination of the things the audience *does*. There are two possible loci of the audience's active contribution: (1) attending to and (2) interpreting the utterance. Attending is at least typically an action—determinate forms of attending, such as listening or looking, are straightforwardly active, as is eavesdropping, the (unintended by the utterer) equivalent of the audience's part in communication. And, at least in some cases, the open-ended process of communicative interpretation involves conscious entertaining of hypotheses, especially when interpretation runs into difficulty.[17]

If we turn to neighboring disciplines, we find research that explicitly invokes the collectivist nature of communication to be more common. For example, psycholinguist Herbert Clark sets out the thesis of his 1996 book *Using Language* as follows.[18]

> Language use is really a form of joint action. A joint action is one that is carried out by an ensemble of people acting in coordination with each other. As simple examples, think of two people waltzing, paddling a canoe, playing a piano duet, or making love. . . . Doing things with language is [. . .] different from the sum of a speaker speaking and a listener listening. It is the joint action that emerges when speakers and listeners—or writers and readers—perform their individual actions in coordination, as ensembles.
>
> (Clark 1996: 3)

Clark calls the actions individuals perform as their parts in joint actions (e.g., playing the flute as one's part in the flute–piano duet) *participatory actions*. These are to be distinguished from merely individual actions (e.g., practicing the flute part of the piano–flute duet). Joint actions are performed by means of participatory actions in the following way.

JA: Ensemble A-and-B is doing joint action k if and only if:

0. the action k includes 1 and 2;
1. A intends to be doing A's part of k and believes that 0;
2. B intends to be doing B's part of k and believes that 0.

(Clark 1996: 61)

Speaker meaning (which Clark calls *signaling*) is an essentially participatory action described by SM.[19]

SM: In presenting (a signal) s to A, speaker S means for A that p if and only if:

0. the communicative act r includes 1 and 2;
1. S presents s to A intending that p as part of r;
2. A recognizes that p as part of r.

(Clark 1996: 131)

For example, Amir presents the utterance "Please sit down" (*s*) to Berit, meaning that she is to sit down (*p*). Amir presents the utterance as a part of their joint action expecting Berit to do her part, namely, recognize that he meant for her to sit down, in part by recognizing that he made the utterance with the intention in 1.

Allwood (1995) points out, against Clark, that one-sided communicative acts are possible, citing examples such as "I warned him but he didn't hear me." It's useful to distinguish two questions in this context. The first, tracing back to Austin (1962), is whether ordinary speech acts—such as requesting, informing, promising—can be performed without the audience's uptake. The second is whether ordinary speech acts are essentially participatory. Allwood's example concerns the first question. The novel part of Clark's account concerns the second.[20] A meaning act such as warning could be the speaker's part in a certain collective action type, and a speaker can count as having performed it, regardless of whether the collective action of which it is a part was itself successfully performed. Analogously, one can serve a tennis ball without its being returned or even noticed by an opponent, even though serving a ball is an essentially participatory act. It is true that Clark's account, as stated, requires that meaning acts be recognized by an audience, but to correct this we need not abandon the collectivist spirit of the account. For example, we may say that in presenting (a signal) *s* to A, speaker S means for A that *p* if and only if S presents *s* *intending* to do a part in an act that consists of 1 and 2.

The more serious problem with SM is that it fails to give sufficient conditions for speaker meaning. For example, it incorrectly counts Herod's showing the head of John the Baptist to Salome (Grice 1957) as an example of speaker meaning. There is a collective action consisting of (i) Herod's presenting the head to Salome intending that she come to believe that John the Baptist is dead and (ii) Salome's recognizing that John the Baptist is dead. Herod makes his gruesome utterance intending to do his part and expecting Salome to do hers. But he does not *mean that* John the Baptist is dead by presenting his head.

The reason Clark's account fails can perhaps be traced back to his general account of joint action. Clark's stock examples of joint actions used to motivate the account (waltzing, paddling a canoe, singing a duet) are all collective intentional actions. But the conditions in JA (and, by extension, SM) suffice at most for the performance of a collective action. To see this, suppose that *k* is a collective action that can be performed either intentionally or unintentionally, e.g., two of us walking out of a talk together. Suppose that each of us intends that she and some other person walk out together because each is embarrassed to be the only person to leave before the talk is finished. Each waits until someone else seems ready to go and then gets up to leave. If we leave the talk in this way, the conditions in JA are satisfied. But we are not thinking that we are cooperating with the other. Instead each is taking advantage of someone else's independent behavior to further her own goal of leaving together. We have performed a collective action but not a collective *intentional* action.

It is thus worth pursuing the thought that Clark's account fails not for being too collectivist but for not being collectivist enough. Specifically, it treats speaker meaning as a part of a collective rather than a collective *intentional* action. It's only the latter that sees communication as a manifestation of the distinctive capacity of our minds for collective intentionality.

So, is communication a collective *intentional* action type? It may seem obvious that it's not, because speakers can communicate by, for example, making lying assertions.

But even if communication isn't necessarily a collective intentional action, its account may have to appeal to a *core* practice that is. For example, an account may take the core practice to be communication between a sincere speaker and a trusting audience, and explain non-core cases as conceptually dependent on the core practice. For example, a lying asserter typically intends to get her addressee to believe that she is engaging in the core practice. This type of account still makes irreducible appeal to collectivist notions such as that of a we-intention. So let's call an account of communication *collectivist* if it ultimately draws on the concept of a we-intention.

Two familiar observations about the utterer's meaning support collectivist accounts: (i) that the utterer's meaning is incompatible with certain kinds of deception and (ii) that there is a difference between meaning something and intentionally letting it be known. Both features of speaker meaning, puzzling for an individualist, can be shown to follow from the general features of collective intentional action. In addition, empirical research about the development of communication in children supports the collectivist account. I describe these considerations in favor of the collectivist account in turn.

Deception. Strawson (1964) and Schiffer (1972) observed that the utterer's meaning is incompatible with the kind of deception illustrated by the following case.[21] Anna cannot bring herself to ask Bes, who has overstayed his welcome, to leave. If she could fake a yawn, she could get him to think that she is tired, but she knows that she can't do so convincingly. Instead, she fakes a yawn intending, not that Bes take it as a real one, but that he think that he was intended to take it as a real one. Bes is intended to reason like this (without realizing that he is intended to reason like this): "Anna is clearly trying to fake a yawn, wanting me to think that she's tired. I see through it, but I don't want to stay where I'm not welcome." If Anna fakes a yawn with these intentions, she does not *mean* that she is tired.

What does the incompatibility of the utterer's meaning with this kind of deception show about communicative action? The lesson typically drawn is that the utterer has to intend his intention to produce a response to be *transparent*, where transparency is interpreted epistemically—as common knowledge or a weaker replacement, such as mutual manifestness.[22] Nothing short of *common* knowledge (or *mutual* manifestness) will do. Anna intends (i1) to produce a response in Bes (a belief that she is tired) and intends (i2) for him to recognize intention (i1). Requiring only a further intention (i3) for Bes to recognize intention (i2) does not help. For if (i3) itself is not intended to be recognized, this complicated intention is still deceptive (given that the pattern is general), and so not an intention by which Anna means something.[23]

However, we readily consider communication successful when the audience recognizes the communicative intention, regardless of whether the utterer believes that she does. A fanciful example is that of reading a message in a bottle. A more mundane case is a text message which is read, but to which the sender receives no reply. The sender might not know whether communication occurred, but knows it is possible. These are successful cases of communication of the type the sender intends, but sender and reader do not have common knowledge that the reader recognizes the sender's intention. So requiring the speaker to intend that it be common knowledge or mutually manifest that she has a meaning intention (whose content subsumes that requirement) is too strong, as an account embedding this requirement would exclude many ordinary cases of communication. One might attempt to save the account by positing that communication succeeds when the utterer's meaning intention is *recognized*, rather than *satisfied*. But this amounts to special pleading for communicative action. In acting with a meaning intention, the utterer aims to communicate with an audience. It is odd to consider the attempt successful despite the intention with which he acts remaining unsatisfied.

We get out of this difficulty if we reinterpret the lesson of the deception cases. Anna's intention is not just sneaky—it is sneaky because it's manipulative. She does not intend that Bes come to think that she is tired as a result of them doing something *together intentionally*. She intends to do something *to* rather than *with* Bes. So an account that takes communication to be a collective intentional action can explain why Anna's yawn is not an instance of utterer meaning. Since she does not make her utterance (the yawn) with an intention to participate in a collective intentional action which results in Bes acquiring a certain belief, her act is not an instance of utterer meaning.[24]

Meaning vs letting know. As Grice noted in his landmark 1957 paper, there is a difference between meaning something and openly and intentionally letting someone know that same thing. Compare starting to pack my suitcase in front of you with telling you "I am leaving now." In both cases I convey the same information. So what is gained if, instead of merely letting you know something, I tell you (or, e.g., if instead of letting you know that I want you to do something, I request that you do it)? Many philosophers, especially those writing on testimony, have pointed out that in telling, and not in letting know, the speaker enters into a specific relationship with an addressee. The core of this relationship has been thought to consist in different things: the speaker's giving her word and inviting the addressee to take it (Elgin 2005), the speaker's giving an assurance to the addressee (Moran 2005), the speaker's inviting the addressee's trust (Hinchman 2005), and so on. But on all accounts, the relationship is normatively significant in the sense that it entails that a speaker has certain obligations to the addressee.

On individualist accounts of speaker meaning, it is mysterious how a communicative act might create such obligations. But if we take *telling* to be the speaker's part in a collective intentional action, we are able to view them as an example of the sort of obligations that agents committed to a collective activity generally have to each other.[25] What is the content of these obligations? Minimally, agents who intend to perform a collective action owe it to each other to act as they had planned or (absent special understanding and a prior explicit plan) in a way appropriate to the joint activity in question. Assume, for the sake of illustration, that telling, as a speaker's part in a certain communicative action, is appropriately performed when the speaker utters *p*, when *p* is true. If so, the speaker owes it *to the addressee* to utter truthfully, as his part in their joint action. This is yet another example where the collectivist view of communication enables us to explain a linguistic phenomenon as an instance of a general phenomenon in collective intentional action.

Origins of communication. Tomasello takes human communication to be a 'fundamentally cooperative process' on several levels. For example, interlocutors collaborate in structuring the conversational context as information that is jointly believed and perceptual environment that is jointly attended to (Tomasello 2008: 73–82). Moreover, he says, they 'create the joint intention of successful communication' (107).

Tomasello describes research concerning the development of communication in children that supports the collectivist account. Children begin engaging in cooperative pointing—a prototypical complete communicative act for Tomasello (2008: 62–6)—at around 12 months of age. This is surprising, as the behavioral form (the characteristic extending of the index finger) emerges as early as 3 months of age, and the young children have some of the prosocial motives that prompt communicative behavior. Tomasello argues that cooperative pointing can emerge only after children acquire the capacity for collective intentionality, specifically the ability to create common ground with others.[26] The prerequisites of collective intentionality emerge between 9 and 12 months of age (Tomasello 2008: Sections 4.1 and 4.2), which is also when cooperative pointing emerges. This suggests that children's capacity for communicative pointing relies on the capacity for collective intentionality.[27]

3. LINGUISTIC MEANING

In what follows, I briefly describe an account of linguistic meaning that builds on the collectivist account of communication. Consider the following example of a meaning-conferring agreement. Revere and the sexton of the Old North Church (Newman) agree that Newman will hang one lantern in the belfry if the British are coming by land, so that Revere can alert the countryside. We can describe their agreement as an adoption (among others) of the following joint action plan.

P1:

(i) Just on the precondition that the British are coming by land at t, S performs action type α (in this case, of hanging one lantern in the belfry) and

(ii) R attends to S at t to determine whether (i)

If Newman and Revere act together intentionally in accordance with P1, then in doing α (whatever it may be), Newman means that the British are coming by land. If each comes to have a standing we-intention that they act in accordance with P1 in the appropriate circumstance, α *means*, for them, that the British are coming by land. In having these intentions, Revere and Newman confer a *status function* onto α. This is a function that an object can only have if there is collective acceptance that it is to have that function. For example, being a 20-dollar bill is a status function, for a piece of paper has this function only because those involved in monetary transactions collectively accept that it is to have this function.[28] And so is *meaning that the British are coming by land*, as the action type of hanging a lantern only has this function because Revere and Newman collectively accept that it is to have it. According to Searle, the imposition of a status function is 'the radical movement that gets us from such simple social facts as that we are sitting on a bench together or having a fistfight to such institutional facts as money, property, and marriage . . .' (1995: 41). If this picture is correct, it is also the movement that gets us from non-conventional communication to conventional language.

Generalizing, we can say that for a signal to have a meaning is for it to have a status function in core communication. This in turn is for it to fill the α-role in the following type of plan.

PC:

(i) on the precondition that C at t, S performs action type α and

(ii) R attends to S to determine whether (i).

P1 above is a determinate form of PC with respect to the position of precondition C.

It does not matter to the parties what object fills the α-role, as long as they coordinate on the same object. In this sense, linguistic meaning is arbitrary. When they do coordinate, this amounts to their having conditional we-intentions to use that object in the role of α in a certain determinate form of PC. They therefore enter into a kind of agreement on an arbitrary solution to a coordination problem, i.e. adopt a *convention*.

This account of linguistic meaning employs the notions of we-intention and status function, which are the fundamental building blocks of institutional reality. It represents language as continuous with the rest of social reality, providing us with our final example of the explanatory power of the collectivist approaches to language use.

CONCLUSION

As the preceding discussion illustrates, many traditional questions in philosophy of language seem to admit of promising resolutions once thoroughgoing individualism, which forms the implicit background of the traditional debates, is identified and rejected. This is not surprising once we recognize that language use is, at least centrally, a collective intentional action. The collectivist account of conversation enables us to articulate the sense in which conversations are necessarily cooperative. The collectivist account of communication preserves the key insights of Grice's seminal work but is immune to standard objections to Gricean analyses of communicative and meaning intentions, which cannot be answered without rejecting the individualist construal of the project. It also has significant explanatory power in enabling us to embed the analysis of meaning in a broader account of joint action and the social reality.

ACKNOWLEDGEMENTS

Thanks to Bill Butchard and Kirk Ludwig for comments and suggestions on earlier drafts.

RELATED TOPICS

Collective Action and Agency (Ch. 1), Non-Reductive Views of Shared Intention (Ch. 2). Reductive Views of Shared Intention (Ch. 3), Interpersonal Obligation in Joint Action (Ch. 4), Common Knowledge (Ch. 14), Status Functions (Ch. 23).

REFERENCES

Allen, J.F. and Perrault, C.R. (1980) "Analyzing Intention in Utterances," *Artificial Intelligence* 15 (3): 143–78.
Allwood, J. (1995) "An Activity Based Approach to Pragmatics," *Gothenburg Papers in Theoretical Linguistics* 76: 1–38.
Austin, J.L. (1962) *How to Do Things with Words*, Oxford: Oxford University Press.
Asher, N. and Lascarides, A. (2003) *Logics of Conversation*, Cambridge: Cambridge University Press.
Bratman, M. (1987) *Intention, Plans, and Practical Reason*, Cambridge, MA: Harvard University Press.
——— (1992) "Shared Cooperative Activity," *Philosophical Review* 101 (2): 327–41.
——— (1999) "I Intend that We J," in *Faces of Intention: Selected Essays on Intention and Agency*, Cambridge: Cambridge University Press.

——— (2014) *Shared Agency: A Planning Theory of Acting Together*, Oxford: Oxford University Press.

Carassa, A. and Colombetti M. (2009) "Joint Meaning," *Journal of Pragmatics* 41 (9): 1837–54.

Chomsky, N. (1966) *Cartesian Linguistics: A Chapter in the History of Rationalist Thought*, Cambridge: Cambridge University Press.

Clark, H.H. (1996) *Using Language*, Cambridge: Cambridge University Press.

Clark, H. and Marshall, C. (1981) "Definite Reference and Mutual Knowledge," in A. Joshi, B.H. Weber and I.A. Sag (eds) *Elements of Discourse Understanding*, Cambridge: Cambridge University Press.

Davis, W.A. (1998) *Implicature: Intention, Convention, and Principle in the Failure of Gricean Theory*, Cambridge: Cambridge University Press.

Elgin, C.Z. (2005) "Word Giving, Word Taking," in D. Wood and J. Medina (eds) *Truth: Engagements Across Philosophical Traditions*, New York: Blackwell.

Fodor, J. (1983) *Modularity of Mind*, Cambridge, MA: MIT Press.

Gilbert, M. and Priest, M. (2013) "Conversation and Collective Belief," *Perspectives in Pragmatics, Philosophy & Psychology*.

Ginzburg, J. (2012) *The Interactive Stance*, Oxford: Oxford University Press.

Grice, H.P. (1957) "Meaning," *Philosophical Review* 66 (3): 377–88.

——— (1969) "Utterer's Meaning and Intention," *Philosophical Review* 78 (2): 147–77.

——— (1989) "Logic and Conversation," in *Studies in the Way of Words*, Cambridge, MA: Harvard University Press.

Grosz, B.J. and Kraus, S. (1996) "Collaborative Plans for Complex Group Action," *Artificial Intelligence* 86 (2): 269–357.

Grosz, B.J. and Sidner, C.L. (1990) "Plans for Discourse," in P.R. Cohen, J.L. Morgan and M.E. Pollack (eds) *Intentions in Communication*, Cambridge, MA: MIT Press.

Harman, G. (1974) "Review of *Meaning* by Stephen R. Schiffer," *The Journal of Philosophy*, 71 (7): 224–9.

Hinchman, E. (2005) "Telling as Inviting to Trust," *Philosophy and Phenomenological Research* 70 (3): 562–87.

Hobbs, J.R. (1985) "On the Coherence and Structure of Discourse," Technical report CSLI-85-37, Center for the Study of Language and Information, Stanford University.

Jankovic, M. (2014) "Communication and Shared Information," *Philosophical Studies*, 169 (3): 489–508.

Lewis, D. (1969) *Convention: A Philosophical Study*, Cambridge MA: Harvard University Press.

——— (1979) "Scorekeeping in a Language Game," *Journal of Philosophical Logic* 8 (1): 339–59.

——— (1975) "Languages and Language," in K. Gunderson (ed.) *Minnesota Studies in the Philosophy of Science*. Minneapolis: University of Minnesota Press.

Ludwig, K. (2007) "Collective Intentional Behavior from the Standpoint of Semantics," *Noûs* 41 (3): 355–93.

——— (2016) *From Individual to Plural Agency: Collective Action 1.*, Oxford: Oxford University Press.

——— (2017) *From Plural to Institutional Agency: Collective Action 2.*, Oxford: Oxford University Press.

Miller, S. (2016) "Assertions, Joint Epistemic Actions and Social Practices," *Synthese* 193 (1): 71–94.

Moore, R. (2016) "Gricean Communication, Joint Action, and the Evolution of Cooperation," *Topoi*: 1–13, doi:10.1007/s11245-016-9372-5.

Moran, R. (2005) "Getting Told and Being Believed," *Philosophers' Imprint* 5 (5): 1–29.

Pinker, S. (2009) "The Evolutionary Social Psychology of Off-Record Indirect Speech Acts," *International Journal on Humanistic Ideology* 1: 59–89.

Pinker, S., Nowak, M.A. and Lee, J.J. (2008) "The Logic of Indirect Speech," *Proceedings of the National Academy of Sciences* 105 (3): 833–8.

Poesio, M. and Traum, D.R. (1997) "Conversational Actions and Discourse Situations," *Computational Intelligence* 13 (3): 309–47.

Potts, C. (2008) "Indirect Answers and Cooperation: on Asher and Lascarides's 'Making the Right Commitments in Dialogue'," *Workshop on Implicatures, University of Michigan Linguistics and Philosophy, November 21–3, 2008*.

Roberts, C. (1996) "Information Structure in Discourse: Towards an Integrated Formal Theory of Pragmatics," *Working Papers in Linguistics-Ohio State University Department of Linguistics*: 91–136.

——— (2017) "Speech Acts in Discourse Context," in D. Fogal, D. Harris and M. Moss (eds) *New Work on Speech Acts*, Oxford: Oxford University Press.

Sabbagh, M.A. and Baldwin, D. (2005) "Understanding the Role of Communicative Intentions in Word Learning," in *Joint Attention: Communication and Other Minds: Issues in Philosophy and Psychology*, Oxford: Oxford University Press.

Schiffer, S.R. (1972) *Meaning*, Oxford: Clarendon Press.

Searle, J.R. (1990) "Collective Intentions and Actions," in P.R. Cohen, J.L. Morgan and M.E. Pollack (eds) *Intentions in Communication*, Cambridge, MA: MIT Press.

——— (1995) *The Construction of Social Reality*, New York: Free Press.

Solan, L.M. and Tiersma, P.M. (2005) *Speaking of Crime: The Language of Criminal Justice*, Chicago: University of Chicago Press.

Sperber, D. and Wilson, D. (1986) *Relevance: Communication and Cognition*, Cambridge, MA: Harvard University Press.

Stalnaker, R. (2002) "Common Ground," *Linguistics and Philosophy* 25 (5–6): 701–21.

Strawson, P.F. (1964) "Intention and Convention in Speech Acts," *Philosophical Review* 73 (4): 439–60.

Thomason, R.H. (1990) "Accommodation, Meaning, and Implicature: Interdisciplinary Foundations for Pragmatics," in P.R. Cohen, J.L. Morgan and M.E. Pollack (eds) *Intentions in Communication*, Cambridge, MA: MIT Press.

Tomasello, M. (2008) *Origins of Human Communication*, Cambridge, MA: MIT Press.

Traum, D. and Allen, J. (1994) "Discourse Obligations in Dialogue Processing," in *Proceedings of the 32nd Annual Meeting of the ACL*: 1–8.

Traum, D. and Hinkelman, E. (1992) "Conversation Acts in Task-Oriented Spoken Dialogue." *Computational Intelligence* 8 (3): 575–99.

Tuomela, R. (2002) "Collective Goals and Communicative Action." *Journal of Philosophical Research* 27: 29–64.

Tuomela, R. and Miller, K. (1988) "We-intentions." *Philosophical Studies*, 53 (3): 367–89.

Wittgenstein, L. (2010) *Philosophical Investigations*, Oxford: John Wiley & Sons.

NOTES

1. See, e.g., Bratman (2014) and Ludwig (2016).
2. See Chapters 2 and 3 of this volume.
3. See Davis (1998: 114–17); Pinker et al. (2008); Pinker (2009); Sperber and Wilson (1986: 162); and Asher and Lascarides (2003: 391). Allen and Perrault (1980) does not appeal to the Cooperative Principle, but offers an account of cooperation as the detecting and removing of obstacles in the plans of others and shows how cooperativeness so understood can generate Quantity implicatures.
4. See also Roberts (1996 and 2017) for a model of discourse that sees conversations as collaborative activities that aim toward joint goals construed as questions implicitly or explicitly posed that the conversation aims to resolve.
5. For more on the notion of a collective action type see Ludwig (2016) and Chapter 1 of this volume.
6. I follow Searle (1990); Bratman (1992, 1999, 2014); and Ludwig (2007, 2016). See Chapters 2 and 3 of this volume for a discussion.
7. Must I intend to help you do your part? Bratman (1992: 336–7) imagines a case of unhelpful singers who intend to sing a duet together though neither would ever help the other, but delight in her partner's failure. If neither singer makes a mistake, and they sing the duet, they do it together intentionally. This suggests that parties to a collective intentional activity do not need to intend to help each other. What sense can we make of the intention that *we J* in such a case? It seems best to think of this as a limiting case in which I intend your activity insofar as I intend to do my part (and in this sense enable you to play your role in our joint action) and do not intend to interfere with your doing your part. But this is truly a limiting case. For unhelpful singers any deviation from their initial plan is enough for each to abandon the intention. But intentions are typically more stable than this, and so parties to a shared intention maintain it under a more robust set of circumstances. This is why an intention to help others do their part is generally associated with shared intention.
8. This, I think, is what Bratman, e.g., in Bratman (1992: 339) calls "pre-packaged cooperation."

9. The fact that quantity implicatures fail in adversarial conversations shows that the assumption of helpfulness is essential for them, but not for, say, relevance implicatures.

10. Wittgenstein's (2010) idea of a language game is perhaps the earliest ancestor of this kind of idea. Lewis's (1979) also lends itself to the idea of conversations as collective actions governed by the rules for updating the shared information participants in a conversation are required to keep track of. There is a lot of work following this idea of Lewis both in linguistics and philosophy under the heading of Discourse Representation Theory.

11. Constitutive rules and conventions should be distinguished in general. It is a rule of chess that a pawn moves a certain way, and one is not playing chess if one is not acting in accord with this rule. It is a convention that thus-and-such a piece of wood serves as a pawn—it is arbitrary and we could use any object as a pawn as long as we agree on the same one.

12. This explanation draws on Potts (2008).

13. Though this is disputed by some, for example, Chomsky (1966).

14. Though work that employs notions from the research of collective intentionality in the study of communication and speech acts is emerging. See Miller (2016); Gilbert and Priest (2013); Tuomela 2002; Carassa and Colombetti (2009); and so on.

15. This follows from the observation that collective intentional action is not simply a collection of individual actions. See Chapters 1–3 of this volume for discussion.

16. This requires a revision of Lewis's (1969) general account of convention—conventions that govern use of language cannot be regularities in action as there is nothing that an audience does.

17. The thesis that *communicative* interpretation is active is compatible with viewing semantic interpretation as modular, and therefore automatic. Semantic interpretation is not the totality of communicative interpretation. For example, the utterance has to be recognized as having a certain illocutionary force. Considerations that help one determine whether an utterance of "you should do some community service" is an order (e.g., when said by a judge) or a suggestion (when said by a friend) do not seem to belong to a module. They seem to be in principle unbounded, whereas modular inference is standardly taken to operate on a proprietary body of information—see, e.g., Fodor (1983).

18. See also Traum and Hinkelman (1992), who analyze discourse into a sequence of what they call *core speech acts* (such as informing, suggesting). Core speech acts are "multiagent collaborative achievements, taking on their full effect only after they have been grounded, i.e., acknowledged" (Poesio and Traum 1997: 317).

19. It is unclear whether SM generalizes to non-imperative signs. Consider replacements for "*p*" when the symbol has an indicative meaning, e.g., "the British are setting out by sea." Then we have to say that S presents s to A intending that the British are setting out, but that is not the right intention, and it is not what A recognizes.

20. Though Clark himself sometimes conflates the two issues, e.g., in Clark (1996: 137–9).

21. For responses, see Grice (1969); Schiffer (1972); Sperber and Wilson (1986); and Harman (1974).

22. For common knowledge see Schiffer (1972). Standardly: a group of people commonly know p just in case they all know p, they all know that they know p, they all know that they know that they know p, and so on. For mutual manifestness see Sperber and Wilson (1986). It is mutually manifest to a group of people that p just in case it is manifest to them that p, it is manifest to them that it is manifest to them that p, and so on. A proposition is manifest to someone just in case 'he is capable at that time of representing it mentally and accepting its representation as true or probably true' (Sperber and Wilson 1986: 31). For a criticism of these views see Jankovic (2014).

23. And so more generally, for any intention (i_n), for the audience to recognize intention (i_{n-1}), as long as (i_n) itself is not intended to be recognized, there is no utterer's meaning.

24. Why, more precisely, does Anna's intention not count as an intention to participate in a collective intentional action? In terms of Bratman's (2014) account, she does not intend that Bes acquire the belief as a result of *meshing sub-plans* of their intentions (see Jankovic (2014) for an explanation along these lines), in terms of Ludwig's (2016) account, she does not intend that they act in accordance with a *shared* plan (see especially chapter 14), etc.

25. The observation that participants in a collective activity have these obligations is due to Gilbert (e.g., 1989). There has been a debate over whether these obligations necessarily accompany collective intention, but it is not disputed that they typically accompany it. See Chapter 4 of this volume for a discussion.

26. Tomasello's collectivist account of communication provides a basis for an account of the evolution of human communication on which it requires our species-specific capacity for shared intentionality. See Tomasello (2008: ch. 5–7) for an accessible presentation. For a criticism pertinent to the topic of this chapter see Moore (2016).

27. An obvious objection is that the dependence goes the other way around, that the development of collective intentionality is due to the development of the infants' capacity to communicate. For Tomasello's response to this sort of objection, see Tomasello (2008: ch. 4.2.2).

28. For more on the notion of status function see Searle (1995), Chapter 23 of this volume, and Ludwig (2017).

29

Collective Intentionality in the Law

Gideon Yaffe

1. INTRODUCTION

The law specifies a large diversity of government responses to the intentional behavior of citizens, often specifying a different response, or no response, to happenings that are not the products of agency. For instance, a contractual term by which the parties intended to be bound is far more likely to be enforced; if the testator of a will intended a particular person to inherit his property, the courts are far more likely to give the property to that person; whether injuries caused were also intended might be crucial both for determining liability for those injuries and for determining the size of the damage award; a person who drives past a bank might be guilty of attempted bank robbery, but only if he intended to rob the bank; someone in possession of a large quantity of cocaine is guilty of a much more serious crime if he intended to distribute it; what Congress intended when they drafted a statute often determines whether that statute applies to a particular case; what the long-dead framers of the Constitution intended to refer to with the words "cruel and unusual" is central to the question of whether or not a particular kind of punishment, such as the death penalty, or "chemical castration," can be administered by a state government. And so on. In all of these cases, what the government is authorized to do, under the law, varies with the intentionality of the behavior in question.

In all of these diverse contexts, the law sometimes specifies a government response to individual intentional behavior, sometimes to behavior of a group. Both individuals and groups can make contracts, and so in so far as contract law predicates government behavior on the intentions of contractors, it cares about both individual and collective intentionality. And this is hardly unique to contract law. In the law, we care both whether *the CEO* intended to defraud the investors and whether *the company* did. We care both whether *the driver* intended to rob the bank and whether *the gang* did. We care both whether *Thomas Jefferson* intended the term "cruel and unusual" to include the death penalty, and whether *the Continental Congress* did.

Law often encodes philosophical theory. The law frequently contains an implicit theory of a concept that it employs—or often multiple implicit theories, sometimes warring with one another, sometimes living amicably in non-overlapping domains. These theories are difficult to uncover, vary by jurisdiction and sometimes within jurisdictions, and they change over time. As a clear illustration, note that the law encodes a theory of the person—an account of the necessary and sufficient conditions for an entity to be a person. But laws banning homicide—the killing of another *person*—employ a theory of the boundaries of that concept quite different from laws banning driving in the carpool lane without another *person* in the car. In many states, it is murder to kill a 39-week-old fetus, but not legal for a woman in her thirty-ninth week of pregnancy to drive in the carpool lane accompanied only by the fetus she is carrying. The fetus is a person for the sake of one set of laws, but not another. The well-known decision in *Citizens United v. FEC* (558 U.S. 310 (2010)) found that the Constitutional protections for the freedom of speech of people applied to corporations. But for many other purposes in law, corporations would not count as people. The same point applies to many legal concepts. Outcomes are needed, cases must be decided, and so those tasked with doing so apply a philosophical theory that helps them to reach decisions, often without knowing they are, and often without anticipating the implications of that theory for future cases. And so the law comes to contain accounts of the necessary and sufficient conditions for being a weapon, a marriage, a will, a person, a cause, an injury, an intention, etc.

The same is true of the notion of collective intentionality. Here the term is being used to refer to the large collection of instances in which, broadly speaking, a group of people function as an agent.[1] The law implicitly contains multiple theories of the necessary and sufficient conditions for collective intentionality. Because there is so much variation and complexity across domains of law in its conceptions of collective intentionality the focus here is narrowed to collective intentionality *in criminal law*, where punishment is at stake, and so where the law's implicit theory of collective intentionality quite often determines whether the government will deprive a group of people of their livelihoods, their liberty, and sometimes even their lives. As will be suggested here, the criminal law encodes a collection of theories of the nature of collective intentionality.

2. COLLECTIVISM OR INDIVIDUALISM?

Criminal law is the only area of law concerned with the allocation of punishment. Other areas of law are concerned, instead, with allocations of goods, such as money, and allocations of entitlements, such as the right to use a piece of land, or the right to make decisions for a child. Punishment, however, is, in a meaningful sense, only ever suffered individually, rather than collectively. If two people commit a crime together, they cannot choose to have one, and not the other, serve the sentence for the crime. If one of them, and not the other, is unjustly treated while in prison it is only the one, and not the other, who has standing to complain. If one earns an early release through good behavior, the other remains imprisoned. Prisoners are, in an important sense, on their own.

The distinctively individual quality of punishment encourages the thought that criminal liability is incurred not thanks to the intentional behaviors of groups but thanks, instead, to the intentional behaviors of individuals (who often happen to be members of groups with which society is concerned). In fact, the paradigm instances of justified punishment are, indeed, predicated on the individual behavior of the person punished. Ordinarily, we punish A for crime Σ because A was the perpetrator of Σ. We punish A for the crime of stealing a car because *A stole a car*. The explanation for the appropriateness, or fittingness, of the punishment appeals to the fact that the punished one's behavior is of the type for which the punishment is issued. If *all* justified criminal punishment is like this, then there is no reason to think that criminal law encodes *any* theory, much less multiple theories, of collective intentionality. Consider, then, the following two conflicting views:

> *Individualism*: A is justifiably criminally punished for a crime of type Σ *only if* A tokened Σ.

> *Collectivism*: A is sometimes justifiably criminally punished for a crime of type Σ that A did not token *if* A is a member of a collective that is justifiably attributed with tokening Σ.

Individualists hold that all criminal liability derives from the individual criminal behavior of those we punish. Collectivists hold that while this is often true, it is not always true. Sometimes, by contrast, a person incurs criminal liability for something *he did not do* thanks to the fact that he is part of a group of people to whom it is rightly attributed.

Collectivists bear a burden: they must identify a relation (or multiple distinct relations) that can hold between people such that, when it does, each of those people can justifiably incur criminal liability for behaviors attributable to the group. This article makes the case for collectivism about criminal law by arguing that several criminal law doctrines which justifiably mandate punishment do so in a way that can be adequately explained only by attributing the law with a supporting theory of collective intentionality, a theory of the ties that can bind people so tightly as to support imposition of punishment for things that they did not, individually, do.

3. DISTINGUISHING COMPLICITY, JOINT PERPETRATION AND VICARIOUS LIABILITY

Statutes defining crimes provide a list of "elements": conditions that need to be shown beyond a reasonable doubt by the prosecution in order to establish the defendant's guilt. These elements are divided into two classes. The "*actus reus*" elements of the crime are all of those conditions involved in the crime not including the mental states of the defendant. The "*mens rea*" elements of the crime are the mental states of the defendant that need to be present for guilt. So, for instance, consider the following statute from the state of Colorado, in which first degree arson is defined:

> A person who knowingly sets fire to. . .any. . .occupied structure of another without his consent commits first degree arson.
>
> (Colorado Criminal Code 18-4-102)

The *actus reus* elements of first degree arson include (1) an act of setting a fire, (2) where the object set on fire is a structure, (3) that is occupied, (4) the structure belongs to someone else, (5) that person does not give consent to the structure being set on fire. And there are five *mens rea* elements, corresponding to these five *actus reus* conditions: the defendant must believe, or "know," that each of these five things is true when he acts. Someone, for instance, who thinks there's a 50–50 chance the structure is occupied is not guilty of first degree arson, in Colorado, although he might be guilty of some other crime.

One might think that all of those that the law labels as arsonists—all those who are legally marked as having violated the statute—actually set fire to an occupied structure. But this is not true. Say that A1 gives B1 a jug of lighter fluid which B1 uses to light an occupied structure. In that case, A1 might be guilty of arson as an accomplice. Or say that A2 and B2 together blow a wildfire toward an occupied structure until the structure lights. In that case, it might be that A2's conduct would not have sufficed to light the structure on its own, and neither would have B2's, but their joint efforts did succeed in lighting it. Still, under the law, A2 might have committed arson. Or, finally, imagine that A3 is the owner of an inspection business and that his employee, B3, sets an occupied structure on fire while inspecting a property. Even though A3 might have been miles away at the time, and might not have lit the fire had he been the one doing the inspection that day, A3 might, in that case, still be guilty of arson. In all three of these cases, A would be found guilty and punished as an arsonist even though it is not true that what he did met the description of arson provided by the statute.

Criminal law students can tell you that the first of these is a case of *complicity*, the second *joint perpetration*, and the third *vicarious liability*. Collectivists are apt to think of these labels as marking different kinds of "togetherness," or collective intentionality. So understood, the legal terms refer to three types of relations that can hold between parties thanks to which it is justified to hold all the members of the resulting collective criminally responsible for crimes attributable to the collective. There are, we might say, three distinct kinds of "glue" linking the parties together. In complicity, the link is constituted by two things: aid and individual intention; A1 helps B1 to commit arson and does so with an intention to further B1's criminal activity.[2] In joint perpetration, we might say that the link is metaphysical. The link is such that the most perspicuous answer to the question, "Who performed the act?" refers to a collective of which each agent is a member—e.g. "Who set the structure on fire?" "A2 and B2 did it together." The act is like an attribute possessed by the collective, but not by any individual member of the collective.[3] And in vicarious liability, the link is one of normative authority. A3 has authority over B3 when it comes to professional conduct. Since B3's crime was perpetrated while engaged in conduct over which A3 had such authority, A3 is sufficiently associated with B3 for it to be the case that the behavior in which B3 engaged can be attributed to the collective, in this case the company, of which A3 and B3 are both a part. At least, that is how the collectivist would describe these three legal doctrines. As we will see shortly, the collectivist description of these doctrines can be contested.

Although we sometimes find more than one of these three things in any given case—sometimes the boss also provides aid, for instance—it is possible, and often the case, that we find only one. It is easy to see that we can have either complicity or joint perpetration without vicarious liability. Vicarious liability requires relations of authority between the parties that may be entirely absent. But we can also have vicarious liability without either complicity or joint perpetration. The vicariously liable often lend no aid at all. They might even actively hinder the commission of the crime by the subordinate, as when they tell their subordinates that they will be fired if they engage in illegal activity on the job. And the vicariously liable are often not joint perpetrators since their association with the crimes of those over whom they have authority does not derive from either their conduct or their mental states, while joint perpetration must depend in some way on those two things.

Further, complicity is neither necessary nor sufficient for joint perpetration. The accomplice is often not a joint perpetrator. For one thing, joint perpetration would seem to require some kind of coordination between the parties, but an accomplice can be associated with another's crime without that other's awareness or acquiescence. The aid need not even be welcomed or accepted for complicity, while some kind of pro-attitude toward the other's role, at least a commitment to not get in the way, is essential for joint perpetration. Further, joint perpetrators might not intend to aid the other parties at all and so might not be accomplices. We can see this in cases of joint perpetrators who are competitors. Say that A4 and B4 are playing a game of chicken: they drive their cars toward each other at high speed and whoever jumps out first is the loser. When their cars smash together, killing an innocent third party, A4 and B4 are the joint perpetrators of the killing. It captures more of the truth to say, "*They* killed someone" than to say either "A4 killed someone" or "B4 killed someone," even if those two latter sentences are also true (are they?). It seems misleading to suggest that one *helped* the other to kill someone. But even if there is some extended sense in which A4 aided B4, or in which B4 aided A4, A4 and B4 both lack the intentions that are essential to complicity. Neither intends to help the other kill anyone, even if he does in fact provide such aid (which can be doubted). Here we have joint perpetrators neither of whom is anyone's accomplice.

4. TOWARD A COLLECTIVIST THEORY OF COMPLICITY

Does A's criminal liability in the examples given so far really derive, as suggested by the collectivist, from the law's implicit acceptance of a theory of collective intentionality? Set aside, for a moment, joint perpetration and vicarious liability and consider this question with respect to complicity. Should we think of complicity—the intentional aiding of another's crime—as a form of collective intentionality?[4] Individualists hold, in contrast, that the rationale for holding accomplices to be criminally liable is that they have made an individual, intentional causal contribution to the violation of a legally protected interest.[5] From this point of view, when A5 holds the victim while B5 rapes her, it is misleading to suggest that A5's crime is *rape*. Rather, A5's crime is *aiding* rape, perhaps as wrongful as rape itself, but a distinct crime. If A5 were to ask, "What did I do wrong?", the right answer would be "You helped someone to commit rape," not "You raped someone." How can we adjudicate between this individualist position and the collectivist position, according to which an accomplice is criminally liable because his aid makes him part of a collective attributable with criminal behavior?

Under current law, accomplices are found guilty of the crimes they aid; that is how the law labels their crimes (LaFave 2010). They are also sentenced for those crimes, rather than for some other, distinct crimes, such as the crimes of aiding others to commit such crimes. We do also have some statutes explicitly banning *aiding*, sometimes under the name "criminal facilitation," such as the relatively recent federal American statute banning the lending of material support to terrorism (18 U.S.C. §2339B). Such statutes do not ban the crimes aided; other statutes do that. Those who commit terrorist acts, for instance, need not have lent material support to terrorism; they have violated (multiple) statutes distinct from those banning the lending of material support. But criminal facilitation statutes are rare creatures and there are many forms of aid that we punish where there is no such statute. And this is a good thing. It seems that A5 has done something worth punishing severely even if the statutes banning rape do not also specify that it is a crime to aid another to commit rape. Even if the statute says only what it is to commit rape, it would seem that we are justified in punishing A5.

The collectivist position suggested here—the position according to which accomplices are criminally liable thanks to the fact that the crimes of those they aid are properly conceptualized as the product of a collective of which the accomplice is a part—explains this easily. Complicity, on the collectivist view, unites a group of individuals to which the crime, a crime such as rape, can be attributed. And so it makes good sense to hold members of that collective criminally liable for that crime, rather than for some form of criminal aiding. While it might be misleading to say that A5 and B5 together raped someone—it is not a case of joint perpetration, after all—it is true that the collective consisting of A5 and B5 are attributable with rape, and that is why the members of the collective are to be punished *for rape*.

Those attracted to the individualist position about complicity—the position according to which accomplices are criminally liable thanks to what they did individually rather than thanks to their role in a collective that includes the person they aid—deny that our current practice of finding accomplices guilty of the crimes of those they aid, *taken at face value*, is justified. Many of those aiders who we wish to hold criminally liable have not individually violated any explicit prohibition. A5, for instance, has not sexually penetrated anyone, and that is an element of the crime of rape. Hence, if we are trying to hold A5 criminally liable *as an individual*, rather than as a member of a collective that includes both him and B5, then we cannot hold A5 responsible *for rape*; he has not committed rape.

The advocate of the individualist position has, at this point, two options. Option 1: deny that it is justified to hold A5 criminally liable *for anything having to do with rape* (assuming that there is no statute banning *aiding* rape, in contrast to statutes banning rape itself). Of course, he might be guilty of a crime in having involuntarily restrained another person. He might even be guilty of kidnapping on those grounds. But there would be no sense in which the non-consensual sexual penetration of another is something for which he is properly held criminally liable. Option 2: insist that our practice is not to be taken at face value. It *seems* that we are holding A5 criminally liable for rape, but his actual crime is distinct; it is the crime of *aiding rape*.

Option 1 is no option at all: it simply must be justified to hold A5 criminally liable for either rape or something very closely related to rape, something that includes in its essence the harm suffered by the victim. Option 2, however, seems to be in conflict with the Principle of Legality, which states that it is never justified to hold someone criminally liable unless he has violated the law. If the only relevant statute on the books bans rape, and there is no statute banning aiding the commission of rape, and if A5 is in fact being held criminally liable for *aiding* rape, rather than for the crime itself, then it appears that to hold A5 criminally liable is to violate the Principle of Legality. If that line of reasoning stands, then Option 2 is no more of an option than Option 1, for it is simply obvious that it is justified to hold A5 criminally liable for something closely related to rape.

The advocate of the individualist position need not throw in the towel, however. Option 2 can be coherently accepted by adding that when the legislature passes a criminal statute, it also, implicitly, criminalizes the behavior of anyone who aids anyone else to engage in the conduct that the statute bans. Thus, statutes banning rape actually generate at least two prohibitions: they explicitly prohibit rape, and they implicitly prohibit aiding rape. Given this further idea, Option 2 now seems possible. It is consistent with the Principle of Legality to hold A5 criminally liable, and asserting this does not require taking A5 to be guilty of rape, as on the collectivist position. The crime of aiding rape will do, for that is also against the law thanks to statutes banning rape. Such statutes, it is asserted, ban more than they appear to ban.

Are the collectivist and the individualist positions about complicity equally defensible, then? Are they equally compatible with (1) the undeniable fact that it is justified to hold A5 criminally liable, (2) our practice of *officially asserting* that accomplices are liable for the crimes they aid, and (3) the Principle of Legality? The two views are not quite on an equal footing. The collectivist position is stronger, and for two reasons. First, the individualist position, for the reasons described above, cannot accept (2) at face value, but must reinterpret it. Under the individualist position, we only *say* that accomplices are guilty of the crimes they aid; what we *mean* is that they are guilty of the crime of aiding those crimes. But if this is so, why do we even have crimes such as lending material support to terrorism? Why do we ever feel the need to identify certain forms of aid as worthy of explicit statutory criminalization? This seems like pure redundancy under the view on offer. And, relatedly, why don't we just *say what we mean*? If we do not think A5 is criminally liable for rape, why pretend? Note that there is another case in which statutes seem to ban more than completed behavior of the kind they explicitly describe: they also ban *failed attempts* to engage in that behavior. But in the case of attempts, we say what we mean: we label those who try and fail to commit crimes as *criminal attempters*, and we punish them differently from those who complete crimes.[6] The person who fires a shot at another and misses, is punished for attempted murder, not for murder. The individualist position requires the view that complicity is different in this respect from attempt. But why should it be any different?

There is a second reason to prefer the collectivist to the individualist position. The individualist position requires the claim that whenever a particular form of behavior is criminalized, lending aid to the commission of that crime is also criminalized. It is not obvious why we should accept that claim. It is true that it is prima facie morally wrongful to help someone to engage in morally wrongful behavior. But it is often so much less bad to aid than it is to actually do the wrongful thing, that there would be no reason to expect this derivative way in which aiding is wrongful to justify criminalizing aid whenever the conduct aided is criminal.[7] A6 changes the tire on B6's car with the intention of helping B6 to run down B6's enemy should he get the chance. A week later, B6 does just that. A6's act is wrongful—he should have stayed out of it—but is it anywhere near as wrongful as B6's? The collectivist position can support the intuitively plausible explanation for why A6 has incurred criminal liability: he is part of a collective that ran someone down.

But the individualist position bears the burden of explaining why changing a tire is a crime, considered independently of the way in which that act associates A6 with B6. It is far from clear that it is possible for the individualist position to meet this burden, given that changing the tire made a tiny contribution, in itself, to the violation of a legally protected interest, and given that the contribution was completely replaceable: B6 could easily have changed the tire himself. The point is that to describe what A6 has done in a way that illuminates why what he has done *is a crime*, we need to say something about the glue between A6 and B6. It is not enough to appeal only to the degree to which A6's act made the world worse (it did, but not much), or the moral norm against aiding wrongful conduct that it violated (it did, but morality is one thing, law another). We need to be able to say that A6 is criminally liable *because he was in on it*. The collectivist position allows us to say this, while the individualist position does not.

The conclusion: the collectivist position about complicity is superior to the individualist. In assigning criminal liability to accomplices, the law implicitly accepts the view that by lending aid with the intention to help another to commit a crime, one associates oneself with a collective that is properly held criminally liable for that crime.

5. COLLECTIVISM ABOUT JOINT PERPETRATION AND VICARIOUS LIABILITY

The same conceptual issue just discussed at length in connection with complicity can be raised about both cases of joint perpetration and vicarious liability. Are these really cases in which A is criminally liable thanks to his membership in a collective that is implicated in a crime? Can't such cases be construed, instead, as involving only individual liability? Our examples so far of joint perpetration would seem to encourage this thought. After all, A2, who blows the fire toward the structure with B2, can be thought of as engaging in an act in a context in which certain causal requisites of success are being produced by independent forces. So understood, his act is no different from what it would have been had the wind been blowing the fire toward the structure and he added to it, thereby accomplishing the task of lighting the structure. Since when B2's role is played by the wind, A2 is criminally liable *as an individual*, it seems that we can also construe him to be liable without appeal to any theory of collective intentionality in the case as given. A similar analysis applies in the case of A4 and B4, driving cars toward each other where the collision causes a death. If A4 drove a car toward an unoccupied car that happened to be hurtling toward him—perhaps a tornado vaulted it—and thereby caused a death, he would be liable *for killing someone*, without any appeal to any "glue" between himself and another person. But then it seems that A4's criminal liability in the case as given, where another agent is involved, can be rationalized, also, without appeal to any theory of collective intentionality.

But the examples of joint perpetration given so far are not the only sort, and others are much more difficult to explain without appeal to a theory of collective intentionality. Consider robbery, the crime of non-consensually taking property that belongs to another by force. The element "by force" distinguishes robbery from other forms of theft, and makes it a much more serious crime. A7 hits the victim in the face, which causes him to drop his property, which B7 grabs and runs off with. A7 and B7 would later have split the proceeds from the sale of the property, but they were arrested and so never got the chance.

A7's conduct, taken by itself, does not constitute robbery. He did not take anyone's property; he never came into possession of it, nor did he benefit from the victim's loss of it. But B7's conduct does not constitute robbery either. He did not use force on anyone. But aren't the two of them together guilty of robbery? They are, and should be. This kind of example simply cannot be explained on a purely individualist theory. To say why it is that A7 is guilty of robbery (or, really any kind of theft), we need to appeal to a theory of the significance of what *connects* A7 and B7, what makes them into a collective that is rightly held responsible for robbery.

The case of vicarious liability is even harder to make sense of on purely individualist grounds. The relation between A3, the CEO of the company for which B3 works, and the crimes committed by B3, and in general in cases of vicarious liability, is extremely weak. While you might think that, given that A3 has a certain kind of authority over B3, A3 should have done something, or at least should have tried to do something to prevent B3. But here there is room to repeat the line of reasoning that led to the conclusion that complicity is best understood on a collectivist rather than an individualist conception. After all, the vicariously liable are found guilty of the crimes of those over whom they have authority; they are not found guilty of the crime of *failing to control those over whom they have authority*. The defender of the individualist view thus has two options again, if he is to remain consistent with the Principle of Legality: deny that the vicariously liable ought to be criminally liable at all, or insist that statutes prohibiting crimes such as arson also prohibit failing to control arsonists over whom one has authority. While the first option is significantly more plausible in the context of vicarious liability than in complicity, it is still in conflict with present legal practice. And so it seems a thin basis from which to deny that the law is adopting an implicit theory of collective intentionality when it employs vicarious liability.

The second option encounters all the same problems that the parallel option faced in connection with complicity, most notably the fact that while it might be wrongful not to control those criminals over whom one has authority, it is not nearly as wrongful as it is to commit such crimes oneself. Hence it is an obvious error, too obvious to be the law's, to follow current practice and label those in authority as guilty of the crimes of those over whom they have authority. Even if the CEO did wrong, he isn't, himself, an arsonist. It seems far more perspicuous, again, to adopt the collectivist view: the CEO is part of a collective that is properly attributed with arson, and that is why he is found guilty of it. A3's authority over B3 binds them together in such a way as to make the conduct of the one something attributable to the two together.

6. CONCLUSION

It is one thing to show that the law accepts a theory of collective intentionality, and quite another to show that the theory it accepts is true. Is it true that accomplices are *always* justifiably punished for the crimes of those they aid? Is the tie that binds the accomplice and the principal always so strong as to warrant punishing the accomplice for the crimes of the collective of which he makes himself a part? We can ask parallel questions about joint perpetration and about vicarious liability. We should not expect uniform answers to these questions. Perhaps joint perpetrators are rightly punished while the vicariously liable and the complicit are not. Perhaps. We have not made progress on such normative questions here. But a first step in answering them has been made. It is easy to overestimate the import of the following observation: in all of these cases what the one party does is not, in itself, enough to constitute a crime. This observation, however, turns into an objection to the law's approach only if we grant individualism. If we grant that what a person does must be enough for crime for him to be criminally liable, then we give up the game. But if we accept, as has been urged here, that it can be justified to individually punish each member of a collective for that which is attributable to the group, the question, then, is the subtler and harder one of when the ties that bind do so sufficiently to justify this practice.

RELATED TOPICS

Complicity (Ch. 25), Collective Intentions and Collective Moral Responsibility (Ch. 24), Institutional Responsibility (Ch. 26).

REFERENCES

Bratman, M. (2014) *Shared Agency: A Planning Theory of Acting Together*, Oxford: Oxford University Press.
Duff, R.A. (2007) "Is Accomplice Liability Superfluous?" *University of Pennsylvania Law Review* 156: 444–52.
——— (1996) *Criminal Attempts*, Oxford: Oxford University Press.
Gilbert, M. (2015) *Joint Commitment: How We Make the Social World*, Oxford: Oxford University Press.
Hurd, H. and Moore, M. (2015) "Untying the Gordian Knot of Mens Rea Requirements for Accomplices," *Social Philosophy and Policy* 32: 161–83.
Husak, D. (2012) "Abetting a Crime," *Law and Philosophy* 33: 41–73.
Kadish, S. (1985) "Complicity, Cause and Blame: A Study in the Interpretation of Doctrine," *California Law Review* 73: 323–410.
LaFave, W. (2010) *Criminal Law*, St Paul: West Publishing.
Moore, M. (2007) "The Superfluity of Accomplice Liability," *University of Pennsylvania Law Review* 156: 395–443.
——— (2009) *Causation and Responsibility*, Oxford: Oxford University Press.
Sarch, A. (2015) "Condoning the Crime: The Elusive Mens Rea of Complicity," *Loyola Law Review* 47: 131–78.
Yaffe, G. (2010) *Attempts: In the Philosophy of Action and the Criminal Law*, Oxford: Oxford University Press.
——— (2012) "Intending to Aid," *Law and Philosophy* 33: 1–40
——— (2014) "Criminal Attempts," *Yale Law Journal* 124 (1): 95–156.

NOTES

1. If groups are capable of acting unintentionally, then it will be possible to exhibit "collective intentionality," in the sense in which the term is being used here, while engaging in unintentional behavior.
2. There has been no shortage of work done, both in the academy and in judicial opinions, to try to specify exactly when a person possesses the mental state needed for complicity. See *United States v. Peoni* (100 F.2d 401 (1938)), *Rosemond v. United States* (134 S.Ct. 1240 (2013)), Yaffe (2012), Husak (2012), Hurd and Moore (2015), Sarch (2015).
3. In one set of joint perpetration cases, there is an element of the *actus reus* of the crime that cannot be present unless realized by a collective. For instance, in crimes of conspiracy—conspiracy to commit murder, or conspiracy to commit fraud, for instance—the *actus reus* of the crime includes an *agreement*

to commit a crime. The act of agreeing can only be jointly perpetrated—nobody can agree all by himself. The result is that all conspiracy cases are joint perpetration cases. There are, in addition, a set of hard questions about *mens rea* in joint perpetration cases. If the act is jointly performed, must the *mens rea* be jointly possessed? And what does it even mean for a mental state, such as an intention, to be jointly held? For discussion see, generally, Bratman (2014), Gilbert (2015).

4. Perhaps the most famous collectivist description of accomplice liability is Kadish (1985).

5. See Moore (2009: ch. 13); Moore (2007). For a particularly illuminating commentary, see Duff (2007).

6. For relevant discussion, see Duff (1996), Yaffe (2010, 2014: note 1).

7. One might take a different tack. One might think that aiding crime demonstrates the same indifference to the reasons to refrain from crime that engaging in crime demonstrates. This is true of attempting crime. Those who attempt crimes are indifferent to the reasons to refrain in just the way that those who complete crimes are. In fact, elsewhere I've claimed that this similarity between attempt and completion is what accounts for the fact that attempts are implicitly criminalized whenever completions are. See Yaffe (2010: ch. 1). But on reflection we do not find the same similarity between doing and aiding. For instance, there are powerful reasons not to inflict certain kinds of insults on the bodies of others. But aiders don't inflict such insults and so the reasons not to inflict such insults are not reasons to refrain from aiding. Or, to put the point more carefully, explaining why the reasons not to inflict such insults are reasons not to aid requires accepting a collectivist position under which the aider is associated with the collective that inflicts such insults and thus has those very reasons not to aid. Of course, such a line of thought cannot be used to support the individualist position.

30

Collective Intentionality and Methodology in the Social Sciences

Deborah Perron Tollefsen

As this Handbook suggests, the topics that fall under the heading of collective intentionality are diverse, ranging from ontological, to epistemological, to ethical. However, because collective intentionality studies social phenomena, the disputes that have arisen regarding its methodology are often viewed as similar, to some extent, to the disputes that occurred during the latter part of the nineteenth century and the early twentieth century over the proper methodology of the social sciences. I refer here to well-worn debates between methodological individualism and methodological holism. In the first section, Methodological Individualism and Methodological Holism, I discuss the extent to which philosophers within the field of collective intentionality have adopted an individualistic approach to explaining social phenomena. Along the way, I make a number of different distinctions in the hope of clarifying and categorizing positions. In the second section, Naturalizing Collective Intentionality, I consider a more recent methodological trend.

1. METHODOLOGICAL INDIVIDUALISM AND METHODOLOGICAL HOLISM

a. History

Max Weber is credited as being the father of methodological individualism, though the term was actually coined by his student, Joseph Schumpeter (1908, 1909). According to Weber, although we talk about social groups, collectives, teams, etc. as if they were agents, in sociological explanation these groups must be viewed as 'solely the resultants and modes of organization of the particular acts of individual persons, since these alone can be treated as agents in a course of subjectively understandable action' (Weber 1922: 13).

As Joseph Heath points out (2015), Weber's commitment to *verstehende* (or interpretive) patterns of explanation is what underlies his methodological individualism. In order to understand the social world we need to understand the actions that brought it about. Actions are intentional and only individuals have motives, intentions, and desires. The social sciences, for Weber, are the sciences of the human spirit. They strive to understand humans and in a way very different from how we might understand the natural world. We cannot understand human action simply in virtue of causes and effects. Understanding requires getting at the subjective motives and only individual human beings have motives.

Weber's methodological individualism is often juxtaposed with Emile Durkheim's holist approach (2014). Methodological holism can be defined as the negative claim that social scientific explanation need not appeal solely to individual psychological states (and relations between individuals). Although Durkheim does not explicitly reject explanations in terms of individual mental states, his reference to collective representations and the ability of such representations to control individual actions has been described as holist.

In a series of articles published in the 1940s (1944a, 1944b, 1945) and later in *The Open Society and its Enemies* (1966), Karl Popper associated holistic explanation with totalitarian ideologies and advocated for methodological individualism as a response. His student J.W.N. Watkins (1952) did much of the work of defending methodological individualism and is credited with bringing the principle to the attention of philosophers. According to Watkins

> the principle of methodological individualism means that the ultimate constituents of the world are individual people who act more or less appropriately in light of their dispositions and understanding of their situation . . . we shall not arrive at rock-bottom explanations of such large scale (social) phenomena until we have deduced an account of them from statements about the dispositions, beliefs, resources and inter-relations of individuals.
>
> (1957: 105–6)

Watkins appears to have been motivated by reductionist principles. The hope was to find a methodology that would allow one to reduce complex social phenomenon to individual psychological phenomena—reducing the social to the psychological.

Debates about the proper methodology of the social sciences seemed to have petered out by the 1970s but in the 1980s the debate was given new life. Jon Elster argued for a version of methodological individualism while defending rational choice theory. He did so in the process of critiquing functionalist theories of economic change, in particular Marxist economic theories. Elster was motivated by the Weberian point that explanation in the social sciences needs to appeal to the intentional actions of individuals. 'To explain social institutions and social change is to show how they arise as the result of the actions and interaction of individuals. This view, often referred to as methodological individualism, is in my view trivially true' (Elster 1989: 13).

b. Clarifying Methodological Individualism

The discussions surrounding methodological individualism and holism have become so voluminous that it is difficult to ascertain clearly what the respective positions in the debate actually are. Alan Carter (1990) distinguishes 12 different versions of collectivism, individualism and what he calls interrelationism. Steven Lukes (1968) made some headway in clarifying things by pointing out that much of the debate confuses methodological and ontological claims. Ontological holism is the view that there are social entities that exist and these entities are something over and above a mere aggregate of individuals. Ontological individualism is the view that there are no non-reducible social entities— only individuals exist. Methodological holism and individualism are claims about the proper methodology of the social sciences. Although ontological commitments often motivate methodological ones, as evidenced by Watkins, they need not. One could agree that only individuals exist but deny that all social facts can be explained solely in terms of individual psychological states. Likewise, one could argue that groups exist but provide an explanation of them solely in terms of individual psychological states and the relations between them. That is, one could be an explanatory reductionist without being an ontological eliminativist.

Methodological individualism should also be distinguished from atomism. According to atomism, it is possible for human beings to develop all the capacities characteristic of human beings in complete isolation from other humans. There is no incoherence, for the atomist, in the possibility of a solitary individual. Many methodological individualists acknowledge that the individual psychological states that serve to explain social facts presuppose social facts. Mannheim (1936) agrees, for instance, that the individual beliefs about banks that explain economic social facts presuppose social institutions such as financial institutions. But this does not mean that explanation cannot be given in terms of the individuals' states and relations between individuals. The opposite of atomism is often called holism, not to be confused with methodological holism. Holism is the view that human agents depend non-causally on their social relations with one another for the possession of distinctive human capacities. They only have these capacities (for instance, the capacity to think) as social beings. Wittgenstein is an example of a holist in this sense.

Finally, methodological individualism ought to be distinguished from what Margaret Gilbert calls "singularism" (1989). Singularism is the thesis that social facts, concepts, events, are explainable solely in terms of the conceptual scheme of singular agency. This conceptual scheme starts with the individual, autonomous agent, and sees them as acting solely in terms of their own individual goals and preferences. Rational choice theory is dominated by the conceptual scheme of singular agency. Cooperation problems are analyzed by focusing on each individual's expected utility. Susan Hurley (2003) and others have argued that this singularism leads us to the absurd conclusion that social interaction is not rational. To avoid such an absurd conclusion we have to see that in the context of human social interaction people often use team reasoning (Sugden 1993; Bacharach 2006; see also Chapter 18, this volume). When a player reasons as a team member he or she attempts to maximize the objective function of a set of players. This involves finding strategies that maximize the team's joint payoff, and then if the strategy is unique, pursuing the individual strategy that is a component of it. In other words, team reasoners reason from the plural perspective and not the singular perspective.

As I have defined it above, methodological individualism is the thesis that social phenomena (facts, objects, events, states, etc.) should be explained solely in terms of individual intentional states and the relations between those individuals. Whether those individuals ought to be viewed as singular agents acting entirely for their own reasons or whether they should be viewed as acting on or from team reasons remains open. Thus, the rejection of singularism is not necessarily a rejection of methodological individualism.

For example, John Searle and Raimo Tuomela are examples of authors who reject singularism but not methodological individualism.

c. Methodological Individualism and Collective Intentionality

Methodological individualism, as it developed in the late nineteenth and early twentieth century, was a thesis about the proper methodology of the social sciences. Understood this way, very few, if any, of the scholars working within the field of collective intentionality argue for methodological individualism. This is because they are not philosophers of social science advocating for a universal methodology but rather philosophers offering accounts of various types of social facts and phenomena. Some philosophers working in the area may indeed feel that *all* explanation of social facts needs to appeal to individual psychological states and the relation between individuals, but few, if any, have argued for this in any sustained way. They have, however, provided analyses of certain types of social phenomena in terms of individual mental states and the relations between individuals. Does this make them methodological individualists?

We can clarify things here by distinguishing *methodological individualism* as a theory about the proper methodology of the social sciences and methodological individualism *as a method*. As a method, individualism seeks to explain social facts in terms of the psychological states of individuals and the relations between those individuals. One who adopts the method of individualism need not be committed to thinking that it is a method that must be used to explain all social facts. Henceforth when I talk of methodological individualism I will be referring to the method rather than the meta-principle.

The field of collective intentionality is populated with scholars who have adopted methodological individualism. Consider the "Big Four." Searle's theory of the construction of social reality is based on individual intentional states (of a certain sort) and the application of status functions on the basis of those intentional states (1990, 2009). The psychological states appealed to in Searle's theory are we-intentions and we-beliefs but nonetheless they are the intentional states of individuals. Likewise, Raimo Tuomela's account of group belief, for instance, is explained in terms of individual intentional states (of a certain sort) and the relationships between individual agents within a group (conditions of common knowledge, role relationships, and so on) (1995). Tuomela's we-mode is the way in which an individual perceives his relationship to the group (2006). Michael Bratman's work on shared intention (1993, 2014) clearly identifies a set of individual intentional states and the interrelation between these states as constituting the phenomenon under question. Finally, even Margaret Gilbert provides an account of social groups and other social phenomena in terms of individual intentional states and the relationship between individuals within a group (Gilbert 1989, 1994, 2013). Gilbert's explanandum is often a group property or state (group belief, for instance) but the explanans makes reference to individual intentional states and the relation between them. But what about joint commitments? According to Gilbert, these are the commitments of groups not individuals. It is true that joint commitments are not reducible to the personal commitments of individuals. But even this element of her account is giving an explanation in terms of individual intentional states and the relationship between them. Joint commitments arise when individuals express their willingness to be jointly committed with others as a body. This is an account of the construction or establishment of joint commitments that makes reference solely to individual intentional states and the relation between members of the group (for more on the notion of joint commitment see Chapter 10, this volume). Thus, even joint commitments, which are irreducible to individual commitments, have their causal roots in individual actions/intentions.

The reasons for adopting methodological individualism vary. Gilbert, as I mentioned, seems to be inspired by Weber and the importance of *understanding* for the social sciences. The social world is not a natural kind. It is a function of human perception. Understanding it requires getting at those perceptions. For Gilbert, those perceptions involve seeing ourselves as part of plural subjects and party to joint commitments. It is the perceptions of individuals that explain the unity found in social groups. Tuomela and others such as Seumas Miller (2001) who are coming to collective intentionality from action theory seem motivated by causal explanatory concerns. Individual action is explained in terms of the mental states that cause them. This too seems to be Searle's motivation. Understanding the social world means understanding the causes that contribute to it and how it arises from a physical world. Joint or group action must, therefore, be explained in terms of the mental states that cause it. If only individuals have mental states, then our explanation needs to appeal to them. Here we see ontological individualism entering as well. Only individual human beings are agents with psychological states.

The form of methodological individualism we find in the standard approaches to collective intentionality can be further refined. In *On Social Facts*, Gilbert adopts what she describes as a Weberian approach to social phenomena. She calls it *intentionalism*. According to intentionalism, social phenomena are constituted by individuals' perceptions. They must 'see themselves in a certain way' (1989: 12). Specifically, they must see themselves as connected.

> Some theorists would propose that the essential mark of a human collectivity is an externally perceivable organization or structure, or systematic relations between the parts, that is, the human members. While there is doubtless something to be said for the view that human collectivities may be viewed externally as systems of structures, I shall argue that according to our intuitive conception they are not systems from an external point of view only. The participants must see themselves as bound together in a highly specific way. This suggests that an *explanation* (her emphasis) for the existence of objective systemic features in a collective may be found in an internal sense of unity. This would not be surprising, in so far as we accept that human beings are powered by their own perceptions of the situation.
>
> (Gilbert 1989: 13)

Intentionalism is a view about what constitutes or makes up the social world and so it is an ontological claim but from it derives an explanatory one. If social facts are not natural kinds but made up or constituted by individuals' perceptions of their world, then an explanation of those *social* kinds needs to appeal to individuals' perceptions (i.e. individual psychology) of themselves vis-à-vis others.

Intentionalism, as Gilbert describes it, is a form of methodological individualism in that it insists that explanation needs to appeal to individual psychology. But the individual psychological states to which one appeals have to do with how individuals perceive themselves vis-à-vis other group members. This differs slightly from a methodological individualist who might explain a social fact (the rise of inflation, for instance) by appeal to individual economic behavior caused by individual beliefs that make no reference to how they perceive themselves within a group.

We can see the commitment to intentionalism in a variety of theories. Searle (1990), for instance, argues that a necessary condition for collective intention is that the other 'must have . . . a similar awareness of you as an agent like themselves' (1990: 415). Tuomela's we-intentions and we-beliefs are had only when there is common knowledge that others have them. Bratman's shared intentions require that members form them because of and in accordance with the intentions of other participants within the group. Participants must view their individual intentional states as interdependent (Bratman 1993). In Miller's (2001) account of joint action, collective ends must be mutually known to participants. The participants must see themselves as sharing these ends with others.

Thus far I have distinguished methodological individualism from intentionalism by pointing out that intentionalism requires that *members view themselves in a particular way vis-à-vis other group members*, either as joint committed with others (Gilbert), as potential contributors to a group action (Searle), as sharing mental states (Tuomela), as intending to *J* along with others (Bratman) or as sharing collective ends (Miller). Methodological individualism does not specify that the psychological states appealed to in the explanation of social facts be those that capture an individual's perceptions of themselves and their relation to others within a group. Intentionalism, then, is a form of methodological individualism (understood as a method and not a thesis about the proper methodology of the social sciences).

What about those who advocate for the existence of group agents? Aren't these theorists best thought of as holists, if not of the ontological then the methodological sort? Christian List and Philip Pettit (2011) have argued that certain groups are agents and are the appropriate subject of attitude ascription such as beliefs. List and Pettit are clear that they are not arguing that groups exist over and above the individuals that comprise them. They are not ontological holists. They do, however, acknowledge that explanations in terms of group attitudes are sometimes explanatorily powerful. To that extent they adopt a form of methodological holism. They reject the idea that all explanation of social phenomenon should appeal to individual intentional states and the relations between them. But group attitudes, according to Pettit and List, are created by various judgment aggregation methods. Insofar as Pettit and List appeal to the votes of individuals within a group, they seem to return to the individual. Indeed, their account of group agency has been criticized for being too individualistic (Rovane 2014).

Recent work by Bryce Huebner (2014) can be viewed as a rejection of intentionalism. According to Huebner genuine collective mentality arises, if it arises at all, only when groups implement the cognitive architecture found at the level of individual minds and they engage in flexible, goal-directed behavior that is robustly predictable from the intentional stance. He turns homuncular functionalism on its head and argues that the "organizational structure" of the individual mind can be writ large within groups. According to this view, individuals don't need to view themselves as part of a group in order to give rise to collective mental phenomena. They simply need to be organized in the right way. Of course, in virtue of their organization, they will, no doubt, form beliefs and attitudes about their relations to one another. But such beliefs will not be sufficient for group mentality nor are they necessary. Huebner also seems to reject individualism as a methodology. He argues that explanation at the level of group mentality will sometimes be explanatorily powerful.

Finally, we can see a form of holism in the work of Georg Theiner (2010, 2013). Theiner has argued that group minds emerge from the interaction of individual minds. The form of emergence he argues for is consistent with mechanistic explanation. However, Theiner argues that appeal to group cognition is explanatorily powerful and appeals to the work of Edwin Hutchins (1991, 1995) in order to establish this. If we look at the group as a cognitive system, in its own right, there are, according to Hutchins, certain phenomena that are better explained from this perspective. Robert Rupert has offered a number of critical challenges to this approach (2011).

d. Singularism and Collective Intentionality

What about singularism? Recall, singularism is the thesis that social facts, concepts, events, are explainable solely in terms of the conceptual scheme of singular agency. This conceptual scheme starts with the individual, autonomous agent, and sees them as acting solely in terms of their own individual goals and preferences. Gilbert clearly rejects singularism. Individuals act, from the perspective of the groups of which they are a part. Individual reasons are often derived from the group's reasons. Likewise, Searle and Tuomela seem to reject singularism. The ability of individuals to form we-intentions and we-beliefs and reason on the basis of these collective attitudes seems to challenge the idea of an individual acting solely on the basis of their own individual goals and preferences. Reasoning from the we-perspective is necessarily a rejection of singularism and reasoning from the we-perspective requires seeing yourself as bound in a certain way to others.

Gilbert (2013) identifies Michael Bratman's account of shared intention (1993) as singularist. Bratman accepts that shared intentions influence the practical rationality of individuals. When people form a shared intention to act, they are no longer constrained simply by their own individual goals and preferences but this acknowledgment does not mean relinquishing the conceptual scheme of singular agency. On standard rational choice theories the Prisoner's Dilemma requires for its resolution *that members view themselves in a particular way vis-à-vis other group members*. At the very least they need to view themselves as sharing the same options and that they are in conditions of common knowledge. But as the history of rational choice theory shows, this is consistent with holding singularism in which the individuals make their choices on the basis of their own individual preferences.

2. NATURALIZING COLLECTIVE INTENTIONALITY

a. From the Armchair

A standard method in philosophy is to reflect on a concept and attempt to provide the necessary and sufficient conditions for its application. The conditions are generally motivated by reflection on a number of different cases, and intuitions about cases are used as evidence for the adequacy of the analysis. It is not surprising, then, that those working within collective intentionality would also adopt this approach.

In *On Social Facts* (1989) Margaret Gilbert describes herself as providing a conceptual analysis of our everyday collectivity concepts. Her concern has been with explicating and justifying the use of our "everyday" collectivity concepts. Conceptual analysis provides necessary and sufficient conditions for the application of a concept. It should be distinguished from the ontological project of "giving truth-makers." Conceptual analysis doesn't tell us about what exists, it just tells us about the content of concepts we use to describe what exists (Rodriguez-Pereyra 2005). In recent work, Gilbert (2013), describes herself as providing analyses of the *core* of our collectivity concepts but continues to provide sufficient and necessary conditions. She also gives necessary and sufficient conditions for the existence of joint commitments so she seems no longer focused entirely on conceptual analysis.

Raimo Tuomela has also attempted to provide necessary and sufficient conditions but the conditions he provides are not the conditions for the correct application of a concept but for the existence of certain social facts. So, for instance, Tuomela provides necessary and sufficient conditions for group belief (1995). We might contrast Gilbert and Tuomela then by saying that Tuomela is interested in giving ontological conditions whereas Gilbert's work sometimes, but not always, seems focused on the conditions for the application of concepts.

Searle and Bratman, too, seem more interested in providing the conditions for the existence of certain social facts (or events) rather than conceptual analyses. Bratman, for instance, provides a functionalist account of shared intention. He begins by identifying the function of shared intention and then asks what configuration of individual intentional states can play that role (Bratman 1993). He also provides only sufficient conditions for shared intention, as he notes the possibility of shared intention being realized by other configurations of individual psychological states.

The philosophical method of identifying necessary and sufficient conditions through the use of thought experiments has been challenged in recent years. Inspired by Quine's naturalism (1969), many philosophers have adopted a more empirical approach to philosophical questions. Some working in collective intentionality have also adopted a more naturalized approach where they appeal to empirical research in the cognitive and behavioral sciences. In some cases, this appeal is meant to provide support for philosophical analyses; in other cases, it challenges philosophical analyses.

b. Empirical Approaches

How do people coordinate their bodies and minds in order to bring about the fulfillment of a shared goal? This is a question that has greatly exercised those working in collective intentionality. Because most approaches to this question begin by reflecting on individual action, theories of joint action model themselves on individual human action. The dominant theory of individual action within action theory has been the causal theory of action. The causal theory of action has it that action is something that is caused by the right antecedent psychological states. In particular, intention is thought to shape and inform the actions of individuals. This has set off the hunt for shared or group intentions that shape and inform joint or group actions. But there is more to individual human action than personal level states such as intention. There is a variety of lower level mechanisms that guide and inform individual human action. According to those who have adopted a more naturalized methodology, we need to take these mechanisms into account when providing a theory of joint action. The field of collective intentionality is becoming increasingly interdisciplinary as philosophers, cognitive scientists, and social scientists try to provide a more empirically informed theory of the ways people do things together.

Research on shared task representations and motor resonance, for instance, has led to a more nuanced understanding of the psychological states involved in joint tasks. Recent research suggests that when individuals participate in a joint action they incorporate other's action capabilities into their own planning (Richardson et al. 2007; Sebanz et al. 2006; Sebanz and Knoblich 2009). Further, just as temporal feedback about one's own action is used to anticipate action control, in a joint task, feedback from others' actions is used in anticipatory action control (Knoblich and Jordan 2003).

Research on alignment points to lower level mechanisms that facilitate joint actions. Alignment refers to the dynamic "matching" between the behavioral or cognitive states of two or more people over time. Gestures, eye gaze, word choice, and various other behavioral features may become coordinated in human interaction. A recent study has shown that this synchrony holds across a host of these behavioral channels simultaneously during a single naturalistic interaction (Louwerse et al. 2012) and that it correlates with task-related performance variables. In this study, the researcher's video- and audio-recorded two people interacting while one directed another in a navigational task. Videos were coded for communicative behaviors across dozens of dimensions spanning a range of complexity, from low-level facial expressions (e.g. furrowing the eyebrows, smiling) to high-level linguistic contexts (e.g. explanation, asking questions). The researchers found that, on average, partners exhibited systematic temporal alignment across many of the channels. In addition, the extent of that alignment predicted how long they had been interacting (i.e. the longer the interaction, the higher the alignment) and task difficulty (i.e. the more difficult the directions, the higher the alignment). People working together appear to become a tightly coupled interactive system, adapting over time and in the face of challenges. These finding and many others suggest that there is an alignment system that facilitates joint action (Tollefsen and Dale 2011). Personal level shared intentions of the sort Bratman and others have identified are only one part of the story of joint action.

Our understanding of joint action has also been enriched by considering joint action from a developmental perspective (Tomasello and Rakoczy 2003; Tomasello et al. 2005; Chapter 33, this volume). Research on the development of shared attention (Carpenter and Liebal 2011), the emergence of helping behavior (Warneken and Tomasello 2009), as well as the understanding of commitment (Grafenhain et al. 2009) and social norms (Rakoczy and Tomasello 2009) suggests that humans are hard-wired for collective intentionality.

Finally, experimental philosophers have turned their attention to topics in collective intentionality. In a series of studies, Joshua Knobe and Jesse Prinz (2008) explored people's judgments about the appropriateness of attitude ascriptions to corporations. Their results suggest that people are much more likely to attribute propositional attitudes to groups than conscious states such as pain. In a recent study, Jenkins and colleagues (2014) showed that when subjects were confronted with ascriptions of attitudes to corporations the same parts of the brain responsible for theory of mind were activated as when subjects were confronted with ascriptions of attitudes to individuals. Tollefsen et al. (2014)

ran a series of experiments that suggest that categorization of actions as joint actions is a dominant form of categorization. That is, people are more likely to categorize actions in this way than in terms of similarity of action type. We-ness or jointness appears to be a salient feature of human action.

3. CONCLUSION

Historically, methodological individualism developed as a meta-theory about the proper methodology of the social sciences. Although the position was often confused with ontological theses, the basic idea was that all explanation of social phenomena should be given in terms of individual psychological states and the relations between individuals. Those working within the field of collective intentionality have not argued for methodological individualism. However, they have adopted the method of individualism in which certain social phenomena are explained by appeal to the psychological states of individuals and the relations between individuals. As we have seen, there are some working within the field of collective intentionality that have argued that an explanation of certain social phenomena in terms of the psychological states of groups (group belief and group intention) is legitimate. This represents a more holist methodology. Some theorists embrace a more ecumenical approach and acknowledge that sometimes explanation will require getting at the "lower level" and appealing to the psychological states of individuals, and other times it will require "higher level" explanations. Tuomela, for instance, in his recent book acknowledges that viewing groups from the intentional stance will sometimes be explanatorily powerful (Tuomela 2013).

As we have seen, there are variations in the content and type of mental states to which the individualist appeals. Intentionalism is the view that certain social phenomena require for their explanation an appeal to individuals' *perceptions of themselves* vis-à-vis group members. Members must see themselves as jointly committed, or as sharing goals or intentions. Under intentionalism, the heart of the social world is to be found in individuals' awareness of how they relate to others. One might question whether group agency requires such self-reflection. Couldn't group agency arise from the organization of individual agents, without the requirement that they perceive themselves in a certain way vis-à-vis others? Singularism is the view that social phenomena should be explained solely in terms of singular agency where that refers to a conceptual scheme that sees the individual as acting from their own individual preferences and goals. As we have seen, singularism is challenged by many of the current theories of collective intentionality. We-intentionality, the we-mode, we-beliefs, and shared intentions are all constructions that involve viewing the world from a plural perspective or, at the very least, appreciating the role of the other in action and deliberation. Traditional rational choice theory, individualistic in its method because of its appeal to the psychological states of individuals, also exhibits singularism. The field of collective intentionality, though predominately individualist in its method, rejects singularism.

Georg Palante, a staunch critic of Durkheim wrote, '. . . It is to individual psychology that one must always return. It remains—whether one wishes it or not—the key which opens all doors' (1903: 60). Those working within collective intentionality have, for the most part, followed Palante's directive. One might even argue that those who acknowledge groups as agents—as bearers of mental states— do so only under the assumption that groups mimic the psychology of the individual. So, it is individual psychology to which they return.

The interdisciplinary nature of collective intentionality has expanded the methodological approaches to understanding the social world beyond conceptual and ontic analyses. Empirical research on shared task representations, for instance, is informing philosophical approaches to joint action. Likewise, empirical discussions of cooperation and coordination are being informed by philosophical discussions of we-intentionality.

RELATED TOPICS

Collective Action and Agency (Ch. 1), Non-Reductive Views of Shared Intention (Ch. 2), Reductive Views of Shared Intention (Ch. 3), Team Reasoning (Ch. 17), Social Construction and Social Facts (Ch. 20).

REFERENCES

Bacharach, M. (2006) *Beyond Individual Choice: Teams and Frames in Game Theory*, Princeton, NJ: Princeton University Press.

Bratman, M. (1993) "Shared Intention," *Ethics* 104 (1): 97–113.

——— (2014) *Shared Agency: A Planning Theory of Acting Together*, New York: Oxford University Press.

Carpenter, M. and Liebal, K. (2011) "Joint Attention, Communication, and Knowing Together in Infancy" in A. Seemann (ed.) *Joint Attention: New Developments in Psychology, Philosophy of Mind, and Social Neuroscience*, Cambridge, MA: MIT Press.

Carter, A. (1990) "On Individualism, Collectivism and Interrelationism," *Heythrop Journal* 31 (1): 23–38.

Durkheim, E. (2014) *The Rules for Sociological Method: and Selected Texts on Sociology and Method*, (ed.) (transl.) Stephen Lukes, New York: Free Press.

Elster, J. (1989) "From Here to There; or, If Cooperative Ownership Is So Desirable, Why are There So Few Cooperatives?" *Social Philosophy and Policy* 6 (2): 93–111.

Gilbert, M. (1989) *On Social Facts*, Princeton, NJ: Princeton University Press.

——— (1994) "Remarks on Group Belief," in F. Schmitt (ed.) *Socializing Epistemology: The Social Dimensions of Knowledge*, Lanham, MD: Rowman & Littlefield.

——— (2013) *Joint Commitment: How We Make the Social World*, New York: Oxford University Press.

Grafenhain, M., Behne, T., Carpenter, M. and Tomasello, M. (2009) "Young children's Understanding of Joint Commitments," *Developmental Psychology* 45: 1430–43.

Heath, J. (2015) "Methodological Individualism," in E.N. Zalta (ed.) *The Stanford Encyclopedia of Philosophy* (Spring 2015 edition), http://plato.stanford.edu/archives/spr2015/entries/methodological-individualism/

Huebner, B. (2014) *Macrocognition: A Theory of Distributed Minds and Collective Intentionality*, New York: Oxford University Press.

Hurley, S. (2003) "The Limits of Individualism Are Not the Limits of Rationality," *Behavioral and Brain Sciences* 26 (2): 164–5.

Hutchins, E. (1991) "Social Organization of Distributed Cognition," in L. Resnick, J. Levie, and S. Teasley (eds) *Perspectives on Socially Shared Cognition*, Washington, DC: The American Psychological Association.

——— (1995) *Cognition in the Wild*, Cambridge, MA: MIT Press.

Jenkins, A., Dodell-Feder, D., Saxe, R. and Knobe, J. (2014) "The Neural Bases of Directed and Spontaneous Mental State Attributions to Group Agents," *PLoS ONE* 9 (8): e105341.

Knobe, J. and Prinz, J. (2008) "Intuitions about Consciousness: Experimental Studies," *Phenomenology and Cognitive Science* 7: 67–83.

Knoblich, G. and Jordan, J.S. (2003) "Action Coordination in Groups and Individuals: Learning Anticipatory Control," *Journal of Experimental Psychology: Learning, Memory and Cognition* 29 (5): 1006–16.

List, C. and Pettit, P. (2011) *Group Agency: The Possibility, Design, and Status of Corporate Agents*, New York: Oxford University Press.

Louwerse, M.M., Dale, R., Bard, E.G. and Jeuniaux, P. (2012) "Behavior Matching in Multimodal Communication Is Synchronized," *Cognitive Science* 36 (8): 1404–26

Lukes, S. (1968) "Methodological Individualism Reconsidered," *The British Journal of Sociology* 19 (2): 119–29.

Mannheim, K. (1936) *Ideology and Utopia*, London: Routledge.

Miller, S. (2001) *Social Action: A Teleological Account*, New York: Cambridge University Press.

Palante, G. (1903) *Combat pour l'individualism*, Paris, France: F. Alcon.

Popper, K. (1944a) "The Poverty of Historicism I," *Economica* 11: 86–103.

——— (1944b) "The Poverty of Historicism II," *Economica* 11: 119–37.

——— (1945) "The Poverty of Historicism III," *Economica* 11: 69–89.

——— (1966) *The Open Society and Its Enemies*, London: Routledge and Kegan Paul.

Quine, W.V. (1969) "Epistemology Naturalized," in *Ontological Relativity and Other Essays*, New York: Columbia University Press.

Rakoczy, H. and Tomasello, M. (2009) "Done Wrong or Said Wrong? Young Children Understand the Normative Directions of Fit of Different Speech Acts," *Cognition* 113 (2): 205–12.

Richardson, M.J., Marsh, K.L. and Baron, R.M. (2007) "Judging and Actualizing Intrapersonal and Interpersonal Affordances," *Journal of Experimental Psychology: Human Perception and Performance* 33: 845–59.

Rodriguez-Pereyra, G. (2005) "Why Truth-makers," in H. Beebee and J. Dodd (eds) *Truth-makers: The Contemporary Debate*, Oxford: Oxford University Press.

Rovane, C. (2014) "Group Agency and Individualism," *Erkenntnis* 79 (9): 1663–84.

Rupert, R. (2011) "Empirical Arguments for Group Minds: A Critical Appraisal," *Philosophy Compass* 6 (9): 630–9.

Schumpeter, J. (1908) *Das Wesen und Der Hauptinhalt Der Theoretischen Nationalökonomie*, Leipzig: Duncker & Humbolt.

——— (1909) "On the Concept of Social Value," *Quarterly Journal of Economics* 23: 213–32.

Searle, J. (1990) "Group Intentions and Actions," in P. Cohen, J. Morgan and M. Pollack (eds) *Intentions and Communication*, Cambridge, MA: MIT Press.

——— (2009) *Making the Social World: The Structure of Human Civilization*, New York: Oxford University Press.

Sebanz, N. and Knoblich, G. (2009) "Prediction in Joint Action: What, When, and Where," *Topics in Cognitive Science* 1: 353–67.

Sebanz, N., Bekkering, H. and Knoblich, G. (2006) "Joint Action: Bodies and Minds Moving Together," *Trends in Cognitive Science* 10 (2): 70–4.

Sugden, R. (1993) "Thinking as a Team: Towards an Explanation of Nonselfish Behavior," *Social Philosophy and Policy* 10 (1): 69–89.

Theiner, G. (2013) "Transactive Memory Systems: A Mechanistic Analysis of Emergent Group Memory," *Review of Philosophy and Psychology* 4 (1): 65–89.

Theiner, G. and O'Connor, T. (2010) "The Emergence of Group Cognition," in A. Corradini and T. O'Connor (eds) *Emergence in Science and Philosophy*, New York: Routledge.

Tollefsen, D. and Dale, R. (2011) "Naturalizing Joint Action: A Process-Based Approach," *Philosophical Psychology* 25 (3): 385–407.

Tollefsen, D., Kreuz, R. and Dale, R. (2014) "Flavors of Togetherness: Experimental Philosophy and Theories of Joint Action," in J. Knobe and S. Nichols (eds) *Oxford Studies in Experimental Philosophy*, Oxford: Oxford University Press.

Tomasello, M. and Rakoczy, H. (2003) "What Makes Human Cognition Unique? From Individual to Shared to Collective Intentionality," *Mind and Language* 18 (2): 121–47.

Tomasello, M., Carpenter, M., Call, J., Behne, T. and Moll, H. (2005) "Understanding and Sharing Intentions: The Origins of Cultural Cognition," *Behavioral and Brain Sciences* 28 (5): 675–91.

Tuomela, R. (1995) "Group Beliefs," *Synthese* 91 (3): 285–318.

——— (2006) "Joint Intention: We Mode and I Mode," in P. French and H. Wettstein (eds) *Midwest Studies in Philosophy* 30: 35–58.

——— (2013) *Social Ontology*, New York: Oxford University Press.

Warneken, F. and Tomasello, M. (2009) "Varieties of Altruism in Children and Chimpanzees," *Trends in Cognitive Sciences* 13 (9): 397–402.

Watkins, J.W.N. (1952) "The Principle of Methodological Individualism," *British Journal for the Philosophy of Science* 3 (10): 186–9.

——— (1957) "Historical Explanation in the Social Sciences," *British Journal for the Philosophy of Science* 8 (30): 104–17.

Weber, M. (1922) *Economy and Society* (ed.) G. Roth and C. Wittich, Berkeley: University of California Press, 1968.

VII

The Extent, Origins, and Development of Collective Intentionality

Introduction to Part VII

Marija Jankovic and Kirk Ludwig

The study of collective intentionality is an interdisciplinary pursuit. Philosophical theories of collective intentionality inform and are informed by empirical research. Especially lively areas of interaction are those that concern the development of collective intentionality in children, the evolution of collective intentionality, and, related to both of these, the extent to which collective intentionality is present in non-human animals.

In Chapter 31, "Development of Collective Intentionality," Hannes Rakoczy describes research from cognitive sciences on the early development of collective intentionality in children. Rakoczy notes that this research employs pre-theoretical notions of collective intentionality, and as such may yield results that reveal certain philosophical accounts to be better or worse suited to accommodate the empirical findings. For example, young children show a capacity for certain forms of collective intentionality, but most reductionist accounts take collective intentionality to require complex higher-order representations. This tension requires resolution in one of several possible directions.

In Chapter 32, "Collective Intentionality in Non-Human Animals," Robert A. Wilson questions what has become a dominant view of collective intentionality, that it is a capacity that belongs to humans only. The main obstacle to attributing collective intentionality to non-human animals, according to Wilson, is the expectation that, roughly, there is no collective intentionality without individual minds. One manifestation of this expectation is the construction of collective intention from we-intentions of individuals. Wilson points to social insects—wasps, bees, ants—which engage in a range of actions that require the coordination of thousands of individuals, but where the individual parts cannot be said to have much of a mind. To properly describe such behaviors, Wilson argues, we either need to accept that there can be collective action without collective intention or that collective intention need not be composed of individual we-intentions. Wilson suggests the latter response, which opens up the possibility that there are forms of collective intentionality that are distinct from those found in humans.

In Chapter 33, "Origins of Collective Intentionality," Jan M. Engelmann and Michael Tomasello present an account of the evolution of collective intentionality. Tomasello is a prominent supporter of the thesis that collective intentionality is a distinctively human cognitive capacity. Engelmann and Tomasello describe the evolution of full-blown collective intentionality as involving a particularly important "middle step," the evolution of the capacity to engage in small-scale, temporary, face-to-face interactions, such as taking a walk together. They hypothesize that this capacity evolved due to the pressure to engage in collaborative hunting, which forced humans to evolve two distinctive kinds of cognitive skill. First, they evolved the capacities required to view others as collaborators, such as joint attention and joint intention. This led to the development of new social relationships in which agents see each other as members of a "we" rather than independent agents. This middle-step was the key for the later development of the capacities needed to create institutional and cultural reality, and to enter into moral relationships.

31

Development of Collective Intentionality

Hannes Rakoczy

1. INTRODUCTION

When and how does collective intentionality develop? This question has come into the focus of research in cognitive development in recent years with the establishment of collective intentionality as a phenomenon to be studied empirically by the cognitive sciences. In the last two decades, cognitive science has been investigating, from an ontogenetic point of view, how collective intentionality emerges and develops in humans and how it relates to other forms of intentionality, and from a comparative point of view, whether or to which degree it might mark one of the cognitive foundations of human uniqueness. The present chapter will give an overview of this research on the emergence and early development of different forms of collective intentionality in human ontogeny, with an eye to the comparative question of which of these kinds of collective intentionality might be shared with other species and which might be uniquely human.

Historically, the empirical interest of the cognitive sciences in collective intentionality arose as a consequence of the establishment of collective intentionality as a separate field of study in the, by now, classical philosophical literature of the 1980s and 1990s (Bratman 1992; Gilbert 1990; Searle 1990; Tuomela & Miller 1988). The empirical phenomena studied and the questions asked have been drawing much inspiration from the different philosophical accounts. Importantly, however, most empirical approaches start off from pre-theoretical folk notions of collective intentionality and thus remain theoretically neutral vis-à-vis the different philosophical accounts of how to best explicate these folk notions—much like, for example, how cognitive science research of people's "theory of mind" investigates how people ascribe mental states to others and themselves without thereby committing to any one specific position in the philosophy of mind. So, while the cognitive science of the development of collective intentionality does neither have to wait until an agreed upon philosophical analysis comes forth (if this ever happens) nor to commit to any one of the currently debated accounts, the empirical results of developmental and other cognitive science research might well have implications for the philosophical debates. It might turn out, for example, that different accounts are suitable to varying degrees for describing one or the other form of developing shared[1] intentionality.

In the following, we first review empirical milestones in the emergence and early development of different forms of collective intentionality, and then discuss potential implications for conceptual analyses and philosophical disputes.

2. WHAT MIGHT THE EARLIEST FORMS OF COLLECTIVE INTENTIONALITY BE?

When trying to uncover the primordial forms of collective intentionality in evolution or ontogeny, empirical research is faced with a fundamental methodological problem: how to distinguish truly collective intentionality from merely individual intentionality or even simpler non-intentional forms of social coordination? As has been stressed in the philosophical literature, two instances of socially coordinated activities by two or more participants (e.g. people walking beside each other (Gilbert 1990) or running to a shelter (Searle 1990)) may look identical from some perspectives—yet, with human adults, in cases of doubt we could just ask the participants what they were doing and get informative answers ("I am taking a walk" vs "we are taking a walk"). In the absence of language in small children and non-human animals, distinguishing true collective intentionality from simpler phenomena is a complicated and controversial endeavor, with different approaches differing in their rigor. While liberal approaches tend to set the bars for collective intentionality relatively low, considering, for example, the coordinated hunting behavior of hyenas an expression of true collective intentionality (Searle 1990), other approaches would be more cautious and set the bars considerably higher, doubting whether the social coordination in distributed hunting, for example, requires collective rather than merely complex individual intentionality (Rakoczy & Tomasello 2007).

Concerning human ontogeny, the earliest forms of coordinated social activities that might be considered by liberal accounts as primordial forms of collective intentionality can be found early in the first year of life. From around 2 months, infants engage in proto-conversational dyadic interactions with caregivers that reveal a contingent turn-taking structure such that infants, for example, smile or vocalize contingently upon the caregiver's actions. From the point of view of very liberal approaches, such forms of interaction have been interpreted as an instance of true and primary intersubjectivity or cooperation (Trevarthen & Hubley 1978). Such interpretations, however, are very controversial and not widely shared. Basically, it is simply not clear why contingent interaction per se should reveal anything about cooperation or sharedness in any more stringent sense. Furthermore, we do not have any evidence that children this young have any grasp of other agents' intentionality, and it is hard to see how an infant should be able to share intentionality and build joint cooperative intentions or other attitudes in the absence of any grasp of the cooperators' intentionality[2].

It is therefore more promising, according to widespread consensus, to look for the earliest forms of true collective intentionality later in ontogeny once children have acquired some basic grasp of other agents' intentionality. A prominent picture of the mind has it that the logically and ontogenetically most basic forms of the mental are generally supposed to be those at the fringes of the head, so to speak, namely perception (on the cognitive side) and intentional action (on the conative side). Following this picture, it can plausibly be expected that the primary forms of individual intentionality of second order should be ascription of perception and intentional action, and that the primary forms of shared intentionality should be shared perception and shared intentional action. The next sections, therefore, deal with the early development of shared perception (joint attention) and shared action, respectively.

3. JOINT ATTENTION

From around 9 months, there are reliable signs that children begin to operate with a basic grasp of other agents' intentionality, often termed "perception-goal psychology" (in contrast to the later developing fully fledged belief-desire folk psychology); they understand what others perceive of their surroundings and what intentions they pursue in their actions (Tomasello et al. 2005; Wellman 2002). And it is from around this time that earliest forms of joint attention emerge as well (see Chapter 10, this volume). Intuitively, joint attention involves two (or more) subjects looking[3] at some object or situation together. For example, wondering what is left for dinner, A and B might open their fridge and look at its contents together ("Let's see what we have left"). What makes such an episode one of truly joint attention? It is not sufficient that each of them looks at the same target, nor that, asymmetrically, one sees the other looking somewhere and follows her gaze to the same target. It is not even sufficient, more symmetrically, that each looks at the same target while knowing that the other does so as well (otherwise I would be jointly attending to many football games with many friends all around the world whenever we watch the same game, and know of each other that we do so, in front of different and very remote TV sets). Rather, in some intuitive sense that conceptually proves notoriously difficult to spell out, both have to attend to the same target in joint and coordinated ways.

Ontogenetic Origins of Joint Attention

Concerning development, when in ontogeny do we see the emergence of joint and coordinated attention-sharing? A basic methodological problem here is the following: while in adults and older children, linguistic data (such as "Let's see what we have left") usually disambiguate whether a given episode reflects merely parallel or truly joint attention, we have to rely on purely pre-verbal indicators and manifestations of joint attention in infants.

Empirically, earliest forms of social coordination of attention that have been considered to manifest joint attention emerge from around 9–12 months of age (Carpenter et al. 1998). Children begin to passively follow the gaze of others and actively direct it to objects and situations. This is not only asymmetrical following or directing of individual attention, however, since infants alternate their gaze between partner and object, check the partner's attention and actively coordinate and align the partner's attention and their own by communicative (gestural) means. Furthermore, some studies have directly analyzed "sharing" and "knowing" looks by the infant towards the partner that intuitively appear to be preverbal analogues of "Let's look . . ." or "We're looking . . ." (Hobson & Hobson 2007).

Additional evidence suggests that the social gaze coordination emerging at this time manifests truly joint attention rather than mere attention-following or manipulation. In their proto-declarative pointing (pointing out situations or states of affairs without any further instrumental ends in mind but simply for the sake of "telling" the social partner), infants expect certain—joint attentional—responses (Liszkowski et al. 2007a, 2007b); when an infant points out a situation to a partner (e.g. that there is a ball over there), she will only be satisfied (and thus stop pointing) when the adult not only looks at the specific situation, but alternates gaze in coordinated ways between the situation and the infant (as if saying "Yes, I saw it, it's the ball we're talking about"). And infants keep track of what was in the focus of joint attention with a given partner (a proxy of what was mutual knowledge among them) over time: they understand one and the same ambiguous communicative act (such as "can you give it to me" vis-à-vis several objects) systematically differently as a function of the previous joint experience they had with the interlocutor (Moll et al. 2008); when one interlocutor and the child had previously jointly engaged with object A, the child gives this object to the interlocutor, but gives to another interlocutor object B to which they both had previously jointly attended.

Older children use joint attention in systematic and sophisticated ways for action planning; when the child and a partner (in a Stag Hunt coordination game) each faced the choice of pressing button A to get a moderate reward, or to press button B to get a higher reward, but only if both pressed B, 4-year-old children actively alternated gaze with the partner and decided for B only when the partner emitted alternating, coordinated and "knowing" looks between the child and the apparatus (Wyman et al. 2013).

Comparative Perspectives on Joint Attention

In sum, children from around 1 year begin to engage in the kinds of attention-sharing with others that plausibly reflect truly joint attention given the systematic interpersonal coordination at a given time and over time—and thus a primordial form of perceptual we-intentionality. From a comparative point of view, this understanding of perceptional intentionality and engaging in shared perceptual we-intentionality in children reveals very interesting commonalities and differences with the cognitive capacities of non-human primates. Concerning commonalities, great apes and some monkeys reliably engage in gaze-following and manipulate others' gaze for instrumental purposes in proto-imperative pointing. And they take into account what others see or have seen for strategic individual action planning (e.g. foraging food that competitors cannot see (Hare et al. 2000)). There are crucial differences, however, in that non-human primates seem not to enter into any form of truly joint attention given the absence of systematic gaze alternation and coordination, "knowing" looks, proto-declarative pointing and the like (Carpenter & Call, 2013; Tomasello et al. 2005).

4. JOINT ACTION

The most obvious and natural case of collective intentionality clearly is acting together. It is cooperative activities that most philosophical accounts of collective intentionality focus on. And it is cooperative activities that present the clearest case for the development of collective intentionality as well.

Ontogenetic Origins of Joint Action

Natural observation and experimental results suggest that children begin to reliably engage in intentional cooperative activities with others in the course of the second year, both in joint instrumental action aimed at some further end, and in joint playful actions that serve as ends in themselves (Tomasello & Hamann 2012). At first, from around 14–18 months, children coordinate and communicate successfully with others in simple collaborative actions involving some basic division of labor (for example, retrieving a reward from an apparatus where one needs to open a flap so that the other can grasp the object (Brownell & Carriger 1990; Warneken et al. 2006)). In subsequent development in the second and third year, the joint-ness of the actions becomes much clearer, and the interpretation of children's social coordination as true shared intentionality much less ambiguous. Cooperation now manifests a suite of features all pointing towards true we-ness. Children not only coordinate and communicate in acting with one another, they also seem to have some basic understanding of the basic structure of complementary roles underlying the division of labor—as indicated in their so-called "role reversal imitation"; when they learn a novel collaborative activity comprising the complementary roles A and B by performing A (while the partner performs B), they do not just acquire egocentric information about their part, rather, they then spontaneously switch roles and perform B as well (Carpenter et al. 2005). Concerning roles, children do not just coordinate in taking up complementary roles, but respond in sophisticated ways when a partner fails in her fulfillment of the role: they try to reassign the role to her communicatively (by pointing out to her the object to be acted upon or the location where to act), help her to fulfill it and generally try to re-engage her for the cooperation (Warneken et al. 2006). And they do so specifically when the partner is still generally willing to participate in the cooperation yet unable to fulfill the role, but not when the partner is unwilling to cooperate (Warneken et al. 2012). From around age 3, children show explicit signs of feeling committed to the pursuit of a cooperative activity. When, in a recent study, children were involved in a mildly interesting cooperative activity with a partner, and then seduced by the option of doing something much more exciting, they often hesitated and then excused themselves before leaving the joint action (Grafenhain et al. 2009). They also indicate a sense of commitment to the successful pursuit of the joint project in other ways. Hamann and colleagues (Hamann et al. 2012) had pairs of peers cooperate by operating apparatus with complementary roles. Successful fulfillment of the roles resulted in rewards for each player. Crucially, however, the reward for player A was issued earlier than the reward for player B, so that from the point of view of A, she could basically stop at that point. This is exactly what happened in a control condition in which the two players acted separately in parallel. In the cooperation condition, however, player A still continued her part until player B's reward was issued as well. Similarly, when the apparatus issued a joint reward for the two players together, children took great pains to distribute it equally (but did not do so in a control condition in which two agents acted individually and in parallel (Hamann et al. 2011)).

Subsequent Developments

In subsequent development, children's grasp of cooperation, its division of labor, role structure and its normative aspects becomes more and more sophisticated. For example, 4-year-olds have completely agent-neutral conception of complementary action roles that can be freely filled by any agent at any time, and flexibly use such a conception for future planning of cooperative activities and their parts therein (Fletcher et al. 2012; Rakoczy et al. 2014). Generally, however, the development of shared intentional activities from children's earliest joint games to fully fledged adult cooperation is currently not well understood yet.

(Sub-Personal) Cognitive Underpinnings of Shared Action

Cognitive science has recently begun to investigate the fine-grained cognitive underpinnings of shared cooperative activities. Theoretical work has introduced distinctions between a hierarchy of representations of shared intentions at different levels, ranging from personal-level conceptualized future-directed intentions to act together to sub-personal motor representations of coordinated social behavior such as how to move one's leg in relation to a dancing partner's leg movements (Pacherie 2008, 2011). And experimental work with adults has shown that such sub-personal motor representations of shared activities are formed and operate swiftly and spontaneously below the threshold of subjects' awareness (Sebanz et al. 2006). From a developmental point of view, little is currently known about the ontogeny of the cognitive underpinnings of shared action. But the first study on this recently has suggested that the same kinds of fine-grained sub-personal motor representations of shared actions as found in adults might be in operation even in preschool-aged children (Milward et al. 2014).

Comparative Perspectives on Joint Action

Much recent research suggests that great apes (and perhaps other non-human primates) have some basic understanding of others' individual intentionality, and systematically use this understanding of what others perceive and intend for strategic purposes in competitive interactions (Call & Tomasello 2008). Yet whether they go beyond such individual intentionality of second order and engage in truly shared intentionality in the form of joint action is highly controversial. Experimental findings suggest that apes are quite skillful in social coordination with others, perhaps even involving something like division of labor (Melis et al. 2006). Whether such coordination amounts to true cooperation remains questionable, however, given that apes do not show the characteristic signatures of acting together that we find in children such as re-engagement of partners, reassignment of roles, sharing of rewards, helping others to fulfill their role or excusing oneself (Tomasello & Hamann 2012). More systematic research is needed to shed more light on the question of whether or to which degree basic forms of joint action are uniquely human or shared with other primates.

5. ROOTS OF INSTITUTIONAL REALITY

According to many conceptual analyses, there is a particular and peculiar sub-form of collective intentionality that underlies our institutional and societal life. In contrast to basic forms of cooperative action such as, say, walking together, this form of collective intentionality is essentially conventional, rule-governed and fact-creating. One prominent approach has it that the logical structure of this form of collective intentionality can be best captured by the notion of status function assignment and the complementary notion of an institutional fact (Searle 1995; Chapters 20–3, this volume). Status functions pertain to objects or actions simply because we collectively treat them as having these functions: nothing in a slip of paper is inherently valuable, nothing in a given person inherently makes her a president. Things are money or presidents because of our collective practices. Such institutional facts (that a given object is money or a president) of the form "this X counts as Y in a given context C" are socially constructed facts in contrast to raw facts that hold independently of any particular collective practice or perspective. And they are essentially normative: the status collectively assigned to an object normatively licenses certain forms of treating it while making other kinds of action inappropriate. The fact that something is a queen in chess, say, entitles one to use it in certain ways but not in others. Being a teacher or a president, entitle both the holder of the role and interactors to certain actions but not to others.

The Early Ontogeny of Status Function Assignment

When and where do we find the first and primary forms of such collective intentionality with status assignment in ontogeny? Clearly, young children seem to have no grasp whatsoever of most of the standard examples of institutional facts such as those pertaining to political power, linguistic meaning or economic matters. But children from very early on do engage in activities that can be considered to share the basis logical structure of status assignment and institutional reality, namely games of various sorts. From their second year on, children begin to engage in pretend play and in simple non-pretense rule games. In pretend play—say, in pretending that a wooden block is an apple—objects are assigned fictional status ("the block counts as 'apple' in the context of our pretense") in much the same way objects are assigned serious status (this X counts as Y in context C) in institutional practices generally. And children from around ages 2 to 3 have been found to grasp the basic logical structure of fictional status assignment in joint pretense and its inferential and normative consequences. They not only engage in solitary and isolated acts of pretending, but they pick up, understand and respect the stipulations of the joint pretense scenario set up by a play partner (such as "this wooden block is our 'apple', and this pen is our 'knife'") and guide their own actions in the course of the pretense accordingly. In particular, they produce acts that are normatively appropriate, inferentially licensed by the fictional status assignment. For example, they pretend to cut the wooden block with the pen, handle the pen "carefully" because it is "sharp" etc. (Harris & Kavanaugh 1993; Rakoczy et al. 2004). And not only do they act appropriately themselves, but also indicate an awareness of the normative structure of such practice more actively; when a third person joins the game, but makes a "mistake," i.e. does not respect the pretense status of an object, they protest and criticize her (Rakoczy 2008; Wyman et al. 2009a). And children's awareness and enforcement of the normative implications of fictional status assignment is already sensitive to the context-relativity typical of status assignment. One form of context-relativity pertains to multiple statuses: That an X counts as a Y_1 in a given context C_1 leaves open the possibility that the very same object can have some other status (Y_2) in some other context C_2. A given card may be a trump in one kind of card game but a lousy card in another. Similarly, one kind of object may at the same time have one kind of fictional status in one pretense game, and a different one in another game. Children at age 3 understand this multiple fictional status, flexibly switch between contexts and adapt their actions accordingly (Wyman et al. 2009b). A related form of context-relativity is the following: given that X counts as Y in C, within the context C there are normative implications as to how to treat X such that a given action may constitute a mistake, but outside of the context C no such implications hold so that the very same kind of act may be perfectly fine. Again, children aged 2–3 understand this form of context-relative normativity; they protest against the very same kinds of act when performed in a context in which it constitutes a mistake in light of the status assignment in this context, but do not do so when the same kind of act is performed outside of this context, for example when the agent had announced "I'm not joining your game, I'll be doing something else" prior to acting (Rakoczy et al. 2008; Wyman et al. 2009a).

So by the third year of life, children have entered into the basics of this remarkable practice of games of pretending, collectively treat objects they know to be Xs as Ys, follow and respect the implications of the proto-constitutive rules of the game, and normatively criticize deviations from the rules. In embryonic and isolated form we thus have here the basic structure of institutional reality in the games of 2-year-olds. Of course this is a long way from money, marriage and universities, but the seeds are there, and so joint pretending quite plausibly can be considered the central cradle for, and the entering gate into institutional life. In fact, it may be no coincidence that pretense and other games constitute a, if not the, cradle for growing into institutional reality more generally. A fundamental problem in coming to participate in institutional life is its holistic structure: most forms of status (e.g. political) cannot be understood without understanding many other forms of status intimately connected (e.g. economic, power relations etc.). So how and where should a child ever be able to break into this circle? Games may do the trick. First, they are in some intuitive sense "non-serious," and however this elusive notion is to be spelled out, one aspect of this is that it is quarantined from the rest of institutional life to a considerable degree. Second, while the contexts of many forms of institutional reality are abstract and far-reaching both spatially and temporally (currency areas etc.), the contexts of simple joint pretense games are very tangible, short-lived and action-based ("in this pretense we're doing right here and now . . ."). Third, setting up fictional status, even in very young children, is intimately linked with language in a way that is typical for institutional reality more generally. One (if not the) paradigmatic form of status assignment is declarative speech acts of the form "This (X) is now a Y" such as "You are now husband and wife" or "From now on, this ship is called MS. Hildegard" (Searle 2010). In their joint pretense, children routinely set up the scenario by declaring things like "this (block) is now the apple, and this (pen) is the knife," often with specialized grammatical marking to signal the non-literal force of the speech act (Kaper 1980). Ontogenetically, thus, pretense declarations such as "this is now the apple" may well be the foundation for serious status declarations such as "you are now husband and wife." Such a general picture of pretense as an ontogenetic foundation for institutional reality is in the spirit of a fascinating account by Kendall Walton (1990) that ascribes a similar foundational role to pretense as a basis for all kinds of representational art.

Comparative Perspectives on Status Function Assignment

From a comparative point of view, there is no convincing evidence in any non-human species for any kind of social practice with status function assignment. Concerning play, there are widespread forms of rough and tumble and other kinds of sensorimotor play in non-human primates and other mammals. But there is no convincing and solid evidence (beyond highly ambiguous natural observation anecdotes) for true pretend play or other types of rule-governed games (Gómez 2008). But do not many animals respect social status in serious domains, for example, in the form of dominance hierarchies etc.? The problem here is that there are at least two radically different notions of social status, dominance etc. On an institutional reading, dominance status—say, in a corporation—is a matter of convention and collective assignment. Yet, on a brute reading, dominance status is a purely causal notion (cashed out, in the end, by physical force and the like). So, while there is ample evidence that non-human animals are sensitive to social status in the latter sense, there is basically no evidence to suggest they respect the former.

6. OUTLOOK

The cognitive science of collective intentionality and its development is a relatively recent phenomenon. So, while we have learned about potential roots, earliest forms and developmental courses of different forms of collective intentionality in many respects we have just begun to scratch the surface, with many conceptual and empirical challenges for future research.

Conceptual Challenges

Empirical approaches to studying collective intentionality and its development, as mentioned in the introduction, usually start off from our pre-theoretic notions of collective intentionality and need not take a stance in the debate between different philosophical attempts at conceptual analysis of "collective intentionality" and related notions. However, the empirical results of developmental cognitive science may well have implications for the plausibility of different such accounts. For example, when attempting to describe the earliest ontogeny of shared cooperative activities, reductionist accounts that analyze shared intentionality in terms of complex forms of higher-order individual intentionality in much the same way as Gricean accounts analyze meaning in terms of individual higher-order communicative intentions (Bratman 1992, 2014) run into trouble. This trouble can be captured with the following schematic trilemma (Breheny 2006; Rakoczy 2006):

1. shared intentionality presupposes higher-order recursive propositional attitudes
2. young children do not yet have such attitudes, but
3. young children manifest shared intentionality.

So, which of the inconsistent triad should be given up? The most plausible solution lies in a refinement and qualification of (i): While full-blown and complex adult shared intentionality might in fact presuppose such attitudes, there are developmentally (and evolutionarily) primary and less complex forms of shared intentionality (Butterfill 2012; Pacherie 2013).

A related set of questions concerns the developmental relations of second-order individual intentionality and collective intentionality more generally. Gricean approaches, notably Bratman's (1992), assume that second-order individual intentionality is necessary and sufficient for collective intentionality (the latter is just a complex and coordinated form of the former), and thus the development of collective intentionality is just the development of a certain complex form of individual intentionality. In contrast, anti-reductionist accounts such as Searle's (1995), assuming that collective intentionality is a primitive phenomenon, seem to imply that second-order individual intentionality is not only not sufficient, but also not necessary for collective intentionality and thus that the two kinds of intentionality might develop without intimate relations to each other. Yet, from a developmental point of view, there might be an interesting third way: second-order individual intentionality and collective intentionality may be intimately related (such that some form of the former is necessary without being sufficient for the latter) and thus develop in close tandem with each other. For example, it may be that joint attention and cooperation—as basic forms of collective intentionality—present the primary contexts in which individual intentionality of second order (ascribing perceptual perspectives, goals etc. to interaction partners) develops (Moll & Meltzoff 2011).

Empirical Challenges

From an empirical point of view, many fundamental questions concerning the development of collective intentionality remain to be addressed: Ontogenetically, what are the origins and roots of collective intentionality? Once basic forms of collective intentionality are in place in early childhood, how do more complex forms develop, such as collective belief? Once children participate in basic forms of joint status assignment and institutional life, how do they develop a more sophisticated and reflective grasp of the logical structure of institutional, observer-dependent facts and their categorical difference to brute facts? More generally, how is development to be characterized? Are there discrete and qualitatively distinct stages of development (e.g. Tomasello et al. 2012)? Are there qualitatively different systems and/or processes, for example for minimalist vs full-blown collective intentionality, as is often assumed in other areas of cognitive development such as numerical or social cognition (Apperly & Butterfill 2009; Carey 2009)?

From the point of view of comparative psychology, more systematic research concerning commonalities and differences in the development of individual and collective intentionality of human and non-human primates is needed. Is collective intentionality as it develops from the second year in human ontogeny per se uniquely human? Or can basic collective intentionality, at least in rudimentary form, be found in non-human primates as well, yet with clear limits when it comes to collective intentionality with status assignment and institutional practices?

RELATED TOPICS

Collective Action and Agency (Ch. 1), Coordinating Joint Action (Ch. 6), Joint Attention (Ch. 9), Social Construction and Social Facts (Ch. 20), Collective Intentionality in Non-Human Animals (Ch. 32), Origins of Collective Intentionality (Ch. 33).

REFERENCES

Apperly, I.A., & Butterfill, S.A. (2009) "Do Humans Have Two Systems to Track Beliefs and Belief-Like States?" *Psychological Review* 116 (4): 953–70.

Bratman, M.E. (1992) "Shared Cooperative Activity," *The Philosophical Review* 101 (2): 327–41.

——— (2014) *Shared Agency: A Planning Theory of Acting Together*, Oxford: Oxford University Press.

Breheny, R. (2006) "Communication and Folk Psychology," *Mind and Language* 21 (1): 74–107.

Brownell, C., & Carriger, M.S. (1990) "Changes in Cooperation and Self-Other Differentiation During the Second Year," *Child Development* 61: 1164–74.

Butterfill, S. (2012) "Joint Action and Development," *The Philosophical Quarterly* 62 (246): 23–47.

Call, J., & Tomasello, M. (2008) "Does the Chimpanzee Have a Theory of Mind? 30 Years Later," *Trends in Cognitive Sciences* 12 (5): 187–92.

Carey, S. (2009) *The Origin of Concepts*, New York: Oxford University Press.

Carpenter, M., & Call, J. (2013) "How Joint is the Joint Attention of Apes and Human Infants?" in J. Metcalfe & H.S. Terrace (eds) *Agency and Joint Attention*, New York: Oxford University Press.

Carpenter, M., Nagell, K., & Tomasello, M. (1998) "Social Cognition, Joint Attention, and Communicative Competence from 9 to 15 Months of Age," *Monographs of the Society for Research in Child Development* 63 (4): 176.

Carpenter, M., Tomasello, M., & Striano, T. (2005) "Role Reversal Imitation and Language in Typically Developing Infants and Children With Autism," *Infancy* 8 (3): 253–78.

Fletcher, G.E., Warneken, F., & Tomasello, M. (2012) "Differences in Cognitive Processes Underlying the Collaborative Activities of Children and Chimpanzees," *Cognitive Development* 27 (2): 136–53.

Gilbert, M. (1990) "Walking Together: a Paradigmatic Social Phenomenon," *Midwest Studies in Philosophy* 15: 1–14.

Gómez, J.C. (2008) "The Evolution of Pretence: From Intentional Availability To Intentional Non-Existence," *Mind & Language* 23 (5): 586–606.

Grafenhain, M., Behne, T., Carpenter, M., & Tomasello, M. (2009) "Young Children's Understanding of Joint Commitments," *Developmental Psychology* 45 (5): 1430–43.

Hamann, K., Warneken, F., Greenberg, J.R., & Tomasello, M. (2011) "Collaboration Encourages Equal Sharing in Children but Not in Chimpanzees," *Nature* 476 (7360): 328–31.

Hamann, K., Warneken, F., & Tomasello, M. (2012) "Children's Developing Commitments to Joint Goals," *Child Development* 83 (1): 137–45.

Hare, B., Call, J., Agnetta, B., & Tomasello, M. (2000) "Chimpanzees Know What Conspecifics Do and Do Not See," *Animal Behaviour* 59 (4): 771–85.

Harris, P.L., & Kavanaugh, R.D. (1993) "Young Children's Understanding of Pretense," *Monographs of the Society for Research in Child Development* 58 (1)[231]: v–92.

Hobson, J., & Hobson, P. (2007) "Identification: the Missing Link Between Joint Attention and Imitation?" *Development and Psychopathology* 19 (2): 411–31.

Kaper, W. (1980) "The Use of Past Tense in Games of Pretend," *Journal of Child Language* 7 (1): 213–15.

Liszkowski, U., Carpenter, M., & Tomasello, M. (2007a) "Pointing Out New News, Old News, and Absent Referents at 12 Months of Age," *Developmental Science* 10 (2): F1–7.

——— (2007b) "Reference and Attitude in Infant Pointing," *Journal of Child Language* 34 (1): 1–20.

Melis, A.P., Hare, B., & Tomasello, M. (2006) "Chimpanzees Recruit the Best Collaborators," *Science* 311 (5765): 1297–1300.

Milward, S.J., Kita, S., & Apperly, I.A. (2014) "The Development of Co-Representation Effects in a Joint Task: Do Children Represent a Co-Actor?" *Cognition* 132 (3): 269–79.

Moll, H., & Meltzoff, A.N. (2011) "Joint Attention as the Fundamental Basis of Understanding Perspectives," in A. Seemann (ed.) *Joint attention: New developments in psychology philosophy of mind, and social neuroscience*, Cambridge, MA: MIT Press.

Moll, H., Richter, N., Carpenter, M., & Tomasello, M. (2008) "Fourteen-Month-Olds Know What 'We' Have Shared in a Special Way," *Infancy* 13 (1): 90–101.

Pacherie, E. (2008) "The Phenomenology of Action: a Conceptual Framework," *Cognition* 107 (1): 179–217.

——— (2011) "Framing joint action," *Review of Philosophy and Psychology* 2 (2): 173–92.

——— (2013) "Intentional Joint Agency: Shared Intention Lite," *Synthese* 190 (10): 1817–39.

Rakoczy, H. (2006) "Pretend Play and the Development of Collective Intentionality," *Cognitive Systems Research* 7: 113–27.

——— (2008) "Taking Fiction Seriously: Young Children Understand the Normative Structure of Joint Pretend Games," *Developmental Psychology* 44 (4): 1195–1201.

Rakoczy, H., & Tomasello, M. (2007) "The Ontogeny of Social Ontology: Steps to Shared Intentionality and Status Functions," in S.L. Tsohatzidis (ed.) *Intentional Acts and Institutional Facts: Essays on John Searle's Social Ontology*, Berlin: Springer Verlag.

Rakoczy, H., Tomasello, M., & Striano, T. (2004) "Young Children Know That Trying Is Not Pretending: A Test of the 'Behaving-as-If' Construal of Children's Early Concept of 'Pretense'," *Developmental Psychology* 40 (3): 388–99.

Rakoczy, H., Warneken, F., & Tomasello, M. (2008) "The Sources of Normativity: Young Children's Awareness of the Normative Structure of Games," *Developmental Psychology*, 44 (3): 875–81.

Rakoczy, H., Gräfenhain, M., Clüver, A., Schulze Dalhoff, A., & Sternkopf, A. (2014) "Young Children's Agent-Neutral Representations of Action Roles," *Journal of Experimental Child Psychology* 128: 201–9.

Searle, J. (1990) "Collective Intentions and Actions," in P. Cohen, J. Morgan, & M. Pollack (eds) *Intentions in Communication*, Cambridge, MA: MIT Press.

——— (1995) *The Construction of Social Reality*, New York: Free Press.

——— (2010) *Making the Social World: The Structure of Human Civilization*, Oxford: Oxford University Press.

Sebanz, N., Bekkering, H., & Knoblich, G. (2006) "Joint Action: Bodies and Minds Moving Together," *Trends in Cognitive Sciences* 10 (2): 71–6.

Tomasello, M., & Hamann, K. (2012) "The 37th Sir Frederick Bartlett Lecture: Collaboration in Young Children," *The Quarterly Journal of Experimental Psychology* 65 (1): 1–12.

Tomasello, M., Carpenter, M., Call, J., Behne, T., & Moll, H. (2005) "Understanding and Sharing Intentions: the Origins of Cultural Cognition," *Behavioral and Brain Sciences* 28 (5): 675–735.

Tomasello, M., Melis, A.P., Tennie, C., Wyman, E., & Herrmann, E. (2012) "Two Key Steps in the Evolution of Human Cooperation: the Interdependence Hypothesis," *Current Anthropology* 53 (6): 673–92.

Trevarthen, C., & Hubley, P. (1978) "Secondary Intersubjectivity: Confidence, Confiding and Acts of Meaning in the First Year of Life," in A. Lock (ed.) *Action, Gesture and Symbol*, London: Academic Press.

Tuomela, R., & Miller, K. (1988) "We-intentions," *Philosophical Studies* 53: 367–89.

Walton, K.L. (1990) *Mimesis as Make-Believe*, Cambridge, MA: Harvard University Press.

Warneken, F., Chen, F., & Tomasello, M. (2006) "Cooperative Activities in Young Children and Chimpanzees," *Child Development* 77 (3): 640–63.

Warneken, F., Gräfenhain, M., & Tomasello, M. (2012) "Collaborative Partner or Social Tool? New Evidence for Young Children's Understanding of Joint Intentions in Collaborative Activities," *Developmental Science* 15 (1): 54–61.

Wellman, H. (2002) "Understanding the Psychological World: Developing a Theory of Mind," in U. Goswami (ed.) *Blackwell Handbook of Childhood Cognitive Development*, Malden, MA: Blackwell Publishers.

Wyman, E., Rakoczy, H., & Tomasello, M. (2009a) "Normativity and Context in Young Children's Pretend Play," *Cognitive Development* 24 (2): 146–55.

——— (2009b) "Young Children Understand Multiple Pretend Identities in Their Object Play," *British Journal of Developmental Psychology* 27: 385–404.

——— (2013) "Non-Verbal Communication Enables Children's Coordination in a 'Stag Hunt' Game," *European Journal of Developmental Psychology* 10 (5): 597–610.

NOTES

1. While "shared" and "collective" intentionality are used largely interchangeably in the philosophical literature, some psychological approaches use the two notions to refer to different forms of joint intentionality (e.g. Tomasello et al. (2012); see Chapter 33, this volume). In the present chapter, I will follow the philosophical literature and use "shared" and "collective" synonymously.

2. Strong anti-reductionist accounts of collective intentionality such as Searle's (1990, 1995) may be read as allowing for exactly this possibility: if collective intentionality is understood as a primitive *sui generis* form of intentionality quite separate from any individual mode of intentionality, then one could imagine

a creature capable of forming we-intentions without being able to ascribe individual intentions to her cooperators. In our view, this is a very implausible possibility, and anti-reductionist accounts ought to claim, not that collective intentionality is completely separate from individual intentionality of higher order, but rather that some form of individual intentionality of higher order, while necessary, may not be sufficient for collective intentionality (Rakoczy & Tomasello 2007).

3. . . . or attending in some other sense modality. For simplicity's sake, we focus on visual perception here.

32

Collective Intentionality in Non-Human Animals

Robert A. Wilson

1. INTRODUCTION

'Collective intentionality', write Schweikard and Schmid in their recent Stanford Encyclopedia of Philosophy review of the topic, 'is the power of minds to be jointly directed at objects, matters of fact, states of affairs, goals, or values" (Schweikard and Schmid 2013). As Schweikard and Schmid's broader overview indicates, and as reflected in the current volume, collective intentionality has been primarily deployed in recent discussions of *human* cognition and sociality. In particular, over the past 20 years, collective intentionality has been used to explore putatively distinct forms of human cooperation and conflict, the role of institutions in human social life, and even the broader nature of social reality itself (Gilbert 1996; Searle 1995; Tomasello 1999; Tuomela 2007).

Whatever else it may be, collective intentionality has come to be conceived as some kind of crowning achievement of our species, and perhaps of our closest ancestors and living relatives, a sort of keystone accomplishment that brings in its wake new forms of sociality. Collective intentionality builds on and utilizes forms of individual cognition that are themselves distinctively human, whether they be metacognitive, modular, or general purpose. In that context, questions about how collective intentionality both develops ontogenetically and evolved phylogenetically are important, albeit secondary. They are questions about how individuals move, or the species moved, from a state without collective intentionality to a state with collective intentionality. Two recent publications on collective intentionality from influential researchers exemplify this perspective on collective intentionality.

In his *Making the Social World: The Structure of Human Civilization* (2010), John Searle emphasizes the importance that collective intentionality plays in human sociality through its role in creating *institutional reality*, elaborating on a view Searle first articulated at length in his *Constructing the Social World*, where he had noted that he used "social facts" and "collective intentional facts" so as to be coextensive (Searle 1995: 122).

For Searle, the collective acceptance or recognition of what he calls "status functions" assigned to brute physical facts is what creates institutional reality, and it is institutional reality that marks off distinctive forms of human sociality. Such collective mental phenomena 'of the sort we get in organized societies are themselves dependent on and derived from the mental phenomena of individuals' (Searle 2010: 4) and, for Searle, all 'intentionality, whether collective or individual, has to exist inside individuals' heads' (2010: 44). So according to Searle, distinctive human sociality is institutionally mediated, where institutional reality is brought into existence through forms of collective intentionality, which itself derives from in-the-head individual intentionality.

Michael Tomasello's *A Natural History of Human Thinking* (2014) concurs with Searle's view of the significance of collective intentionality for human sociality, and defends a particular, two-step evolutionary trajectory for the rise of collective intentionality that links it tightly to the origins of human culture. Although individual intentionality is possessed by humans and our closest living relatives in the primate order, Tomasello takes what he calls *joint attention* to be distinctively human, resting on forms of sharing or small-scale collaborative behavior between restricted numbers of individuals. Joint attention, in turn, becomes extended as 'group life as a whole became one big collaborative activity, creating a much larger and more permanent shared world, that is to say, a culture' (Tomasello 2014: 5). This new collaboration, together with the conventional, institutional, and normative forms of communication it involves, are what Tomasello calls *collective intentionality*, a kind of *group-mindedness* (2014: 5–6) that only human beings and their recent ancestors possess.

The anthropocentric perspective reflected in such views of collective intentionality are manifest more generally in the recent literature. For example, neither Schweikard and Schmid's (2013) article on collective intentionality, nor Chant, Hindriks and Preyer's introduction to their collection *From Individual to Collective Intentionality* (2014) even so much as mention non-human animal cognition. From such perspectives, an article on collective intentionality in non-human animals could be very brief, except insofar as it might help to delineate what collective intentionality is not. In short: there isn't any collective intentionality in the non-human animal world to be found.

We could, of course, break the visual silence here, avoiding the professional embarrassment that one should feel in writing on a non-topic, by discussing all the phenomena that one might think involve collective intentionality in non-human animals but don't really, or forms of proto-collective intentionality, or perhaps collective proto-intentionality, that one can find in non-human animals. Even so, I think it would be hard to completely suppress the thought that one was whistling in the dark, and that summers really are for something else.

Perhaps, at the end of the day, that's what readers will think this paper does. Fortunately for me at least (even if not for my summer), I think there is much more to be said in a positive and constructive vein about collective intentionality itself in non-human animals. Doing so involves probing at the concept of collective intentionality fairly directly (Section 2), considering the various forms that collective intentionality might take (Section 3), showing some sensitivity to the history of appeals to that concept and its close relatives (Section 4), and raising some broader questions about the relationships between sociality, cognition, and institutions by discussing two different possible cases of collective intentionality in non-human animals: that of the social insects (Section 5) and that of highly social mammals, such as canines (Section 6). If the discussion here is on track, then the widely shared perspective on collective intentionality exemplified by the work of Searle and Tomasello needs to be reconsidered.

2. COLLECTIVE INTENTIONALITY: THE WHAT AND THE WHERE

Although "intentionality" is a philosophical term of art, something that is often forgotten, the phenomena that it refers to are commonplace, particularly in how we think about the mental activities of individuals. Much of that activity is directed at, about, or represents how things are, were, or might be, in the world. Our mental lives are suffuse with activities—believing, desiring, imagining, remembering, pretending, fearing—that are representational or intentional in this way. Thus, intentionality is integral to the folk conception of individual minds. Indeed, intentionality was taken by Franz Brentano (1874) to be sufficiently central to having a mind that he famously characterized it as 'the mark of the mental'.

The primary ground for thinking that individuals have mental states with intentionality is epistemic and explanatory: such states are required for us to systematically grasp why human agents do what they do. Challenges issued to the claim that individuals have mental states with intentionality, such as behaviorism and eliminative materialism, lost out as viable alternatives in the philosophy of mind and cognitive science, which long ago made peace with an appeal to the intentionality of mental states as an integral part of the explanatory toolkit needed to understand human behavior and action (R.A. Wilson 1999).

Discussions of *collective* intentionality arose more recently from the same kind of epistemic ground within the theory of action (Searle 1990), but from the outset faced the same challenge that individual intentionality has bettered over time. This continuing challenge to the idea of collective intentionality is reflected in the more tentative way in which collective intentionality is often introduced into discussions of collective human action: might we need to posit intentionality that goes beyond the familiar forms of individual intentionality in order to explain at least some human social behaviors and actions?

More particularly, much human social behavior is cooperative, shared, or joint. We do things *together*: we work and play, we walk and talk, we celebrate and mourn, we laugh and cry. There seems little reluctance to view ourselves as undertaking such behaviors or actions together, to accept collective action, in addition to individual action. Even though collective action requires (and has received) further philosophical analysis, those who want to deny that there is such a thing as collective action face an uphill battle. Collective actions, such as building a fire together or holding hands, are no more ontologically dubious than the corresponding individual actions.

Not so with the underlying states that explain such collective behavior or action itself. Collective psychology, group minds, shared and joint cognition of various kinds—intentions, commitments, beliefs—all seem to invoke a mental ontology that goes beyond that of our common-sense thinking about minds and intentionality, and beyond the comfort zone that individual intentionality has found for itself in contemporary philosophical thinking about the mind.

For this reason, a major issue permeating the collective intentionality literature is whether one can provide an adequate account of the phenomena to be explained while restricting oneself to what Schweikard and Schmid (2013) call the *individual ownership claim*: 'collective intentionality is had by the participating individuals, and all the intentionality an individual has is his or her own'. If the individual ownership claim is true, then we seem at least primed to reduce collective intentionality to individual intentionality, plus some other non-intentional remainder. And if distinctively human cooperative, shared, or joint behavior and action is made possible by collective intentionality, so conceived, then we have a reductionist framework for understanding those aspects of human social life.

I want to suggest several ways in which one might adjust this overall perspective on collective intentionality that makes space for collective intentionality in the non-human animal world, but which also appeals to a form of the individual ownership claim. This is a particular form of what I have, elsewhere (R.A. Wilson 2001, 2004), called the *social manifestation thesis*. I begin with two reminders, the first about two forms of collective action, the second about the variety there is to collective intentionality itself.

3. FROM COLLECTIVE INTENTIONALITY TO COLLECTIVELY ACTING

The phrase "collective intentionality" itself can take on a reifying tendency: to think of intentionality as a thing of some kind that collectives or groups have or possess. Since collective action—or, better, collectively acting—is taken to be a relatively unproblematic phenomenon, an *explanandum* in search of an *explanans*, I want to suggest that we begin by reminding ourselves of two forms that collectively acting might take, neither of which are simply summative of the actions of individuals in the corresponding group. We might call these the *distributive* and the *joint* or *shared* forms of collectively acting.

A collective or group of individuals acts *distributively* when the components of the overall action are distributed across the actions of those individuals. A crowd's gathering at one time, and later dispersing, are two distributed forms of collectively acting, something that a group does through the actions of individuals. But distributive group action can also involve specialized individual actions, such as when a group builds a shelter or catches some food, where each individual does something distinctive that contributes to the overall group accomplishment.

In distributive collective action, the group does something that no individual in the group herself does, except insofar as she contributes to the collective action itself. To take a simplified example, one beaver finds and transports waterlogged debris to a particular site in a creek; a second beaver then places that material in the growing dam. The collective action of building a shelter—a beaver lodge or dam—is distributed across this pair of actions. To find and transport that material, or to arrange it, is to build a shelter only insofar as these component actions form part of the collective action.

For there to be *joint* or *shared* collective action, there needs to be not simply distributive collective action but in addition some kind of coordinating glue that makes it an action that is completed *together* intentionally. When a team of contractors builds my house, or a restaurant cooks me a meal, there is not simply distributed collective action but the kind of coordination and cooperation that makes for joint or shared collective action. One hypothesis is that joint or shared *intentionality*, particularly shared *intentions,* is what provides this coordinating glue. Such shared intentions have been central to the literature on collective intentionality, where they are often called "we-intentions": first-person plural intentions.

Finally, I turn to the second of my promised reminders. Although collective *intentions* feature prominently in the literature on collective intentionality, intentions are just one of many mental states that might be possessed by individuals or by collectives. An intention is a particular kind of propositional attitude or mental act, one related in specific ways to consciousness, planning, and behavior. But groups, like individuals, may also choose, plan, try, remember, perceive, sense, believe, desire, enjoy, or regret. At least in principle, each of those mental activities can exemplify collective intentionality. Indeed, it has been these forms of putative group-level intentionality that were postulated in both the biological and social sciences in the more distant past of our attempts to understand collective action via the idea of a group mind.

4. GROUP MINDS AND THE SOCIAL MANIFESTATION THESIS

As the evolutionary biologist David Sloan Wilson (1997a, 1997b) pointed out 20 years ago in the context of his successful revival of group selection as a viable mechanism for evolutionary change, the idea that groups of individual organisms, including human agents, have minds of some kind was once widely accepted in the social sciences. Wilson pointed to a number of the founders of sociology and anthropology, such as Emile Durkheim and William McDougall, as proponents of the idea that human groups, as well as human individuals, could literally have minds of some kind. To capture a broad set of views that one might argue are found in the works of such figures, I characterized the corresponding view as follows:

> *Group mind hypothesis*: groups of individual organisms can have or can be thought of as having minds in something like the way in which individual organisms themselves can have minds.
>
> (R.A. Wilson 2004: 267; cf. R.A. Wilson 2001: S263)

Wilson argued that group-level adaptations included not only physical activities but cognition, since 'groups can also evolve into adaptive units with respect to cognitive activities such as decision making, memory, and learning' (D.S. Wilson 1997a, S128). Here Wilson took himself to be advocating a form of the group mind hypothesis with respect to both human and non-human animals.

In exploring both the kind of claim that Wilson makes about the history of the social sciences and the contemporary revival of that tradition that he was himself advocating, I argued that such revivalist enthusiasm is somewhat misplaced (R.A. Wilson 2001, 2004: ch.11–12). This is because much of the relevant literature here is more plausibly viewed as advocating not the group mind hypothesis but what I called the *social manifestation thesis*:

> *social manifestation thesis*: individuals have properties, including psychological properties, that are manifest only when those individuals form part of a group of a certain type.
>
> (R.A. Wilson 2004: 281; cf. R.A. Wilson 2001: S265)

According to the social manifestation thesis, it is individuals rather than groups that have psychological properties and thus minds, but the social groups to which those individuals belong play some kind of important role in the possession of those properties. That role was not simply as a background condition or as a causal trigger for cognition, but partially constitutive or realizing of the manifestation of cognition itself. Having offered, in the previous chapters in the book, a sustained—some might say prolonged—articulation and defense of the idea that individual cognition was *extended* (R.A. Wilson 1994; Clark and Chalmers 1998; Clark 2008), I intended the social manifestation thesis to be read as a particular form of the hypothesis of extended cognition:

> *hypothesis of extended cognition*: individual cognition sometimes (regularly, often, always?) involves the operation of systems that physically extend beyond the body of the individual cognizer.

(see also Adams and Aizawa 2008; Rupert 2009;
Wilson and Clark 2009; R.A. Wilson 2014)

Offering a more deflationary alternative to the group mind hypothesis, this version of the social manifestation thesis has been explored in the contexts of human remembering (Barnier et al. 2008), moral psychology (Sneddon 2011), and more general discussions of human collective intentionality (Huebner 2013; Rupert 2014; Theiner 2014).

The basic idea in positing the social manifestation thesis, especially when married with the hypothesis of extended cognition, was to pose a challenge to those who viewed an ontology populated by group minds and collective intentionality as having the kind of explanationist justification already mentioned. By accepting an enriched view of individual cognition—seeing it as embodied, embedded, extended, and enactive, and recognizing the social dimensions to this "4E" view of human cognition—and showing that such a view could account for at least paradigm cases of putative collective intentionality, the challenge to the proponent of group minds was to identify phenomena that require, in addition or instead, human *group-level* cognition. That challenge has been taken up, both directly and indirectly, in recent defenses of the group mind hypothesis (e.g. Theiner 2014; Huebner 2013).

As should be clear, the social manifestation thesis itself does not entail the hypothesis of extended cognition. As such, that thesis admits of versions that are individualistic not only about the *bearers* of cognitive states but about the nature of those states themselves. That is, one could accept the social manifestation thesis and hold both that the bearers of intentional states are individuals *and* that those states supervene on the intrinsic, physical properties of their bearers. Such readings of that thesis are compatible with the dominant perspective on collective intentionality articulated by Schweikard and Schmid's individual ownership claim that we also find in Searle and Tomasello.

Drawing on an analogy to a riffing jazz musician, Tomasello captures the role of the social context in modern human cognition in saying that '[h]uman thinking is individual improvisation enmeshed in a sociocultural matrix' (2014: 1). Starting from self-contained individual intentionality, Tomasello's shared and collective intentionality are elaborations on such head-bound cognition, elaborations that are shaped by and shape new emerging forms of human sociality marked by heightened cooperativeness. If Tomasello accepts the social manifestation thesis, it is likely to be an individualistic view of that thesis, in both senses.

We have already seen that Searle thinks that 'intentionality, whether collective or individual, has to exist inside individuals' heads' (2010: 44). Searle's antipathy to the extended mind, reflecting his long-standing commitment to individualism about mental states, was apparent recently in his off-hand comment that 'it upsets me when I read the nonsense written by my contemporaries, the theory of extended mind makes me want to throw up' (Boag 2014). This report of Searle's (natural?) digestive state reflects his own strong and long-standing commitment to individualism about mental states, and thus any version of the social manifestation thesis that he accepts is also likely to be doubly individualistic. If Searle rejects the social manifestation thesis, it is likely because he finds the very idea of socially manifested intentional states to be too close to the other nonsense written by his contemporaries that he can't stomach.

The final point to make here is that since the 4E view of human cognition makes intentionality very much something that is neither contained within nor bounded by the head of the individual cognizer, it sits at best uneasily with the project of providing a reductive account of collective intentionality (cf. Rupert 2005). On this view, individual cognition itself is *constitutively social*, and so there is no reductive pathway leading, either ontogenetically or evolutionary, from pre-social individual intentionality to collective intentionality to sociality. Reflection on the sociality and cognition of non-human animals can make this claim both more concrete and readily defensible.

5. NON-HUMAN ANIMALS, SOCIALITY, AND COGNITION: THE SOCIAL INSECTS

In the mobile living world, sociality is pervasive, and it is easy to understand why. Living agents that move around need to have means of responding (relatively) rapidly to features of their local environments that can change (relatively) quickly because of the movement of the agent. This is why sensory systems are ubiquitous in the mobile living world (cf. MacIver 2009). When you are moving around, your proximal environment tends to change more rapidly in ways that are relevant to your survival and reproduction than it does when you have a sedentary way of life. This is why mice have elaborate, quick-time sensorimotor systems, but trees do not.

And any mobile living agent, unless it is extremely unfortunate or unusual, will often encounter other mobile living agents that are endowed with something like the same capacities and powers that it has, in part because it will be reproduced by, and often with, other such agents. For a mobile living agent to track, respond to and even anticipate the behavior of other mobile agents requires even more sensory or cognitive sophistication than simply to track, respond to and even anticipate other kinds of environmental resources.

Social interactions in the non-human animal world take many overlapping forms. They can be, among other things, reproductive, cooperative, competitive, predatorial, protective, domineering, resource-securing, mutualistic, exploitative, parasitic, pathogenic, altruistic, or sacrificial. Many of these forms of sociality take place with very little cognitive mediation, given that they occur between critters whose individual cognitive power is likely quite limited. Much of this sociality is merely aggregative in that it is the outcome simply of aggregated individual behaviors that require little coordination with conspecifics. Jellyfish, like real fish, tend to form social aggregates; such jellyfish blooms, unlike the fish schools they may superficially resemble, fall into this category. But as perhaps suggested by the brief discussion of distributive collective action, some forms of sociality in non-human animals have generated versions of the group mind hypothesis, something missed by an exclusive focus on human agency and collective intentionality.

Alongside what I have called the *collective psychology* tradition that postulates group minds in human social groups, there is an independent *superorganism* tradition that posits group minds in special sorts of non-human animal social groups (R.A. Wilson 2004: 274–80). As the name suggests, these special groups are sometimes referred to as superorganisms, a term coined by the Harvard entomologist William Morton Wheeler in 1920 as part of a series of reflections on insect colonies (Wheeler 1911, 1920, 1923, 1926). Although the ascription of mental states to such colonies does not form a central part of the early part of the superorganism tradition, more recently entomologists have articulated and defended the group mind hypothesis, particularly with respect to honey bees (Seeley et al. (1991); Seeley (1995, 1997, 2003); Seeley and Visscher (2003); see also Huebner (2013: 230–33)).

Consider the *Hymenoptera*—the wasps, ants and bees—which, together with the termites, are commonly known as the "social insects." As their moniker suggests, the *Hymenoptera* exhibit much sociality—from nest-cleaning behavior to hive temperature regulation requiring the coordination of the behaviors of thousands of bees. Although individual wasps, ants, and bees clearly have some kind of intentionality, the clearest forms it takes are perceptual or sensory in nature, and only dubiously involve what we might call *cognition central*: belief, reason, and thought.

Despite this, social insect colonies as a whole or in sizeable part, accomplish impressive outcomes that are very naturally described by attributing perceptual or sensorimotor properties to those groups of organisms. These include the perceptual and communicative abilities involved in gathering information about food sources and the motoric capacities to utilize resources and avoid predators and dangers in the world. Some of these abilities, such as the ability of a bee colony to locate distance sources of nectar and regulate the relative number of foragers and hiver workers in accord with the richness of the source, or the ability of a termite colony to rapidly repair damage to its nest, manifest both some level of intentionality and a degree of concern over the integrity of the colony. Yet it is very implausible to think that these are possessed by *individual* members of the hive, nest, or colony. In short, the behavior of at least some groups is such that it seems directed at self-preservation, where the self here is a colony, and the means of achieving that goal involves group-level decision-making that draws on collectively distributed perception and sensing.

The relevant, putative mental activities here—for example, perceiving, remembering, deciding, monitoring—are *group-only* traits, traits possessed only by a group, and not by the individuals that comprise the group. For that reason, appealing to the social manifestation thesis as an explanatory alternative to the group mind hypothesis is much less plausible than it is in the case of human cognition, where the traits under consideration are *multi-level traits*, traits that either individuals or groups could, in principle possess.

How is this relevant to collective intentionality? If, following Schweikard and Schmid (2013), collective intentionality just is 'the power of minds to be jointly directed', there is no collective intentionality without individual minds. Georg Theiner has suggested more directly that what he calls "hive cognition" is not really an example of the group mind hypothesis, defined as the view that 'there are collective types of minds that comprise two or more singular minds among their constitutive parts' (2014: 301). Since there are no singular minds among the constitutive parts of a beehive, there is no more collective intentionality in these cases than there is collective intentionality in a single brain that is constituted by the non-minded activities of millions of single neurons (cf. Tomasello 2014: 33). Rather, what we have in hive cognition, as in a brain, is a division of labor between many parts of some greater individual, and it is that individual—the hive or the brain—that is the cognitive agent. In short, hive cognition is not collective but *individual* cognition.

What strikes me as right about this response is that it rests on the point that the integration of the individuals in social insect colonies makes very much for an entity that is at least organism-like, one of our paradigms of individuals with intentionality (Wilson and Barker 2017). But that is also true of the human social groups that have been central to the core work on collective intentionality, which is why they have been considered to be *persons* (e.g. Pettit 2003) or "true believers" (Tollefsen 2002), and the subjects of moral responsibility. If the individual-like character of human social groups is not only no barrier to entertaining the question of whether there might be collective intentionality at play, but one of the signs that we are considering human social groups of the right kind in taking up that issue, then the individual-like character of hives, nests, swarms, and colonies of social insects should be viewed in just the same way.

Theiner views being composed of components that are themselves intentional agents as a necessary condition for some entity to be a candidate for collective intentionality. Can we accept this condition and still view hive cognition as exemplifying the group mind hypothesis? I think so, since it is plausible to view individual members of the hive as having some limited form of intentionality, just not the rich level of intentionality that seems to emerge in the hive's actions. But should we accept Theiner's condition, or (for that matter) Schweikard and Schmid's characterization of collective intentionality as 'the power of [individual] minds to be jointly directed'? Once we recognize that the singular or individual-level intentionality can be significantly distinctive in both its "propositional" and "attitudinal" dimensions from that at the collective level, such views seem to me more plausible—more plausible, but also less apt for ruling out hive cognition as a form of collective intentionality.

In defending hive cognition as exemplifying a type of collective intentionality or group mind, Bryce Huebner (2013: 230–33) has noted that social insects should be thought of as exemplifying *minimally collective mentality*, and that it would be misleading to think of them as having mental states such as beliefs and desires. Despite lacking what I have previously called *full-blown* minds, they nonetheless possess or participate in some relatively constrained sets of focal processes or abilities, such as decision-making, planning, or monitoring (R.A. Wilson 2004: 290–1). Since it is this kind of minimal-mindedness that has been contested in discussions of group minds in human social groups, the fact that hive minds lack the full range of intentional states that individual cognizers possess is no reason to deny them group-mindedness. And if there can be group minds without individual intentionality of the appropriate kind—perhaps just more restricted forms of individual intentionality—then the idea that collective intentionality must derive, in some way, from individual intentionality, cannot be correct.

Although so far I have been shifting between talk of group minds and collective intentionality, it is at this point that a defender of the standard view of collective intentionality, according to which collective intentionality derives from individual intentionality, might insist on a firm distinction here. The thought here is that whatever we say about group minds in social insects is completely independent of what one should say about genuinely *collective* intentionality in humans and their closest biological relatives. As Tomasello says,

> Cooperation by itself does not create complex cognitive skills—witness the complex cooperation of the cognitively simple eusocial insects and the cooperative child care and food sharing of the not-so-cognitively-complex New World monkeys, marmosets and tamarins.
>
> (Tomasello 2014: 33)

While Tomasello is certainly correct that the enriched "we-intentionality" whose ontogeny and phylogeny he explores is missing in eusocial insects and other non-human animals—individual intentionality here is, at best, very limited—it is less clear that one can simply bracket off the corresponding forms of collective action, whether they be merely distributive or joint and shared. Indeed, if one can have both of these forms of collective action in psychologically more impoverished circumstances, as I want now to suggest, such we-intentionality cannot hold the key to understanding of acting collectively.

6. SOCIAL PLAY AND TERRITORY MARKING: HIGHLY SOCIAL MAMMALS

In past work (R.A. Wilson 2007) I have argued that social play and territory marking in non-human animals such as canids poses another kind of challenge to the picture of collective intentionality as requiring an enriched, individualistic form of intentionality. Although part of that argument was directed at particular claims—about sociality, institutional reality, and status functions—central to John Searle's (1995) answers to the questions "what is social reality?" and "what are social facts?", part of the argument suggests that there can be a kind of joint or shared intentionality amongst non-human animals that stops short of the full-blown sharing of we-intentions that now form a deep bedrock in our own sociality.

Social play of the kind that is readily observed in domestic dogs (and less-easily observed in non-domestic dogs) involves multiple individuals responding to one another's recognizably play-signaling behaviors, such as arched bows, mock bites, tail-nipping, and back-rolling. Social play in canids, like social play in human children, is not simply behavior, but behavior that is recognized by the participants in it *as play*, as something that both or all participants undertake. Like territory marking, social play functions via individual intentionality that is sensitive to the social context in which the activity takes place. Here shared intentionality gains purchase, I want to suggest, not so much through the generation of playful or territory-marking activity, but through its *reception as playful or territory-marking*. When other conspecifics stop treating a behavior as playful, play ends, just as their ignoring of a scent as marking out territory takes away that scent's territory-marking function.

Both social play and territory marking in canids and, I think, other highly social mammals, are collective acts involving participants with at least some kind of second-order intentionality. I also think that such activities involve some level of joint or shared intentionality since they require that mere behaviors and scents be taken by participants as signals of the respective intentionality-laden activities of play and territory marking. In this respect, they are representative of a large class of non-human animal behavior, including grooming in primates and collective food-sharing in bats, that are generated and underwritten by individual-level intentionality that is other-directed in the way that we-intentionality is. Such multilevel traits—play, territory marking, grooming, and food sharing—could be explained as either an appeal to group-level intentionality or to individual-level intentionality. As such, the challenge posed by the social manifestation thesis to proponents of the group mind hypothesis remains live: do we need to posit intentionality at the group level, as I suspect we do need to in the case of social insects, in order to explain this collective behavior, or can we make do with an appeal to individual-level, socially manifested intentionality?

To come back to the conception of collective intentionality exemplified by Searle and Tomasello, note that whatever intentionality there is in such cases, it is related to neither "institutional reality" nor the enriched forms of we-intentionality central to their conceptions of collective intentionality. This itself does not imply either that collective intentionality plays a special role in structuring institutional facts, or that there are no forms of shared intentionality that are distinctively human. But it does suggest that we need a view of the relationship between sociality and intentionality, both individual and collective, that departs from the individualistic tradition to which both Searle and Tomasello are committed.

7. CONCLUSION

The relationships between sociality, collective intentionality, and individuals can inform how we think of each of these three relata. I have suggested that Schweikard and Schmid's individual ownership claim, that 'intentionality is had by the participating individuals, and all the intentionality an individual has is his or her own' can be satisfied in at least many cases by accepting the social manifestation thesis, particularly by non-individualistic versions of that thesis. Collective intentionality might well be possessed by individuals without itself being individualistic.

Collectively acting is widespread in the non-human animal world. Some of this collective action is merely distributive, but some of it is very likely also shared or joint, in the senses in which I have introduced those terms. This does not itself imply that collective intentionality has a corresponding range, but it does mean that the very same explanationist motivation for positing collective intentionality in human groups applies to non-human animals.

The significance of the social insects in the present context is that they represent a range of cases in which we have both merely distributed and shared or joint collective action without much individual intentionality at all. Thus, we either allow that such collective action can take place without collective intentionality at all, or that there is collective intentionality without we-intentions.

The significance of social play and territory marking in highly social mammals, such as canids, is that they represent cases in which we have shared or joint collective action with individual intentionality that stops short of the full-blown, institution-laden forms of we-intentionality that structure much of our own social life. Thus, we either allow, as with the case of social insects, that such collective action can take place without collective intentionality at all, or that there is collective intentionality of some type that exists independent of distinctively human psychology and institutional reality.

RELATED TOPICS

Collective Action and Agency (Ch. 1), Collective Memory (Ch. 11), Groups as Distributed Cognitive Systems (Ch. 18), Social Construction and Social Facts (Ch. 20), Development of Collective Intentionality (Ch. 31), Origins of Collective Intentionality (Ch. 33).

REFERENCES

Adams, F. and Aizawa, K. (2008) *The Bounds of Cognition*, Oxford: Blackwell.

Barnier, A., Sutton, J., Harris, C. and Wilson, R.A. (2008) "A Conceptual and Empirical Framework for the Social Distribution of Cognition: The Case of Memory," *Cognitive Systems Research* 9 (1–2): 33–51.

Boag, Z. (2014) "Searle: It Upsets Me When I Read the Nonsense Written by My Contemporaries," *New Philosopher* January 25, 2014. www.newphilosopher.com/articles/john-searle-it-upsets-me-when-i-read-the-nonsense-written-by-my-contemporaries/ Retrieved July 24, 2014.

Brentano, F. (1874) *Psychology from an Empirical Standpoint*, translated by A.C. Rancurello, D.B. Terrell and L. McAlister, London: Routledge, 1973.

Chant, S.R., Hindriks, F. and Preyer, G. (eds) (2014) "Introduction: Beyond the Big Four and the Big Five," in *From Individual to Collective Intentionality: New Essays*, New York: Oxford University Press: 1–9.

Clark, A. (2008) *Supersizing the Mind: Embodiment, Action, and Cognitive Extension*, New York: Oxford University Press.

Clark, A. and Chalmers, D. (1998) "The Extended Mind," *Analysis* 58: 10–23.

Gilbert, M. (1996) *Living Together: Rationality, Sociality, and Obligation*, New York: Rowman and Littlefield.

Huebner, B. (2013) *Macrocognition: A Theory of Distributed Minds and Collective Intentionality*, New York: Oxford University Press.

MacIver, M. (2009) "Neuroethology: From Morphological Computation to Planning," in P. Robbins and M. Aydede (eds), *Cambridge Handbook of Situated Cognition*, New York: Cambridge University Press.

Pettit, P. (2003) "Groups with Minds of Their Own," in F. Schmitt (ed.) *Socializing Metaphysics: The Nature of Social Reality*. New York: Rowman and Littlefield.

Rupert, R. (2005) "Minding One's Own Cognitive System: When is a Group of Minds a Single Cognitive Unit?" *Episteme: A Journal of Social Epistemology* 1 (3): 177–88.

——— (2009) *Cognitive Systems and the Extended Mind*, New York: Oxford University Press.

——— (2014) "Against Group Cognitive States," in S.R. Chant, F. Hindriks, and G. Preyer (eds) *From Individual to Collective Intentionality: New Essays*, New York: Oxford University Press.

Schweikard, D.P. and Schmid, H.B. (2013) "Collective Intentionality," in E.N. Zalta (ed.) *The Stanford Encyclopedia of Philosophy* (Summer 2013 edition), http://plato.stanford.edu/archives/sum2013/entries/collective-intentionality/.

Searle, J. (1990) "Collective Intentions and Actions," in P. Cohen, J. Morgan, and M.E. Pollack (eds) *Intentions in Communication*, Cambridge: Bradford Books.

——— (1995) *The Construction of Social Reality*, New York: Free Press.

——— (2010) *Making the Social World: The Structure of Human Civilization*, New York: Oxford University Press.

Seeley, T. (1995) *The Wisdom of the Hive*, Cambridge, MA: Harvard University Press.

——— (1997) "Honey Bee Colonies are Group-Level Adaptive Units," *The American Naturalist* 150 (sup.): 22–41.

——— (2003) "Consensus Building During Nest-Site Selection in Honey Bee Swarms: The Expiration of Dissent," *Behavioral Ecology and Sociobiology* 53: 417–24.

Seeley, T. and Visscher, P. (2003) "Choosing a Home: How the Scouts in a Honey Bee Swarm Perceive the Completion of Their Group Decision Making," *Behavioral Ecology and Sociobiology* 54: 511–20.

Seeley, T., Camazine, S. and Sneyd, J. (1991) "Collective Decision-Making in Honey Bees: How Colonies Choose Among Nectar Sources," *Behavioral Ecology and Sociobiology* 28: 277–90.

Sneddon, A. (2011) *Like-Minded: Externalism and Moral Psychology*, Cambridge, MA: MIT Press.

Theiner, G. (2014) "A Beginner's Guide to Group Minds," in J. Kallestrup and M. Sprevak (eds) *New Waves in Philosophy of Mind*, Boston, MA: Palgrave Macmillan.

Tollefsen, D. (2002) "Organizations as True Believers," *Journal of Social Philosophy* 33 (3): 395–411.

Tomasello, M. (1999) *The Cultural Origins of Human Cognition*, Cambridge, MA: Harvard University Press.

Tomasello, M. (2014) *A Natural History of Human Thinking*, Cambridge, MA: Harvard University Press.

Tuomela, R. (2007) *The Philosophy of Sociality: The Shared Point of View*, New York: Oxford University Press.

Wheeler, W.M. (1911) "The Ant-Colony as an Organism," reprinted in his *Essays in Philosophical Biology*, Cambridge, MA: Harvard University Press, 1939.

Wheeler, W.M. (1920) "The Termitodoxa, or Biology and Society," reprinted in his *Essays in Philosophical Biology*, Cambridge MA: Harvard University Press, 1939.

Wheeler, W.M. (1923) *Social Life Among the Insects*, New York: Harcourt Brace.

Wheeler, W.M. (1926) "Emergent Evolution and the Development of Societies," modified version reprinted his *Essays in Philosophical Biology*, Cambridge, MA: Harvard University Press, 1939.

Wilson, D.S. (1997a) "Altruism and Organism: Disentangling the Themes of Multilevel Selection Theory," *American Naturalist* 150 (supp.): S122–34.

——— (1997b) "Incorporating Group Selection into the Adaptationist Program: A Case Study Involving Human Decision Making," in J. Simpson and D. Kendrick (eds) *Evolutionary Social Psychology*, Hillsdale, NJ: Erlbaum.

Wilson, R.A. (1994) "Wide Computationalism," *Mind* 103: 351–72.

——— (1999) "Philosophy: Introduction," in R.A. Wilson and F.C. Keil (eds) *The MIT Encyclopedia of the Cognitive Sciences*, Cambridge, MA: MIT Press.

——— (2001) "Group-Level Cognition," *Philosophy of Science* 68 (supp.): S262–73.

——— (2004) *Boundaries of the Mind: The Individual in the Fragile Sciences: Cognition*, New York: Cambridge University Press.

——— (2007) "Social Reality and Institutional Facts: Sociality Within and Without Intentionality," in S.L. Tsohatzidis (ed.), *Intentional Acts and Institutional Facts: Essays on John Searle's Social Ontology*, Dordrecht: Springer.

——— (2014) "Ten Questions Concerning Extended Cognition," special issue of *Philosophical Psychology*, edited by T. Sturm and A. Estany, 27 (1): 19–33.

Wilson, R.A. and Clark, A. (2009) "How to Situate Cognition: Letting Nature Take Its Course" in P. Robbins and M. Aydede (eds) *Cambridge Handbook of Situated Cognition*, New York: Cambridge University Press.

Wilson, R.A. and Barker, M.J. (2017) "The Biological Notion of Individual," in E.N. Zalta (ed.) *The Stanford Encyclopedia of Philosophy* (Spring 2017 edition), http://plato.stanford.edu/archives/spr2017/entries/biology-individual/

33

The Middle Step: Joint Intentionality as a Human-Unique Form of Second-Personal Engagement

Jan M. Engelmann and Michael Tomasello

Over the past two decades, a small group of philosophers of action have singled out for special attention human social interactions characterized by what may be called shared intentionality or collective intentionality (e.g. Bratman 1992, 2014; Gilbert 1990, 2014; Searle 1995, 2006). In our own empirical research attempting to identify those aspects of human cognition and sociality that are unique to the species (i.e. not possessed by humans' closest primate relatives), we have come to see skills and motivations of shared intentionality as key (e.g. Tomasello 2014, 2016; Tomasello et al. 2005).

In attempting to give both a phylogenetic and ontogenetic account of the origin of these uniquely human capacities, we believe that an important distinction must be made. On the one hand there are capacities for jointly acting with a partner, jointly attending to things with her, and perhaps jointly committing to do certain things. Prominent examples from the literature include Bratman's (1992) cooperators painting a house together and Gilbert's (1990) friends taking a walk together. We may call such face-to-face interactions joint intentionality. On the other hand there are capacities for acting collectively within a social group or culture, relying on an understanding and sensitivity to such supra-individual constructions as cultural conventions, norms, and institutional reality. Prominent examples from the literature include Searle's (1995) customer at a French café, weighted down by all of the institutional realities involved in the simple purchase of a cup of coffee. We may call these more impersonal, institutional interactions collective intentionality. We reserve the term "shared intentionality" as the more general term to cover both of these modes of uniquely human social engagement.

Much recent attention has been paid to processes of collective intentionality, often under the rubric of "social ontology" (e.g. see new journal of the same name). Here we would like to focus instead on joint intentionality because we believe that indeed collective intentionality is made possible in human phylogeny and ontogeny by a prior step of joint intentionality. In addition, in the current literature it is almost exclusively the cognitive dimensions of shared intentionality that are emphasized, whereas here we emphasize the new types of social relationships that these kinds of interaction create.

1. THE MIDDLE STEP

It is obvious that humans are different from other animals in a number of important ways. They differ from even their closest living relatives, the great apes, on such things as communication and teaching, technology and subsistence, and norms and institutions. While many of these differences are readily observable, it is not easy to say exactly what is their underlying psychological basis. According to the shared intentionality hypothesis (Tomasello 2014, 2016), human distinctiveness is traceable to novel and unique ways of social engagement, including the formation of shared intentions. On this account, humans first started to veer onto their distinctive evolutionary pathway when they began to put their heads together with others in acts of shared intentionality, and in the process created everything from concrete acts of collaborative problem solving to complex cultural institutions. While the social life of even our nearest living relatives, chimpanzees and bonobos, is characterized by individual intentions, humans routinely coordinate with others to form intricate modes of collective intentions and enduring cultural practices.

How did humans become such an ultra-cooperative species, able to engage with and relate to their conspecifics in ways that even their closest relatives do not? The shared intentionality hypothesis holds that it is not plausible to assume that early humans evolved directly from great ape societies to full-blown human cultures and collective intentionality in one giant leap. Rather, it posits a two-step sequence in the evolution of modern day humans: joint intentionality followed by collective intentionality. The crucial middle step consists in second-personal engagement with specific others. Said another way, human cultures were made possible by an earlier evolutionary step in which humans coordinated their intentions with specific others in relatively simple acts of collaboration. Before humans started to interact with one another as members of the same cultural group and took part in the complex set of conventional practices and beliefs that define such a group, they formed with particular others dyadic units that were both temporary and local: temporary, because these units were constituted by and restricted to the joint activity itself, and once this activity was over, so was the unit; local, because these temporary units were limited to two agents interacting and their various ways of relating to one another and did not directly involve third parties.

Like all significant changes in evolution, the move from the individual intentionality of chimpanzees to the joint intentionality of early humans took place in the context of substantial ecological changes. More specifically, environmental pressures (mostly increased food competition with other species) forced humans to adopt ever more cooperative lifestyles and so the main subsistence strategy of early humans shifted from solitary to collaborative foraging. According to the shared intentionality hypothesis, the key ecological change propelling humans onto their unique evolutionary pathway involved a novel and unique subsistence strategy. To understand how the foraging of early humans differed from that of their most recent ancestors, we must first look at the foraging pattern of the last common ancestor of humans and other great apes, who lived somewhere in Africa approximately 6 million years ago. To characterize the subsistence strategy of this ancestor, we use as a contemporary model the foraging of humans' nearest living relatives, chimpanzees and bonobos. Crucial for current purposes, both chimpanzees and bonobos procure the majority of their diet—which consists mostly of fruit, other vegetation, and insects—individually. In a prototypical foraging episode, a small traveling party visits a fruit tree, individuals disperse to different parts of the tree, grab one or several pieces of fruit, and then separate from the others by a few meters to eat. There is one exception to this general great ape pattern of solitary foraging: chimpanzees' hunting of monkeys, typically red colobus monkeys. While chimpanzees seem to be quite adept at hunting monkeys, with more than 50 percent of hunts resulting in kills (Muller & Mitani 2005), two lines of evidence suggest that chimpanzees are not specially adapted for such collaborative procurement of food. First, the extent to which these hunts are cooperative in nature is unclear, with most researchers emphasizing the apparent lack of active behavioral coordination of participants (for an exception, see Boesch 1994; Muller & Mitani 2005). Moreover, and more importantly, it is doubtful whether the meat procured during hunts actually constitutes an important part of the chimpanzees' diet. Perhaps surprisingly, chimpanzees do not preferentially hunt in the dry season when other food sources are scarce, but in the rainy season when fruit and vegetation are more abundant (Watts & Mitani 2002).

While the last common ancestor thus likely procured the majority of her diet individually, early humans had to substantially modify, if not reinvent, their foraging strategies. According to Dunbar (1996) and Tomasello (2014), what might have happened is that soon after the emergence of the genus *Homo* around 2 million years ago, early humans were faced with a rapid expansion of terrestrial monkeys who outcompeted humans for their normal fruits and vegetation, resulting in selective pressure to move to a new foraging niche. The niche that early humans eventually came to inhabit, most likely by way of a transitional phase of scavenging, consisted in collaborative hunting of large game, requiring the active coordination of participants. According to paleoanthropological evidence, systematic large game hunting was probably in place by around 400,000 years ago in the common ancestor to Neanderthals and modern humans, *Homo heidelbergensis* (Stiner 2013).

Collaborative hunting was not optional for early humans in the same way it is for chimpanzees and was not restricted to specific seasons of the year. On the contrary, with few or no satisfactory fallback options, collaboration for food became *obligate*. One of the most significant repercussions of the transition from individual to obligate collaborative foraging consisted in the fact that early humans were now interdependent with their hunting partners in a strong sense. It was not only that they needed partners to succeed during hunting events and to acquire the nourishment necessary for survival, systematic hunting of large game requires participants' active coordination and a willingness to defer one's own interests to the interests of others (at least to some extent). So early humans came to care ever more about recruiting the right type of partners, i.e. partners that possessed the right kind of attitudes and that could be trusted. In contrast, the group hunting of chimpanzees only creates interdependence of a weak sort. Chimpanzees are clearly interdependent with one another during the hunt itself—their chances of capturing a monkey on their own tend towards zero—but they are neither dependent on the hunt for survival nor do they seem to engage in much partner choice (Tomasello 2014). Thus, the ecological revolution that occurred somewhere in Africa around half a million years ago saw early humans evolve from a common ancestor who was interdependent with their group members only in a weak sense to a species that depended on standing in the good graces of their group members 100 percent, no way out, and so had to evolve a suite of psychological mechanisms and motivations to successfully deal with this novel environmental and social context. Most importantly and fundamentally, it forced early humans to evolve new ways to engage with others second-personally involving the formation of joint goals structured by joint attention ("joint intentionality," discussed in Section 2). These novel cognitive representations, in turn, led humans to relate to those around them in new ways involving the formation and maintenance of second-personal social relationships ("social relationships," discussed in Section 3).

2. COGNITIVE REVOLUTION: JOINT GOALS AND JOINT ATTENTION

The foraging niche inhabited by early humans, obligate collaborative foraging, presented individuals with many, and one especially pressing challenge: agents had to find novel ways to coordinate their behavior with others. The primeval scene, according to Tomasello et al. (2012), is best understood in terms of the stag hunt scenario from game theory (Skyrms 2004). In this scenario, two hungry agents are on the lookout for food and can follow either of two mutually exclusive options. Alternative 1 is for each agent to pursue an individual, low-cost, and safe goal on her own: the "hare" (e.g. low-calorie vegetation). Alternative 2 consists in the agents coordinating their interests, abandoning their hares, and collaborating to acquire a high-payoff but difficult-to-obtain "stag" (e.g. large game). The payoff matrix is usually defined in a way that each agent individually prefers to abandon the hare and collaboratively pursue the stag (the agents' interests are aligned), but this is not sufficient for cooperation, given the possible uncertainty about the other's likelihood of joining in. Going for the stag involves giving up the hare, and so agents have to find a way to coordinate their individual interests and form a joint goal. According to the shared intentionality hypothesis, early humans evolved the cognitive mechanism of joint intentionality to coordinate these earliest forms of small-scale collaboration. Joint intentionality can be best understood in terms of a dual-level structure of simultaneous sharedness and individuality both on the level of the intention—a joint goal but with individual roles—as well as on the level of the attention structuring this goal—a joint attention but with individual perspectives (Tomasello 2014).

Joint Goals and Individual Roles

For two agents to form a joint goal to capture a stag, they both have to individually have the goal of capturing the stag with the other, and, crucially, they have to have mutual knowledge of the other's goal. Two individual goals to capture the stag only amount to a parallel goal and are not sufficient for the creation of a joint goal. Note that even two individual goals to capture the stag with the other cannot do the job. What is needed in addition is to bring these individual goals into our common ground so that we both know that the other wants to capture the stag with us.

Young children show first signs of forming joint goals of this type when they are still mostly prelinguistic, at around 18 months of age. Warneken and colleagues (2006) had infants of this age engage with an experimenter in a cooperative activity, such as playing a social game that required both partners to play their role at the same time. At a pre-defined point, the experimenter suddenly retreated from the joint activity, by, for example, putting his hands on the floor and stopping playing his part. Children even at this young age produced communicative attempts to re-engage the experimenter, potentially showing an awareness of a shared, joint goal. In contrast, and tellingly, chimpanzees exposed to the same sequence of events did not show any signs of trying to re-engage the recalcitrant partner but instead tried to find ways to achieve the goal on their own. Just slightly older children stay committed to a joint activity even if doing so is costly for them and thus show an understanding not just of a joint goal but also its underlying joint commitment. Hamann et al. (2012) had dyads of 3-year-old children engage in a reward-retrieval collaborative activity that required both partners' efforts for success. Midway through the activity, one child surprisingly got access to her part, but only her part, of the reward. Nonetheless, the lucky children continued engaging in the collaborative activity until the not-so-fortunate child could access her reward as well. These findings lend support to the contention that young children at this age conceptualize cooperative activities not in individual terms but in terms of a "we," including what Bratman (1992) calls mutual responsiveness to the intentions and actions of the other.

Joint Attention and Individual Perspectives

Agents pursuing joint goals naturally attend to events and objects that are relevant to the task at hand and coordinate not only their actions, but also their attention. In the hypothesis of Tomasello (2014), this suggests that joint actions, joint goals, and joint attention must have co-evolved together and that collaborative activities provide a natural scaffold for the first emergence of joint attention as they structure attention in a "top-down" manner.[1] Joint attention not only shares the common ground prerequisite with joint goals—in order for us to jointly attend to an object experiencing it at the same time is not sufficient, we also have to know that we are doing this—but also its dual-level structure. During joint attentional activities, interactants share their attention but keep their individual perspectives. Human children start engaging in such activities (rolling a ball back and forth or building a tower) between the ages of 9 and 12 months. Despite specific and systematic attempts by Tomasello and Carpenter (2005), joint attentional activities could not be elicited in human-raised chimpanzees.

In much the same way that each partner in a joint collaborative activity occupies an individual role, each participant in joint attentional engagement perceives the shared object from her individual perspective. One prediction of the current account, arguing that the capacity to engage in joint attention first emerged in the context of joint collaborative activities, is that human children should show their first understanding of different perspectives in precisely such cooperative interactions. This prediction is supported by the finding of Tomasello and Haberl (2003) that young infants understand that others can have perspectives that differ from their own at 1 year of age. After an adult and a child had played together with two objects, the adult left the room and a research assistant entered and started to play with the child with a third object. When the adult returned to the room and saw the three objects, he exclaimed "Wow! Cool!" and asked "Can you give it to me?" Infants passed the correct (the third) object to the adult, showing an understanding of the fact that the object was new from the adult's perspective although it wasn't from the child's. Just a little later, at 3 years of age, children show evidence not only of such level 1 perspective taking (understanding whether others can see something) but also of level 2 perspective taking (understanding that others see something in a different way). In a study by Moll et al. (2013), children correctly inferred which of two objects an adult referred to by asking for the blue one, although it only appeared blue to the adult who looked at it through a color filter.

Joint attention, joint action, and common ground: The step from the individual intentionality of chimpanzees and bonobos to the joint intentionality of early humans, brought about by a change in subsistence strategy from relying almost exclusively on solitary foraging to obligate collaborative foraging, equipped early humans with a unique set of cognitive mechanisms adapted to coordinate actions and attention with others toward joint goals. This constitutively involved a dual-level cognitive structure for joint collaborative activities—involving joint goals and individual role, as well as for joint attentional activities—involving joint attention and individual perspectives.

Once these novel forms of second-personal engagement were in place, they modified not only the collaborative interaction itself, but also restructured the social relationships of the interacting parties. Agents participating in joint collaborative activities began to relate to one another in new ways, involving second-personal moral attitudes such as trust, blame, resentment, responsibility, and forgiveness.

3. SOCIAL REVOLUTION: NEW FORMS OF INTERPERSONAL RELATIONSHIPS

One of the main effects of engaging with others in collaborative activities regulated by the dual-level cognitive structure of joint intentionality was the development of new types of interpersonal relationships: agents began to relate to each other not only as independent agents, but also as an "I" to a "you" in the context of our "we." To fully appreciate how this dual-level organization of relating to one another structured the social relationships of early humans in novel ways, we first take a look at the social life, and, in particular, the main (non-kin based) social relationship, friendship, of the last common ancestor, using as contemporary models our nearest living relatives.

Social Relationships in Chimpanzees and Bonobos

Both chimpanzees and bonobos live in large social groups comprising individuals of both genders (so-called multi-male, multi-female groups). Daily life is structured by fission-fusion dynamics in which small parties of individuals separate from the group, forage together for periods varying from a few days to weeks, and reunite with other group members at later points. A further complexity of chimpanzee and bonobo social groups results from the fact that group composition is transitory with females immigrating to neighboring groups during early adolescence (males spend their whole lives in the same group). Most essential for current purposes, during their ontogenies, individuals form with others various kinds of social relationships, both short- and long-term. As shown by Langergraber et al. (2007), such social relationships are not restricted to kin interactions but involve unrelated partners as well. While traditionally research has focused on male-male bonds (Muller & Mitani 2005), recent research has shown not only that female-female bonds are common (Langergraber et al. 2009), but that even bonds between sexes exist (Langergraber et al. 2013). In addition to establishing and maintaining such social bonds or friendships with group members, chimpanzees also represent the affiliative relations of others. Much of the intricacy of chimpanzee social interaction results from the fact that individuals track and react to social relationships among third parties. In a recent playback study, for example, chimpanzee subjects heard recordings of aggressive barks of a bystander who had witnessed a previous fight between the subject and an opponent (Wittig et al. 2014). What varied according to condition was whether or not the bystander was a bonding partner of the former opponent. Chimpanzees clearly differentiated between these two conditions, moving away more often when they heard barks from a close relation of the former opponent.

Chimpanzees react to others' social relationships and, in addition, they also engage in various behaviors to initiate and maintain such relationships themselves. Observational evidence indicates that the main dyadic cooperative behaviors of chimpanzees, grooming, food sharing, and coalitionary support, are differentially directed toward preferred bonding partners. For instance, male chimpanzees extend as much as 66–81 percent of their grooming toward their top three bonding partners (reviewed in Muller & Mitani 2005). The exchange of meat follows a similar pattern. Mitani and Watts (2001) have shown that chimpanzees use meat sharing as a social tool to develop and maintain bonds with important partners by non-randomly directing their sharing toward them. Finally, there is the finding of de Waal and Luttrell (1988) providing evidence that coalitionary support among chimpanzees most commonly takes place in a reciprocal fashion among bonding partners. Taken together, these results present unequivocal evidence that chimpanzees have strong and enduring intentions to help their friends.

In addition, in a recent experimental study, Engelmann, Herrmann, and Tomasello (2015) have shown that chimpanzees not only show spontaneous trust in conspecifics, but can also establish and maintain trusting relationships with members of their own social group. In a second study, using the same basic setup, chimpanzees were selectively paired with either a closely bonded partner or a non-bond partner (bonding relationships were defined using observational data on such behaviors as grooming, proximity, and co-feeding). The results showed that chimpanzees were more likely to trust their friends than their non-friends (Engelmann & Herrmann 2016).

Close social relationships are defined in terms of such attitudes and intentions to preferentially trust, help, support, and share with friends; a second, no less important, part of interpersonal relationships consists in forming and holding each other to certain expectations (Scanlon 2008; Wallace 2013). Put differently, we not only preferentially trust and help our friends, we also expect our friends to behave toward us in similar ways.

Little work has directly addressed the question of whether great apes form and hold special expectations of their friends and experience reactive attitudes when such expectations are disappointed. But a reinterpretation of two studies by Brosnan et al. using the inequity aversion task (2005, 2010) suggests that they do indeed. The basic result is that chimpanzees reject food given to them by a human experimenter (food they would otherwise readily accept) if a conspecific gets better food for the same or even less effort. The authors interpret this finding in terms of social comparison, and thus ultimately as a burgeoning sense of fairness. However, a different interpretation, suggested by Roughley (2015) and Tomasello (2016), is that the chimpanzees' reaction in those studies is not based on a comparison of how they have been treated compared to a conspecific, but rather based on how they are being treated by the human experimenter with whom they share a cooperative relationship. A recent study lends support to this alternative interpretation. Engelmann et al. (in press) contrasted two conditions in which food is either distributed by a machine or a cooperative partner and found that chimpanzees indeed react negatively only in the latter context. Furthermore, chimpanzees show negative emotional reactions to their food-distributing partner independent of whether a conspecific was present or not, further supporting the hypothesis that the inequity aversion task reveals special expectations of cooperative partners and not fairness considerations. The social disappointment displayed by chimpanzees in the inequity aversion task is thus distinctively interpersonal, and, in Tomasello's (2016) words, might take the form of: "I am angry that you are treating me without sympathy."

The general picture of chimpanzee and bonobo social relationships can be summarized as follows. Both species monitor and react flexibly to the social relationships of those around them. In addition, chimpanzees have robust and selective intentions to behave cooperatively toward their bond partners, including a tendency to preferentially trust those partners. Last but not least, there is suggestive evidence that chimpanzees form special expectations toward their partners, refusing to engage in cooperative interactions when they are treated in ways that run counter to expected regard. We will now turn to the question of how the step from individual to collaborative foraging, and the concurrent transition from individual to joint intentionality, transformed the social relationships of early humans. In the previous section, we discussed how early humans evolved new cognitive adaptations, most importantly and fundamentally the dual-level cognitive structure of joint intentionality. We will now see how this ability of early humans to represent two agents simultaneously, an "I" and a "we," transformed the friendships of chimpanzees (based on sympathy) to the social relationships of early humans (which, in addition, were based on joint commitments as well).

Social Relationships in Early Humans

Once early humans related to one another not only directly, as independent agents, but also indirectly, as an "I" to a "you" via a common "we," this constituted the first instantiation of a supra-individual entity with the capacity of regulating each individual's behavior. And once this "we" took a special form, namely the form of a joint commitment (see Gilbert 1990, 2014), initiated by an overt and explicit act of cooperative communication, this opened the door to a novel second-personal moral psychology including such distinct attitudes as trust, obligation, duty, blame, resentment, and forgiveness.

The key point is that once a collaborative activity is initiated by an overt and explicit act of cooperative communication, everything is out in the open and in our common ground, and our behavior toward each other is regulated not only in terms of our individual intentions and preferences, but also by referring to a "we" that is created both by us and for us. While chimpanzee friends are committed to their social relationships in a certain sense because both individuals feel sympathy for each other, early humans were more committed still and trusted each other in a deeper way, because, as a result of the joint commitment, they felt that they truly *ought* to stick with each other as they now had acquired a special responsibility toward the other. They felt, in other words, that they *owed* it to one another. But this meant also that they came to expect certain behaviors from their partners, and non-fulfillment resulted in a novel form of reactive attitude, resentment.

Once the interpersonal relationships of early humans were based not just on sympathy, but on joint commitments as well, the intentions and expectations constitutive of such relationships were structured in novel ways. While chimpanzees help their friends based on the motive of sympathy, the partnership of early humans involved being moved both by sympathy and responsibility. When social relationships are initiated by joint commitments, the involved agents stand to each other in a relation of responsibility or accountability. If, in a collaborative activity that was initiated by an implicit or explicit joint commitment, you ask me for help, I might fulfill the request out of sympathy for your plight; additionally, I might help you because I feel that I owe it to you, that you can reasonably demand it from me—from the perspective of our "we" that was formed by the joint commitment. The flip side of this is that early humans formed and held their partners to specific and distinct standards of behavior, experiencing resentment in cases where these expectations were disappointed. If our collaborative activity is structured and regulated by a joint commitment, I have a claim on you following through with it, to you not simply turning your back and abandoning me (Gilbert 1990).

This understanding of a joint commitment can already be seen in young children. In an experimental study, when 3-year-old children were jointly committed to a collaborative task, and then one child surprisingly got access to her rewards early, most children still continued the collaborative task until the partner got access to her rewards as well (Hamann et al. 2012). Importantly, children were more likely to do so when the collaborative activity was structured by a joint commitment compared to a control condition in which the partner just asked them for help outside of any collaboration or commitment. This provides conclusive evidence that joint commitments present young children with an additional motive and intention to help their partner (over and above sympathy as in the control condition), which arises from an understanding that they have a special responsibility to their partner in such contexts.[2] It is important, to repeat, that this intention is causally linked to the partner holding a reasonable expectation that she will be helped and, furthermore, that the partner has standing to reproach in cases of disappointment. Such reproach voices resentment, which in turn expresses my authority to hold you to certain expectations and make claims on you (Darwall 2006). This authority of course is nothing but a representation of the fact that it was "you" *and* "I" that formed this joint commitment and so we both have standing to hold each other accountable. This can be seen clearly in a study by Warneken and colleagues (2011). Two 3-year-old children collaboratively produced a resource, and when one child took more of her fair share, the disadvantaged child often responded with an expression of resentment: "Hey!" or "Katie!" Most of the greedy children relented right away, showing an appreciation of the fact that their partner had standing to hold them answerable and could reasonably demand a fair share of the acquired resource.

When an interaction between two agents is structured by a joint commitment, and one party unilaterally defects, the disadvantaged party not only has special standing to reproach, but also to reinstate the commitment by forgiving the contrite partner.

Forgiveness represents a critical component of joint commitments, as expectations and demands can be disappointed and so partners have to find ways to restore their joint commitment and thus their relationship. Forgiving someone entails the forgoing of resentment and the expectation that the partner will not behave in such ways again in the future, and serves to reestablish trust (Hieronymi 2001). Chimpanzees often reconcile after fights, and such behavior can plausibly be understood as attempting to repair important social relationships (de Waal 1989). What is underlying such cases of reconciliation is likely a form of "strategic forgiveness." I forgive you because I know that I am dependent on you and I will likely need you in the future and so continued fighting would be detrimental to my individual goals. "Real forgiveness," on the other hand, involves the belief that a wrongdoer will not behave in similar ways in the future and thus reinstates the joint commitment.

Offended parties can forgive partners that have wronged them and in this way the key attitude for any collaborative activity, trust, can be restored. I have to trust you to remain committed to our joint goal even in the face of other temptations or unforeseen obstacles. Otherwise, if, for whatever reason, I cannot form such a trusting belief toward you, the only reasonable decision is to opt for the hare (using the stag hunt jargon, see previous section). A trusting belief, i.e. a belief that you will do what I am trusting you to do, can take many different forms. Take the case of the previously mentioned study suggesting that chimpanzees trust members of their social group (Engelmann et al. 2015), and, in particular, those individuals that they are closely bonded with (Engelmann & Herrmann 2016). Chimpanzees in this study could decide between a no-trust option (resulting in immediate access to low-quality food) and a trust option (which moved a box of high-quality food to a partner). Crucially, the partner could only access half of the high-quality food and could then either send back the other half, or not (by briefly pulling a rope). Chimpanzees and partners interacted for several rounds and so it is reasonable to assume that it was not in the partner's strategic interest to violate the subject's trust since (i) being trustworthy was low-cost and (ii) partners could not benefit in any way from not reciprocating trust (it might even have been detrimental as subjects might not have chosen the trusting option in the next round). The trust experienced by the truster in this setup falls into a class of trusting beliefs that can reasonably be described as "strategic": I trust you because I know that it is in your immediate strategic interest to behave trustworthily.

Early humans, in addition to such strategic forms of trust, likely also developed unique forms of "normative trust." Thus, when young children play a trust game similar to the one just described for chimpanzees (Harbaugh et al. 2003), they can also establish trust in situations in which it would pay for the partner not to reciprocate (because she can access all of the rewards and interactions are not repeated, they are one-shot). No one has attempted a similar study with chimpanzees (where the trustee can eat all of the rewards), because as everyone who has observed chimpanzees regularly can attest, the results would be clear: chimpanzee trustees would not reciprocate, would eat all of the food, and trust would break down over trials. It is likely that children can form trusting relationships even under such risky circumstances, where the interests of truster and trustee are not aligned (as in "strategic trust"), because they approach the situation with their skills and motivations for joint intentionality. And so the trustee does reciprocate the subject's trust, even though she could benefit from not doing so, because she cannot help but see the truster as having a valid claim to a share of the reward. This distinct form of a trusting belief can be called "normative trust": I trust you because we stand to each other in a relation of mutual accountability, and I know that you have a claim on me treating you in a fair way and vice versa.

The social relationships of early humans, then, were structured in novel ways as a consequence of relating to others via a joint commitment in the context of a joint cooperative activity. Forming a joint goal in a certain way, namely by implicitly or explicitly agreeing on a specific joint intention, fundamentally reworks the ways in which two agents relate to one another. For these two agents now stand to each other in a relation of mutual accountability. Standing to each other in such a relation implies a distinct form of responsibility to the other and failing to live up to this responsibility results in legitimate protest from one's companion. Chimpanzees and bonobos form complex and long-term social relationships involving such attitudes as sympathy, strategic trust, reconciliation, and, interrelated with those attitudes, presumably form specific expectations toward closely bonded partners. However, our nearest great ape relatives do not hold their partners to these expectations, they do not consider themselves having a valid claim in requesting a certain type of behavior. This is because the social relationships of chimpanzees and bonobos are underlined by individual intentionality and sympathy, not by joint intentionality and commitment. It is this small but nonetheless significant step in human evolution, from the individual intentionality of our nearest primate relatives to the joint intentionality of early humans, that fundamentally restructured the ways those early representatives of our species treated each other, involving such attitudes as responsibility, normative trust, forgiveness, and resentment.

4. CONCLUSION

Current philosophical accounts of shared intentionality focus on collective intentionality and the human ability to act together as a social group or culture and in the process create such collective entities as conventions, norms, and institutions (e.g. Searle 2006). The current chapter presents a phylogenetic perspective on shared intentionality and maintains that human evolution likely did not proceed in one big step from the individual rationality of our last common ancestor to the collective intentionality of modern humans. There were, rather, many small in-between steps and we have attempted to characterize one particularly important "middle step": joint intentionality as human-unique form of second-personal engagement. Before humans began to relate to one another as members of the same culture and developed locally distinct sets of traditions that distinguished them from other such groups, they likely had already gone through a previous step that involved a specific and distinct form of dyadic interaction. On Tomasello's account (2014, 2016), the phylogenetic origins of such second-personal interactions lie in (and were indeed restricted to) joint collaborative activities. Since these early cooperative endeavors were underlined by local and temporary joint commitments between two collaborative partners, the commitment dissolved as soon as the collaborative event was over.

But if the essence of a moral relationship consists in committing oneself and holding the other to a mutually known expectation that is created by us and for us, and involves the deferral of individual to common interests, then the early humans we are picturing here are doing something very much like this. And although many developments await early humans on their way toward a fully "objective" morality underlined not only by skills for joint but also collective intentionality, much of the content of universal claims and demands is already foreshadowed in the second-personal judgments we have characterized here. In Strawson's (1962: 84) words: '*The generalized or vicarious analogues of the personal reactive attitudes rest on, and reflect, exactly the same expectation or demand in a generalized form*'. As compared to a full-blown and "objective" morality, the second-personal morality we are picturing here is restricted in at least two ways. For one thing, it is restricted temporally. The joint commitments underlying early humans' ways of relating to one another second-personally were limited to the joint collaborative activity and dissolved as soon as the collaborative hunt was over. A full-blown morality, on the other hand, applies across time and situations. For another, the second-personal morality we have described is restricted in terms of its reference circle. It involved only two agents and was constituted by the intentions and behaviors that these two agents could reasonably demand of each other. This is different from a group-minded, cultural morality that applies to everyone equally and so involves behaviors and intentions that each person, even uninvolved third parties, can reasonably demand from one another; that is, in one word, agent-independent. Tomasello (2014, 2016) argues that the next key step in human evolution, from joint to collective intentionality, was brought about by ratcheting up the interdependence from the level of the collaborating dyad to the level of the entire group. This likely happened in the wake of separate and distinct cultural groups contesting over limited resources—a process that has been called "cultural group selection" and which led to individuals collaboratively creating various forms of conventional cultural practices.

RELATED TOPICS

Interpersonal Obligation in Joint Action (Ch. 4), Joint Attention (Ch. 9), Joint Commitment (Ch. 10), Development of Collective Intentionality (Ch. 31).

REFERENCES

Boesch, C. (1994) "Cooperative Hunting in Wild Chimpanzees," *Animal Behaviour* 48 (3): 653–67.
Bratman, M. (1992) "Shared Cooperative Activity," *Philosophical Review* 101 (2): 327–41.
——— (2014) *Shared Agency: a Planning Theory of Acting Together*, Oxford: Oxford University Press.
Brosnan, S.F., Schiff, H.C., & de Waal, F.B.M. (2005) "Tolerance for Inequity May Increase With Social Closeness in Chimpanzees," *Proceedings of the Royal Society of London B Biological Sciences* 272 (1560): 2005/2002/2005.
Brosnan, S.F., Talbot, C., Ahlgren, M., Lambeth, S.P., & Schapiro, S.J. (2010) "Mechanisms Underlying Responses to Inequitable Outcomes in Chimpanzees *Pan troglodytes*," *Animal Behaviour* 79 (6): 1229–37.
Darwall, S.L. (2006) *The Second-Person Standpoint: Morality, Respect, and Accountability*, Cambridge MA: Harvard University Press.
de Waal, F.B.M. (1989) *Peacemaking Among Primates*, Cambridge, MA: Harvard University Press.
de Waal, F.B.M., & Luttrell, L.M. (1988) "Mechanisms of Social Reciprocity in Three Primate Species: Symmetrical Relationship Characteristics or Cognition?" *Ethology & Sociobiology* 9 (2–4): 101–18.
Dunbar, R.I.M. (1996) *Grooming, Gossip and the Evolution of Language*, London: Faber and Faber.

Engelmann, J.M., Clift, J., Herrmann, E., & Tomasello, M. (in press) "Social Disappointment Explains Chimpanzees' Behavior in the Inequity Aversion Task." *Proceedings of the Royal Society B: Biological Sciences* 284 (1861): 20171502.

Engelmann, J.M., & Herrmann, E. (2016) "Chimpanzees Trust Their Friends," *Current Biology* 26 (2): 252–6.

Engelmann, J.M., Herrmann, E., & Tomasello, M. (2015) "Chimpanzees Trust Conspecifics to Engage in Low-Cost Reciprocity," *Proceedings of the Royal Society B: Biological Sciences* 282 (1801): 20142803.

Gilbert, M. (1990) "Walking Together: A Paradigmatic Social Phenomenon," in P.A. French, T.E. Uehling, Jr., & H.K. Wettstein (eds) *The Philosophy of the Human Sciences*, Notre Dame: University of Notre Dame Press.

Gilbert, M. (2014) *Joint Commitment: How We Make the Social World*, New York: Oxford University Press.

Greenberg, J.R., Hamann, K., Warneken, F., & Tomasello, M. (2010) "Chimpanzee Helping in Collaborative and Noncollaborative Contexts," *Animal Behaviour* 80 (5): 873–80.

Hamann, K., Warneken, F., & Tomasello, M. (2012) "Children's Developing Commitments to Joint Goals," *Child Development* 83 (1): 137–45.

Harbaugh, W.T., Krause, K., Liday, S.G., & Vesterlund, L. (2003) "Trust in Children," in E. Ostrom, & J. Walker (eds) *Trust, Reciprocity and Gains from Association: Interdisciplinary Lessons from Experimental Research*, New York City: Russell Sage Foundation.

Hieronymi, P. (2001) "Articulating an Uncompromising Forgiveness," *Philosophy and Phenomenological Research* 62 (3): 529–55.

Langergraber, K., Mitani, J.C., & Vigilant, L. (2009) "Kinship and Social Bonds in Female Chimpanzees (*Pan Troglodytes*)," *American Journal of Primatology* 71 (10): 840–51.

Langergraber, K., Mitani, J.C., Watts, D., & Vigilant, L. (2013) "Male-Female Socio-Spatial Relationships and Reproduction in Wild Chimpanzees," *Behavioral Ecology and Sociobiology* 67: 861–73.

Langergraber, K., Mitani, J.C.C., & Vigilant, L. (2007) "The Limited Impact of Kinship on Cooperation in Wild Chimpanzees," *Proceedings of the National Academy of Sciences of the United States of America* 104 (19): 7786–90.

Mitani, J.C., & Watts, D.P. (2001) "Why Do Chimpanzees Hunt and Share Meat?" *Animal Behaviour* 61 (5): 915–24.

Moll, H., Meltzoff, A., Mersch, K., & Tomasello, M. (2013) "Taking Versus Confronting Visual Perspectives in Preschool Children," *Developmental Psychology* 49 (4): 646–54.

Muller, M.N., & Mitani, J.C. (2005) "Conflict and Cooperation in Wild Chimpanzees," in P. Slater, C. Snowdon, T. Roper, H.J. Brockmann, & M. Naguib (eds) *Advances in the Study of Behavior* 35, San Diego, CA: Academic Press.

Roughley, N. (2015) "Resentment, Empathy and Moral Normativity," in N. Roughley, & T. Schramme (eds) *Forms of Fellow Feeling. Sympathy, Empathy, Concern and Moral Agency*, Cambridge: Cambridge University Press.

Scanlon, T.M. (2008) *Moral Dimensions: Permissibility, Meaning, Blame*, Cambridge, MA: Harvard University Press.

Searle, J.R. (1995) *The Construction of Social Reality*, New York: Free Press.

——— (2006) "Social Ontology: Some Basic Principles," *Anthropological Theory* 6 (1): 12–29.

Skyrms, B. (2004) *The Stag Hunt and the Evolution of Sociality*, Cambridge: Cambridge University Press.

Stiner, M. (2013) "An Unshakable Middle Paleolithic? Trends Versus Conservatism in the Predatory Niche and Their Social Ramifications," *Current Anthropology* 54: 288–304.

Strawson, P.F. (1962) "Freedom and Resentment," *Proceedings of the British Academy* 48: 1–25.

Tomasello, M. (2014) *A Natural History of Human Thinking*, Cambridge, MA: Harvard University Press.

——— (2016) *A Natural History of Human Morality*, Cambridge, MA: Harvard University Press.

Tomasello, M., & Haberl, K. (2003) "Understanding Attention: 12- and 18-Month-Olds Know What Is New for Other Persons," *Developmental Psychology* 39 (5): 906–12.

Tomasello, M., & Carpenter, M. (2005) "The Emergence of Social Cognition in Three Young Chimpanzees," *Monographs of the Society for Research in Child Development* 70 (1): 1–132.

Tomasello, M., Carpenter, M., Call, J., Behne, T., & Moll, H. (2005) "Understanding and Sharing Intentions: The Origins of Cultural Cognition," *Behavioral and Brain Sciences* 28 (5): 675–735.

Tomasello, M., Melis, A.P., Tennie, C., Wyman, E., & Herrmann, E. (2012) "Two Key Steps in the Evolution of Human Cooperation: the Interdependence Hypothesis," *Current Anthropology* 53 (6): 673–92.

Wallace, R.J. (2013) "The Deontic Structure of Morality," in D. Bakhurst, B. Hooker, & M.O. Little (eds) *Thinking About Reasons. Essays in Honour of Jonathan Dancy*, Oxford: Oxford University Press.

Warneken, F., Chen, F., & Tomasello, M. (2006) "Cooperative Activities in Young Children and Chimpanzees," *Child Development* 77 (3): 640–63.

Warneken, F., Lohse, K., Melis, A.P., & Tomasello, M. (2011) "Young Children Share the Spoils After Collaboration," *Psychological Science* 22 (2): 267–73.

Watts, D.P., & Mitani, J.C.C. (2002) "Hunting Behavior of Chimpanzees at Ngogo, Kibale National Park, Uganda," *International Journal of Primatology* 23 (1): 1–28.

Wittig, R., Crockford, C., Langergraber, K., & Zuberbühler, K. (2014) "Triadic Social Interactions Operate Across Time: A Field Experiment With Wild Chimpanzees," *Proceedings of the Royal Society B: Biological Sciences* 281 (1779): 20133155.

NOTES

1. The alternative is bottom-up joint attention in which we, for example, both hear a sudden and loud noise, and know that the other must have heard it as well.

2. When pairs of chimpanzees were tested in the same situation, the lucky individual (who got access to her rewards early) simply abandoned the partner and left with her food (Greenberg et al. 2010).

VIII

Semantics of Collectivity

Introduction to Part VIII

Marija Jankovic and Kirk Ludwig

Natural languages have developed multiple ways of talking about collectivity. Many languages contain plural nouns (such as "we" and "the students"), singular collective nouns (such as "the team," "the committee,") collective action verbs (such as "cooperate" and "gather"). The study of the semantics of these expressions has significance for the broader study of collective intentionality. It has implications for social ontology, in that it can reveal that our ordinary discourse is committed to certain social entities. This can in turn have ramifications for theories of specific aspects of collective intentionality insofar as they embrace or make a point of eschewing such commitments.

In Chapter 34, "Logic and Plurals," Salvatore Florio and Øystein Linnebo present two approaches to the logical analysis of sentences containing plural expressions. The singularizing approaches paraphrase away the plural vocabulary in the final logical analysis of the sentences containing them. The pluralist approaches preserve the distinction between singular and plural expressions, even in the final analysis. Florio and Linnebo describe the standard implementation of the pluralist approach, *plural logic,* and outline some arguments against singularizing approaches.

In Chapter 35, "Plural and Collective Noun Phrases," Katherine Ritchie examines the semantics of plural and singular collective nouns in natural languages. Since formal semantics often takes the form of a regimentation (i.e. a logical analysis) of the natural language sentences, the main approaches to the semantics of plural and singular collective nouns mirror the approaches to the logical analysis of plural vocabulary. The singularist theories take these nouns to refer to singular entities such as sets or mereological sums. The pluralist theories take them to pick out several individuals plurally. Ritchie argues that the view that takes singular collective nouns to be polysemous between a singular and a plural meaning best captures the linguistic data.

An important singularist approach to plural vocabulary is based on Donald Davidson's event analysis of action sentences. On this analysis, a simple action sentence, e.g. "Brutus walks," is to be analyzed as (roughly) the statement that there is an event of walking of which Brutus is the agent. In Chapter 36, "Actions and Events in Plural Discourse," Kirk Ludwig outlines a number of advantages for the Davidsonian event analysis of *plural* action sentences. The event analysis allows us to develop a singularist semantics by analyzing the plural subject as several agents of a single event. For example, "We walked" is to be analyzed as claiming that there was a walk (an event) of which each of us is an agent. It explains the ambiguity between distributive and collective readings of plural action sentences as one of scope rather than a lexical ambiguity, and has the resources to explain so-called intermediate readings.

34

Logic and Plurals

Salvatore Florio and Øystein Linnebo

1. THE LOGICAL ANALYSIS OF PLURAL EXPRESSIONS

Many natural languages contain plural vocabulary such as "we", "those", "the philosophers", "cooperate", and "gathered". What is the correct logical analysis of sentences involving such vocabulary?

Before we can attempt to answer the question, we need to comment briefly on how we understand logical analysis. Logical analysis generally proceeds by paraphrasing sentences of natural language in a way that provides a more perspicuous representation of logically relevant features of those sentences. Often, the paraphrase is given in a formal language that is equipped with a deductive system and a model-theoretic semantics. However, as Quine observes, 'to paraphrase a sentence of ordinary language into logical symbols is virtually to paraphrase it into a special part still of ordinary or semi-ordinary language [. . .]' (Quine 1960: 159). This is because, in many important cases, the sentences of the formal language are obvious counterparts of particular sentences of natural language (or natural language augmented with some mathematical locutions). The process of paraphrasing into a more logically perspicuous fragment of natural language is known as *regimentation*.

Though the logical study of plurals is a relatively recent phenomenon, semantic questions concerning plurals were already entertained by the founders of modern logic.[1] Frege himself, for instance, addressed the question of the proper logical analysis of sentences with a plural subject, such as (1).

(1) Socrates and Plato are philosophers.

He wrote:

[W]e have two thoughts: Socrates is a philosopher and Plato is a philosopher, which are only strung together linguistically for the sake of convenience.

Logically, Socrates and Plato is not to be conceived as the subject of which being a philosopher is predicated.

(Frege 1980: 40)

In effect, Frege proposes to analyze (1) as (2).

(2) Socrates is a philosopher and Plato is a philosopher.

However, he realizes that this strategy is not always available. Sentences such as (3) and (4) are not amenable to the conjunctive analysis proposed for (1).

(3) Bunsen and Kirchhoff laid the foundations of spectral analysis.
(4) The Romans conquered Gaul.

Frege remarks:

Here we must regard *Bunsen and Kirchhoff* as a whole. "The Romans conquered Gaul" must be conceived in the same way. The Romans here are the Roman people, held together by custom, institutions, and laws.

(Frege 1980: 40)

While Frege provided no additional indications as to the nature of the objects that should serve as "wholes" in the logical analysis of plurals, the subsequent literature has offered a number of alternatives. Sets, mereological sums, and groups are just some of the more popular candidates. By way of illustration, let us briefly consider the appeal to sets. The most famous advocate of this approach is Quine. One of the sentences he grapples with is known as the *Geach-Kaplan sentence*.[2]

(GK) Some critics admire only one another.

According to Quine, by 'invoking classes and membership, we can do justice to [the Geach-Kaplan sentence]' (Quine 1982: 293). The regimentation Quine proposes may be informally glossed as (5).[3]

(5) There is a non-empty set such that any member of the set is a critic who admires some other member of the set.
(6) $\exists s(\exists x(x \in s) \ \& \ \forall x(x \in s \rightarrow C(x)) \ \& \ \forall x \forall y[(x \in s \ \& \ x \text{ admires } y) \rightarrow (y \in s \ \& \ x \neq y)])$

To understand what is distinctive about Quine's position, consider the following sentence, which appears to be a set-theoretic truism.

(7) There are some sets that are self-identical, and every set that is not a member of itself is one of them.

It is reasonable to demand that no proper regimentation of this sentence render it obviously false.[4] However, a strict application of Quine's method of set-theoretic paraphrasing would turn (7) into (8), which is inconsistent with standard set-theoretic principles.

(8) There is a non-empty set such that every member of it is a self-identical set, and every set that is not a member of itself is a member of it.

James Higginbotham aptly labels this problem *the paradox of plurality* (Higginbotham 1998: 17).

In linguistics, an influential approach to plurals is that of Godehard Link, who uses mereological sums to analyze plurals. In his framework, the formal language contains a special mereological relation ($\leq$), corresponding to the notion of individual parthood: being an *atomic* part of. This notion is not to be confused with that of material parthood: being a *material* part of. For example, while *Annie* is an atomic part of the mereological sum (in the individual sense) of Annie and Bonnie, she is not an atomic part of it in the material sense. So the plurality of Annie and Bonnie is the mereological fusion of Annie and Bonnie *taken as atomic individuals*. Let "$\oplus$" stand for the binary operation of mereological fusion relative to individual parthood. Let $\sigma x.\varphi(x)$ be the mereological fusion of the individuals satisfying the formula $\varphi(x)$.[5] Then we may formalize some basic plural sentences as displayed below (see Link 1983, 1998 as well as Moltmann 1997 and Champollion 2017 for more details and applications of the framework).

(3) Bunsen and Kirchhoff laid the foundations of spectral analysis.
(3*) $F(b \oplus k)$
(9) The Romans conquered Gaul.
(9*) $C(\sigma x.R(x), g)$
(7) There are some sets that are self-identical, and every set that is not a member of itself is one of them.
(7*) $\exists x\,[\forall y\,(y \leq x \rightarrow (\text{Set}(y)\,\&\,y = y))\,\&\,\forall y\,((\text{Set}(y)\,\&\,y \notin y) \rightarrow y \leq x)]$

A final "singularizing" strategy we should mention is based on Davidson's analysis of predication (hence also plural predication) in terms of events, broadly understood to include states (see Higginbotham and Schein 1989; Schein 1993; and Chapter 36, this volume). This approach enables us to eliminate a plural subject by reducing it to the single co-agents of the underlying event. To illustrate it, let us look at the treatment of one of Frege's examples.

(3) Bunsen and Kirchhoff laid the foundations of spectral analysis.
(3**) There is an event e of laying the foundations of spectral analysis such that Bunsen is a co-agent of e, Kirchhoff is a co-agent of e, and there is no other co-agent of e.

Are these "singularizing" strategies successful? Many philosophical logicians believe that the answer is negative. Some of their main arguments will be outlined in Section 6. First we will consider an altogether different analysis of plurals.

2. TAKING PLURALS AT FACE VALUE

George Boolos championed an approach to plurals that completely rejects Frege's attempt to render plural discourse in terms of "wholes."

Abandon, if one ever had it, the idea that use of plural forms must always be understood to commit one to the existence of sets [. . .] of those things to which the corresponding singular forms apply. There are, of course, quite a lot of Cheerios in that bowl, well over two hundred of them. But is there, in addition to the Cheerios, also a set of them all? [. . .]

It is haywire to think that when you have some Cheerios, you are eating a set [. . .] [I]t doesn't follow just from the fact that there are some Cheerios in the bowl that, as some who theorize about the semantics of plurals would have it, there is also a set of them all.

(Boolos 1984: 448–9)

In fact, Boolos's rejection of the singularizing approach has a distinguished pedigree featuring, most prominently Russell (1938) (see Klement 2014). Russell distinguishes between a *class as one* and a *class as many*. A class as one is a multiplicity of objects thought of as a single whole, as is done in traditional first-order set or class theory. In contrast, a class as many is a multiplicity of objects *as such*. There is no single entity that represents, collects, or goes proxy for the objects that make up the multiplicity. Russell emphasizes the usefulness of the second way of thinking about multiplicities. In more recent history, Black (1971) and Simons (1982, 1997) have advocated a treatment of plurals in the spirit of classes as many.[6]

What is the broader significance of Boolos's attack on singularizing analyses and of Russell's much earlier non-singularizing approach based on the notion of classes as many? At the heart of their remarks is the simple idea that plurals should be taken at face value. That is, we should allow certain forms of plural discourse in the regimentation of natural language. Frege, Quine, and others were simply wrong to think that plurals needed to be paraphrased away. Rather, plurals deserve to be regimented in their own terms by employing a type distinction between singular and plural expressions in the regimenting language. The standard implementation of this proposal is known as *plural logic*.

3. THE LANGUAGE OF PLURAL LOGIC

We first introduce a formal language that may be used to regiment a wide range of natural language uses of plurals. This language captures Boolos's and Russell's suggestion and will enable us to represent many valid patterns of reasoning that essentially involve plural expressions. The language is known in the philosophical literature as PFO+, which is short for *plural first-order logic plus plural predicates*. In one variant or another, it is the most common regimenting language for plurals in philosophical logic.[7]

Start with the standard language of first-order logic. We expand this language by making the following additions.

A. Plural variables ($vv, xx, yy, \ldots$, and variously indexed variants thereof) and plural constants ($aa, bb, \ldots$, and variants thereof), roughly corresponding to the natural language pronoun "they" and to plural proper names, respectively.
B. Quantifiers that bind plural variables ($\forall xx, \exists yy, \ldots$).
C. A binary predicate $\prec$ for plural membership, corresponding to the natural language "is one of" or "is among". This predicate is treated as logical.

D. Symbols for collective plural predicates with numerical superscripts representing the predicate's arity: P^1, P^2, ..., Q^1, ... (and variously indexed variants thereof). Examples of collective plural predicates are "... cooperate", "... gather", "... meet", "... outnumber ...". For economy, we leave the arity unmarked.

The fragment of PFO+ containing items A-C, i.e. PFO+ minus plural predicates, is known as PFO. Table 34.1 below summarizes which linguistic items are added to the standard language of first-order logic to obtain PFO+.

The recursive clauses defining a well-formed formula of PFO+ are the obvious ones. However, some clarifications about the language are in order.

First, one may require a rigid distinction between the argument places of predicates. An argument place that is open to a singular argument could be reserved *only* to such arguments. A similar restriction could be imposed on argument places open to plural arguments. Would this rigid distinction between singular and plural argument places reflect a feature of natural language? Different natural language predicates suggest different answers. Some predicates are flexible and are capable of combining felicitously with both singular and plural terms. Examples include "own a house", "lifted a boat", or, as in Frege's example, "laid the foundations of spectral analysis". (Of course, the conjugations of the verbs will have to be adjusted.) Other predicates appear to lack this flexibility and combine felicitously *only* with plural terms, e.g. "cooperate with one another" and "are two in number". There is an interesting linguistic question as to the source of these felicity judgments: are they of syntactic, semantic, or pragmatic origin? We don't wish to take a stand on these matters. For our purposes, we can leave things open, noting that the two kinds of argument place—apparently flexible and apparently inflexible—suggest different regimentation strategies, namely to admit flexible plural predicates, or not.

Second, collective plural predicates are contrasted with distributive ones, such as "are prime", "are students", "have visited Rome". Roughly speaking, these are predicates that apply to a collection if and only if they apply to each of its members. How best to make this precise will depend on one's stand on the issue of flexible plural predicates mentioned just above. If all plural predicates are allowed to be flexible, then a plural predicate P is distributive just in case the following is analytic (or near enough):

$$P(xx) \leftrightarrow \forall x \, (x < xx \rightarrow P(x))$$

Table 34.1 Linguistic Items Added to the Standard Language of First-Order Logic to Obtain PFO+

	natural language equivalent	symbolization
plural variables	they$_1$, they$_2$, ...	vv, vv_0, ... xx, ...
plural constants	the Hebrides, the Channel Islands	aa, bb, ..., aa_1, ...
plural quantifier	there are some (things)	$\exists vv\, \exists xx$, ...
plural membership	is one of, is among	$<$
collective plural predicates	are two, cooperate, met, wrote together	$T(vv)$, $C(vv)$, $M(vv)$, $WT(vv, x)$

In the presence of inflexible plural predicates, however, a slight modification is needed. Then a plural predicate P is distributive just in case its singular analogue P^s is such that the following is analytic (or near enough):

$$P(xx) \leftrightarrow \forall x(x < xx \rightarrow P^s(x))$$

If P has no singular analogue (as is arguably the case for "cooperate with one another" and "are two in number"), then P is collective by default.[8] Distributive plural predicates in this sense may thus be obtained by paraphrase from their corresponding singular forms. For this reason, distributive plural predicates may be omitted from PFO+ without any loss of expressibility—although admittedly with some violence to style.

It might be helpful to close this section by providing some basic examples of regimentation in PFO+.

(10)   Some students cooperated.
(10′) $\exists xx\, (S(xx)\, \&\, C(xx))$
(11)   Bunsen and Kirchhoff laid the foundations of spectral analysis.
(11′) $\exists xx\, (\forall y\, (y < xx \leftrightarrow (y = b \vee y = k))\, \&\, L(xx))$
       (GK) Some critics admire only one another.
(12) $\exists xx\, (\forall x(x < xx \rightarrow C(x))\, \&\, \forall x \forall y[(x < xx\, \&\, A(x,y)) \rightarrow (y < xx\, \&\, x \neq y)])$

4. THE THEORY OF PLURAL LOGIC

As a formal language, PFO+ comes equipped with logical rules of inference and axioms aimed at capturing correct reasoning in the fragment of natural language regimented by this formal language. The rules associated with the singular vocabulary—logical connectives and quantifiers—are the usual ones, i.e. introduction and elimination rules for each logical expression. Plural quantifiers are associated with introduction and elimination rules mirroring those for the singular quantifiers. Two principles may be added. One captures the fact that pluralities are not empty:

(Non-empty) $\forall xx\, \exists y\, y < xx$

The other is an indiscernibility principle. It expresses the fact that coextensive pluralities satisfy the same formulas:

(Indiscernibly) $\forall xx\, \forall yy\, (\forall x(x < xx \leftrightarrow x < yy) \rightarrow (\varphi(xx) \leftrightarrow \varphi(yy)))$

Finally, there is a principle sanctioning which pluralities there are. This is the axiom schema of *plural comprehension*. For any formula $\varphi(x)$ of PFO+ containing x free, we have the axiom stating that, if $\varphi(x)$ is satisfied by at least one thing, then there are some things which include all and only things that satisfy $\varphi(x)$. The formula $\varphi(x)$ may contain parameters. So, in symbols, we have the universal closure of the following axiom schema:

(P-Comp) $\exists x\, \varphi(x) \rightarrow \exists xx\, \forall y\, (y < xx \leftrightarrow \varphi(y))$

The notion of derivation is defined inductively in the usual way as an appropriate sequence of formulas.

5. THE SEMANTICS OF PLURAL LOGIC

The formal language of plural logic also comes equipped with a model-theoretic semantics that captures the notion of logical consequences in terms of models (also called interpretations or structures): a sentence φ is the logical consequence of some premises just in case there is no model of the language in which the premises are true and φ is false. So the central task is to characterize a suitable notion of model and a correlative notion of truth in a model (also called satisfaction).

Traditional model-theoretic semantics is based on set theory. A model is defined as an ordered pair (d, f), where d is a non-empty set representing the domain of discourse of the model (i.e. what there is according to the model) and f is an interpretation function from the non-logical terminology of the language to set-theoretic constructions based on d.[9] Let $[\![E]\!]_f$ be the denotation of the expression E according to the function f. A natural setup is one in which a proper name denotes an object in the domain and a monadic predicate denotes a subset of the domain. So for any proper name a and singular predicate S, the sentence $S(a)$ is true in the model (d, f) if and only if $[\![a]\!]_f \in [\![S]\!]_f$.

There is an obvious way of extending this semantics to PFO and PFO+. The interpretation function f can be augmented so that plural constants are assigned non-empty subsets of the domain and (monadic) plural predicates are assigned sets of subsets of the domain. The treatment of plural predication is then parallel to that of singular predication: for any plural term aa and plural predicate P, the sentence $P(aa)$ is true in the model (d, f) if and only if $[\![aa]\!]_f \in [\![P]\!]_f$. Plural membership is treated as logical in that it is not subject to reinterpretation, always corresponding to set-theoretic membership. That is, a sentence of the form $b \prec aa$ is true in the model (d, f) if and only if $[\![b]\!]_f \in [\![aa]\!]_f$.

On the semantics just developed, plural logic has metalogical properties that distinguish it from first-order logic. It is not compact, hence it is incomplete, and it fails to have the Löwenheim-Skolem property.[10]

However, the set-theoretic model theory for PFO and PFO+ has received two main criticisms. First, since plural terms are taken to denote sets, the semantics is said to introduce ontological commitments that are arguably absent in ordinary discourse. Second, by construing domains as sets, the set-theoretic model theory rules out models whose domain is too big to form a set. This means that there are no models that correspond to some intuitive interpretations of the language, such as those with a domain of quantification encompassing absolutely everything.[11]

As a reaction to these criticisms, an alternative approach to the semantics of PFO and PFO+ has gained increasing popularity. Instead of letting the values of plural terms be subsets of the first-order domain, the semantic values of plural terms are represented by plural terms in the metalanguage. A plural term now stands for *many* objects. To state this view, one needs of course to make use of plural resources in the metalanguage. This semantic proposal traces back to Boolos (1985) who insisted that the value of a plural variable not be a set (or any kind of set-like object). For him a plural variable has many values from the ordinary, first-order domain and thus ranges plurally over it.

The semantics based on Boolos's new approach may be called *plurality-based* to highlight the contrast with the set-based semantics described above.

How are the criticisms to the set-based semantics avoided on the plurality-based approach? First, since plural terms no longer denote sets, the charge of introducing spurious ontological commitments to sets does not arise. A plural term denotes many objects as such, without the need of collecting those objects into a single entity. Second, by using plural resources in the metalanguage one may define a domain of quantification to be *some things* rather than a set. In turn, this enables one to capture a domain of quantification encompassing absolutely everything. That would be the domain consisting of the things such that everything is among them, which can be obtained by plural comprehension. Therefore, the plurality-based semantics sidesteps the two main criticisms leveled against the set-based approach.

In closing this section, we would like to make two further remarks. First, the plurality-based semantics sanctions the same metalogical properties as the set-based semantics. In particular, the resulting logic is not compact, is incomplete, and it fails to have the Löwenheim-Skolem property. Second, these metalogical properties, both in the case of the plurality-based semantics and in the case of the set-based semantics, depend on a *standard* treatment of quantification according to which plural quantifiers range over *all* subpluralities or *all* non-empty subsets of the first-order domain. But there is a *non-standard* (i.e. Henkin) treatment of plural logic. By allowing quantification over some but not all subpluralities of the first-order domain, or some but not all subsets of the first-order domain, we obtain respectively a Henkin plurality-based semantics and a Henkin set-based semantics (see Florio and Linnebo 2016).

6. ARGUMENTS AGAINST SINGULARIZING STRATEGIES

Plural logic provides an appealing alternative to the singularizing strategies surveyed in the first section. But is the resort to plural logic inevitable? Can we successfully analyze plurals by paraphrasing them away according to one of those strategies? Singularizing approaches face some serious objections. *The argument from incorrect existential consequences* points out that, for a broad range of singularizing approaches, some translations will have first-order existential consequences that the initial plural sentences appear not to have. In those cases, we are able to transition *as a matter of logic* from *some objects* to some sort of "collection" or single object that comprises, or somehow represents, those objects. But a number of examples suggest that this transition is not always licit. Consider these two sentences.

(13) Bill and Hillary are two. (Yi 1999).
(14) Russell and Whitehead wrote *Principia Mathematica*. (Oliver and Smiley 2001).

Set-theoretic and mereological paraphrases offer translations along the following lines.

(15) {Bill, Hillary} is two-membered.
(16) Russell⊕Whitehead wrote* *Principia Mathematica*.

where "wrote*" stands for the appropriate mereological rendering of the predicate "wrote". Thus, in both cases, the translation has a singular existential consequence, (17), that is intuitively neither a consequence of (13) or (14).

(17) There is a set or there is a mereological sum.

Boolos proposed a famous variant of this argument when he remarked that 'I am eating some Cheerios' does not logically entail 'I am eating a set' (Boolos 1984: 72).

Another argument is *the paradox of plurality* introduced in Section 1. It purports to show that plausible singularizing strategies are bound to regiment intuitively true sentences of the object language as logical falsehoods (Boolos 1984; Lewis 1991; Schein 1993; Higginbotham 1998; Oliver and Smiley 2001; Rayo 2002; McKay 2006; Oliver and Smiley 2013).

While the paradox of plurality threatens a wide array of singularizing strategies, it does not threaten all of such strategies. Notably, the mereological approach can escape the paradox. The paradox assumes that the relation regimenting plural membership is not reflexive. Unlike the set-theoretic singularist, the mereological singularist need not grant this assumption. She can model plural membership by means of the reflexive relation of individual parthood ($\leq$).

However, the very feature that immunizes the mereological approach from the paradox of plurality makes it vulnerable to another sort of objection. According to this objection, mereology doesn't have the resources to represent the more complex structure associated with plural expressions, thus validating intuitively invalid inferences. In particular, the mereological singularist faces difficulties when regimenting plural talk involving the very mereological notions that are at the core of her regimentation strategy. In such cases, there can be more structure than can be represented by the mereological strategy (see, e.g. Schein 1993; Oliver and Smiley 2001; and Rayo 2002).

The criticisms against singularizing strategies have varying degrees of force. Whether or not they are ultimately compelling, we hope that this brief exposition will suffice to appreciate the standard motivations for plural logic.

7. LOGICALITY AND PLURAL LOGIC

One of the central disputes about plural logic concerns its status as *logic*. Does the logical system outlined above qualify as "pure logic"? Since the debate about what counts as pure logic is vast, we cannot do full justice to it here. Rather, we focus on three important marks of logicality: topic-neutrality, formality, and epistemic access.

The requirement of topic-neutrality is based on a simple, intuitive idea, namely that logical principles should be applicable to reasoning about any subject matter. In contrast, other principles are only applicable to particular domains of individuals. The laws of physics, for instance, concern the physical world and cannot be applied to reasoning about natural numbers or other abstract entities. Plural logic seems to satisfy this intuitive notion of topic-neutrality. The validity of the principles of plural logic does not appear to be restricted to specific domains of individuals.

Another mark of logicality is formality. Logical principles are often thought to hold in virtue of their form, and not of their content. There are different ways of articulating the notion of formality, some of which are connected to the notion of topic-neutrality just discussed (see MacFarlane 2000). However, the following conditions are commonly associated with formality. The first is that formal principles are ontologically innocent: they do not commit us to the existence of particular objects. The second is that formal principles are unable to discriminate between objects: they cannot single out particular objects or classes thereof.

Is plural logic ontologically innocent? In particular, are plural quantifiers ontologically innocent? The traditional answer to these questions is affirmative. Plural logic indeed originated as an ontologically innocent alternative to second-order logic, a system that adds to first-order logic quantification into predicate position (Boolos 1984, 1985). This view is sustained by the plurality-based semantics developed in Section 5. According to that semantics, plural quantifiers do not range over a special domain of plural entities. They range plurally over entities in the domain of the singular quantifiers and thus do not introduce commitments beyond those incurred by the first-order quantifiers.[12] However, both earlier critics of the ontological innocence of plural logic (e.g. Parsons 1990; Hazen 1993; and Shapiro 1993) and more recent ones (Linnebo 2003; Florio and Linnebo 2016) have emphasized that the conclusion follows only if ontological innocence is understood in terms of commitments to objects, i.e. to entities in the range of the first-order quantifiers. However, there is a broader notion of ontological commitment tied to the presence of existential quantifiers of any logical category in a sentence's truth conditions. According to this notion, plural locutions incur additional ontological commitments even on a plurality-based semantics. The resulting view is an analogue of that espoused by Frege when he held that quantification into predicate position incurs its own distinctive kind of commitment, not to objects but rather to (what he called) concepts.

Another condition on formality is that formal principles should not discriminate between objects. A standard way of making the condition precise is to claim that logical principles are those that remain true no matter how the non-logical expressions of the language are reinterpreted. This presupposes a distinction between logical and non-logical expressions of the language, which is typically captured by defining logical notions in terms of isomorphism invariance (e.g. Tarski 1986; Sher 1991; McGee 1996) and then characterizing as logical the expressions that are suitably related to logical notions.[13] The notions corresponding to plural quantification and plural membership come out as logical on this account.

The last mark of logicality we would like to consider concerns *epistemic access*. It is often thought one must be able to grasp and accept logical principles (or logical notions) without relying on non-logical principles (or non-logical notions). Moreover, logical truths, if knowable, must be knowable independently of non-logical truths. In the context of plural logic, the prime suspect has been plural comprehension (see Linnebo 2003). The claim is that our knowledge and acceptance of plural comprehension is mediated by our knowledge and acceptance of set theory.

8. PLURAL LOGIC AND SECOND-ORDER LOGIC

Both plural logic and second-order logic have found a number of philosophical applications. As first shown by Boolos, monadic second-order logic can be interpreted in PFO. The converse is true as well: PFO can be interpreted in monadic second-order logic. So, from a syntactic point of view, the two theories are equivalent. In light of this equivalence, one question (also relevant in the context of collective intentionality) is whether there is a genuine choice between them. When considering particular applications, are they interchangeable? Could plural logic be replaced by second-order logic in the formalization of talk about collections or collective entities? Or should one system be preferred over the other?

One reason to keep the two systems separate concerns natural language. Plural logic is typically motivated by the need to capture natural language plurals while avoiding the problems incurred by the singularizing strategies. Second-order logic can be said to enjoy a parallel motivation. There are examples strongly suggestive of variable binding of predicate positions (e.g. "John is everything we wanted him to be," see Higginbotham 1998: 3; see also Rayo and Yablo 2001), which includes predicate positions of plural predicates ("John and Mary are everything we wanted them to be"). Thus plural logic and second-order logic might be needed as distinct formalisms for the regimentation of natural language.

Another reason to keep the two systems separate is that, as naturally interpreted, the semantic values of plural and second-order terms seem to have different modal profiles. While pluralities are modally rigid, properties are not. Compare the following sentences, where "them" in (18) refers to Annie and Bonnie.

(18) Annie is one of them but might not have been.
(19) Annie is a philosopher but might not have been.

While (18) appears to be false, (19) appears to be true. This is symptomatic of the fact that we regard pluralities as modally rigid: if x is one of xx, then necessarily x is one of xx. In the jargon of possible worlds, we may say that pluralities retain their members across worlds (for more details, see Rumfitt 2005; Williamson 2010; Uzquiano 2011; an unorthodox view is defended by Hewitt 2012). Not so for all properties. Some properties do not retain their extension across worlds. For instance, the property of being a philosopher has a non-empty extension but might have had an empty one.

ACKNOWLEDGEMENTS

For helpful discussion, we would like to thank Hannes Leitgeb, Gil Sagi, and Florian Steinberger. We gratefully acknowledge the support of the Munich Center for Mathematical Philosophy at Ludwig-Maximilians-Universität München and of the Center for Advanced Studies in Oslo.

RELATED TOPICS

Plural and Collective Noun Phrases (Ch. 35), Actions and Events in Plural Discourse (Ch. 36).

REFERENCES

Black, M. (1971) "The Elusiveness of Sets," *Review of Metaphysics* 24: 614–36.
Boolos, G. (1984) "To Be Is to Be a Value of a Variable (or to Be Some Values of Some Variables)," *Journal of Philosophy* 81: 430–50.

——— (1985) "Nominalist Platonism," *Philosophical Review* 94: 327–44.

Burgess, J. and Rosen, G. (1997) *A Subject with No Object. Strategies for Nominalistic Interpretations of Mathematics*, Oxford: Oxford University Press.

Champollion, L. (2017) *Parts of a Whole: Distributivity as a Bridge Between Aspect and Measurement*, Oxford: Oxford University Press.

Enderton, H.B. (2002) *A Mathematical Introduction to Logic*, San Diego: Academic Press.

Florio, S. and Linnebo, Ø. (2016) "On the Innocence and Determinacy of Plural Quantification," *Noûs.* 50: 565–83.

Frege, G. (1980) *Philosophical and Mathematical Correspondence*, Oxford: Basil Blackwell.

Hazen, A. (1993) "Against Pluralism," *Australasian Journal of Philosophy* 71: 132–44.

Hewitt, S. (2012) "Modalising Plurals," *Journal of Philosophical Logic* 41: 853–75.

Higginbotham, J. (1998) "On Higher-Order Logic and Natural Language," in T. Smiley (ed.) *Philosophical Logic*, Oxford: Oxford University Press.

Higginbotham, J. and Schein, B. (1989) "Plurals," in J. Carter and R.-M. Dechaine (eds) *Proceedings of the North East Linguistics Society*, Amherst: Graduate Linguistics Students Association, University of Massachusetts.

Klement, K. (2014) "Early Russell on Types and Plurals," *Journal for the History of Analytical Philosophy* 2: 1–21.

Kreisel, G. (1967) "Informal Rigour and Completeness Proofs," in I. Lakatos (ed.) *Problems in the Philosophy of Mathematics*, Amsterdam: North Holland.

Landman, F. (2000) *Events and Plurality*, Dordrecht: Kluwer Academic Publishers.

Lewis, D. (1991) *Parts of Classes*, Oxford: Basil Blackwell.

Link, G. (1983) "The Logical Analysis of Plurals and Mass Terms: A Lattice-Theoretical Approach," in R. Bäuerle, C. Schwarze, and A. von Stechov (eds) *Meaning, Use and the Interpretation of Language*, Berlin: De Gruyter.

——— (1998) *Algebraic Semantics in Language and Philosophy*, Stanford: CSLI Publications.

Linnebo, Ø. (2003) "Plural Quantification Exposed," *Noûs* 37: 71–92.

——— (2010) "Pluralities and Sets," *Journal of Philosophy* 107: 144–64.

MacFarlane, J. (2000) What Does It Mean to Say That Logic Is Formal? Ph.D. thesis, University of Pittsburgh.

McCarthy, T. (1981) "The Idea of a Logical Constant," *Journal of Philosophy* 78: 499–523.

McGee, V. (1996) "Logical operations," *Journal of Philosophical Logic* 25: 567–80.

McKay, T.J. (2006) *Plural Predication*, Oxford: Oxford University Press.

Moltmann, F. (1997) *Parts and Wholes in Semantics*, Oxford: Oxford University Press.

Oliver, A. and Smiley, T. (2001) "Strategies for a Logic of Plurals," *Philosophical Quarterly* 51: 289–306.

——— (2013) *Plural Logic*, Oxford: Oxford University Press.

Parsons, C. (1990) "The Structuralist View of Mathematical Objects," *Synthese* 84: 303–46.

Quine, W.V.O. (1960) *Word and Object*, Cambridge, MA: MIT Press

Quine, W.V.O. (1982) *Methods of Logic*, Cambridge, MA: Harvard University Press.

Rayo, A. (2002) "Word and Objects," *Noûs* 36: 436–64.

Rayo, A. and Yablo, S. (2001) "Nominalism Through De-Nominalization," *Noûs* 35: 74–92.

Rayo, A. and Williamson, T. (2003) "A Completeness Theorem for Unrestricted First-Order Languages," in J.C. Beall (ed.) *Liars and Heaps*, Oxford: Oxford University Press.

Resnik, M. (1988) "Second-Order Logic Still Wild," *Journal of Philosophy* 85: 75–87.

Rumfitt, I. (2005) "Plural Terms: Another Variety of Reference?" in J.L. Bermúdez (ed.) *Thought, Reference, and Experience: Themes from the Philosophy of Gareth Evans*, Oxford: Oxford University Press.

Russell, B. (1938) *The Principles of Mathematics*, New York: Norton.

Sagi, G. (2015) "The Modal and Epistemic Arguments Against the Invariance Criterion for Logical Terms," *Journal of Philosophy* 112: 159–67.

Schein, B. (1993) *Plurals and Events*, Cambridge, MA: MIT Press.

Schwarzschild, R. (1996) *Pluralities*, Dordrecht: Kluwer Academic Publishers.

Shapiro, S. (1993) "Modality and Ontology," *Mind* 102: 455–81.

Sher, G. (1991) *The Bounds of Logic: A Generalized Viewpoint*, Cambridge, MA: MIT Press.

Simons, P. (1982) "Plural Reference and Set Theory," in B. Smith (ed.) *Parts and Moments: Studies in Logic and Formal Ontology*, München: Philosophia Verlag.

——— (1997) "Higher-Order Quantification and Ontological Commitment," *Dialectica* 51: 255–71.

Tarski, A. (1986) "What Are Logical Notions?" *History and Philosophy of Logic* 7: 143–54.

Uzquiano, G. (2011) "Plural Quantification and Modality," *Proceedings of the Aristotelian Society* 111: 219–50.

Williamson, T. (2010) "Necessitism, Contingentism, and Plural Quantification," *Mind* 119: 657–748.

Winter, Y. and Scha, R. (2015) "Plurals," in S. Lappin and C. Fox (eds), *The Handbook of Contemporary Semantic Theory*, Oxford: Wiley-Blackwell.

Yi, B.-U. (1999) "Is Two a Property?" *Journal of Philosophy* 96: 163–90.

——— (2002) *Understanding the Many*, London: Routledge.

——— (2005) "The Logic and Meaning of Plurals. Part I." *Journal of Philosophical Logic* 34: 459–506.

——— (2006). "The Logic and Meaning of Plurals. Part II." *Journal of Philosophical Logic* 35: 239–88.

NOTES

1. For historical details, see Oliver and Smiley (2013: ch. 2).
2. As shown by Boolos, who credits David Kaplan, there is no paraphrase of this sentence comprising only singular vocabulary and the predicates occurring in it (Boolos 1984: 432–3).
3. See Resnik (1988) for a similar view.
4. According to the view defended in Linnebo (2010), (7) is false—but only for non-obvious reasons having to do with the "definiteness" of any plurality, contrasted with the "indefiniteness" of the notion of a self-identical set.
5. If desired, both fusion constructions can be defined in terms of the parthood relation by exploiting the fact that the fusion is the smallest object whose parts include the things to be fused.
6. Again, for historical details, see Oliver and Smiley (2013: ch. 2).
7. For systems that employ the notation for variables adopted here, see Rayo (2002) and Linnebo (2003). An ancestor of this notation is found in Burgess and Rosen (1997). Variants include variables in boldface (Oliver and Smiley), capitalized (McKay), or pluralized with the letter "s" (Yi).
8. Notice that our definition of distributivity takes the form of (analytic) equivalences. Some authors (e.g. McKay 2006: 6) tie distributivity solely to the left-to-right implication. For discussion and references, see Oliver and Smiley (2013: 112–13). For an overview of linguistic treatments of distributivity, see Winter and Scha (2015).
9. The logical terminology is not subject to reinterpretation. Its meanings are characterized inductively through the characterization of the notion of truth in a model.
10. For an explanation of these properties, see any advanced introduction to logic, e.g. Enderton (2002).
11. Since the completeness theorem fails for plural logic with standard semantics, the famous Kreisel "squeezing argument" (Kreisel 1967) is not available. See Rayo and Williamson (2003) for discussion.
12. Note that the picture is different if one adopts the set-based semantics or attempts to regiment plurals along one of the singularizing strategies presented in the first section.
13. Denoting a logical notion has been claimed to be necessary but not sufficient for the logicality of an expression. An additional semantic connection would be required (as argued, for instance, by McCarthy (1981) and McGee (1996); see also Sagi (2015) for a critical evaluation of these arguments).

FURTHER READINGS

The classic references for Boolos's pioneering work on plural logical are Boolos (1984) and Boolos (1985). More recent developments include Yi (1999), Oliver and Smiley (2001), Rayo (2002), Linnebo (2003), Yi (2005) and Yi (2006). There are three philosophical monographs on plurals, all embracing plural logic: Yi (2002), McKay (2006), and Oliver and Smiley (2013). The latter is the most comprehensive philosophical treatment of the subject to date.

There is also a rich literature on plurals in linguistic semantics. Among the most influential works, often adopting a singularizing approach, are Link (1998), Schein (1993), Schwarzschild (1996), and Landman (2000).

35

Plural and Collective Noun Phrases

Katherine Ritchie

This chapter examines the semantic behavior and treatments of plural terms and collective noun phrases. The semantics of plurals and collective nouns should be of interest to those working on collective intentionality more generally for at least two reasons. First, we will see that two sorts of formal semantic treatments have been developed to capture varieties of plural predication. The first involve a predicate taking a singular group-like entity as argument, while the second involves taking some individuals (as many rather than as a group) as argument. Choice of treatment or superiority of one over the other may have ontological ramifications for debates about collective intentionality and action. Second, the apparent truth of certain sentences is sometimes used as evidence for the existence of some feature. For example, "The Spurs are disappointed to have lost to the Clippers" might be used as evidence for the view that a corporation or a team can have emotions. Looking more closely at the semantics and plurals of collective nouns may increase one's understanding of the support (or lack thereof) linguistic data can offer.

The chapter is structured as follows. In Section 1 I discuss the sorts of plural terms and collective nouns that will be the focus of this chapter. In Section 2, we turn to canvassing a range of data a semantic treatment should capture. In Section 3 we examine semantic treatments of plural terms. In Section 4 the treatments of collective nouns are discussed and it is argued that collective nouns have dual meanings. In Section 5 concluding remarks are drawn. While most of the literature on plurals and collective nouns involves the use of formal semantic and logical tools, here I will keep the discussion as informal as possible.

1. THE EXPRESSIONS

Plural terms come bare (*birds, students*), bound by quantifiers (*some birds, all the students*), in numeral constructions (*three birds*), with definite articles (*the judges*) and as conjunctions of expressions (*Dante, Alice, and Esme*). Here our examination will focus on definite plural noun phrases and conjunctive plural expressions in subject position.[1] The discussion is limited due to space and is limited to these two construction types as they have been focused on most in the philosophical literature.

A syntactically singular collective noun can also arise in a variety of constructions (e.g. *a team, some committee, every flock, the crowd*). Further they manifest behavior that varies depending on features of the entities in the collections picked out. Collective nouns can pick out groups of inanimates (*deck, fleet*), groups of non-human animates (*swarm, pride*), unorganized groups of humans (*mob, crowd*) and organized groups of humans (*team, committee*). The behavior of collective nouns varies according to whether groups of inanimates, non-human animates, or humans are picked out. For example, corpus studies (e.g. Levin 2001) have shown that collective nouns denoting human groups allow plural agreement most often, followed by those denoting non-human animate groups and last, by those denoting inanimate groups, which rarely or never allow plural agreement. Given issues of space and that the focus of this Handbook is on collective intentionality, I will center our discussion on collective nouns that denote groups of humans. Even more specifically, our inquiry here will focus on collective nouns that pick out organized groups of humans such as *team* and *committee*.

2. DATA

Predicates can apply to plurals and collective nouns distributively or collectively. An application of a predicate is **distributive** if it applies to each (or perhaps most) of the entities referred to by the plural expression. *Eat lunch, smile, tall, fall asleep*, and *human* are paradigmatic examples of predicates with distributive interpretations. An application of a predicate is **collective** if it applies to some entities together. Predicates such as *gather*,[2] *surround, walk together, met in 1984*, and *six in number* are naturally interpreted collectively. To illustrate the distinction further, consider the following sentences:

1. The students/Dante, Irene, and Ebony/The committee ate lunch.
2. The judges/Sonia, John, and Ruth/The Supreme Court walked into the room together.
3. The judges/Sonia, John, and Ruth/The Supreme Court surrounded the building.

In 1 the predicate is naturally interpreted as applying to the subjects individually. It is true if each student or each of Dante, Irene and Ebony or each of the members of the committee ate lunch. In contrast, the predication in 2 and 3 is most naturally understood as collective. They require that the judges or Sonia, John, and Ruth or the Court together satisfy the predicate. Sentence 2 fails to require, for example, that Sonia individually walked into the room together and 3 is true even if no individual member of the Supreme Court surrounded the building. I'll call predicates such as that in 1 **distributive predicates** and predicates such as those in 2 and 3 **collective predicates**. In labeling predicates themselves as distributive or collective, I adopt the convention that predicates are lexically marked as distributive or collective. While this convention is not uncontroversial, it has been widely adopted by linguists and philosophers (e.g. Link 1983; McKay 2006; Bennett 1974; Schwarzschild 1996; Scha 1981).[3]

Other predicates—often called **mixed** predicates—have easily accessible distributive and collective interpretations. Examples include *carry a table upstairs, weigh 400 lbs,* and *write a decision.* Consider the following sentences:

4. The movers/Nick, Sara, and Sabrina carried a table upstairs.
5. The team carried a table upstairs.

Sentence 4 has two obvious interpretations. On its collective interpretation it means that the movers or Nick, Sara, and Sabrina worked together to carry a table upstairs. Alternatively, each of the movers or each of Nick, Sara, and Sabrina might have carried a (possibly distinct) table upstairs. Context can make one or the other reading more salient. In contrast to 4, 5 has only a collective reading. It does not have a reading on which the team members each are said to have carried a table upstairs. The unavailability of a distributive reading in 5 generalizes to all cases of mixed predicates combined with collective nouns. For instance, when *weighs 400 lbs, lifted a piano,* or *composed an opera* are combined with a singular collective noun they too fail to allow for distributive interpretations.

Schwarzschild (1996) makes a similar point employing a collective noun that denotes a collection of inanimates. He notes that while (A) has a clear interpretation involving distributive predication, (B) does not.

(A) These cigarettes can be smoked in under two minutes.
(B) This pack can be smoked in under two minutes.

Given this example Schwarzschild states 'it is a property of collectives that they are generally not amenable to distributive readings' (1996: 181). Given examples such as 1 above we see that this claim is too strong, but Schwarzschild's observation provides further evidence that mixed predicates cannot be interpreted distributively when combined with collective noun phrases.

Distributive, collective, and mixed predicates have additional differences. Some might be interpreted as syntactic. Distributive and mixed predicates can be grammatically combined with ordinary non-collective singular subjects. In contrast, collective predicates do not easily combine felicitously with singular non-collective subjects.[4] The following examples show this.

6. Meg ate lunch.
7. Meg carried the table upstairs.
8. ? Meg walked into the room together.
9. ? Meg surrounded the building.

Sentences 6 and 7 are grammatical, felicitous, and might be true. Sentence 8 is marked and plausibly ungrammatical. Sentence 9 might be interpreted as ungrammatical, false (at least in all normal circumstances), or somehow pragmatically inappropriate.

Other differences in distributive and collective predicates are plausibly semantic in nature. Instances of distributive predication have a feature that Link (1983) calls the Cumulative Reference Property (CRP).[5] The feature can be captured as follows:

CUMULATIVE REFERENCE PROPERTY [CRP]: If P is a distributive predicate and some thing(s) X are P and some other thing(s) Y are P, then the X and Y are P.[6]

For example, suppose that Nancy and Molly are pianists and that Farrah and Linda are pianists. Then, Nancy, Molly, Farrah, and Linda are pianists. The CRP applies when predication is distributive and fails to apply with collective predication. For example, the collective predicate *are in a circle* fails to manifest CRP. Suppose that both "the boys are in a circle" and "the girls are in a circle" are true. From this we cannot conclude that "the boys and the girls are in a circle"; CRP fails to apply.[7]

Distributive and collective instances of predication also differ in their entailments. Instances of distributive predication have distributive entailments. Instances of collective predication lack these entailments. Distributive entailments can be captured by the following condition:

DISTRIBUTIVE ENTAILMENT [DE]: If P is an instance of distributive predication and X is a plural or collective noun phrase, P(X) is true if and only if for all x that are among X or are members of X, P(x).[8]

We saw that the predication in 1 is distributive. Given DE it entails that each of the individual students (or each of Dante, Irene, and Ebony or each of the members of the committee) ate lunch. DE fails to apply to instances of collective predication, so, for example, 2 fails to require that Ruth walked into the room together.[9]

The formulation of DE requires that distributive predicates distribute universally. One might argue that this condition should be weakened. Let's look at an example. Suppose the relevant students are a, b, c, d, e, f and g. The sentence "The students ate lunch" is uttered when situation A obtains and when situation B obtains.

> Situation A: a, b, c, d, e and f each ate lunch.
> Situation B: a, b, c, d, e, f and g each ate lunch.

A and B differ with respect to whether student g ate lunch. In Situation A the predicate is satisfied non-maximally while in Situation B it is satisfied maximally. One might, however, take the utterance to be true in both situations.[10]

Nonmaximality behavior could be captured semantically or pragmatically. Semantic strategies might appeal to altering the quantifier in DE to allow for exceptions (e.g. Brisson 2003) or by positing that the denotations of plural and collective terms are (or are sometimes) distinct from extensional lists of individuals (e.g. Landman 1989b). Alternatively, one might argue that, strictly, when plurals or collective nouns are arguments of instances of distributive predication, they require the universal entailments DE as formulated specifies. However, we are apt to take an utterance of "the students ate lunch" to be reasonable in Situation A, so we mistakenly judge it to be true. Here I will not attempt to adjudicate whether a semantic or pragmatic strategy is superior. Next, I turn to data specific to collective noun expressions.

In addition to predicates that apply to collective nouns distributively and collectively, some predicates apply in a third distinct way. Take the following examples:

10. The Committee on Ways and Means is old. It's been around since 1789!
11. The committee was reduced in size after the government shutdown.
12. The team was founded in 1902.
13. The group is large. It has over 50 members!

The predicates in 10–13 apply to the denotations of the subject expression as a whole, rather than to the members of the collections picked out by the collective noun phrases. For example, 12 says that the team as a whole or as an institution was founded in 1902. It fails to require that any team member was founded in 1902 (or at all). The uses of the predicates in 10–13 fail to meet DE. In that way they pattern with instances of collective predication. Further, they can combine felicitously with singular subjects in ways that collective predicates usually cannot. They do not seem to involve the sort of joint or togetherness condition that typifies collective predication. For instance, when a group surrounds, writes together, or even collectively weighs 500 lbs the members jointly or taken together satisfy the predicate. The predicates in 10–13 are not like this. We have evidence that predicates like those in 10–13 are to be understood in a way distinct from distributive and collective predication. So, I argue that we have evidence that collective nouns allow for a third sort of predication, call it **group-level predication**.[11] Finally, I turn to data on collective nouns and agreement.

It has been noted, at least since Jespersen (1914), that collective nouns allow for singular and plural agreement. Further, it has long been known that agreement possibilities vary among English dialects and features of the denotation of the collective noun. For example, British English allows for plural agreement on verb phrases (VPs) and pronouns, while American English rarely (if ever) allows for plural VP agreement, but does allow for plural pronoun agreement. Consider the following sentences.

14. The team **is/are** old.
15. The Supreme Court is in session. **It/They** will likely rule on *Burwell v. Hobby Lobby* today.
16. After every game, the winning team dumps Gatorade on **its/their** coach.
17. Inspections may come sooner if the department indicates that **it is/they are** ready for evaluation.

In British English both singular and plural VP agreement in 14 are acceptable. The variation in agreement corresponds to a variation in the interpretations the sentences are given. When agreement in 14 is plural, it is taken to mean that the team members are old. When the agreement is singular it is said to have two interpretations—one on which the team was formed long ago and one on which the individual members are old. In British English the choice of verb number can, but need not always, constrain the interpretation of the predication.

As exemplified in 15–17, bound and unbound singular and plural pronoun agreement is felicitous with collective nouns that pick out collections of humans. This holds across in all forms of English. In contrast, collective nouns that pick out collections of non-human animates (e.g. *swarm*, *pride*) allow plural agreement less frequently, and collective nouns that pick out collections of inanimates (e.g. *fleet*) rarely or never felicitously allow plural agreement.[12] We have come to the end of our discussion of linguistic data involving plurals and collective nouns. Next, let's turn to semantic accounts of plurals and collective nouns.

3. SEMANTIC TREATMENTS OF PLURALS

Semantic treatments of plural expressions can be broadly divided into two classes based on whether a plural term is taken to pick out a set/sum of entities or many entities.

I'll follow Oliver and Smiley (2001) in calling the former treatments Singularist and the latter treatments Pluralist. They are so-called as Singularist treatments take plural terms to pick out singular entities[13] and Pluralist treatments take plural terms to pick out many individuals plurally.[14] Here I briefly explicate how a version of each represents plural terms and can capture distributive and collective predication. There are many points where theorists diverge.[15] Here I adopt one simplified version of each type of theory.

On a Singularist approach the denotation of plural expressions is either sets or sums. For example, in a Singularist treatment *Dante, Irene, and Ebony* will denote either the set {Dante, Irene, Ebony} or the sum Dante+Irene+Ebony. Here I examine a Singularist treatment (based on Link (1983)) that employs sums. The Singularist who employs sums uses a domain structured by the sum formation operator and the individual-part relation. Ordinary individuals are called atomic individuals or atoms. The sum formation operator, "+", takes two atoms or non-atomic sums and yields their sum. A domain of atoms closed under sum formation yields all the sums of those individuals. For example, if a domain includes the atoms Dante, Irene, and Ebony, the sum formation operation will deliver the sums Dante+Irene, Dante+Ebony, Irene+Ebony and Dante+Irene+Ebony. These entities are available to serve as the denotations of plural terms. The domain of atoms and sums is structured according to the individual-part (or i-part) relation. The i-part relation, symbolized as "≤", meets the following biconditional:

$$a \leq b \quad \text{iff} \quad a + b = b.$$

This captures that, for example, Dante is an i-part of Dante+Irene+Ebony given that the sum of Dante and Dante+Irene+Ebony is just the sum Dante+Irene+Ebony.

Definite plural terms of the form 'the F' pick out the largest sum of entities satisfying the predicate F. For example, if there are four students, a, b, c and d, *the students* picks out the sum a+b+c+d. Following Link (1983) "the Fs" can be represented as σxFx.

A Pluralist adds a plural existential quantifier ∃*xx*, and plural universal quantifier, ∀*xx*, to first-order logic.[16] The first is read "some things are such that," the second, "all things are such that." They are plural as they can take multiple individuals as argument. Pluralists do not take this to involve quantifying over plural objects (e.g. sums or sets), but to involve many individuals as many serving as arguments. Pluralists employ domains with only ordinary singular individuals (e.g. Dante). The Pluralist uses the "among"-relion, which allows one to say that some thing or things are among some things. More formally, "the *xxs* are among the *yys*" is formalized as "*xxAyy*." Conjunctive plural terms can be written, (following McKay (2006)) using constants and brackets. For example, the plural term Dante, Irene and Ebony is written ⌊*d, i, e*⌋. A Pluralist treatment of definite plural terms could be formulated following a Russellian analysis with plural quantifiers.[17] "The Fs" would be formalized as [∃*xxFxx* & ∀*yy*(*Fyy*→ yyAxx)]. Next I turn to the treatments of predication.

To capture distributive and collective predication, predicates in the Singularist language are differentiated according to whether they take both individuals and sums or only sums. The first accords with distributive predication, the second with collective predication. The difference can be marked with a "*" on distributive predicates. Mixed predicates could be taken to be ambiguous. The "*" operator is defined to capture DE and CRP. According to the definition of the operator, if *F applies to a sum, *F truly applies to every atomic i-part of the sum. Collective predicates fail to have distributive entailments as they are not modified by the operator. The "∗" operator closes the domain of the predicate under sum formation. Given this, if ∗F(a) and ∗F(b), then ∗F(a+b). In this way CRP is met for distributive predicates.

The Pluralist captures collective predication through predicates whose single argument places can be satisfied by multiple individuals. Collective predication is not reducible to predication of each individual. Instead, some things together as many satisfy a predicate. Distributive predication is captured using the "among"-relation and a quantifier. For example, 1 with a conjunctive plural term in which "E" represents *eat lunch* is represented as

$$1'. \ \forall x \, (xA\lfloor d,i,e\rceil \rightarrow Ex)$$

Informally 1′ says that anything that is among Dante, Irene, and Ebony is such that she or he eats lunch. Mixed predicates could again be taken to be ambiguous. DE is captured in instances of distributive predication due to the use of the universal quantifier. Since collective predicates are not reducible to quantifier expressions, which are relied on to meet DE, they correctly fail to meet it. In simple cases, CRP is captured through conjunction introduction or through universal instantiation and conjunction introduction. We have seen a sketch of the way a Singularist and a Pluralist can capture plural predication. Next, we examine whether one treatment is superior.

One might appeal to semantic or logical reasons to try to argue for the superiority of a Singularist or Pluralist approach. First, it has been argued that a Pluralist approach is superior as it can avoid Russellian-style paradoxes that a Singularist theory cannot.[18] However, using sums rather than sets avoids Russell's Paradox. So, the Singularist we have been considering sidesteps this worry. Further, the sentence "there are some sums which are all and only the sums that are not i-parts of themselves" is false, as all sums are i-parts of themselves so the same sort of paradox does not arise for sums.[19]

Second, one might argue that only one style of treatment can handle the full range of semantic data. There is not space here to go through the variety of constructions one might argue cannot be captured by both theories, but the similarity of the two treatments gives us some evidence that they are equally capable. For example, both appeal to a part-style relation (either i-part or among). Where the Singularist uses a domain closed under sum formation, the Pluralist appeals to plural reference and quantification. Of course this is not an argument that the two are equally semantically capable, but it gives us some evidence that they are.[20]

Metaphysical arguments have also been given in favor of a Pluralist treatment. An appeal to ontological parsimony favors a Pluralist treatment. Intuition can also be appealed to in favor of a Pluralist treatment. For example, Boolos states that 'it is haywire to think that when you have some Cheerios, you are eating a set' (1984: 72). Here I will not attempt to further adjudicate the debate between Singularism and Pluralism. Next, we turn to a discussion of semantic treatments of collective nouns.

4. SEMANTIC TREATMENTS OF COLLECTIVE NOUNS

Semantic data involving collective nouns appear to pull us toward the view that collective nouns denote many entities *and* toward the view that they denote singular entities. For example, we saw that, like plurals, they allow for collective and (some) distributive predication. Yet, as we saw in 10–13, they appear to denote wholes when serving as arguments for other predicates. Further, we saw that collective nouns allow for singular and plural agreement. In accordance with the data, treatments of collective nouns have tended to take their denotations to be either the same as plural term denotations (Bennett 1974; Munn 1998; Elbourne 1999) or to be whole singular entities of some sort (Barker 1992; Schwarzschild 1996; Landman 1989b).[21] In choosing either a singular or a plural denotation, one must account for the data that pushes in the other direction. For example, if the denotation of a collective noun is singular, one needs to account for the possibility of plural agreement and distributive predication. Given the mixed data, instead of opting for one or the other denotation for collective nouns, one might argue that collective nouns have dual denotations. Since expressions with multiple meanings are often taken to be ambiguous, it would be prima facie natural to take collective nouns to be ambiguous.[22]

Ambiguous expressions require that a use selects one meaning. For example, in 18 *duck* can have its bird-meaning or its crouching-meaning, but not both.

18. Sue saw her duck and I did too.[23]

If collective nouns are ambiguous, a single token of a collective noun should allow for only one meaning to be utilized. However, a single token of a collective noun can allow for both a group as a whole meaning and a group as many meaning. For instance, we saw that a token of a collective noun can allow for both singular and plural agreement in examples 14–17. Sentence 19 involves a collective noun combined with predicates that rely on the group as a singular entity and on group members.

19. The team, which is composed entirely of freshmen, is young, but talented.

Since a single token can utilize multiple meanings, collective nouns should not be taken to be ambiguous. Instead, we should take both meanings to be had by each collective noun. I will call expressions that have multiple meanings in this way **polysemous**.[24] Next I turn to a brief sketch of a semantics of collective nouns that captures the data canvassed in Section 2.

On the semantics being developed, collective nouns are polysemous between a singular group-meaning and a plural members-meaning. The two are connected so that the group-meaning delivers the varied group members (the various members-meanings) across worlds and times.[25] One way to think of the connection between the group and members meaning is in terms of a group-meaning involving an entity with a structure. Teams, committees and courts seem to be entities with structures.[26] They are functionally organized in terms of roles and the relations that members bear to one another. On this picture, the members of a group at a time are the individuals who bear the relations required by the group's structural-functional organization. Since different members can play the roles in the group's structure, this view allows for variation in members of a group across worlds and times. Next let's briefly examine how the data can be captured by a view on which collective nouns are polysemous.

Distributive predicates, such as *eat lunch*, apply to individual people, so such predicates will select for the members-meaning of a collective noun. In order to keep the treatments of plurals and collective nouns similar, collective predicates, such as *gather*, could be taken to apply to the denotation of the members-meaning (i.e. the many members).[27]

Finally, group predication will be captured by a predicate applying to a collective noun's group-meaning. Singular agreement will be captured through concord with a collective noun's group-meaning, while plural agreement can be explained due to the members-meanings of collective nouns.[28] While brief, this will have to suffice for an explication of how a semantic treatment that takes collective nouns to be polysemous might go.

5. CONCLUDING REMARKS

We have seen that plurals and collective nouns allow for varied predication that bring with them varied entailments and that collective nouns allow for both plural and singular agreement. I have described Singularist and Pluralist semantic treatments of plural terms. I also canvassed some arguments that have been given in favor of Pluralist treatments and for the view that the two sorts of treatments are equally adequate. Finally, I argued that collective nouns are polysemous between a plural members meaning and a singular group meaning. In arguing for views in social ontology and in collective intentionality, action, and emotion, the semantics of plural terms and collective nouns may prove informative.

RELATED TOPICS

Social Groups (Ch. 21), Collective Intentionality and Language (Ch. 28), Logic and Plurals (Ch. 34).

REFERENCES

Barker, C. (1992) "Group Terms in English: Representing Groups as Atoms," *Journal of Semantics* 9/1: 69–93.
Bartsch, R. (1973) "The Semantic and Syntax of Number and Numbers," *Syntax and Semantics* 2: 51–93.
Bennett, M. (1974) *Some Extensions of a Montague Fragment of English*, Doctoral Dissertation, UCLA.
Boolos, G. (1984) "To Be is to Be the Value of a Variable (or Some Values of Some Variables)," *Journal of Philosophy* 81: 430–50.
Brisson, C. (2003) "Plurals, All, and the Nonuniformity of Collective Predication," *Linguistics and Philosophy* 26: 129–84.
Champollion, L. (2010) *Parts of a Whole: Distributivity as a Bridge between Aspect and Measurement*, Doctoral Dissertation, University of Pennsylvania.
Corbett, G. (2000) *Number*, Cambridge: Cambridge University Press.
De Vries, H. (2015) *Shifting Sets, Hidden Atoms: The Semantics of Distributivity, Plurality and Animacy*, Doctoral Dissertation, Utrecht University.
Dowty, D. (1987) "A Note on Collective Predicates, Distributive Predicates and All," in *Proceedings of ESCOL '86*: 97–115.
Elbourne, P. (1999) "Some Correlations between Semantic Plurality and Quantifier Scope," *Proceedings of NELS* 29: 81–92.
Hoeksema, J. (1983) "Plurality and Conjunction," in A. ter Meulen (ed.) *Studies in Model Theoretic Semantics*, Dordrecht: Foris.
——— (1988) "The Semantics of Non-Boolean 'and'," *Journal of Semantics* 6: 19–40.
Hossack, K. (2000) "Plurals and Complexes," *British Journal for the Philosophy of Science* 51 (3): 411–43.
Jespersen, O. (1914) *A Modern English Grammar on Historical Principles*, London: Allen & Unwin.

Landman, F. (1989a) "Groups I," *Linguistics and Philosophy* 12 (5): 559–605.

——— (1989b) "Groups II," *Linguistics and Philosophy* 12 (6): 723–44.

Lasersohn, P. (1995) *Plurality, Conjunction and Events*, Dordrecht: Kluwer Academic Publishers.

Levin, M. (2001) *Agreement with Collective Nouns in English*, Lund: Lund Studies in English.

Link, G. (1983) "The Logical Analysis of Plurals and Mass Terms: A Lattice Theoretic Approach," in R. Bauerle, C. Schwarze, and A. von Stechow (eds) *Meaning, Use and Interpretation of Language*, Berlin: Gruyter.

McKay, T. (2006) *Plural Predication*, Oxford: Clarendon Press.

Moltmann, F. (1997) *Parts and Wholes in Semantics*, Oxford: Oxford University Press.

Munn, A. (1998) "First Conjunct Agreement: Against a Clausal Analysis," *Linguistic Inquiry* 30 (4): 643–68.

Nicolas, D. (2007) "Can Mereological Sums Serve as the Semantic Values of Plurals?" Unpublished manuscript, http://jeannicod.ccsd.cnrs.fr/ijn_00176868>.

Oliver, A. and Smiley, T. (2001) "Strategies for a Logic of Plurals," *Philosophical Quarterly* 51 (204): 289–306.

——— (2005) "Plural Descriptions and Many-Valued Functions," *Mind* 114/456: 1039–68.

——— (2013) *Plural Logic*, Oxford: Oxford University Press.

Pearson, H. (2011) "A New Semantics for Group Nouns," in M. Byram Washburn, K. McKinney-Bock, E. Varis, A. Sawyer and B. Tomaszewicz (eds) *Proceedings of the 28th West Coast Conference on Formal Linguistics*, Somerville, MA: Cascadilla Proceedings Project.

Quine, W.V. (1960) *Word and Object*, Cambridge, MA: MIT Press.

Rayo, A. (2002) "Word and Objects," *Noûs* 36/3: 436–64.

Ritchie, K. (2013) "What are Groups?" *Philosophical Studies* 166 (2): 257–72.

——— (2015) "The Metaphysics of Social Groups," *Philosophy Compass* 10 (5): 310–21.

——— (2016) "Can Semantics Guide Ontology?" *Australasian Journal of Philosophy* 94 (1): 24–41.

Russell, B. (1905) "On Denoting," *Mind* 14 (56): 479–93.

Scha, R. (1981) "Distributive, Collective and Cumulative Quantification," in J. Groenendijk, T. Janssen and M. Stokhof (eds) *Formal Methods in the Study of Language*, vol. 2., Amsterdam: Mathematisch Centrum.

Schein, B. (1993) *Plurals and Events*, Cambridge, MA: MIT Press.

Schwarzschild, R. (1996) *Pluralities*, London: Kluwer Academic Publishers.

——— (2011) "Stubborn Distributivity, Multiparticipant Nouns and the Count/Mass Distinctions," in S. Lima, K. Mullin and B. Smith (eds) *Proceedings of the 39th Meeting of the North East Linguistic Society (NELS 39)*, vol. 2. Amherst, MA: GLSA.

Suerland, U. and Elbourne, P. (2002) "Total Reconstruction, PF Movement, and Derivational Order," *Linguistic Inquiry* 33 (2): 283–319.

Winter, Y. (1997) "Choice functions and the Scopal Semantics of Indefinites," *Linguistics and Philosophy* 20: 399–467.

——— (2000) "Distributivity and Dependency," *Natural Language Semantics* 8: 27–69.

——— (2002) "Atoms and Sets: A Characterization of Semantic Number," *Linguistic Inquiry* 33: 493–505.

Winter, Y. and Scha, R. (2015) "Plurals," in S. Lappin and C. Fox (eds) *Handbook of Contemporary Semantics*, vol. 2., Malden, MA: Wiley-Blackwell.

Yi, B.-U. (2005) "The Logic and Meaning of Plurals, Part I," *Journal of Philosophical Logic* 34 (5/6): 459–506.

Zwicky, A. and Sadock, J. (1975, "Ambiguity Tests and How to Fail Them," *Syntax and Semantics* 4: 1–36.

NOTES

1. Additional complications arise when plural terms are in subject and object position, as in "Three students gave four presentations." Such cases are often taken to involve cumulative readings. See, e.g. Scha (1981) and Winter (2000) for discussion of such cases and how they relate to collective and distributive predication.

2. Here I mean to highlight the intransitive use of *gather*. The transitive use of *gather* as in "The judges gathered their papers" can be interpreted distributively.

3. Not everyone agrees that predicates should be marked lexically. Some have argued that distributive and collective interpretations are available for all predicates given the right context (e.g. Winter and Scha 2015; Josh Dever (pc); Marija Jankovic (pc)).

4. If all predicates have distributive and collective interpretations in some context or other, syntactically singular subjects should be able to grammatically combine with predicates that I have labeled collective. For instance, while *surround* and *gather* are classified as collective, sentences such as "The wall surrounded the city" and "The storm gathered in the sky" are grammatical and easily interpretable.

5. He cites Quine (1960: 61) as the source of this observation.

6. The CRP might need to be modified to include a contextual parameter to correctly handle context-sensitive predicates. For instance, in context c1 it might be true that Nancy and Molly are tall and in context c2 it might be true that Farrah and Linda are tall. However, if c1 and c2 have different standards for tallness, it might be false that Nancy and Molly and Farrah and Linda are tall. Given this, the CRP could be modified to apply only when a context is fixed.

7. McKay (2006: 7) argues that the CRP does not apply to all distributive predicates. He cites predicates such as "being fewer than four in number" and "being of just one gender" as examples that involve distributive predicates for which the CRP does not hold. While I agree that the CRP fails in these cases, it seems the readings are collective rather than distributive. For example, in saying "the students are fewer than four in number" one is not saying that each student is fewer than four in number, but that collectively they are. The same holds for the other predicates McKay considers.

8. We will see in the next section different ways semantic theories might understand what it takes for x to be among the Xs, so as of now this is a somewhat rough formulation.

9. Instances of collective predication also have entailments which one might call participates-in entailments or subentailments (Dowty's 1987 terminology). For example if "the students surrounded the table" is true and Kai is one of the students, then Kai took part in surrounding the table. For reasons of space these won't be further addressed here.

10. Definite plural expressions seem to have looser truth conditions than conjunctive plural expressions. Although, see Landman (1989a and 1989b) for a discussion of cases in which he argues that conjunctive plural terms can be true in non-maximal situations.

11. De Vries (2015) calls predicates such as in 10 "'group-level' atom predicates." Here I classify the sort of predication, rather than the predicates, as the predication seems similar in all of 10–13 and some of the predicates can also be classified as distributive when combined with plural terms and, in some cases (e.g. *old* and *large*) collective nouns. The predicates in 10–13 pattern with predicates that Schwarzschild (2011) calls stubbornly distributive predicates. Such predicates take only singularities (such as Bob or the Cleveland Cavaliers), rather than sets or many things (such as the students or Chris and Luke). They also pattern with what Winter (2002) calls atom predicates. He takes such predicates to only apply to atoms, rather than sets.

12. See Levin (2001) for corpus data to support the difference between British, American, and Australian English and for differences between agreement with collective nouns based on animacy and humanity. See also de Vries (2015) for a discussion of animacy and collective nouns.

13. Singularists usually take the denotation of plural terms to be sets or sums. For proponents of a set approach see, e.g. Bartsch (1973), Bennett (1974), Schwarzschild (1996), Landman (1989a, 1989b). For proponents of lattice-theoretic sum approaches see, e.g. Link (1983). See Landman (1989a) for an argument that plural terms can also pick out groups, entities that are atomic in ways that sets and sums are not.

14. For proponents of Pluralist approaches see, e.g. Boolos (1984), Hossack (2000), Oliver and Smiley (2001, 2005, 2013), Yi (2005), McKay (2006), Schein (1993), Moltmann (1997).

15. For example, ambiguities have been posited in the denotations of subject expressions (e.g. by Landman (1989a and 1989b)) and in predicates (e.g. by Link (1983) and Lasersohn (1995)). Others have appealed to covers, developed by Schwarzschild (1996) to avoid ambiguities in predicates. Distinctions regarding, for example, how to handle distributive predication, have been implemented with quantifiers (following Link (1983)), via meaning postulates (following Scha (1981) and Hoeksema (1983)), and through a combination of the two (see, e.g. Dowty (1987); Hoeksema (1988); Winter (1997, 2000); Champollion (2010); and de Vries (2015)).

16. Alternatively, these are sometimes represented as $\exists X$ and $\forall X$.

17. This departs from Russell (1905) in allowing for definite expressions to have meaning in isolation.

18. For exposition and arguments see, e.g. Boolos (1984), Schein (1993), Oliver and Smiley (2013).

19. See Rayo (2002) and Nicolas (2007) for discussion of ways for a Singularist to avoid paradox.

20. For arguments that the Singularist cannot capture the full range of semantic data see, e.g. Schein (1993), Oliver and Smiley (2001, 2013), McKay (2006), Yi (2005). For arguments that the two styles of treatment are equally semantically capable see Ritchie (2016).

21. See Pearson (2011) for an alternative view.

22. Schwarzschild (1996) has suggested that collective nouns in British English are ambiguous between a plural and a singular denotation. Suerland and Elbourne (2002) have argued that collective nouns in British English are semantically plural while those in American English are semantically singular.

23. This observation and a very similar example come from Zwicky and Sadock (1975).

24. Other expressions that are often taken to be polysemous can require multiple meanings in a single token. For example, "Anne broke the window and then climbed through it" and "After finishing the bottle, we recycled it" are felicitous and utilize multiple meanings of *window* and *bottle*.

25. Formally the connection between the group and members meaning can be captured via a function or a relation.

26. See Ritchie (2013 and 2015) for a development of a view on which groups are structured wholes.

27. Some have argued that collective predication of plural terms should be handled by taking plurals to denote groups (e.g. Landman 1989a, 1989b). If one opts for this strategy with plurals, it would be natural to do the same in one's treatment of collective nouns and take collective predication to involve predication of groups rather than members.

28. One might appeal to syntactic and semantic features to help explain why plural VP agreement is dispreferred in some dialects of English. See, e.g. Corbett (2000).

36

Actions and Events in Plural Discourse

Kirk Ludwig

1. INTRODUCTION

Plural discourse may be understood syntactically or semantically, depending on whether one focuses on grammatically plural terms (*we, they, those, them, the men, some politicians, all tigers, most philosophers, two columns,* etc.) or simply on terms that refer to collectives or groups,[1] whether grammatically plural or singular (*the Foreign Legion, the Supreme Court, the British Parliament, the Paris mob,* etc.). This chapter is concerned with plural discourse in the grammatical sense. The goal of the chapter is to urge the value of the event analysis of the matrix of action sentences in thinking about logical form in plural discourse about action. Among the claims advanced are that:

1. The ambiguity between distributive and collective readings of plural action sentences is not lexical ambiguity, either in the noun phrase (NP) or in the verb phrase (VP), but an ambiguity tracing to the scope of the event quantifier introduced by the action verb.[2]
2. This allows us to analyze collective action sentences in a way that commits us only to individual agents acting when we say that groups act, without denying that there are groups as such or that we talk about them as such.
3. Intermediate readings, that seem to be neither purely distributive nor purely collective, can be explained in terms of the same apparatus.

The following methodological principles guide the inquiry:

i) We should respect common sense.
ii) We should not multiply senses beyond necessity.
iii) We should make use of tools already developed and introduce new devices only if needed.

iv) We should develop an account of the structure and content of discourse about collective actions on the basis of an account of the structure and content of discourse about individual actions.

Section 2 develops the event analysis of singular action sentences. Section 3 applies it to plural discourse about action and Section 4 summarizes.

2. THE EVENT ANALYSIS OF ACTION SENTENCES

The standard event analysis of [1], introduced to provide a handle on the logic of adverbs, is given in [1a].[3]

[1]　Brutus stabbed Caesar [violently] [with a knife] [on the Ides of March].
[1a]　$(\exists e)$(agent(e, Brutus) & stabbing(e) & object(e, Caesar) & with(e, a knife) & on(e, the Ides of March)).

There is an event e such that Brutus is agent of e, e is a stabbing, e's object is Caesar, e was done with a knife, and e was done on the Ides of March.

[1a] treats adverbs as contributing predicates of an event variable bound by a quantifier introduced by the action verb, and separates out the thematic role of agent and object. This analysis explains why [1] implies each of the sentences got from it by dropping one or more of the adverbial modifiers (i.e. modifier drop entailment), as well as why it follows from [1] that there was a stabbing (see note (c) below), that someone was stabbed (which can happen without there being an agent), that someone did something, that something happened to someone, and that something happened.

[1a] is deficient in four respects, however. First, it ignores tense. Second, it does not secure that there was a stabbing of which Brutus was the sole agent.[4] If Brutus built the first half of a boat and Cassius the second half, neither gets to say he built a boat, though they can say that they did. Third, we need to add a parameter that captures the contribution of the verb to determining what specific agency relation the agent is to bear to the event he brings about. For example, being an agent of someone's death is not sufficient for me to have killed him. If I hire an assassin to kill him, it is the assassin who kills him and not me. Fourth, we require a second quantifier over events to capture the distinction between the primitive action the agent performs and the different consequences, which may be captured by different verbs, of what he thereby brings about. Otherwise, we have to identify the action performed with the value of the single event variable. But if Booth shot Lincoln with a gun and pulled the trigger with his finger, and it was one and the same action, we get the result that Booth shot Lincoln with his finger.[5]

I represent the result of adding all the appropriate modifications at once in [1b].

[1b]　$(\exists e)[\exists t: t < \text{now}](\exists f)([\text{agent}(f, t, \text{Brutus})$ & $\text{directly}(f, e)]$ &
　　$[\text{only } y = \text{Brutus}][\exists t': t' < \text{now}](\exists f')[\text{agent}(f', t', y)$ & $\text{directly}(f', e)]$ &
　　$\text{stabbing}(e)$ & $\text{object}(e, \text{Caesar})$ & $\text{with}(e, \text{a knife})$ & $\text{on}(t, \text{the Ides of March}))$.

There is an event e, there is a time t before the present, and there is an event f such that: Brutus is a primitive agent of f at t & f brings e about directly & only Brutus is a primitive agent of an event before the present that brings e about directly and e is a stabbing and Caesar is an object of e and e is done with a knife and t was during the Ides of March.

Notes:

a) Tense I treat as a restricted quantifier over times, related in one way or another to utterance time, binding argument places implicit in the predicates, excepting the present tense which is equivalent to putting an indexical whose value is the time of utterance in the temporal argument position of the verb.

b) I locate the temporal argument place in the agency relation, for intuitively someone did something characterized by some consequence *when* he performed a primitive action that led to it. Suppose I put poison in your curry this summer. I die in an automobile accident in the fall. You first use the curry for a winter stew and die as a result. What I did to kill you occurred in the summer. I wasn't doing anything when you died.

c) In the representation of logical form, I use the present participle of the action verb to represent what we understand to be the type of event which one's primitive action brings about (where *bringing about* is a determinable of which causation is just one determinate), where the type is neutral with respect to whether anyone brought it about. Some action verbs have intransitive forms that express the appropriate event type. For example, if I melted the chocolate, then chocolate melted. The chocolate could have melted, though, without anyone melting it. But not all verbs have appropriate intransitive forms. I press the present participle into service for this purpose uniformly. The primitive action in the case of [1] is the movement of the arm and hand that holds the knife. The consequent event is (roughly) the insertion into an object of another object, which results in the violent parting of the matter that constitutes it.

d) The verb "stabs" requires, like "kill", a form of direct agency in which what I do to bring about the result does not go primarily through the agency of another (hiring another to stab someone is not to stab him). I represent this as a two-place predicate "directly(f, e)."

e) The requirement that there be a sole agent of the event for a singular action sentence I represent by the conjunct:

[only y = Brutus]$(\exists t': t' < now)(\exists f')$[agent$(f', t', y)$ & directly(f', e)].

For convenience, I will introduce the following abbreviation:

agent$_d$(f, t, e, just Brutus)

$=_{df}$
[agent(f, t, Brutus) & directly(f, e)] & (only y = Brutus)$(\exists t': t' < now)(\exists f')$
[agent(f', t', y) & directly(f', e)].

f) With a quantifier over times, I treat "on the Ides of March" as a predicate of the temporal variable rather than an event variable.

g) I call the quantifier binding the event variable "f" in the agency relation, the primitive action quantifier and, the other, the consequent event quantifier.

We represent the form of the matrix for an arbitrary action sentence whose verb is inflected for the past tense, which has a direct object, and is modified by an adverb, as in [M], where for notational convenience I include an argument place for the object O in the event type predicate.

x V-ed O F-ly

[M] $(\exists e)[\exists t: t < now](\exists f)(agent_d(f, t, e, just\ x)\ \&\ V\text{-}ing(e, O)\ \&\ F(e))$

The next question is how the matrix interacts with plural NPs in the subject position.

3. PLURAL ACTION SENTENCES

It is well known that many plural action sentences admit of an ambiguity between a plural and a distributive reading [2–4]. Some, in contrast, seem to have only a distributive reading [5–6], and some seem to have only a collective reading [8–11]. Arguably, some admit readings that are neither purely distributive nor purely collective [11–12].

[2] They lifted a piano.
[3] Antony and Cleopatra built a pleasure barge.
[4] The players sang the national anthem.

[5] They played solitaire.
[6] The quarterbacks pass the ball.

[7] They surrounded the house.
[8] Some protesters gathered in the park.
[9] We met in the library.
[10] The Justices ruled that segregation is unconstitutional in *Brown v. Board of Education*.

[11] Rodgers, Hart and Hammerstein wrote musicals.[6]
[12] Helen and Bill and Bud and Pearl contributed $100 to charity.

The distributive reading in [5–6] seems forced by the meaning of the VP, and likewise the collective reading in [7–8] seems forced by the meaning of the VP. We return to these later.

But in general the distributive/collective readings are not due to the meaning of the verb because that is the same on both readings of [2–4]. One might postulate an ambiguity in the VP (Hoeksema 1983; Dowty 1986; Link 1987; Lasersohn 1989, 1995) but this fails because [13], unlike [14], is not zeugmatic, that is, in [13], in contrast to [14,] there is not the slightest hint of infelicity as the one meaning is distributed across clauses (Zwicky and Sadock 1975).

[13] They lifted the piano together and individually.

[14] He bored a hole and his audience.

The matrix of [2] is [2m]. On the distributive reading, it is clear that the truth conditions are that each of them satisfies the matrix. This requires us to read the NP as a restricted quantifier over members of the group picked out by the plural subject term (call this *a distributive quantifier*), as in [2d].

[2m] $(\exists e)[\exists t: t < now](\exists f)(agent_d(f, t, e, just\ x)$ & $lifting(e, a\ piano))$.

[2d] $[Each\ x\ of\ them](\exists e)(\exists t: t < now)(\exists f)(agent_d(f, t, e, just\ x)$ & $lifting(e, a\ piano))$.

Each of them lifted a piano.

How should we understand the collective reading? One popular option is to take the NP to be ambiguous (Lakoff 1972; Link 1983; Gillon 1987; Landman 1989; Gillon 1990; Link 1991; Gillon 1992).[7] The most straightforward way is to take it on the collective reading to be a bare plural referring term, as opposed to a distributive quantifier, that occupies directly the agency relation in the matrix. This would commit us to the existence of genuine group agents in accepting the truth of sentences such as [2] on the collective reading. But the NP ambiguity thesis is implausible, unnecessary, unable to handle all of the data. It is implausible because it commits us to group agents per se even when two people do something together unintentionally (e.g. block a doorway). It cannot handle all the data because, for example, if we use "they" in [15] to refer to a group as such, as shown in [15'], the reading of [15] on which they jointly carry the piano upstairs and each gets a cookie, is unavailable.[8]

[15] They carried the piano upstairs and got a cookie as a reward.

[15'] $(\exists e)[\exists t: t < now](\exists f)(agent_d(f, t, e, just\ them)$ & $carrying(e, a\ piano)$ & $to(e, upstairs)$ & $(\exists e')getting(e', they, a\ cookie))$.

They carried the piano upstairs together and got a cookie collectively.

Finally, it is unnecessary because the use of a distributive quantifier together with a difference in how we treat the scope of the consequent event quantifier yields the collective reading. The idea is to give the event quantifier wide scope over the distributive quantifier, so that instead of saying that for every one of them there was an event of lifting of which he was the agent, we say there was an event of lifting of which each of them was an agent. This has to be developed in stages though, to get it exactly right. First we drop the NP into the argument position in the matrix as in [2']. We expand [2'] as in [2''] (adjusting form for grammatical position), but now introduce a variable for a group (using capital letters) in the clause requiring there be a single appropriate agent.

[2'] $(\exists e)[\exists t: t < now](\exists f)(agent_d(f, t, e, just\ them)$ & $lifting(e, a\ piano))$.

[2''] $(\exists e)[\exists t: t < now](\exists f)([agent(f, t, they)$ & $directly(f, e)]$ & $(only\ Y = them)(\exists t': t' < now)(\exists f')[agent(f', t', y)$ & $directly(f', e)]$ & $lifting(e, a\ piano))$.

We take the appearance of "they" as a restricted quantifier over members of the group, "(Each x of them)," represented for convenience as "$(they_x)$" and pull it out but give it narrow scope with respect to the consequent event quantifier as in [2‴].

[2‴] $(\exists e)\ (they_x)\ [\exists t: t < now](\exists f)([agent(f, t, x)\ \&\ directly(f, e)]\ \&$
(only Y = them)$(\exists t': t' < now)(\exists f')[agent(f', t', y)\ \&\ directly(f', e)]\ \&$
lifting(e, a piano)).

There remains the question how to treat the other appearance of "them" in the clause requiring there be a single agent in the relevant way of the consequent event. The uniqueness clause says that only groups identical with *them* are agents in the relevant way of the event: (Only Y = them). We first observe that since we are committed to taking the agency relation to relate only individuals to events, we must add a distributive quantifier after "(only Y = them)," namely, "(for all y in Y)," which we abbreviate as "Y_y." This gives us "(only Y = them)$(Y_y)(t: t < now)(f)[agent(f, t, y)\ \&\ directly(f, e)]$". This says that only groups identical with them are such that any member y of it is at any time before the present such that y is a direct agent of e. We can achieve a further simplification. For saying only groups identical with them are such that any member of it is a direct agent of an event is equivalent to saying that only members of them are such that they are direct agents that event. So we can rewrite "(only Y = them)(Y_y)" as "(only y in them)". This ensures that no agents other than members of the group are agents of the consequent event in the relevant way. This finally gives us [2c]. Again, we can abbreviate, as shown.

[2c] $(\exists e)[they_x][\exists t: t < now](\exists f)([agent(f, t, x)\ \&\ directly(f, e)]\ \&\ (only\ y\ in\ them)$
$(\exists t': t' < now)(\exists f')[agent(f', t', y)\ \&\ directly(f', e)]\ \&\ lifting(e, a\ piano)).$

$=_{df}$

$(\exists e)[they_x][\exists t: t < now](\exists f)(agent_d(f, t, e, x, them)\ \&\ lifting(e, a\ piano)).$

There is an event e such that each of them at some time did something that contributed directly to e, and e is an event of a piano going up.

Clearly, if [2c] is true, then so is [2], and vice versa. So we have intuitively the right truth conditions for [2] on the collective reading. Thus, the distributive/collective ambiguity traces to a scope ambiguity. This analysis handles [15], repeated here, straightforwardly, in [15a].

[15] They carried the piano upstairs and got a cookie as a reward.
[15a] $(\exists e)[they_x][\exists t: t < now](\exists f)(agent_d(f, t, e, x, them)\ \&$
carrying(e, a piano) & to(e, upstairs) &
$(\exists e')[\exists t': t' > t](receiving(e', t', x, a\ cookie))).$

Some event e is such that each of x them is such that: at some time t, x is a direct agent of e at t and e is the piano going upstairs and there is an e' and a time t' later than t such that e' is an event of x receiving a cookie at t' as a reward.

The initial quantifier over members of the group binds the argument place in the scope of the event quantifier in the second embedded conjunct, and so makes room for the reading on which there is a separate getting of a cookie for each.

Let me now treat [3] and [4], repeated here, to illustrate how the account extends to other plural NPs.

[3] Antony and Cleopatra built a pleasure barge.
[4] The players sang the national anthem.

For the collective reading of [3] one could take the conjunctive NP to be a special type of referring term receiving the clause [RC] (where for now we take the metalinguistic variables to range over ordinary proper names):

[RC] For any N_1, N_2, N_3, . . . for any X,
      Ref(CONJ(N_1, N_2, N_3, . . .)) = X
      iff
      Ref(N_1) is in X and Ref(N_2) is in X and Ref(N_3) is in X . . . and nothing else is.[9]

Then we would analyze [3] on the collective reading as in [3c] ("{A and B}" refers to the group of A and B.).

[3c] $(\exists e)$[{Antony and Cleopatra}$_x$][$\exists t$: t < now]$(\exists f)$(agent$_d$(f, t, e, x, {Anthony and Cleopatra}) & building(e, a pleasure barge)).

In the case of the collective reading of [4], we treat "The players" as introducing a group description and distributive quantifier over members of the group of players: (The X: X is a group each member of which is a player)(every x of X). Let's abbreviate the restriction in the first to "players(X)." Then we have:

[4c] $(\exists e)$[the X: players(X)][X_x][$\exists t$: t < now]$(\exists f)$(agent$_d$(f, t, e, x, X) & singing (e, the national anthem)).

But if the ambiguity in [2–4] is a scope ambiguity, why does there not seem to be an ambiguity in [5–6] and [7–10] (repeated here)?

[5] They played solitaire.
     [Each x of them](x played solitaire).

[6] The quarterbacks passed the ball.
     [the X: quarterbacks(X)](X_x)(x passed the ball).

[7] They surrounded the house.
     $(\exists s)$[Each x of them][$\exists t$: t < now]$(\exists f)$(agent$_d$(f, t, s, x, them) & surrounding(s, them, the house)).[10]

[8] Some protesters gathered in the park.
     $(\exists e)$[the X: protesters(X)][X_x][$\exists t$: t < now]$(\exists f)$(agent$_d$(f, t, e, x, X) & gathering(e, X, the park)).

[9] We met in the library.
     $(\exists e)$[Each x of us][$\exists t$: t < now]$(\exists f)$(agent$_d$(f, t, e, x, we) & meeting(e) and in(e, the library)).

[10] The justices ruled that segregation is unconstitutional in *Brown v. Board of Education*.

$(\exists e)[the\ X: justices(X)][X_x][\exists t: t < now](\exists f)(agent_c(f, t, e, x, X)\ \&$
$ruling(e)\ \&\ content(e, segregation\ is\ unconstitutional)\ \&$
$in(e,\ Brown\ v.\ Board\ of\ Education)).$[11]

The answer is that one of the semantically available readings is dismissed out of hand because the content of the predicate ensures that it is false. Thus, the collective reading of [5] requires that there be an event of playing solitaire of which there are multiple agents in the way required by the predicate, but the predicate requires that there be just one. Similarly, the distributive reading of [9] requires that each person be an agent by himself of an event type requiring two agents. The same goes for [10]. [7] and [8], however, are different. These are often classified incorrectly as involving predicates that semantically require groups. But this isn't so. An amoeba can surround its food, and the elastic Mr. Fantastic of the Fantastic Four of comic book fame could presumably surround the house by himself. Even gathering is something that a single agent of an appropriate sort could do. An amoeba (or Mr. Fantastic) could gather itself (himself) together in a smaller area. It is just that for many typical applications involving groups the members of the group cannot individually bring about what the verb expresses, and so we hear only the collective reading.

This brings us to the intermediate cases [11]–[12], repeated here.

[11] Rodgers, Hart and Hammerstein wrote musicals.
[12] Helen and Bill and Bud and Pearl contributed $100 to charity.

Rodgers, Hart and Hammerstein did not write any musicals together. Two did, but the three did not, and neither did each of them individually. But it has been suggested that there is a reading of [11] which is true (Gillon 1987) because Rodgers and Hart wrote musicals together and Rodgers and Hammerstein did too. In the case of [12], we are to imagine a reading on which Helen and Bill together contributed $100 to charity and Bud and Pearl together likewise, but not all of them together or individually, or in other groupings.

Supposing that there is a literal reading of [11] true in the circumstances (as opposed to something that in light of background information we succeed in finding a point to), how do we get the right reading? In answering this, let's take up [12] first. Here the answer is an extension of our earlier approach to conjunctive NPs involving names. Let the metalinguistic quantifiers in our reference clause [RC], repeated here, range over both ordinary and what we will call conjunctive names.

[RC] For any N1, N2, N3, . . . for any X,
Ref(CONJ(N1, N2, N3, . . .)) = X
iff
Ref(N_1) is in X and Ref(N_2) is in X and Ref(N_3) is in X . . . and nothing else is.

Then we read the NP in [12] as:

(Helen and Bill) and (Bud and Pearl).

Then apply our earlier pattern to this to get [12′]:

[12′] [{(Helen and Bill) and (Bud and Pearl)}$_x$]($\exists$e)[X$_x$][$\exists$t: t < now]($\exists$f)(agent$_d$(f, t, e, x, X)] & contributing(e, a charity, \$100)).

So we first treat the NP as a distributive quantifier over groups in a group, then in the scope of the event quantifier we have a distributive quantifier over members of each of them in turn.[12]

Now the solution to [11] is clear. To get the right reading, we read "Rodgers, Hart and Hammerstein" as "Rodgers × (Hart and Hammerstein)" which is "(Rodgers and Hart) and (Rodgers and Hammerstein)."

Is there a reading of [11] on which it is open what groups among Rodgers, Hart, and Hammerstein wrote musicals? Let's change the example to [16] illustrate the idea here. Is there a reading of [16] on which there is more than one event of meeting and none involve all six girls, but every one of six girls is involved in one meeting at the library with at least one of the others?

[16] Six girls met in the library.

Plausibly there is a reading of [16] on which it means that each of the girls met with one or more of the others in the library.

For a clue to what to say about this, we turn to a different construction involving a verb that expresses a collective action but which takes singular NPs that refer to individuals as subjects, as in [17].

[17] Helen got married.

Helen couldn't have got married alone. We understand "Helen got married" to mean that Helen married someone. I take marriage to be a state of two people, and marrying to be being an agent of coming to be in the state of marriage.[13] With these points in hand, I suggest the logical form of [17] is [17′].

[17′] ($\exists$s)[$\exists$X: Helen is in X][X$_x$][$\exists$t: t < now]($\exists$f)([agent(f, t, s, x, X) & constitutes(f, s)] & ($\exists$y: y is in X)marrying(s, Helen, y)).

We allow more agents of the marrying than those between whom it is, e.g. a judge or a minister, and take the contributions to it to be (at least in part) constitutive rather than merely causal. However, the position in "marrying(s, x, y)" occupied by "x" is understood to be that of a participant in the state of marriage that results.

This shows that intransitive verbs taking singular NPs that imply the involvement of others have to be implicitly completed with a quantifier, either fixed by semantic rules attaching to the sentence form or supplied contextually.

We apply the idea of implicit quantificational structure to [16]. [16] appears to admit of a number of different readings. We may read it as "Six girls met together in the library," which requires a single meeting event involving all six. Another is "Six girls met each other," for nine pairwise meetings. Another is that every one of them met at least one or more of the others—the target interpretation here. These readings just represent different ways of filling in quantification structures not fixed by the surface form. How we read it is sensitive to context. The last of these readings is given by:

[16′] [∃X: six-girls(X)][X_x](∃e)[∃t: t < now](∃f)(agent(f, t, e, x) & meeting(e) & (∃Y ≠ X: x is not in Y, every member of Y is in X, and no member of Y is not in X)(with(e, x, every z in Y or some z in Y) & in(e, the library)).

This approach can be pursued with [11] if it is thought to leave matters more open than the suggested approach. Thus, it appears that the intermediate readings can be expressed easily enough using just the materials provided by the event analysis, and the ambiguities involved can be understood to be due to various ways in which we are free to complete the quantificational scheme required by the semantic structure of the predicates.[14]

Thus, on this approach, the answer to the question what it is for a group to do something collectively or jointly is for each of them, and no one else to be an agent of one event (or state) by way of some individual contribution (of a specified kind) to its coming about.

4. SUMMARY

In summary, the event analysis of the matrix of action sentences provides resources for giving a straightforward and intuitively compelling account of ambiguities in plural actions sentences between distributive, collective, and intermediate readings. Collective action, on this account, is simply a matter of there being multiple agents of a single event through individual contributions to them. An immediate consequence is that collection action may fail to be intentional under any description. The approach is deflationary in the sense that, while it accepts groups in our ontology, it assigns the role of agent only to individuals who are members of those groups, which is the commonsense view. It has the virtue of making use in the account only of materials that we are already committed to, of minimizing multiplication of senses, and of handling the data better than views that locate the ambiguity in the plural NPs or in the VPs.

RELATED TOPICS

Collective Action and Agency (Ch. 1), Reductive Views of Shared Intention (Ch. 3), Groups as Distributed Cognitive Systems (Ch. 18), Logic and Plurals (Ch. 34), Plural and Collective Noun Phrases (Ch. 35).

REFERENCES

Barsch, R. (1973) "The Semantics and Syntax of Number and Numbers," in J. Kimball (ed.) *Syntax and Semantics*, New York: Seminar Press.
Davidson, D. (1967) "The Logical Form of Action Sentences," in N. Rescher (ed.) *The Logic of Decision and Action*, Pittsburgh: University of Pittsburgh.
——— (1985) "Adverbs of Action," in B. Vermazen and M. Hintikka (eds) *Essays On Davidson*, Oxford: Clarendon Press.

Dowty, D. (1986) "Collective Predicates, Distributive Predicates and *All*," paper read at *Proceedings of the Third Eastern States Conference on Linguistics*, at Ohio State University.

Gillon, B. (1987) "The Readings of Plural Noun Phrases in English," *Linguistics and Philosophy*, 10: 199–219.

——— (1990) "Bare Plurals as Plural Indefinite Noun Phrases," in H. Kyburg, R.P. Loui and G.N. Carlson (eds) *Knowledge Representation and Defeasible Reasoning*, Dordrecht: Kluwer.

——— (1992) "Towards a Common Semantics for English Count and Mass Nouns," *Linguistics and Philosophy* 15 (6): 597–639.

Hausser, R. (1974) "Syntax and Semantics of Plural," paper read at *Papers of the 19th Regional Meeting of the Chicago Linguistic Society*, at Chicago.

Hoeksema, J. (1983) "Plurality and Conjunction," in A.G.B. ter Meulen (ed.) *Studies in Modeltheoretic Semantics*, Dordrecht: Foris.

Lakoff, G. (1972) "Linguistics and Natural Logic," in G. Harman and D. Davidson (eds) *Semantics of Natural Language*, Dordrecht: Kluwer.

Landman, F. (1989) "Groups, I," *Linguistics and Philosophy*, 12: 559–605.

Lasersohn, P. (1989) "On the Readings of Plural Noun Phrases," *Linguistic Inquiry* 20: 130–4.

——— (1995) *Plurality, Conjunction and Events*, Dordrecht: Kluwer Academic Publishers.

Link, G. (1983) "The Logical Analysis of Plurals and Mass Terms: a Lattice-Theoretic Approach," in R. Bauerle, C. Schwarze and A. von Stechow (eds) *Meaning, Use, and the Interpretation of Language*, Berlin: de Gruyter.

——— (1987) "Generaized Quantifiers and Plurals," in P. Gardenfors (ed.) *Generalized Quantifiers: Logical and Liinguistic Approaches*, Dordrecht: Springer.

——— (1991) "Plural," in D. Wunderlich and A. von Stechow (eds) *Handbook of Semantics*, Berlin: de Gruyter.

Lombard, L.B. (1985) "How Not to Flip the Prowler: Transitive Verbs of Action and Actions," in E. LePore and B. McLaughlin (eds) *Actions and Events: Perspectives on the Philosophy of Donald Davidson*, Oxford: Blackwell.

Lønning, J.T. (2011) "Plurals and Collectives," in J. van Benthem and A. ter Meulen (eds) *Handbook of Logic and Language*, Amsterdam: Elsevier.

Ludwig, K. (2007a) "Collective Intentional Behavior from the Standpoint of Semantics," *Noûs*, 41 (3): 355–93.

——— (2007b) "Foundations of Social Reality in Collective Intentional Behavior," in S.L. Tsohatzidis (ed.) *Intentional Acts and Institutional Facts: Essays on John Searle's Social Ontology*, Dordrecht: Springer.

——— (2010) "Adverbs of Action," in T. O'Connor and C. Sandis (eds) *Blackwell Companion to the Philosophy of Action*, Oxford: Wiley-Blackwell.

——— (2014) "Proxy Agency in Collective Action," *Noûs*, 48 (1) 75–105.

——— (2016) *From Individual to Plural Agency: Collective Action 1*, Oxford: Oxford University Press.

——— (2017) *From Plural to Institutional Agency: Collective Action 2*, Oxford: Oxford University Press.

McCawley, J. (1968) "The Role of Semantics in a Grammar," in E. Bach and R. Harms (eds) *Universals in Linguistic Theory*, New York: Holt, Rinehart & Winston.

Oliver, A. and Smiley, T. (2001) "Strategies for a Logic of Plurals," *The Philosophical Quarterly* 51 (204): 289–306.

——— (2013) *Plural Logic*, Oxford: Oxford University Press.

Parsons, T. (1980) "Modifiers and Quantifiers in Natural Language," *Canadian Journal of Philosophy* 6: 29–60.

Pietroski, P. (2002) *Causing Actions*, New York: Oxford University Press.

Schein, B. (1993) *Plurals and Events*, Cambridge, MA: MIT Press.

——— (2002) "Events and the Semantic Content of Thematic Relations," in G. Preyer and G. Peter (eds) *Logical Form and Language*, Oxford: Clarendon Press.

——— (2006) "Plurals," in E. Lepore and B. Smith (eds) *The Oxford Handbook of Philosophy of Language*, Oxford: Oxford University Press.

——— (2010) "Event Semantics," in D.G. Fara and G. Russell (eds) *The Routledge Companion to Philosophy of Language*, New York: Routledge.

Vendler, Z. (1984) "Agency and Causation," *Midwest Studies in Philosophy: Causation and Causal Theories* IX: 371–84.

Zwicky, A. and Sadock, J. (1975) "Ambiguity Tests and How to Fail Them," in *Syntax and Semantics*, New York: Academic Press.

NOTES

1. By *a group*, I mean whatever it is that we use plural terms such as "we," "they," "those," etc., to refer to—things such as couples, pairs, collections. But I do not have a topic-neutral conception of them. Groups, as I understand them, are neither sets nor (mereological) sums (where individuals are treated as parts of the sum, which is another, complex, individual). So though the approach sketched here to plural action sentences is Singularist in the sense of Oliver and Smiley (2013), it conforms to neither of the Singularist views they criticize. (See the discussion also in Chapters 34 and 35 of this volume, which discuss only set and sum versions of Singularism.) Why are groups not sets? They differ in what can be predicated of them truly. While a group of boxes (those boxes) may weigh 250 kg and take up space, no set does, as opposed to the collection of its members. There is an empty set, but no empty group. There is a singleton set, but all groups have at least two members. However, like sets, groups are individuated by their members, and groups can have groups as well as individuals as members. It makes sense to talk, for example, of those pairs of dancers who advanced to the final round of the competition. Intuitively groups are constructed hierarchically, starting with groups of individuals, then groups of groups of individuals, and so on. The relation of "is a member of" (or "is in" or "is one of") relates only lower to higher orders in the hierarchy. Therefore, groups do not give rise to paradoxes analogous to those of unrestricted set abstraction. The foregoing shows that groups are not sums because while groups can have groups as members, they do not thereby have the members of those groups as members, and thus the membership relation is distinct from the parthood relation. Talk of institutional groups, which may seem not to be individuated by their members since they can change over time and could have been different than they are, can be explained in terms of a socially constructed membership relation, which is a time-relative status function, and the ontology of groups required by plural referring terms (Ludwig 2014, 2017).

2. I have argued for this in Ludwig (2007a, 2007b, 2016). See Schein (1993, 2002, 2006, 2010) for extensive work on plurals in the event framework. My analysis of action sentences differs in the treatment of tense, the introduction of a quantifier over primitive events, the treatment of the verb as introducing a constraint on the form of agency expressed, and some other details. Oliver and Smiley (2001, 2013) discuss this general type of approach and trace it back to McCawley (1968) and Barsch (1973).

3. The *locus classicus* is Davidson (1967). See Ludwig (2010) for a review of the basic considerations in favor of the event analysis and Ludwig (2016) for a fuller defense of this approach to plural action sentences. See Ludwig (2017) for an extension to grammatically singular group action sentences.

4. This requirement is typically overlooked. I introduced it in Ludwig (2007a), but Oliver and Smiley (2001) anticipated me. There are differences in the implementation because of the complications introduced by the third and fourth points in this paragraph.

5. I borrow the example from Pietroski (2002) who suggests introducing an additional quantifier. The problem was first raised in an unpublished paper by John Wallace (reported in Parsons (1980)), and later independently by Vendler (1984) and Lombard (1985). Davidson proposed informally essentially the solution that Pietroski does, in Davidson (1985).

6. The example is from Gillon (1987) who suggests it has an intermediate reading, neither all together nor each individually.

7. I don't say that the NP ambiguity thesis is incorrect in every case. For example, some predicates apply indifferently to individuals and groups, and in these cases the ambiguity is plausibly due to an ambiguity between a distributive quantifier and a simple referring term. "The boxes weigh 150 kg" is ambiguous between a distributive and collective reading, but on the collective reading it is the boxes collectively that we say weigh 150 kg.

8. Adapted from Lønning (2011: 1021). Oliver and Smiley (2001, 2013) make this point, attributing it to Lasersohn (1995: ch. 7, section 3), who attributes it to Dowty (1986). Hausser gives the example (noted in Lasersohn) of "Horses gather and graze" in Hausser (1974). As Oliver and Smiley point out, it is not an option to distribute "they" first and then interpret it differently in each place because that yields the wrong result for something like "Some of the boys carried the piano upstairs and got a cookie as a reward."

9. What if every name in a conjunctive name names the same thing? As it stands [RC] requires the referent to be a singleton group, but there are none. For this case we need another clause, but I will forgo adding it in this context. This requires also making the distributive quantifier a bit more complex. See Ludwig (2016: ch. 10) for discussion.

10. I take "surround" here to be an action verb but directed at bringing about a state rather than an event, the same state that trees or a moat are in when they surround a house or a castle, where here "surround" is not used as an action verb.

11. I subscript the agency relation here with "c" to indicate that the form of agency required includes that the justices do something that partially constitutes the ruling being made and not merely contribute causally.

12. Some NPs may mix names of groups and individuals, e.g. Helen and (Bud and Pearl) contributed $100 to charity. This requires some modifications to the treatment. See Ludwig (2016: ch. 10) for further discussion of refinements needed for this and other cases, and a different treatment for conjunctive NPs with numerals.

13. We also say that the minister married Bud and Pearl, but this expresses a different role in the act, that of officiating. If the minister marries Pearl, he enters into the marriage state. If he married Bud and Pearl, he enters them into the marriage state (with their cooperation). We might say, the minister married Pearl, meaning he officiated, but this is short for he married her to someone. Thanks to Katherine Ritchie for the observation.

14. See Ludwig (2016: ch. 10, especially note 25) for more discussion of the context sensitivity of hidden quantificational structure, and some other constructions, such as reciprocals and cumulative readings.

Index

Printed in Great Britain
by Amazon